INDEX TO
CHILDREN'S
SONGS

INDEX TO
CHILDREN'S
SONGS

A TITLE, FIRST LINE, AND SUBJECT INDEX

Compiled by
Carolyn Sue Peterson
and
Ann D. Fenton

THE H. W. WILSON COMPANY • NEW YORK 1979

Printed in the United States of America

Library of Congress Cataloging in Publication Data

Peterson, Carolyn Sue
   Index to children's songs.

   1. Children's songs—Indexes.   2. Songs—Indexes.
I. Fenton, Ann D., joint author.   II. Title.
ML128S3P48 016. 784624   79-14265
ISBN 0-8242-0638-X

Contents

Preface   vii

A List of Books Indexed   ix

Title and First Line Index   1

Broad Topic Guide to Subject Index   163

Subject Index   169

Preface

INDEX TO CHILDREN'S SONGS is an index to more than 5,000 songs and variations contained in 298 children's books published between 1909 and 1977. The list of song books indexed includes those titles that appeared in *Children's Catalog* (both 12th and 13th editions) and in *Elementary School Library Collections* (both 9th and 10th editions). In addition, the list includes other song books, both in and out of print, that are commonly found in school libraries and public libraries. A few collections, published primarily as adult books but containing a large number of children's songs, have also been included. Only song books that contain music as well as lyrics have been indexed, with the exception of a few individual songs published in picture book format without music.

The Index is divided into three parts. The first part, the LIST OF BOOKS INDEXED arranged alphabetically by author, contains complete bibliographical information on every song book, and assigns every one a location code.

The TITLE AND FIRST LINE INDEX, contains song titles and first lines in one alphabet. First lines are printed in *italic* to distinguish them from titles, which are printed in roman. Each entry includes a title, or a first line, followed by a location code and page number. For example:

> Troy, the Drummer Boy 167:30
> *True love, true love, don't lie to me* 148:186

The location code (which always precedes the colon) is a reference to the List of Books Indexed. In the example above, the song Troy, the Drummer Boy can be located by finding number 167 in the List of Books Indexed, which turns out to be the number for *Hop, Skip and Sing* by Lois Metz. The number after the colon tells you on what page of this song book Troy, the Drummer Boy can be found. Similarly, the song for which "True Love, true love, don't lie to me" is the first line can be located first by finding the book numbered 148 in the List of Books Indexed, then by turning to page 186 of that book.

Variations, whether of song title or first line, are treated as separate entries; however, the most common variation is treated as the main entry and contains *see also* references to the other variations. Where there are more than four *see also* references, the main title entry is used instead of location codes. For example:

> The Little Dustman 71:52, *see also:* 125:90
> The Little Horses 189:90, *see also:* All the Pretty Little Horses

The SUBJECT INDEX lists song titles only, under more than 1,000 subject headings and cross references, alphabetically arranged. The subject headings and cross references allow the user to find songs in a very wide range of categories, such as

ACTION SONGS   HOLIDAYS
COOKS AND COOKING   INDIANS OF NORTH AMERICA
COWBOYS   OPERAS AND OPERETTAS
CHRISTMAS SONGS   SPIRITUALS
ELVES   TALL TALES
GAMES

For users who have less specific topics in mind as they begin a search for songs, the Subject Index is preceded by a separate section, the Broad Topic Guide to the Subject Index, which contains about forty-five more general catagories under which are listed relevant headings from the Subject Index.

In the Subject Index an asterisk precedes those song titles whose lyrics are in a foreign language. A song whose lyrics are both in its original language and in an English translation, will have not only a first-line entry for each version, but two title entries as well. For example:

> *Gille Beag, 'O/Little Lad, Oh 89:133
> *Little Lad, Oh/Gille Beag, 'O 89:133

In both the Title and First Line Index and the Subject Index, articles are retained at the beginning of entries but are disregarded in the alphabetizing. However, in the case of languages other than English, if a title or first line begins with an article, the entry is filed according to that article. Abbreviations are filed as if spelled in full; contractions are filed as one word; hyphenated words are filed as separate words. Entries beginning with O and Oh have been interfiled under Oh.

It should be noted that the spellings of titles and first lines always conform to the style in the collection indexed even when this departs from standard spelling: thus, Pretty Dolly Madison (instead of Dolley), and Robin Hood and Allen-A-Dale (instead of Allan-A-Dale).

INDEX TO CHILDREN'S SONGS should prove a practical reference tool for all those who wish to find the music or lyrics of songs for children and young people—librarians, teachers in elementary and secondary schools, music instructors, children's entertainers, camp counsellors, parents, and young people themselves. In particular, the wide range of headings in the Subject Index will be useful to anyone who must prepare programs for special occasions, whether in school or elsewhere.

CAROLYN SUE PETERSON
ANN D. FENTON

A List of Books Indexed

1. Abisch, Roz and Boche Kaplan. Sweet Betsy from Pike. Dutton, 1970.
2. Abisch, Roz. 'Twas in the Moon of Wintertime; the First American Christmas Carol. Prentice-Hall, 1969.
3. Adams, Adrienne. Bring a Torch Jeannette, Isabella. Scribner, 1963.
4. Adams, Pam. Old Macdonald Had a Farm. Grosset, 1976.
5. Adams, Pam. There Was an Old Lady Who Swallowed a Fly. Grosset, 1975.
6. Adams, Pam. This Old Man . . . Grosset, 1975.
7. Adshead, Gladys L. Seventeen to Sing. Oxford, 1946.
8. Alexander, Cecil Frances. All Things Bright and Beautiful. Scribner, 1962.
9. Aliki. Go Tell Aunt Rhody. Macmillan, 1974.
10. Aliki. Hush Little Baby; A Folk Lullaby. Prentice-Hall, 1968.
11. Antey, John W. Sing and Learn; Simple Songs and Rhythms That Retarded Children Can Enjoy While Learning Basic Lessons. Day, 1965.
12. d'Aulaire, Ingri and Edgar Parin d'Aulaire. The Star Spangled Banner. Doubleday, 1942.
13. Baker, Laura Nelson. The Friendly Beasts. Parnassus, 1957.
14. Bancroft, Jessie H. Games. Revised and Enlarged Edition of Games for the Playground, Home, School, and Gymnasium. Macmillan, 1937.
15. Bangs, Edward. Steven Kellog's Yankee Doodle. Parents' Magazine. 1976.
16. Berger, Donald P. Folk Songs of Japanese Children. Tuttle, 1968.
17. Bertail, Inez. Complete Nursery Song Book. Lothrop, 1954.
18. Bichel, Earl. How Many Strawberries Grow in the Sea? A Songbook of Mother Goose Rhymes. Follett, 1969.
19. Bierhorst, John. Songs of the Chippewa. Farrar, 1974.
20. Bley, Edgar S. The Best Singing Games for Children of All Ages. Sterling, 1959.
21. Boni, Margaret Bradford. The Fireside Book of Favorite American Songs. Simon, 1952.
22. Boni, Margaret Bradford. The Fireside Book of Folk Songs. Simon, 1947.
23. Bonne, Rose. I Know an Old Lady. Rand, 1961.
24. Botkin, B. A. A Treasury of American Folklore. Crown, 1944.
25. Boy Scouts of America. Boy Scout Songbook; Ballads of the Trail. Boy Scouts of America, 1970.
26. Boy Scouts of America. Cub Scout Songbook. Boy Scouts of America, 1969.

27. Brand, Oscar. Singing Holidays; The Calendar in Folk Song. Knopf, 1957.

28. Brand, Oscar. Songs of '76; A Folksinger's History of the Revolution. M. Evans, 1972.

29. Brand, Oscar. When I First Came to This Land. Putnam, 1974.

30. Broomfield, Robert. The Twelve Days of Christmas. McGraw-Hill, 1965.

31. Bryan, Ashley. Walk Together Children; Black American Spirituals. Atheneum, 1974.

32. Calvert, Captain James, USN. A Promise to Our Country. Whittlesey, 1961.

33. Carmer, Carl. America Sings; Stories and Songs of Our Country's Growing. Knopf, 1942.

34. Carryl, Charles Edward. A Capital Ship; or The Walloping Window-blind. Whittlesey, 1963.

35. Cazden, Norman. The Abelard Folk Song Book. Abelard, 1958. Part 1. Songs for Everyday

36. Part 2. Songs for Saturday Night

37. Chase, Richard. American Folk Tales and Songs and Other Examples of English-American Tradition as Preserved in the Appalachian Mountains and Elsewhere in the United States. Dover, 1956, 1971.

38. Chase, Richard. Billy Boy. Golden Gate Junior Books, 1966.

39. Chase, Richard. Hullabaloo and Other Singing Folk Games. Houghton, 1949.

40. Child, Lydia Maria. Over the River and Through the Wood. Coward, 1974.

41. Coleman, Satis N. and Alice G. Thorn. Singing Time; Songs for Nursery and School. Day, 1929.

42. Colum, Padraic. A Treasury of Irish Folklore. Rev. ed. Crown, 1962.

43. Conover, Chris. Six Little Ducks. Crowell, 1976.

44. Crofut, William. The Moon on the One Hand; Poetry in Song. Atheneum, 1975.

45. DeAngeli, Marguerite. Book of Favorite Hymns. Doubleday, 1963.

46. Depew, Arthur M. The Cokesbury Game Book. Rev. ed. Abingdon, 1960.

47. DeRegniers, Beatrice Schenk. Catch a Little Fox; Variations on a Folk Rhyme. Seabury, 1970.

48. Devlin, Harry. The Walloping Window Blind; An Old Nautical Tale. Van Nostrand, 1968.

49. Dietz, Betty Warner and Thomas Choonbai Park. Folk Songs of China, Japan, Korea. Day, 1964.

50. Di-George. The Twelve Days of Christmas. Heineman, 1967.

51. Domanska, Janina. Din Dan Don It's Christmas. Morrow, 1975.

52. Domanska, Janina. I Saw a Ship A-Sailing. Macmillan, 1972.

53. Domanska, Janina. If All the Seas Were One Sea. Macmillan, 1971.

54. Ehret, Walter. The International Book of Christmas Carols. Prentice-Hall, 1963.

55. Eisenberg, Helen and Larry Eisenberg. The Omnibus of Fun. Association Press, 1956.

56. Emberly, Ed. London Bridge Is Falling Down. Little, 1967.

57. Emberly, Barbara. One Wide River to Cross. Prentice-Hall, 1966.

58. Emberly, Barbara. Simon's Song. Prentice-Hall, 1969.

59. Engvick, William. Lullabies and Night Songs. Harper, 1965.

60. Felton, Harold W. Cowboy Jamboree: Western Songs and Lore. Knopf, 1951.

61. Fife, Austin E. and Alta S. Fife. Cowboy and Western Songs: A Comprehensive Anthology. Potter, 1969.

62. Fowke, Edith. Ring Around the Moon. Prentice-Hall, 1977.

63. Fowke, Edith. Sally Go Round the Sun; Three Hundred Children's Songs, Rhymes and Games. Doubleday, 1970.

64. Fowke, Edith and Joe Glazer. Songs of Work and Protest. Dover, 1960, 1973.

65. Gardner, Horace J. Let's Celebrate Christmas; Parties, Plays, Legends, Carols, Poetry, Stories. Ronald, 1940.

66. Garson, Eugenia. The Laura Ingalls Wilder Songbook; Favorite Songs from the "Little House" Books. Harper, 1968.

67. Gick, Georg J. and Marlys Swinger. Shepherd's Pipe Songs From the Holy Night: A Christmas Cantata for Children's Voices or Youth Choir. Rev. ed., 2nd ed. Plough, 1969.

68. Girl Scouts of the USA. Brownies' Own Songbook. Girl Scouts of America, 1968.

69. Girl Scouts of the USA. Girl Scout Pocket Songbook: For Juniors, Cadettes, Seniors and Leaders. Girl Scouts of America, 1956.

70. Girl Scouts of the USA. Skip to My Lou. Girl Scouts of America, 1958.

71. Girl Scouts of the USA. Sing Together. Girl Scouts of America, 1957.

72. Girl Scouts of the USA. Sing Together. 3rd ed. Girl Scouts of America, 1973.

73. Glass, Paul. Singing Soldiers (A History of the Civil War in Song). Grosset, 1975.

74. Glass, Paul. Songs and Stories of the North American Indians. Grosset, 1968.

75. Glazer, Tom. Eye Winker, Tom Tinker, Chin Chopper; Fifty Musical Fingerplays. Doubleday, 1973.

76. Glazer, Tom. On Top of Spaghetti. Grosset, 1966.

77. Goldstein, Rose B. Songs to Share. United Synagogue Book, 1949.

78. Gordon, Dorothy. Around the World in Song. Dutton, 1932.

79. Gordon, Dorothy. Sing It Yourself. Dutton, 1960.

80. Gordon, Margaret. A Paper of Pins. Seabury, 1975.

81. Graboff, Abner. Old MacDonald Had a Farm. Scholastic, 1970.

82. Gretz, Susanna. Ten Green Bottles. Puffin, 1976.

83. Harbin, E. O. The Fun Encyclopedia. Abingdon, 1968.

84. Hardendorff, Jeanne B. Sing Song Scuppernong. Holt, 1974.

85. Harewood, Countess of (Maria Donata) and Ronald Duncan. Classical Songs for Children. Potter, 1965.

86. Hartzler, Arlene and John Gaeddert. The Children's Hymnary. Faith and Life, 1968.
87. Hausman, Ruth L. Hawaii: Music in Its History. Tuttle, 1968.
88. Hawkinson, Lucy. That New River Train. Albert Whitman, 1970.
89. Haywood, Charles. Folk Songs of the World. Day, 1966.
90. Hazen, Barbara. Frere Jacques. Lippincott, 1973.
91. Heide, Florence Parry. Songs to Sing About Things You Think About. Day, 1971.
92. Henderson, York and others. Parents' Magazine's Christmas Holiday Book. Parents' Magazine. 1972.
93. Higgins, Don. Papa's Going to Buy Me a Mockingbird. Seabury, 1968.
94. Hoffmann, Hilde. The Green Grass Grows All Around. Macmillan, 1968.
95. Hogrogian, Nonny. The Thirteen Days of Yule. Crowell, 1968.
96. Horder, Mervyn. On Christmas Day: First Carols to Play and Sing. Macmillan, 1969.
97. Humpty Dumpty's Magazine. Little Songs for Little People. Parents' Magazine, 1968.
98. Hurd, Michael. Sailors' Songs and Shanties. Walck, 1965.
99. Hurd, Michael. Soldiers' Songs and Marches. Walck, 1966.
100. Ickis, Marguerite. The Book of Games and Entertainment the World Over. Dodd, 1969.
101. Ingzel, Marjorie. Table Graces for the Family. Nelson, 1964.
102. Ipcar, Dahlov. The Cat Came Back. Knopf, 1971.
103. Ivimey, John W. The Complete Version of Ye Three Blind Mice. Warne, 1909.
104. Jacobs, Frances E. Finger Plays and Action Rhymes. Lothrop, 1941.
105. Jeffers, Susan. All the Pretty Horses. Macmillan, 1974.
106. Jeffers, Susan. Three Jovial Huntsmen. Bradbury, 1973.
107. Jenkins, Ella. The Ella Jenkins Song Book for Children. Oak, 1966.
108. Johnson, James Weldon and J. Rosamond Johnson. Lift Every Voice and Sing: Words and Music. Hawthorne, 1970.
109. Jones, Bessie and Bess Lomax Hawes. Step It Down; Games, Plays, Songs, and Stories from the Afro-American Heritage. Harper, 1972.
110. Justus, May. The Complete Peddler's Pack: Games, Songs, Rhymes, and Riddles from Mountain Folklore. University of Tennessee Press, 1967.
111. Kapp, Paul. A Cat Came Fiddling and Other Rhymes of Childhood. Harcourt, 1956.
112. Kapp, Paul. Cock-A-Doodle-Doo! Cock-A-Doodle-Dandy! Harper, 1966.
113. Karasz, Ilonka. The Twelve Days of Christmas. Harper, 1949.
114. Kaufman, William I. UNICEF Book of Children's Songs. Stackpole, 1970.
115. Keats, Ezra Jack. Little Drummer Boy. Macmillan, 1968.
116. Keats, Ezra Jack. Over in the Meadow. Four Winds, 1971.

117. Keeping, Charles. Tinker, Tailor; Folk Song Tales. World, Brock-hampton Pr. 1968.

118. Keller, Charles. Glory, Glory, How Peculiar. Prentice-Hall, 1976.

119. Keller, Keith. The Mickey Mouse Club Scrapbook. Grosset, 1975.

120. Kellogg, Steven. There Was an Old Woman. Parents' Magazine, 1974.

121. Kent, Jack. Jack Kent's Twelve Days of Christmas. Parents' Magazine, 1973.

122. Key, Francis Scott. The Star-Spangled Banner. Crowell, 1966.

123. Klink, J. L. Bible for Children. Volume One: The Old Testament with Songs and Plays. Westminster, 1968-69.

124. Klink, J. L. Bible for Children. Volume Two: The New Testament with Songs and Plays. Westminster, 1968-69.

125. Knudsen, Lynne. Lullabies from Around the World. Follett, 1967.

126. Kraus, Richard G. Square Dances of Today, and How to Teach and Call Them. Ronald, 1950.

127. Krythe, Maymie R. Sampler of American Songs. Harper, 1969.

128. Landeck, Beatrice. More Songs to Grow On; A New Collection of Folk Songs for Children. Morrow, 1954.

129. Landeck, Beatrice. Songs to Grow On. Morrow, 1950.

130. Landeck, Beatrice and Elizabeth Crook. Wake Up and Sing! Folk Songs from America's Grass Roots. Morrow, 1969.

131. Langstaff, John. Frog Went A-Courtin'. Harcourt, 1955.

132. Langstaff, John. Gather My Gold Together. Doubleday, 1971.

133. Langstaff, John. The Golden Vanity. Harcourt. 1972.

134. Langstaff, John. Hi Ho the Rattlin' Bog: And Other Folk Songs for Group Singing. Harcourt, 1969.

135. Langstaff, John and Nancy Langstaff. Jim Along, Josie; A Collection of Folk Songs and Singing Games for Young Children. Harcourt, 1970.

136. Langstaff, John. Oh, A-Hunting We Will Go. Atheneum, 1974.

137. Langstaff, John. Ol' Dan Tucker. Harcourt, 1963.

138. Langstaff, John. On Christmas Day in the Morning! Harcourt, 1959.

139. Langstaff, John. Over in the Meadow. Harcourt, 1957.

140. Langstaff, John. The Season for Singing: American Christmas Songs and Carols. Doubleday, 1974.

141. Langstaff, John and Carol Langstaff. Shimmy Shimmy Coke-ca-Pop! A Collection of City Children's Street Games and Rhymes. Doubleday, 1973.

142. Langstaff, John. Soldier, Soldier, Won't You Marry Me? Doubleday, 1972.

143. Langstaff, John. The Swapping Boy. Harcourt, 1960.

144. Langstaff, John. Sweetly Sings the Donkey. Atheneum, 1976.

145. Langstaff, John. Two Magicians. Atheneum, 1973.

146. Larkin, Margaret. Singing Cowboy; A Book of Western Songs. Oak, 1963.

147. Larrick, Nancy. The Wheels of the Bus Go Round and Round. Golden Gate, 1972.

148. Leisy, James. Good Times Songbook. Abingdon, 1974.
149. Lenski, Lois. At Our House; A Read-and-Sing Book. Walck, 1959.
150. Lenski, Lois. Davy and His Dog. Walck, 1957.
151. Lenski, Lois. A Dog Came to School. Walck, 1955.
152. Lenski, Lois. I Like Winter. Walck, 1950.
153. Lenski, Lois. On a Summer Day. Walck, 1953.
154. Lenski, Lois. Songs of Mr. Small. Oxford, 1954.
155. Lenski, Lois. We Are Thy Children. Crowell, 1952.
156. Lenski, Lois. When I Grow Up; A Read-and-Sing Book. Walck, 1960.
157. Lloyd, Ruth and Norman Lloyd. American Heritage Songbook. American Heritage, 1969.
158. Lomax, John A. and Alan Lomax. Best Loved American Folk Songs (Folk Song: USA). Grosset, 1947.
159. Lomax, John A. and Alan Lomax. Cowboy Songs and Other Frontier Ballads. Rev. and enl. Macmillan, 1938.
160. Lyons, John Henry. Stories of Our American Patriotic Songs. Vanguard, 1958, 1942.
161. MacKay, Ruth. They Sang a New Song; Stories of Great Hymns. Abingdon, 1959.
162. McLaughlin, Roberta. The Small Singer. Bowmar, 1969.
163. Makeba, Miriam. The World of African Song. Quadrangle, 1971.
164. Malcolmson, Anne. Song of Robin Hood. Houghton, 1947.
165. Matterson, Elizabeth. Games for the Very Young. American Heritage, 1969.
166. Metz, Lois Lunt. Action Songs and Rhythms for Children. Denison, 1963.
167. Metz, Lois Lunt. Hop, Skip and Sing; A Collection of 25 Songs and Rhythms Based on the Interests and Activities of Children. Denison, 1959.
168. Millen, Nina. Children's Games from Many Lands. New and rev. ed. Friendship, 1965.
169. Miller, Carl S. Sing, Children, Sing; Songs, Dances and Singing Games of Many Lands and Peoples. Time Books, 1973.
170. Miller, Mitch. Sing Along With Mitch. Bernard Geis, 1961.
171. Mills, Alan. The Hungry Goat. Rand, 1964.
172. Milne, A. A. The Pooh Song Book. Dutton, 1961.
173. Milne, A. A. Fourteen Songs from "When We Were Very Young." Dutton, 1925
174. Milne, A. A. The Hums of Pooh. Dutton, 1930.
175. Mitchell, Donald. Every Child's Book of Nursery Songs. Crown, 1968, 1969. (Also Published as Faber Book of Nursery Songs.)
176. Mitchell, Donald and Roderick Biss. Gambit Book of Children's Songs. Gambit, 1970.
177. Mulac, Margaret E. The School Game Book. Harper, 1950.
178. Nelson, Esther L. Dancing Games for Children of All Ages. Sterling, 1973.
179. Nic Leodhas, Sorche. Always Room for One More. Holt, 1965.

180. Nic Leodhas, Sorche. Kellyburn Braes. Holt, 1968.
181. Nic Leodhas, Sorche. The Laird of Cockpen. Holt, 1969.
182. Nic Leodhas, Sorche. A Scottish Songbook. Holt, 1969.
183. Niles, John Jacob. Folk Carols for Young Actors. Holt, 1962.
184. Noble, T. Tertius. A Round of Carols. Walck, 1964.
185. Oberhansli, Trudi. Sleep, Baby, Sleep. Atheneum, 1967.
186. Paterson, A. B. Waltzing Matilda. Holt, 1970.
187. Pauli, Hertha. Silent Night; The Story of a Song. Knopf, 1943.
188. Poston, Elizabeth. The Baby's Song Book. Crowell, 1972.
189. Poston, Elizabeth. The Children's Song Book. Bodley Head, 1961.
190. Poston, Elizabeth. The Second Penguin Book of Christmas Carols. Penguin, 1970.
191. Poulsson, Emilie. Finger Plays for the Nursery and Kindergarten. Lothrop. 1921.
192. Price, Christine. One Is God. Warne, 1970.
193. Price, Christine. Widdecombe Fair; An Old English Folk Song. Warne, 1968.
194. Prieto, Mariana. Play It in Spanish; Spanish Games and Folk Songs for Children. Day, 1973.
195. Quackenbush, Robert. Clementine. Lippincott, 1974.
196. Quackenbush, Robert. Go Tell Aunt Rhody. Lippincott, 1973.
197. Quackenbush, Robert. The Holiday Song Book. Lothrop, 1977.
198. Quackenbush, Robert. The Man on the Flying Trapeze; The Circus Life of Emmett Kelly, Sr. Lippincott, 1975.
199. Quackenbush, Robert. Old MacDonald Had a Farm. Lippincott, 1972.
200. Quackenbush, Robert. Pop Goes the Weasel and Yankee Doodle. Lippincott, 1976.
201. Quackenbush, Robert. She'll Be Comin' Round the Mountain. Lippincott, 1973.
202. Quackenbush, Robert. Skip to My Lou. Lippincott, 1975.
203. Quackenbush, Robert. There'll Be A Hot Time in the Old Town Tonight. Lippincott, 1974.
204. Raebeck, Lois. Who Am I? Follett, 1970.
205. Raph, Theodore. The Songs We Sang; A Treasury of American Popular Music. Barnes, 1964.
206. Raposo, Joe and Jeffrey Moss. The Sesame Street Song Book. Simon, 1971.
207. Ray, Florence. Singing Days of Childhood; Songs, Poems, Finger Plays and Rhythms for the Young Child. Denison, 1958.
208. Read, Donald. Songs of the United Nations Singers. Dodd, 1965.
209. Reed, W. L. The Second Treasury of Christmas Music. Emerson, 1968.
210. Reed, W. L. The Treasury of Christmas Music. Emerson, 1961.
211. Rice, Dorothy. The Gypsy Laddie. Atheneum, 1972.
212. Ritchie, Jean. From Fair to Fair; Folk Songs of the British Isles. Walck, 1966.

213. Ritchie, Jean. Jean Ritchie's Swapping Song Book. Walck, 1964.
214. Robbins, Ruth. Baboushka and the Three Kings. Parnassus, 1960.
215. Robinson, Adjai. Singing Tales of Africa. Scribner, 1974.
216. Rockwell, Anne. El Toro Pinto and Other Songs in Spanish. Macmillan, 1971.
217. Rockwell, Anne. Savez-vous Planter les Choux? and Other French Songs. World, 1969.
218. Rodgers, Richard and Oscar Hammerstein. The Rodgers and Hammerstein Song Book. Simon, 1968. 2nd ed.
219. Rogers, Fred. Mister Rogers' Songbook. Random, 1970.
220. Roseberry, Eric. The Faber Book of Carols and Christmas Songs. Transatlantic, 1969.
221. Rounds, Glen. The Boll Weevil. Golden Gate, 1967.
222. Rounds, Glen. Casey Jones; The Story of a Brave Engineer. Golden Gate, 1968.
223. Rounds, Glen. The Strawberry Roan. Golden Gate, 1970.
224. Rounds, Glen. Sweet Betsy from Pike. Children's Pr. 1973.
225. Sackett, S. J. Cowboys and Songs They Sang. Scott, 1967.
226. Sandburg, Carl. The American Songbag. Harcourt, 1927.
227. Sanders, Mary A. Our Songs. Published by An Roos, Printed by Kipe-Dependable, 1968. (Dist. by Girl Scouts of America)
228. Schackburg, Richard. Yankee Doodle. Prentice-Hall, 1965.
229. Schreiter, Rick. The Derby Ram; A Ballad. Doubleday, 1969.
230. Seeger, Pete. American Favorite Ballads. Oak, 1961.
231. Seeger, Pete and Charles Seeger. The Foolish Frog. Macmillan, 1973.
232. Seeger, Ruth Crawford. American Folk Songs for Children in Home, School and Nursery School. Doubleday, 1948.
233. Seeger, Ruth Crawford. American Folk Songs for Christmas. Doubleday, 1953.
234. Seeger, Ruth Crawford. Animal Folk Songs for Children. Doubleday, 1950.
235. Sendak, Maurice. Maurice Sendak's Really Rosie. Harper, 1975.
236. Serwadda, W. Moses. Songs and Stories from Uganda. Crowell, 1974.
237. Seuss, Dr. The Cat in the Hat Song Book. Random, 1967.
238. Shideler, Ross. Staffan: An Old Christmas Folk Song. Parnassus, 1970.
239. Siegmeister, Elie. Work and Sing; A Collection of the Songs That Built America. Scott, 1944.
240. Silber, Irwin. Songs of Independence. Stackpole, 1973.
241. Simon, Henry W. A Treasury of Christmas Songs and Carols. 2nd ed. Houghton, 1973.
242. Slaughter, Jean. And It Came to Pass. Macmillan, 1971.
243. Smith, Edward. The Frogs Who Wanted a King. Four Winds, 1977.
244. Society of Brothers. Behold That Star; A Christmas Anthology. Plough, 1966.

245. Society of Brothers. Sing Through the Day. Plough, 1968.
246. Spier, Peter. The Erie Canal. Doubleday, 1970.
247. Spier, Peter. The Fox Went Out on a Chilly Night. Doubleday, 1961.
248. Spier, Peter. London Bridge Is Falling Down. Doubleday, 1967.
249. Spier, Peter. Star Spangled Banner. Doubleday, 1973.
250. Stobbs, William. A Frog He Would A-Wooing Go. Bodley Head, 1969.
251. Street, Julia M. Candle Love Feast. Coward, 1959.
252. Sullivan, Sir Arthur Seymour. Gilbert and Sullivan Song Book. Random, 1955.
253. Tashjian, Virginia A. Juba This and Juba That; Story Hour Stretches for Large or Small Groups. Little, 1969.
254. Tashjian, Virginia A. With a Deep Sea Smile; Story Hour Stretches for Large or Small Groups. Little, 1974.
255. Taylor, Mark. Bobby Shafto's Gone to Sea. Golden Gate, 1970.
256. Taylor, Mark. The Bold Fisherman. Golden Gate, 1967.
257. Taylor, Mark. Jennie Jenkins. Little, 1975.
258. Taylor, Mark. Old Blue, You Good Dog You. Golden Gate, 1970.
259. Taylor, Mark. The Old Woman and the Pedlar. Golden Gate, 1969.
260. Thomas, Marlo, et al. Free to Be . . . You and Me. McGraw, 1974.
261. Titra, Stephen. Be Nice to Spiders, Be Kind to Snakes. Hubbard, 1973.
262. Tobitt, Janet E. The Ditty Bag. Girl Scouts of America, Rev. 1960.
263. Troughton, Joanna. The Little Mohee; An Appalachian Ballad. Dutton, 1971.
264. Tudor, Tasha. Take Joy! The Tasha Tudor Christmas Book. World, 1966.
265. U.S. Committee for UNICEF. Hi Neighbor, Book I. United Nations, n.d.
266. U.S. Committee for UNICEF. Hi Neighbor, Book II. United Nations, n.d.
267. U.S. Committee for UNICEF. Hi Neighbor, Book III. United Nations, n.d.
268. U.S. Committee for UNICEF. Hi Neighbor, Book IV. Hastings, 1961.
269. U.S. Committee for UNICEF. Hi Neighbor, Book V. Hastings, 1962.
270. U.S. Committee for UNICEF. Hi Neighbor, Book VI. Hastings, 1963.
271. U.S. Committee for UNICEF. Hi Neighbor, Book VII. Hastings, 1964.
272. Van der Horst, Brian. Folk Music in America. Watts, 1972.
273. Vinson, Lee. The Early American Songbook. Prentice-Hall, 1974.
274. Von Schmidt, Eric. Come for to Sing. Houghton, 1963.
275. Walt Disney Productions. The Walt Disney Song Book. Golden, 1971.
276. Walt Disney Productions. Walt Disney's 50 Happy Years/ 50 Happy Songs; Disney Favorites. Charles Hansen, 1973.

277. Warner, James. Songs That Made America. Grossman, 1972.
278. Warren, Fred. The Music of Africa. Prentice-Hall, 1970.
279. Wasner, Franz. Trapp Family Book of Christmas Songs. Pantheon, 1950.
280. Watson, Nancy Dingman. Carol to a Child and a Christmas Pageant. World, 1969.
281. Watson, Wendy. Fisherman Lullabies. World, 1968.
282. Wenning, Elisabeth. Christmas Mouse. Holt, 1959.
283. Wessells, Katharine Tyler. The Golden Song Book. Golden, 1945.
284. Wheeler, Opal. Sing for Christmas. Dutton, 1943.
285. Wheeler, Opal. Sing Mother Goose. Dutton, 1945.
286. White, Florence and Kazuo Akiyama. Children's Songs from Japan. Edward B. Marks, 1960.
287. Wildsmith, Brian. The Twelve Days of Christmas. Oxford, 1972.
288. Wiltrout, Dorothea. Let's Sing and Play. Children's, 1959.
289. Winn, Marie. The Fireside Book of Children's Songs. Simon, 1966.
290. Winn, Marie. The Fireside Book of Fun and Game Songs. Simon, 1974.
291. Winn, Marie. What Shall We Do and Allee Galloo! Harper, 1970.
292. Yolen, Jane. The Fireside Song Book of Birds and Beasts. Simon, 1972.
293. Yolen, Jane. Rounds about Rounds. Watts, 1977.
294. Yulya. Bears Are Sleeping. Scribner, 1967.
295. Yurchenco, Henrietta. A Fiesta of Folk Songs from Spain and Latin America. Putnam, 1967.
296. Zeitlin, Patty. Castle in My City; Songs for Young Children. Golden Gate, 1968.
297. Zemach, Harve. Mommy, Buy Me a China Doll. Follett, 1966.
298. Zemach, Margot. Hush, Little Baby. Dutton, 1976.

Title and First Line Index

"A" alligators all around 235:39
A B C D E F G 17:41
A B C tumble down D 17:138
A Canoa Virou/My Little Boat 168:139
A Cantar a una Niña/To Teach a Young Girl to Sing 216:12
A–Cubbing We Will Go 26:46
A–Fishing 168:26
A–Gardening We Will Go 26:84
A–Hunting We Will Go 17:134, 63:36, 135:118, 136, 165:192, see also: 14:349, 20:82, 47
A is for axes, we very well know 35:12
A–Jump 162:105
A la Claire Fontaine/At the Spring of Sparkling Water 217:42
A la entrada del pueblo ya la salida 69:160, 216:18
A la Media Noche/At the Hour of Midnight 54:286
A la Niñita Nana 54:252, 279:108, see also: 89:161, 216:31
A la niñita, nanita 54:252, 89:161, see also: 216:31, 279:108
A la Puerta del Cielo/At the Gate of Heaven 72:142
A la Rue 277:149
A la ru-ru-ru, my baby dearest 279:106, see also: 54:308, 100:154
A la ru, ru, ru, my little boy 100:154, see also: 54:308, 279:106
A la rururu, my lovely Jesus 54:308, see also: 100:154, 279:106
A la rururu, niño chiquito 54:308, 100:154, 279:106
A la Víbora/To the Serpent 295:24
A mi burro a mi burro 289:64
A. R. U. 226:190
A–Roving 22:168, 36:24, 71:77, 72:78, 98:29, 176:34
A stands for Americans, who never will be slaves 28:36
A–Tisket, A–Tasket 20:51, 165:195, 238:20, 266:176, see also: 14:351, 17:106, 24:806, 63:11, 197:42
A-tisket, a-tasket, a green and yellow basket 20:51, 283:20, 289:176, see also: A–Tisket, A–Tasket
A vinticinc de Desembre, fum, fum, fum 89:162, see also: Fum, Fum, Fum
A–Walkin' and A–Talkin' 35:30

AB–C–DEF–GHI 206:10
Abalone 72:98, 226:333
Abdul, the Bulbul Ameer 226:344, see also: 25:34
The Abe-iad 73:50
Abe Lincoln he stood at the White House gate 73:64
Abe Lincoln was a citizen of very small reknown 73:50
Abelaph'amanpondo ayavuke kusen 163:65
Abena 114:41
Aber heidschi bumbeidschi, small brother 245:89
Abide With Me 25:114, 45:61
Ablakomba/Through My Window 89:188
Abolitionist Hymn 64:167
About a maiden I'll sing a song 290:186
About my Dixie, o won't you come and sing 69:40
About the age of sixteen, I joined a jolly band 33:234, see also: 159:359, 159:361
About the year of one, two, three 62:98
Above a plain of gold and green 262:63
Above is red, below is red 87:17
Above, on the Mountain/Da Droben Vom Berge 54:174
Above the world the winter stars 86:180
Abraham the Faithful 123:51
Abraham's Daughter 27:17, 73:102
Abram danced on Simhat Torah 77:46
Abuku tata nietataa 286:39
Accept Our Offering 86:194
Ach Ja 55:510, 83:495, see also: 178:30
Ach Yah! 178:30, see also: 55:510, 83:495
Acres of Clams 64:138
Across the Western Ocean 226:412
Across the wide ocean on good Christmas Eve 207:55
Ada Jones, Agnes Jones, Albert Jones 59:62
Adam Had Seven Sons 129:99, 232:174
Adams and Liberty 157:28
Adam's Fall 240:79, see also: 28:49
Adelita 226:300, 226:301
Adelita se llama la ingrata 226:301
Adelita's the name of the lady 226:300
Adeste Fideles/O Come All Ye Faithful 22:244, 54:318, 92:171, 148:266, 241:148, 279:18, 283:50, see also: O Come All Ye Faithful

INDEX TO CHILDREN'S SONGS

The Adopted Monkey/Le Singe Adopté 243:45

A'don Olom 25:120

Adoración/Adoration 89:55

Adoration/Adoración 89:55

Advent tells us Christ is near 86:161

Affair at Newport 28:114, *see also:* 240:155

After the Ball 21:35, 205:228

After the Ball Was Over (parody) 290:130

After the ball was over, she lay on the sofa and sighed 290:130

After the children and the shepherds 67:57

An Afternoon Like This 49:107

Afton Water 176:26, *see also:* 22:106, 205:95

Agatha Fry she made a pie 260:60

Age of Not Believing 276:65

An aged longhorn bovine lay dying on the river 61:310, *see also:* 159:325

Aguinaldo/"Mary," Said St. Joseph 140:28

Ah-a-a-a-a-a-h 237:unpaged

Ah! Ah! Ah! 89:224

Ah, ah you've come back 89:31

Ah, fun with music, fun with music 119:96

Ah got a hook and you got a line, Honey 21:106, *see also:* Crawdad

Ah, How the Moon Is Shining 262:69

Ah lu lu, lullaby, the stars are in the sky 125:23

Ah, My Belov'd Dunaii/Ai, Dunaii Moy 89:176

Ah-nee-nen-way-way ah-nee-nen-way-way 19:39

Ah! S'eeria it un lièvre au gite 243:16

Ah! si no fos p'es carreto 89:163

Ah! Vous Dirai-je, Maman/Oh! Shall I Tell You, Mother 217:12

Ah wune kune cha o wuni 69:15

Ah ya Zane, ah ya Zane 89:207

Ah yah, tair um bam, boo wah 226:455

Ah! your days are over, good horse 89:163

Ah'm goin' whah nobody knows my name 226:225

Ah'm gonna build mahself a raft 226:234

Ahora Voy a Cantarles/Now I'm Going to Sing 216:8

Ai, Dunaii Moy/Ah, My Belov'd Dunaii 89:176

Ai! Yeve lyang chu lai lyang wang wang 49:20

Aia la o Pele i Hawaii, ea 87:14

Aia O Pele I Hawaii/Pele Is at Hawaii 87:14

Aici l'estelo de Nadal 54:124

Aiken Drum 111:44, 162:36, 175:130, 188:104, 189:28, 289:96

Ain' Go'n to Study War No Mo' 226:480, *see also:* Down By the Riverside

Ain' No Mo' Cane on dis Brazis 158:320

Ainahau 87:40

Ainsi Font, Font, Font/They Do Like This 217:23

Ain't Gonna Rain 226:141

Ain't it a glorious day? Right as a mornin' in May 276:55

Ain't It a Shame? 148:10

Ain't It Hard to Be a Farmer 109:212

Ain't my brother or my sister, but it's me, oh Lord 148:350

Ain't That a Rocking All Night 233:42

The Air Force 27:126

Airplane, Airplane 154:28

Airplanes, airplanes all in a row 165:72

Aizu Komori Uta/Aizu Lullaby 49:22

Aizu Lullaby/Aizu Komori Uta 49:22

Ajaaj/Drum Song 89:31

Ajjamal Wanna/Caravan Song 89:244

Ajukkari tong baeka 49:41

Akai mosen shikitsumete 286:70

Akanyonyi 236:54

Akanyonyi kaabaze 236:34

Akela's Council 26:64

Akela's Pack 26:51

Akhsham Oldu/Behold the Sun 89:208

Al Animo/Cheer Up 194:24, *see also:* 168:112

Al animo, al animo, la fuente se rompio 168:112, 194:24

Al Canto de una Laguna/At the Edge of a Lagoon 216:22

Al Olivo Subí/I Climbed the Olive Tree 216:26

Al pasar el arroyo de Santa Clara 295:68

Al Quebrar la Piñata/On Breaking the Piñata 295:79

Al Ya Zane/Oh Thou Zane 89:207

The *Alabama* 73:186

The *Alabama* and *Kearsarge* 73:189

Alabama Bound 230:44

Alabama Girl 126:107

The Alabama's gone, hurrah, to "Davy Jones' Locker" far 73:189

Alas! my love, you do me wrong 72:108, 148:142, 176:20, 189:98, 205:18, 261:52, 262:80

Alaska, or Hell of the Yukon 61:83

Alegría/Happily Singing 54:293

Algy met a bear; the bear met Algy 144:19

Ali, Alo 72:130

Ali, alo for Maschero ali, ali, alo 72:130

Alicante hasucedido la torre 216:7

Alice B. 226:28

Alice in Wonderland 275:47

Alice in Wonderland, how do you get to Wonderland 275:47

Alknomook 273:114, *see also:* 61:116

All around the British marched 200, *see also:* Pop! Goes the Weasel

2

All around the cobbler's bench 17:136, 66:72, 75:64, 135:115, 157:45, 205:132, 283:33, 289:100, 292:88, *see also:* Pop! Goes the Weasel

All Around the Kitchen 128:100, 130:44, 232:94, 291:6

All Around the Maypole 83:492

All at Once You Love Her 218:286

All By Myself 204:25

All clap your hands! One two three! 204:11

All Creatures of Our God and King 161:29

All day, all night you hear them say 130:23

All day long on the prairie in the saddle I ride 146:132, *see also:* 60:90, 159:67

All day on the prairie in the saddle I ride 159:67, *see also:* 60:90, 146:132

All day o'er the prairies alone I ride 61:332

All for Baby 191:40

All Glory, Laud, and Honor 22:294, 86:56, 161:106

All God's Children Got Shoes 148:14, *see also:* 25:103, 31:9, 129:16

All God's Chillun Got Wings 129:16, *see also:* 25:103, 31:9, 148:14

All good children now are sleeping 241:223

All Good Gifts Around Us 86:197

All hail, superior sex, exalted fair 28:109

All Hail the Power of Jesus' Name 22:283, 25:116, 157:32

All hail to the days that merit more praise 158:32

All Hail to the Morning 140:82

All Hid 109:185

All I want in this creation 158:96

All in the wood there was a tree 27:90, *see also:* Green Grass Grows All Around

All Is Silent 71:112, 72:168, 293:84

All mein Gedanken, die ich hab, die sind bei dir 22:114

All Men Are Brothers 77:20

All music has such silver ways 85:224

All My Heart This Night 54:59, 184:50

All Night, All Day 55:278, 69:28

All Night Long 226:448, *see also:* 53:136

All of Us 149:6

All our land is draped in mourning 73:72

All out on the railroad, 's all out on the sea 134:39, 213:36

All people give greetings to friends on the street 162:72

All people that on earth do dwell 45:7, 86:125

All Poor Men and Humble 96:1, 244:96

All praise to Thee, my God, this night 86:170, *see also:* 71:106, 72:51, 176:104, 189:60

All Quiet Along the Potomac Tonight 73:197, 157:132

All secretly the moon comes up 189:144

All the Blue Bonnets Are Over the Boarder 66:50

All the Boys in Our Town 63:69

All the dames of France are fond and free 205:27, *see also:* 42:604, 61:171, 66:112

All the Ducks 135:25, *see also:* 227:37

All the ducks are swimming in the water 135:25, 227:37

All the Fish Are Swimming in the Water 128:30, 130:100

All the fish are swimming in the water 162:85

All the Pretty Li'l Horses 59:42, *see also:* All the Pretty Little Horses

All the Pretty Little Horses 105, 129:53, 158:14, 277:23, 289:22, *see also:* 59:42, 176:54, 188:136, 189:90, 232:178

All the singing, ringing sounds have made my heart aglow 67:45

All the World Is Sleeping 125:70

All-the-Year-Carol 189:78, *see also:* 220:94

All Things Bright and Beautiful 8, 45:32, 86:11

All Things Must Perish 293:6, *see also:* 62:20, 69:50

All Things on Earth 62:20, *see also:* 69:50, 293:6

All things shall perish from under the sky 69:50, *see also:* 62:20, 293:6

All together, here we go, clap, clap, clap 68:9

All Through the Night 21:337, 59:20, 125:72, 205:60, 289:26

All thy wonders are far beyond telling 87:71

All up and down, my honey, all up and down we go 24:810

All Ye Jolly Huntsmen 212:22

All you that pass along, give ear unto my song 36:72

Alla en el rancho grande 216:23

Alle elsker Lordag asten 148:84

Alle Jahre Wieder/As Each Happy Christmas 86:44, 279:70

Alle Jahre wieder Kommt das Christuskind 86:44, 279:70

Allee Allee-o 39:46, 135:54, 289:182, *see also:* 63:37, 165:113, 291:16

Allee Galloo 291:72

Alleluia 55:255, 86:150, 241:224 (*Alleluia, Alleluia, Alleluia*)

Alleluia 86:134 (*Alleluia, alleluia, Amen, Amen*)

Alleluia, Alleluia, Alleluia! The Spring, the Spring again is here 189:68, *see also:* 27:54

Alleluia, alleluia, Amen, Amen 86:134
Allelujah 55:254, 71:14, 72:175, 101:33
Allelujah, Allelujah, Amen, Amen 55:254, 71:14, 72:175, 101:33
Alleluya, alleluya! O praise Him, o praise Him 262:156
Alles Schweiget 293:84
Alligator, hedgehog, anteater, bear 234:80, 289:41
Alligators All Around 235:39
Allons enfants de la patrie 64:183, *see also:* 22:223
Ally Bally 135:35
Almost Day 130:41 *(Christmas is coming and its almost day)*
Almost Day 233:76 *(Chicken crowing for midnight)*
Almost Done 158:324
Aloha Oe/Farewell to Thee 87:99
Alone on the prairie at the dawn of early day 207:122
Alone with my herd, when the day becomes long 68:21
Along the Hwang-no River where young men walk and dream 218:314
Alouette 20:84, 22:124, 25:90, 26:24, 23:68, 148:18, 262:73
Alphabet in the Air 112:35
Alphabet Song 17:41
Alpine Song 245:8
Als Ich Bei Meinen Schafen Wacht/While By My Sheep I Watched at Night 54:146, 241:136
Although You Are Still Weak and Helpless/Quoique Soyez Petit Encore 54:116
Always Room for One More 179
Am I a Soldier of the Cross? 66:138
Am Weihnachtsbaum die Lichter Brennen/The Christmas Tree With Its Candles Gleaming 54:150
Amampondo/Pondo Man 163:65
Amazing Grace 148:20, 157:56, 158:344, 272:10
Amazing grace (how sweet the sound) 148:20, 157:56, 158:344, 272:10
Ambo, ato, matarile, rile, rile 169:60, 269:38, 295:37
America 273:154 *(Amid surrounding foes)*
America 25:44, 26:88, 66:90, 69:4, 71:4, 72:32, 127:73, 148:22, 157:118, 160:32, 197:76 *(My country, 'tis of thee)*
America 240:49 *(To thee the tuneful anthem soars)*
America, Commerce, and Freedom 273:118
America the Beautiful 25:46, 26:86, 37:34, 69:2, 71:5, 72:24, 127:184, 148:24, 128:216, 160:70, 161:35, 197:74, 205:351
America, thou fractious nation 28:31

An American Frigate 27:124, 28:123
An American frigate, a frigate of fame 240:132, *see also:* 35:16
An American frigate called Richard by name 27:124, 28:123
An American frigate from Baltimore came 35:16, *see also:* 240:132
American "Heart of Oak" 273:38
The American Hero 240:115, 273:40
American Rule Britannia 240:58
American Taxation 28:4, 240:36
American Vicar of Bray 240:157
America's flag of red, white and blue 207:83
Amid surrounding foes Thou dost my table spread 273:154
Amid the Roses Mary Sits 209:59
Among the Little White Daisies 110:48
Anacreontic Song 273:88
Anatomical Song 129:118
An ancient long-horned bovine 159:325, *see also:* 61:310
And are ye sure the news is true? 176:38, 262:138
And as, my friend, you ask me what makes me sad and still 159:125, *see also:* 61:218, 146:120
And did those feet in ancient time 64:182
And God Said 86:6
And I Ran Away/Et Moi de M'Encourir 217:61
And it's ladies to the center, and it's gents around the row 158:103, *see also:* 61:272, 61:273, 61:274
And now, May the Great Master of all Scouts 26:94
And so you ask me, little friend, why I am silent, sad and still 61:218, *see also:* 146:120, 159:125
And there were in the same country shepherds abiding in the field 209:70
And Thou Shalt Love 77:30
And We Hunted and We Hunted 234:36, *see also:* 27:62, 106, 128:122, 292:190
And when the Child was born at Bethlehem, where he lay 241:100
Angan Phuli/Jasmine Flower in Bloom 89:218
Angel Band 233:74
The Angel Gabriel 220:72, 241:42, *see also:* 209:33
The Angel Gabriel from God was sent to Galilee 241:42, *see also:* 209:33, 220:72
The Angel Gabriel from Heaven Came 209:33, 220:72, *see also:* 241:42
The angel voice that bids you "good-night" 276:31
Angelina Baker 157:92

Angels and Shepherds 220:100, *see also:* 54:236, 279:116

Angels From Heaven/Menyböl Ar Angyal 54:240

Angels, from the Realms of Glory 45:21, 54:49, 96:2, 148:28, 210:12, 241:144, 264:118

Angels O'er the Fields Were Singing/Les Anges Dan Nos Campagnes 54:96, *see also:* 241:102, 279:89

The Angels' Song 126:22

Angels We Have Heard on High 22:234, 92:144, 241:102, 264:120, 279:89, 284:123

Angelus ad Virginem/Carol of the Annunciation 189:70

The Angler's Song 189:120

The Animal Fair 25:38, 26:17, 62:33, 226:348, 289:152, 292:188, *see also:* 254:121

The Animal Song 234:80, 289:41

The Animals Go to Sleep 41:14

The Animals Wake Up 41:15

Anio/On to War 89:32

Anio! Anio! Anio! Anio! 89:32

Anna Elise 112:3

Anna Elise, she jump'd with surprise 112:3

Annem kuyudan 266:57

Annie Breen 159:225

Annie Laurie 22:110, 205:85

Annie the Miller's Daughter 20:19

Anong laking hirap kung pakaiisipin 89:296

Another good cow-puncher has gone to meet his fate 159:82

Another Man Done Gone 158:326

The Answers 59:38

The Ant and the Grasshopper/La Fourmi et la Sauterelle 243:34, *see also:* 79:65

The ant-workers yonder dwell, ever dwell 89:309

Antagata Dakosa?/Where Do You Come From? 286:50

Anthem of the ILGWU 64:78

Anthony Wayne 28:126, *see also:* 240:100

The Ants Come Marching 63:82, 118:24, *see also:* 147:10

The Ants Go Marching One By One 147:10, *see also:* 63:82, 118:24

Anton, Anton, Anton Firulero 114:75

Anton Firulero 114:75

Anyone can be a fool and do things which are wrong 119:108

Anything Can Happen Day 119:100

Anytime Perica wishes that her husband go to meeting 262:18

Apple blossoms pink and white 207:94

The Apple-Cheeked Rider 154:120

Apple Dumplings 166:22

The Apple Tree 189:58 *(This beauty doth all things excel)*

Apple Tree 41:17 *(Apple tree, big apple tree)*

The Apple Tree/Pliot Mola Lule 89:193 *(The apple tree, with white blossoms)*

Apple tree, big apple tree 41:17

The apple tree with white blossoms 89:193

The apple trees are standing with their trunks so brown 41:43

The Apples 227:10

Apples mellow, pumpkins yellow 86:183

Apples, peaches, bananas, who'll come and buy 41:40

April Rain 97:unpaged

Aquí bien lejos, Aquí bien lejos de nuestra patria 89:98

Ar go eat you wan 215:50

Ar-Rouzana 157:35

Arbor Day Song 197:49

The ardent, romantic, the charming god of song 157:102

Are matsumushiga naite iru 286:30

Are you in a box? No, I'm Not! 204:9

Are You Sleeping 25:31, 26:42, 62:11, *see also:* Frère Jacques

Are you sleeping, are you sleeping 17:72, 25:31, 26:42, 62:11, 90, 148:102, 289:186, *see also:* Frère Jacques

Arirang 49:40, 72:153, 114:22

Arise, arise you pretty fair maid 212:76

Arise, ye sons of France to glory 64:183, *see also:* 22:223

The Arizona Boys and Girls 159:256

Arizona Home 61:296

Arkansas Traveler 22:58

Armenian Lullaby 125:130

The Army Bean 73:168, *see also:* 99:47

Arnold Is as Brave a Man 24:55

Aroi, aroi, aroi, aroi, di aroi 89:295

Aroi Toyong/Oh, Beloved 89:295

Around, around, around in the circle let us go 266:36

Around, around our circle runs a pointed Elfin Cap 245:56

Around her neck she wore a yellow ribbon 170:22

Around the Campfire Bright 25:121

Arre, Burriquito/Hurry, Little Donkey 295:75

Arroyo Claro/Clear-Running Stream 188:62

Arroz Con Leche 168:136, *see also:* 216:10, 295:28

As Collinet and Phebe sat, beneath a poplar grove 273:82

As Cub Scouts we'll always be happy 26:50

As Each Happy Christmas/Alle Jahre Wieder 86:44, 279:70

As evening fell, they said to Him 124:147

As Farmer John from his work came home 62:34, *see also:* 71:94

As Granny arose in the morning so soon 28:7

As I came in by Tara Market 212:86

As I came down the Bowery one evening in July 22:160

As I came down the new cut road 33:82, *see also:* Old Dan Tucker

As I came over yonder hill 234:46

As I came past by Garrick, and by the bridge of Dee 262:45

As I came through Sandgate 135:16, 262:68, *see also:* 89:302

As I came to Sandgate, to Sandgate, to Sandgate 89:302, *see also:* 135:16, 262:68

As I 'rived in St. Louis on April the tenth 35:52, *see also:* 129:90, 130:64, 148:314, 274:12

As I rode down to Laredo, Laredo 225:56, *see also:* Streets of Laredo

As I rode out in the streets of Laredo 272:18, *see also:* Streets of Laredo

As I rode over London low, it's there I heard the news 37:179

As I Roll My Rolling Ball 262:49

As I Roved Out 212:72

As I sat on a sunny bank 140:25, 190:128, 233:79, *see also:* I Saw Three Ships

As I strolled out one morning all in the bloom of spring 35:22

As I walked down the new-cut road 24:905

As I walked forth in my father's garden 35:32, *see also:* 213:60, 226:68

As I walked one rainy morn' 89:209

As I walked out by de light ob de moon 78:91

As I walked out in Petticoat Lane 35:98, *see also:* 22:26, 37:112

As I walked out in the streets of Laredo 21:212, 24:859, 148:362, 158:206, 159:417, 226:263, 230:41, *see also:* Streets of Laredo

As I Walked Out One Holiday 232:89

As I Walked Out One May Morning 27:106

As I walked out one morning along the highway 35:91

As I Walked Through London City 134:60

As I was a-gwine on down the road 22:66, 226:94, *see also:* 20:72, 126:48

As I was a-ridin' one mornin' for pleasure 24:853, 292:41, *see also:* Git Along Little Dogies

As I was a-ridin' the streets of Laredo 277:61, *see also:* Streets of Laredo

As I was a-walkin' down Paradise Street 226:404, *see also:* Blow the Man Down

As I was a-walking along the seashore 27:236, *see also:* 24:824, 37:128, 61:135, 263

As I was a walking, one morning for pleasure 71:86, 197:81, 226:268, *see also:* Git Along Little Dogies

As I walked out one morning for pleasure 61:207, 159:6, *see also:* Git Along Little Dogies

As I was goin' to Ballynure, the day I well remember 42:593

As I Was Going to Banbury 134:88

As I was going to Darby 27:60, 229, 292:49, *see also:* 37:134, 62:36, 129:44, 234:58

As I was going up London Hill 291:15, *see also:* 135:122

As I Was Going Up Pippin Hill 18:14, 112:15

As I Was Going Up the Hill 18:40, *see also:* 111:79

As I Was Going Up the Stairs 112:38

As I was lumb'ring down de street 24:841, 128:80, 157:86, 205:119, *see also:* Buffalo Gals

As I was out walking, a-rambling one day 61:6, *see also:* 159:183

As I was out walking alone one fine day 263, *see also:* 24:824, 27:236, 37:128, 61:135

As I was out walking for pleasure one day 61:135, *see also:* 24:824, 27:236, 37:128, 263

As I was out walking one morning for pleasure 225:18, *see also:* Git Along Little Dogies

As I was passing by Tom Sherwin's bar room 61:322, *see also:* Streets of Laredo

As I was snapping out broncs on the old Flying U 61:189, *see also:* 61:187, 223, 225:32

As I was walking down by the seaside 292:172

As I was walking down the road 110:20

As I was walking down the street, down the street, down the street 63:12, 148:50, 230:34, *see also:* Buffalo Gals

As I was walking down the street, heigh-ho, heigh-ho, heigh-ho 165:182, 178:24, *see also:* 283:41

As I was walking down the street, Heigh-o! Heigh-o! Heigh-o! 283:41, *see also:* 165:182, 178:24

As I was walking down the street one dark and dreary day 147:44

As I Was Walkin' Down Wexford Street 226:35

As I was walking on the quay, Hoo-dah to my hoo-dah 262:38

As I Was Watching By My Sheep 244:274

As I went a-walking all by the seashore 24:824, *see also:* 27:236, 37:128, 61:135, 263

As I went a-walking one morning in May 36:92

As I went down to Darby Town 37:134, 129:44, *see also:* Darby Ram

As I went down to Derbyshire 62:36, *see also:* Darby Ram

As I went down to Louisville some pleasure for to find 61:153

As I went lumb'ring down the street, down the street, down the street 66:58, *see also:* Buffalo Gals

As I went out one morning to take the morning air 36:52, 37:138, 148:232, 158:46, 277:71

As I went out sailing 'twas in the spring time 37:128, *see also:* 24:824, 27:236, 61:135, 263

As I went over London Hill 135:122, *see also:* 291:15

As I went to market, on one market day 234:58, *see also:* Darby Ram

As I went up the mountainside 241:52

As it fell on an holy day 79:47

As it fell out on a sun-shining day 164:52

As it was rather warm, I thought the other day 73:136

As Joseph Was A-Walking 86:36, 220:68, 241:46, 279:44

As Lately We Watched/Die Hirten auf dem Felde 54:170

As long as deep within the heart the soul of Judea is turbulent and strong 22:194

As Mary and Joseph were a-walking the green 232:182, *see also:* Cherry Tree Carol

As near beauteous Boston lying 240:52

As Pants the Hart 45:24

As shepherds in Jewry were guarding their sheep 140:92, 190:108, *see also:* 233:32

As the blackbird in the spring beneath the willow tree 205:396, *see also:* 73:234

As the Frightened Baby Jesus/Como Busca el Tierno Infante 54:298

As the Sun Goes Down 72:144

As Tommy Snooks and Bessie Brooks 111:77

As Tommy was walking one fine summer's day 62:89

As we come marching, marching in the beauty of the day 64:70

As we greet each Easter morn 167:20

As we sailed on the water blue, Whisky Johnny! 226:403, *see also:* 21:246, 98:24

As we work we sing a song 25:90, *see also:* 64:106, 69:49, 148:424, 290:196

As With Gladness Men of Old 54:48, 210:13

As you go through yonder town, Rose Marie and thyme 37:112, *see also:* 22:26, 35:98

As you look at the picture that hangs on the wall 61:184, *see also:* 60:82, 128:46, 146:116, 159:356

As you walk, my dearest dear, and you lend to me your hand 61:273, *see also:* 61:272, 61:274, 158:103

Aserrin, aserran, all the woodsmen of San Juan 262:17

Aserrin, aserran, los maderos de San Juan 262:17

The Ash Grove 55:258, 71:36, 72:124, 176:14

The Ash-grove how graceful, how plainly 'tis speaking 55:258, 176:14, *see also:* 71:36, 72:124

Assembled round the patriots grave 273:74

Astonishing, Astonishing 91:10

Astri, Mi Astri/Astri, My Astri 208:49

Astri, My Astri/Astri, Mi Astri 208:49

At a Cowboy Dance 61:287

At a Georgia Camp Meeting 21:45

At dawn of day, I met them on the way 241:105, *see also:* 54:126

At dawn of day I saw a man stand by a grog saloon 226:104, 277:131

At evening when I go to bed 245:99

At Halloween 207:24

At his post the Little Major dropp'd his drum that battle-day 73:194

At midnight when cattle are sleeping 61:327, 159:122

At Summer Morn 262:125

At summer morn the merry lark heralds in the day 262:125

At the Beach 207:129

At the bottom of the tub hides my cake of soap 91:46

At the Crèche 140:18, *see also:* 54:282

At the Dawn of Easter Day 86:64

At the Door a Babe Is Knocking 209:9

At the Edge of a Lagoon/Al Canto de una Laguna 216:46

At the end of this my day, Lord 155:28

At the entrance of the city 216:45

At the foot of yon mountain, where the fountain doth flow 159:181, *see also:* 37:152, 61:161

At the Foot of Yonder Mountain 37:152, *see also:* 61:161, 159:181

At the foot of yonder mountain where often lay snow 61:161, *see also:* 37:152, 159:181

At the Gate of Heaven/A la Puerta del Cielo 72:142

At the Gates of Heaven Above/Sus in Poarta
Raiului   54:238
At the Hour of Midnight/A la Media Noche
54:286
At the Lemonade Stand   166:44
At the Spring of Sparkling Water/A la Claire
Fontaine   217:62
At their father's gate, they stand   89:176
*At thy door I'm knocking, by the pale moon-
light*   22:74, *see also:* Au Clair de la Lune
At Willie's wedding on the green   182:50
At Work Beside His Father's Bench   86:51
Atago mountain, Huhai, huhai, huhata
49:29
Atago yama, Huhai, huhai, huhata   49:29
Attention, pray give, while of hobbies I sing
240:183
Au Clair de la Lune   22:74, 71:69, 148:30,
188:40, 217:13, 283:57, *see also:* 217:54
Au fond d'un puits par aventure   243:38
*Auf, auf nun, ehs Hiarten, nid schlaft's ma
so lang*   54:170
Auf dem Berge da gehet der Wind   279:74,
see also: 241:86
Auf dem Berge da Weht der Wind   241:86,
see also: 279:74
Auf einem Baum ein Kuckuck   20:86
Auf Wiedersehen, My Dear   170:59
Auhea wale oe E ke aloha la   87:66
Auld Lang Syne   22:76, 25:89, 27:2, 46:207,
148:32, 170:62, 197:10, 205:50, 290:216
The Auld Man   182:41
Aunt Hessie's White Horse/Tant Hessie Se
Witperd   189:140
Aunt Jemima   46:226
Aunt Jemima, look at uncle Jim   46:226
Aunt Rhody   230:45, *see also:* Go Tell Aunt
Rhody
Auntie Nextdoor/Tonari-no Obasan
286:48
Auprès de Ma Blonde/Near to My Fair One
21:340
Aura Lee   73:234, 205:396
Aurelia's charms and magic art   157:100
Australia   71:34
Australia, my lads, is a very fine place
71:34
Automation   64:146
Autumn   86:183
Autumn Dance   162:42
Autumn Is Here   245:109
*Autumn is here and the leaves are all chang-
ing*   245:109
Autumn leaves are falling down   77:50
The Autumn Leaves Have Fallen Down
165:61
Autumn Nights By the River   261:40
Autumn Song   77:50 (*Autumn leaves are
falling down*)

Autumn Song   227:22 (*From the boughs
o'er head the leaves are floating down*)
Autumn Voices   72:136
Autumn, winter, summer, spring   245:106
Autumn's Message   207:27
*Aux risques de l'orage pourquoi vous expos-
er?*   243:2
Avalon   170:49
Ave Maria (Mozart)   241:225
Aw nw aa ja aa hajee   89:31
Awake   233:62
Awake, Awake   35:3
Awake, awake, oh, pretty maid   128:70, *see
also:* 27:102, 134:31, 213:80
Awake, awake, ye drowsy sleepers   35:3
Awake, my soul, to joyful lays   233:62
Away, away, we're bound for the mountain
292:103
Away down South where grows the cotton
73:11
Away down yonder in the Yankety Yank
290:164, *see also:* 147:38, 231
Away in a Manger   45:19, 54:60, 65:89,
86:35, 92:146, 96:3, 125:102, 140:85,
156:50, 190:52, 210:15, 241:166, 264:110,
279:54, 283:49, 284:23
*Away out in old Texas, that great Lone Star
State*   159:116
Away to Rio   78:9, *see also:* 22:140, 176:110,
239:14
Away up high in the Sierry Petes   61:202,
146:76, *see also:* 225:52
Away with These Self-Loving Lads   85:29
Awo   236:42
Ay, Chiapanecas, ay, ay!   162:107
*Aye-aye-aye-aye, in China they never grow
chilly*   290:100
Aye ban a farmer in Minnesota   64:110
Aye, Wakin' O!   182:25
Ayer salio la lancha Nueva Esparta   216:4
Ayo ay, oh baby don't you cry   114:44
Azert Hogy én Huszár Vagyok/Look at Me,
a Gallant Hussar   89:187

B

B for Barney   134:16
Baa, Baa, Black Sheep   17:147, 175:84,
188:102, 189:20, 283:24, 285:49
The Babe   54:308, *see also:* 100:154,
279:106
The Babe in Bethl'em's Manger   220:54, *see
also:* 241:28
The Babe in Bethlehem's manger laid
220:54, 241:28
A Babe Is Born   209:46, 241:39

Babe of Bethlehem   140:74, 190:37, 233:37
The Baboon Climbs the Hill   292:213, *see also:* 289:52
The baboon climbs the hill with a sickle tail   289:52, 292:213
Baboushka   214
Baboushka sits before the fire upon a winter's night   214
The Baby and the Moon   125:36
Baby born in Bethlehem, oh, when I get in glory   233:34
Baby Born Today   190:142, 233:28, *see also:* 67:28, 140:56
The Baby Bumblebee   63:135
Baby Bunting   59:33, *see also:* Bye Baby Bunting
Baby Bye, Here's a Fly   59:74
Baby Dear   232:141
Baby dear, baby dear, don't you cry   232:141
A Baby in the Cradle/Ein Kindlein in der Wiegen   43:178
Baby Mine   114:60
Baby mine, a star is peeping in the sky   41:48
The Baby Prune   63:134
Baby-Sitter Sense   166:50
Baby Sitter's Lullaby/Vigndig A Fremd Kind   289:32
Baby-sitters must use lots of sense   166:50
Baby's Birthday   125:12
Back in the Saddle Again   25:70
Back of the Bread   72:44
Back of the bread is the flour and back of the flour is the mill   72:44
Back there, behind my father's, Lon la, londigga, da   188:110
Backward, turn backward, film guy in your flight   61:313
Backward, turn backward oh time in thy flight   66:28
Backward, turn backward, oh time with your wheels   61:313
The Bad Boy   159:161
Bad Faith/Whai Lyang Shin   49:17
Bad Man from the Brazos   159:138, *see also:* 61:104
Bad news has come to town—bad news is carried   158:118, *see also:* 240:33, 273:16
The Baffled Knight   176:58
Bafti Hindi   89:206, 114:52
Bahyahn Mongol/Rich Mongolia   208:45
Bailando el Gato/Dancing the Gato   89:88
Baile de los Pollos/The Chicken Dance   194:30
Baile de Nadal   89:162, *see also:* Fum, Fum, Fum
The Bailiff's Daughter of Islington   71:37
Bajabula Bonke/I Became Ill   163:95

The Baker-Girl/La Panaderita   216:45, *see also:* 89:160
The Baker Maiden/La Panaderita   89:160, *see also:* 216:45
Bakhchalarda/In My Garden   89:178
Baking Apples   41:9
Bali Ha'i   218:142
The Ball/El Baile   208:62
Ballad of Billy the Kid   61:266, 61:268, 159:140
Ballad of Bunker Hill   240:114
Ballad of Chicken Soup   235:56
Ballad of Davy Crockett   275:90, 276:86
Ballad of Jane McCrea   28:96
Ballad of Jesus Christ/Ballade de Jésus Christ   54:114
Ballad of Sergeant Champe   28:150, *see also:* 240:107, 273:52
Ballad of the American War   240:170
Ballad of Trenton   26:86, *see also:* 240:121
Ballade de Jésus Christ/Ballad of Jesus Christ   54:114
Ballet of the Boll Weevil   21:81, 226:252, *see also:* Boll Weevil
Ballinderry   42:596, 134:66
Balloons for Sale   162:68
Ballynure Ballad   42:593
Baloo, Lammy   54:56, 241:14, *see also:* 125:64
Baloo Loo, Lammy   125:64, *see also:* 54:56, 241:14
Balulalow/A Cradle Song   210:88
Bam Chi, Chi, Bam   130:102
Bamboo Fairies   68:36
Bamboo fairies in the tree   68:36
Bamboo leaves are swayed by the breeze   286:81
Banana Bird   63:139
Banbury Ale   290:194
The Band   162:66
Band of Angels   129:54
A band of sweet blue violets all on an April day   227:8
The Band Played On   205:245
Bang Bang Bang   290:218
The Banks of Sacramento   226:112, *see also:* 33:210
The Banks of Sweet Dundee   35:24
The Banks of the Dee   28:74, 240:61, 273:30
The Banks of the Dee (parody)   240:62, 273:32, *see also:* 28:77
The Banks of the Little Eau Pleine   157:42
The Banks of the Sacramento   33:210, *see also:* 226:112
Barbara Allen   22:104, 157:69, 176:115, 169:21, 272:11, *see also:* 21:316, 24:820, 66:122, 226:56, 230:79

Barbary Allen   66:122, *see also:* Barbara Allen
Barbra Allen   226:56, *see also:* Barbara Allen
Barb'ry Ellen   21:316, *see also:* Barbara Allen
Bare Necessities   275:68, 276:60
Barges   72:96
Barley, barley, buckwheat straw   63:38, *see also:* 135:108, 232:72
Barley Harvesting/Mugi Kari   286:76
Barn Jesus/Child Jesus   54:190
Barnacle Bill   162:62
Barney and Katey   89:137
The Barnyard Song   68:27, 75:10, 128:34, 129:76, *see also:* 27:96, 37:171, 55:265, 109:193, 132:unpaged, 232:104, 254:108, 289:47, 292:13, 292:18
Barnyards O'Delgaty   212:86
Baruh adonai bayom   77:28
Baruh attah adonai   77:14
The Bashful Courtship   37:140
A basket! A basket! I found a little basket   197:42, *see also:* A-Tisket, A-Tasket
A Basque Lullaby   71:38, 125:114
The Bathroom   149:22
Battle Cry of Freedom   73:36, 157:122, 160:56
Battle Cry of Freedom (southern version)   73:38
Battle Hymn of the Republic   21:145, 22:220, 25:94, 26:89, 64:172, 71:10, 72:30, 73:5, 99:53, 127:132, 148:34, 128:126, 160:64, 277:57
Battle of New Orleans   240:213
Battle of Saratoga   240:124
Battle of the Kegs   28:94, 240:93, 273:46
Battle of Trenton   240:121
Batudde mu ddy iro   89:283
Bau pe wena, kisi pe wena   168:76
The bawl of a steer to a cowboy's ear   61:236, 159:281, *see also:* 60:36, 146:53, 159:15
Be a Cool Ghoul   167:44
Be Alive   261:6
Be Game, Be Fair   26:50
Be Kind to Your Webfooted Friends   26:12, 118:32, 292:158
Be Nice to Spiders   261:22
Be one little, be two little, we'll all go down the meadow   262:46
Be Prepared   25:56
Be present at our table, Lord   86:213
Be still, my puvwai, I nae iki ne   87:42
Be Thou My Vision   86:136
The Beacon-Light of Home   66:12
The Beanie Song   68:23
Beans, Bacon, and Gravy   64:132

The Bear and The Two Gascons/L'Ours et les Deux Gascons   243:26
Bear in the Hill   292:106
The Bear Is Pointing at the Sun   74:49
The Bear Went Over the Mountain   17:16, 75:12, 147:14, 290:72, 292:110
Bears Are Sleeping   294
Beauregard   73:86
Beautiful as a star hanging in the sky   19:15
The Beautiful Briny   276:68
A beautiful castle I've built for thee   66:98
Beautiful Dreamer   205:151
Beautiful dreamer, wake unto me   205:151
Beautiful Is Our Lodge   19:15
Beautiful Maiden   114:70
Beautiful Soup   112:12
Beautiful soup, so rich and green   112:12
Because   205:282
Because you come to me with naught save love   205:282
Bed in Summer   227:36
Bed Is Too Small   69:48
Bed of Hay   67:64
The Bedroom   149:24
Bedtime Song   125:42
Bedtime Stories   207:21
The Bee   162:23
Been in the Pen So Long   226:220
Been on the hummer since ninety-four   226:190
Beeper Booper   237:unpaged
Bees   7:27
Before the leaves are brown and dead   7:32
Before the Lord We Bow   86:14
Beggar's Double Sack/La Besace   243:50
Begone, Dull Care   262:70
Begone, Pernicious Tea   28:29
Behold a Branch Is Growing/Es Ist ein Ros Entsprungen   279:58, *see also:* 54:166, 210:30, 241:84, 264:86
Behold How Many Lights/Miren Cuantas Luces   216:52
Behold That Star   54:78, 140:62, 140:110, 244:1
Behold the moon shining thro' the dark night   89:164
Behold the Reaper/Es Ist ein Schnitter   89:142
Behold the Sun/Akhsham Oldu   89:208
Bein' Green   206:82
Believe Me, If All Those Endearing Young Charms   21:280, 205:60
The Bell   71:105, 72:172, *see also:* 293:16 *(The bell doth toll, its echoes roll)*
The Bell   67:88 *(I ring it far and near)*
Bell Bottom Trousers   205:371
The Bell Cow   128:40

The Bell Doth Toll   71:105, 72:172, 293:16
Bell Song   69:13
Bella Notte   275:62, 276:49
Bella ragazza dala treccia bionda   208:39
Belle Brandon   61:138
Bellflower, bellflower, lovely little bellflower   49:36
Bellflower Taryong/Toraji Taryong   49:36
The Bellman's Song   184:10, *see also:* 208:72, 210:68, 220:92
Bells   162:67
Bells Over Bethlehem/Campana Sobre Campana   54:278
The Beloved   67:40
Belt Red As Flame/Czerwony pas   208:58
Ben Bolt   66:18
Bend With the Wind   162:32
Bendemeer's Stream   22:20
Beneath a Weeping Willow's Shade   273:96
Bengawan Solo/Solo River   265:14
Berceuse Française   78:41, *see also:* 59:51
Berger, Secoue Ton Sommeil Profond/ Shepherd, Shake Off Your Drowsy Sleep   54:122
Beside the Nodle River/Nodle Kangbyon   49:38
Beside Thy Cradle Here I Stand/Ich Steh an Deiner Krippe Hier   54:163, 210:16, 241:156
Bessie Bell and Mary Grey   62:88
The Best Book of All   86:85
Bethel   123:72
Bethlehem   220:60, *see also:* 210:39
Betsy B.   35:74
Betsy Liner   83:510
Betty Botter   112:8, *see also:* 18:12
Betty Botter bought some butter   18:12, 112:8
Betty Botter's Batter   18:12, *see also:* 112:8
Beware!   66:110
Beyond those mountains lives a beautiful maiden   163:56
Bibbidi-Bobbidi-Boo   275:39, 276:37
The Bible Helps Me   86:81
Bible Stories   36:107, 290:156, *see also:* 178:70
The Bicycle   245:26
Bicycle Built for Two   21:19, 148:40, *see also:* 26:19, 83:493, 205:234
Biddy Biddy Burkey/Widewidewenne   188:126
Biddy Biddy Burkey's the name of my turkey   188:126
Bide Ye Yet   182:47
Big, big elephant, stalking down the path   207:107
Big Black Train   162:96
The Big Corral   128:84, 239:26
Big-Eye Rabbit   128:36

Big Mr. Small   151:8
Big old owl with eyes so bright   232:124, *see also:* Blue Tail Fly
The Big Procession   135:103
The Big Ranch/El Rancho Grande   216:47
Big Rock Candy Mountains   21:112, 24:884, 158:278, 230:66
The Big Sheep   234:58, *see also:* Darby Ram
A Big Ship Sailing   291:16, *see also:* Allee Allee-O
The big ship sails through the Alley, Alley O   165:113, *see also:* Allee Allee-O
The Big Sunflower   21:202, 66:114
Big Tall Indian   41:26, 162:43
Big Yellow Bus   162:102
Bigerlow   226:174, *see also:* 24:843, 158:149
The Bigler   158:149, *see also:* 24:843, 226:174
The Bigler's Crew   24:843, *see also:* 158:149, 226:174
Bill Bailey, Won't You Please Come Home?   21:88, 148:42, 170:44, 205:272
Bill Grogan's Goat   289:151
Bill Peters, the Stage Driver   159:391
Bill Peters was a hustler from Independence town   159:391
Bill Venero   159:197, *see also:* 61:129, 146:42
The Billboard   147:44
Billy Barlow   232:80, 274:18, *see also:* 20:11
Billy, Billy goat, my joy, think upon your little boy   114:59
Billy Boy   17:66, 36:28, 38, 62:111, 66:56, 62:112, 71:38, 135:42, 197:22, 205:53, 283:52, *see also:* 27:22
Billy Goat   114:59
Billy has a birthday   11:19
Billy Magee Magaw   290:70, 292:142, *see also:* Three Ravens
Billy Pringle   175:150
Billy Pringle had a little pig   175:150
Billy the Kid   61:266, 61:268, 159:140
Billy Venero heard them say   61:129, 159:197, *see also:* 146:42
Billy Veniro   61:129, 146:42, *see also:* 159:197
Billy was a bad man and carried a big gun   61:268, 159:140, *see also:* 61:266
Bingo   26:22, 39:52, 46:201, 63:91, 75:13, 126:93, 129:101, 147:16, 253:94, 289:54, *see also:* 17:131 (There was a farmer had a dog)
Bingo   59:59 (The miller's mill-dog lay at the door)
The Binschgauer folk on a pilgrimage set forth   89:149
The Binschgauer Pilgrimage   89:149

Bintil Shalabeya/Fairest Maid   89:206
The Birch Tree   71:80, 72:152
The Bird/El Pájaro   295:10
Bird, bird, you pretty thing   16:20
The Bird-Catcher   85:93
A bird doesn't grow sorghum   236:27
Bird in a Cage   226:213 *(Bird in a cage, love)*
The Bird in the Cage/Kagome Kagome   169:45, 286:38, *see also:* 16:20, 266:46 *(The bird in the cage)*
The Bird of Night   44:44
The Bird Song   69:18, 157:76, 262:44, *see also:* 36:56, 129:40, 158:18, 289:68, 292:122 *(Hi, says the blackbird sitting on a chair)*
Bird Song/Ntyilo   163:36 *(I heard a sound from the bush)*
The Bird With Silver Wings   154:26
The Birds   184:18, *see also:* Carol of the Birds
Birds' Christmas Feast   207:55
Birds' Courting Song   129:40, 289:68, *see also:* Bird Song
Birds fly back to their nests at twilight time   114:34
Birds Have Wings   7:28
The Birds' Lullaby   125:48
Birds of a Feather   112:57
Birds of a feather flock together   112:57
The Birds' Song   292:122, *see also:* Bird Song
The Birthday Cake   207:10
The Birthday of a King   241:204
Birthday Presents   245:121
Birthday Roundelay   245:107
A Birthday Song   41:25 *(We'll all sing together)*
Birthday Song   11:18 *(Billy has a birthday)*
Birthday Song   77:61 *(I'm five years old today)*
Birthday Song   130:24 *(How do you feel one year older)*
Birthday Song   162:56 *(On this bright and happy day)*
Birthday Song   197:124 *(Oh, Birthday Pal, we sing-a-ling-a-ling)*
Bist einmal kommen, du Heiland der Welt   279:84
Black, black, black is the color of my true love's hair   158:56, 277:33, *see also:* 36:108, 272:12
The Black Cats Come   166:34
Black Is the Color   36:108, 158:56, 272:12, 277:33
Black Sheep, Black Sheep   234:57
The Black Tail Range   60:86, 146:142, 159:292

Black the night and high the wind   281:60
The blackbirds are singing, the blackbirds are dancing   74:17
Blackeyed Susie   158:96
The Blacks go down, down, baby   141:78
The Blacksmith   85:171
The blacksmith I hear, the clanging and clashing   262:31
The Blantyre Explosion   64:60
Blazing campfires make our spirits light   25:64
Bless Our Cub Scouts   26:93
Bless This Table   72:173
Bless Us, O Jesus   124:148
Blessed Be That Maid Marie   54:41
The Blessings of Mary   190:61, 233:58, *see also:* The Seven Joys of Mary
Blest art Thou, O Lord, our God   77:26
Blest Be the Tie That Binds   161:91
Blest eternal Buddha—abandoned wife and child   89:231
Blind Man Lay Beside the Way   226:452
Bling Blang   130:74
Bliss   85:135
Blood on the Saddle   61:112, 290:170, *see also:* 61:113, 159:288
The Bloody Cowboy   61:113, *see also:* 61:112, 159:288, 290:170
Blow, Blow Thou Winter Wind   85:50
Blow, Boys, Blow   33:42, 232:161
Blow, my boys, I long to hear you   33:42, *see also:* 232:161
Blow on the Sea Shell   262:13
Blow the Man Down   22:152, 25:105, 36:54, 71:40, 72:77, 78:7, 87:22, 98:24, 148:46, 176:106, 197:79, 205:116, 226:404, 230:39, 277:113
Blow the Trumpet and Bang the Drum   96:4
Blow the Wind Southerly   72:126
Blow Up a Balloon   162:68
Blow, Ye Winds   24:829, 71:84, 72:71, *see also:* 64:112, 158:44
Blow Ye Winds, Westerly   128:50, *see also:* Boston Come All-ye
Blowin' in the Wind   72:8
Blue Bells of Scotland   22:60, 205:66
Blue Bird   141:35, *see also:* 20:20, 63:24, 110:44, 168:184, 232:118, 289:174 *(Bluebird, blue bird, on my window)*
Blue Bird/Parangsai   49:34 *(Blue bird, blue bird, lovely blue bird)*
Blue bird, blue bird, lovely blue bird   49:34
Blue bird, blue bird, through my window   141:35, *see also:* Blue Bird
Blue Flower/Lan Hua-Hua   87:50
The Blue Juniata   66:92
Blue Monday/Der Blaue Montag   89:147
Blue Mountain   61:239

Blue Mountain Lake   158:168
The Blue Tail Fly   27:10, 129:42, *see also:* 22:72, 178:26, 205:110, 230:12, 232:124
The Blue-tail Fly   22:72, 205:110, 230:12, *see also:* 27:10, 129:42, 178:26, 232:124
Bluebeard   290:148
Bluebell, Bluebell   20:20, *see also:* Blue Bird
Bluebell, bluebell, through my window 20:20, *see also:* Blue Bird
Bluebird   289:174, *see also:* Blue Bird
Bluebird, Bluebird   168:184, *see also:* Blue Bird
Bluebird, bluebird, on my window 63:24, 289:174, *see also:* Blue Bird
Bluebird, bluebird through my window 63:24, 110:44, *see also:* Blue Bird
De Blues Ain' Nothin'   226:234
Bo-san, Bo-san   16:16, 286:44
The Board Is Spread   101:33
Boar's Head Carol   54:34, 210:63, 241:18, 264:96, 292:112
The Boar's head in hand bear I 54:34, 210:63, 241:18, 264:96, 292:112
The Boasting Drunk in Dodge   159:135
A Boat, A Boat   290:192, 293:58
The Boatman Dance   33:114
The boatmen dance, the boatmen sing 33:114
The Boatmen's Song   239:58
Boats Sail on the Rivers   245:75
Bob-a-Needle   109:164
Bob-a-needle, Bob-a-needle is a-running 109:164
Bob Roebuck is my sweetheart's name 73:252
Bob Stanford   159:295
Bob Stanford, he's a Texas boy 159:295
Bobby Shafto   255, 289:87, *see also:* Bobby Shaftoe
Bobby Shaftoe   17:105, 59:50, 135:34, 162:94, 175:30, 285:64, *see also:* 255, 289:87
Bobcat! Wolf! Bear and Scout!   26:66
Bobo waro fero Satodeh   148:84
Bog in the Valley-O   72:127, *see also:* Green Grass Grows All Around
Bogando a la Luz del Sol/Rowing Toward the Sunlight   89:103
Boggy Creek   159:41, *see also:* Buffalo Skinners
Bohemian Carol   262:103
Bold Brennan on the Moor   22:28, *see also:* 35:72
The Bold Fisherman   27:208, 128:116, 239:20, 256
The Bold Grenadier   36:92
Bold Robin Hood   37:124
The Bold Soldier   35:42

The 'Bold Trellitee'   35:46, 35:48, *see also:* 22:172, 89:128, 133
The Bold Volunteer   27:36, 28:141
The Boll Weevil   24:916, 33:170, 64:98, 158:236, 221, 226:8, 239:40, 274:38, 277:29, 292:204, *see also:* 21:81, 226:252
The boll weevil is a little bug 33:70, 64:98, 292:204, *see also:* Boll Weevil
Bolsum Brown   226:355
Bolumbu   100:77
The Bombardment of Bristol   240:119
Boney   98:17
Boney was a warrior, Way-ay Yah 98:17
Bonnie Black Bess   61:15, 61:16, 159:217
The Bonnie Blue Flag   21:142, 73:16, 127:141, 157:124
The Bonnie Blue Flag With the Stripes and Stars   73:19
Bonnie Charlie's now a'wa' 176:32, 262:144
Bonnie George Campbell   22:24
Bonnie Maggie Lauder   182:15
The Bonny Banks of Virgie-O   134:52
Bonny Barbara Allen   24:820, *see also:* Barbara Allen
Bonny Doon   66:124, *see also:* 21:284
The Bonny Earl o' Moray   134:54
A bonny fine maid of noble degree, Maid Marian called by name 164:48
The Bonny Laboring Boy   35:22
The Bonny Wee Window   62:134
Boom ba de um boom, boom ba de um boom 55:257
Boom Boom   162:66
Boom, Boom, Ain't It Great to Be Crazy? 178:72, 289:143
Boom! Boom! Gee, It's Great to Be Scouting 25:53
The Border   114:18
Border Affair   61:146
Border Ballad   61:236, *see also:* 60:36, 146:53, 159:15, 159:281
The Border Lament   89:132
Born Is He, Little Child Divine   209:10
Born Is Jesus, the Infant King/Il Est Né, le Divin Enfant   279:92
Born on a mountain top in Tennessee 275:90, 276:86
Boscastle   83:508
The boss came up to me with a five-dollar bill 64:28
The bosses are taking it on the chin, parlez-vous 64:31
Bossy Cow   112:30
Bossy Cow, Bossy Cow, where do you lie? 112:30
The Boston Burglar   159:203
Boston Come—All-Ye   22:154, 33:18, 69:33, 71:85, 72:70, *see also:* 128:50

INDEX TO CHILDREN'S SONGS

The Boston Massacre 28:20

Boston Tea Tax Song 240:53, *see also:* 28:26

Botany Bay 21:247, 176:88

Bought Me a Cat 232:104, *see also:* Barnyard Song

Bouncing along comes the gay Easter Bunny 7:18

Bouncing Bet and Black-eyed Susan 97:unpaged

Bound for the Promised Land 21:256, 158:350, *see also:* 157:58

Bound to Go 157:136

Bow Belinda 126:105, *see also:* 39:32, 135:93, 178:52

Bow Bow Bow Belinda 178:52, *see also:* 39:32, 126:105, 135:93

Bow, bow, bow Belinda, Bow, bow, bow Belinda 126:105, 178:52, *see also:* 39:32, 135:93

Bow, bow, O Belinda! Bow, bow, O Belinda! 39:32, *see also:* 126:105, 135:93, 178:52

Bow Down, O Belinda 135:93, *see also:* 39:32, 126:105, 178:52

Bow down, O Lord, thine ear 273:130

Bow down, old Betsy Liner 83:510

Bow Down Your Head and Cry 159:159

Bow Wow, Says the Dog 18:24, 112:2

Bow-Wow-Wow 17:78

Bow-wow-wow, whose dog art thou? 17:78

The Boy and the Schoolmaster/L'Enfant et le Maître d'Ecole 243:35

A Boy He Had an Auger 226:343

A Boy Is Born in Bethlehem/Puer Natus in Bethlehem 54:316, *see also:* 220:111, 279:12

Boy Scouts of America 25:50

A Boy Scout's Prayer 25:62

A boy was born in Bethlehem 220:111, *see also:* 54:316, 279:12

The Boys' Carol/Personent Hodie 220:104

Boys' Chorus 85:196

Boys, Keep Your Powder Dry 73:148

The boys' sticks will come to life at the river Yo Homm! 163:45

Brady 226:198

Brahms' Lullaby 17:63, 289:18, *see also:* 71:122, 72:58, 85:176, 125:89, 283:60

Brand new state! Brand new state, gonna treat you great 218:54

Brave news is come to town 112:63

Brave Paulding and the Spy 240:104, *see also:* 28:138

Brave Wolfe 158:118, 240:33, 273:16

Bread and Roses 64:70

Break Forth, O Beauteous Heavenly Light/Brich an, du Schönes Morgenlicht 54:162, 210:18, 241:124

Break the News to Mother 21:41

The breezes went steadily through the tall pines 240:98, *see also:* 28:80

Brennan on the Moor 35:72, *see also:* 22:28

Brethren in Peace Together 72:147

Brich an, du Schönes Morgenlicht/Break Forth, O Beauteous Heavenly Light 54:162, 241:124

A bridal garland for thy head 85:207

Brigham Young 159:399

Bright blue flow'r as blue as day 87:50

Bright Morning Stars Are Rising 233:15

The bright new moon of Heshvan 77:48

Bright New Year 97:unpaged

Bright Phoebe 35:87

The Bright Sunny South 35:18

Brightest and Best 54:88, *see also:* 140:78, 210:20, 233:36

Brightest and best of the sons of the morning 54:88, 210:20, 233:36, *see also:* 140:78

Brightly, Brightly Gleam the Sparkling Rills 262:153

Bring a Torch, Jeannette, Isabella 3, 54:128, 217:64, 241:98, 264:72, 279:94, *see also:* 22:242, 184:36, 217:50

Bring Him Back Dead or Alive 61:250

Bring Me Li'l Water, Silvy 72:74, 130:79

Bring the Bricks/Hava L'Venim 89:203

Bring the good old bugle, boys 73:223, 157:130

Bring Them With You or Be Victorious/Zenizenabo 163:31

Bring your pail and shovel. Come with me 207:129

Bringing in the Sheaves 157:166

The British Grenadiers 22:198, 240:142

The British Light Infantry 240:153

A British Tar 98:52

A British tar is a soaring soul 98:52

Broder Manyo 89:66

Broder Manyo is dead an' gone 89:66

The Broken Troth 262:77

Bronc Peeler's Song 159:83

The Brooklet 262:72

The Broom o' the Cowdenknowes 182:37

Brother, Come and Dance With Me 75:14, 227:28

Brother Ephraim sold his cow and bought him a commission 240:71

Brother John (parody) 64:29

Brother Rabbit 135:28

Brother Rabbit and Mister Railroad's Taters 109:207

Brother James 188:180, 217:55, *see also:* Frère Jacques

Brother, Tell Me of the Battle 73:280

Brown-eyed Lee 146:72, 159:214

The Brown Girl or Fair Eleanor 226:156

The Brown Girl she has houses and lands 226:156
Brownie 172:140, 173:26
Brownie Friend-Maker Song 68:32
Brownie Hiking Song 68:28
Brownie Magic 68:7
Brownie Smile Song 68:47
The Brownies' Song 68:10
Bruce the Goose 91:39
Bubbles and Bubbles 114:10
Buckee, Buckee, Biddy, Bene 59:63
Buckee Bene 59:63
Buckeye Jim 21:277, 158:12, 277:83
Bucking Bronco 61:165, 159:267, *see also:* 61:166, 146:59
Buckingham Palace 172:128, 173:14
Buckskin Joe 159:170
Bucura t'e Tintirim/Oh, Rejoice, Thou Frightful Grave 89:192
Buenos dias amigos, come sing with me 162:104
Buenos dias mi señorio 169:27, 269:26
Buenos noches, Mariquita, yo vengo con mucho pena 54:303
Buffalo Boy 290:88
Buffalo Gals 20:28, 24:841, 61:278, 66:58, 126:97, 148:50, 158:104, 205:119, 230:34, *see also:* 63:12, 128:80, 157:86, 283:41
The Buffalo Hunters 61:4, 159:343
The Buffalo Range 61:341
The Buffalo Skinners 24:854, 64:120, 146:92, 158:174, 159:335, 226:270, 230:63, 277:137, *see also:* 159:41
A bug all black and shiny 97:unpaged
The buildings are so bright and tall 91:22
Buildings gray and sidewalks gray and smoke is in the air 261:44
Built My Lady a Fine Brick House 232:170
The Bull Rider Song 61:189, *see also:* 61:187, 223, 225:32
The Bullfrog 97:unpaged
The Bullwhacker 159:396
A bully ship and a bully crew 21:306, 158:140, *see also:* 262:38
Bumblebees Are Humming 245:37
The Bumpkin 262:14
Bunde San Antonio 169:16
Bunker Hill 28:46
Bunkhouse Orchestra 61:282
Bunnies zip and bunnies zoom 245:45
Bunny Bunny, little Easter bunny 41:39
Buon Giorno 69:50
Burgoyne with thousands came 240:128
Burgoyne's Defeat 28:100
Burgoyne's Disgrace 240:128
Burn, little candles, burn, burn, burn 162:48
The Burrowing Yankees 28:63, 240:152

Bury Me Not on the Lone Prairie 158:208, *see also:* Oh, Bury Me Not on the Lone Prairie
Bury Me Out on the Prairie 159:300, *see also:* 61:177
The Bus Song 75:16, *see also:* 147:6, 165:73, 291:46
Busy busy little bees 7:27
Busy Christmas Time 207:47
Busy Little Bushytail 207:28
But black is the color of my true love's hair 272:12, *see also:* 36:108, 158:56, 277:33
Butsu Butsu Mame/Red Beans 286:39
Buttercups and Daisies 17:109
Butterflies 261:34
Butterfly 114:62 *(Little Butterfly, my friend)*
The Butterfly 85:145 *(I dance in the sunshine)*
The Butterfly's Wedding/Les Noces du Papillon 217:63
Buy a Broom 66:34
Buy a Pretty Pony 234:65, *see also:* 245:100
Buy all the old furniture; clo's, rags 239:89
Buy My Dainty Fine Beans 293:70
The buzzards are singing, the buzzards are flying 74:18
Bwalobera Nkere/The Frogs 89:283
By an old Swiss mill, on a sparkling rill 25:92
By and By 157:149
By Clyde's bonny banks where I sadly did wander 64:60
By day the shadows slip away 125:38
By my faith but I think you're all makers of bulls 28:53, 240:64
By myself oh all alone 16:30
By the Blazing Council Fire 25:126
By the Clear Running Fountain 71:67
By the light of moonshine, my good friend Pierrot 188:40, *see also:* Au Clair de la Lune
By the Light of the Moon 217:54, *see also:* Au Claire de la Lune
By the Light of the Silvery Moon 170:56
By yon bonnie banks and by yon bonnie braes 22:80
Bye and bye, stars in the heav'n 233:12
Bye, Baby Bunting 17:110, 125:40, 175:14, 188:14, 283:58, *see also:* 59:33, 285:102
Bye baby bunting, daddy's gone a-hunting 17:110, 59:33, 125:40, 175:14, 188:14, 283:58, *see also:* 285:102
Bye Bye Blackbird 170:17
Bye-lo, Baby, Bunting 285:102, *see also:* Bye Baby Bunting
Bye low, bye low, Baby's in the cradle sleeping 125:54

Bye-o-baby baby, bye-o baby bye 129:13

By'm By 129:18, 226:453, *see also:* 135:44, 157:156, 232:71, 289:13

By'm by, by'm by, Stahs shinin', numbah, numbah one 129:18, 226:453, *see also:* 135:44, 157:156, 232:71, 289:13

By'M Bye 157:156, 232:71, 289:13, *see also:* 129:18, 135:44, 226:453

By'm bye, by'm bye, stars shining 157:156, 232:71, 289:13, *see also:* 129:18, 135:44, 226:453

By'n Bye 135:44, *see also:* By'M Bye

C

C. C. Rider 226:246, *see also:* 158:68, 226:247

C. C. Rider, just see what you have done! 226:247, *see also:* 158:68, 226:246

Ca, Ca, Ca 236:77

Cabin in the Wood 26:32, *see also:* 55:270

Cactus—Mr. Small's Pony 154:32

Cadima 107:42

Cadet Rousselle 217:44

Cae la tarde, lentamente sobreel mar 21:259

The Caissons Go Rolling Along 197:103

Cakes and Custard 18:48

Cakes are beautiful to see 207:10

California 226:110

The California Brothers 61:38

California Here I Come 170:46

California Joe 146:136, 159:346

California Stage Company 159:393

Call all hands to raise the anchor 69:44

Call 'em Names, Jeff 73:53

Call John the Boatman 71:99, 72:162

Call Me on the Telephone 166:36

Caller Herrin' 292:174

Calliope 226:349

Calliope Song 55:264

Calm on the Listening Ear of Night 241:143

The Cambric Shirt 37:112, *see also:* 22:26, 35:98

Cambridgeshire May Song 212:76

Cameroon 163:83

A camp meeting took place, by the colored race 21:45

Camp Menu Song 25:22

Campana Sobre Campana/Bells Over Bethlehem 54:278

The Campbells Are Coming 66:48, 205:106, 184:204

Campfire Medley 25:122

Camporee or Jamboree Hymn 25:64

The Camptown ladies sing this song, Doodah! doo-dah! 22:64, 66:36, 157:90, 205:126, *see also:* 126:67, 230:40

Camptown Races 22:64, 66:36, 126:67, 157:90, 205:126, 230:40

Can a Growing Child Like Me 86:199

Can Ye Sew Cushions 27:110, *see also:* 71:82, 78:29, 125:68

Can You Count the Stars? 86:3, 125:80

Can you see the deer he's munching leaves you hear 114:16

Can You Show Me How the Farmer? 17:32

Can You Tell 261:16

Can you tell me what the boys do 165:178

Can you tell what's for supper 261:16

Can you walk on two legs, two legs, two legs? 165:143

Canaday-i-o 64:118

Canadian Friendship 107:16

The Canary 41:20

Cancao a Lua/Song to the Moon 89:164

Can'cha Line 'Em 158:274

Canción del Marinero Hondureño/Song of the Honduran Sailor 89:74

Canco de's Batre/Threshing Song 89:163

The Candle 67:83 *(A candle let me be)*

The Candle 162:67 *(A little candle cries)*

A candle let me be, to shine before the manger 67:83

Candles are gleaming, snow is on the ground 162:76

Candles of Hannukah 162:48

Candy Man 134:21, 274:42

Caney Mi Macaro 107:40

The Cannibal King 25:10

The Cannibal King with a big nose ring 25:10

The Canoe 41:33

Canoe Round 293:60, *see also:* 62:19

Canon of the Mimes 241:229

Cans't tell who lost the battle, off in the council's field? 73:148

Can't You Dance the Polka? 22:160

Can't you see Aunt Hessie's white horse 189:140

Cantemos/We Are Singing 54:296

Canticle 262:108

Cantique de Noël/O Holy Night 54:107, *see also:* 241:197

Canto Lucumi de Iya/Lucumi Cult Song 89:59

Canzone d'i Zampognari/Carol of the Bagpipers 54:242, 241:100, *see also:* 279:100

Cape Cod Chantey 129:82, *see also:* 290:110

Cape Cod Girls 290:110, *see also:* 129:82

Cape Cod girls they have no combs 129:82, 290:110

A Capital Ship 34, 289:126, *see also:* 48

A capital ship for an ocean trip was the "Walloping Window Blind" 34, 48, 289:126

Cap'n I Believe 226:363

Captain Jinks 66:63, 70:28, 126:65, 135:96

Captain Kidd 21:332

"Captain, oh captain, take me on board 35:48, *see also:* 22:172, 35:46, 89:128, 133

Captain said to big old John Henry 33:178, *see also:* John Henry

The captain sailed a ship, boys, and she put out to sea 33:186

Captain Small sails over the sea 154:25

The Captain's Shanty 290:118

The Capture of Major Andre 28:138, *see also:* 240:104

Capture of Burgoyne 273:44

The Captured Bird/Poymanaya Pteechka 289:62

The Car Song 235:8

The Caravan Song 69:54 *(Let us go walking together)*

Caravan Song/Ajjamal Wanna 89:244 *(Slowly winding through the desert)*

The Careful Bunny 207:100

Carefully on Tiptoe Stealing 252:16

Carefully Taught 218:169

Careless Love 22:46, 24:901, 126:69, 158:64, 205:365, 226:21, 230:11, 272:16

The Carite Fish/El Carite 216:42

Carol For East and West 209:61

Carol of Beauty 184:64

Carol of Service 184:68

Carol of the Annunciation/Angelus ad Virginem 189:70

Carol of the Bagpipers/Canzone d'i Zampognari 54:242, 241:100, 279:100

Carol of the Beasts 128:62, *see also:* 13, 54:24, 86:47, 138:unpaged

Carol of the Birds 54:124, 54:268, 128:60, 140:96, 183:22, 184:18, 209:119, 241:61, 264:94, 284:61, 292:126

Carol of the Children of Bethlehem/Lied der Kinder zu Bethlehem 279:84

Carol of the Flowers 241:66, 284:93

Carol of the Hay/Sliczna Panienka 54:216

Carol of the Nuns of Saint Mary's, Chester 279:16

Carol of the Seekers 244:28

Carol to a Child 280:unpaged

Carousel 20:59

The Carousel Waltz 218:64

The Carpenters 245:59

The carpenters are working 245:59

Carpenters use saws and nails 261:12

Carrousel/Karusellen 89:168, 100:50

The Carrion Crow 89:131, 134:56, 175:160, 188:152, 292:148

Carry Me Back to Old Virginny 22:84, 127:176, 205:186

Carry on, sister, high up the hill 209:48

Casey Jones 22:142, 158:264, 158:266, 176:148, 222, 226:366

Casey Jones (parody) 64:43

Casey Junior 275:26, 276:8

Casey would waltz with a strawberry blonde 205:245

Castle in My City 296:8

Castle Island Song 273:26, *see also:* 28:22

The Cat Came Back 102

A Cat Came Fiddling Out of a Barn 111:51

Cat in the Plum Tree 144:11

Cat in the Sack/Katten i Saekken 208:19

Catch a Little Fox 47, *see also:* A-Hunting We Will Go

The Caterpillar 191:36

Caterpillars 261:32

Caterpillars on the run 261:32

Cats have kittens, doggies have pups 206:25

Cattle Call 61:302

Cattleman's Prayer 61:338, *see also:* 159:329

Caught today a mosquito bigger than a horse, oh 84:50

Caux Carol 210:90

Ce matin, j'ai rencontré le train 54:126, *see also:* 241:105

Celebrons la naissance 54:92, 279:21

The Cellar 149:26

A certain man traveled to Jericho 155:18

C'est la mère Michel qui a perdu son chat 217:26

C'était la fille au Roi Français 89:150

Chacarera 70:17, 197:37

Chacarera, Chacarera, I've been told by a hummingbird 197:37, *see also:* 70:17

Chacarera, Chacarera, Me ha contado un picaflor 197:37, *see also:* 70:17

Chacun à ses avantages 243:50

Chahcoal Man 226:459

Chairs to Mend 46:228, 71:104, 72:164, 289:186, 293:64, 293:66, *see also:* 111:58

Chaparral Song 25:82

The Chaparreres/Las Chaparreras 89:71

A Charge to Keep I Have/He Kihapai No Ka'u 87:30

Charles Ives's Carol 190:82, 190:84

Charleston Gals 24:905

The Charleston Song 28:131

Charley, Charley 111:66

Charley, Charley, stole the barley 111:66

Charlie Is My Darling 71:42, 176:30, 205:72, *see also:* 134:14, 226:117, 232:137

Charlie Over the Water 75:18

Charlie Rutledge 159:82

Charlie's neat and Charlie's sweet 213:28, see also: 24:813, 66:76, 226:161
Charlottie liv'd on a mountain top 226:58, see also: 24:825, 27:244, 35:50, 159:231
Chaw Mah Lee/My Beloved 169:67, 267:54
Che Che Koole 178:65, see also: 169:23
Chebogah 83:494
Chechekoolay, chechekoolay 169:23, 178:65
Cheeks as red as the blooming rose 157:74, 213:44, see also: 134:50
Cheeks of Rose 17:139
Cheer Up/Al Animo 194:24, see also: 168:112
Cheer up, cheer up, the platter has broken 194:24, see also: 168:112
Cheer up, friends and neighbours, now it's Easter tide 184:60
The Cheerful Horn 27:194
The cheerful horn, it blows in the morn 27:194
Chen hsian hsian na ke lan hsian hsian 87:50
Cherries Are Ripe 262:26
Cherries Ripe 17:27
Cherries ripe, cherries ripe, who will buy my cherries ripe? 17:27
Cherry Blossoms/Sakura Sakura 286:73, see also: 72:141
The Cherry Tree Carol 140:26, 232:182, 264:76, 284:55, see also: 190:70, 233:24
Cherry Trees/Sakura 72:141, see also: 286:73
Cherry trees, cherry trees bloom so bright in April 72:141, see also: 286:73
The Cheshire Hunt 71:41
Chester 21:242, 28:147, 157:20, 197:25, 240:83, 273:140
Chester Schottische 126:95
Chevaliers de la Table Ronde 176:98
Cheyenne 159:245
Chi chi pappa, chi pappa 266:47
Chi Ya V'luzi Ne Kalina Bula?/Was I Not a Flower in the Meadow? 89:177
Chiapanecas 162:107
Chick, Chick Little Chickies 114:48
The Chicken/El Pollo 295:15
Chicken crowin' on Sourwood Mountain 46:214, see also: Sourwood Mountain
Chicken crowing for midnight 233:76
The Chicken Dance/Baile de los Pollos 194:30
Chicken-hahk oh! Chicken-hahk oh! 100:108
Chicken Hawk 100:108
Chicken Reel 226:116
Chicken Soup With Rice 235:60

Chickens a-crowing on Sourwood Mountain 37:148, 134:38, 158:84, 226:125, see also: 24:897, 46:214, 226:320
The Child 67:37
The Child and the Star 17:11
Child in the Manger 209:11
A Child Is Born in Bethlehem/Et Barn er Fodt I Betlehem 54:192
A Child Is Born in Bethlehem/Puer Natus in Bethlehem 279:12, see also: 54:316, 220:111
Child Jesus/Barn Jesus 54:190 (*Child Jesus in a manger lay*)
The Child Jesus 241:88, see also: 54:284, 197:117 (*Mother dear, a Child at our doorstep*)
Child of God 190:88, 233:40, see also: 140:64 (*If anybody asks you who I am*)
A Child of God 155:27 (*A child of God shall be planted like a tree*)
A child of God shall be planted like a tree 155:27
A Child This Day Is Born 210:11, 241:4
Children Can 219:45
Children From Everywhere 124:152
Children, go and I will send thee 124:68
Children, go where I send thee 54:82, 118:unpaged, 140:46, 190:68, see also: 213:88, 233:69
Children, guess what I have here 20:16, 71:56, 72:138, see also: 75:52, 254:119, 289:170 (*I Am a Gay Musician*)
Children in a far-flung ring 124:152
Children of Jerusalem Sang the Praise 86:128
Children of the Heavenly King 233:62
Children, Sabbath, Sabbath is today 77:38
Children's Chorale 86:166
The Children's Friend 86:104
The Children's Prayer 125:98, 262:149
The Children's Song 71:7
Children's Song of the Nativity 184:39, see also: 96:7, 209:82
The Children's Zoo 162:19
Child's Prayer 177:86 (*Dear Lord, look down upon us*)
A Child's Prayer 86:202 (*We thank Thee, loving Father*)
Child's Song 44:78 (*I have a garden of my own*)
A Child's Song 85:222 (*In our garden, tiny garden*)
The Child's Testament/Den Lillas Testamente 89:169
Chilly autumn mornings, what do I see? 207:32
Chim Chim Cher-ee 275:48, 276:51
Chim chiminey, chim chiminey, chim chim cher-ee! 275:48, 276:51

Chimes of Dunkirk 46:202

China 273:152

Chinene Nye/What Is Big? 168:18

Chinese Baby Song 17:134, 59:27

A Chinese Christmas Cradle Song/Shiao Bao-Bao 209:68

Chinese Cradle Song 78:77, *see also:* 125:10

The Chinese Fan 68:16

Chinese Grace 86:212

Chip-chop, chip-chop, Chipper, Chopper Joe 165:173

The Chipmunk's Day 42:30

Chippy, Get Your Hair Cut 157:44, 226:158, *see also:* 135:15, 226:158, 232:142

Chiquirriquitín/O My Loveliest One 54:280

The Chisholm Trail 60:4, 146:20, 146:23, *see also:* Old Chisholm Trail

The Chivalrous Shark 176:126

Chonan Samgori, Hung! Hung! 49:35

Choo, choo, choo, the train will soon be going 41:29

The Choo-Choo Train 289:94

Chook-a-choo! Chook-a-choo! We are starting 227:21

Chopo 61:191

Choral Grace 86:211

The Christ-Child Lay on Mary's Lap 184:47, 209:117, 244:64

The Christ Child's Lullaby 59:31

Christ Is Born This Evening/Gdy Się Chrystus Rodzi 54:210, *see also:* 279:124

Christ Is Risen 86:63

Christ, the Babe was giv'n to all 284:119

Christ the Lord Is Risen Today; Alleluia 86:67, 197:40

Christ the Lord Most Glorious 140:40, 140:118

Christ was born in Bethlehem 86:41, 157:65

Christ Was Born on Christmas Day 241:68

The Christening 172:138, 173:24

The Christian Year 86:161

Christians, Awake 210:21, 241:114

Christians, awake, salute the happy morn 210:21, 241:114

Christmas 207:58

Christmas Bells 41:6

Christmas bells are ringing in the morning air 207:49

Christmas Bells Ring Out Glad News 86:43

Christmas Comes Anew/Noël Nouvelet 54:118, *see also:* 220:78

Christmas Cookies 207:48

Christmas cookies, I can tell 207:48

Christmas Cradle Song 100:154, *see also:* 54:308, 279:106 (A la ru, ru, ru, my little boy)

Christmas Cradle Song 210:92 *(Still and dark the night)*

Christmas Dance 89:162, 216:51, *see also:* Fum, Fum, Fum

Christmas Day 220:64, *see also:* 138:unpaged, 197:121

Christmas Day in the Morning 233:79, *see also:* I Saw Three Ships

Christmas Day is come; let's all prepare for mirth 241:48

Christmas Eve 65:92 *(Watching in the meadows o'er their flocks by night)*

Christmas Eve 166:76 *(Candles are gleaming)*

Christmas Eve Canon 241:223

Christmas Every Day 67:50

Christmas in lands of the fir tree and pine 54:64

Christmas in the Air 207:49

Christmas Is Coming 27:248, 68:8, 128:54, 178:23, 210:94, 241:225, 293:76 *(Christmas is coming, the goose is getting fat)*

Christmas Is Coming 162:49 *(Christmas is coming, Christmas is coming)*

Christmas is coming and it's almost day 130:41

Christmas is coming, Christmas is coming! 162:49

Christmas is coming the goose is getting fat 27:248, 68:8, 128:54, 178:23, 210:94, 241:225, 293:76

Christmas Is Here Again 89:170, 262:42, *see also:* 54:193, 241:168, 279:112

A Christmas Lullaby 207:50

Christmas Mouse 282

The Christmas Nightingale/Die Weihnachtsnachtigall 279:62

Christmas Piece 209:70

Christmas Polka 262:42, *see also:* 54:193, 89:170, 241:168, 279:112

Christmas Shoes and Stockings 207:54

A Christmas Song 220:86 *(Winds through the olive trees)*

Christmas Song/Zu Weihnachten 279:66 *(I stand beside thy cradle here)*

A Christmas Spiritual 209:48

The Christmas Tree 241:164, *see also:* O Tannenbaum *(O Christmas tree, o Christmas tree)*

Christmas Tree 162:52 *(Christmas tree, Christmas tree, beautiful sparkling Christmas tree)*

Christmas tree, Christmas tree, beautiful sparkling Christmas tree 162:52

The Christmas Tree With Its Candles Gleaming/Am Weihnachtsbaum die Lichter Brennen 54:150

Christopher Columbo 27:200, *see also:* 197:88

Christopher Columbus didn't have a compass 27:202

Christopher Robin goes hoppity, hoppity 172:124, 173:10

Christopher Robin Is Going 172:79, 174:65

Chtic, Aby Spal, Tak Zpívala/Sweet Mary Sings Her Babe to Sleep 54:234

Chug-a-Lug-a-Lug 291:20

Chug Chug Chug 162:96

"Chug, chug, chug," the tractor goes 288:12

Chum, Chummy Lou 83:489

Church in the Wildwood 25:117, *see also:* 21:164

The Church of God Is Everywhere 86:68

Cicerenella/Tarantella of Posilipo 78:47

Cielito Lindo/Pretty Skies Above 197:36, 216:27, 226:298, 230:23

Cigarettes Will Spoil Yer Life 226:335

Cinderella, Cinderella, all I hear is Cinderella 276:36

Cindy 24:899, 158:94, 176:122, 205:146, 230:61

Ciranda/Dancer, Little Dancer 168:141, 169:9, 266:13

Ciranda, ciandinha 168:141, 169:9, 266:13

Circle Singing Games 177:75

Circle to the left, the Old Brass Wagon 33:98, 226:159, *see also:* 55:506

Circles 206:14

The Circus 207:112

The Circus Comes to Town 26:71

The Circus Seal 207:111

The circus swings I love to see 207:108

The City 91:22

The City Rat and the Country Rat 17:96 (*Once a rat who loved the city*)

The City Rat and the Country Rat/Le Rat de Ville et le Rat des Champs 243:29 (*Le rat de ville au rat des champs*)

City Time 91:28

Ciu Ciu Bèllo 169:41, 265:24

Clams 239:88

Clams, clams, ten cents for your clams 239:88

Clang! Clang! The fire truck comes 154:30

Clap, clap, clap your hands 232:86, 289:160

Clap Singing Game 177:76

Clap With Me 162:6

Clap Your Hands 232:86, 289:160 (*Clap, clap, clap your hands*)

Clap Your Hands 26:27 (*Clap your hands! Clap your hands!*)

Clap your hands so gaily, gaily, gaily 104:51

Clap your hands, stamp your feet 162:63

Clapping Game 68:9

The Clay Pot and the Iron Pot/Le Pot de Terre et le Pot de Fer 243:2

Clean Hands 11:12

Cleano 130:16

Clear Rock's Chisholm Trail 159:37, *see also:* 234:70

Clear-Running Stream/Arroyo Claro 188:62

Clear the Track 239:18

Clementine 22:82, 25:76, 26:16, 61:100, 148:52, 195, 205:213, 230:27, 290:162

The Click Song/Qongqothwane 163:28

Click Your Heels/Podkóweczki Dajcie Ognia 89:182

Climb Ev'ry Mountain 218:246

Climb ev'ry mountain, search high and low 218:246

Clinch Mountain 37:142, *see also:* 24:855, 158:218, 159:163, 226:307, 230:69

The Clock 288:22

The Clock Song 291:36

The Clocks 68:48, 262:33

Close to the patches of old winter snow 207:86

Close Your Eyes 59:77

The Closet Key 232:169

Clouds 261:38

The Clouds at Kona/Kona Kai Opua 87:27

Clouds go drifting by, lazy in the sky 162:100

Clouds of gray are in the sky 125:50

Clouds of October in skies of blue 207:31

A clown, a clown, I think I'll be a clown 219:17

The Clown in Me 219:17

A clown there was, the best I've seen 207:109

The Coasts of High Barbary 22:166

Cobbler, Cobbler 17:47, 165:174, 285:84

Cobbler, cobbler, mend my shoe 17:47, 165:174, 285:84

Cobbler's Dance 245:58

Cocaine Lil 226:206

The Cock/Qhude 163:76

Cock-A-Doodle-Doo 17:138, 111:76, 135:50, 175:116, 285:86, 289:98

Cock-a-doodle-doo! My dame has lost her shoe 17:138, 111:76, 135:50, 175:116, 285:86, 289:98

Cock-a-doodle-doo! Wake up! Wake up! 207:106

Cock-A-Doodle-Doodle-Do 112:1

The Cock and the Fox/Le Coq et le Renard 243:36

Cock-doodle doodle doo and cock-doodle dandy 112:1

The Cock Crows 114:37

Cock Robin 37:177, 134:58, *see also:* 135:32, 289:74, 292:138

Cock Robin and Jenny Wren 188:148

The Cockeyed Mayor of Kaunakakai 87:84

Cockles and Mussels 22:22, 262:89

The Cockroach 21:110, 197:38, 226:291

Cocky Doodle Doodle Do 130:44, *see also:* 128:100, 232:94, 291:6

Cocky Robin 135:32, 289:74, *see also:* 37:177, 134:58, 292:138

Coffee Grows on White Oak Trees 39:42, 158:100

The coffee that they give us, they say is mighty fine 158:124, *see also:* 27:226

Cold December's winds were stilled 54:266

Cold Is the Morning 241:63

Coldly the night winds winging 210:139

Cole Younger 61:262

Colin 262:147

Collinet and Phebe 273:82

The Colorado Trail 159:7, 225:62, 226:462

Columbia, the Gem of the Ocean 26:86, 157:116, 160:36, *see also:* 197:65

Come/Woza 163:68

Come A-Hunting 26:43

Come all girls pay attention to my voice 61:23

Come all my boys and listen, a song I'll sing to you 24:843, 158:149, *see also:* 226:174

Come all of you, my brother scouts, and join me in my song 159:354

Come all of you people, I pray you draw near 159:256

Come all ya young fellers that follow the sea 205:116, *see also:* Blow the Man Down

Come all ye bold fishermen 289:72, 292:168

Come all ye British heroes, I pray you lend your ears 240:209

Come all ye handsome comely maids that live near Carlow dwelling 42:604, *see also:* 61:171, 66:112, 205:27

Come all ye jolly fellows, how would you like to go 64:118

Come all ye jolly good shanty boys, come listen to my song 239:36

Come all ye jolly huntsmen who want to hunt the fox 212:22

Come all ye jolly shepherds that whistle through the glen 182:43

Come all ye jovial shanty boys 21:222, *see also:* 24:847, 35:6, 158:170, 226:394

Come all ye lads and lasses and hear my mournful tale 42:612

Come all ye railroad section men, an' listen to my song 64:88, 226:360

Come All Ye Shepherds/Nesem Vám Noviny 220:100, 279:116, *see also:* 54:236

Come all ye sons of freedom throughout the state of Maine 277:73

Come all ye true-born shanty boys, wherever you may be 24:847, 226:394, *see also:* 21:222, 35:6, 158:170

Come, all ye young fellows that follow the sea 197:79, *see also:* Blow the Man Down

Come, all ye young sailor men, listen to me 22:154, 33:18, 69:33, 71:85, 72:70, 128:50

Come all you bold Americans, the truth to you I'll tell 240:139

Come all you bold Britons, wherever you be 240:18

Come All You Bold Canadians 240:194

Come all you bold ox teamsters 21:250

Come all you bold robbers and open your ears 159:142, *see also:* 159:144

Come all you bold sailors that follow the Lakes 226:176

Come, all you bold undaunted men, you outlaws of the day 159:209

Come all you brave Americans and unto me give ear 28:138, 240:104

Come all you brave gallants and listen awhile 164:58

Come, all you brave soldiers, both valiant and free 28:68, 240:84

Come all you brave young shanty boys 226:389

Come All You Fair and Tender Ladies 158:58, 230:24, *see also:* 36:16

Come all you fair and tender ladies, take warning how you court young men 36:16, 158:58, 230:24

Come all you fine fellows with hearts so warm and true 226:392

Come all you good fellers, wherever you be 158:168

Come all you good old boys and listen to my rhymes 159:187

Come all you good old farmers that on your plow depend 35:62, *see also:* 21:298, 226:162

Come all you good people wher-e'er you be 240:148

Come all you good workers, good news to you 64:54, 230:94, 239:90

Come all you jolly cowboys and listen to my song 24:854, *see also:* The Buffalo Skinners

Come, all you jolly cowboys, don't you want to go 60:36, 146:53, *see also:* 61:235, 159:15, 159:281

Come all you jolly cowboys that follow the bronco steer 159:27

Come all you jolly fellows, wherever you may be 158:170, *see also:* 21:222, 24:847, 35:6, 226:394

Come all you jolly freighters that has freighted on the road 159:394, *see also:* 61:50

Come all you jolly freighters who travel upon the road 61:50, *see also:* 159:394

Come, all you jolly river lads, I'll have you to draw near 35:6, *see also:* 21:222, 24:847, 158:170, 226:394

Come all you jolly skinners and listen to my song 159:335, *see also:* Buffalo Skinners

Come all you Lachlan men 176:80

Come you ladies and you gentlemen and listen to my song 64:100

Come all you little riders that gamble all day 61:20, *see also:* 61:18, 234:68

Come all you Louisiana girls and listen to my noise 159:339, *see also:* 158:44

Come all you melancholy folks and listen unto me 159:220

Come all you men of Arkansas, a tale to you I'll sing 159:225

Come all you Mississippi girls and listen to my noise 61:25

Come all you old cow-punchers, a story I will tell 159:355

Come all you old-time cowboys and listen to my song 159:41, 230:63, *see also:* Buffalo Skinners

Come all you old-timers and listen to my song 159:25

Come All You Playmates 63:95

Come all you playmates, come out and play with me 63:95

Come all you pretty fair maids, these lines to you I write 61:4, *see also:* 159:343

Come all you pretty girls, to you these lines I'll write 159:343, *see also:* 61:4

Come all you pretty maidens, some old and some younger 36:96

Come all you range riders and listen to me 159:185, 159:280

Come all you rounders that want to hear 22:142, 158:266, 176:148, 222, 226:366, *see also:* 158:264

Come all you roving cowboys, bow down your head and hand 61:163

Come, all you sly and crafty rogues 36:32

Come all you sons of Erin, attention now I crave 226:398

Come all you sons of freedom that run the Saginaw stream 158:166

Come all you sporting bach'lors 158:52

Come all you Texas cowboys, and warning take of me 61:92, *see also:* 60:48, 146:66, 159:22

Come all you Texas rangers, wherever you may be 33:234, *see also:* 159:359, 159:361

Come, all you Virginia girls and listen to my noise 36:66

Come all you woolly waddies, let's go to Harrington's ranch 159:244

Come All You Worthy Gentlemen 210:22

Come, all you young companions, and listen unto me 146:109, 159:212

Come all you young fellows so young and so fine 64:49

Come all you young fellows that follow the sea 78:7, *see also:* Blow the Man Down

Come, all you young men all, let nothing fright you 273:16, *see also:* 158:118, 240:33

Come all you young men all, let this delight you 240:33, *see also:* 158:118, 273:16

Come all you young waddies, I'll sing you a song 61:110

Come, all young girls, pay attention to my noise 226:129

Come, all young men and maidens, come listen to my song 36:68

Come along, get you ready, wear your bran', bran' new gown 21:30, 157:191, *see also:* 126:57, 203

Come along, girls, we're going to Boston 129:78, *see also:* 39:36, 63:39, 135:98, 157:47

Come along now, come along now 16:27

Come along, o come along, my little honey 189:156

Come, and go to Bethlehem 245:118

Come and Go With Me 148:54

Come and have a cup of tea 162:76

Come, and I will sing to you 129:63, 190:64, *see also:* Green Grow the Rushes, Ho!

Come and let me tell you 'bout the rising of the Saviour 27:74

Come and Let Us Dance 71:106

Come and Play With Me 162:75

Come and see my playhouse 162:75

Come and take a ride with me upon my magic pony 245:28

Come Arise! 245:28

Come away to the skies, my beloved, arise 140:84, 190:41, 233:61

Come away! To the woods! I see acorns 207:35

Come away with me Lucile 205:317, *see also:* 157:203

Come Bring With a Noise 112:42

Come, buy of poor Kate, primroses I sell 273:112

Come, come, come and see turkey gobblers in a tree 162:46

Come, come, come fireflies come! 286:24, see also: 16:32

Come, Come, Ye Saints 21:300

Come, each death-doing dog who dares venture his neck 240:145

Come, Fair Rosina 273:90

Come, faithful people, come away 124:192

Come, Fellow Workers 22:228

Come Fireflies/Hotaru Koi 286:24, *see also:* 16:32

Come, Follow 71:104, 72:163, 148:57, 293:78

Come, frontier men, awake now, by mountain and by lake now 28:116

Come gather around me, my comrades and friends 61:319 ·

Come Gently Spring 85:120

Come, girls! Let's deck the shelf 286:70

Come, give me your attention, and see the right and wrong 61:125

Come, Hear the Wonderful Tidings 54:236, see also: 220:100, 279:116

Come Here and Sing 176:17

Come here! Come, firefly 16:32, see also: 286:24

Come hither, brother tradesmen, and hear the news I bring 240:162

Come Home, Father 157:174

Come, Holy Spirit, Come 86:71

Come In and Shut the Door 66:94

Come in! Come in! Come in! We greet you! 68:4

Come in Out of the Draft 73:136

Come, Jeremy, Etan! 197:44

Come Jiroyan, come Taroyan 49:24

Come, join hand in hand, brave Americans all 21:238, 27:182, 28:9, 157:16, 240:44, 273:20

Come join in our temperance army 157:51

Come ladies, come ladies, come gentlemen and all 61:18, see also: 61:20, 234:68

Come, lads, your glasses fill with glee 273:72

Come Lasses and Lads 79:51, 227:42

Come let us all a-maying go 239:127

Come, Let Us Be Joyful 46:200, 70:15

Come let us be joyful and mingle our song 114:90

Come, let us go to the dance, see how lovely 22:78, 72:106, see also: 295:66

Come Let's Go A'Planting 100:64

Come list ye, landsmen, all to me, to tell the truth I'm bound 292:178

Come, listen a while you gentlemen all 164:16

Come, listen all you gals and boys, I'm just from Tuckyhoe 21:290

Come listen and I'll tell you how first I went to sea 28:120

Come listen kind friends, and I'll sing you a song 35:64

Come listen, my cocks, to a brother and friend 240:164

Come listen to a ranger, you kind-hearted stranger 159:369

Come, listen to me closely, while I rehearse a ditty 27:211

Come, listen to me, you gallants so free 164:42

Come listen to my story, I'll not detain you long 61:46

Come, listen to my story, ye landsmen, one and all 226:178

Come, Little Sennerin 245:12

Come, love, let us live happily 163:68

Come maidens fair, altogether come 70:10, 100:126, 168:57

Come, My Dear Old Lady/Ya Viene la Vieja 54:254

Come My Love 126:91

Come my love and go with me 126:91

Come, my lute, and gently sighing 85:143

Come, O Children, Sing to Jesus 86:66

Come, O Sabbath Day 25:113

Come, Oh Come, Dear Children All 244:166

Come, Oh Love/Shule Aroon 21:344, 89:136

Come On and Join In to the Game 75:19, 289:158, 291:4

Come on and show me, Hi-dee-roon 291:8, see also: 72:105

Come on and sing with me 72:105, see also: 291:8

Come On Boys and Girls and Hush Your Talkin' 178:13, see also: 232:134

Come on, boys, and hush your talking 232:134, see also: 178:13

Come on brave boys, let us be brave, for liberty and law 240:28

Come on Girls (Boys), We're Going to Boston 178:36, see also: Going to Boston

Come on, hurry and let's go down 110:19

Come on, my hearts of tempered steel 28:153

Come on out, o, come on out 286:48

Come on, you lads of old Lorraine 22:188

Come on young men and ladies, mothers and fathers too 24:891

Come Out and Play 245:19

Come out and play. What a snowy day! 207:77

Come out, the sun is high, the wind is fair 262:84

Come Out to Play 18:46

Come Out, Ye Continentalers 27:34, 28:107

23

Come over the sea in my boat with me 227:16

Come play this game with me 288:6

Come Quickly, New Year/Hayaku Koi Koi Oshogatsu 286:85

Come rise up brother Minute Men and let us have a chorus 240:86

Come, rouse up, my lads, and join this great cause 273:38

Come Running, You Shepherds/O Laufet Ihr Hirten 54:154

Come, Saints and Sinners 21:349

Come See 130:34

Come see my little baby 130:34

Come see the lovely way in which he's coming 169:17

Come Shake Your Dull Noodles 28:11, 240:45, 273:22

Come, sheathe your swords, my gallant men 28:150, 240:107, 273:52

Come sit by my side, little darling 61:158

Come soldiers all in chorus join 240:118

Come, Son 176:76

Come, son, said his mother, rock our little baby 176:76

Come, stack arms, men, pile on the rails 73:84

Come Surfing with Me/Ku'u Ipo I Ka He'e Pu'eone 87:36

Come Swallow Your Bumpers 28:13, *see also:* 240:47, 273:24

Come swallow your bumpers, ye tories and roar 240:47, *see also:* 28:13, 273:24

Come take a ride, come take a ride 162:70

Come, tell me now. Come, tell me now 208:67

Come, they told me (pa-rum-pum, pum, pum) 115

Come, Thou Almighty King 45:31, 86:15, 161:85, 273:158

Come Thou Long Expected Jesus 161:54

Come to see Jinny Jo, Jinny Jo, Jinny Jo 63:32, *see also:* 17:39, 68:12, 100:90

Come to the barnyard, Olga 68:26

Come to the Farm 162:15

Come to the top of the path in the garden 262:85

Come to the Window 245:94

Come Unto Me 155:31

Come unto me, all ye children 155:31

Come unto me ye heroes whose hearts are true and bold 240:124

Come up, horsey, hey, hey 234:27

Come, wife and children, let us see the light 210:101

Come With Hearts Rejoicing 86:124

Come with us sweet flow'rs 284:91

Come with your shining white fire 19:21

Come Ye Children, Praise the Savior 85:129

Come ye people bright and gay, carousel is running 20:59

Come, Ye Thankful People, Come 45:44, 86:179

Comin' Round the Mountain One By One 178:40

The Coming Feast 207:41

Comment allez-vous 107:16

Common Bill 62:130, 226:62

Commonwealth of Toil 64:14

Como Busca el Tierno Infante/As the Frightened Baby Jesus 54:298

Complete Version of Ye Three Blind Mice 103, *see also:* 17:25, 25:29, 26:41, 62:10, 148:391, 175:52, 188:82, 189:14, 283:66, 292:192, 293:98

Con real y medio, con real y medio 262:22

Congo Tay 130:82

The Congress 240:150

The Constitution and the Guerrière 240:191

The Convict 159:90

Coo, Coo 71:107 *(Coo, coo, coo, coo. How I love you)*

Coo-Coo (Peacock Song) 226:237 *(Coo-coo, coo-oo-oo, Coo-Coo, coo-oo-oo)*

Cookie, you see nobody pass here? 130:48

Cool Breezes/Liang Fung Lyao Lyao 49:18

Coon Can 226:310

Coonie's Got a Pretty Tail 292:97

Coonshine 109:132

Coonshine, baby, coonshine, Coonshine on the sly 109:132

The Cooper of Fife 20:25, *see also:* Wee Cooper of Fife

The Coqui sings a lullaby 69:32

Corde Natus Ex Parentis/Of the Father's Love Begotten 54:314

The Cordwood Cutter 35:14

The Cork Leg 78:25

Corn-Grinding Song/Ockaya 68:13, 89:38 *(Lovely! See the cloud, the cloud appear)*

The Corn-Grinding Song 197:85 *(Ioho, wonder water)*

Corn in the Wind 245:64

The Cornfields/Los Maizales 270:50, *see also:* 169:55

Cornish May Song 208:70

Cornwallis Burgoyned 240:137, 273:56

The Cornwallis Country Dance 28:156, 240:135, 273:54, 277:16

Cornwallis led a country dance 28:156, 240:135, 273:54, 277:16

Corporal Schnapps 73:115

Cossack's Lullaby 262:93, *see also:* 125:18

The Cottager to Her Infant 59:61

Cottleston, Cottleston, Cottleston pie 172:27, 174:13, 289:121
Cottleston Pie 172:27, 174:13, 289:121
Cotton Eyed Joe 128:20, 274:6, 289:25
Cotton Field 189:142
Cotton-Picking Song 239:45
The Counting Lesson 191:56, *see also:* 162:23
Counting Song/Kazoe Uta 286:86
Counting the Goats 292:56
Counting Valentines 162:53
Country Clodhoppers 262:78
The Court of King Carraticus 290:10
Coventry Carol 22:252, 54:19, 220:114, 241:26, 264:116, 279:32, *see also:* 190:105, 210:46
Covered Wagon Song 69:39
The Cow 44:14 *(The friendly cow all red and white)*
The Cow 17:115 *(Thank you, pretty cow that made)*
The Cow-bosses are good-hearted chunks 159:51
A Cow Camp on the Range 159:71
The Cow Chase 28:134
Cow on the Railroad Track 118:28
A cow will moo when it's disturb'd 112:20
The Coward 227:11
The Cowboy 159:139 *(Oh, a man there lives on the western plains)*
The Cowboy 159:168 *(It was only a few short years ago)*
The Cowboy 60:90, 146:132, 159:67 *(All day on the prairie in the saddle I ride)*
Cowboy Again for a Day 61:313
The Cowboy and His Love 159:311
The Cowboy at Church 159:272
The Cowboy at Work 159:83
Cowboy Carol 210:96
A Cowboy Dance Song 159:241
A cowboy he lay on the prairie 159:306
Cowboy Jack 159:230
Cowboy Lullaby 277:135
Cowboy Small wears dungarees 154:34
Cowboy Song 83:466, 288:25
Cowboy Spring 189:116, *see also:* 27:50
Cowboy Tune 207:120
The Cowboy Up to Date 159:296
Cowboys 207:123
The Cowboy's Christmas Ball 159:246
Cowboys, come and hear the story of Roy Bean in all his glory 159:147
The Cowboy's Dance Song 159:251, *see also:* 61:284
The Cowboy's Dream 158:210, 159:44, *see also:* Cowboy's Heaven
Cowboy's Gettin'-Up Holler 159:3, *see also:* 289:24

The Cowboy's Heaven 60:72, 146:106, 225:66, *see also:* 25:74, 26:74, 158:210, 159:44
Cowboy's Home Sweet Home 61:243
The Cowboy's Lament 146:30, *see also:* 60:16, 69:22, 159:421, 262:51 *(My home's in Montana)*
The Cowboy's Lament 24:859, 60:16, 159:417, *see also:* Streets of Laredo *(As I walked out in the streets of Laredo)*
The Cowboy's Life 61:235, 159:281, *see also:* 60:36, 146:53, 159:15
A cowboy's life is a dreary, dreary life 60:36, 61:235, 159:15, *see also:* 146:53, 159:281
The Cowboy's Meditation 61:327, 159:122
A Cowboy's Prayer 61:343
The Cowboy's Ride 61:298
The Cowboy's Soliloquy 61:332
The Cowboy's Sweet Bye and Bye 25:74, 26:74, *see also:* Cowboy's Heaven
The Cowboy's Vision 61:329
The Cowman's Prayer 159:329, *see also:* 61:339
Crab Is a Better Man 130:76
Cradle Hymn 65:89, 125:102, *see also:* Away in a Manger
Cradle Hymn 233:41, *see also:* Hush, My Babe *(Hush, my babe, lie still and slumber)*
Cradle Song 184:62, *see also:* Hush, My Babe *(Hush! my dear, lie still and slumber)*
Cradle Song 220:24, *see also:* Joseph Dearest Joseph
Cradle Song 41:48 *(Baby mine, a star is peeping in the sky)*
Cradle Song (Brahms) 71:122, 72:58, 85:176, 125:89, *see also:* 17:63, 283:60, 289:18 *(Lullaby and good night, in the sky stars are bright)*
Cradle Song 85:24 *(My little sweet darling, my comfort and joy)*
The Cradle Song (Blake) 59:41 *(Sleep, sleep, beauty bright)*
Cradle Song (Kwakiutl Indians) 79:17 *(Sleep oh, sleep oh, sleep oh)*
Cradle Song (Mozart) 85:101, *see also:* Lullaby *(Lullay, my prince, lullaby)*
Cradle Song (Schubert) 85:140 *(Lulla, lulla, pretty little darling)*
A Cradle Song/Balulalow 210:88 *(O my deir hert, young Jesus sweit)*
Crane, oh, crane 169:69
The Cranky Soap 91:46
The Crawdad 21:106, 24:896, 27:160, 230:86, *see also:* 129:30, 148:58, 158:107, 292:182

The Crawdad Hole   129:30, *see also:* Crawdad

Crawdad Song   148:58, 158:107, 292:182, *see also:* Crawdad

The Crawfish Man   129:21, *see also:* 262:35

Crazy Carrousel   166:66

Crazy Song to the Air of "Dixie"   226:342

The Creation   123:22

Creep, Mouse, Creep   135:111

Crested Crane/Ntuha Ntuha   265:56, *see also:* 169:69

Cricket Voices/Mushi-no Koe   286:30

Cripple Creek   24:898, 134:48

Cripple Creek girls; don't you want to go to Somerset?   134:48, *see also:* 24:898

Cro cro cro cro cro   266:25

The Crocodile   62:48, *see also:* 26:36, 89:33, 234:72 *(She sailed away on a bright and sunny day)*

The Crocodile   59:29, *see also:* 112:39 *(How doth the little crocodile)*

The Crocodile   290:168 *(One day when I was sailing)*

The Crocodile   292:178 *(Come list ye, landsmen, all to me)*

Crocodile Song   26:36, 89:33, 234:72, *see also:* 62:48

The crooked paths go every way   44:52

The Crooked Trail to Holbrook   159:27

The Crops Have Been Gathered   125:22

Cross-eyed Gopher   234:20

Cross Patch   112:16

Cross Patch, draw the latch   112:16

Cross your little fingers   68:7

The Crow/Karasu   286:26

The Crow and the Fox/Le Corbeau et le Renard   243:2

The Crow-Fish Man   262:35, *see also:* 129:21

Crow on the Cradle   292:146

Crown Him with Many Crowns   45:43

Crows in the Garden   130:107

Cruel Baboon/Mfene Sandhleni   89:286

The Cruel War Is Raging   72:12

The Cruiskeen Lawn   42:609

Cry a pint   237:unpaged

Cuando la perico quiere que el perico vaya amisa   262:18

Cuando los San Juaninos bajan el aqua   89:88

Cuando uno quierea une Yesta una no lo quiere   21:110, 226:291, *see also:* 197:38

Cub Days   26:51

Cub days, cub days, dear old golden pal days   26:51

Cub friendships, pure and deep   26:62

Cub Pledge   26:62

Cub Scout Advancement Song   26:46

Cub Scout Booster Song   26:46

The Cub Scout circus comes to town   26:71

The Cub Scout Hymn   26:64

Cub Scout Marching Song   26:59

Cub Scout Prayer   26:95

Cub Scout Travelers   26:77

Cub Scout Welcome Song   26:8

Cub Scouting Song   26:57

Cub Scouting We Will Go   26:57

Cub Scouts All   26:57

Cub Scouts all join in the song, Doo-dah, Doo-dah!   26:75, 26:76

Cub Scouts, Cub Scouts, help the pack to go   26:57

Cub Scouts in Blue   26:63

Cub Scouts U.S.A.   26:61

Cubbing Along Together   26:60

Cubbing in the Morning   26:56

Cubs Are Always Happy   26:50

Cubs Are Fair   26:52

Cubs! Cubs! All Cubs are fair   26:52

Cubs, it's time we're parting   26:92

Cubs Whistle While They Work   26:58

Cuc-A-Nandy   212:64

The Cuckoo   177:91 *("Cuckoo, Cuckoo," sings the cuckoo all day long)*

Cuckoo   17:40, 289:66 *(Cuckoo, Cuckoo, calls from the wood)*

The Cuckoo/Le Cou-Cou   27:52, 157:77, 217:60, *see also:* 59:23, 292:130 *(The cuckoo is a funny bird)*

The Cuckoo   71:107 *(Down yonder in the woodland, the cuckoo sings today)*

A Cuckoo and an Owl   144:13

Cuckoo, Cuckoo, calls from the wood   17:40, *see also:* 289:66

"Cuckoo, Cuckoo," sings the cuckoo all day long   177:91

Cuckoo is acalling   289:66, *see also:* 17:40

The Cuckoo is a funny bird, she sings as she flies   27:52, *see also:* 59:23, 157:77, 217:60, 292:130

The Cuckoo Is a Pretty Bird   59:23, 292:130, *see also:* 25:52, 142:77, 197:60

The Cuckoo, she's a pretty bird   142:77, *see also:* 27:52, 59:23, 217:60, 292:130

Cuckoo Waltz   226:160

The 'Cumberland' Crew   35:20, *see also:* 73:183

Cumberland Gap   33:154, 230:67, 277:79

Cumberland Gap is a noted place   33:154, 277:79, *see also:* 230:67

Cumberland Mountain Bear Chase   292:103

The *Cumberland*'s Crew   73:183, *see also:* 35:20

Curly Locks   17:86, 175:106, 285:68

Curly Locks, Curly Locks, will you be mine?   17:86, 175:106, 285:68

Curtains of Night   61:245

The Cushion Dance 176:57
Custer's Last Charge 61:127
A Customer 154:22
Cut the Oats 100:49, 168:100
Cutting Down the Pines 35:8
The Cutty Wren 64:175
Cyclone Blues 159:294
Czerwony Pas/Belt Red as Flame 208:58

D

Da Droben Vom Berge/Above, On the Mountain 54:174
Da re demo do yo bi gasuki 148:84
Daddy Shot a Bear 135:53, 234:78
Daddy Wouldn't Buy Me a Bow Wow 197:68
Daddy's Gone to Town 125:30
Daddy's Whiskers(1) 197:70
Daddy's Whiskers(2) 197:71
Dagestan 89:179
Dainty Little Butterfly 245:42
Daisies 245:99
Daisy Bell 21:19, 205:234, *see also:* 26:19, 83:493, 148:40
Daisy, Daisy 26:19, 83:493, 148:40, *see also:* 21:19, 205:234
Daisy, Daisy, give me your answer, do 26:19, 83:493, 148:40, *see also:* 21:19, 205:234
Dakota Hymn 69:25, 71:88, 72:69
Dakota Land 61:62, 159:410, 226:280, *see also:* 61:63, 61:64
Dame Get Up 17:123, 129:52, 138:unpaged, 188:150
Dame get up and bake your pies 17:123, 129:52, 138:unpaged, 188:150
Dame, Lend Me a Loaf 293:74
The Damper Song 26:34, *see also:* 253:90
Dan Taylor 159:261
Dan Taylor is a jolly cuss, a frisky son-of-a-gun 159:261
Dance a Baby, Diddy 17:74, 188:18
Dance a baby, diddy, what can mammy do wid 'e 17:74, 188:18
Dance all night with your bottle in your hand 134:42
Dance Carol 279:112, *see also:* 54:193, 89:170, 241:168, 262:42
Dance in a Circle 162:62
Dance Like a Lady 296:23
Dance, Little Baby 111:78
Dance, Little Maiden 245:32
Dance of Greeting 83:497
Dance the bonny lad up, and dance the bonny lad down 212:64

Dance, Thumbkin, Dance 17:42, 111:29
Dance to the Merry Piper's Sound 245:50
Dance to Your Daddy 27:142, 111:42, 281:56
Dance With Gladness/Doos Ya Lellee 89:248
Dance your dance, Imilla 114:66
Dancer, Little Dancer/Ciranda, Cirandenha 168:141, *see also:* 169:9, 266:13
Dancing 104:50
Dancing Dollies 128:98
The Dancing Lesson 227:28, *see also:* 75:14
Dancing like the leaves falling from the trees 162:42
Dancing Song of the Skunk 74:29
Dancing the Gato/Bailando el Gato 89:88
Dandelion Buttons 207:93
Daniel 109:146
Daniel Saw the Stone 123:305
Danny is his first name 291:38
Dans Cette Etable/In That Poor Stable 210:39, *see also:* 220:60
Dans la forêt lointaine 217:35
Dans le jardin d'mon père 21:340
Dans les Chantiers Nous Hivernerons 176:62
Dans un amas d'épaisse boue 243:48
Danse Juba/Juba Dance 89:57
Daphe Bird 114:26
The Darby Ram 27:60, 37:134, 129:44, 292:49, *see also:* 62:36, 229, 234:58
Dark As a Dungeon 64:49
Dark brown is the river, golden is the sand 69:43
Dark night, I see nothing 216:47
Dark the night is, total blackness 89:96, *see also:* 169:14, 216:24, 267:46
The Darkness Is Falling/Es Wird Scho Glei Dumpa 279:82, *see also:* 54:172
Darlin' Corey 21:274, 158:310, 230:73
Darling, I am growing old, silver threads among the gold 21:231, 170:27
Darling Nelly Gray 21:132, 126:59
Dashing Away with the Smoothing Iron 134:14, *see also:* Charlie Is My Darling
Dashing through the snow, in a one horse open sleigh 54:70, 92:163, 127:220, 148:200, 264:114, 283:64, *see also:* 17:63, 241:171
Dat Sunshine Special comin' around de bend 226:246, *see also:* 158:68, 226:247
Daughters, Will You Marry? 290:76
Davi Ayele no bu lo 215:44
David, the king, was grieved and moved 273:142
David's Lamentation 273:142
Davy Crockett 33:106
Day and Night 125:38

Day by day, Lord, for three things I pray 189:59

The day is broke, my boys, march on 28:84, 27:32

Day is done, gone the sun 25:126, 26:92, 69:10, 71:12, 72:53, 148:370, 197:62, *see also:* 277:45

Day is done, sinks the sun 277:45, *see also:* Taps

Day Is Dying in the West 22:288

Day is over, time for rest 149:24

The day is so lovely, the world is so fair 86:145

A Day of Joy and Feasting 241:8

The day on which you were born were born all the flowers 295:62, *see also:* 169:49, 226:292, 262:21, 268:41

The day that my dear came to us 226:292

A Day to Ski 207:73

Dayenu 27:84, 197:46

The daylight is gone, the daylight is gone 74:15

The daylight will come, the sunshine is bright 74:22

The Days of '49 158:180, 159:378

Days of the Week 104:52, *see also:* Here We Go Round the Mulberry Bush

De Bezem 262:120

De Blanca Tierra/From Lands Far Away 89:90, *see also:* 262:19

De Blanca Tierra/From the White Earth 262:19, *see also:* 89:90

De deux chiens frères et jumeaux 243:46, 243:54

De grand matin j'ai rencontre le train 241:105

De la gent magote sottement épris 243:45

De la Sierra Morena, cielito lindo 197:36, 216:27, 226:298, 230:23

De Nederige Geboorte/The Simple Birth 54:182

De Rommelpot/The Rommelpot 89:140

De Tierra Lejana Venimos/Song of the Wise Men 54:288, *see also:* 140:22

De tierra lejana venimos a verte 140:22, *see also:* 54:288

De tus encantos, celestial Paloma Azul 89:72

The Dead Horse 98:39, 226:406

The Deaf Woman's Courtship 37:136, 69:19, 129:100, 213:72, 262:119, 290:75, *see also:* 20:26, 46:223, 83:470

Dear countrymen, attend the tale 240:170

Dear George and Martha Washington, long years ago 207:84

Dear Lord and Father of Mankind 45:30, 148:60, 161:67

Dear Lord, guide us Girl Scouts today 69:5, 71:29

Dear Lord Jesus, Hear My Prayer 86:165

Dear Lord, look down upon us, we bow our heads in prayer 177:86

Dear Lord, We Give Our Youth to Thee 86:118

Dear Nightingale, Awake/Lieb Nachtigall, Wach Auf 54:158, *see also:* 279:62

Dear Old Girl 205:292

Dearest love, do you remember, when we last did meet 73:267

Dearest Sun 245:4

Death of General Wolfe 273:18

The Death of Jesse James 61:258, *see also:* Jesse James

The Death of Mother Jones 64:58

Death Song of an Indian Chief 273:108

Debreczenbe Kéne Menni/The Turkey 289:86

Debwangue 89:260

Deck the Halls 22:254, 54:53, 92:148, 148:62, 220:102, 241:2, 262:165, 264:98, 279:30, 284:39

Deep and Wide 26:27

Deep Blue Sea 230:76

Deep blue sea, baby, deep blue sea 230:76

Deep in the caverns of our mountain 245:63

Deep in the forest in cool shady grove 89:172

Deep in the forest stands a little hill 176:130, *see also:* Green Grass Grows All Around

Deep in the hundred acre wood where Christopher Robin plays 275:66, 276:82

Deep in the Woods 197:48, *see also:* Green Grass Grows All Around

Deep in the woods there was a hill 197:48, *see also:* Green Grass Grows All Around

Deep River 31:27, 157:142

Deep river, my home is over Jordan 157:142, *see also:* 31:27

The Deer Begins His Travels 74:13

The deer is traveling, the deer is traveling 74:13

The Deer Song 234:34, 292:80

Deilig Er den Himmel Blaa/Lovely Is the Dark Blue Sky 54:188

Delia, Delia, why didn't you run? 24:911

Delia Holmes 24:911

Delilah was a woman fine and fair 123:178

Deliver the Goods 239:92

Den Lillas Testamente/The Child's Testament 89:169

Dendenmushi/The Snail 286:21

Dendenmushi, mushi Katatsumuri 286:21

The Dens of Yarrow 35:40

Der Blaue Montag/Blue Monday 89:147

Der Kuckuck 20:86

Der Montag, der Montag der muss gefeirt werden 89:147

Derby Ram 229, *see also:* Darby Ram

Dere's a little wheel a-turnin' in my heart 157:146, 227:27, *see also:* 129:10

Dere's a star in de Eas' on Christmas morn 209:22, *see also:* Rise Up, Shepherd and Follow

Derrière de Chez Mon Père/My Father's Apple Tree 188:110

Derry Down 27:164, *see also:* 28:51, 240:67, 273:36

Dese Bones Gwine to Rise Again 89:42, 197:94, 226:470, *see also:* 290:40

The Desert 91:20

The Desperado 159:137, 290:63

The despot's heel is on thy shore 73:22, 127:149, 160:50

The Destruction of the Tea 240:52

Det Kimer Nu Til Julefest/The Happy Christmas Comes Once More 54:186

Deta Deta/The Moon Is Coming Out 286:62

Deta, deta tsuki ga 286:62

Deux Gascons manquaient d'argent 243:26

Deux mulets faisaient un voyage 243:20

The Devil and the Farmer's Wife 36:74, 230:58

The devil, in hell, we are told, was chained 61:83

The devil was given permission one day 61:82

The devil, we're told, in Hell was chained 61:80, *see also:* 159:317

Devilish Mary 36:60, 37:154, 62:142, 230:70, *see also:* 157:14

The Devil's Nine Questions 27:214, *see also:* 37:110, 134:85

The Devil's Questions 37:110, 134:85, *see also:* 27:214

The Dew Is Dry at Midday/Seba Alaso Trodje 89:234

Dewdrops on Leaves/D'Purle vum Da 89:146

Dey tell me Joe Turner he done come 226:241

Diamond Joe 159:65

Dickey-Bird Song 75:20, *see also:* Two Little Blackbirds

Dicky Ducky Daddle 162:13

Did You Ever, Ever, Ever? 226:329

Did you ever, ever, ever, in your leaf, life, loaf 226:329

Did You Ever Go Fishing? 112:28

Did you ever go fishing on a bright, sunny day? 112:28

Did you ever go to meeting, Uncle Joe, Uncle Joe 130:68, 135:18, 234:66, *see also:* 128:23

Did you ever hear about Cocaine Lil? 226:206

Did you ever hear tell of sweet Betsy from Pike 22:62, 158:176, 159:388, *see also:* Sweet Betsy from Pike

Did you ever hear the story 'bout Willy, the Weeper? 22:54, 226:204

Did You Ever See a Lassie? 14:344, 17:36, 20:33, 63:21, 165:180, 283:36, 289:162

Did you ever see a muskrat Sally Ann? 230:53

Did you ever see the longest dog in the world 167:38

Did you ever see two Yankees 205:307

Did you ever think about Red Riding Hood's red hood? 162:72

Did you ever think, as the hearse rolls by 226:444, 290:178, *see also:* 62:109

Did you ever think when you see a hearse 62:109, *see also:* 226:444, 290:178

Did You Feed My Cow? 107:18, *see also:* 232:112, 234:56, 292:20, 292:44

Did You Go to the Barney? 232:112, *see also:* 107:18, 234:56, 292:20, 292:44

Did You See My Wife? 111:71

Diddle, Diddle Dumpling 285:97, *see also:* 162:88, 175:162

Diddle, diddle dumpling, my son John 285:97, *see also:* 162:88, 175:162

Didn't it rain-a, rain-a, rain-a, rain-a, rain-a, rain-a, rain? 129:118

Didn't My Lord Deliver Daniel? 31:17, 157:140

Die Abendglocke/The Evening Bells 21:322

Die Binschgauer Wallfahrt/The Binschgauer Pilgrimage 89:149

Die Gedanken Sind Frei 64:178

Die Hirten auf dem Felde/As Lately We Watched 54:170

Die Kinder an der Krippe 86:42, *see also:* 54:142, 241:162, 279:72

Die Könige/The Kings 241:215, *see also:* 210:121

Die Lorelei 176:68

Die Weihnachtsnachtigall/The Christmas Nightingale 279:62

The Dieting Dragon 162:12

Digging, digging, this is how we dig the ground 291:56

A Dillar, a Dollar 285:79

Diller, Diller Dollar 110:18

Diller, diller dollar, Danny is a scholar! 110:18

A diller, a dollar, a ten o'clock scholar 285:79

Dime, Lluvia/Tell Me, Rain   216:17
Din Dan Don It's Christmas   51
Din, din, din, es hora de partir   54:300
Din, din, din, we must be on our way   54:300
Din Don   188:170
Din, don, din, don, dan, campanitas sona-ran   188:170
Ding-A-Ling-A-Ling   162:52
Ding, ding, ding, a winter holiday   162:47
Ding-ding-ding! Alarm bell rings   154:31
Ding, Dong Bell   17:49, 147:13, 175:174
Ding, dong, ding, dang, dong, little bells are ringing on   188:170
Ding! Dong! Ding! Dong! Church bells sing an Easter song   162:57
Ding Dong Merrily on High   96:5, 210:22
The Dining Room   149:16
Dink's Song   158:66, 230:88
Dip and Fall Back Low   130:52
Dipidu   114:46
Dis Mornin', Dis Evenin', So Soon   226:18
The Disheartened Ranger   159:369
Dites-Moi   218:134
Dites-moi pourquoi la vie est belle   218:134
Diudlidiudliem   71:57
Diw' Laiwinas/Two Little Boats   89:174
Dixie   22:192, 25:101, 26:15, 99:53, 127:112, 157:120, 160:42, *see also:* 73:8
Dixie Girls   141:90
Dixie Land   73:8, *see also:* Dixie
Dixie, The Land of King Cotton   73:20
Do, Do, L'Enfant Do   59:51, *see also:* 78:41
Do, Do, Pity My Case   24:805, 232:136
Do I Love You Because You're Beautiful   218:290
Do, Lord, oh do, Lord, oh do remember me   55:279, 148:64
Do, Lord, Remember Me   55:279, 148:64
Do Not Cry   19:43
Do Not Cry, My Child/Yeke, Omo Mi   89:270, 267:14, *see also:* 169:50, 208:47
Do not jump on ancient uncles   290:142
Do-Re-Mi   218:234
Do Unto Others   155:10
Do You Hate Your Teachers Dear   147:22
Do you have a playmate? Oh, yes!   162:73
Do You Know How to Plant Cabbages?   217:53, *see also:* 165:85, 168:164
Do you know the muffin man   135:27, *see also:* The Muffin Man
Do you know the tale of Abraham   123:51
Do you plant your cabbages in the right way   165:85, *see also:* 168:164, 217:53
Do Your Ears Hang Low   63:139, 118:19
Do your share to help us keep our classroom clean and looking neat   11:21
Dobe Bill, he came a-riding   159:172

Dobrou Noc/Sweetheart, Good Night   208:13
Doctor, Doctor   63:68
Doctor, doctor, can you tell, what will make poor Sheila well?   63:68
Doctor Faustus   112:18
Doctor Faustus was a good man   112:18
Doctor Foster   175:126
Doctor Foster went to Gloucester   175:126
The doctor of the road is the beetle   163:28
Dodge City, the End of the Trail   159:133
The Dodger   24:875, 64:150
Dodo, Baby, Do   125:108, *see also:* 78:41
Dodo, l'enfant do, l'enfant dormira tantere   78:41, *see also:* 59:51
Doe—a deer, a female deer, Ray—a drop of golden sun   218:234
A Dog Came to School   151
Dog Jumps Through the Window   189:21
Dog Tick   232:127
The Dog Who Sees His Reflection in the Water/Le Chien Qui Se Voit dans L'Eau   243:4
The Dogie Song   25:84, 71:86, *see also:* Git Along Little Dogies (*As I was a-walking, one morning for pleasure*)
Dogie Song   159:51 (*The cow-bosses are good-hearted chunks*)
Dogs are barking, dogs are barking   89:235
Dollar, Dollar   20:10, 110:31
Dollar, dollar, how you wander   20:10, 110:31
Dolls' Festival/Hina Matsuri   286:70
Dolly by by dolly lullaby   85:219
Dolly's Lullaby   85:219
Don-Don Ba Ji   169:63, *see also:* 269:50
Don Gato/Sir Cat   295:4, *see also:* 216:3
Don' Let Yo' Watch Run Down   226:370
Doña Blanca   168:28, 295:30
Dona Gal   61:232, *see also:* 61:231, 61:233, 159:8, 232:69
Doña Maria   295:55
Doña Maria doesn't go out of the house   295:55
Doña María no sale de casa, porque los pollos le comen la masa   295:55
Dona Nobis Pacem   55:254, 69:11, 176:47, 201:224, 262:34, 293:112
Donana   114:86
Donde está la Ma Teodora?   216:19
Donde Están las Llaves?/Where Are the Keys to the Castle?   188:54, *see also:* 189:154
Done found my lost sheep   233:20
Doney Gal   61:231, 61:232, 159:8, *see also:* 232:69
Donkey, Donkey, Old and Gray   285:42
Donkey Riding   71:81, 72:117, 78:11, 128:88

Donkeys and Carrots   293:92
Donkeys are in love with carrots   293:92
Donkeys Love Carrots   144:23
Donkeys love to munch on carrots   144:23
Don't Cry Little Dolly   162:78
Don't Fence Me In   170:72
Don't Grow Weary, Boys   159:259
Don't pull off my boots and pull off my hat   159:223
Don't stop a moment to think, John   73:112
Don't Swat Your Mother   290:176
Don't Want to Go Home   68:37, 262:25
Don't you hear my needle sing Zing!   130:36
Don't You Hear the Lambs a-Crying?   233:19
Don't You Push Me Down   130:54
Doodle Dandy   134:92
Doodle, doodle, doodle dandy, cornstalks rum and a home-made brandy   134:92
"The door is shut fast and everyone's out"   44:68
The Door of My Heart   155:15
Doos Ya Lellee/Dance With Gladness   89:248
Dormi, dormi, o bel Bambin   54:248, 190:30, 221:94
Dormy Dormouse   144:17
Dormy, dormy dormouse, sleeps in his little house   144:17
Dors, Ma Colombe/Sleep Little Dove   54:120, *see also:* 184:44
Dos y Dos Son Cuatro/Two and Two Are Four   194:36
A Dose for the Tories   240:162
D'où Viens-tu, Bergère?/Whence Art Thou, My Maiden   54:133, *see also:* 279:96
D'où viens-tu, bergère, d'ou viens-tu   54:133, 279:96
The Double-Breasted Mansion on the Square   61:76
Doughnuts   239:88
Douglas Mountain   59:70
The Dove   292:132
The dove she is a pretty bird   292:132
Dove si sta jersira   89:156, *see also:* 157:71, 232:140
Down at the Station Saga   55:263, *see also:* 25:30, 26:45, 75:21, 165:67
Down at the station early in the morning   55:263, *see also:* 25:30, 26:45, 75:21, 165:67
Down By the Bay   63:98
Down By the Greenwood Sidey-O   232:87
Down By the Old Millstream   290:66
Down By the River   141:22
Down by the river there lived a maiden   61:100, *see also:* Clementine

Down by the river where the green grass grows   141:22
Down By the Riverside   27:230, 148:66, *see also:* 64:202, 83:473, 226:480, 230:50
Down By the Station   25:30, 26:45, 75:21, 165:67, *see also:* 55:263
Down By the Station(adaptation)   41:28
Down by the station early in the morning   25:30, 75:21, 165:67, *see also:* 26:30, 55:263
Down Came A Lady   232:51
Down came a lady, down came two   232:51
Down Came an Angel   157:65, *see also:* 86:41
Down, Down Derry Down   226:118
Down, Down, Down   24:867, 158:188
Down goes the bright sun bearing his light   125:32
Down here, down here, there's no hiding place down here   262:145
Down in a Coal Mine   33:122, 64:47, 128:14
Down in front of Casey's old brown wooden stoop   157:188, 205:240, *see also:* 148:328
Down in St. Louis at 12th and Carr   226:198
Down in some lone valley in a lonesome place   21:278, 157:75, 213:92
Down in the canebrake, close by the mill   277:129
Down in the cellar where the furnace burns coal   149:26
Down in the garden lived a snail   162:26
Down in the grass, curled up in a heap   165:95
Down in the jungles lived a maid   21:68
Down in the Valley   22:99, 24:902, 25:99, 46:224, 61:162, 148:70, 158:62, 205:79, 226:148, 230:33
Down in the valley, the valley so low   22:99, 46:224, 148:70, 226:148, 230:33, *see also:* Down in the Valley
Down in the valley, sing hallelu   233:46
Down in the Willow Garden   158:302
Down in Yon Forest   27:82, 190:58, 210:23
Down on Penny's Farm   64:100
Down South on the Rio Grande   159:362
Down the Avenue   288:8
Down the green fields we'll jig it, we'll jig it   212:55
Down the Mississippi steamed the Whippoorwill   61:42
Down the River   20:75, 27:156, 197:82
Down where the patriot army, near Potomac's side   73:180
Down yonder green valley where streamlets meander   71:36, 72:124, *see also:* 55:258, 176:14
Down yonder in the woodland, the cuckoo sings today   71:107

The Doxology 21:312, 22:287, 45:7, 86:213, 148:74, 157:12, 161:11

D'Purle vum Da/Dewdrops on Leaves 89:146

Draw a Bucket of Water 14:345, 39:24, 109:80, 135:78

The Dream 273:116

A Dream Is a Wish Your Heart Makes 276:35

Dream Song 19:35

Dreamland 125:107

Dreamland opens here sweep the dream path clear 72:99, 79:37

The Dreary Black Hills 61:65, 146:95, 159:372, 226:264, 277:125

Dreary Life 60:36, 146:53, *see also:* 61:235, 159:16, 159:281

Drei Kon'ge wandern aus Morganland 241:215, *see also:* 210:121

Dreidel Song 68:30

Dressing 91:5

The Drifter 159:76

Drill, Ye Tarriers, Drill! 22:138, 64:87, 72:88, 239:80, 290:52

Drink that rotgut, drink that rotgut 159:136

Drink to Me Only with Thine Eyes 22:90, 71:116, 72:48, 205:89, 273:106

Drinking Song 159:136

Drip, drip, drip 237:unpaged

Drip, drip, drop, little April shower 276:26

Drivin' Steel 226:150

Drivin' steel, drivin' steel, drivin' steel, boys, is hard work, I know 226:139

Driving Saw-Logs on the Plover 226:396

Drool Song 25:40, *see also:* 63:124

Drum Song/Ajaaj 89:31

The Drummer Boy of Shiloh 73:200

Drummers Drumming A Round 237:unpaged

The Drunkard's Doom 226:104, 277:131

The Drunken Sailor 22:176, 176:108, 205:33, *see also:* 39:35, 98:25, 239:10

Dry as dust is the desert 91:20

The Dry-Landers 159:306

Du Gronne, Glitrende Tre, God-Dag/You Green and Glittering Tree, Good Day 54:198

Du lieber, heil'ger, frommer Christ 241:174

Dubula/Shoot 163:54

The Duck and the Hen 17:73

The Duck and the Kangaroo 112:53

The Duck Dance 14:346, *see also:* A Ship A-Sailing

Duck, o duck, dear duck of the meadow 70:23

Duck of the Meadow 70:23

The Ducks 227:37, *see also:* 135:25

Ducks in the Millpond 232:122

Ducks in the mill-pond eating up moss 159:259

Ducks on a Pond 290:197

Duérmete Mi Niño/Sleep My Child 194:16

Duérmete, Niño lindo, en los brazos dei amor 277:149

Dulce Dulce 107:44

Dumb, Dumb, Dumb 78:22

Dumbarton's Drums 99:35

Dumbarton's drums beat bonnie o 99:35

Dumplin's 130:48

Duncan and his brother was playing pool 226:198

Dunderbeck 290:158

The Durant Jail 158:316, 159:176

The Durant jail beats no jail at all 158:316, 159:176

The dust hangs thick upon the trail 158:311

Dutch Lullaby 33:74

Dwarf Song 245:63

Dyd da fo i ti, seren oleu 89:134

D'ye ken John Peel with his coat so gay 22:92, 176:48, 205:374

The Dying British Sergeant 240:148

The Dying Cowboy 25:78, 61:314, 159:48, 225:48, *see also:* Oh, Bury Me Not on the Lone Prairie

The Dying Cowboy of Rim Rock Ranch 61:325, 159:98

The Dying Desperado 159:223

The Dying Hogger 226:186

The Dying Outlaw 61:319

The Dying Ranger 159:366

Dze(r) dzoo diow/Purple Bamboo Flute 208:12

Dziasiaj w Betlejem/O Come Rejoicing 54:206

E

E Arrivato L'Ambasciatore 188:118

E! E! E! 89:304

E he ya! Bomi wanne bomiwanne 49:43

E he ya! Springtime, springtime 49:43

E Hii E/I Rock Thee 87:18

E hii leie, E hii leie 87:18

E, Ie, Ie 89:269

E ka gentle breeze e pa mai nai 87:47

E Lala E Liyo 89:259

E Mi Son Chi in Barchetta/In My Little Boat 89:155

The E-RI-E 21:282, 158:146, 226:180, 290:44, *see also:* 230:87, 277:39

Each Campfire Lights Anew 72:37

Each frog has a single mouth 49:14
Each little flower that opens, each little bird that sings 86:11, *see also:* 8, 45:32
Each man must find a pasture green 276:78
Each praying Jew begins anew 77:42
The Eagle 44:48
The eagle is flying around and around 74:59
Early in the Morning 155:2
Early in the morning down by the station 41:28, *see also:* Down By the Station
Early in the Spring 61:181, 61:182
Early in the summer when you pass 207:93
The Early Morning 44:18
Early Mornings/Mañanitas 226:292
Early on a Monday morning, high up on the gallows tree 21:116, 64:194, 226:42
Early One Morning 36:48, 176:18
Early one morning, in the homelands 163:100
Early one morning, just as the sun was rising 36:48, 176:18
Early one morning, the weather being fair 62:129
Early to Bed 71:105, 293:26
The Earth Needs the Raindrops 245:80
An earthly nourrice sits and sings 292:184
East Coast Line 109:97
East Side West Side 148:328, *see also:* 157:188, 205:240
East side, west side, all around the town 148:328, 157:188, 205:240
Easter 207:101
Easter Alleluya 262:156
Easter Basket 197:42
Easter Bells 162:57
Easter bells make music in the steeples high 207:98
Easter Bunny Song 245:114
Easter Bunny's coat is soft, Nimble are his legs 207:100
Easter Carol 184:60 *(Cheer up, friends and neighbors)*
An Easter Carol 86:59 *(Easter flowers are blooming bright)*
Easter flow'rs are blooming bright 86:59
Easter Greeting 245:113
The Easter Hare 245:115
Easter Hats 207:99
Easter Hymn 167:20 *(As we greet each Easter morn)*
Easter Hymn 197:40, *see also:* 86:67 *(Christ the Lord is risen today; Alleluia)*
Easter Is Here 7:18
An Easter Message 207:98
Easter Rabbit 162:58
Easter Time 86:61

Easy Rider 158:68, *see also:* 226:246, 226:247
Easy rider, see what you done done, Lawd, Lawd 158:68, *see also:* 226:246, 226:247
Eating Goober Peas 99:48, *see also:* 27:132, 73:166, 157:128, 277:85
Echameese toro pinto 216:1
Eche mis perros al monte 216:28
Echo Yodel 55:254
Edelweiss 218:252
Edelweiss, Edelweiss, ev'ry morning you greet me 218:252
Educated Feller 61:194, *see also:* 60:30, 61:194, 146:50, 159:78, 159:81, 225:38
Edward, Edward 89:137
Eency Weency Spider 20:81, 232:126, 289:92, 291:44, *see also:* 46:216, 63:103, 75:22, 147:26, 292:202
Eentsy Weentsy Spider 75:22, *see also:* Eency Weency Spider
Ef I had wings like Norah's dove 158:66, *see also:* 230:88
Eggs in nests turn into birds 91:33
Eglantine 275:81
Eglantine! Eglantine! Oh, how you'll shine! 275:81
Ego Sum Pauper 69:53
Eh-nee-wek kah-yea neen 19:33
Ehre Sei Gott/Glory to God 241:233
Eia, Eia 241:207
The Eight Hour Day 64:26
Eight Hours 21:215
Eileen Aroon 42:599
Ein' Feste Burg 21:324
Ein Jäger aus Kurpfalz/A Hunter from Kurpfalz 89:145
Ein Kindlein in der Wiegen/A Baby in the Cradle 54:178
Ein Mannlein steht im Walde, ganz still und stumm 79:71
Ein Schafermadchen Weidete 78:61
El-a-noy 21:298, 226:162, *see also:* 35:62
El Abandonado 226:295
El Baile/The Ball 208:62
El Cant dels Ocells 54:268, *see also:* Carol of the Birds
El Carite/The Carite Fish 216:4
El Charro/The Bumpkin 262:14
El Conejo de Esperanza/The Rabbit of Hope 194:20
El Coqui 69:32
El Cuando/O When, O When? 22:122
El Desembre Congalat/The Icy December 54:266
El día en que tu naciste nacieron todas las flores 226:292, 295:64, *see also:* Las Mañanitas
El Juego del Pañuelo/The Handkerchief Game 194:18

El Lobo/The Wolf   70:27
El Marido y la Piedra/The Husband and the Stone   89:78
El Mino Jesús/The Child Jesus   241:88, *see also:* 54:284, 209:110
El Noi de la Mare/The Son of Mary   54:260
El Pájaro/The Bird   295:10
El Patio de Mi Casa/The Patio of My House   295:40
El Pollo/The Chicken   295:15
El Quele le/The White Hawk   262:118
El Rancho Grande/The Big Ranch   216:23
El Rei Herodes/King Herod   54:264
El Rorro   54:308, 100:154, 279:106
El Sabado ama todo el mundo   148:84
El Santo Niño/The Holy Child   54:284, *see also:* 209:110, 241:88
El Sapo/The Toad   216:20
El sapo es un animal   216:20
El Señor don Gato/Sir Tomcat   216:3, *see also:* 295:4
El Sol y la Luna/The Sun and the Moon   216:14
El Sol se llama Lorenzo   216:14
El Tesoro de Santa Clara/The Treasure of the Santa Clara   295:68
El-thahlib   169:19
El Toro Pinto/The Spotted Bull   216:1
El Tortillero/The Tortilla-Seller   89:96, 169:14, 216:24, 267:46
El Vito   295:26
El Zancudo/The Mosquito   216:28
El Zapatero/The Shoemaker   78:88
Elenka   89:191
The Elephant   169:12
Elephant Fair   109:62
The elephant is big and strong   165:103
The Elephant Present   59:60
Elephant's Bath   207:107
Elephants can be lots of fun   59:60
Elephants Marching   63:80
Eletelephony   44:64
Eleven Cent Cotton   21:98, 64:104
Eleven Slash Slash Eleven   61:212
The Elfin Cap   245:56
Elizabeth's Carol   245:35
Elk Woman, Elk Woman, something is burning   74:31
Ellsworth Avengers   73:180
Elu honkwa lonan iyane!   89:38, *see also:* 68:13
Emancipation   73:26
Emilia   89:165
En Avant, Grenadiers/Forward March, Grenadiers   89:45
En Belén Tocan a Fuego   54:276, 295:76, *see also:* 89:276
En el mil nueve cientos y diez   226:303
En el Portal a Belén   54:282, 140:18

En la punta del manzano   295:10
En Nombre del Cielo/Pray Give Us Lodging   54:306
En Passant par la Lorraine/While Passing Through Lorraine   176:66, 217:36, *see also:* 208:23
En passant près d'un petit bois   217:38
En Roulant Ma Boule Roulant   89:34
En Salamanca/In Salamanca   295:51
En silencio te estoy adorando   89:55
En Sumag Palacio/In My Spacious Palace   89:97
En veure despuntar el major illuminar   54:268, *see also:* Carol of the Birds
Enchanted by your heav'nly beauty, sky-blue dove   89:72
End of a Lollypop   26:16
Engine, Engine   112:16
Engine, Engine Number Nine   112:16
The English Soldiers   63:34
Enkomo Zee-Gah-Baba   107:38
Enraptured I Gaze   21:244, 157:25
Ento Shinku/Faraway Island   49:32
Entre le boeuf et l'âne gris   54:100, 241:82
Eph Kate was a cow-punchin' boy   159:110
Epigram on Singers   176:141
Er is ein kindekin geboren op d'aard   54:182
Era una Vez/There Was Once   89:62, 216:34
Era una vez un barco chiquitito   89:62
Erie Canal   230:87, 277:39, *see also:* 21:282, 158:146, 226:180, 290:44 *(We were forty miles from Albany)*
Erie Canal   22:37, 69:34, 197:78, 226:171, 239:60, 246, 262:74, 292:38, *see also:* 33:58 *(I've got a mule and her name is Sal)*
Erin's Green Shores   35:86
Es Ist ein Ros Entsprungen   54:166, 210:30, 241:84, 279:58
Es Ist ein Schnitter/Behold the Reaper   89:142
Es regnet auf der Brucke, und es werd nass   188:144
Es Wird Scho Glei Dumpa/The Twilight Is Falling   54:172, 279:82
Esa, esa, Essa Hoi sasa   286:28
The Escape of Old John Webber   240:25
Eskimos   207:77
Está Sí Que Es Nochebuena/Yes! It Is Christmas Eve   295:78
Estaba una calandria pendiente de un balcon   295:7
Estant a la cambra amb so fill almat   54:264
Estas son las mañanitas   169:49, 262:21, *see also:* 226:292, 268:41, 295:62
Estabael Señor don Gato   216:3, *see also:* 295:4

Estilo 89:100

Et Barn er Fodt I Betlehem/A Child Is Born in Bethlehem 54:192

Et Moi de M'Encourir/And I Ran Away 217:38

The Etiquette 240:168

Evalina? (Pizza, Pizza, Mighty Moe) 109:64

Even in the City 261:44

The Evening Bells/Die Abendglocke 21:322

Evening Glow/Yu-Yake Koyake 286:64

Evening Hymn. Tallis's Canon 86:170, 189:60, *see also:* 71:106, 72:51, 176:104 (Glory to Thee, my God, this night)

Evening Hymn 125:106 (Hear us, Father, as we pray)

Evening Hymn 85:34 (Now, now that the sun has veil'd his light)

Evening Is a Little Boy 59:37

The Evening Is Coming 17:33, 289:38

Evening Prayer 155:28

Evening shadows spreading 'round me 16:41

The Evening Star 262:109

Evensong 77:26 (Blest art Thou, O Lord, our God)

Evensong 155:29 (Softly the evening, softly the night)

Ever Since Uncle John Henry Been Dead 226:376

Ever sweet my memory, I dream of you, my dear 87:42

Every Monday Morning (More About John Henry) 232:156, *see also:* John Henry

Every morning at half-past four 64:68

Every morning at seven o'clock 72:88, 239:80, *see also:* 22:138, 64:87, 290:52

Every Night When the Sun Goes In 22:120, 72:92, 176:94

Every Time I Feel the Spirit 148:78

Every time I think of Liza 72:107

Everybody Loves Saturday Night 64:200, 148:82, *see also:* 89:279

Everybody up and bow, back in place and you know how 107:50

Everybody's Dixie 73:11

Everybody's Fancy 219:10

Everyone Makes Mistakes 206:78

Everything Grows Together 219:12

Everywhere, Everywhere, Christmas Tonight 54:64

Ev'ry body loves the spring 49:15

Ev'ry flower, soft and gay smiling gently, seems to say 86:18

Ev'ry morning at seven o'clock 22:138, 53:87, 290:52, *see also:* 72:88, 239:80

Ev'ry one has gone to bed 166:10

Ev'ry op'ning bud and flow'r in loveliness blooming 87:76

Ev'ry person in the nation 71:46, 72:128

Ev'rybody clap with me 166:6

Everybody clap your hands, clap your hands, clap your hands 166:31

Ev'rybody Has a Laughing Place 275:36

Ev'rybody Loves Saturday Night/Mofe Moni S'mo Ho Gbeke 89:279, *see also:* 64:200, 148:84

Ev'rybody Wants to Be a Cat 275:70, 276:56

Ev'rybody wash your hands 206:46

Ev'ryone sings your fame, Maremma, Maremma 262:47

Ev'rything is laughing, singing 112:17

Ev'rything is over and I'm feeling bad 205:312, *see also:* 148:246

Exultation 140:84, 233:61, *see also:* 190:41

Eye Winker 75:24

Eye winker, Tom Tinker, nose smeller 75:24

Eyes like the morning star, cheek like a rose 159:7, 225:62, 226:462

Ezekiel Saw the Wheel 148:86, *see also:* 226:488

Ezekiel, You and Me 226:488, *see also:* 148:86

Ezek'l saw de wheel, Ezek'l saw de wheel 226:488, *see also:* 148:86

F

A Face 206:63

A face can be up, a face can be down 206:63

Faint Heart Never Won Fair Lady 252:40

Fair and Free Elections 27:218

Fair Annie of Lochyran 226:99, *see also:* 110:24, 226:98, 230:65

A fair good morrow, lovely maiden 89:134

The Fair-Haired Child 42:598

Fair Julian Bond 35:26, 35:28

Fair ladies and maids of all ages 73:163

Fair Lady of the Plains 61:121, 146:148

Fairest daughter of the King of France 89:150

Fairest Isle 85:41, 189:102

Fairest isle, all isles excelling 85:41, 189:102

Fairest Lord Jesus 22:289, 45:36, 86:116, 148:90

Fairest Maid/Bintil Shalabeya 89:206

Fairest of all pretty maids 89:206

The Fairies 227:40

The Fairy Flute 245:30

The Fairy Ship   17:61, 68:25, *see also:* A Ship A-Sailing
Fais Do-Do   33:130
Fais Dodo, Colin   59:71
Fais do-do, fais do-do, fais do-do   33:130
Faith of Our Fathers   25:114, 45:35, 86:70
Falade Ben Baixo/We'll Speak Very Softly   54:271
Falling down, gently down, see the softly falling snow   167:48
Falling Leaves   41:44
Falling Snow   167:48
Famed Are the Roughriders/Kilakila Na Roughrider   87:88
The Famine   114:43
Fancie   85:251
Fancy   85:255, 85:257
Far and wide as the eye can wander   22:212, 64:192
Far Away in Old Judea   86:52
The Far, Far West   159:416
Far from my country   89:98
Far in the Wood   245:97
The Far Northland   25:91, 69:38
Far off in northern lands, so cold   166:52
Faraway Island/Ento Shinku   49:32
The Farce   28:112
The farce is now finished, your sport's at an end   28:112
Fare Thee Well   46:228, 69:10, 71:12, 72:172
Fare thee well, luck go with thee   46:228, 69:10, 71:12, 72:172
Fare Thee Well, You Sweethearts   28:153
Fare You Well   35:49
Fare you well, green fields, soft meadow, adieu!   159:88
Fare you well, my own true love, and 'tis fare you well for awhile   35:49
Farewell and adieu to you, Spanish ladies   21:330, 27:204, 262:65
Farewell, fair ladies, I'm a-leavin' Cheyenne   61:227, *see also:* Goodbye, Old Paint
Farewell, farewell, my pretty maid, Fare-thee-well for a while   226:98, *see also:* 110:24, 226:99, 230:65
Farewell Father, Friend and Guardian   73:72
Farewell, Little Fishes   292:177
Farewell to Old England for ever   176:88, *see also:* 21:247
Farewell to Old England the beautiful   21:247, *see also:* 176:88
Farewell to Thee/Aloha Oe   87:99
Farm Boy's Bonny   20:66
The Farm Windmill   207:104
The Farmer   226:282, *see also:* 24:879, 64:96, 230:57, 239:42
The Farmer and the Crow   262:43
"The farmer and the miller have work'd," the mother said   191:72
Farmer Brown, he had a dog, and Bingo was his name   63:91, *see also:* Bingo
A Farmer came to camp one day   73:160
The Farmer Comes to Town   24:879, 239:42, *see also:* 64:96, 226:282, 230:57
Farmer Gray   126:75
The farmer he drove to the fir tree woods   262:43
A farmer he lived in the West Country   71:44
The Farmer in the Dell   14:347, 17:8, 20:70, 63:13, 157:46, 283:9, 289:180
The Farmer Is the Man   64:96, 230:57, *see also:* 24:879, 226:282, 239:42
De farmer say to de weevil: "What you doin' on de square?"   226:252, *see also:* Boll Weevil
Farmer's Boy   212:48
Farmer's Carol   210:101
The Farmer's Daughter   71:44
The Fatal Curse of Drink   290:166
The Fate of John Burgoyne   240:127
Father/Taticek   189:148
Father and I went down to camp   21:240, 26:14, 28:36, 127:14, 157:21, 160:20, 205:36, 240:76, 273:42, 277:15, *see also:* Yankee Doodle
Father, as the morning sun   86:163
Father Bless Our School Today   86:158
Father, dear Father, come home with me now!   157:174
Father got a deerskin, brought it home to me   207:39
Father is somewhere, Mother is somewhere   74:43
Father, O Father dear, be with your children here   189:148
Father of all God   25:111, 101:34
Father, unto Thee we raise hearts and voices full of praise   71:17, 72:41
Father, We Thank Thee for the Night   25:115, 45:40, 86:141
Father, We Thank You for Your Word   86:208
Father's at the Sea   281:57
A Favorite Christmas Hymn   273:156, *see also:* Hark the Herald Angels Sing
Fe nas pilon pilet, pilet nans pilon!   89:57
The fearful struggle's ended now, and peace smiles on our land   73:292
The Federal Constitution and Liberty Forever   273:62
Feed-My-Cow   172:108
Feed the Birds   97:unpaged
Felix the Soldier   240:32
The Female Patriots   28:109

36

Fengyang drum, Fengyang gong 89:232
The Ferry 71:118
The Ferry Boat 41:31
The ferry boat wheels go round and round 41:31
Ferry me across the water, do, boatman, do 71:118
Feuilles, oh/Leaves, oh 208:29
Fhola Li Na Mulanda/Snuff Is Very Guilty 89:275
Fiddle-de-dee, fiddle-de-dee the Fly has married the Bumblebee 17:77, 68:29, 128:44, *see also* 59:28, 188:20, 292:200
Fiddle-Dee-Dee 17:77, 59:28, 188:20, 292:200, *see also:* 68:29, 128:44
Fiddle Hi Ho 97:unpaged
Fiddle-I-Fee 37:171, 292:18, *see also:* Barnyard Song
The Fiddlers Are Playing 176:74
Fiddler's Fair 110:40
Fiddlers playing, how they call me 176:74
Fie, do not look at me, you maduna 163:72
Fie, Nay, Prithee, John 176:51
The Fightin' Booze Fighter 61:102
A Filipino Hombre 226:434
Fillimeeooreay 230:43, *see also:* Pat Works on the Railway
Fine Knacks for Ladies 85:26
The Fine Old English Gentleman 117:unpaged
A fine wooden sword that's trusty and broad 85:167
Fingers like to wiggle waggle 165:120
Finlandia 262:155
Finnegan's Wake 42:611
The Finnish Forest/Suomen Salossa 89:172
Fire Down Below 98:34, 129:84, 232:162, *see also:* 134:64
Fire! Fire! 134:64, *see also:* 97:34, 129:84, 232:162
Fire in the galley, fire down below 98:34, *see also:* 129:84, 134:64, 232:162
A Fire Is Started in Bethlehem 54:276, *see also:* 89:276, 295:76
Fire Truck 154:30 *(Clang, clang! The fire truck comes)*
The Fire Truck 162:98 *(Hurry, hurry, drive the fire truck)*
Firefly 162:21 *(I'm a little firefly, flit, flit, flit)*
Firefly 245:48 *(A little light is going by)*
Fireman Brave 154:31
Fire's Burning 62:14
Fireworks for the Fourth 166:64
The First Bouquet 207:86
First comes the Easter Bunny Papa 245:114
The First Courier 86:37

The first day of Christmas my true love sent to me 30, 190:148, 210:64, 233:72, 287, *see also:* Twelve Days of Christmas
First Day of the Week 124:243
The first good joy that Christmas brings 241:192
The First Good Joy That Mary Had 22:262, 54:14, 148:322, 210:65, 220:30, 241:193, *see also:* Seven Joys of Mary
The first grasshopper jumped over the second grasshopper's back 292:210
First he walks upon his toes 165:146
The first joy of Mary was the joy of one 140:14, 140:116, 279:46, *see also:* Seven Joys of Mary
The first king was tall and dressed in red 155:24
First lady swing with the right hand gent 61:278, *see also:* Buffalo Gals
The First Noel 65:100, 264:102, 279:25, *see also:* The First Nowell
The first Noel, the angel did say 65:100, 264:102, 279:25, *see also:* First Nowell
The First Nowell 22:256, 54:26, 92:150, 96:12, 148:92, 184:30, 210:66, 220:20, 241:6, 242:unpaged, 284:51, *see also:* 65:100, 264:102, 279:25
The first Nowell the angel did say 22:256, 54:26, 92:150, 96:12, 148:92, 184:30, 210:66, 220:20, 241:6, 242:unpaged, 284:51, *see also:* 65:100, 264:102, 279:25
The First Snowfall 207:66
The first time I saw little Weevil 221, *see also:* Boll Weevil
The first young gent to the opposite lady 61:171, *see also:* 42:604, 66:112, 205:27
Fish and Tea 240:67, *see also:* 27:164, 28:51, 273:36
A Fish Net/He 'UPENA 87:16
Fishermen's Evening Song 262:121
The Fisherman's Song 114:15
The Fishes 292:168, *see also:* 289:72
Fishin' Fun 167:28
Fishing Weather 281:58, *see also:* 18:26
Fishy, Fishy 17:48
Fishy, fishy in the brook 17:48
Five currant buns in a baker's shop 165:30
Five Fat Turkeys Are We 178:42
Five Hills/Tahleeng Tahvahng Toalgoy 208:43
Five hills rising high above the plain 208:43
Five Hundred Miles 72:17, *see also:* 148:252, 158:254
Five Little Ducks 75:26, 165:136
Five little ducks went swimming one day 75:26, 165:136
Five Little Mice 191:44

Five little mice on the pantry floor 191:44
Five People in My Family 206:18
The Flag of Columbia 73:12
The flag of our country is floating on high 27:146
A Flag Salute 207:83
Flashing through the bright sunlight I saw him 262:54
Flat River Girl 226:392
Flat River Raftsman 36:100
The Flea and the Louse/La Pulga y el Piojo 295:12
Flies in the buttermilk, two by two 70:32, 202, see also: Skip to My Lou
Flights of birds are filling the air 208:41
Floating Down the River 135:94, see also: 128:97
The Floating Scow of Old Virginia 66:15
Flow Gently, Sweet Afton 22:106, 205:95, see also: 176:26
Flow, Oh Water, Flow On/Teče Voda Teče 208:15
Flower Carol 184:58
The Flower Drum/Hua Ku Ko 89:232
The flowers are blooming, the flowers are blooming 162:58
Flowers Are Dying 71:113
The Flowers O' the Forest 182:28
The Flowers That Bloom in the Spring 252:46
Flowing River/Río, Río 208:7
Flow'r blossoming, flow'r blossoming 16:47
The flow'rets all sleep soundly 71:52, 125:90
Flute Song 19:25
The Fly and the Ant/La Mouche et la Fourmi 243:10
The Fly and the Bumblebee 68:29, 128:44, see also: 17:77, 59:28, 188:20, 292:200
The Fly and the Coach/La Mouche et le Coche 243:48
Fly, Kite, Fly 207:89
Flying Carp/Koi Nobori 87:52, 286:74
The Flying Cloud 24:845
Foes and Friends 73:264
Fog 162:30
The Foggy Dew 35:34
The Foggy, Foggy Dew 22:32, 205:388, 226:14, see also: 226:460
The folks on t'other side the wave 240:161
Follow, Follow 62:15
Follow me, follow, follow me ev'ryone 89:61
Follow the Drinking Gourd 33:162
Follow the Leader 162:63
Follow Washington 27:32, 28:84
Follow winding paths thru the forest 69:46
Following Christ 86:109

Following the Leader 275:60, 276:28
Following the leader, the leader, the leader 275:60, 276:28
Fond Affection 226:323
Fooba-Wooba John 289:136
Food 11:10
Food is good for us you know, 11:11
The Foolish Frog 147:38, 231, see also: 290:164
A foolish man built his house 155:20
The Fools of Forty-nine 155:381
Foom, Foom Foom! 241:80, see also: Fum, Fum, Fum!
The Foot Traveler 71:45, 72:135
Footsteps on distant trail campward are bending 25:61, 26:93
For a Tender Kiss/Por un Beso de Tu Boca 89:94
For all the glory of the way 262:173
For All the Love 72:43
For all the love that from our earliest days 72:43
For All Thy Gifts 101:32
For Bales 73:192
For battle prepared in their country's just cause 240:153
For day's work and week's work as I go up and down 135:30
For Ev'ry Evil 112:67
For ev'ry evil under the sun 112:67
For food and drink and happy days 86:213
For God so loved us He sent the Savior 86:146
For He Is an Englishman 68:12
For Health and Strength 68:38, 71:13, 72:175, 101:32
For health and strength and daily bread 68:38, 71:13, 72:175, 101:32
For here comes a turkey, very tiny, flying by 216:51
For He's a Jolly Good Fellow 197:100
For I came from Alabama with my banjo on my knee 205:113, see also: Oh Susanna
For It Is a Pleasant Day 112:17
For one long week I have not seen her 85:173
For our home and daily food 86:144
For Simhat Torah 77:46
For Stories Fine and True 86:83
For Sukkot 77:44
For the Beauty of the Earth 45:48, 86:10, 148:96, 262:151
For the Golden Corn 245:111
For the sun in heav'n that wakens 262:108
For this new morning with its light 86:166
For this our daily food, for health and happiness 262:173

For Thy gracious blessings, for Thy wondrous word 72:63

For you I will build a wondrous bath 208:35

Ford Song 118:16

The Forest 91:19

The Forge 262:31

Forgive Me, God 86:204

Forth from its scabbard, pure and bright 73:78

Fortuosity 276:73

Forward America 25:49

Forward America, it's my home and country 25:49

Forward March Grenadiers/En Avant, Grenadiers 89:45

Forward march, grenadiers! He who gets shot will get no rations 89:45

Forward ye sons of men who with might and main 25:60

Found a Peanut 63:138, 118:8, 147:24, 254:114

Found My Lost Sheep 254:20

The Fountain/La Fuente 168:112, *see also:* 194:24

The Four Brothers 188:24, *see also:* Riddle Song

The Four Generals/Los Cuatro Generales 22:218

4-H Field Song 55:257

Four in a Boat 20:23, 63:31

The four insurgent gen'rals 22:218

Four Jolly Blacksmiths 72:90

Four Little White Doves 33:202

The Four Loves 175:66, *see also:* 71:112, 292:90

The Four Marys 148:98

Four Nights Drunk 230:22

Four Pence a Day 64:134, *see also:* 117:unpaged

Four weary years of toll and blood 73:295

The Four Winds 18:26, *see also:* 281:58

Fourpence a Day 117:unpaged, *see also:* 64:134

The Fox 269:62 *(The sly fox, passed, passed)*

The Fox 129:46, 148:100, 230:80, 292:86, *see also:* 62:41, 234:32, 247, 262:41 *(The fox went out on a chilly night)*

The Fox and the Goose/Fuchs, Du Hast Die Gans Gestohlen 289:60 *(Fox, you stole our goose last night)*

The Fox and the Goose 62:41, *see also:* Fox Went Out on a Chilly Night *(The fox roved out on a very dark night)*

The Fox and the Grapes 62:43 *(A sly young fox one day did spy)*

The Fox and the Grapes/Le Renard et les Raisins 243:42 *(Un renard dent la génie)*

The Fox and the Wolf/Le Renard et le Loup 243:38

Fox in a Box 20:82, *see also:* A-Hunting We Will Go

The fox roved out on a very dark night 62:41, *see also:* Fox Went Out On a Chilly Night

The Fox Went Out On a Chilly Night 148:100, 230:80, 247, 292:86, *see also:* 62:41, 129:46, 234:32, 262:41

The fox went out on a starlit night 129:46, *see also:* Fox Went Out On a Chilly Night

A Fox Went Out One Starry Night 262:41, *see also:* Fox Went Out On a Chilly Night

Fox, you stole our goose last night 289:60

Foxlease Vesper 71:17, 72:41

Frankie and Albert 158:312, 226:76, *see also:* Frankie and Johnny

Frankie and Albert were sweethearts, ev'rbody knows 226:76, *see also:* Frankie and Johnny

Frankie and Johnnie 21:65, 226:78, 226:79, 230:64, *see also:* Frankie and Johnny

Frankie and Johnny 226:78, 226:79, *see also:* 21:65, 158:312, 226:76, 226:82, 226:84, 226:86, 230:64

Frankie and Johnny were lovers 21:65, 226:78, 226:79, 230:64, *see also:* Frankie and Johnny

Frankie Blues 226:82, *see also:* Frankie and Johnny

Frankie was a good woman 158:312, 226:82, *see also:* Frankie and Johnny

Fraternal 209:80

Fray Felipe, Fray Felipe 148:102, 293:43

Free America 240:57, 273:28, *see also:* 27:120, 28:43

Free Amerikay 27:120, 28:43, *see also:* 240:57, 273:28

Free At Last 31:21, 157:139

Free Little Bird 232:120

Free to Be . . .You and Me 260:16

Freedom calls in the time of need 73:86

Freighting from Wilcox to Globe 61:50, 159:394

Freiheit/Salute to Freedom 22:210

French Cathedrals 71:101, 72:165, 293:38

French Slumber Song 78:41, 125:108

The Frenchmen came upon our coast 28:129

Frère Jacques/Are You Sleeping? 17:72, 62:11, 90, 148:102, 176:73, 188:180, 217:17, 217:55, 283:21, 289:186, 293:42, *see also:* 25:31, 26:42

A friend sent me an alligator from the sea
162:70

The Friendly Beasts   13, 54:24, 86:47,
138:unpaged, *see also:* 128:62

The friendly cow all red and white   44:14

Friends and Neighbors   35:38

Friends come and tell me: Where is our rose?
85:218

*Friends, if you will listen, I'll sing to you a
song*   35:8

Friends, listen to what I tell you   89:78

Frightful giant snake!   89:265

A frog and a skunk and a nice little duck
68:42

The Frog and the Crow   188:72

The Frog and the Mouse   129:32, *see also:*
Frog Went A-Courtin'

A Frog, He Would A-Wooing Go   17:34,
175:140, 188:34, 250, 283:28, *see also:*
Frog Went A-Courtin'

The Frog in the Bog   63:134

The Frog in the Spring   292:118

The Frog in the Well   62:44, *see also:* Frog
Went A-Courtin'

Frog Round   69:14, 71:107, 72:167, *see also:*
289:187, 293:100

The Frog Song   289:187, *see also:* 69:14,
71:107, 72:167, 293:100

Frog Went A-Courtin'   79:27, 131, 135:64,
205:30, 232:116, *see also:* 17:34, 20:62,
35:88, 62:44, 62:46, 129:32, 148:104,
162:11, 175:140, 188:34, 226:143, 230:56,
250, 261:62, 274:22, 283:28, 289:58,
292:116

A Frog Went Walking   162:11, *see also:*
Frog Went A-Courtin'

Froggie Went A-Courtin'   20:62, 148:104,
230:56, 261:62, 292:116, *see also:* Frog
Went A-Courtin'

Froggie Went Courting,   274:22, *see also:*
Frog Went A-Courtin'

Frogman Frogman   167:32

The Frogs   293:100, *see also:* 69:14, 71:107,
72:167, 289:187 *(Hear the lively song of
the frogs in yonder pond)*

The Frogs/Bwalobera Nkere   89:283 *(You
who sit in the room)*

Frogs/Show Ha Mo   49:14 *(Each frog has a
single mouth)*

The Frog's Flute/Kaeru-no Fue   286:32

The Frogs Who Want to Have a King/Les
Grenouilles Qui Demandent un Roi
243:18

*From a distant home, the Savior we come
seeking*   54:288, *see also:* 140:22

From Daylight to Darkness   74:15

From Greenland's Icy Mountains   157:55

From Heaven Above to Earth I Come
54:161, 86:30, 161:96, *see also:* 241:150,
279:64, 280:115

From Heaven High   241:150, 279:64, *see
also:* 54:161, 86:30, 161:96, 280:115

From Heaven High I Come to You
280:115, *see also:* 54:161, 86:30, 161:96,
241:150, 279:64

From Heav'n O praise the Lord!   273:126

From Heav'n on high, O angels, sing!
54:152

*From Heav'n there came to earth a Baby so
small*   54:182

From la Sierra Morena/Cielito Lindo
197:36, *see also:* 216:48, 226:298, 230:23

From Lands Far Away/De Blanca Tierra
89:90, *see also:* 262:19

*From lands that lie beyond the rim of dawn
and deserts wild*   209:88

*From Louis, Monsieur Gerard came to Con-
gress in this town, sir*   28:114, 240:155

From Nippon Bridge/Kochae-Bushi
89:237

From out of the wood did the cuckoo fly
128:60, 184:18, 292:126, *see also:* Carol of
the Birds

From Out the Forest a Cuckoo Flew/Ze-
zulka Z Lesa Vylítla   54:230

From Sky Above   262:52

From Starry Skies Descending/Tu Scendi
dalle Stélle   279:98, *see also:* 54:244

From Starry Skies Thou Comest/Tu Scendi
dalle Stélle   54:244, *see also:* 279:98

*From Teutchland I come with my light-
wares all laden*   66:34

*From the boughs o'er head the leaves are
floating down*   227:22

*From the calm Pacific waters to the rough
Atlantic shore*   21:208, 157:163, *see also:*
205:368, 230:85

*From the Dark Mountain Ridges, pretty
skies above*   216:48

From the Eastern Mountains   241:130

From the feast there came a farmer   46:203,
see also: 55:521

*From the great Atlantic Ocean to the wide
Pacific shore*   205:368, *see also:* 21:208,
157:163, 230:85

*From the Halls of Montezuma to the shores
of Tripoli*   197:102, 205:358, 277:121

From the hills of San Francisco   206:98

From the land of the shining mountains
69:47

*From the plain there comes a creaking
sound*   262:30

*From the reed a little flower fell into the
river, oh*   114:84

From the White Earth/De Blanca Tierra
262:19, *see also:* 89:90

From the wilds of the North comes the young voyageur 22:36

From this desert I know you are leaving 61:159

From this valley they say you are going 22:146, 25:73, 61:157, 158:220, 159:298, 205:380, 226:130, *see also:* 55:514, 126:55

From way down south on the Rio Grande 159:362

The Frozen Girl 27:244, *see also:* 24:825, 35:50, 159:231, 226:58

Fsyeh lyubyat soobawtnyee vyeacher 148:84

Fuchs, Du Hast Die Gans Gestohlen/The Fox and the Goose 289:60

Fuhng Yahng Flower Drum/Fuhng Yahng hwah goo 208:10

Fuhng Yahng hwah goo/Fuhng Yahng Flower Drum 208:10

Fuller and Warren 146:127, 159:205

Fum, Fum, Fum/Foom, Foom, Foom 54:258, 125:121, 197:115, 221:80, 279:104, 295:84, *see also:* 89:162

Fun with Music 119:96

A Funeral Dirge on the Death of General George Washington 273:74

Funiculi, Funicula 22:43

The Funniest Clown 207:109

Funny Clown 162:70

Funny little shadow 162:64

A funny man lives on our block 91:38

Funny Money Riddle 68:42

A Funny, Silly Clown 288:6

Fuzzy Caterpillar 296:34 *(Fuzzy, fuzzy caterpillar crawling, crawling by)*

The Fuzzy Caterpillar 207:26 *(Fuzzy little caterpillar, why do you roam?)*

Fuzzy, fuzzy caterpillar crawling, crawling by 296:34

Fuzzy little caterpillar, crawling, crawling on the ground 191:36

Fuzzy little caterpillar, Why do you roam? 207:26

Fuzzy Wuzzy Caterpillar 162:20

G

Gaaer Jeg Udi Skoven/In Forest and Meadow 89:166

The Gaberlunzie Man 182:9

Gabriel 261:8

Gabriel and me set upon to take a journey 261:8

Gabriel to Mary came, A gentle message bare he 189:70

Gage's Proclamation 28:31

The Gal I Left Behind Me 159:58, *see also:* 42:604, 61:171, 66:112, 205:25

The Gallant Fisherman/Pescator dell'Onda 89:158

Gallant sailor from Honduras who proudly sails the high seas 89:74

The Gallant Ship 62:98, 291:73, *see also:* 135:79

Gallants attend and hear a friend 240:93, 273:46, *see also:* 28:94

Gallop quickly, gallop quickly 262:150

Galloping Horses 129:74

The Galway Piper 71:46, 72:128

The Gambling Suitor 37:146

The Gamboling Man 226:313, *see also:* 24:889, 226:312

Gamboling on the gumbo with the gambits all in gear 290:140

Gannon killed a man in Denton in the year of forty-five 61:250

The Garden 206:116

The Garden Hymn 37:158

The Garden of Jesus 184:56

The Garden of Paoakalani/Kuu Pua I Paoakalani 87:47

The Gas Station 154:12

Gasta la molinera ricos collares 295:59

Gather Around the Christmas Tree 54:68

The Gathering/Kaduguwai 89:303

Gathering Nuts in May 128:102, *see also:* Nuts in May

A gay little spotted bird sat high upon a green lemon tree 168:127

The Gazelle/Gbodi 89:281

Gbodi/The Gazelle 89:281

Gbodi mangi were 89:281

Gdy Sie Chrystus Rodzi/Christ Is Born This Evening 54:210, 279:124

Gebet an den Heiligen Christ/Prayer to the Christ Jesus 241:174

Gee, But I Want to Go Home 158:124, *see also:* 27:226

Gee, Mom I Want to Go Home 27:226, *see also:* 158:124

Geeft wat om den rommelpot 89:140

Gee-up, gee-up little horse, you don't cost a pennyworth 188:30

Gelobet 69:52

Gentil Coquelicot/Pretty Poppies 217:20

Gentle Annie 157:110

Gentle Jesus, Meek and Mild 86:24

Gentle Mother/Yasashii Okasan 286:54

Gentle Mother holds me dearly as I close my eyes 286:54

The Gentle Shepherd 189:86

Gentle spring revives the earth 85:178

A gentleman came to our house 37:140

Gently caresses the breeze in the morning 89:103

Gently flow the waters of Ouliastai 89:230

Gently Flowing Stream/Shao Hua Tang Shui 49:20

Gently gliding, my little canoe 41:33

Gently Sleep 125:20

Gently the Breezes 71:47

George Britton 159:18

George Washington, first president, by Adams was succeeded 27:222

George Washington, Lincoln 207:80

Georgie Porgie 17:38, 175:152, 188:146

Georgie Porgie, pudding and pie 17:38, 175:152, 188:146

Gerakina 169:25, 267:38

Gerakina went for water 169:25, 267:38

Gerry's Rocks 24:847, *see also:* 21:222, 35:6, 158:170, 226:394

Gesù Bambin L'e Nato/Jesus, the New-Born Baby 54:246

Get a flag and then wave it 'way up high 166:64

Get Along, Cayuse, Get Along 33:226

Get along home Cindy, Cindy 158:94, 176:122, 205:146, 230:61, *see also:* 24:899

Get Along, Little Dogies 225:18, *see also:* Git Along Little Dogies

Get out your gun and whistle up your dog 292:98, *see also:* 24:893, 158:26, 213:68, 289:46

Get ready, my brother and we will start to run 74:58

Get Thee Behind Me, Satan 64:28

Get you a partner, Chum, Chummy Lou 83:489

Getting to Know You 218:200

The Ghost of John 293:46, *see also:* 289:190

Giant Snake/Ssemusota 89:265

Giddiap 162:81

Giddiap, giddiap, giddiap, horsey 162:81

Gideon's Band 290:46

Gille Beag'O/Little Lad, Oh 89:133

The Gingerbread Boy 41:45

Gira, Gira Tondo/Ring-A-Ring-A Round-O 188:48, 189:25

A girl and a boy walked over the hill 207:126

The Girl I Left Behind Me 42:604, 61:171, 66:112, 205:27, *see also:* 159:58

The Girl in the Lane 111:48

A Girl Scout wakes at dawn of day 71:104

Girl Scouts Are We 71:18

Girl Scout's Goodbye Round 71:103

Girl Scout's Round 71:104

Girl Scouts Together 69:6, 71:22, 72:34

The Girl that Wore a Waterfall 61:175

The Girl Warrior/La Doncella Guerrera 295:53

Girls and Boys Come Out to Play 17:9, 175:60, 188:56, 189:34

Girls Clap, Boys Clap 204:11

A Girl's Name/Nomthini 163:56

Girls, O girls, I'm goin' to Boston! 39:36, *see also:* Going to Boston

Git Along Little Dogies 24:853, 26:73, 60:60, 61:207, 146:98, 146:102, 158:204, 197:81, 292:41, *see also:* 22:162, 25:84, 56:86, 129:92, 159:4, 225:18, 226:268

Git yo' little sage hens ready 61:287

Give a Little Whistle 275:19, 276:16

Give ear to my song, I'll not tell you a story 240:167

Give ear unto a maid that lately was betrayed 240:20

Give me a home in the far, far West 159:416

Give me some men, who are Scout hearted men 25:68

Give me that old time religion 157:165

Give Me Three Grains of Corn, Mother 226:41

Give My Regards to Broadway 205:307

Give peace to our hearts, O God, give peace 155:32

Give the Fiddler a Dram 134:42

Give to Our God Immortal Praise 86:9

Glad to Have a Friend Like You 260:119

Gladjens Blomster/Joyful Blossoms 208:65

A Gladsome Hymn of Praise 86:126

Glee Reigns in Galilee 22:284

The gloomy night before us flies 27:188, 64:188

Gloria 54:181 *(Gloria, gloria, to God on High)*

Gloria, Gloria 71:17 *(Gloria, gloria, in excelsis)*

Gloria, Gloria, Gott in der Höh 54:181

Gloria, Gloria, in excelsis 71:17

Gloria, Gloria, To God on high! 54:181

Gloria in Excelsis Deo! 244:10

Glorious Things of Thee Are Spoken 86:69

Glory, Glory How Peculiar 118:6

Glory to God/Ehre Sei Gott 241:233

Glory to God in the Highest 155:22, 241:233

Glory to the Mountain 141:38

Glory to Thee 176:104, *see also:* 71:106, 72:51, 86:170, 189:60

Glory to Thee, my God, this night 71:106, 72:51, 176:104, 189:60, *see also:* 86:170

The Glory Trail 61:335

Gloucestershire Wassail 54:32, 241:22, *see also:* 89:130, 184:12, 210:74, 220:96

Glow Worm 21:72

Glunk, Glunk went the little bullfrog one day 147:41

Go and Tell Aunt Nancy 135:61, *see also:* Go Tell Aunt Rhody

Go Away, Little Fairies 125:74

Go Bring Me Back My Blue-Eyed Boy 226:324

Go Down, Moses 22:316, 31:13, 64:168, 148:108, 158:372, 197:45, 205:178

Go From My Window 21:317

Go get me some of your father's gold 226:60, *see also:* 158:304

Go Get the Ax 226:332, 289:150, *see also:* 197:33

Go in and out the window 63:22, 75:27, 109:77, 110:52, *see also:* Round and Round the Village

Go on, Old 'Gator 234:74

Go rolling, rolling down the hill 288:14

Go round and round the village 14:375, 75:27, 283:25, *see also:* Round and Round the Village

Go Round to the Rocks/Jikele Maweni 163:45

Go Tell Aunt Abbie 62:51, *see also:* Go Tell Aunt Rhody

Go Tell Aunt Nancy 158:16, *see also:* Go Tell Aunt Rhody

Go Tell Aunt Rhody 9, 17:104, 59:15, 72:89, 148:110, 196, 274:26, 289:69, 292:150, *see also:* 37:176, 62:51, 135:61, 158:16, 188:176, 230:45

Go Tell It on the Mountain 31:7, 54:84, 92:156, 140:58, 148:112, 190:79, 197:116, 233:29, 241:34, 242:unpaged, 261:50

Go to Bethlehem 245:118

Go to Jane Glover 71:103, 293:50

Go to Sleep 41:19 *(Little boys, little girls, go to sleep)*

Go to Sleep 107:68 *(Go to sleep, go to sleep, hush a bye and go to sleep)*

Go to Sleep 245:100, *see also:* 234:65 *(Go to sleep, go to sleep, go to sleep, little baby)*

Go to sleep, baby child, go to sleep my li'l baby 59:42

Go to sleep, go to sleep, go to sleep, little baby, 245:100, *see also:* 234:65

Go to sleep go to sleep, hush a bye and go to sleep 107:68

Go to sleep, go to sleepy, Go to sleepy little baby 234:65, *see also:* 245:100

Go to sleep upon my breast 125:70

Go to Sleepy 226:454, 232:176, 262:122, *see also:* 109:8

Go to sleepy, baby bye 232:176, *see also:* 109:8, 226:454, 262:122

Go to Sleepy, Little Baby 109:8, *see also:* 226:454, 232:176, 262:122

Go to sleepy, little baby, Fo'de booger man ketch you 109:8, 226:454, 262:122, *see also:* 232:176

Go 'Way F'om Mah Window 226:377

The Goat 62:38, *see also:* 171

The goat has a fine pair of horns on his head 208:2

The Goat Paths 44:52

Gobble, Gobble 162:46

Goblins, on the night of Halloween 207:34

God Be in My Head 111:30, 161:124

God Bless America 25:45, 72:33

God bless America, Land that I love 25:45, 72:33

God bless our noble army! 73:176

God bless the master of this house 134:26, 210:24

God Bless the Old Sixth Corps 73:176

God Did So Love the World 86:80

God don't want no coward soldiers 226:479

God has created a new day 25:111, 262:174

God Hath Given Us Harvest 86:178

God Himself Is With Us 86:187

God Is Always with Us 77:28

God Is Great 55:253

God is great and God is good 55:253

God Is Love/Gott Ist Die Liebe 86:146

God Is the Loving Father 86:20

God made all the food we eat 86:206

God made the light in a heavenly wise 123:22

God Made the Shy, the Wild Ones 245:34

God My Father, Loving Me 86:114

God, my heart prepared is 21:315

The God of Abraham Praise 86:13

God of my justice when I call 240:17

God of Our Fathers 45:49

God of our fathers, whose almighty hand 45:49

God, Our Loving Father 71:24, 72:46, 135:31

God Rest You Merry, Gentlemen 22:260, 54:18, 92:152, 148:114, 184:16, 210:24, 220:18, 241:10, 279:28, 284:67

God Save America 240:81

God save our gracious King 22:208

God Save Our States 28:166, *see also:* 240:82, 273:50

God save our thirteen states 28:166, *see also:* 240:82, 273:50

God Save the King 22:208

God Save the South 73:30

God Save the Thirteen States 240:82, 273:50, *see also:* 28:166

God Sees the Little Sparrow Fall 86:26

God the Master of All Pagans 273:134

God tole Hezykiah in a message from on high 24:914, *see also:* 148:228, 232:152

God Who Made the Earth 86:25

God, Whose Name Is Love 86:17

God's a Father Kind and True 86:18

God's Garden 123:26

God's Goin' to Set This World on Fire 226:478

Goin' Down the Road Feeling Bad 64:128, 148:116, 158:242

Goin' Down to Town 226:145, *see also:* 232:158

Goin' for a Ride 206:48

Goin' to Boston 39:36, 157:47, *see also:* 63:39, 129:78, 135:98, 178:36

Goin' to lay down my sword and shield 64:202, *see also:* Down by the Riverside

Goin' to Leave Ol' Texas 69:21, *see also:* 21:108, 61:182, 159:57, 277:35

Goin' to run all night, goin' to run all day 230:40, *see also:* 22:64, 66:36, 126:67, 157:90, 205:126

Going Down to Town 232:158, *see also:* 226:145

Going homeward through the darkness 169:15, 267:46, *see also:* 89:96, 216:24

Going Over the Sea 63:84

Going to Bethlehem/Vamos a Belén 54:303

Going to Boston 63:39, 129:78, 135:98, *see also:* 39:36, 157:47, 178:36

Going to Chicago 63:26

Going to Leave Old Texas 61:182, *see also:* 21:108, 69:21, 159:57, 277:35

Going to Study War No More 64:202, *see also:* Down By the Riverside

Going West 61:150

The Gol-Darned Wheel 159:269

Golden Cradle 125:60, *see also:* 42:613

Golden Mornings 184:48

The Golden Rule 86:87

Golden Slippers 126:63

Golden Slumbers 71:120, 72:56, 79:53, 111:72, 175:34

Golden slumbers kiss your eyes 71:120, 72:56, 79:53, 111:72, 175:34

Golden Tresses/La Treccia Bionda 208:39

The Golden Vanity 22:172, 89:128, 133, *see also:* 35:46, 35:48

The golden waves of ears of barley 286:76

Golden Years Are Passing By 66:38

The Golux's Song 59:19

Gombei Is Sowing/Harvest Song 78:83

The Gondolier's Song 162:48

Gone Is Autumn 71:113, 72:175

Gone to bed is the setting sun 262:35

Goneh 169:65

Goneh, mbeedoh, moosakahree 169:65

Gonigetagina/I Wonder 89:37

Gonigetagina agadendamodog 89:37

Gonna jump down, turn around, pick a bale of cotton 20:39, 25:21, 75:62, *see also:* Pick a Bale of Cotton

Gonna lay down my sword and shield 148:66, *see also:* Down By the Riverside

Goober Peas 27:132, 73:166, 157:128, 277:85, *see also:* 99:48

The Good Boy 226:203

Good-by Liza Jane 226:51

Good-by Old Paint 25:77, 33:218, 158:214, 159:12, 239:28, *see also:* Goodbye Old Paint

Good-by to my pals of the prairie 159:98, *see also:* 61:325

Good-bye, Brother 226:477

Good-bye, brother, good-bye, brother, if I don't see you more 226:477

Good-bye, girls, I'm going to Boston 135:98, 157:47, *see also:* 39:36, 66:39, 129:78, 178:36

Good-bye, Old Glory 73:295

Good Bye to America 28:165

Good-bye to my pals of the prairie 61:325, *see also:* 159:98

Good Christian Men, Rejoice 22:240, 54:12, 184:40, 210:26, 284:127

Good day, Good day to you, Good day, O dipidu 114:46

Good evening, dear little Mary 54:303

Good Evening, Shining Silver Moon 245:82

Good friends and all, on you I call 62:50

Good King Arthur 18:28, 112:7, 188:142, *see also:* 17:100

Good King Dagobert/Le Bon Roi Dagobert 217:58

Good King Wenceslas 22:246, 54:17, 65:90, 92:154, 148:118, 184:22, 210:27, 220:22, 241:16, 279:38, 284:79

Good Morning 11:25 (*Good morning, good morning, what is your name*)

Good Morning 177:93 ("*Good morning, good morning," it's such fun to say*)

Good Morning 77:12 (*Thank you for the sun*)

Good Morning, Dear Children 245:5

Good morning, Farmer Small 154:22

Good morning! Good morning! Good morning, dear children 245:5

"Good morning, good morning," it's such fun to say 177:93

Good morning, good morning, what is your name 11:25

Good morning, Mister Postman, here again today 207:81

Good Morning to You 17:123, 289:11

A good morning to you, my master 114:78, *see also:* 169:27

Good morning to you, sei, matatero 169:26, *see also:* 114:78

Good Mother Hen sits here on her nest 191:20

Good News 148:122

Good news! Chariot's a-comin' 148:122

Good Night   59:53 (*Here's a body, there's a bed*)

Good Night   71:49 (*Good night, good night, companions all*)

Good Night   71:106 (*Good night, good night, time sends a warning call*)

Good-Night   125:82 (*Good-night, good-night, far flies the light*)

Good Night, Beloved   71:58

Good Night Canon   71:106, 72:51, *see also:* 86:170, 176:104, 189:60

Good Night, Cub Scouts   26:91

Good Night, Cubbers   26:91

Good Night Flowers   97:unpaged

Good night, flowers, good night, trees 97:unpaged

Good night, good night, companions all 71:49

Good-night, good-night, far flies the light 125:82

Good night, good night, time sends a warning call 125:55

Good Night, Ladies   170:111, 290:212

Good Night, My Baby   125:24

Good-Night Song   68:48

Good Night to You All   125:34, 262:86, 293:106

The Good Old Man   71:89

The Good Samaritan   155:18

Goodbye, Julie   232:60

Goodbye, my little sweet one   262:21

Goodbye, My Lover, Goodbye   162:92, 290:214

Goodbye, Old Glory   73:295

Goodbye, Old Paint   33:218, 60:106, 61:227, 128:86, 135:14, 146:169, 225:70, 232:62, *see also:* 25:77, 158:214, 159:12, 239:28

Goodbye to the cracking of the pistol 61:325, *see also:* 159:98

Goody Bull   28:15, *see also:* 240:40, 273:58, 289:133

Goody Bull and her daughter together fell out   28:15, 240:40, 273:58, *see also:* 289:133

Goosey, Goosey, Gander   17:7, 111:64, 175:32, 285:60

Goosey, goosey gander, whither do you wander?   17:7, 175:32, 285:60, *see also:* 111:64

The Gospel Train   72:85, 148:126

The gospel train is coming, I hear it just at hand   72:85, 148:126

Got a whale of a tale to tell ya, lads   276:79

Got Dem Blues   226:232

Got dem blues, but I'm too mean, lordy, I'm too damn'd mean to cry   226:232

Gott Ist Die Liebe/God is Love   86:146

Grace   25:111, *see also:* 262:174

Grace After Meals   77:16

Grace Before Meals   77:14

Grace Song   25:111, 101:34

Gracious Spirit, Dove Divine   86:72

Grafted into the Army   73:133

The grain field is mowed and the meadows are empty   83:496, *see also:* 208:17

The Grand Old Duke of York   26:25, 63:37, *see also:* Noble Duke of York

A Grand Time in Cubbing   26:52

Grandest place in the world to see is a shop full of toys, a shining Christmas tree 207:53

Grandfather Frog   162:12

Grandma, Grandma, have you heard? 197:57, *see also:* Hush, Little Baby

Grandma Grunts   79:21, 262:51

Grandma Grunts said a curious thing 79:21, 262:51

Grandma makes 'em, from a special recipe 166:22

Grandma's Spectacles   75:28

Grandpa and I   207:17

Grandpa came to our house one day 207:17

Granny Wales   28:7

Grasshopper   292:210 (*The first grasshopper jumped over the second grasshopper's back*)

Grasshopper   177:84 (*Grasshopper, grasshopper, jumping up and down*)

The Grasshopper   288:10 (*A grasshopper hopped on a sweet potato vine*)

The Grasshopper and the Ant/La Cigale et la Fourmi   79:65, *see also:* 243:34

A grasshopper hopped on a sweet potato vine   288:10

Grasshoppers Three   62:18, 292:208

Grasshoppers three a-fiddling went   62:18, 292:208

Gray Clouds Engulf the Sky/Yehrgeenkun Ahmbel Eh   89:181

The Gray Goose   134:89, 234:38, 274:28, 292:152, *see also:* 24:907, 129:48, 158:20, 277:49

Great A, Little A   285:61

Great Americans   207:80

Great Big Dog   78:93

Great big dog come a runnin' down de river 78:93

Great big standing clocks go tick tock, tick tock   68:48

Great Big Stars   233:14

Great Day (parody)   64:40

Great Gawd, I'm Feelin' Bad   226:238

Great Gittin' Up Mornin'   158:364

Great Granddad   27:140, 60:66, 89:41, 146:83, 159:302

Great granddad when the land was young 27:140, 60:66, 89:41, 146:83, 159:302

The Great Meat Pie 148:130

The great meat pie was a tidy size, and it took a week to make it 148:130

The great Pacific railway, for California hail! 226:358

The Great Round-Up 159:327, *see also:* 61:330

The Great Silkie of Sule Skerry 292:184

Great Tom Is Cast 71:103, 176:29, 293:21

Great Wall, stretching mile on mile 22:204

A Greater King Than They 155:24

Green Bottles 290:32, *see also:* 82, 147:30, 148:376

Green Corn 130:46, 134:36

Green corn, come along Charley 130:46, 134:36

Green Fields Jig 212:55

The Green Grass Grows All Around 94, 192, 290:19, *see also:* 27:90, 62:72, 72:127, 109:197, 132:unpaged, 134:11, 176:130, 197:48, 213:20

Green Gravel 63:25, 110:54, 135:80, 175:124, *see also:* 109:70

Green gravel, green gravel, your grass is so green 63:25, 109:70, 110:54, 135:80, 175:124

The Green Green Grass 149:42

Green, Green, the Crab Apple Tree 109:70, *see also:* 63:25, 110:54, 135:80, 175:124

Green, green the riverside grasses, Shiao Bao Bao 209:68

Green Grow the Lilacs 22:174, 148:132, 157:70, *see also:* 66:96

Green Grow the Rushes, Ho! 22:116, 25:100, 27:76, 71:50, 72:112, 148:134, 190:64, *see also:* 129:63, 176:146, 213:66

Green Grows the Laurel 66:96, *see also:* 22:174, 148:132, 157:70

The Green Mountaineer 28:40

Green Sally Up 109:26

Green Sally up, Green Sally down 109:26

The green worm sleeps in silk 59:26

Greenfields 21:354, 157:54, 226:154

The Greenland Fisheries 24:832, 292:170

Greenland Glaciers 166:52

Greens 226:347

Greens, greens, good old culluhed greens 226:347

Greensleeves 72:108, 148:142, 176:20, 189:98, 205:18, 261:52, *see also:* 262:80 *(Alas, my love, you do me wrong)*

Greensleeves 128:68, 220:42, *see also:* 210:68 *(The old year now away is fled)*

Greer County 159:407

Greeting 85:178

Greeting Song 262:27

Greetings 162:72

Greetings of Peace/Hevenu Shalom A'Leychem 266:36, *see also:* 72:149, 169:39, 208:36

Gregory Griggs 112:11

The Grey Goose 24:907, 129:48, 158:20, 277:49, *see also:* 134:89, 234:38, 274:28, 292:152

The Grey Mare 62:136

The grey speckled birdie was playing 114:76

Grizzly Bear 274:10, 292:108

The grizzly bear is huge and wild 59:58

Ground Hog 24:893, 158:26, 213:68, 289:46, 292:98

The ground is white. The sun is bright 207:73

The ground so cold and bare last night 207:66

A group of jolly cowboys, discussing plans at ease 27:112, 61:221, 159:74, 226:260, *see also:* 126:79

A group of jolly cowboys on the Franklin range one night 61:242

Growing Up 261:20 *(How do you know when you've grown up)*

Growing Up 172:126, 173:17 *(I've got shoes with grown-up laces)*

Grün, Grün, Grün 262:123

The Guajira/La Guajira 89:58

Guan Pazek/Stepping on the Dog 168:75

Guava Berry Song 114:90

Guess Who 207:65

Guide Me, O Thou Great Jehovah 22:286

Guillo, pran ton tamborin, Toi, pran tai fleute Robin 241:176

Gum-Ball Machine 166:18

The Gum-Tree Canoe 66:117

Gunpowder Tea 240:189

Gūri Gūri Karayō/I Will Rock Thee 89:216

Gus 112:14

Gustaf's Toast 46:204, 70:39

Guten Abend, gut' Nacht, mit Rosen bedacht 86:139

Gwei Cho shan dwo yo dwo lin 49:19

Gwine to lay down my burden, down by the riverside 83:473, *see also:* Down By the Riverside

Gwine to Ride Up in the Chariot 55:277

The gypsies they came to my lord Cassile's yett 211, *see also:* 22:70, 148:144, 226:311, 227:12

Gypsy Davy 226:311, *see also:* 22:70, 148:144, 211, 227:12

The Gypsy Laddie 211, *see also:* 22:70, 148:144, 226:311, 227:12

The Gypsy Rover 148:144, *see also:* 22:70, 211, 226:311, 227:12

The gypsy rover came over the hill, and down thro' the valley so shady 148:144, see also: 22:70, 211, 226:311, 227:12
Gypsy Song 69:14, 262:124
A gypsy's life is free and gay, O faria 69:14, 262:124

H

Ha-aaa 197:84
Ha-Ha, This-A-Way 75:87, 128:11, 135:74, 289:166, see also: 17:110, 27:192, 130:86, 189:50, 232:168
Ha, Ha, Thisaway 27:192, 130:86, see also: Ha-Ha, This-A-Way
Ha hacido en un portal 140:18, see also: 54:282
Ha! Sanju gotanno 49:32
Ha! We're casting off to sail to Sendai 49:32
Ha'a heo e ka ua i na pali 87:99
Hacia Belén se encaminan 54:293
Had a dog and his name was Blue 234:30, 261:58, 292:72, see also: 158:24, 258, 277:147, 289:55
Had a little dog, his name was Right 234:26
Had a little fight in Mexico, wasn't for the girls, the boys wouldn't go 61:23
Had a Little Rooster 128:34, see also: Barnyard Song
Had He (Moses) done nothing more than take us out of Egypt 197:46, see also: 27:84
Haenschen Klein/Little Hans 168:94
Hail, blessed morn! See the Great Mediator 140:78, see also: 54:88, 210:20, 233:36
Hail, Columbia 21:266, 27:185, 66:84, 157:26, 160:26, 205:46, 240:187, 273:68
Hail! Hail! Scouting Spirit 25:67
Hail, Hail the Gang's All Here 25:4, 26:7
Hail, Mary 124:26
Hail Mary, Full of Grace 220:56
Hail the blest morn, see the great Mediator 233:36, see also: 54:88, 140:78, 210:20
Hail the fam'd expert Roughriders 87:88
Hail thee, Joy! All hail divinest 71:27, 72:54
Hail to Cubbing 26:62
Hail to the Scouts 71:26
Hail, Waimea!/Hole Waimea 87:26
Hail you! and where did you come from? 233:55
Hajej, Nynej, Ježišku/Rocking Carol 54:226, 279:118
Hajimete Karausu 16:41

Hakone Hachiri/Hakone Mountain Road 49:30
Hakone Mountain Road/Hakone Hachiri 49:30
Hal-Le-Lu 277:47
The Halcyon Days of Old England 240:167
Hale in the Bush 28:80, see also: 240:98
Halelujah, Halelujah! Praise ye the Lord 262:113
Halfway Down 172:122, 173:8
Halfway down the stairs is a stair where I sit 172:122, 173:8
Halfway up the mountain I found a little purse 16:44
Halkada Boynundan/Here We Go Loop the Loop 266:57
Hallelu 55:280
Hallelu, Hallelu, Hallelu, Hallelujah, Praise ye the Lord 55:280
Hallelu, Hallelu, O my Lord I'm gwine ter see my mother again 277:47
Hallelujah 148:146
Hallelujah, Bum Again 24:883
Hallelujah, I'm a Bum 22:102, 24:882, 64:126, 226:184, 239:54
Halloween 41:46
Halloween Goblins 207:34
Hallowe'en Is Very Queer 7:38
Halloween Marching Song 207:33
Halloween Sounds 162:41
Ham and Eggs 25:26, 26:26
Hambone 109:36, 274:36
Hambone, Hambone, pat him on the shoulder 109:36, see also: 274:36
Hambone, Hambone, where you been? 274:36, see also: 109:36
The hammer keeps a-ring-in' on somebody's coffin 226:473
Hammer Man 226:139
The Hammer Song 230:19
Hand Game Guessing Song 74:51
Hand in hand, strolling along 286:60
Hand in hand you see us well creep like a snail into his shell 14:378, 100:96
Hand Shadow Song 114:16
The Handcart Song 277:107
The Handkerchief Game/El Juego del Pañuelo 194:18
Hands that are clean, I know you'll agree 11:13
A handsome young airman lay dying, 226:437
Hang down your head, Tom Dooley 148:392, 158:300, 205:402
Hanging Johnny 98:24
Hanging Out the Linen Clothes 226:117, 232:137, see also: 71:42, 134:14, 176:30, 205:72

Hangman 226:385, *see also:* 24:822, 176:60, 226:72

Hangman, hangman, slack up on your rope 226:385, *see also:* 24:822, 176:60, 226:72

The Hangman's Tree 24:822, *see also:* 176:60, 226:72, 226:385

Hanohano Hawaii, moku o kea we 87:60

Hanukkah Song 22:292, 197:110

Happily Singing/Alegría 54:293

Happiness 172:117, 173:3

Happy Birthday to Little Sally Spingel Spungel Sporn 237:unpaged

Happy Bride/Tarancuta 208:60

The Happy Burro 97:unpaged

Happy Christmas Comes Once More/Det Kimer Nu Til Julefest 54:186

Happy Hannukah 207:61

Happy Happy Birthday 204:15

Happy happy birthday to Mary Lou 204:15

Happy Holiday 97:unpaged

Happy Holiday, to one and all 97:unpaged

Happy Is the Miller 20:35, *see also:* 17:118, 63:28, 135:82, 227:26

A happy little chappy at the club one day 84:42

The Happy Miner 159:383

Happy New Year 41:1 *(Happy New Year, everyone here)*

A Happy New Year 27:4 *(The old year now does pass away)*

A Happy New Year 77:40 *(L'shanah tovah)*

Happy New Year, everyone here 41:1

Happy Talk 218:163

Happy talk, keep talkin' happy talk 218:163

The Happy Wanderer 25:80, 26:70

Harangue sur harangue, que sert tant de discours? 243:35

Hard Crackers Come Again No More 73:146

Hard Times in the Mill 64:68

Hard Times in the Mount Holly Jail 24:887

Hard Traveling 64:124, 230:89

Hard upon the beach oar, she moves too slow 33:90

The Hare and the Frogs/Le Lièvre et les Grenouilles 243:16

The Hare and the Tortoise/Levraut et la Tortue 243:24

Hares on the Mountain 292:92

Hark! Hark! his matin praise, in warblings sweet the lark doth raise 262:81

Hark, Hark the Dogs Do Bark 59:57, 111:41, *see also:* 17:70

Hark, Hark! The dogs do bark, beggers are coming to town 17:70, *see also:* 59:57, 111:41

Hark, hark the dogs do bark, but only one in three 59:57, *see also:* 17:70, 111:41

Hark! Hark! The dogs do bark! The beggars are coming to town 111:41, *see also:* 17:70, 59:57

Hark! Hark! the herald angels sing 273:156, *see also:* Hark! The Herald Angels Sing

Hark! Hark! The Lark 262:160

Hark! roars the bellows, blast on blast 262:133

Hark! The Herald Angels Sing 22:264, 54:46, 65:96, 92:158, 148:148, 210:28, 241:158, 242:unpaged, 264:88, 279:42, 284:75, *see also:* 273:156

Hark the Robbers 291:82

Hark the robbers walking through 291:82

Hark! the vesper hymn is stealing 262:171

Hark to the Angels 220:82

Hark to the angels from heaven calling: "Shepherds wake, shepherds wake!" 220:82

Hark to the Chimes 71:13, 72:172, 101:32

The Harrington Barn Dance 159:244

Harry McGarry 291:22

The Hart He Loves 292:90, *see also:* 71:112, 175:66

The Hart He Loves the High Wood 71:112, *see also:* 175:66, 292:90

Haru Ga Kita/Spring Song 100:15, *see also:* 286:69

Haru nga kita, haru nga kita 100:15, *see also:* 286:69

Haru wa hayo kara 286:34

Haruga kita haruga kita! 286:69, *see also:* 100:15

Harvest Home 189:122

Harvest Is Over/Marken er mejet 208:17, *see also:* 83:496

Harvest Song/Gombei Is Sowing 78:83

Has anybody seen my mouse 172:118, 173:4

Has la Tarara a garden of flowers 295:61

Haste Away to the Wedding 46:225

Haste Thee, Nymph 71:101

Hasten Now, O Shepherds/Vamos, Pastorcitos 54:310

The Hasty Crab Barber 286:34

Hatikvah/The Hope 22:194

Hato Popo/Pigeons 286:17

Hatt'i di, hatti di 55:254

Haukie, taukie combah, haukie taukie combah 26:33

Haul Away, Joe 22:145, 98:18, 128:87, 134:69, 272:13, 290:48

Haul Away the Bowlin' 98:12, *see also:* 227:12, 239:13, 274:34

Haul on the Bowline 227:12, 239:13, 274:34, *see also:* 98:12

Haunted Wood   61:118

Hava L'Venim/Bring the Bricks   89:203

Havah Nagilah   266:36

Have a Little Dog   232:114

Have Courage to Say No   109:204

Have courage, young girls, to say no   109:204

Have the stars come floating down to me and entered all?   67:9

Have we not one Father? All men are brothers   77:20

Have ye seen owt o' my bonny lad   134:72

Have you any bread and wine?   39:26, 129:114, 135:88

Have you any work for the tinker, Mistress   71:102

Have you ever seen my new toy, my new toy, my new toy?   177:73

Have you ever tried to be alive   261:6

Have you heard of the ship called the good Reuben James   230:84

Have You Seen But a White Lily Grow   189:100

Have you seen my dolly?   165:56

Have You Seen My Love?   189:22

Have You Seen the Ghost of John?   289:190, 293:46

Have you seen the little ducks swimming in the water   165:81

Have your tickets ready, come to the circus   207:112

Hawaii, isles of beauty, where skies are blue and love is true   87:81

Hawaii Ponoi/Hawaii's Own True Sons   87:58

Hawaii's Own True Sons/Hawaii Ponoi   87:58

Hay Aquí, Madre, un Jardín/Mother, There Is a Garden   216:11

Hayaku Koi Koi Oshogatsu/Come Quickly, New Year   286:85

Hay-Hoo! Hay-Hoo!/Jeu! Jeu!   216:51, *see also:* 89:79

Haying Song   169:59, 268:61

Hayom yom hulad'ti   77:61

Hayseed   226:50

A hayseed one day to himself did say   226:50

He aloha wau ia oe   87:34

He clasps the crag with crooked hands   44:48

He Haku hoi ko'u, E imi a hahai   87:30

He has a big bushy tail, rings all around   166:60

He Is Born, The Holy Child/Il Est Né, Le Divin Enfant   54:94, 220:46, *see also:* 279:92

He is born the Holy One! Let thy joyful music ring!   54:94, 220:48, *see also:* 279:92

He is born within a stable   54:282, *see also:* 140:18

He is king of kings, He is Lord of Lords   31:51

He Kihapai No Ka'u/A Charge to Keep I Have   87:30

He Knew the Earth Was Round-O   197:88, *see also:* 27:200

He Leadeth Me   45:52

He leaves unplowed the furrow   159:371

He Mele O Ke Kahuli/Song of the Land Shell   87:15

He Moa Kane/A Strutting Rooster   87:17

He Shall Feed His Flock   241:201

He Smiles Within His Cradle   184:51, 210:29

He taught me about the woods   261:46

He that is down needs fear no fall   112:62

He 'Upena/A Fish Net   87:16

He walked up and down the street 'till the shoes fell off his feet   226:185

He was a desperado from the wild and woolly West   159:137, 290:63

He was just a lonely cowboy   159:230

He was only a common puncher, such as the punchers were   159:105

He was only a lavender cowboy   61:114, 159:304

He was prime fav'rite out our way   24:838

He who heav'n created   279:16

He, Whom Joyous Shepherds Praised/Quem Pastores Laudavere   279:14, *see also:* 54:317, 220:58

He wiggled his whiskers and looked up at me   245:39

He will not slumber, He will not sleep   77:34

Head and Shoulder, Baby   109:33

Head and shoulder, baby, one, two, three   109:33

Head and Shoulders   26:35, 63:46, *see also:* 55:266, 165:125

Head and shoulders, knees and toes   26:35, 63:46, *see also:* 55:266, 165:125

Head, Shoulders   55:266, *see also:* 26:35, 63:46, 165:125

Head, Shoulders, Knees and Toes   55:267

The Heads   240:165, *see also:* 28:82

Heads and shoulders, knees and toes   165:125, *see also:* 24:35, 55:266, 63:46

Hear All the Angels Singing   245:125

Hear it raining, raining, raining   245:70

Hear Me, Dearest/Kad se Jangin   89:190

Hear, O Shepherds/Oj Pastiri   241:70

Hear Our Prayer, O Lord   86:200

Hear the bells! Ding, dong! Ding, dong!   207:101

Hear the bells! Jingle, jingle bells!   207:58

Hear the lively song of the frogs in yonder pond 69:14, 71:107, 72:167, 293:100, *see also:* 289:187

Hear the mimes! In olden times 241:229

Hear us, Father, as we pray 125:106

Heard from Heaven Today 233:53

The Hearse Song 62:109, 226:444, *see also:* 290:178

Heart of Oak 98:51

Hearts and flowers, ribbons and bows 207:79

Hearts of Oak Are We Still 240:42

Heave Away 226:407

Heave away, heave away! I'd rather court a yellow gal 226:407

Heaven Bell Ring 190:112, 233:77

Heaven Is So High 148:150

The Heavenly March 157:58, *see also:* 21:256, 158:350

Heav'nly Father, we sing praises 207:43

Heaven's Gate Has Opened 244:187, 245:116

The Heavens Resound 262:157

Hechalutz l'man avodah 69:49, 148:424, *see also:* 25:90, 64:106, 290:196

Hector Protector 111:21

Hector Protector was dress'd all in green 111:21

The Hedge-Rose 85:141

Hehler vehrden elsker luhrdahgskvel 148:84

Heidschi Bumbeedschi 245:89

Heigh-Ho 275:9, 276:1

Heigh-ho, Heigh-ho, to make your troubles go 275:9, 276:1

Hej Pada Pada/Raindrops 289:36

Hej Te Cigany!/Hey, You Gypsy 208:32

Hell in Texas 61:80, 159:317

The Hell-Bound Train 61:337, 159:236

Hello 107:14 *(Hello, hello, hello, and how are you)*

Hello 91:4 *(Hello, hello, hello, won't you be my friend?)*

Hello, Girls 226:128

Hello girls, listen to my voice 226:128

Hello! Hello! 25:6, 26:10, 69:10, 71:11, 72:160

Hello, hello, hello, and how are you 107:14

Hello! hello! hello! hello! 26:10, 69:10, 71:11, 72:160

Hello, Hello, Hello, We're glad to meet you 25:6

Hello, hello, I can hardly hear you 162:74

Hello, hello, hello, won't you be my friend? 91:4

Hello, hello, who's there? It is the Easter Hare! 245:115

Hello, Ma Baby! 157:194, 205:258

Hello, Mister Robin in the tree 97:unpaged

Hello, Young Lovers 218:189

Help me wind my ball of wool 165:32

Help us fill the rommelpot 89:140

Helpers 11:20

Helping 260:60

The Hen and Chickens 191:20

Hen Fell Out of the Roost/O-LU-WE 265:57

The Hen Who Laid Golden Eggs/La Poule aux Oeufs d'Or 243:14

Henery, My Boy 62:113, *see also:* 89:39

Henry, My Son 89:39, *see also:* 62:113

Her Kommer Dine Arme Smaa/Thy Little Ones, Dear Lord, Are We 54:196

Her name is Mary 197:56, *see also:* 205:327

Herdgirl's Song 68:21

Herdsmaid's Song 176:78

The Herdsman 25:93, 71:65, 72:119

The herdsman is merry, he sings all day long 25:93, 71:65, 72:119

Here a Torch 184:36, *see also:* Bring a Torch, Jeanette. Isabella

Here a torch, Jeannette, Isabella 184:36, *see also:* Bring a Torch, Jeannette, Isabella

Here are grandma's spectacles 75:28

Here are the robbers coming through 63:31

Here are two Valentines for you 167:14

Here Awa', There Awa' 182:34

Here Come the Dukes 110:46, *see also:* Three Dukes

Here come the dukes a-riding 110:46, *see also:* Three Dukes

Here come three dukes a-riding 39:16, 100:92, 227:18, *see also:* 110:46, 135:84, 213:40

Here come three kings a-riding 63:36

Here come three witches a-riding 197:93

Here Come Two Dukes A-Riding 135:84, 213:40, *see also:* 39:16, 100:92, 110:46, 227:18

Here Comes a Knight A-Riding 168:152

Here comes a policeman, riding a bicycle 165:71

Here comes one Johnny Cuckoo 109:73

Here Comes Sally! 135:87

Here Comes the Circus 119:102

Here comes the doughnut man 239:88

Here comes the little donkey 216:42

Here comes the snail 286:21

Here followeth the dire fate of Burgoyne and his army great 28:100

Here I sit with my power, I bring the South Wind t'ward me 74:60

Here I sit on Buttermilk Hill 134:94, 240:87, 273:84, *see also:* Johnny Has Gone for a Soldier

Here in Bethlehem this evening, springs a mighty flame from Heaven 54:276, *see also:* 89:276, 295:76

Here in Our Father's House 86:74

Here Is the Beehive 162:23, *see also:* 191:56

Here is the beehive. Where are the bees? 162:23, 191:56

Here Is the Church 75:30

Here is the church, here is the steeple 75:30

Here Is the Little Door 210:103

Here Lies a Tree 172:75, 173:61

Here, Rattler, here! Here, Rattler, here 130:32

Here Sits a Monkey 232:175

Here sits a mousie in her little housie 63:26

Here Stands a Red Bird 63:20

Here 'twixt the ass and oxen mild 54:100, *see also:* 241:82

Here We Come A-Caroling 264:82, *see also:* Wassail Song

Here we come a-caroling among the leaves so green 264:82, *see also:* Wassail Song

Here we come advancing, advancing 100:111

Here We Come A-Wassailing 96:6, 128:66, 148:154, 209:12, 220:62, 284:47, *see also:* Wassail Song

Here we come a-wassailing among the leaves so green 22:270, 27:6, 54:35, 92:186, 96:6, 128:66, 148:154, 184:8, 189:130, 197:8, 209:12, 220:42, 262:112, 279:36, 284:47, *see also:* 264:82

Here we come gath'ring nuts in May 14:367, 128:102, 165:191, 188:38, 189:36, *see also:* 63:32, 175:78

Here we come looby loo 188:42, 189:42, *see also:* Looby Loo

Here We Come on Our Ponies 135:102

Here we come, the big procession 135:103

Here We Come With Gladness 86:193

Here we dance Looby-loo, here we dance Looby-light 14:363, 283:46, *see also:* Looby Loo

Here we go gathering nuts in May 63:32, 175:78, *see also:* Nuts in May

Here We Go Looby-loo 17:14, 63:18, 147:18, 165:194, *see also:* 39:6, 188:42, 189:42, 283:46

Here We Go Loop the Loop/Halkada Boynundan 266:57

Here We Go on Our Ponies 178:6

Here We Go Over the Mountain Two By Two 168:183, *see also:* 63:17, 70:11

Here We Go Round the Mountain 63:17, 70:11, *see also:* 168:183

Here we go round the mountain, two by two 63:17, 70:11, *see also:* 168:183

Here we go round the mulberry bush 14:366, 17:90, 20:9, 63:16, 75:50, 168:108, 175:78, 188:66, 189:40, 289:172, *see also:* 104:52, 283:17, 291:2

Here we go 'round the old soap-gourd 213:48

Here we go, Santy Maloney 135:123

Here We Go to the Pumpkin Shop 7:36

Here we go with a hoppity hop 7:36

Here's a ball for Baby, big and soft and round 191:40

Here's a body, there's a bed 59:53

Here's a health to the jolly blacksmith 262:24

Here's a pony galloping 41:42, *see also:* 162:82

Here's a tree with trunk so brown 165:93

Here's the ambassador, he's arriving from his mountains and by the valleys 188:118

Here's the start of a bright new year 97:unpaged

Here's to the birds that fly above 26:50

Here's to the Boy Scouts 25:69

Here's to the Ranger 159:371

Here's to the squire that goes on parade 27:36, 28:141

Here's what happen'd when Willie Ware 112:35

Here's Your Mule 73:160

Hermosas doncellas que al prado venis 295:43

Herne the Hunter 85:188

Herod Dead/Mòrto Erode 279:102

A Herring in Salt 182:31

The Herring Song 292:172

He's a Tramp 276:48

He's a tramp but they love him 276:48

He's Gone Away 226:3

He's Gone to the Arms of Abraham 73:126

He's Got the Whole World in His Hands 25:102, 31:19, 55:278, 72:83, 75:31, 148:156, 205:399

Het Kwezelken/Little Hypocrite 21:320

Hevebe Song 79:15

Hevebeta, come come Hevebeta! 79:15

Hevenu Shalom A'leychem 72:149, 169:39, 208:36, 266:36

Hexlein/Little Witch 78:63

Hexlein, willst du tanzen? 78:63

Hey, Betty Martin 129:72, 135:120, 157:44, 226:158, *see also:* 33:194

Hey! boys, I want the linin' bars! 239:74

Hey, cross-eyed gopher, punch him in the ribs 234:20

Hey-Day-Day 83:471

Hey Dee Roon 72:105, *see also:* 291:8

Hey Diddle Diddle 17:5, 175:67, 283:32, 285:83

Hey, diddle diddle, the cat and the fiddle 17:5, 175:67, 283:32, 285:83

Hey Diddle Dumpling, My Son John 162:88, 175:162, 285:97

Hey, hey, hey! Sea Lion! 100:54, 168:161

Hey, Ho! 25:29, 26:43, 62:14, 64:201, 71:105, 72:163, 148:158, 293:30

Hey, ho! nobody at home 25:29, 26:43, 62:14, 64:201, 71:105, 72:163, 148:158, 293:30

Hey Ho, To the Greenwood 176:99, 292:82, 293:96

Hey, jim along, jim along, Josie 63:38, 135:108, 232:72

Hey Liley, Liley Lo 130:28

Hey, Little Boy 292:20, *see also:* 107:18, 232:112, 234:56, 292:44

Hey, little boy. Yes, Ma'am. Did you go to the barney 292:20, *see also:* 107:18, 232:112, 234:56, 292:44

Hey, Little Lassie 70:21

Hey Lollee 148:160

Hey Lollee, lollee, lollee, Hey Lollee, lollee lo 148:160

Hey, Look Me Over (parody) 26:56

Hey, Pretty Little Bird 292:124, *see also:* 232:179, 277:27

"Hey," said the blackbird, sittin' on a chair 292:122, *see also:* The Bird Song

Hey, the Little Rusty Dusty Miller 111:59

Hey there, young fellow, stop sitting on the tree 89:272

Hey, You Gypsy!/Hej, te cigany! 208:32

Hi-Dee-Roon 291:8, *see also:* 72:105

Hi! Hi! Hi! there, Cub! 26:7

Hi Ho, Jerum 36:70, *see also:* 62:101, 64:148

Hi Ho! Nobody Home 25:29, 26:43, 62:14, 64:201, 71:105, 72:163, 148:158, 293:30

Hi! Ho! The Rattlin' Bog 134:11 *see also:* Green Grass Grows All Around

Hi, Marsha Peter 55:260

"Hi!" said the blackbird sitting on a chair 157:76, 289:68, *see also:* Bird Song

"Hi!" said the little leatherwing bat 36:56, 158:18, *see also:* Bird Song

"Hi!" says the black bird sitting on a chair 69:18, 129:40, 157:76, 262:44, *see also:* 36:56, 158:18, 289:68, 292:122

Hi! There, Cub! 26:7

Hi, Thunder! 245:72

Hi ya! Go to sleep baby 49:22

Hi yo hi yo ip si ni yah 69:26, 197:84, 262:107

Hickety, Pickety, My Black Hen 188:50, 189:13, 285:73, *see also:* 175:137

Hickory, Dickory, Dock 17:113, 75:32, 135:117, 175:68, 188:172, 283:10, 285:25, 292:196

Hickory, dickory, dock! The mouse ran up the clock 17:113, 75:32, 135:117, 175:68, 188:172, 283:10, 285:25, 292:196

Hide and Seek 41:16 *(John has gone away)*

Hide and Seek/Kakurembo 286:41 *(People who play hide and seek)*

Hie upon Hielands and laigh upon Tay 22:24

Higgledy, Piggledy, My Black Hen 175:137, *see also:* 188:50, 189:13, 285:73

High, Betty Martin 33:194, *see also:* 129:72, 135:120, 157:44, 226:158

High ho, the boatmen row, floatin' down the river 239:58

High in the sky I go, walking in the sky I go 19:35

High Middle Low 206:66

High on a hill was a lonely goatherd 218:240

High on the giddy bending mast 85:109

High Sheriff tol' de deputy 24:909, 158:308

The High-Toned Dance 61:284, *see also:* 159:251

High up, high on the mountain 69:8, 71:15, 72:38

Highbridge 226:155

Highland Lullaby 85:169

Highland Mary 66:126

Hiking 25:57

Hiking Song 227:34, *see also:* 25:65, 26:65

Hill an' Gully 134:20

Hill an' Gully rider, Hill an' Gully 134:20

Hill you ho, boys; let her go, boys 134:70

The Hills of Glenshee 35:92

The Hills of Mexico 61:89

Himmel und Erde müssen vergehn 293:56, *see also:* 69:50

Hina Matsuri/Dolls' Festival 286:70

Hiney lo yanum v'lo yeshan 77:34

Hinky Dinky, Parlee-voo 126:61, 158:122, 170:61, 205:348, 226:440

Hinky Dinky Parlez Vous (parody) 64:31

Hippity Hop 17:47, *see also:* 165:139

Hippity hop to the barber shop 17:47, *see also:* 165:139

Hippity hop to the candy shop 165:139, *see also:* 17:47

Hiraita, Hiraita/Open, Open 16:47, 286:36

Hirten, auf um Mitternacht/Shepherds, Up! 279:80

His grandfather's hat is too big for his head 27:220

His hair was black, his eye was blue 21:344, *see also:* 89:136

His Jewels 189:66

His name is Mister Snow and an upstanding man is he 218:73

His sword-blade gleams and his eyelight beams 28:126, 240:100

Hitori de Sabishii 16:30

Ho, all to the borders, Vermonters come down 28:40

Ho, boys, ho for California, O! There's plenty of gold so I've been told 33:210, 226:112

Ho, boys, is you right? Done got right 158:274

Ho! Every Sleeper Waken 262:67, 293:104

Ho for California 239:64

Ho! Ho! For the Pack 26:58

Ho!ho! Hotaru koi 16:32, 286:24

Ho! my comrades see the signal 73:214, *see also:* 230:20

Ho ra nei ro nen nei ro 49:22

Ho, Ro, The rattlin' bog, the bog down in the valley-o 72:127, *see also:* Green Grass Grows All Around

Ho, sleepers, arise! The sun's in the skies 71:60

Ho, there you are Mister Postman! 41:24

Ho, there you are, Punchinello 128:96, *see also:* 63:14, 109:106, 135:113, 178:7

Ho! young rider, Apple-cheeked one 262:120

The Hobbies 240:183

Hog-drivers, hog-drivers, hog-drivers we air 24:810, *see also:* 27:24

Hog Drovers 27:24, *see also:* 24:810

Hog-Eye 226:380

Hog-eye gal am a debbil of a gal 226:380

The Hog-Eye Man 24:836, 226:410

A hogger on his death-bed lay 226:186

Hohai Bushi/Hohai Song 49:29

Hohai Song/Hohai Bushi 49:29

Hojita de Guarumal/Little Leaf of the Guarumal 216:13

The Hokey-Pokey 148:164, 178:34, 289:168

Hold, Men, Hold! 241:178

Hold the Fort 73:214, 230:20

Hold the Fort (parody) 64:36

Hold the Wind 124:104

A Hole in the Bucket 290:74, *see also:* 197:32

Hole in the Ground 62:72, *see also:* Green Grass Grows All Around

Hole Waimea/Hail, Waimea! 87:26

Holland 273:150

The Holly and the Ivy 54:22, 184:20, 210:67, 220:34, 241:40, 264:71, 279:34, 284:43

Hollyhock Ladies 166:16

Holy Babe 233:70

The Holy Baby 124:68

Holy Bible, Book Divine 86:78

The Holy Boy 209:105, 241:210

The Holy Child 54:284, 197:117, 209:110, *see also:* 241:88

The Holy Family 189:76

Holy, Holy, Holy 45:29, 86:127, 148:166, 161:102

Holy, holy, holy, Lord God almighty 45:29, 86:127, 148:166, 161:102

Holy Joseph and Mary the Maid/Sant Josep i la Mare de Deu 54:262

Home Came the Old Man 37:118

The Home of the Soul 66:140

Home on the Range 22:164, 25:75, 26:72, 60:42, 61:296, 71:90, 72:97, 146:166, 158:212, 159:424, 170:101, 205:361, 230:26

Home, Sweet Home 22:52, 127:61, 157:98 *(Mid pleasures and palaces)*

Home, Sweet Home 159:124 *(We were lying on a prairie)*

Homes 86:152

Honey-Ant Song of Ljaba/Makerenben 89:309

Honey, honey bee ball, I can't see y'all. All hid? 109:185

Honey, you can't love one 128:78, *see also:* 88, 148:250, 230:74

Honey, You Look So Sweet 130:26

Honkaen kesskella mokkini seisoo 89:172

Honor to one who guides our village shrine so dear 286:82

Honor to Sheridan 163:82

Honza, I Love You 262:61

Hoo, hoo! Here we go. Off to the picnic 207:129

Hoo, hoo! Hoo, hoo, Mother! 207:22

Hoosen Johnny 129:34, 135:36, 226:164, *see also:* 234:54, 292:46

Hop and skip a little, sing a little, say a little rhyme 167:8

Hop, Chop, My Little Horse 17:124

Hop, Hop, Hop 17:121

Hop! Hop! Hop! Pony goes clip-clop 17:121

Hop, Old Squirrel 232:109

Hop, Skip and Sing 167:8

Hop Up, My Ladies 128:23, 130:68, 135:18, 234:66

Hope 85:132 *(Thou who art near when holy night is falling)*

The Hope/Hatikvah 22:194 *(As long as deep within the heart)*

Hopping Music 11:34

Hoppity 172:124, 173:10

Hora kalee jo raba thee 89:195

Hora Nero, Nen Nero 16:35

A Horrible Tale 290:188

A horrible tale I have to tell of sad disasters that befell 290:188

A horse and a flea and the three blind mice 289:143, *see also:* 178:72

Horse and the Buggy 109:175

Horse and the buggy, sail away, 109:175

Horse Named Bill   226:340, 289:154, 292:28

The Horse Named Napoleon   62:35

The Horse Wrangler   159:119, *see also:* 61:198, 226:274, 277:67

Horsemen are coming from North and the West   74:42

The Horsemen in the Cloud   74:42

The Horses Run Around   25:32

Horsey, Horsey   72:94

Hos Bilezik/Pretty Bracelet   70:20

"Hosanna!" Be the Children's Song   86:186

Hosanna in the Highest   124:192

Hosanna, Loud Hosanna   86:57

Hoshanah! hoshanah!   77:44

Hoshanah! we celebrate Sukkot   77:44

Hot Cross Buns   17:122, 135:105, 175:64, 188:100, 285:54

Hot Mutton Pies   71:103

Hot Stuff   240:145

A Hot Time in the Old Town   126:57, 157:191, *see also:* 203

Hotaru Koi/Come Fireflies   16:32, 286:24

Hotte, Hotte Reiterpferd   188:30

The Hound and Her Neighbor/La Lice et sa Compagne   243:41

The hours I spent with thee, dear heart   205:342

The Hours of the Clock/Las Horas del Reloj   295:34

The House Carpenter   226:66, *see also:* 35:82

The House of the Mouse   245:38

House of the Rising Sun   230:18

The House on the Rock   155:20

How Are You, Conscript?   73:139

How beautiful is the green earth   86:149

How blest the life a sailor leads   273:118

How blithe was I each morn to see my swain come o'er the hill!   182:37

How Brightly Shines the Morning Star/Wie Schön Leuchtet der Morgenstern   54:164, 241:132

How Creatures Move   18:8

How dear to my heart are the scenes of my childhood   21:178

How delightful to see in the evenings in spring   129:36, 134:102, 292:54

How Do You Do?   25:5, 26:8

How do you do, ev'rybody, how do you do?   25:5, 26:8

How do you do? How do you do?   162:19

How do you feel one year older   130:24

How do you know when you've grown up   261:20

How do you like to go up in a swing   245:20

How do you think I began in the world?   277:63, 292:62

How does a caterpillar go?   165:44

How Does My Lady's Garden Grow?   17:98, 175:40, 188:92, *see also:* Mary Mary Quite Contrary

How Doth the Little Crocodile   59:29, 112:39

How-D'ye-Do?   274:30

How far away are you?   218:278

How Far Is't to Bethlehem   96:7, 184:39, 209:82

How Firm a Foundation   21:352, 45:54

How gaily we frolic   85:148

How Good and Joyous   114:50

How goodly it is and how pleasant   72:147

How Happy the Soldier   240:143, 273:86

How I love the clouds o'er Kona's sea   87:27

How little you good people know   27:130

How many beautiful girls Madama Dore   265:23, *see also:* 188:86

How Many Days Has My Baby to Play?   285:45

How many lovely daughters, Madama Dore   188:86, *see also:* 265:23

How many miles to baby land?   17:18

How Many Miles to Bethlehem?   233:22

How many more nights to sleep till the bright New Year?   286:85

How Many Raindrops   162:27

How many roads must a man walk down   72:8

How Many Strawberries Grow in the Sea?   18:5, *see also:* 112:23

How much wood would a woodchuck chuck   144:9

How nice are those mice! said the cat   296:10

How oft I dream of childhood days   226:114

How Old Are You?   128:21, 232:56

How old are you, my pretty little miss?   128:21, 232:56

How pleasant bobbing along, bobbing along on the bottom of the beautiful briny sea   276:68

How Shall I Find Thee   85:65

How Shall I Fitly Meet Thee?/Wie Soll Ich Dich Empfangen   241:152

How Shall the Young Direct Their Way   86:86

How Stands the Glass Around   240:144, 273:14

How sweet is the horn that blows in the morn   71:41

How Sweet to Be a Cloud   172:21, 174:7

How tedious and tasteless the hours   21:354, 157:54, 226:154

How the Corn Grew   191:64

How the stars do stare tonight   67:26

How wonderful is Maytime   262:29

Hua-Hua'i/Wander Here With Me   87:34

Hua Ku Ko/The Flower Drum 89:232

Hugh 91:31

Hullabaloo 39:6, *see also:* Looby-Loo

Hullabalooby looby, hullabalooby light
39:6, *see also:* Looby-Loo

Humpty Dumpty 17:102, 175:104,
188:174, 283:47, 285:56

Humpty Dumpty sat on a wall 17:102,
175:104, 188:174, 283:47, 285:56

A Hundred Million Miracles 218:296

A Hundred Years Ago 226:485

A hundred years is a very long time, Oh, yes!
226:485

Hung Taryong 49:35

The Hungry Cat and the Grumbling Mouse
112:64

A hungry cat look'd out one day 112:64

The Hungry Goat 171, *see also:* 62:38

Hungry, hungry, I am hungry
237:unpaged

Hunt the Squirrel 24:806, *see also:*
A-Tisket, A-Tasket

A Hunter from Kurpfalz/Ein Jäger aus
Kurpfalz 89:145

The Hunters of Kentucky 157:34, 226:427

Hunting 14:349, *see also:* A-Hunting We
Will Go

A Hunting Tale 61:8

Huntsman's Song 85:179

The Huntsmen 59:54

The Huron Indian Carol 140:38, *see also:* 2,
54:76, 161:79

Hurrah for Harry McGarry 291:22

Hurrah for the choice of the nation 27:14,
157:51, 226:167

Hurry, hurry, drive the fire truck 162:98

Hurry, Hurry, Hurry 237:unpaged

Hurry, Hurry to the Stable 209:12

Hurry, Little Donkey/Arre, Burriquito
295:75

Hurry on, my weary soul 233:53

Hurry Up, Liza Jane 128:18

The Husband and the Stone/El Marido y la
Piedra 89:78

Hush-a-ba, Birdie 262:125, *see also:* 112:44

Hush-a-ba, Birdie, croon, croon 262:125,
see also: 112:44

Hush-A-Baw Birdie 112:44, *see also:*
262:125

Hush-a-baw, Birdie, croon, croon 112:44,
see also: 262:125

Hush-a-by, baby, and go to sleep 125:85

*Hush-a-by, hush-a-by, go to sleep, go to
sleep* 125:74

Hush-a-Bye 281:55 (*Hush-a-bye baby
down by the sea*)

Hush-a-bye, Baby 135:110 (*Hush-a-bye,
baby, thy cradle is green*)

Hush-a-bye, Baby 175:85, 188:88
(*Hush-a-bye, baby, on the tree top*)

Hush-a-bye baby down by the sea 281:55

Hush-a-bye, baby, on the tree top 175:85,
188:88

Hush-a-bye, baby, thy cradle is green
135:110

Hush a bye, don't you cry 129:55, 289:22
see also: All the Pretty Little Horses

Hushabye Swing 207:91

*Hush, do you hear? Hear the loons singing
up in the sky* 19:19

*Hush, hush baby mine close thine eyes thou
must not peep* 78:41, *see also:* 125:108

Hush! Hush! Shush! Shush! 237:unpaged

Hush, hush the waves are rolling in 281:62

Hush, hush, You're my good child 286:63

Hush, Little Baby 10, 59:52, 75:33, 178:56,
213:84, 232:147, 261:56, 274:20, 289:12,
298, *see also:* 63:90, 125:134, 129:97,
135:52, 197:57

Hush, My Babe 54:87, 140:24, 140:113,
283:62, *see also:* 184:62, 190:43, 190:45,
233:41

Hush, my babe, lie still and slumber 54:87,
140:24, 140:113, 190:45, 233:41, 283:62,
see also: 184:62, 190:43, 241:116

Hush, My Baby/Ninni, Baba 169:30,
268:19

Hush my baby, go to sleep 125:30

Hush my bunny go to sleep 296:42

Hush! my dear, lie still and slumber
184:62, 190:43, 241:116, *see also:* Hush,
My Babe

Hush my honey, hush my honey 294

Hush 'n' Bye 232:178, *see also:* All the
Pretty Little Horses

Hush Now, My Children 208:47, *see also:*
89:270, 169:50, 267:14

Hush pretty baby, sleep pretty baby 16:35

Hush Song 281:59

Hush Up, baby, don't say a word 135:52,
see also: Hush, Little Baby

Hush-You-Bye 176:54, *see also:* All the
Pretty Little Horses

Hush-you-bye, don't you cry 158:14,
176:54, 188:136, 189:90, 277:23, *see also:*
All the Pretty Little Horses

Hushabye Swing 207:91

Huzza for Liberty 273:72

Hvar har du va't sa lange 89:169

Hymn of Thanksgiving 27:234, *see also:*
21:338, 45:56, 205:24

Hymn to Buddha/Wou Liang   89:231

I

I ain't gonna grieve my Lord no more 147:46, 290:93

I ain't got no father 61:229, 159:290, *see also:* Poor Lonesome Cowboy

I Ain't Gwine Study War No More 83:473, *see also:* Down By the Riverside

I always watch the traffic light 177:90

I am a bold cowboy, from Midland I came 159:268

I am a brave man, acting like a bear 74:50

I am a cowboy by my trade. Joe Johnson is my name 159:221

I am a cowboy. See me ride 207:123

I am a fine musician 75:52, *see also:* Musicians

I Am a Gay Musician 289:170, *see also:* Musicians

I am a highway bandit man, Cole Younger is my name 61:262

I am a jolly driver of the Salt Lake City line 61:30, *see also:* 61:32

I am a jolly soldier, enlisted years ago 240:116

I am a jovial collier lad, as blithe as blithe can be 64:47, *see also:* 33:122, 128:14

I am a little beggarman, and begging I have been 117:unpaged

I am a little pony, prancing up and down 177:83

I am a Mormon bishop and I will tell you what I know 159:401

I Am a Musician 254:119, *see also:* Musicians

I Am a Pilgrim 148:168

I am a Pilgrim, walking in the woods 207:44

I am a poor and a foreign stranger 35:68, 148:304, *see also:* Wayfaring Stranger

I am a poor strange girl whose fortune is bad 37:181, *see also:* 36:64, 61:13, 230:21, 232:110

I am a poor unlucky chap, I'm very fond of rum 35:4

I Am a Poor Wayfaring Stranger 22:34, 35:68, 148:304, *see also:* Wayfaring Stranger

I am a Pretty Little Dutch Girl 63:88

I am a roving cowboy off from the Western plains 60:86, 146:142, 159:292

I am a roving gambler, I gamble down in town 24:889, *see also:* 226:312, 226:313

I am a roving gambler, I've gambled all around 226:312, *see also:* 24:889, 226:313

I am a roving pedlar man 36:98

I am a roving traveler and go from town to town 226:313, *see also:* 24:889, 226:312

I am a shoemaker by my trade 239:52

I am a Texas cowboy and I am far away from home 61:91, 61:93, *see also:* 60:48, 146:66, 159:22

I am a vaquero by trade 159:73

I am a wandering cowboy, from ranch to ranch I roam 159:305, *see also:* 146:144

I am alone in my little boat 89:155

I am, as you know, a Madison belle 157:182

I am feeling sort of happy since I proved up on the farm 61:70

I Am Fur From My Sweetheart 159:259

I Am Like a Bear 74:50

I am lonesome since I crossed the plains 61:171 *see also:* 42:604, 66:112, 205:27

I am looking rather seedy now while holding down my claim 61:68, 159:405, 226:89, *see also:* 61:72

I am merry, loving Lailow 208:1

I Am Quite Big, But My Lisbeth Is Wee 245:21

I Am So Glad on Christmas Eve/Jeg Er Saa Glad Hver Julekveld 54:202

I am the ass, and blind for life 67:34

I Am the Captain of the Pinafore 252:10

I Am the Monarch of the Sea 252:14

I am the shepherd's song 67:80

I Am the Very Model of a Modern Major-General 252:26

I asked the white seagull 49:27

I Became Ill/Bajabula Bonke 163:95

I been having some hard traveling, I thought you know'd 64:124, 230:89

I Been Wukkin' on de Railroad 22:148, *see also:* I've Been Workin' on the Railroad

I believe that on this day 86:157

I Bought Me a Rooster 289:47, *see also:* Barnyard Song

I Bring the Rain 74:60

I brought my love a cherry that has no stone 37:156, *see also:* The Riddle Song

I build my house upon de rock, oh, yes, Lord! 157:36

I Built My Love a Big Fine House 213:24

I buyed me a little dog, its color it was brown 234:28, *see also:* 274:32

I Cain't Say No 218:35

I came from Salem City with my washpan on my knee 66:46

I came home the other night as drunk as I could be 230:22

I came to Alabama wid my banjo on my knee 157:94, 230:46, 283:38, *see also:* Oh Susanna

I came to town de udder night 21:304, 157:84, *see also:* Old Dan Tucker

I can beep a beeper 237:unpaged

I can dance upon my toes, tra-la-la-la-la 165:141

I Can Figure Figures 237:unpaged

I Can Fly 162:101

I can knock with my two hands 165:119

I can only sing the high part 206:66

I can play a trumpet, a trumpet, a trumpet 104:53

I can plink a plinker 237:unpaged

I can sing: tra-la-la-la-la 91:26

I can take the wildest bronco in the tough old wooly West 159:269

I Can't Do That Sum 289:130

I can't play an accordeen, I can't pla-ay a fiddle 83:466, *see also:* 288:25

I Can't Stay in Egypt Lan' 89:54

I Catch-a da Plenty of Feesh 226:409

I Climbed the Olive Tree/Al Olivo Subí 216:47

I come from Alabama with my banjo on my knee 22:40, 25:107, 126:89, 227:35, *see also:* Oh Susanna

I Could Spend a Happy Morning 172:55, 174:41

I Couldn't Hear Nobody Pray 148:170

I courted pretty Polly the livelong night 158:304, *see also:* 226:60

I danced in the morning when the world was begun 140:36

I dance in the sunshine so freely and lightly 85:145

I don't know what the village wants of me 208:60

I Don't Like No Railroad Man 226:326

I Don't Want No More of Army Life 63:140

I Don't Want to Be a Gambler 226:465

I don't want you to come courting 208:62

I Don't Want Your Millions, Mister 64:160

I dream of Jeanie with the light brown hair 22:100

I dream'd a dream next Tuesday week 112:29

I dreamed a dream the other night 22:132, *see also:* 158:142

I dreamed I saw Joe Hill last night 22:48, 64:20

I Dreamed Last Night of My True Love 226:149

I dreamed of my true love last night 37:132

I dreamed that I had died and gone to my reward 64:76

I drop my thumb, pick it up, pick it up 130:18

I Enjoy Being a Girl 218:308

I expect ev'ry one of my crowd 218:153

I feel so yaw-yaw-yaw today 237:unpaged

I Found a Horseshoe 226:382

I Found a Little Dog 296:40

I Found a Million Dollar Baby 170:91

I found my love in Avalon 170:49

I Gave Her Kisses One 63:142

I Gave My Love a Cherry 277:105, *see also:* Riddle Song

I gave my love a cherry that has no stone 22:25, 69:21, 135:46, 148:310, 205:39, 230:72, 262:152, 277:105, *see also:* Riddle Song

I give myself very good advice 276:44

I Give Thee Thanks With All My Heart 86:92

I Go to Bethlehem/Sel Bych Rád K Betlému 54:232, 241:184, *see also:* 245:120

I go walking into ever'y puddle 207:88

I Goes to Fight Mit Sigel 73:118

I Got a Gal at the Head of the Holler 24:897, 226:320, *see also:* Sourwood Mountain

I got a girl and she loves me 24:898, *see also:* 134:48

I Got a Letter from Jesus 226:487

I Got a Letter This Morning 232:144

I got a shoe, you got a shoe 148:14, *see also:* 25:103, 31:9, 83:476, 129:16

I got sheep, I got all live stock 129:90, *see also:* 35:52, 130:64, 148:314, 274:12

I Got Shoes 25:103, 31:9, *see also:* 83:476, 129:16, 148:14

I got to Kansas City on a Frid'y 218:24

I had a bird and the bird pleased me 75:10, *see also:* Barnyard Song

I had a cat and the cat pleased me 68:27, 129:76, 292:18, *see also:* Barnyard Song

I had a dog and his name was Blue 289:55, *see also:* Old Blue

I had a gal that called me, "Dear" 27:174, *see also:* I've Been Workin' on the Railroad

I Had a Little Cat 132:unpaged, *see also:* Barnyard Song

I had a little cat, and the cat pleased me 37:171, 132:unpaged, *see also:* Barnyard Song

I had a little dog, the color it was brown 274:32, *see also:* 234:28

I had a little engine, but it wouldn't go 165:70

I Had a Little Husband 111:26

I had a little nut tree 18:18, 135:41, 175:92, 188:98, 189:12, 283:54, 285:16, *see also:* 17:145, 59:24, 227:5, 289:108

I Had a Little Rooster 292:13, *see also:* Barnyard Song

I Had a Little Wife 111:28

I had a penny, a bright new penny 172:137, 173:22

I had a true love but she left me 226:71

I Had an Old Rooster 109:193, *see also:* Barnyard Song

I Had But Fifty Cents 84:46

I Had Four Brothers 17:22, 189:26, *see also:* Riddle Song

I had four brothers over the sea 17:22, 188:24, 189:26, *see also:* The Riddle Song

I hate to see de ev'nin' sun go down 21:120

I have a bonnet trimmed in blue 212:18

I Have a Dog 26:18

I have a garden of my own 44:78

I have a head and eyes that see 204:31

I Have a Little Doll/Yo Tengo una Muñeca 194:28

I have a little dreydl 128:59, 197:111

I Have a Little House 296:24

I have a little pony, and Cactus is his name 154:32

I Have a Little Puppy Dog 112:10

I have a pretty parakeet that says "Qwa-qwa!" 167:18

I have a ship on the ocean 21:296, *see also:* 27:196

I Have a Song to Sing, O! 252:56, 262:57

I have a string of red beads 163:78

I Have Confidence 218:230

I have confidence in sunshine 218:230

I have heard talk of bold Robin Hood 164:98

I have just come from the salt, salt sea 226:66, *see also:* 35:82

I have laid a herring in salt 182:31

I have led a good life, full of peace and quiet 226:203

I have made a pretty nest 165:155

I have reached the land of drought and heat 61:62, 61:63, 61:64, *see also:* 159:410, 226:280

I have some fine new shoes 77:23

I Have Some Good Tobacco/J'ai du Bon Tabac 217:60

I have ten little fingers and they all belong to me 75:72

I hear de bell a-ring-in', I see de captain stand 277:101

I hear my true love, he's swinging his hammer 85:171

I Heard the Bells on Christmas Day 54:58, 148:172, 190:86, 241:126

I heard the merry lark at dawn 71:110, 72:169

I Held a Lamb 245:40

I just came down from Louisville some pleasure for to find 61:154

I kama zimba, zimba, zimba 72:146

I know a little burro who's happy as can be 97:unpaged

I know a little lady from Baltimore 128:104

I Know a Little Puppy 26:18, 254:111

I know a little puppy, he hasn't any tail 254:111, *see also:* 26:18

I know a little pussy, her coat is silver gray 165:94

I know a maiden fair to see, take care! take care! 66:110

I Know a Place 72:45

I Know a Rose Tree Springing 210:30, *see also:* 54:166, 241:84, 264:86, 279:58

I Know an Old Lady Who Swallowed a Fly 23, 75:34, 289:116, 292:216, *see also:* 5, 120, 148:378

I Know It's Spring 162:58

I Know Moonlight 226:451

I Know My Love 36:4, 42:601

I Know the Lord's Laid His Hands on Me 83:469

I know very well that spring has come 207:90

I Know Where I'm Going 42:596, 72:125, 148:174, 176:133

I know you! I walked with you once upon a dream 275:64, 276:41

I know you've heard of Washington 197:26

I Lay on My Chest 172:71, 174:57

I learned a lovely song today 207:18

I learned Spanish from a girl who lived down Sonora way 61:147

I Like It 162:105

I like the leaves, I like the trees 162:105

I Like to Be Told 219:49

I Like to Do the Highland Fling 167:42

I Like to Live on the Farm 154:19

I like to sing about Mister Small 154:40

I like to take a horse and buggy as I go riding through the town 72:94

I like to walk in winter, watching snowflakes blow 207:67

I like to watch the circus seal oh oh oh! 207:111

I Like Winter 152

I like winter, I like snow 152

I live for the good of my nation 159:278, *see also:* 61:10, 157:50

I live for the good of the nation 157:50, *see also:* 61:10, 159:278

I lost my shoe, my new red shoe 288:8

I Love God's Tiny Creatures 86:19

I Love Little Pussy 17:116, 175:86, 283:15, 285:66

I love little pussy, her coat is so warm 17:116, 175:86, 283:15, 285:66

I Love Little Willie 63:147

I love my little cat, I do 197:68

I Love My Rooster 55:265, 254:108, *see also:* Barnyard Song

I love my rooster, my rooster loves me 27:96, 254:108, *see also:* Barnyard Song

I love not Colorado where the faro table grows 159:415

I Love Sixpence 188:46, *see also:* 175:97

I love sixpence, jolly little sixpence 188:46, *see also:* 175:97

I Love That Word Hello 26:11

I love the freedom up in the sky 74:20

I Love the Mountains 26:21, 148:176

I love the wild streams as they foaming leap 262:66

I love to go a-wandering, along the mountain track 25:80, 26:70

I love to hear that word "hello" 26:11

I love to hear the pealing bells 71:98, 72:166, *see also:* 62:12

I love to row in my big blue boat 165:111

I Love to Tell the Story 45:38

I Love to Think that Jesus Saw 86:21

I Love Trash 206:95

I Love You Truly 205:337

I made a little boy of gingerbread dough 41:45

I made this pipe for you, and in a secret way 74:44

I made up my mind in the early morn 24:858, 61:180, 146:62, 225:64, *see also:* 159:52, 226:285, 239:32

I made up my mind to change my way 61:180, 159:52, 219:32, *see also:* 24:858, 146:62, 225:64, 226:285

I married a wife in the month of June 36:36, *see also:* 37:122, 62:143, 128:114

I married my wife in the month of June 37:122, 128:114, *see also:* 36:36, 62:143

I married my wife in the month of May 62:143, *see also:* 36:36, 37:122, 128:114

I met an engine on a hill 26:77

I Met Her in the Garden Where the Praties Grow 226:463

I met her in the morning, won't you go my way? 134:68

I met her on the mountain 205:402, *see also:* 148:392, 158:300

I met the boss; he wanted me to go 159:24

I need someone nice to be nice to 206:74

I Never Felt Such Love 55:276

I Never Will Marry 230:29

I once dressed up and went to town 230:70, *see also:* 36:60, 37:154, 62:142, 157:14

I once had a gal and I loved her well 159:228

I once had a horse and his name was Napoleon 62:35

I once had a sweetheart but now I've got none 66:96, *see also:* 22:174, 148:132, 157:70

I once knew a fellow who had twelve teeth 237:unpaged

I once knew a maiden who lived on the plains 61:121, *see also:* 146:148

I once was young and gallant and drove a span of grays 61:76

I only wish that I might dream 123:72

I-pal Chyongchyun Ka/Sweet Sixteen 49:42

I pass the shoe from me to you 20:90, 289:173, *see also:* 55:250, 70:18, 83:491

I pick up my hoe an' I go 189:142

I Planted Watermelons/Ja Posejah Lubenice 169:71, 270:63

I pledge allegiance, pledge allegiance 32:28

I Points to Mineself 25:12

I points to mineself, vas is das here, das is mine top-notcher, ya mama dear 25:12

I promise to do my best to do 26:62

I put my arm around her waist 36:26, *see also:* A-Roving

I put my dolly's dress on 130:20

I raised a dog and his name was Blue 158:24, 277:147, *see also:* Old Blue

I Ride an Old Paint 24:857, 60:24, 128:82, 146:34, 157:154, 158:216, 225:41, 226:12, 230:25, 292:26

I ride my bicycle silver and red 207:116

I rock the cradle for my boy 125:26

I Rock Thee/E Hie E 87:18

I rock thee, child dear, I rock thee, child dear 87:18

I rode a line on the open range 61:299, 159:93

I rode up to London all on St. Stephen's Day 212:12

I Roll the Ball 75:37

I roll the ball to Daddy 75:37

I rolled and tumbled in the snow 207:75

I said I will look to my ways 273:128

I sail over the ocean blue, I catch-a da plenty of feesh 226:409

I saw a fair Mayden syttin and sing 210:112

I saw a peanut stand, heard a rubber band 275:23, 276:10

I saw a redbird in the air 110:36

I Saw a Ship A-Sailing 18:6, 52, *see also:* A Ship A-sailing

I saw a ship a-sailing, a-sailing on the sea 14:346, 17:61, 18:6, 33:346, 52, 116:97, *see also:* 68:25, 188:58

I saw a sled of beautiful red, very fine! 207:70

I saw a youth and maiden on a lonely city street 21:58

I saw Adam leave the garden, with an apple in his hand 230:31

I Saw an Old Man 112:36

I saw an old man put shells in his pocket 112:36

I saw one day, the last of May 63:139

I Saw Three Ships 17:52, 54:52, 92:160, 96:8, 129:58, 138, 140:25, 148:180, 184:15, 189:128, 210:31, 241:12, 262:166, 264:93, 284:91, *see also:* 188:168, 190:128, 233:79

I saw three ships come sailing by 17:52, 54:52, 92:160, 96:8, 129:58, 138, 140:25, 148:180, 184:15, 188:168, 189:128, 190:128, 210:31, 233:79, 241:12, 262:166, 264:93, 284:91

I saw you toss the kites on high 44:4

I say good bye to my puppy 207:13

I say the Rock Island Line is a mighty good road 148:314, *see also:* 35:52, 129:90, 130:64, 274:12

I see the Mailman, Maily man, Mailer man 130:73

I See the Moon 111:80

I see the moon, and the moon sees me 111:80

I See You/Jag Ser Dig 189:134

I see you, I see you, Tra la la la la la 189:134

I sent a letter to my love 165:195, *see also:* A-Tisket A-Tasket

I set my dogs loose on the hill 216:48

I should like to ride, I know, with a little Eskimo 207:71

I Sing a Song of the Saints of God 86:111

I Sing for the Animals 74:40

I sing for the Deer, I sing for the Otter 74:40

I Sing Of a Maiden 209:84

I Sing the Birth Was Born Tonight 209:14

I Sing the Mighty Power of God 86:12

I sing you one O, Green grow the rushes O 148:134, *see also:* Green Grow the Rushes, Ho!

I snum I am a Yankee lad 240:53, *see also:* 28:26

I snum I am a Yankee man and I'll sing to you a ditty 28:26, *see also:* 240:53

I soldered in the stable and I soldered in the hall 117:unpaged

I spoke to a shoemaker for to make me a pair of shoes-es 78:89

I Spy 177:85

I stand beside Thy cradle here 279:66

I started on a journey just about a week ago 84:22

I started on the trail on June twenty-third 226:266, *see also:* 60:102, 61:307, 146:162, 159:19

I started out a'courtin' and I knew where to go 61:24

I stood on the Atlantic ocean, on the wide Pacific shore 230:85, *see also:* 21:208, 157:163, 205:368

I struck the trail in seventy nine 159:58, *see also:* 66:112

I struck the trail in seventy-two 66:112, *see also:* 159:58

I think I sing this little song 64:62

I think of my darling as the sun goes down 72:144

I think of my son when the moon goes down 49:12

I Think When I Read That Sweet Story of Old 45:8, 86:108

I thought I heard the old man say 64:114, *see also:* 98:40, 134:73

I thought one spring that just for fun 61:198, 159:121, *see also:* 226:274, 277:67

I told the Sun that I was glad 245:14

I Took a Notion Now 62:129

I took my girl to a fancy ball 84:46

I touch your hand and my arms grow strong 218:159

I trace these gardens o'er and o'er 73:104, *see also:* Johnny Has Gone For A Soldier

I used to have an old grey horse 226:145, *see also:* 232:158

I used to live on Cottonwood and owned a little farm 159:403

I uster own the Double D; I'm punchin' steers today 159:294

I Vow to Thee, My Country 71:8

I wake in the morning early and always 245:15

I Walk With My Little Lantern 245:91

I Walked the Road Again 35:4

I wander sadly to and fro oppressed with grief and care 85:151

I wander'd today to the hill, Maggie 21:183, 205:158

I Wan'na Be Like You 276:62

I Want a Girl 25:33

I Want to Be a Clown 167:12

I Want to Be a Farmer 128:76

I Want to Be Like Jesus 155:5

I Want to Go to Morrow 84:22

"I want to talk to Clover Bloom" said Buttercup one day 227:14

I want to tell you of a trip I did take 159:18

I wanted much to go to war 73:142

I Wanted to Die in the Desert 159:323

I warm my son upon my breast 209:87

I was a bachelor, I lived by myself 226:460, *see also:* 22:32, 205:388, 226:14

I was a high-born gentleman, she was a high-born lady 226:311, *see also:* 22:70, 148:144, 211, 227:12

I Was Born About Four Thousand Years Ago 62:103, *see also:* 36:84, 158:30, 226:330

I Was Born About Ten Thousand Years Ago 158:30, 226:330, *see also:* 36:84, 62:103

I was born almost ten thousand years ago 36:84, *see also:* 62:103, 158:30, 226:330

I was born in Boston city 159:203

I was born long ago in eighteen ninety-one 64:132

I was dreaming of a campfire 26:68

I Was Glad 86:73

I was hanging round town and just wasting my time 223, 225:32, *see also:* 61:187, 61:189

I was laying around town just spending my time 61:187, 61:189, *see also:* 223, 225:32

I was on the drive in Eighty working under Silver Jack 159:234

I was out walking an' a-ramblin' one day 159:183, *see also:* 61:6

I Was Riding Through the Country 141:36

I was standing round a defense town one day 64:90

I was teaching a young girl to sing 216:44

I Was There 36:84, *see also:* 62:103, 158:30, 226:330

I was young and happy, my heart was light and gay 61:289

I wear my pink pajamas in the summer when its hot 25:41

I went down, down, down to the factory 64:146

I went down into my garden 217:56

I went down to feed my cow 172:108

I went down to old Joe's house 20:78, *see also:* Old Joe Clark

I went down to sandy hook toder arternoon 157:80

I Went Down to the Depot 226:374

I went down to the elephant fair 109:62

I went down to the river, poor boy 159:159

I Went Downtown 112:46

I went downtown to see Missus Brown 112:46

I went out one pleasant evening by the seashore 21:200

I went to John Whipple and asked for a job 35:102

I went to school one morning and I walked like this 165:145

I went to the animal fair 25:38, 26:17, 62:33, 226:348, 254:121, 289:152, 292:188

I went to the dance and the animals come 130:114

I Went to the Movies Tomorrow 290:121

I went to visit a farm one day 165:77

I Whistle a Happy Tune 218:184

I will drink, I will gamble, I will play wild again 159:166

I Will Give My Love an Apple 27:28, *see also:* The Riddle Song

I will long remember well upon those mountains I did dwell 61:155

I will nevermore deceive you or of happiness bereave you 157:180

I will open the door of my heart 155:15

I Will Rock Thee / Gūri Gūri Karayō 89:216

I will sing about my lover who has gone to sea 72:129

I will sing you a one-O 176:146, *see also:* Green Grow the Rushes, Ho!

I will sing you a song and it won't be very long 157:186

I will sing you a song of that beautiful land 66:140

I Will Tell You My Troubles 61:75

I will tell you of a fellow 226:62, *see also:* 62:130

I Will Toss Up the Sticks 74:61

I wish I had a load of rails 63:139

I Wish I Had the Shepherd's Lamb 292:52

I Wish I Was a Little Bird 226:338, *see also:* 129:19

I wish I was a little sparrow 36:16, *see also:* 158:58, 230:24

I wish I was a mole in the ground 24:900, 234:25, 253:96

I Wish I Was a Single Girl 36:87, *see also:* 157:67, 158:48

I wish I was an apple, a hanging in the tree 24:899, *see also:* 158:94, 176:122, 205:146, 230:61

I wish I was in de land ob cotton 22:192

I wish I was in de land of cotton 25:101, 26:15, 73:8, 157:120, 160:42, *see also:* 99:53, 127:112

I wish I was in Dixie, Hooray! Hooray 99:53, *see also:* Dixie

I wish I was in St. Law County 73:11

I wish I was in the land of cotton 127:112, *see also:* Dixie

I Wish I Was Single Again 36:102, 62:140, 226:47, *see also:* 20:30, 158:50

I Wish I Were a Little Bird 129:19, *see also:* 226:338

I wish I were an apple, an apple on a tree 110:23

I wish I were on yonder hill 89:136, *see also:* 21:344

I wish you a Merry Christmas 227:32, *see also:* We Wish You a Merry Christmas

I Wonder 276:40 *(I wonder, I wonder, I wonder)*

I Wonder/Gonigetagina 89:37 *(Oh, I wonder at her)*

I Wonder as I Wander 140:90, 183:10, 190:96, 209:15

I wonder, I wonder, I wonder why each little bird has someone to sing to 276:40

I wonder what he'll think of me! 218:90

I Wonder What's Become of Sally 170:97

I Wonder When I Shall Be Married 36:22, 157:66, 262:126

I Wonder Who's Kissing Her Now 21:102

I Would Follow Jesus 86:112

I Would Like to Be as Tall as the Moon/ Quisiera Ser Tan Alta Como la Luna 295:47

I wouldn't marry a farmer, he's always in the dirt 66:119

I Wrote a Letter to My Love 63:11, *see also:* A-Tisket, A-Tasket

Ia Puna, pain a ala 87:43

Ibo of Nigeria 215:17

Ich bin ein Musikanter 55:268

Ich Ging Emol Spaziere/One Day I Went A-Walking 89:144

Ich Steh an Deiner Krippe Hier/Beside Thy Cradle Here I Stand 54:163, 241:156, 279:66

Ich weiss nicht, was soll es bedeuten 176:68

Ichi Kake, Ni Kakete 16:55

The Icy December/El Desembre Congelat 54:266

I'd Like to Be in Texas When They Round-Up in the Spring 159:321

I'd Like to Be Like Dad 219:43

I'd Like to Be Like Mom 219:43

I'd like to introduce you to a goose you haven't met 91:39

I'd love to be a shepherd boy tonight 86:37

I'd Rather Be a Panther 234:75

Ida, Sweet as Apple Cider 21:94, 205:287

Idyl of the Plains 61:85

Iesu No Ke Kahuhipa/Saviour, Like a Shepherd Lead Us 87:97

If a steamship weighed ten thousand tons 289:130

If All the Raindrops 289:140

If All the Seas Were One Sea 53, 111:34

If All the World Were Paper 17:84, 135:26, 175:128

If an S and an I and an O and a U 84:30

If anybody asks you who I am 140:64, 190:88, 233:40

If buttercups buzzed after the bee 28:159, 289:133, *see also:* 240:40, 273:58

If each little kid could have fresh milk each day 64:198

If I could drive steel like John Henry 226:150

If I could have a windmill, a windmill, a windmill 55:267, 165:84

If I could I surely would stan' on de rock where Moses stood 226:476, 230:78, *see also:* 148:274

If I Die a Railroad Man 226:362

If I Had a Boat 154:24

If I had a hammer, I'd hammer in the morning 230:19

If I had a little boat 154:24

If I Had a Tractor 154:18

If I had a wee house and a canty wee fire 182:47

If I Had the Wings of a Turtledove 290:90

If I had wings like Noah's dove 230:88, *see also:* 158:66

If I lived out on a prairie 91:18

If I Loved You 218:80

"If I may trust your love," she cried 159:313

If I should die and be buried at sea 37:157, *see also:* 128:22, 157:40

If I were a little bird, high up in the sky 165:153

If it should please kind fortune once more to set me free 35:28, *see also:* 35:26

If it's padi then say it's padi 114:24

If Mary goes far out to sea 290:136

If my old top were a dancing man 189:138

If people ask me, I always tell them 172:135, 173:21

If Rabbit Was Bigger . . . 172:63, 174:49

If yo' brother done you wrong take him to yo'self alone 226:248

If You Are Near 85:83

If you can't answer my questions nine 27:214, 37:110, 134:85

If you don't quit monkeying with my Lulu 159:263

If you evah go to Houston, you better walk right 226:217, *see also:* Midnight Special

If you go in you're sure to win 252:40

If you listen a while, I'll sing you a song 226:416

If you listen I'll sing you a sweet little song 205:263, *see also:* 170:85

If you miss the train I'm on 72:17, *see also:* 148:252, 158:254

If you throw paper in the street 26:83

If you want higher wages, let me tell you what to do 64:22

If you want to know where the privates were 226:442

If you were a beech tree, what would you do? 165:96

If You Were a Kitty 296:20

*If you'll come gather round me, I'll sing you
a song* 159:307

*If you'll listen awhile I'll sing you a song
and as it is short it won't take me long*
159:384

*If you listen a while, I'll sing you a song of
the glorious land of the free* 226:416

*If your mind is in a dither, and your heart
is in a haze* 276:37

If You're Happy and You Know It 25:16,
26:39, 63:44, 147:20, 253:91

Iga' ma Lo Ta'ndo/Song of Love 89:274

Igqira Lendle-la 163:28

Ihr Kinderlein kommet, o kommet doch all!
54:142, 86:42, 241:162, 279:72

Il court, il court, le furet 217:48

Il Est Né, le Divin Enfant/He Is Born, the
Holy Child 54:94, 220:46, 279:92

Il était un petit homme 217:18

Il était un petit navire 217:14, *see also:*
89:62

Il Etait une Bergère/There Was a Shepherdess 217:32

Il faut te marier 217:46

Il Me Dhu Vetrim 212:91

Il Mio Bel Castello/I'm the King of the Castle 189:152

Il Pleut, Bergère/It Is Raining, Shepherdess
217:22

I'll buy a horse and steal a gig 17:95, 70:13

*I'll cover my eyes while you go hide and
then I'll look for you* 177:85

*I'll eat when I'm hungry, I'll drink when
I'm dry* 24:855, 37:142, 158:218,
159:163, 226:307, 230:69

I'll give to you a paper of pins 17:93, 20:42,
62:114, 68:22, 80, 134:18, 148:300, 290:78

*I'll go up on the mountain top and plant me
a patch of cane* 128:18, 226:132

I'll Play Something for You 27:252

I'll race you down the mountain 130:56

*I'll sing to you a good old song, made by a
good old pate* 117:unpaged

I'll sing to you about a man 197:88, *see
also:* 27:200

I'll Sing You a Song 111:11

I'll sing you a song, a good song of the sea
148:46

I'll sing you a song and it's not very long
24:874, 158:230, 230:42

I'll sing you a song, e'en though a sad tale
61:124

I'll sing you a song of the fish of the sea
71:70, 72:76

I'll sing you a song that has often been sung
159:399

I'll sing you a song, tho' not very long
111:11

*I'll sing you a song, though it may be a sad
one* 61:123, 159:344, 277:119

I'll sing you a true song of Billy the Kid
61:266, 159:140 *see also:* 61:268

*I'll sing you one-ho! Green grow the rushes,
ho* 22:116, 27:76, 71:50, 72:112, *see also:*
Green Grow the Rushes, Ho

I'll Take You Home Again, Kathleen
157:170, 170:106, 205:181

I'll tell you a story about Jack-a-Nory
111:39

*I'll tell you a story that is no sham, in Hol-
land liv'd a merchant man* 78:25

*I'll tell you a story that will thrill you, I
know* 159:356, *see also:* 60:82, 61:184,
128:46, 146:116

I'll tell you a story, there's one that I know
60:82, 128:46, 146:116, *see also:* 61:184,
159:356

I'll tell you of a fellow I have seen 62:130

I'll tell you the story of Jonathan Tweed
64:162

I'll tell you the tale of a burglar bold 84:12

I-lu ho-tci, ho-tci-o-nu mi 27:84, 197:46

*I'm a blizzard from the Brazos on a tear,
hear me hoot* 159:138, *see also:* 61:104

I'm a Brownie in a beanie 68:23

*I'm a buzzard from the Brazos on a tear,
hear me toot!* 61:104, *see also:* 159:138

I'm a Citizen in Cub Scouts 26:64

I'm a cowboy, a lonesome cowboy 288:24

I'm a Cowboy a-Ropin' 167:26

*I'm a decent boy just landed from the town
of Ballyfad* 64:152

I'm a fairy doll on the Christmas tree
165:54

I'm a Frogman. Rubber fins upon my feet
167:32

I'm a gay puncher, fresh from the Pecos Flat
61:303, 159:95

I'm a girl, and by me that's only great
218:308

I'm a happy miner, I love to sing and dance
159:383

*I'm a heart-broken raftsman, from Green-
ville I came* 36:100

I'm a howler from the prairies of the West
159:137, *see also:* 290:63

I'm a Jack-o'-lantern with a great big grin
75:40

I'm a jolly Jack-o-lantern 207:33

I'm a lazy old frog, a grandfather frog
162:12

I'm a little acorn nice and round 63:137

I'm a Little Dutch Girl 63:40

I'm a little Eskimo. Taku is my name
207:77

I'm a little firefly, flit, flit, fan 162:21

I'm a Little Teapot   63:106, 75:36, 165:31, 291:50

I'm a little teapot short and stout   63:106, 75:36, 165:31, 291:50

I'm a lonely bullwhacker on the Red Cloud Line   159:396

I'm a nice guajira, born on Melena   89:58

I'm a Nut   63:137

I'm a Person   204:9

I'm a Poor Lonesome Cowboy   60:76, 61:229, 61:230, 146:112, 159:290, 225:46, 226:273

I'm a rambler and a gambler, and a long ways from home   159:266

I'm a rambling wretch of poverty   226:44

I'm a stranger in your city, my name is Paddy Flynn   226:214

I'm a turtle, I'm a turtle walking very slow   177:85

I'm a wisp of manger straw   67:67

I'm a Witch   162:38

I'm a Yankee Doodle Dandy   157:212, 205:301

I'm A-Goin' Down This Road Feelin' Bad   24:875

I'm Alabama bound, I'm Alabama bound   230:44

I'm an Indian Chief in a wigwam high   288:28

I'm as free a little bird as I can be   232:120

I'm as restless as a willow in a windstorm   218:260

I'm a-tellin' you the truth and not lying nor joking   159:245

I'm a-trampin', trampin', tryin' to make heaven my home   83:464, 148:394

I'm a'walkin' down the track, I got tears in my eyes   158:254, *see also:* 72:17, 148:252

I'm back in the saddle again   25:70

I'm bound to follow the longhorn cows   60:102, 146:162, 159:19, *see also:* 61:307, 226:266

I'm bringing home a baby bumble bee   63:135

I'm Called Little Buttercup   252:8

I'm Captain Jinks of the Horse Marines   66:63, *see also:* 70:28, 126:65, 135:96

I'm dreaming now of Hallie   21:156, 205:142

I'm five years old today   77:61

I'm goin' away for to stay a little while   226:3

I'm Goin' Chop Crab   89:266

I'm goin' down the road feelin' bad   64:128, 148:116, 158:242

I'm goin' to leave Ol' Texas now   21:108, 69:21, *see also:* 61:182, 159:57, 277:35

I'm Going Away to See Aunt Dinah   109:142

I'm going down to town   232:158, *see also:* 226:145

I'm going out West before long   61:150

I'm Going to Join the Army   232:95

I'm going to leave Old Texas now   61:182, 159:57, *see also:* 21:108, 69:21, 277:35

I'm go'n' to lay down my sword and shield   27:30, 226:480, 230:50, *see also:* 64:202, 83:473, 148:66

I'm Gonna Leave Old Texas Now!   159:57, 277:35, *see also:* 21:108, 61:182, 69:21

I'm Gonna Pat My Little Old Head   204:17

I'm Gonna Sing When the Spirit Says Sing   148:182

I'm gonna tell you little story 'bout a grizzly bear   274:10, 292:108

I'm Gonna Wash That Man Right Out of My Hair   218:137

I'm gonna wrap myself in paper   130:70

I'm Gwine to Alabamy   24:904

I'm Happy When I'm Hiking   25:65, 26:65, *see also:* 227:34

I'm just a girl who cain't say no   218:36

I'm just a poor wayfaring stranger   24:880, 27:45, 148:304, 158:346, 205:56, 230:15, 262:47, 277:41, *see also:* 22:34, 35:68, 37:162

I'm Late   275:42, 276:42

I'm late, I'm late for a very important date   275:42, 276:42

I'm leaving Cheyenne, I'm off for Montan'   225:70, *see also:* Goodbye, Old Paint

I'm Little White Clover   245:36

I'm looking out of the window   207:78

I'm Looking Over a Four Leaf Clover   170:69

I'm No Fool   119:108

I'm old Mister Brown just from the South   66:43

I'm old Tom Moore from the bummer's shore   158:180, *see also:* 159:378

I'm on My Way   148:184

I'm on my way and I won't turn back   148:184

I'm on your first step siftin' in the sand   107:60

I'm really Rosie and I'm Rosie real   235:33

I'm riding Old Paint, I'm leading Old Dan   61:227, *see also:* Goodbye, Old Paint

I'm riding on that new river train   88, 128:78, 148:250, 230:74, *see also:* 62:126

I'm Sad and I'm Lonely   226:243

I'm so sad I could cry a pint   237:unpaged

I'm so sorry for old Adam   62:102, 115:20, 226:339

I'm spider in his cubbyhole   67:71

I'm Taking Care of You   219:58

I'm the guy they call little Mickey Mouse   119:90

I'm the kid that's all the candy, I'm a Yan-kee Doodle dandy 157:212, 205:301

I'm the King of the Castle/Il Mio Bel Castel-lo 189:152

I'm the man, the very fat man, that waters the workers' beer 64:158

I'm Very, Very Tall 287:86

I'm Wise 68:34

I'm wise, I'm wise, because of the size of my eyes 68:34

I'm with you and you're with me, and so we are all together 72:148, 254:118

Imag-inat-ion 261:12

Imandwa 89:278

Imawa yamanaka 286:58

Imi au Ia Oe/King's Serenade 87:66

In a cabin in the wood 26:32, 55:270

In a cavern, in a canyon, excavating for a mine 22:82, 25:76, 26:16, 148:52, 195, 205:213, 230:27, 290:162, *see also:* 61:100

In a chariot of light from the regions of day 28:58

In a corner of the bedroom is a great big curtain 172:140, 173:26

In a Cottage in Fife 112:6

In a Manger 241:111

In a manger poor sleeps the Christ Child 241:111

In a moldering cave where the wretched re-treat 273:18

In a neat little cottage where Granny did dwell 62:134

In a shady nook one moonlight night 42:608, 79:61

In a snug little field of a neighboring park 71:109

In a stable lies a baby 140:18, *see also:* 54:282

In Alicante it came to pass 216:43

In all my play at home or away 207:114

In Amsterdam there lives a maid 36:24, *see also:* A-Roving

In an Arizona town one day, Billy Venero heard them say 146:42, *see also:* 61:129, 159:197

In and Out the Bonnie Bluebells 245:54

In and out the bushes, up the ivy, into the hole 44:30

In and Out the Window 39:14, 63:22, *see also:* Round and Round the Village

In Bahia/Na Bahia Tem 266:14

In Bethlehem So Lowly/Zu Bethlehem Ge-boren 54:144

In Bethlehem They Light a Fire 295:76, *see also:* 54:276, 89:276

In Bethlehem's Cradle 54:282, *see also:* 140:18

In Carmel Bay the people say, we feed the Lazzaroni 226:333, *see also:* 72:98

In Christ There Is No East or West 86:88

In come Daddy from the plow 234:22

In de vinter, in de vintertime, ven de vin' blows on de vindowpane 226:334, *see also:* 27:242

In de Vinter Time 226:334, *see also:* 27:242

In Doncella Guerrera/The Girl Warrior 295:53

In Dreamland Far Away 66:98

In Dublin's fair city where girls are so pret-ty 22:22, 262:89

In Dulci Jubilo 21:328, 210:32, 220:98, 241:76

In early Spring on the edge of the river bank 286:34

In eighteen hundred and forty one I put me corduroy breeches on 22:150, 64:84, 158:270, 230:43, 239:72, 277:115, *see also:* 27:40, 62:90,

In eighteen hundred and ninety one 62:90, *see also:* Pat Works on the Railway

In eighteen hundred and twenty-four 292:170, *see also:* 24:832

In eighteen hundred forty-one, I put my cord'roy britches on 27:40, *see also:* Pat Works on the Railway

In Enterprise of Martial Kind 252:62

In ev'ry job that must be done, there is an element of fun 276:54

In Fading Light/In stiller Nacht 208:27

In Fairyland 207:94

In Father's Car 207:16

In flakes so feathery light, silently falls the snow 162:34

In Forest and Meadow/Gaaer Jed Udi Skov-en 89:166

In fourteen hundred ninety-two, three ships set out to sea 27:200, *see also:* 197:88

In Freedom We're Born 27:182, 28:9, *see also:* 21:238, 157:16, 240:44, 273:20

In Frisco Bay 118:13

In Frisco Bay there lives a whale 118:13

In good old Colony times 21:252, 157:30

In His Hands 31:19

In January it's so nice 235:60

In Just 44:22

In Just-spring when the world is mud-lus-cious 44:22

In Kansas 61:96, *see also:* 61:97

In Kieldrecht/Te Kieldrecht 89:139

In Lim'rick city he was brought up 21:316, *see also:* Barbara Allen

In London City where I once did dwell 226:57, *see also:* Barbara Allen

In midnight stillness and peaceful slumber 89:165

In Midnight's Silence/Wsrod Nocnej Ciszy 54:218

In Monterey the people say "We feed the lazzaroni" 72:98, see also: 226:333

In my backyard there is some ground 94, see also: Green Grass Grows All Around

In My Bureau Drawer 237:unpaged

In My Father's House 226:483

In My Garden/Bakhchalarda 89:178

In My Little Boat/E Mi Son Chi in Barchetta 89:155

In my little garden bed rak'd so nicely over 191:24

In my little new log cabin home my heart is light and free 61:70

In My Merry Oldsmobile 157:203, 205:317

In My Plane 162:100

In My Spacious Palace/En Sumag Palacio 89:97

In my young days, In my young days we always went our parents' ways 85:105

In Nottingham there lived a jolly tanner 164:22

In Our Aquarium 162:85

In Our Church We Gladly Sing 86:77

In Our Garden 291:56

In our garden, tiny garden 85:222

In Our Rowboat 162:94

In Our Work and in Our Play 86:117

In Plymouth town there liv'd a maid 22:168, 176:34, see also: 36:24, 71:77, 72:78, 98:29

In Poland 227:20

In Poland there's an inn, in Poland there's an inn 227:20

In Prehistoric Times 167:22

In Puget Sound there lives a whale 62:49

In Scarlet Town where I was born, there was a fair maid dwellin' 22:104, 66:122, 176:115, 205:20, 230:79, see also: Barbara Allen

In seventeen hundred seventy-five, our Bristol town was much surprised 240:119

In Stiller Nacht/In Fading Light 208:27

In Summer the Sunshine Is Brightest 72:131

In summertime when days are long 71:77, 72:78, see also: 22:168, 36:24, 98:29, 176:34

In summer time when leaves are green 164:36

In that great gittin' up mornin' 158:364

In That Poor Stable 210:39, see also: 220:60

In that poor stable how charming Jesus lies 210:39, 220:60

In the backyard, in the attic, or the cellar down below 26:47

In the backyard, in the backyard 26:80

In the beginning was the Word 124:17

In the Big Rock Candy Mountains, there's a land that's fair and bright 24:884, see also: 21:112, 158:278, 230:66

In the Bleak Mid-Winter 210:108

In the Blue Ridge mountains of Virginia stood a cow on the railroad track 118:28

In the Boardinghouse 290:174

In the dawn's light faintly gleaming, stand the ancient Kremlin walls 22:206

In the Days of Old Rameses 226:202

In the early morning as I went my way 241:66, see also: 284:93

In the Evening By the Moonlight 25:123, 170:76, 277:141

In the evening when I sit alone a-dreaming 157:200

In the faraway forest, one hears the cuckoo 217:60, see also: 27:52, 59:23, 157:77, 292:130

In the Fashion 172:120, 173:6

In the fire by the stream we see pictures of the past 69:39

In the Forest Lonely 72:68

In the gloom of mighty cities 64:14

In the Good Old Summertime 21:76, 25:98, 205:277

In the land of the Lassen, where timber is tall 25:82

In the little village of Bethlehem, there lay a Child one day 241:204

In the lobby of a big hotel in New York town one day 159:321

In the meadow sleep the lambkins with the ewe in the fold 125:115, see also: 71:38

In the middle of the night, when the moon is dark 166:34

In the moonlight down in the rice field 286:32

In the morning when I waken 86:164

In the Morning, When You Wake 125:116

In the Orchard 41:43

In the Pines 148:186

In the pond my ducklings all are swimming there 68:21

In the prison cell I sit 21:147, 73:172

In the region where the roses always bloom 21:94, 205:287

In the sky the bright stars glittered 21:180, 157:48

In the Snow 207:77

In the spread wings of the black crow 89:217

In the Starlight 66:100

In the Summer of Sixty 159:386

In the Sweet By and By 21:176, see also: 66:150

In the time of David, some call him a king 190:79, see also: Go Tell It On the Mountain

In the top of the apple tree   295:10
In the Town   241:90
In the Valley   140:31, *see also:* 190:100
In the Vinter   27:242, *see also:* 226:334
In the wintertime we go walking in the fields of snow   44:26
In the Woods   207:35
In this land of the free, not a slave shall there be   73:26
In this time of little things, sing, my heart, the story telling   209:113
In winter I get up at night and dress by yellow candle light   227:36
In Winter time I feed the birds   97:unpaged
Inaka nari domo Nambuno kuniwa sa   49:28
Incy Wincy Spider climbed up the water spout   46:216, *see also:* Eency Weency Spider
Independence Day   28:68, 240:84
Indian Harvest   245:110
Indian Lullaby   245:84
Indian muslin, Indian muslin   89:206, *see also:* 114:52
Indian Song   288:28
Indian War Song   28:118
Indians   207:44
The Indian's Death Song   61:116, *see also:* 273:114
The Indian's Over the Border   28:116
Infant Holy, Infant Lowly   220:36
Infant Innocence   59:58
Inkosi Jesus/My Sovereign Jesus   209:87
Inky Dinky Spider   147:26, *see also:* Eency Weency Spider
Inky Pinky 'Pider   63:103, *see also:* Eency Weency Spider
Inside Out   91:8
The Instrument Song   20:16, *see also:* Musicians
An intimate friend of the Czar was I   290:150
Into nga za ma Kwen-Kwe   163:46
Into the ward of the clean, white-wash'd halls   73:228
Into Yam/My Man   163:50
The Invalid Corps   73:142
An Invitation   207:51
An Invitation to North America   240:18
Invocation for Girl Scouts   69:5, 71:29
Ioho, wonder water   197:85
Iraka no nami to   87:52, *see also:* 286:74
Irakano namito kumono nami to   286:74, *see also:* 87:52
Irene, Goodnight   230:48
Irish Carol   241:48
Irish Washerwoman   126:109
The Irishman's Epistle   240:64, *see also:* 28:53

I's the B'y   27:66, *see also:* 134:74
Is There Anybody Here?   31:25
Is there anybody here that loves Jesus?   31:25
Is there, for honest poverty, that hangs his head, and a'that?   64:186
Is this door locked? No, child, no   109:177
Isabeau S'y Promène   176:134
Isabella   65:60
Isabella, go skin in a soakee   89:60
I'se got a little baby, but she's out of sight   157:194, *see also:* 205:258
I'se the B'y That Builds the Boat   134:74, *see also:* 27:66
The Island of Jamaica   36:46
Isn't It Funny   172:17, 174:3
Isn't it funny how a bear likes honey?   172:17
Isn't that dandy neat, Mister Banjo   21:251
It ain't gonna rain, it ain't gonna snow   226:141
It ain't no mo' cane on dis Brazis   158:320
It ain't so much a question of not knowing what to do   218:35
It Came Upon the Midnight Clear   54:62, 65:90, 92:161, 140:102, 148:190, 190:131, 210:40, 210:41, 241:122, 264:84, 279:48, 284:83
It Could Be a Wonderful World   64:198
It Doesn't Really Matter   63:46
It has many doors, it has many doors   87:16
It Is I, the Little Owl   19:31
It is of a fearless highwayman a story I will tell   159:144, *see also:* 159:142
It is of a wealthy farmer, as you shall hear   35:78
It is Raining, Shepherdess/Il Pleut, Bergère   217:56
It Is Spring   27:50, *see also:* 189:116
It is spring, the daisies are busting out   27:50, 189:116
It is the joyful Easter time   86:65
It is wrong, it is wrong, you guessed wrong   74:45
It isn't any trouble just to S-M-I-L-E   25:39, 26:12
It Might As Well Be Spring   218:260
It oft-times has been told that British seamen bold   240:191
It Rained a Mist   162:30, 232:68
It started into raining an' followed with a sleet an' snow   159:11
It Takes a Worried Man   147:40, *see also:* 24:890, 148:422
It takes a worried man to sing a worried song   24:890, 147:40, 148:422
It wobbles and tips, I spill in a puddle   245:26

It Was a Lover and His Lass 85:16, 176:137, 189:104

It was a lucky April shower 170:91

It was a royal gathering 89:303

It was down in old Joe's bar-room on a corner by the square 226:228

It was down to Red River I came 159:14

It was early, early all in the spring 212:33

It was early, early on one spring 61:181, 61:182

It was early one mornin' as I passed St. James Hospital 159:420, *see also:* Streets of Laredo

It was in Juda's land by God's almighty hand 140:31, 190:100

It was in the lovely month of May, I heard a poor soldier lamenting and say 226:137

It was in the merry month of May when I started for Texas far away 226:285, *see also:* Trail to Mexico

It was in the month of October-o that we started out for Saludio 61:35

It was just about a year ago I left my eastern home 61:71

It was last Monday morning, lawd, lawd, lawd 234:38, *see also:* Grey Goose

It was late one summer's evening when I bid L.A. adieu 146:46

It was on a cold winter's night 226:466

It was on a Wednesday night, the moon was shining bright 157:158, 226:420, *see also:* Jesse James

It was one Sunday mornin', Lord, Lord, Lord 129:48, 292:152, *see also:* Grey Goose

It was only a few short years ago 159:168

It was poor little Jesus, yes, yes 158:354, 233:52, *see also:* 54:86, 140:60, 190:90

It was springtime in the Rockies 290:132

It was upon a high, high hill 24:820, *see also:* Barbara Allen

It Will Never Do to Give It Up So 66:43

It wuz one day, I believe in May, when old Si Hubbard to me did say 226:350

Itaskit, Itasket 14:351, 17:106, 197:42, *see also:* A-Tisket, A-Tasket

It's a beautiful day in this neighborhood 219:4

It's A Grand Night for Singing 218:264

It's a grand time we have in Cubbing 26:52

It's a Small World 275:88

It's a very ancient saying, but a true and honest thought 218:200

It's a world of laughter, a world of tears 275:88

It's All Right to Cry 260:93

It's All Wrong 197:89

It's all wrong! All a mistake 197:89

It's an Indian Village 166:14

It's Casey Junior comin' down the track 275:26, 276:8

It's dusk on the prairie. The lamps are aglow 166:30

It's four long years since I reached this land 24:863

It's Fun to Be a Person, Yes-Sir-ee! 204:31

It's Going to Be a Long Vinter 55:260

It's gonna take everybody to win this war 239:92

It's into the city, not far from this spot 35:96

It's Jim Farrow and John Farrow and little Simon, too 159:112

It's Little Joe, the wrangler, he'll wrangle nevermore 159:91, *see also:* 61:215, 146:124

It's Love That Makes the World Go Round 55:269

It's lucky my skin grows with me 91:16

It's not that easy bein' green 206:82

It's of a fearless highwayman a story I'll tell 22:28, *see also:* 35:72

It's of a fierce highwayman a story I will tell 35:72, *see also:* 22:28

It's of a jolly farmer who lived on yonder hill 176:58

It's of a wealthy farmer, lived on the banks of sweet Dundee 35:24

It's of those Texas cowboys a story I'll tell 159:291, 159:342

It's on a dark and stormy night, the snow was falling fast 35:50, *see also:* 24:825, 27:244, 159:231, 226:58

It's on this railroad bank I stand 24:901, *see also:* Careless Love

It's Only a Paper Moon 170:52

It's pretty well met to my own true love 35:82, *see also:* 226:66

It's rain or shine, sleet or snow 232:69, *see also:* 61:232, 61:233, 159:8

It's raining, it's hailing, the stars give no light 33:146, *see also:* On Top of Old Smoky

It's round in your cavy and it's rope out your hack 61:212

It's step her to your weev'ly wheat 24:814, 226:161, *see also:* 66:76, 213:28

It's Such a Good Feeling 219:35

It's the far northland that's a-calling me away 25:91, 69:38

It's the Milkman 107:20

It's the Same the Whole World Over 197:50

It's the Syme the Whole World Over 21:56, 226:200

It's time to end our school day now 11:27

It's time to find your places 166:24

It's Very, Very Funny 172:25, 173:11

It's very, very funny, 'cos I know I had some honey 172:25

It's what did you have for your supper, Jimmy Randall, my son? 232:140, 89:156, *see also:* 157:71

It's with Kitty I'll go for a ramble 212:58

Ivan Skizavitzsky Skivar 25:34, *see also:* 226:344

I've a brand new baby brother 166:56

I've a fine big castle, mata rillay rillay rillay 188:54, *see also:* 189:154

I've a Fine, Bonny Castle 189:154, *see also:* 188:54

I've a message from the Medicine Man 166:42

I've a special secret children ought to know 206:78

I've beat my way wherever any winds have blown 159:289

I've been a moonshiner for sev'nteen long years 157:52, 226:142

I've been a sailor since my birth 290:118

I've been a'wand'rin' all the night 134:31, 213:80, *see also:* 27:102, 128:70

I've Been All Around This World 61:252

I've been ridin' for cattle for the most of my life 61:106

I've been thinking today, as my thoughts began to stray 159:330

I've Been to Haarlem 20:56, 70:9, 129:120, 134:44, *see also:* 39:2

I've been upon the prairie 159:83

I've Been Workin' on the Railroad 25:35, 26:78, 83:506, 129:86, 148:192, 162:95, 197:80, 205:196, *see also:* 22:148, 27:174

I've come shust now to tells you how 73:118

I've got a little baby but she's out of sight 205:258, *see also:* 157:194

I've got a mule [and] her name is Sal 22:37, 33:58, 69:34, 197:78, 226:171, 230:87, 239:60, 246, 262:74, 292:38

I've got a robe, you've got a robe 83:476, *see also:* 25:103, 31:9, 129:16, 148:14

I've got a wife an' a five li'l chillun 158:151

I've Got No Strings 275:21, 276:12

I've got no strings to hold me down, to make me fret or make me frown 275:21, 276:12

I've Got Shoes 83:476, *see also:* 25:103, 31:9, 129:16, 148:14

I've got shoes with grown-up laces 172:126, 173:12

I've Got That Cub Scout Spirit 26:53

I've Got That Scouting Spirit 25:54

I've Got Two 206:22

I've got two eyes 206:22

I've got two legs and so have you 204:23

I've heard the lilting at our ewe milking 182:28

I've lost the closet key 232:169

I've rambled and gambled all my money away 226:284, *see also:* 159:253

I've sung this song but I'll sing it again 64:107, 230:92, *see also:* 130:59

I've traveled about a bit in my time 66:40

I've traveled this wide world over, and now to another I'll go 61:11, *see also:* 157:50, 159:278

I've travelled all over this country 158:184

I've two little hands to work for Jesus 86:120

I've wandered all over this country 64:138

Iya', mo dukpe fo' ba e 89:59

J

J Jump 206:20

"J" jump joyful, jumble around 206:20

Ja Posejah Lubenice/I Planted Watermelons 169:71, 270:63

Ja tudo dorme vai a noite em meio 89:165

Jack-a-Nory 111:39

Jack and Jill 17:83, 75:38, 175:18, 177:90, 188:124, 283:24, 289:88

Jack and Jill went up the hill 17:83, 75:38, 175:18, 177:90, 188:124, 283:24, 289:88

Jack and Joan 85:23

Jack Be Nimble 17:46, 162:88, 285:87

Jack be nimble, Jack be quick 17:46, 162:88, 285:87

Jack, Boy, Ho, Boy 71:100, 293:48

Jack, Can I Ride? 234:76

Jack Donahoe 159:209

Jack Horner 17:11, 175:75, 188:178, 283:16

Jack O' Diamonds 159:253

Jack o' Diamonds, Jack o' Diamonds, I know you of old 159:253

Jack-o-Lantern 75:40 *(I'm a Jack-o-lantern with a great big grin)*

Jack-o'-Lantern 97:unpaged *(Jack-o'-lantern, Jack-o'-lantern, big and yellow)*

Jack-o-lantern grinning wide 207:24

Jack-o'-lantern, Jack-o'-lantern, big and yellow! 97:unpaged

Jack-o'-lanterns 197:96

Jack Sprat 17:70, 175:15

Jack Spratt could eat no fat 17:70, 175:15

Jack Sprat, His Wife and Cat 112:43

Jack, the Piper 111:79, *see also:* 18:40

Jackaro 213:64

The Jacket So Blue 35:76

The Jackfish 135:45

Jackie Rover 36:62
Jack's Yak 91:41
Jackson 226:430
Jackson is on sea, Jackson is on shore 226:430
Jackson Scott, the Astronaut 112:56
Jacky, Come Give Me the Fiddle 112:58
Jacky Jingle 18:34
Jacob's Ladder 21:130, 25:97, 31:11, 69:29, 86:110, 148:198
Jade green shoots explode everywhere 261:30
Jag Ser Dig/I See You 189:134
J'ai descendu dans mon jardin 217:20
J'ai du Bon Tabac/I Have Some Good Tobacco 217:34
The Jam on Gerry's Rocks 21:222, 35:6, 158:170, 226:394, *see also:* 24:847
James Bird 240:200
James Whaland 226:389
Jane Glover 293:50, *see also:* 71:103
January, February 233:50
Jargon 273:144
Jasmine Flowers in Bloom/Angan Phuli 89:218
Jay Gould's Daughter 226:364
Je suis disait la mouche 243:10
Jeanie With the Light Brown Hair 22:100
Jeannette, Isabella 22:242, *see also:* Bring a Torch, Jeannette, Isabella
Jeder eyne hot lieb Shabas ba nacht 148:84
Jedermann liebb Samstag Nacht 148:84
Jeff Davis awoke one morn' from a dream 73:66
Jeff Davis built a wagon 73:48
Jeff Davis' Dream 73:66
Jefferson and Liberty 27:188, 64:188
Jeg Er Saa Glad Hver Julekveld/I Am So Glad on Christmas Eve 54:202
Jehdeh, jehdeh, pochtovsky panahchek 289:80
Jehovah Hallelujah 233:23
Jei me da de gu nyang 49:17
Jemmy Dawson 112:63
Jen jen nei ge ddo ba yo 49:15
Jen ywe li, jen ywe jen 49:16
Jennie Dang the Weaver 182:50
Jennie Jenkins 20:40, 69:20, 75:42, 129:22, 158:54, 257, 262:37, *see also:* 135:62, 291:28
Jennifer Gently 36:36, *see also:* 37:122, 62:143, 128:114
Jenny Jenkins 291:28, *see also:* Jennie Jenkins
Jenny, you can't love one 88, *see also:* 62:126, 128:78, 148:250, 230:74
Jeremiah, Blow the Fire 135:119, 291:34
Jerry, Go an' Ile that Car 64:88, 226:360
Jerusalem 124:316

Jerusalem gaude gaudiomagno 279:9
Jerusalem Guide/Jerusalem Rejoice 279:9
Jerusalem, my guiding star, my mother land adored 124:316
Jerusalem Rejoice/Jerusalem Guide 279:9
Jerusalem the Golden 45:55
Jess, a wild cowboy, loves whisky and beer 159:86
Jesse James 21:224, 60:96, 61:255, 61:257, 61:259, 61:260, 146:154, 157:158, 158:296, 159:152, 159:155, 159:156, 159:157, 226:420, 230:36, *see also:* 61:256, 61:258
Jesse James and His Boys 61:256, *see also:* Jesse James
Jesse James and his boys rode the Dodge City trail 61:256, *see also:* Jesse James
Jesse James was a boy that downed many a man 159:157, *see also:* Jesse James
Jesse James was a lad who killed many a man 21:224, 60:96, 61:255, 146:154, 158:296, 159:152, 230:36, *see also:* Jesse James
Jesse James was a man who traveled through the land 159:155, *see also:* Jesse James
Jess's Dilemma 159:86
Jesu, Redemptor Omnium/Jesus, Redeemer of the World 279:10
Jesus Borned in Bethlea 86:34, 140:16, 140:114, 190:102, 232:181, 233:48
Jesus came in garment lowly 54:114
Jesus Christ Is Born/Gdy Sie Chrystus Rodzi 279:124, *see also:* 54:210
Jesus Christ Is Born Tonight 220:66
Jesus Christ Is Risen Today 45:42, 86:62
Jesus Christ, s'habille in pauvre 54:114
Jesus Christ the Apple Tree 190:93
Jesus, Friend of Little Children 86:96
Jesus From Thy Throne on High 86:143
Jesus healed the sick 86:101
Jesus Holy, Born So Lowly/W Zlobie Lezy 54:204
Jesus, Jesus, Baby dear 54:226, *see also:* Rocking
Jesus, Jesus, Rest Your Head 140:86, 183:28
Jesus, Lead Me Day By Day 86:102
Jesus Liebt Mich Ganz Gewiss/Jesus Loves Me 86:97
Jesus Listens When I Pray 86:138
Jesus, Lover of My Soul 21:335
Jesus Loves Me 45:26, 86:97, 283:61
Jesus Loves Me, Jesus Loves Me 86:103
Jesus loves me, this I know 45:26, 86:97, 283:61
Jesus, our brother, kind and good 13, 54:24, 86:47, 128:62, 138:unpaged
Jesus, Our Friend 86:100
Jesus, Redeemer of the World/Jesu Redemptor Omnium 279:10

Jesus, Saviour, Pilot Me 22:291
Jesus, Tender Shepherd 45:27, 283:63, see also: 86:171
Jesus, tender Shepherd, hear me; 45:27, 86:171, 283:63
Jesus the Christ Is Born 183:16
Jesus, the New-Born Baby/Gesù Bambin L'e Nato 54:246
Jesus Walked in Galilee 37:166
Jesus walked this lonesome valley 86:54, 148:238, see also: 158:352, 226:486
Jesus Was a Loving Teacher 86:99
Jesus who by the water strolled 124:99
Jesus, Won't You Come B'm-By? 226:469
Jeu! Jeu!/Hay-Hoo! Hay-Hoo! 89:79, 216:36
The Jewish Year 77:36
The Jewish year brings joy 77:36
Jig Along Home 130:114
Jiggle, jiggle, jiggle, jiggle 289:89
Jikele Maweni/Go Round to the Rocks 163:45
Jill told Bill that it was lots of fun to cook 260:119
Jim Along, Josie 63:38, 135:108, 232:72
Jim Crack Corn 232:124, see also: Blue Tail Fly
Jim crack corn, I don't care 129:42, see also: Blue Tail Fly
Jim Farrow 159:112
Jim Fisk 226:416
Jim the Roper 146:164
Jimmy Crack Corn 178:26, see also: Blue Tail Fly
Jimmy Randal 157:71, see also: 89:156, 232:140
Jimmy Rose He Went to Town 232:58
Jingle at the Windows 232:173
Jingle Bells 17:63, 54:70, 92:163, 127:220, 148:200, 241:171, 264:114, 283:64
Jinny Jo 63:32, see also: 17:39, 68:12, 100:90
Jiroyanmo Taroyanmo 49:24
Joe Bowers 61:33, 159:375, 230:47
Joe Hill 22:48, 64:20
Joe Turner 226:241
Jog On, Jog On 262:129
The John B. Sails 226:22, see also: 148:344
John Brown Had a Little Indian 135:112, 165:135, see also: 107:24
John Brown Knew a Little Indian 107:24, see also: 135:112, 165:135
John Brown's Baby 20:32, 26:30, 118:31, 253:100, 289:114
John Brown's baby had a cold upon his chest 20:32, 26:30, 118:31, 253:100, 289:114
John Brown's Body 22:222, 64:170, 73:7, 158:120, 230:62, 277:57

John Brown's body lies a mould'ring in the ground 22:222, 64:170, 73:7, 158:120, 230:62, 277:57
John Brown's Ford 26:31
John Brown's Ford had a puncture in its tire 26:31
John Cook 111:15
John Cook had a little grey mare 111:15
John Dory 79:47
John Garner's Trail Herd 159:25
John Grumlie 79:57, see also: Old Grumbler
John Grumlie swore by the light o' the moon 79:57, see also: Old Grumbler
John had great big waterproof boots on 172:117, 173:3
John Hardy 158:306
John Hardy was a desp'rate little man 158:306
John has gone away; where is he now? 41:16
John Henry 22:170, 33:178, 64:82, 89:40, 158:258, 158:260, 158:262, 226:24, 230:82, 232:154, 239:68, 272:15, 274:16, see also: 232:156
John Jacob Jingleheimer Jones 62:67, see also: 25:37, 26:14, 253:106, 289:125
John Jacob Jingleheimer Schmidt 25:37, 26:14, 253:106, 289:125, see also: 62:67
John O'Dwyer of the Glens 42:591
John Peel 22:92, 176:48, 205:374
John Whipple's Mill 35:102
Johnnie Verbeck 25:18
Johnny Appleseed's Grace 101:31
Johnny Bull and many more, soon, they say, are coming o'er 240:189
Johnny Bull, beware, keep at your proper distance 27:172, 240:205
Johnny Cake 61:23
Johnny Come to Hilo 128:22, see also: 37:157, 157:40
Johnny Cuckoo 109:73
Johnny Doolan's Cat 84:39
Johnny, Get Your Hair Cut 135:15, 226:158, 232:142, see also: 157:44, 226:158
Johnny, Git Your Gun 157:45
Johnny Had a Little Dog 17:131, see also: Bingo
Johnny Has Gone For a Soldier 22:69, 134:94, 157:24, 158:117, 240:87, 262:25, 273:84, see also: 73:104
Johnny I Hardly Knew Ye 42:605, see also: 148:204
Johnny, I Hardly Knew You 148:204, see also: 42:605
Johnny Is Gone for a Soldier 73:104, see also: Johnny Has Gone for a Soldier
Johnny! Johnny! 71:100, 72:164

Johnny Jump Around 296:14

Johnny Riley 35:32, *see also:* 213:60, 226:68

Johnny Sands 84:14

Johnny Shall Have a New Bonnet 111:22

Johnny Todd 212:38

Johnny Todd he took a notion for to cross the oceans wide 212:38

Johnny Went Down in the Bucket 62:94

Johnny Works With One Hammer 178:28, *see also:* 75:61, 165:166

Johnny's Gone to Hilo 37:157, *see also:* 128:22, 157:40

Johnny's Jarmanie 37:179

Johnny's So Long at the Fair 62:126, *see also:* Oh, Dear! What Can the Matter Be

Join hands and circle to the left 159:242

The Jolly Cowboy 159:275

A jolly fat frog lived in the river swim, O! 188:72

Jolly Holiday 276:55

Jolly Is the Miller Boy 17:118, 135:82, 227:26, *see also:* 20:35, 63:28

Jolly Miller 110:51, *see also:* 165:200 (*There was a jolly miller and he lived by himself*)

The Jolly Miller 17:76, 283:26 (*There was a jolly miller once lived on the River Dee*)

The Jolly Old Miller 63:28, *see also:* 17:118, 20:35, 135:82, 227:26 (*There's a jolly old miller and he lives by himself*)

Jolly Old Roger 262:60, *see also:* 239:83

Jolly Old Saint Nicholas 54:74, *see also:* 197:122

The Jolly Stage Driver 35:100

The Jolly Thrasher 35:91

Jolting up and down in the little red wagon 129:70

Jomfru, jomfru, jomfru, jomfru, skjaer 89:168

Jonathan you are back today 77:18

Josef, Lieber Josef Mein 54:148, *see also:* 21:326

Joseph and Mary 190:70, 233:24, *see also:* 140:26, 232:182, 264:76, 284:55

Joseph, Dearest Joseph 21:326, 54:148, 210:42, *see also:* 184:42, 220:24

Joseph dearest, Joseph mine, help me cradle the Child divine 21:326, 184:42, 210:42, 220:25, *see also:* Joseph, Dearest Joseph

Joseph Henry Alligator 166:70

Joseph, lieber Joseph mein 21:326, *see also:* 54:148

Joseph was an old man, an old man was he 190:70, 233:24, 264:76, 284:55, *see also:* 140:26, 232:182

Josephine 109:60

Joshua Fit the Battle of [ob] Jericho 22:304, 107:28, 158:374, *see also:* 148:208, 230:37

Joshua Fought the Battle of Jericho 148:208, 230:37, *see also:* 22:304, 107:28, 158:374

Josie 226:84, *see also:* Frankie and Johnny

Josie she's a good girl, as ev'rybody knows 226:84, *see also:* Frankie and Johnny

The Journey/La Jornada 54:300

The Journey 59:45

Joy to the World 22:258, 54:28, 65:95, 92:166, 148:212, 241:146, 242:unpaged, 264:100, 279:56, 284:31

Joy to the world! The Lord is come 22:258, 54:28, 65:95, 92:166, 148:212, 241:146, 242:unpaged, 264:100, 279:56, 284:31

Joyful Blossoms/Gladjens Blomster 208:65

Joyful Easter 86:65

Joyful Greetings 245:107

Joyful, joyful, joyful greetings 245:107

Joyful, Joyful, We Adore Thee 86:132

Juan Murray 159:158

Juanita 21:259, 61:144, 170:25

Juanita, I must leave you. I have come to say farewell 61:144, *see also:* 21:259, 170:25

Juba 109:40, 232:91

Juba Dance/Danse Juba 89:57

Juba this and Juba that 109:40, 232:91

Jubilee 134:39, 213:36

Jubilo 27:134

Juda's Carol 190:100, *see also:* 140:31

Juego de los Pavos/The Turkey Game 194:34

Jump Jim Crow 21:290

Jump Josie 135:94, *see also:* 128:97

Jump, Jump, Jump! 68:6

Jump, jump, jump! Jump over the moon 68:6

Jump, jump! Kangaroo Brown 165:105

Jump That Jody 109:10

Jump that Jody, jump it 109:10

Jumping, Jumping, Jumping, Jumping 178:12

June Is Bustin' Out All Over 218:85

June, Lovely June 262:34

Jungfru Maria till Betlehem gick/Mary the Virgin to Bethlehem Went 279:111

Jungle Mammy Song 226:455

The Juniper Tree 27:88, 232:82

Junk Man 239:89

A Junto Song 240:66

Just a Closer Walk With Thee 148:214

Just a Song at Twilight 66:30, 205:216

Just before brave Custer's charge 61:127

Just Before the Battle, Mother 21:153

Just before the battle the General hears a row 99:48

Just for Once 219:40

Just from the Kitchen 109:52

Just Like a Cowboy 154:34

Just plant a watermelon on my grave
25:40, 63:124
Just whistle while you work   275:12

K

'K Heb mijn wagen volgeladen   21:318
Ka ma tay ka ma tay Cowruh cowruh
107:26
Ka Tam Ma Wui/One Morning I Rose
89:264
Ka vadudu ka guyawe   89:303
Kabak da Boynuma/Striking a Tune
89:180
Kad se Jangin/Hear Me, Dearest   89:190
Kaduguwai/The Gathering   89:303
Kaeru-no Fue/The Frog's Flute   286:32
Kagome Kagome/Bird in the Cage   16:20,
169:45, 266:46, 286:38
Kah-ee-gwoo nee-mah-jah kah-ee-gwoo nee-mah-jah   19:43
Kahuli aku, kahuli mai   87:15
Kahuli calling, hear us afar   87:15
Kaika chitne, kaika chitne   89:235
Kakkai ciraginile nandalalaninran
89:217
Kakurembo/Hide and Seek   286:41
Kakurembo surumono, yotoide   286:41
Kaleeba   236:11
Kana Ma Laune/My Husband   89:214
The Kangaroo   290:106
A kangaroo sat on an oak   290:106
Kangwon Do Arirang   49:41
Kansas Boys   226:129
Kansas City   218:24
A Kansas Cowboy   159:103
The Kansas Line   159:15, *see also:* 60:36,
61:235, 146:53, 159:281
Karasu/The Crow   286:26
Karasu, naze naku no?   286:26
Kari/Wild Geese   286:20
Kari, kari, watare!   286:20
Kariboshi Kiri Uta/Miscanthus Mowing
Song   49:23
Karusellen/Carrousel   89:168
Kasooli w'omwana? Ca, ca, ca   236:77
Kate and Her Horns   36:90
Katey Morey   36:32
Kattan, Kattan/Run, Run   89:257
Katten i Saekken/Cat in the Sack   208:19
Katy Cruel   157:14, *see also:* 36:60, 37:154,
62:142, 230:70
Kazhdi ma rad sabotu vietcher   148:84
Kazoe Uta/Counting Song   286:86
Kee-Chee   69:15

The Keel Row   135:16, 262:68, *see also:*
89:302
Keemo Kyemo   290:108, *see also:* 234:48
'Keenene   236:3
Keep Advancing   26:47
Keep Moving   14:352, *see also:* 26:37,
253:104
Keep the Horseshoe Over the Door   66:21
Keep Your Hand on the Plow   158:376, *see
also:* 157:147, 226:474
The Keeper   71:74, 72:118, 176:9, 230:59,
290:86, *see also:* 148:216, 292:84
The keeper did a hunting go   230:59, *see
also:* Keeper
*The Keeper did a-shooting go and under his
cloak he carried a bow*   71:74, 72:118, *see
also:* Keeper
The Keeper Would A-Hunting Go
148:216, 176:9, 290:86, 292:84, *see also:*
71:74, 72:118, 230:59
Keeping Time   104:51
Kellyburn Braes   180
Kentucky Babe   125:139
Kentucky Moonshiner   157:52, 226:142
Kesailta/'Twas Summer and 'Twas Evening
208:21
The Kettle Is Burning   74:31
Kevin Barry   21:116, 64:194, 226:42
The Keys of Canterbury   27:26
Khoe Li/The Moon   89:256
Khuluma/Speak   163:115
Ki lo naeh lo yaeh   77:57
Kicking Mule   234:62, 292:34
Kids   206:25
Kuni se egera kuna gia nero   169:25
Kilakila Na Roughriders/Famed Are the
Roughriders   87:88
The Killer   159:172
Kimi-ga Yo   286:53
Kind folks, you will pity my horrible tale
277:125, *see also:* 61:65, 146:95, 159:372,
226:264
*Kind friends, if you will listen, a story I will
tell*   146:72, 159:214
*Kind friends won't you listen to my pitiful
tale*   61:65, *see also:* 146:95, 159:372,
226:264, 277:125
*Kind friends you must listen to my pitiful
tale*   146:95, *see also:* 61:65, 159:372,
226:264, 277:125
*Kind friends, you must pity my horrible
tale*   159:372, *see also:* 61:65, 146:95,
226:264, 125
Kind Miss   226:144
Kind miss, kind miss, go ask your mother
226:144
Kindness   155:13
Kindness is the same in any language
155:13

King Arthur   17:100
*The King asked the Queen, and the Queen
   asked the Dairymaid*   172:93
King Hancock sat in regal state   28:131
King Henry Has Set Me Free   62:31
King Herod/El Rei Herodes   54:264
King Herod and the Cock   96:9
King Jesus Hath a Garden   96:10, 210:44
The King May Pass/Que Pase el Rey
   168:149
The King of France   14:355, 17:120, 83:505
*The King of France, with forty thousand
   men*   14:355, 17:120, 83:505
King of Kings   31:51
The King of Love My Shepherd Is   45:11
*The King sent his lady on the first day of
   Yule*   95
King William   39:4, *see also:* 63:24
King William Was King George's Son
   63:24, *see also:* 39:4
King William was King James's son   39:4,
   see also: 63:24
Kingdom Coming   73:93
The Kings/Die Könige   241:215, *see also:*
   210:121
The King's Breakfast   172:93
Kings of Orient   92:168, 184:34, *see also:*
   We Three Kings
The King's Own Regulars   240:89, *see also:*
   27:166, 28:89
King's Serenade/Imi Au Ia Oe   87:66
The Kinkaiders   159:412, 226:278
Kisha/The Train   286:58
Kisses Sweeter Than Wine   230:93
The Kitchen   149:14
Kite String   141:94
Kitty Alone   289:28
Kitty and Puppy   162:86
Kitty Wells   66:132
Kitty White   14:357
*Kitty White so slyly comes to catch the Mou-
   sie Gray*   14:357
Klahpsete/Oh, Weep Mine Eyes   89:194
Kling, Glöckchen/Ring, Little Bells   54:140
Knick Knack   20:44, *see also:* This Old Man
The Knickerbocker Line   35:94
Knock along, Brother Rabbit, knock along
   135:28
Knock at the Door   17:150
Knock Jim Crow   109:57
Kochae-Bushi/From   Nippon   Bridge
   89:237
Koganemushi/Mister   Golden   Beetle
   286:23
Koganemushiwakanemochi da   286:23
Koi Nobori/Flying Carp   286:74, *see also:*
   87:52
Kol Jauns Nevedes Buvau/Quite Young and
   Carefree Was I   89:175

Kolattam/The Stick Dance   70:10, 100:126,
   168:57
Kolyada   128:55
Kommet, Ihr Hirten   54:326
Komoriuta/Lullaby   286:63
Kona Kai Opua/The Clouds at Kona   87:27
Kookaburra   128:108,   148:218,   176:23,
   178:55, 189:136, 262:148, 289:188, 293:86
Korobushka   178:60
Kouh Beh Kouh/On the Road   89:201
Kudala sinyamaze   163:92
Kui Mina Alles Noor Veel Olin/When I Was
   But a Small Young Laddie   89:173
Kum-Ba-Ya   25:108, 55:276, 72:143, 86:198,
   107:36, 148:220, *see also:* 261:54
Kum-ba-ya my Lord Kum-ba-ya   25:108,
   55:276, 72:143, 86:198, 107:36, 148:220,
   see also: 261:54
Kumbaya   261:54, *see also:* Kum-Ba-Ya
Kutsu-ga Naru/Shoes Squeak   286:60
Ku'u Ipo I Ka He'e Pu'eone/Come Surfing
   With Me   87:36
Kuu Pua I Paoakalani/The   Garden of
   Paoakalani   87:47
Kwei Cho's mountains are so high   49:19
Kye Kye Kole   169:23

L

L-O-double L-I-P-O-P spells Lollipop
   118:21
La aurora empieza a brillar   89:100
La Besace/The Beggar's Double Sack
   243:50
La Biritullera   262:40
La Burriquita/The Little Donkey   216:6
La Calandria/The Lark   295:7
La Chacarera/The Little Farm Girl   70:17,
   197:37
La Chaparrita/Little Sweet One   262:21
La Cigale et la Fourmi/The Grasshopper
   and the Ant   79:65, *see also:* 243:34
La Cucaracha   21:110, 197:38, 226:290
*La cucaracha, la cucaracha, Doesn't care to
   travel here*   197:38, *see also:* 21:110,
   226:290
*La cucaracha, la cucaracha, ya no quiere
   caminar*   197:38,   *see   also:*   21:110,
   226:290
La Doncella Guerrera/The Girl Warrior
   295:53
La Fourmi et la Sauterelle/The Ant and the
   Grasshopper   243:34, *see also:* 79:65
La Fuente/The Fountain   168:112, *see also:*
   194:24
La Guajira/The Guajira   89:58

La Gue Declarée/War Is Declared 89:61

La haut, sur la montagne 69:8, 71:15, 72:38

La Imilla 114:66

La Jesucita 22:78, 72:106, 295:66

La Jornada/The Journey 54:300

La la la la la la la 178:51

La lice a sa voisine se fit preter ja dis 243:41

La Lice et sa Compagne/The Hound and Her Neighbor 243:41

La Marche des Rois/The March of the Kings 54:126, 241:105

La Marseillaise 22:223, 64:183

La Mère Michel/Old Lady Mitchell 217:26

La Molinera/The Miller's Wife 295:59

La Mouche et la Fourmi/The Fly and the Ant 243:10

La Mouche et le Coche/The Fly and the Coach 243:48

La Pájara Pinta/The Spotted Bird 168:127

La Paloma Azul/The Sky-Blue Dove 89:72

La Palomita/Little Dove 169:53, 265:45

La Panaderita/The Baker-Girl 89:160, 216:18

La Poule aux Oeufs d'Or/The Hen Who Laid Golden Eggs 243:14

La Poulette Grise/The Old Grey Hen 289:30

La Princesse Mariée à un Anglais/The Princess Wed to an Englishman 89:150

La Pulga y el Piojo/The Flea and the Louse 295:12

La pulga y el piojo se quieren casar 295:12

La Punta y el Tacón/The Tip and Heel Dance 194:32

La Raspe/Mexican Clap Dance 178:45

La Tarara 295:61

La Tejedora de Nanduti/The Weaver of Nanduti 89:98

La Torre de Alicante/The Tower of Alicante 216:7

La Tortue et les Deux Canards/The Tortoise and the Two Ducks 243:22

La Treccia Bionda/Golden Tresses 208:39

La Vidalita 22:108

La Virgencita/The Little Maiden 70:14

La Viudita del Conde Laurel/The Widow of Count Laurel 295:43

Lackey Bill 159:187

A Lad to Prove His Love 114:29

The ladies! Bless the darling creatures 73:11

The Lady and the Pig 46:226, *see also:* 175:76

The Lady and the Swine 175:76, *see also:* 46:226

Lady Bird, Lady Bird 285:58, 292:203, *see also:* 175:89

Lady bird, lady bird fly away home 285:58, 292:203, *see also:* 175:89

Lady come down and see 144:11

Lady Gay 37:116

Lady, lady, lady, lady fair 89:168

The Lady on the Mountain 39:20

Lady Saint Anne/Señora Santa Ana 216:45

Ladybird 85:162

Ladybird, Ladybird 175:89, *see also:* 285:58, 292:203

Ladybug 162:22

Ladybug, ladybug, how do you do 162:22

Lailaw/Lament for an Absent Lover 208:1

The Laird of Cockpen 181

The Laird of Cockpen, he's proud and he's great 181

La-la-la- la la la-la-la la la 69:16

The Lamb 112:59, 189:62

The Lambs 191:16

Lambs Are Sleeping 125:56

The Lame Crane 71:114, 72:170, *see also:* 62:19, 144:25, 176:152, 292:65, 293:52

A Lame, Tame Crane 144:25, *see also:* The Lame Crane

A Lament/Ngoma Kurila 163:42

Lament for an Absent Lover/Lailaw 208:1

The Lamentation of Hugh Reynolds 42:607

Lamkin 176:153

Lan Hua-Hua/Blue Flower 87:50

Land of our birth, we pledge to thee 71:7

Land of the Silver Birch 55:257

The Land We Call Home 69:36

Landlord 141:56

Landlord, Fill the Flowing Bowl 176:100

The Lane County Bachelor 61:58, 226:120, 254:91

Langa More/More Sun 163:108

L'angombe a ati:"Kilumba" 89:278

L'angombe had said: "O sit down!" 89:278

The Lark 292:134 *(The lark it is a handsome bird)*

The Lark/La Calandria 295:7 *(There was a lark hanging from a balcony)*

The lark it is a handsome bird 292:134

Las Chaparreras/The Chaparreras 89:71

Las Horas del Reloj/The Hours of the Clock 295:34

Las Mañanitas/Morning Song 169:49, 226:292, 262:21, 268:41, 295:62

Las Posadas/Thou Art Well Content 54:256

Last evening Cousin Peter came 165:170

The last I was in London, I heard the happy news 35:36

The Last Longhorn 61:310, 159:325

Last Monday morning 'bout half past five 35:14

Last Month O' the Year When Was Jesus Born 190:119

Last night as I lay on the prairie 25:74, 26:74, 60:72, 61:329, 146:106, 158:210, 159:45, 225:66

Last night I had the strangest dream 230:32

Last night the night before-who all is here? 107:58

Last night there were four Marys 148:98

Last Roundup 61:330, *see also:* 159:327

Last Sunday mornin' Lord, Lord, Lord 277:49, *see also:* Grey Goose

Last time on that lazy old river, when last I roamed its quiet shore 61:167

Last Winter Was a Hard One 35:66

Lata Ptaszek po Uticy/The Little Bird 189:150

Late yest're'en I gathered the shellfish 212:91

Lather and Shave 35:96

The launch New Sparta sailed 216:42

L'Autre Jour en Voulant Danser/While I Was Dancing the Other Day 89:152

The Lavender Cowboy 61:114, 159:304

Lavender's Blue 17:6, 62:125, 135:58, 175:54, 188:122, 189:118, 227:15, 262:128

Lavender's blue, dilly dilly, Lavender's green 17:6, 62:125, 135:58, 175:54, 188:122, 189:118, 227:15, 262:128

L'Avvelenato/The Poisoned Lover 89:156, *see also:* 157:71, 232:140

De Lawd he thought he'd make a man 89:42, *see also:* 226:470, 290:40

Laws-a-massey, what have you done 226:134

Lay back in the tall grass 261:38

Lay down boys, take a little nap 230:67, *see also:* 33:154, 277:79

Lay up nearer, brother, nearer for my limbs are growing cold 61:38

Lazy John 135:38, 213:16, 254:112

Lazy John, Lazy John, will you marry me? 135:38, 213:16, 254:112

Lazy Mary 17:101, 289:17

Lazy Mary, will you get up 17:101, 289:17

Lazy Moon 21:84

Lazy moon! Come out soon! 21:84

Lazy Sheep, Pray Tell Me Why 175:132

Le Bon Roi Dagobert/Good King Dagobert 217:28

Le Chien Qui Se Voit dans L'Eau/The Dog Who Sees His Reflection in the Water 243:4

Le Coq et le Renard/The Cock and the Fox 243:36

Le Corbeau et le Renard/The Crow and the Fox 243:2

Le Cou-Cou/The Cuckoo 217:35

Le Furet du Bois Joli/The Weasel from the Lovely Woods 217:48

Le Levraut et la Tortue/The Hare and the Tortoise 243:24

Le Lièvre et les Grenouilles/The Hare and the Frogs 243:16

Le Lion et le Rat/The Lion and the Rat 243:6

Le Loup Berger/The Shepherd Wolf 243:30

Le Loup et la Cicogne/The Wolf and the Stork 243:30

Le Petit Chasseur/The Little Hunter 217:18

Le Petit Navire/The Little Ship 89:62, 217:14

Le Pot de Terre et le Pot de Fer/The Clay Pot and the Iron Pot 243:2

Le Rat de Ville et le Rat des Champs/The City Rat and the Country Rat 243:29

Le Rat et l'Eléphant/The Rat and the Elephant 243:13

Le Renard et le Loup/The Fox and the Wolf 243:38

Le Renard et les Raisins/The Fox and the Grapes 243:42

Le Singe Adopté/The Adopted Monkey 243:45

Le Sommeil de l'Enfant Jésus/The Sleep of the Infant Jesus 54:100, 241:62

Lead a Yell 166:20

Lead, Kindly Light 45:14

Lead, kindly light, a'midth encircling gloom 45:14

Lead On, O King Eternal 45:16

Leadbelly's Chisholm Trail 159:39, *see also:* 61:86

Leap Frog 46:222

Leatherwing Bat 36:56, 158:18, *see also:* The Bird Song

Leave Her, Bullies, Leave Her 226:412

Leave Her, Johnny 64:114, 98:40, 134:73

Leaves in the mortar, a man pounds in the mortar! 89:57

Leaves, Oh/Feuilles, Oh 208:29

Leaves underfoot, leaves overhead 91:19

Leaving on that New River Train 62:126, *see also:* 88, 128:78, 148:250, 230:74

Leba Gado/Leba God 89:102

Leba Gado ko' ya Esinamay' Leba 89:102

Leba God/Leba Gado 89:102

The Leba God is coming 89:102

Led by a Star 209:88

Leemwah 169:64

Leemweh, eeveeree, eetahtoo 169:64

Left hand brass, right hand drum 208:10

Left slide, left slide, here we go 83:494

The Left-Sock Thievers 237:unpaged

A Leg of Mutton Went Over to France 62:100

Legacy 226:155

A Lei for Our Queen/Makalapua. 87:76

Lei Ilima 87:62

The Leis of Hawaii/Na Lei O Hawaii 87:60

Lena 91:34

Lena was a lady who was very thin and lean 91:34

L'Enfant et le Maître d'Ecole/The Boy and the Schoolmaster 243:35

L'Enfant Jésus s'Endort/While Jesus Sleeps 241:108

Leonore 89:141

The Leprechaun 42:608, 79:61

Les ânes aim' les carrottes 293:92

Les Anges Dans Nos Campagnes/Angels O'er the Fields Were Singing 54:96, 241:102, 279:89

Les Belles Pommes D'Api! 227:9

Les Deux Chèvres/The Two Goats 243:23

Les Deux Chiens/The Two Dogs 243:46, 243:53

Les Deux Chiens et Leur Maître/The Two Dogs and Their Master 243:8

Les Deux Mulets/The Two Mules 243:20

Les Grenouilles Qui Demandentun Roi/ The Frogs Who Want To Have a King 243:18

Les Grenouilles Se Lassant 243:18

Les Noces du Papillon/The Butterfly's Wedding 217:46

Les Petites Marionettes 283:55

Let All Mortal Flesh Keep Silence 86:190

Let ev'ry good fellow now fill up his glass 205:103, *see also:* 25:124, 290:208

Let ev'ry good fellow now join in a song 25:124, 290:208, *see also:* 205:103

Let ev'ryone clap hands like me 75:19, 289:158, *see also:* 291:4

Let horrid jargon split the air 273:144

Let loose that spotted bull, son of the dark red cow 216:41

Let man be to man a brother, forgiving one another 209:80

Let me call Bolumbu, "Come down here" 100:77

Let Me Fly 148:222, *see also:* 22:300

Let Me Learn of Jesus 86:98

Let My Little Light Shine 148:224, *see also:* 135:20

Let my prayer be: to do unto others 155:10

Let Simon's Beard Alone 290:192

Let the banners wave for the honored brave 163:82

Let the farmer praise his grounds 42:609

Let the Feet Go Tramp 14:359

Let the Rest of the World Go By 170:94

Let the Savior's Gentle Call 86:91

Let the Words of My Mouth 86:192

Let tyrants shake their iron rod 21:242, 28:147, 157:20, 197:25, 240:83, 273:140

Let us all go together, swimmin' in the "Old Swimmin-Hole" 166:74

Let Us All Sing 237:unpaged

Let Us All Speak Our Minds 64:195

Let Us Be Friends Again/Lomir Sich Iberbetn 89:205

Let Us Break Bread Together 31:23, 55:274, 72:82

Let us close our game of poker 73:146

Let Us Go A-Maying 262:127

Let us go walking together 69:54

Let us honor Lincoln, kind and fair was he 207:82

Let us join our voices clear and strong 71:18

Let Us Light the Candles 129:56

Let us now our voices raise 155:7

Let us put man and woman together 89:64

Let Us Sing Together 55:256

Let us try to roll the R 290:195

Let Us With a Gladsome Mind 86:148

Let's Go Fly a Kite 275:55

Let's go huntin', said Risky to Rob 20:11, 232:80, *see also:* 274:18

Let's go, let's go. Let's look for a treasure trove 167:36

Let's go out to the pack meet 26:51

Let's go to the dance and you'll see how pretty 295:66, *see also:* 22:78, 72:106

Let's go to the orchard of Tontorallere 114:86

Let's Go to the Sea/Vamos a la Mar 216:49

Let's Go to the Zoo 128:42

Let's go zudie-o, zudie-o, zudie-o 109:139

Let's hasten to the field, my dear 89:77

Let's Have a Peal 71:100

Let's Have a Rhythm Band 166:28

Let's Hike to the Woodlands Today 245:23

Let's make pretty valentines 97:unpaged

Let's Make Valentines 97:unpaged

Let's pull together, sing and dance 70:26

Let's start at the very beginning! 218:234

Levee Moan 226:225

The Levee Song 27:174, *see also:* I've Been Workin' on the Railroad

'Leven cent cotton, forty cent meat 21:98, 64:104

Lewee go down, lewee go down 130:85

Liang Fung Lyao Lyao/Cool Breezes 49:18

The Liberty Song 21:238, 157:16, 240:44, 273:20, *see also:* 27:182, 28:9

Liberty Tree 28:58

Lie down, baby, on your pillow 125:14

Lieb Nachtigall, Wach Auf/Dear Nightingale, Awake 54:158, 279:62

Lied der Kinder zu Bethlehem/Carol of the Children of Bethlehem 279:84
Life in a Half-Breed Shack 159:409
Life in a Prairie Shack 61:108
Life Is a Toil 64:136
Life Let Us Cherish 66:24
Life on the Ocean Wave 126:73
A Life on the Vicksburg Bluff 73:211
The Life That's Free 262:66
Lift Every Voice and Sing 108
Lift up your hands, ye heroes 273:28, *see also:* 27:120, 28:43, 240:57
The light from our candles, the bright light of Cubbing 26:64
Light in the darkness, sailor, day is at hand! 66:152
Light, light, light, my little Scotch-ee 226:64
Light My Way to Bed 19:21
Lights 11:14
Lightsome Heart 262:128
Lightsome heart gives trust pleasure 262:128
Like No a Like/Remembrance 89:299
Lili Marlene 22:202
Lilliburlero 176:156
Lilly Dale 157:108, *see also:* 66:128
Lily Dale 66:128, *see also:* 157:108
Lily, Lily Wallflowers 291:76
Lily of the West 61:154
The Limejuice Ship 98:45
The Limerick Song 290:100
Lincoln and Liberty 27:14, 157:51, 226:167
Lincoln came to Washington to view the situation 27:220
The Lincolnshire Poacher 117:unpaged, 176:44
The Linden Tree 67:21 (*Pardon, I'm the linden tree*)
The Linden Tree 125:86 (*A linden tree is standing beside a running stream*)
A linden tree is standing beside a running stream 125:86
Lindo conejo Esperanza, Salio desde está mañana 194:20
Lines and Squares 172:142, 173:28
Lines Written By a Bear of Very Little Brain 172:31, 174:17
Lio Lang Jr Ge/The Vagabond's Song 49:13
The Lion and the Rat/Le Lion et le Rat 243:6
The Lion and the Unicorn 111:54
A lion has a tail and a very fine tail 172:120, 173:6
The lion walks on padded paws 18:8
The lions on the mountains I've drove them to their lairs 159:133

Lippai 54:168, 241:78
Lippai, don't play you're dead! 241:78, *see also:* 54:168
Lippai, get out of bed! "No, I'm asleep" 54:168, *see also:* 241:78
Lippai, steh auf vom Schlaf! "Was ist denn da?" 54:168
Lir I Lir 169:34, 265:13
List to the Bells 46:228
List to the bells, silver-y bells 46:228
Listen, listen, what do you hear? What do you hear? 162:66
Listen, my child, to the lullaby 89:161, *see also:* 54:252, 216:31, 279:108
Listen now while I tell the story 114:43
Listen to me, Bozu! 286:56
Listen to my song, listen to my song 74:49
Listen to the Bells 27:238
Listen to the crickets' songs 286:30
Listen to the Mocking Bird 21:156, 205:142
Listen to the song of the frogs in yonder pond 289:187, *see also:* 69:14, 71:107, 72:167, 293:100
Litterbug Rag 26:83
Little Ah Sid 226:276
Little Ah Sid was a Chinese kid 226:276
Little April Shower 276:26
Little Arabella Miller 75:44, 165:165
Little Arabella Miller found a woolly caterpillar 75:44, 165:165
Little baby gently sleep, do not weep 125:20
The Little Beggarman 117:unpaged
The Little Bells 71:101, 72:164, 293:20
The little bells of Westminster 71:101, 72:164, 293:20
Little Betty Martin 135:120, *see also:* 33:194, 129:72, 157:44, 226:158
The Little Birch Tree 78:69
Little birch tree growing in the meadow 71:80, 72:152
The Little Bird/Lata Ptaszek po uticy 189:150 (*Little birdie, hopping gaily*)
The Little Bird 18:32, *see also:* 111:49, 285:99 (*Once I saw a little bird*)
Little Bird, Little Bird 232:118, *see also:* Blue Bird
A little bird, a little black-eyed bird 236:54
Little bird, little bird, go through my window 232:118, *see also:* Blue Bird
Little Birdie 292:128
Little birdie, hopping gaily, in the street I see you daily 189:150
Little birdie, little birdie, what makes you fly so high? 292:128
Little Bitty Baby 213:88, 233:69, *see also:* 54:82, 132:unpaged, 140:46, 190:68

Little Black Bull   135:36, 234:54, 292:46, see also: 129:34, 226:164

De little black bull came down de medder   129:34, 226:164, 234:54, see also: 135:36, 292:46

The little black bull went down to the meadow   292:46, see also: 129:34, 135:36, 226:164, 234:54

Little Black Train   232:152, see also: 24:914, 148:228

Little Black Train Is A-comin'   24:914, 148:228, see also: 232:152

Little Bo-Peep   17:87, 175:82, 188:60, 189:18, 285:10

A little boy and a little girl in an ecstasy of bliss   62:133

Little Boy Blue   17:10, 175:56, 188:32, 283:23, 285:38

Little Boy Blue, come blow your horn   17:10, 175:56, 188:32, 283:23, 285:38

Little Boy kneels at the foot of the bed   172:145, 173:31

A little boy went walking one lovely summer's day   191:32

Little boys, little girls, go to sleep   41:19

A Little Boy's Walk   191:32

Little Brother in the Cradle   245:83

The Little Brown Bulls   24:849

Little Brown Church in the Vale   21:164, see also: 25:117

Little Brown Dog   234:28, see also: 274:32

Little Brown Jug   20:61, 21:198, 62:93, 126:50, 170:104, 205:172

A Little Brown Sparrow   111:18

A little brown sparrow sat on a green tree   111:18

Little brown sparrow flying around   191:52

The Little Bullfrog   147:41

The Little Bunny   41:39

Little butterfly, my friend, will you come here a minute?   114:62

A little candle cries, the little teardrops fall   162:67

Little Carcol is dancing   168:130

The Little Carol   209:113

A Little Child on the Earth Has Been Born   210:12

Little children, little children, so tired and so weary   125:96, see also: 71:123, 85:101, 125:92

Little children, praise the Lord   86:156

Little children sweet and gay   100:50, see also: 89:168

A Little Child's Thanksgiving   7:8

A Little Cock-Sparrow   18:22, 175:148, 188:128

A little cock-sparrow sat on a green tree   18:22, 175:148, 188:128

Little Cossack   125:18, see also: 262:93

The Little Cradle Rocks Tonight   140:64, see also: 190:88, 233:40

Little Dame Crump   17:130

Little Darling   61:158

Little David   31:3, 123:210

Little David play on your harp   31:3, 123:210

The Little 'Dobe Casa   61:71

Little Dog   150:3

A little dog came to school   151

Little Dog, Little Dog   112:4

Little dog, little dog, what do you there?   112:4

Little Dog Named Right   234:26

A little dog not big at all   150:3

The Little Donkey/La Burriquita   216:42

Little Donkey Close Your Eyes   245:101

Little donkey on the hill   245:101

Little Dove/La Palomita   265:45, see also: 152:53

Little dove, little darling   245:123

Little drops of rain hit the window pane   11:29

Little drops of water, little grains of sand   17:98, 86:119

Little Drummer Boy   115

The Little Dustman   71:52, see also: 125:90

Little Dutch girl, sitting there   167:57

The Little Family   37:183

The Little Farm Girl/La Chacarera   70:17, 197:37

Little Father Horse-washer/Man Paman Goejang Djarang   89:294

Little feathers falling softly   7:11

The little flowers peeped through the ground   245:113

The little flow'rs came through the ground   86:61

Little folk in Holland far, far away   207:54

Little Ghost   197:95

Little Girl   230:28 (Little girl, little girl, don't lie to me)

A Little Girl   162:61 (A little girl was skipping)

Little girl, little boy? Yes, ma'am. Well, did you go down town?   109:54

Little girl, little girl, don't lie to me   230:28

A little girl was skipping, tra la la la la la la la   162:61

Little grasshopper, summer now has passed   79:65

Little Hans/Haenschen Klein   168:94

Little Hans goes alone out into the wide, wide world   168:94

The Little Horses   189:90, see also: All the Pretty Little Horses

A little house was vacant on a branch among the leaves   207:92

The Little Hunter/Le Petit Chasseur 217:55

Little Hypocrite/Het Kwezelken 21:320

Little Jack Horner sat in a corner 17:111, 175:75, 188:178, 283:16

Little Jack Jingle 112:67, *see also:* 18:34

Little Jesus Sleeps in the Hay 245:122

Little Jesus, sweetly sleep 68:45, 184:66, 210:45, 220:28, 241:64, 279:118, *see also:* 54:226

Little Joe, the Wrangler 61:215, 146:124, 159:91

Little Johnny Brown 109:94

Little Johnny Brown, spread your comfort down 109:94

Little King Pippin 111:60

The Little Kitty 62:47

Little Lad, Oh/Gille Beag 'O 89:133

Little Lady from Baltimore 128:104

Little Lamb 162:50

Little lamb, little lamb, lying on the hillside 162:50

Little Lamb, who made thee? 112:59, 189:62

Little Lambkin Sweet 245:98

Little Lap-Dog Lullaby 234:27

Little Leaf of the Guarumal/Hojita de Guarumal 216:44

A little light is going by 245:48

The Little Lost Child 21:48

The Little Maiden/La Virgencita 70:14

A little maiden climbed an old man's knee 21:35, 205:228

Little Major 73:194

Little Mary, child thou art 281:unpaged

Little Miss Muffet 17:85, 175:74, 188:134, 285:81

Little Mohea 24:824, 27:236, 37:128, 61:135, 263

Little Mother Goose 167:34

The Little Nut Tree 17:145, 175:92, 289:108, *see also:* I Had a Little Nut Tree

The Little Old Sod Shanty 61:68, 61:72, 159:405, 226:89

The Little Path 67:75

Little Peter Rabbit 26:30

Little Peter Rabbit had a flea upon his ear 26:30

The Little Pig 79:23, 135:56, 232:102, 234:50, *see also:* Old Woman and Her Pig

The Little Plant 191:24

Little Poll Parrot 111:43

Little Poll Parrot sat in her garret 111:43

Little Polly Flinders 17:150, 175:44, 112:47, 285:100

The Little Pony 291:53

Little Prairie Dog 162:59

The Little Pumpkin 162:40

A little rabbit came to town 162:58

Little Red Bird 176:52, 245:86

Little Red Caboose 46:213, 162:97

Little red caboose, little red caboose, little red caboose behind the train 46:213, 162:97

Little Red Engine 162:99

Little Red Handkerchief 70:19

The Little Red Hen 245:60

The Little Red Wagon 129:70

Little red wagon painted blue 232:166, *see also:* Skip to My Lou

Little Robin Redbreast 17:67, 18:16

Little robin redbreast sat upon a tree 17:67, 18:16

A little robin red breast was sitting in a tree 41:22

Little Sacka Sugar 289:89

Little Sally Walker 109:109, 109:110, 109:111, 291:68, *see also:* Little Sally Water

Little Sally Water 17:132, 100:89, 130:45, 141:34, 169:43, 271:63, *see also:* 109:109, 109:110, 109:111, 291:68

Little Sally Water sitting in a saucer 130:45, 141:34, *see also:* Little Sally Water

Little Sally Water sprinkle in the saucer 100:89, 169:43, 271:63, *see also:* Little Sally Water

Little Sally Waters, sitting in the sun 17:132, *see also:* Little Sally Water

Little Scotch-ee 226:64

Little Seed 130:92

A Little Seed Lay Fast Asleep 86:8

The Little Sergeant 28:70

Little Shadow 162:64

Little Shell 162:24

The Little Ship/Le Petite Navire 217:54, *see also:* 89:62, 216:50

Little ship will go a-fishing 114:56

Little shoes by a white bed 59:45

Little Sir Echo 68:18

Little Sir Echo, how do you do? Hello (hello), hello (hello) 68:18

The Little Skunk 63:138

The Little Sparrow 36:16, *see also:* 158:58, 230:24

Little Squirrel, living there in the hollow tree 191:48

Little Star of Bethlehem! Do we see thee now? 190:82, 190:84

Little star that shines so bright 17:11

The little stones, they came to see me 74:37

Little Sweet One/La Chaparrita 262:21

Little Things 17:98, 86:119

Little Tommy Tinker 26:44, 290:192

Little Tommy Tucker 17:99, 285:88, *see also:* 175:24

Little Tommy Tucker sings for his supper 17:99, 175:24, 285:88

A Little Town 91:21

A Little Town in Switzerland 107:34

A little town with one main street 91:21

The Little Train 154:14

Little Trotty Wagtail 44:10

Little trotty wagtail, he went in the rain 44:10

The Little Vine-Clad Cottage 61:70

Little Wheel A-Turnin' in My Heart 157:146, 227:27, *see also:* 129:10

Little White Daisies 291:38

Little White Duck 75:46, 289:56

Little Witch/Hexlein 78:63

Little witch come dance with me 78:63

Live, live, live, our fields and woodlands need you 71:25, 72:62

Living in Missouri was a bad bold man 61:257, *see also:* Jesse James

The Living Room 149:18

Liza in the Summer Time 226:308

Liza Jane 128:124, 226:132

The Llano Estacado 159:313

Lliw Gwyn Rhosyn Yr Haf/White Rose of My Heart 89:134

Lloyd George Knew My Father 289:112

Lo! A Light Is in the East 244:260

Lo, How a Rose E'er Blooming 54:166, 241:84, 264:86, *see also:* 210:30, 279:58

Lo Que Digo 226:294

Lo, the Winter Is Past 86:182

Loch Lomond 22:80

Lock the Dairy Door! 144:27

Locks and Bolts 37:132

The Logger's Boast 277:73

Lollipop 118:21

Lolly Too Dum 36:52, 37:138, 148:232, 158:46, 277:71

Lolotte 157:150

Lomir Sich Iberbetn/Let Us Be Friends Again 89:205

L'onde transparente au chien represente 243:4

London Bridge 14:360, 17:37, 20:7, 37:189, 56, 63:30, 100:31, 109:181, 165:190, 175:98, 248, 283:43

London Bridge (nonsense version) 188:160, 290:124

London Bridge is all broke down 109:181, *see also:* London Bridge

London Bridge is broken down · 175:98, 188:160, *see also:* London Bridge

London Bridge is falling down, falling down 14:360, 17:37, 20:7, 56, 63:30, 100:31, 109:181, 165:190, 248, 283:43, *see also:* 37:189, 175:98, 188:160

London bridge is falling up 290:124, *see also:* 188:160

London Bridge is washed away 37:189, *see also:* London Bridge

London City 226:324

London City where I used to dwell 226:324

London Hill 121:122, 291:15

London Street Cries 71:102

London's Burning 25:30, 175:20, *see also:* 46:227, 148:321, 283:35, 289:188, 293:36

London's burning, London's burning 25:30, 175:20, *see also:* 46:227, 148:321, 283:35, 289:188, 293:36

The Lone Buffalo Hunter 159:342, *see also:* 159:291

Lone Driftin' Riders 159:307

The Lone Prairie 60:20, 146:38, *see also:* Oh, Bury Me Not on the Lone Prairie

The Lone Star Trail 61:307, 159:19, 226:266, *see also:* 60:102, 146:162

The Lonely Cowboy 61:242

Lonely, forgotten, no one to help him 89:267

The Lonely Goatherd 218:240

The Lonely Robin 207:87

The Lonesome Grove 157:78

Lonesome Road 22:115, 148:236, 226:322

The Lonesome Trail 61:233, *see also:* 61:232, 159:8, 232:69

Lonesome Valley 86:54, 148:238, 158:352, *see also:* 226:486

Long ago the little children gathered close at Jesus' knee 86:104

Long before the rising sun 245:8

Long John 107:52

Long legs, long legs, slowly stalking 165:144

Long Live the Girls of Canada/Vive la Canadienne 208:5

Long, Long Ago 205:99

Long Nail A-Grinding 118:26

Long Time Ago 17:146, 129:26, 130:108, *see also:* 62:47

The Longest Dog in the World 167:38

Longfellow's Carol 54:58, 148:172, 190:86, 241:126

Long-haired preachers come out ev'ry night 24:886, 64:155, 226:222

Longing for Spring 85:107

Loo Loo Loo Loo 74:27

Looby-Loo 14:363, 17:14, 63:18, 147:18, 165:194, 188:42, 189:42, 283:46, *see also:* 39:6

Look, A Star Shines 220:13

Look ahead, look astern, look the weather in the lee 22:166

Look at Me, a Gallant Hussar/Azert Hogy én Huszár Vagyok 89:187

Look at the terrible crocodile 165:104

Look at them farmers comin' to town, sugar babe 158:108

Look at Us 162:103
Look Away to Bethlehem 233:21
Look down, look down, that lonesome road 22:115, 148:236, 226:322
Look down the street, see the peddler come 72:150
Look for the bare necessities 275:68, 276:60
Look in the beanpot see the bubbles rise! 286:39
Look, look away, look away to Bethlehem 233:21
Look one way and the sun is going down 44:34
Look out, you cowards! 163:62
Look what the gazelle does 89:281
Look who is here, Punchinello, follow Sally 109:106, *see also:* 63:14, 128:96, 135:113, 178:7
Look who is here, Punchinelo, funny fellow 63:14, *see also:* 109:106, 128:96, 135:113, 178:7
Look who's here it's the milkman 107:20
Look Wider Still 69:12
Looking for my darling 236:8
The Loons Are Singing 19:19
The Lord Be With Us 86:209
Lord, he thought he'd make a man 226:470, 290:40, *see also:* 89:42
Lord, I thank Thee for this day 155:3
Lord, I Want to Be a Christian 83:477, 86:106
Lord, in this evening hour I pray 26:95
The Lord into his garden comes 37:158
The Lord Is Ever Near 86:140
The Lord is good to me 101:31
The Lord Is My Shepherd 155:30, *see also:* 72:50, 86:23
Lord Jesus hath a garden 184:56
Lord Jesus, may I always be 86:113
Lord Jesus, Thou Art Mine 86:137
Lord Lovel 22:96, 226:70
The Lord of the Dance 140:36
Lord, Remember Me 24:915
Lord This Day Thy Children Meet 86:159
The Lord to earth has come, appearing as a Baby 54:290
Lord, Who Lovest All Thy Children 86:203
The Lord will to the other side 124:126
The Lord's My Shepherd 72:50, 86:23, *see also:* 155:30
The Lord's Prayer 155:14
Lorena 73:231
Los Cuatro Generales/The Four Generals 22:218
Los Diez Perritos/The Ten Puppies 295:17
Los Maizales/The Cornfields 169:55, 270:50

Los maizales brotan con primor fulguran sus hojas de color 169:55, 270:50
Los Pastores/The Shepherds 295:70
Los Reyes Oriente/Song of the Wise Men 140:22, *see also:* 54:288
Lost my partner, what'll I do 158:98, 205:76, 230:90, *see also:* Skip to My Lou
Lost River Desert 61:159
The Lost Sheep 155:17
Lots of Worms 296:26
Lou, Lou Skip to my Lou 37:193, 61:275, 129:104, 289:178, *see also:* Skip to My Lou
A loud day today, a crowded day today 91:28
The loud wind roared, the rain fell fast 273:122
Louisiana Lullaby 72:99, 79:37
L'Ours et les Deux Gascons/The Bear and the Two Gascons 243:26
Lou'siana gals, come and listen to my noise 158:44 *see also:* 159:338
Lousy Miner 24:863
Love Came Down at Christmas 210:46
Love Divine, All Love Excelling 45:60
Love Is a Song 275:86, 276:24
Love is a song that never ends 275:86, 276:24
Love, Look Away 218:304
Love My Daddy, Yes I Do 197:71
Love, oh love, oh careless love 22:46, 126:69, 158:64, 205:365, 226:21, 230:11, 272:16, *see also:* 24:901
Love Somebody, Yes I do 162:53, 226:140
Love Song/Mereu 89:300 *(Tell me who?)*
Love Song/Prom Kut 89:222 *(Oh, fairest of all maidens)*
Love Song/Waiata Aroha 89:301 *(Not until my last breath)*
Lovely Evening 71:109, 72:173
Lovely Is the Dark Blue Sky/Deilig Er den Himmel Blaa 54:188
Lovely ladies who to the meadow go 295:43
Lovely Maiden/Yammil Abaya 89:202
A Lovely Night 218:293
Lovely Rosa/Schöne Rosa 189:144
Lovely! See the cloud, the cloud appear 68:13, *see also:* 89:38
The Lover's Lament 226:126
Love's Old Sweet Song 66:30, 205:216
The Lovesick Cowboy 159:268
Loving Shepherd of Thy Sheep 189:64
Low Bridge Every Body Down 33:58, *see also:* Erie Canal
Lowlands 22:132, 158:142
Lowlands Low 33:186
Lowly Bethlehem 277:109
Lowly, laid in a manger, with oxen brooding nigh 209:105, 241:210

Lubley Fan, Will You Cum Out Tonight 157:86, *see also:* Buffalo Gals

Lucumi Cult Song/Canto Lucumi de Iya 89:59

Lucy Locket 17:38, 175:16, 188:84, 285:22

Lucy Locket lost her pocket 17:38, 175:16, 188:84, 285:22

Lucy Long 126:77

Lula, baby, la, la, whem shell quam 262:127

Lula Gal 232:138

Lulajze Jezuniu/Polish Lullaby 54:220, 241:74, 279:122

Lulajze Jezuniu moja peretko 54:220, 241:74, *see also:* 279:122

Lulay/Serenade 89:296

Luli, Deck the Crib 125:126

Lulla, lulla, pretty little darling 85:140

Lullaby 125:85 *(Hush-a-by, baby, and go to sleep)*

Lullaby/Komoriuta 286:63 *(Hush, hush. You're my good child)*

Lullaby (Mozart) 71:123, 125:92, 125:96, *see also:* 85:101 *(Sleep, little boy, go to sleep)*

Lullaby/Nhim Ne Nhim 89:225 *(Weep not my love)*

Lullaby/Niña, Nana 216:49, *see also:* 54:252, 89:161, 279:108 *(This is a lullaby, lullaby)*

Lullaby/Olilili 163:100 *(Early one morning, in the homelands)*

Lullaby 114:44 *(Ayo, ay, oh baby don't you cry)*

Lullaby 177:92 *(Sleep, my baby, slumber deep)*

Lullaby/Soum, soum 208:25 *(Sleep, sleep, come to my darling)*

Lullaby 262:127 *(Lula, baby, la, la)*

Lullaby 19:11 *(Way way way way way)*

Lullaby, and goodnight, in the sky stars are bright 71:122, 72:58, 125:89, *see also:* 17:63, 85:176, 283:60

Lullaby and good-night with lilies white 85:176, *see also:* Brahms' Lullaby

Lullaby and goodnight, with roses bedight 17:53, 283:60, *see also:* 71:122, 72:58, 85:176, 125:89

Lullaby for Mr. Benjamin B. Bickelbaum 237:unpaged

Lullaby, My Jamie 176:56

Lullaby, my little brother, be still and close your eyes 207:20

Lullaby, my sweet wee Donald 85:169

Lullaby of the Rain 162:31

Lullaby, oh lullaby, flow'rs are closed and lambs are sleeping 125:56

Lullaby to the Animals 296:42

Lullaby, twilight is spreading 71:38, *see also:* 125:114

Lullay My Liking 209:89, 210:109

Lullay, my prince lullaby. Birds to their little nests fly 85:101

Lullay, Thou little tiny Child 54:19, 210:46, 264:116, *see also:* Coventry Carol

Lulle Lullay 190:105, *see also:* Coventry Carol

Lully, lulla, thou little tiny child 220:114, 279:32, *see also:* Coventry Carol

Lully, Lullay 241:26, *see also:* Coventry Carol *(Lully, lullay, thou little tiny child)*

Lully, Lullay (Haydn) 241:222 *(Lully, lullay, lullay, O sisters too)*

Lully, lullay, thou little tiny child 22:252, 241:26, *see also:* Coventry Carol

Lully, Lully, Lu 284:119

Lulu 159:263

A lumberjack whose name was Jack 91:41

The Lumberman in Town 158:172

Lumkani magwalandini l'emka 163:62

Lustukru 262:30

Lydia Pinkham 226:210

M

Ma Fille, Veux-tu un Bouquet?/My Daughter, Would'st Have a Bouquet? 79:66

Ma! Ma! Where is my Pa? 197:98

Ma! Ma! Where Is Papa 197:98

Ma Teodora 216:19

Ma to mate ra no 89:301

Ma ye ma me bajabula 163:95

Ma'am dear, did ye never hear of pretty Molly Brannigan? 42:594

Maçaffie's Confession 159:201

Mackeral, fresh mackerel, chairs to mend 71:104, 72:164, *see also:* 46:228, 289:186

MacTavish 134:49, 290:175

Mad Anthony Wayne 240:100, *see also:* 28:126

Madam, I Have Come A-courting 62:122

Madam I Have Come to Court 62:120

Madama Dore 188:86, 265:23

Madame, I will give to you the keys of Canterbury 27:26

Mademoiselle from Armentieres "Parley Voo" 158:122, 170:31, 205:349, *see also:* 126:61, 226:440

Madre, a la puerta hay un niño 54:284, 241:88, *see also:* 209:110

Maduna/Maduna Clan 163:72

Maduna Clan/Maduna 163:72

Magdil y'shuot Malko 77:16

The Magic Pony 245:28

Magicians Do Tricks 166:58

A Magnet Hung in a Hardware Shop 252:32

Magnificat 262:113

Mag's Song 226:316

Magtanim 169:57, 271:23, see also: Planting Rice

Magtanim Ay Di Biro 87:54, see also: Planting Rice

Magwalandini/You Cowards 163:62

Mahiya Illa Zalab/Song of the Fig Vendors 89:246

Mahnoo ne nah ninga mahjah 69:27

The Maid Freed From the Gallows 226:72, *see also:* 24:822, 176:60, 226:385

The Maid of Monterey 157:114

The Maid of Newfoundland 89:36

The Maid of the Sweet Brown Knowe 42:610

The Maid on the Mountain's Brow 36:68

The Maid on the Shore 36:8

A maiden from the Bosporus with eyes as bright as phosphorus 290:148

Maiden on the Plains 61:121, *see also:* 146:148

Maiden, pray for thy lover now 73:262

The Mail Boat 129:13

Mail Myself to You 130:70

Mailman 130:73

The Mailman/Poctovsky Panáček 289:80

Mailong Sera 168:76

Majestic Hawaii, home of great Keawe 87:60

Makalapua/A Lei for Our Queen 87:76

Make a Hat for Easter 166:38

Make America Proud of You 26:87

Make my living in sandy land 46:211, 70:25, 135:75

Make New Friends 68:38, 69:10, 262:34, 293:11

Makerenben/Honey-Ant Song of Ljaba 89:309

Making a Snowman 207:77

Making Bread 191:72

Making Butter 191:76

Making Rice Cakes/Mochi Tauki Odori 49:24

Malbrouck 21:346, see also: 217:49

Malbrouck has gone to battle 21:346, see also: 217:49

Malbrouck s'en va t'en guerre 21:346, see also: 217:49

Malbrough 217:49, see also: 21:346

Mali kini kouike ana 87:71

The Mallard 62:75

Mama Bake the Johnny Cake, Christmas Comin' 130:42

Mama Have You Heard the News? 226:368

Mama, Mama, have you heard? 93, *see also:* Hush Little Baby

Mama, mama, mama have you heard the news? 226:368

Mama, oh, mama, come wash my face 130:16

Mama, Papa 194:22

Mama Small 154:37

Mama Small is sweet and pretty 154:37

Mamanehe mamanehe 163:42

Mama's Gonna Buy 197:57, *see also:* Hush, Little Baby

Mama's home abakin' bread brown as it can be 296:7

Mambru Se Fué a la Guerra/Mambru Went to War 295:56

Mambru Went to War/Mambru Se Fué a la Guerra 295:56

Mame ye ye ye 89:260

Mamma, 'Kwill 'N Man He/Mother, I Want a Husband 89:276

Mammy Don't 'Low 290:62, *see also:* 197:58

Mammy don't 'low no pickin' and singin' round here 290:62, *see also:* 197:58

Mammy Loves 157:68

Mammy loves and Pappy loves 157:68

Mammy, mammy told me 63:102

The Man 67:42

Man and woman bought a little pig 234:50, *see also:* Old Woman and Her Pig

Man Goin' Roun' 226:447

Man had his first creation in heevin's guarded place 35:70

The Man I Used to Be 218:282

The Man in the Moon 17:107

The Man in the Moon 112:48

The man in the moon as he sails the sky 112:48

The man in the moon came down too soon 17:107

A Man in the Wilderness 112:23, *see also:* 18:5

The man in the wilderness asked me 18:5, 112:23

A Man Named Hods 159:355

A Man of Words 44:72

A man of words and not of deeds 44:72

The Man on the Flying Trapeze 21:191, 170:87, 198, 205:167

Man Paman Goejang Djarang/Little Father Horse-Washer 89:294

Man Smart—Woman Smarter 89:64

The Man That Waters the Workers' Beer 64:158

A man there lives on the Western plain 61:85

A man went out to plant his seed 155:16

A man whose name was Johnny Sands 84:14
The Man With the Gun 175:112
Mañanitas/Early Mornings 226:292
Mangeant a sa guise, un loup grand glouton 243:32
The Manger 67:14
Mango Walk 134:40
A Man's A Man For A' That 64:186
Man's Fate 85:115
Man's Life 62:20, *see also:* 293:28
Man's life is but vain 189:120
Man's Life's a Vapour 62:20, 293:28
Man's will before his fate 85:115
Manthi'ki/Spirit Song 89:273
Many and great, O God, are Thy things 69:25, 71:88, 72:69
The Many, Many Children 86:90
Many Thousan' Gone 22:187, *see also:* 64:173
Many Million Years Ago 59:32
Maori Indian Battle Chant 107:26
Maple Sweet 33:50
March! March! Ettrick and Teviotdale! 66:50
The March of the Kings/La Marche des Rois 54:126, 241:105
March of the Men of Harlech 21:188
March of the Siamese Children 218:195
March went out like a lion, a-whippin' up the water in the bay 218:85
Marche Lorraine 22:188
Marching Along 27:146
Marching Music 11:35
Marching Song 41:7
Marching Through Georgia 73:223, 157:130
Marching to Pretoria 72:148, 254:118
Margot, Dress the Vines 262:117
María Lavava/Mary Washed the Linen 188:156
Maria auf dem Berge/Marie on the Mountain 241:86, 279:74
Maria Durch ein' Dornwald Ging/Maria Walks Amid the Thorn 54:160, 241:96, 279:60
Maria Durch ein' Dornwald Ging/Maria Wandered Through a Wood 54:160, 241:96, 279:60
Maria on the Mountain 241:86, 279:74
Maria Walks Amid the Thorn/Maria Durch ein' Dornwald Ging 54:160, 241:96, 279:60
Maria Wandered Through a Wood/Maria Durch ein' Dornwald Ging 54:160, 241:96, 279:60
Marie in the Meadow 245:25
Marinero hondureño que ya te vas a la mar 89:74
Mariner's Hymn 233:55
The Marines' Hymn 197:102, 205:358, 277:121
Marion's Men 28:144
Marken Er Mejet/Harvest Is Over 83:496, 208:17
Market Man 41:40
Market Square 172:136, 173:22
Marlborough/Malbrough 217:64, 295:56
Marlborough goes off to war 217:64, *see also:* 295:56
Marlbrough/Marlborough 217:49, 295:56
Marlbrough s'en va t'en guerre 217:49, *see also:* 295:56
(Martha) is her first name, first name, first name 110:48
Martyrs Tune 273:128
Mary 197:56, *see also:* 205:327
Mary and Martha 148:240
Mary and Martha jus' gone 'long 148:240
Mary Ann 130:23
Mary Ann McCarthy 290:58
Mary Ann McCarthy went a-fishing for some clams 290:58
Mary Had a Baby 31:15, 54:83, 140:54, 190:73, 209:17, 232:180, 233:47
Mary Had a Little Lamb 17:51, 162:7, 175:58, 283:11, 289:77, 292:48
Mary Had a William Goat 62:39, 226:336
Mary had the little Baby 233:42
Mary, Mary, Quite Contrary 175:171, 177:87, 188:52, 285:12, *see also:* 17:62, 17:98, 175:40, 188:92, 283:16
Mary on the Mountain 241:86, 279:74
"Mary," Said Saint Joseph/Aguinaldo 140:28
Mary, she had a little boy 130:38
Mary, the Maiden, when she bore dear Jesus 54:216
Mary the Virgin to Bethlehem Went/Jungfru Maria till Betlehem Gick 279:111
Mary Was a Red Bird 130:15, *see also:* 129:12, 232:130
Mary Washed Linen/María Lavava 188:156, *see also:* 189:76
Mary, What You Going to Name That Pretty Little Baby? 233:44, *see also:* 140:66, 140:69, 190:114, 190:134, 209:26
Mary wo' three links of chain 158:376, *see also:* 157:147, 226:474
Mary Wore a Red Dress 129:12, *see also:* 130:15, 232:130
Mary Wore Her Red Dress 232:130, *see also:* 129:12, 130:15
Mary Wore Three Links of Chain 157:147, 226:474, *see also:* 158:376
Maryland, My Maryland 73:22, 127:149, 160:50

Maryland, My Maryland(A northern reply) 73:24

The Maryland Resolves 28:33

Mary's a Grand Old Name 205:327, *see also:* 197:56

Mary's Little Boy 130:38

Mary's Lullaby 7:6 *(Tiny precious child)*

Mary's Lullaby 245:123 *(Little dove, Little darling)*

Massa Had a Yaller Gal 24:903

Massachusetts Liberty Song 240:47, 273:24, *see also:* 28:13

Master I Have 111:25

Master I have, and I am his man 111:25

Masters in This Hall 22:268, 54:50, 210:47, 241:36, 241:230

Masters in this hall, hear ye news today 22:268, 54:50, 210:47, 241:36, 241:230

Matatero-tero-la 114:78, 169:27

Matarile 169:60, 269:38, 295:37

Matarile, Rile, Ro 169:60, 269:38, 295:37

Matt Casey formed a social club that beat the town for style 205:245

Matthew, Mark, Luke and John 111:16, 189:84

Maverick the Two-Gun Cowboy 62:97

Maxwelton's braes are bonnie 22:110, 205:85

May all your life be filled with joy 89:195

May Baskets 207:115

The May Carol 27:102, 213:80, *see also:* 128:70, 134:31 *(This morning is the month of May)*

May Day Carol 208:72, *see also:* 184:10, 210:68, 220:92 *(The moon shines bright)*

The May Day Carol 128:70, 134:31, *see also:* 27:102, 213:80 *(Awake, awake, oh pretty)*

May Day in the Morning 189:52, *see also:* 27:104

May God Save the Union 73:28

May I Speak Peace 155:12

The May is in blossom 85:165

May Time 207:119

May time, play time! 207:119

May we be truthful and ever loyal be 71:30, 72:40

Mayibuye/Restore Africa to Its Owners 163:91

Mayree Mack 107:64

May-ree Mack dressed in black 107:64

Mazoo 55:503

Me abandonastes, mujer porque soy muy pobre 226:295

Me an' My Doney-Gal 159:11

Me and my wife live all alone 20:61, 62:93, *see also:* 21:198, 126:50, 170:104, 205:172

Me Johnny Mitchell Man 24:865

Meadowlands 22:200

Meadows and flowers, shrubs and trees 123:26

A mean little man from Phlebean 91:40

The Mean Old Man 91:40

The Measles in the Spring 234:52

Meefooahza ieh rabehtooreemasoo 169:47, 271:35

Meet Me in St. Louis, Louis 205:296

Meet me tonight, lover, meet me 226:216

Mein Hands 20:88

Mein hands bei mein sides 20:88

The Melancholy Cowboy 159:220

Melt the Bells 73:42

Memories 170:29

Memories, memories, dreams of love so true 170:29

Men of Harlech! In the hollow 21:188

Men of the Soil 64:94

Men tell us 'tis fit that wives should submit to their husbands submissively 64:195

Mengedagnan/The Wanderer 169:21, 267:27

Mengedagnan eyezemeriyhedal 169:21, 267:27

Menominee Lullaby 19:37

Menyböl Ar Angyal/Angels from Heaven 54:240

Mereu/Love Song 89:300

The Mermaid 71:78, 72:72, 117:unpaged, 290:160

Merrily Dance the Quaker's Wife 188:120

Merrily, Merrily 46:227, 71:110, 72:165, 293:12, *see also:* 62:12

Merrily, merrily greet the morn 46:227, 62:12, 71:110, 293:12, *see also:* 72:165

Merrily We Roll Along 17:113

Merry Are the Bells 111:40

The merry bells of Christmas ring 41:6

Merry Christmas 241:232 *(Merry Christmas, ev'ryone!)*

A Merry Christmas 227:32, *see also:* We Wish You a Merry Christmas

Merry Christmas, ev'ryone! 241:232

The Merry-Go-Round 17:92 *(Oh, camels and bears and ponies are found)*

Merry-Go-Round 147:39, *see also:* 25:8, 26:10, 73:48 *(The more we get together)*

Merry-Go-Round 70:22 *(Young maid, young maid, young maid, young maid dear)*

Merry Go Round 162:70 *(Come take a ride, come take a ride)*

The Merry Golden Tree 37:120

The Merry Lark 71:110, 72:169

A Merry Life 22:43

The Merry Little Men 191:12

A merry little river went singing day by day 191:68

The Merry Little Robin 245:10

Merry, Merry Christmas 66:142

Merry, merry Christmas ev'rywhere! 66:142

The Merry Mousketeers 119:94

Message from the Medicine Man 166:42

Meunier, Tu Dors/Miller, You Are Sleeping 217:41

Mexican Clap Dance/La Raspe 178:45

The Mexican Waltz 126:99

Mfene Sandhleni/Cruel Baboon 89:286

Mi Abuelo Tenía un Huerto/My Grandfather Had a Garden 295:21

Mi Burro/My Donkey 289:64

Mi Chacra/My Farm 262:19

Mi Compadre Mono/My Godfather Monkey 216:32

Mi marmie ar da pan trobul! 215:51

Mi Pollera/My Hoopskirt 216:2

Mi pollera, mi pollera 216:2

Mi Y'malel 27:256

The Mice 296:10

The Mice and the Cat 291:78

The mice are sound asleep in their holes 291:78

Michael Finnegan 25:41, 36:80, 62:67, 197:30, 289:138

Michael, Row the Boat Ashore 25:95, 72:84, 148:242, 230:75

Mickey Mouse Club! Mickey Mouse Club! 119:92, 275:92, 276:85

Mickey Mouse March 119:92, 275:92, 276:85

Mickey Mouse Theme Song 119:90

'Mid pleasures and palaces though I may roam 22:52, *see also:* 127:61, 128:98

'Mid pleasures and palaces though we may roam 127:61, 157:98, *see also:* 22:52

Midnight on the Ocean 290:138

Midnight, Sleeping Bethlehem 241:72

Midnight Special 21:90, 24:908, 158:318, 226:26, 226:217, 230:55

The Midnight Train 226:325

Midst quiet night a voice from heaven cries 220:85

Mifohaza 169:47

A Mighty Fortress Is Our God/Ein Feste Burg 21:324, 22:278, 45:10

Mighty Lak' a Rose 205:268, *see also:* 125:136

Mighty Like a Rose 125:136, *see also:* 205:268

Mighty pretty motion toodala 232:54, 291:14

Milha bilou loubi shembel 262:144

Milínekej Pan Děkan/Our Village Deacon 89:184

The milkman runs with all his might 149:30

The Mill 191:68

The Mill Was Made of Marble 64:76

Miller, You Are Sleeping/Meunier, Tu Dors 217:62

The miller's milldog lay at the door 59:59

The Miller's Wife/La Molinera 295:59

The Miller's Will 37:144

Millions of Snowflakes 86:181

Min fod, min fod 69:13

A Mince Pie or a Pudding 233:78

Mine eyes have seen the glory 21:145, 22:220, 25:94, 26:89, 64:172, 71:10, 72:30, 73:5, 99:53, 127:132, 127:34, 157:126, 160:64, 277:57

Mine eyes have seen the glory of the downfall of the school 118:6, *see also:* 63:146

Mine heart ish proken into little pits 73:115

A Miner's Life 64:65

Miner's life is like a sailor's 64:65

Mingulay Boat Song 134:70

Minnie and Winnie 59:34

The Minstrel Boy 22:226

The minstrel boy to the war is gone 22:226

The Minuet 207:84

Minuit, Chrétiens/O Holy Night 241:197, *see also:* 54:107

Mir Senne Heil's Lustig/We Are Happy and Merry 89:154

Mira que bonito lo vienen 169:16

The Miracle 67:94

The Miraculous Meal 124:147

Miren Cuantas Luces/Behold How Many Lights 216:38

Miscanthus Mowing Song/Kariboshi Kiri Uta 49:23

Miss Jenny Jones 17:39, 68:12, 100:90, *see also:* 63:32

Miss Julie Ann Johnson, o-ho! 232:60

Miss Lucy 109:173

Miss Lucy, she is handsome 128:16

Miss Mary Mack 107:62, 290:57

Miss McLeod's Reel 126:51

Miss Polly Had a Dolly 63:40

Miss Polly had a dolly who was sick, sick, sick 63:40

Missie Mouse 35:88, *see also:* Frog Went A-Courtin'

Missing 172:118, 173:4

Mississippi Gals 61:25

Missouri Land 61:64, *see also:* 61:62, 61:63, 159:410, 226:280

Missouri, she's a mighty river 61:2, *see also:* Shenandoah

The Mist 281:60

Mistah Rabbit 78:95, *see also:* Mister Rabbit

Mistah Rabbit, Mistah Rabbit, yo' ears mighty long 78:94, *see also:* Mister Rabbit

Mister Bamboo Bug   236:18
Mister Banjo/Monsieur Bainjo   21:251
Mister Brown, Mister Brown, I come to court your daughter   109:99
Mister Buff acts tough and rough   91:36
Mister Crumpit   91:42
Mister Frog Went A-Courting   226:143, 289:58, *see also:* Frog Went A-Courtin'
Mister Golden Beetle/Koganemushi   286:23
Mister Golden Beetle has a lot of gold   286:23
Mister Jumping Jack Man is a funny, funny man   165:171
Mister Rabbit   71:83, 129:80, 158:22, 234:16, 253:102, 292:94, *see also:* 78:95
Mister Rabbit, Mister Rabbit, your ears' mighty long!   71:83, 129:80, 234:16, 253:102, 292:94, *see also:* 78:95, 158:22
Mister Rabbit, Mister Rabbit, your tail's mighty white   158:22, *see also:* Mister Rabbit
Mr. Rat and Miss Mouse   62:46, *see also:* Frog Went A-Courtin'
Mr. Snail/Señor Carocol   168:129
Mister Snow   218:73
Mr. Turtle   162:84
Mister Turtle moves around, See him go   162:84
Mister Urian   85:130
Mr. Wolz   261:46
Mistress Bond   62:52, 175:72, 292:154, *see also:* 188:116
Mistress Mary, Quite Contrary   17:62, 283:16, *see also:* Mary, Mary Quite Contrary
Mistress Mary, quite contrary, how does your garden grow?   17:62, 283:16, *see also:* Mary, Mary Quite Contrary
Mrs. Murphy's Chowder   290:16
Mrs. Nothing-At-All   112:5
Mrs. Pussy, sleek and fat   191:60
Mrs. Pussy's Dinner   191:60
Mixed-up Mother Goose   290:122
Mizerna Cicha/Only a Manger Bed   54:214
Mmm mmm mmm   77:51
Mo' Yet   130:50
Moanish Lady!   226:11
Mochi Tauki Odori/Making Rice Cakes   49:24
The Mocking Bird   125:134, 129:97, *see also:* Hush Little Baby
The Mockingbird   135:52, *see also:* Hush Little Baby
The Mockingbird   44:34 (*Look one way, the sun is going down*)
Modeh Ani   77:11
Modenlaw tiday nar Shake ade Day!   215:66

The Modes of the Court   176:156
The Modes of the Court so common are grown   176:156
Mofe Moni S'mo Ho Gbeke/Ev'rybody Loves Saturday Night   89:279, *see also:* 64:200, 148:84
Mole in the Ground   234:25, *see also:* 24:900, 253:96
Molly Brannigan   42:594
Molly Brooks   37:202
Momma, Momma, Have You Heard?   63:90, *see also:* Hush Little Baby
Mommies are people, people with children   260:48
Mommy, Buy Me a China Doll   297
Mon Ane/My Donkey   217:16
Mon Vieux Moine/My Old Top   189:138
Monday Morning Go to School   232:177
Monday was my wedding day   21:294, 157:96
Monday's child is fair of face   18:44
Money   226:112
The Monkey and the Skunk   166:26
The monkey married the baboon's sister   226:113
The Monkey Palanquin/O-saru-no Kagoya   286:28
Monkey See and Monkey Do   63:17
The monkey stamp, stamp, stamps his feet   63:17
The Monkey's Wedding   226:113
Monsieur Bainjo/Mister Banjo   21:251
Moo-oo, Moo-oo, the cow woke up in the morning   41:15
Moo, Moo, Two by Two   85:227
The Moon/Khoe Li   89:256
The Moon and I   252:52
Moon and Sun   125:94
The Moon Is Coming Out/Deta Deta   286:62
The moon is shining. We glide along   166:48
The Moon Shines Bright   210:68, 220:92, *see also:* 184:10, 208:72
The moon shines bright and the stars give a light   184:10, 208:72, 220:92, *see also:* 210:68
Moon shining bright along the pathway home   148:360
Moon! Sun! Shiny and silver, Moon!   125:94
The moon was shining brightly upon the battle plain   157:114
Moonlight   226:216
Moonlight/Ngarm Saeng Duen   267:54
Moonlight Bay   170:65
Moonlight is gleaming   262:77
The Moonshine Steer   61:199
More About John Henry   232:156

The more I reflect, the more plain it appears 28:163

The More It Snows   172:47, 174:33

More Sun/Langa More   163:108

The More We Are Together   73:48, *see also:* 25:8, 26:10, 147:39

The More We Get Together   25:8, 26:10, *see also:* 73:48, 147:39

The more we get together, together, together 25:8, 26:10, 73:48, 147:39

The Mormon Bishop's Lament   159:401

A Mormon Immigrant Song   159:403

The morn of life is past   292:67

Morning, ev'ning, noon and night   101:32, 262:172

Morning Hymn   189:59

Morning Is Come   71:111, 72:169

Morning is come, night is away   71:111, 72:169

Morning is here, the board is spread 101:33, 262:172

Morning Prayer   155:3

Morning Serenade/Las Mañanitas   295:63, *see also:* 169:49, 226:292, 262:21, 268:41

Morning Song   71:48, *see also:* 245:2 (*The sun is rising out of bed*)

Morning Song/Las Mañanitas   169:49, 262:21, 268:41, *see also:* 295:63 (*With a morning song we greet you*)

Morning Star   128:64

Morning Star, oh cheering sight   128:64

Morrissey and the Russian Sailor   226:398

Mòrto Erode/Herod Dead   279:102

Moscow   22:206

The Mosquito/El Zancudo   216:48

Most Adored/Thorum   89:223

The most chivalrous fish of the ocean 176:126

Most people live on a lonely island 218:142

Mother and I   207:22

Mother dear, a Child at our door step 241:88, *see also:* 54:284, 197:117

Mother Earth, to you we're singing 245:110

Mother Hen   207:102 (*Mother Hen walked proudly*)

Mother Hen   41:36 (*Mother Hen calls to her baby chicks three*)

Mother Hen calls to her baby chicks three 41:36

Mother Hen walked proudly   207:102

Mother Horse and Colt/Ouma   286:16

Mother horse and baby colt are gently grazing in the field   286:16

Mother, I Want a Husband/Mamma, 'Kwill 'N Man He'   89:276

Mother-in-law, today is Shake-head Day! 215:66

Mother Machree   170:40

Mother Mary, what is the matter?   67:28, 140:56, 190:142, *see also:* 233:28

Mother, May I Go Out to Swim?   17:73

Mother, Mother, now I'm married   36:76, *see also:* 37:184

Mother, see! A Child in our dooryard! 197:117, *see also:* 54:284, 209:110, 241:88

Mother, standing at our doorway   54:284, *see also:* 197:117, 241:88

Mother, There Is a Garden/Hay Aquí, Madre, un Jardín   216:44

Mother Was a Lady   21:26

Mother Would Comfort Me   73:256

Mother's Day   86:151

Mother's washing, mother's washing 165:34

Mount, mount for the chase! Let your lassoes be strong   159:227

Mount Vernon   273:76

A Mountain High-Top/Nací en la Cumbre 89:76

A mountain high-top was my birth's dwelling   89:76

Mountain Monkey/O-yama-no O-saru 286:22

Mountain monkey likes the ball   286:22

Mountain Top   226:133

Mousekartoon Time   119:109

Mousie, mousie, little mousie   63:132

Mouth and Eyes   204:19

Moving Picture Cowboy   61:313

Mow the Meadow/Market Er Mejet 83:496, 208:17

Mozart's Lullaby   289:34

Mozhunnale, Pezhe yakiske shunmon? 79:12

Mud!   245:73

Mud is very nice to feel   245:73

Müde Bin Ich, Geh Zur Ruh/Weary, Now I Close Mine Eyes   86:173

The Muffin Man   14:365, 17:46, 129:99, 135:27, 165:195, 168:107, 175:42, 283:53, 289:99

The muffled drum is beating   73:203

Mugi Kari/Barley Harvesting   286:76

Mugiwa sarasara koganeno hona nri 286:76

Mukono yamano   49:23

The Mulberry Bush   14:365, 17:90, 63:16, 75:50, 168:108, 175:78, 289:172, *see also:* Here We Go Round the Mulberry Bush

Mule Skinner's Song   226:400

The Mule Song   35:80

Mules   26:19, 289:148, 292:36

The Mulligan Guard   157:177

Mummers' Song   220:116

Mura Matsuri/Village Festival   286:82

Murano chinjuno kamisamano   286:82

Mushi-no Koe/Cricket Voices 286:30

Music 104:53, *see also:* Musicians

Music Shall Live 69:50, *see also:* 61:20, 293:6

The Musicians 75:52, *see also:* 20:16, 71:56, 72:138, 104:53, 254:119, 289:170

Musieu Bainjo 157:152

Musikanter 55:268

Muskrat 234:21

Muskrat, muskrat, doggone your daddy's soul! 234:21

Müss I Denn?/Must I Then? 22:112, 176:70

Must I Then?/Müss I Denn? 22:112

Must I then, must I then to the city away 22:112

Mustang Gray 61:140, 159:362

Muster Out the Rangers 159:368

My Aunt Has a Lame Tame Crane 62:19, *see also:* A Lame Crane

My Aunt Jane 63:122

My Aunt Jane she called me in 63:122

My beautiful, beautiful blue bird 114:26

My Beloved/Chaw Mah Lee 169:67, 267:54

My beloved, I see you as you dance 169:67, 267:54

My Best Friend Is Jesus 86:105

My best friend is my old bear 91:45

My Billy Boy 27:22, *see also:* Billy Boy

My Body Is God's Temple 86:107

My body lies over the ocean 63:145

My Bonnie 26:21, 55:272, *see also:* 205:202, 253:98

My Bonnie (parody) 290:128, *see also:* 55:272

My Bonnie Lad 134:72

My Bonnie lies over the ocean 26:21, 55:272, 205:202, 253:98

My Bonnie looked into a gas tank 55:272, 290:128

My Bonnie Cuckoo 262:129

My Boy Billy 27:22, *see also:* Billy Boy

My Boy, Tammie 182:56

My Boy Willie 62:112, *see also:* Billy Boy

My brother did a-tell me that you go mango walk 134:40

My brother has a little flute of gold and ivory 245:30

My Buddy 170:20

My country, 'tis of thee 25:44, 26:88, 66:90, 69:4, 71:4, 72:32, 127:73, 148:22, 157:118, 160:32, 197:76

My country, 'tis of thee, land where things used to be 159:319

My daddy is an engineer 148:404, 226:188

My daddy was a miner 117:unpaged, *see also:* 64:134

My Dame had a lame tame crane 71:114, 72:170, *see also:* The Lame Crane

My Dame Hath a Lame, Tame Crane 144:25, 176:152, 292:165, 293:52, *see also:* 62:19, 71:114, 72:170

My darling stayed in the West 89:274

My Daughter, Wouldst Have a Bouquet/Ma Fille, Veux-tu un Bouquet? 79:66

My day in the hills has come to an end 218:220

My Days Have Been So Wondrous Free 273:80

My dearest dear, the time draws near 226:126

My Dolly 130:20

My Donkey/Mi Burro 289:64, *see also:* 217:55

My Donkey/Mon Ane 217:55, *see also:* 289:64

My Dream 112:29

My Dreydl 128:59, 197:111

My Ducklings 68:21

My eyes have seen the glory of the burning of the school 63:146, *see also:* 118:6

My Faith Looks Up to Thee 22:282, 148:244

My Farm/Mi Chacra 262:19

My father died a month ago 111:52

My father died but I don't know how 37:174, *see also:* Swapping Song

My Father Gave Me 62:69

My father, how they rejoiced over my illness! 163:95

My Father Is Dead 188:44, *see also:* Swapping Song

My father is dead, but I can't tell you how 188:44, *see also:* The Swapping Song

My Father Owns 112:4

My father owns the butcher shop 112:4

My father says that children keep growing 218:296

My Father Shot a Kangaroo 292:197, *see also:* 289:142

My Father's Apple Tree/Derriére de Chez Mon Père 188:110

My Father's House 25:119

My Father's Riches 111:52

My Favorite Things 218:226

My foot is in my stirrup, the bridle's in my hand 61:228

My foot's in the stirrup, my pony won't stan' 33:218, 159:12, *see also:* Goodbye, Old Paint

My friend, Pierrot 148:31, *see also:* Au Clair de la Lune

My Gal Sal 148:246, 205:312

My Gal's a Corker 290:98

My Gentle Harp 22:88

My gentle harp once more I waken 22:88

My gen'rous heart disdains the slave of love to be 273:100

My Godfather Monkey/Mi Compadre Mono 216:50

My Good Lord's Done Been Here 31:5

My Good Old Man 20:68, 129:24, 274:40

My Goose 128:101, 144:21, 176:91, *see also:* Why Shouldn't My Goose

My Grandfather Had a Garden/Mi Abuelo Tenía un Huerto 295:21

My Grandma 62:131

My Guitar 162:104

My Hat 83:471, *see also:* 291:54

My Hat It Has Three Corners 83:471, 291:54

My head, my shoulder, my knees, my toes 55:266, *see also:* 26:35, 63:46, 165:125

My Heart Is Heavy with Sadness/Suspira, Coracao Triste 89:91

My Heart Is Sair for Somebody 66:130

My heart is sair, I dare-na tell 66:130

My home is the West 207:120

My home it was in Texas 61:239

My Home's Across the Smoky Mountain 148:248

My Home's in Montana 60:16, 69:22, 159:421, 262:51, *see also:* 146:30

My Hoopskirt/Mi Pollera 216:41

My Horses Ain't Hungry 230:21, 232:110, *see also:* 36:64, 37:181, 61:13

My horses ain't hungry they won't eat your hay 61:13, 232:110, *see also:* 36:64, 37:181, 230:21

My Husband/Kana Ma Laune 89:214

My Jo, Janet 182:21

My kitten walks on velvet shoes 59:13

My Lady Greensleeves 262:80, *see also:* Greensleeves

My Lady's Garden 17:98, 188:92, *see also:* Mary, Mary, Quite Contrary

My landlord ring my front door bell 141:56

My Lantern 245:90

My lantern, my lantern 245:90

My Little Boat/A Canoa Virou 168:139

My little boat turned over when the wind began to blow 168:139

My Little Horse 296:15

My little horse, my little horse with his silver bridle 296:15

My Little New Log Cabin in the Hills 61:70

My little red car goes down the hill 162:77

My little sweet darling 85:24

My Lord, What a Morning 22:314, 140:51, 262:42

My Lord's done just what He said 83:472

My Lords, with your leave an account I will give 28:66, 240:91

My Lord's Writing All the Time 55:275

My love he built me a bonnie bow'r 89:132

My love is a rider, wild bronchos he breaks 61:165, 61:166, 146:59, 159:267

My Love Is Gone to Sea 273:94

My Love Is Like a Dewdrop 35:84

My Lover's a Rider 61:166, *see also:* 61:165, 146:59, 159:267

My lover he is a cowboy, he's brave and kind and true 159:275

My Lover Is a Sailor Boy 262:130

My Love's an Arbutus 176:42

My Lulu 226:378

My Lulu hugged and kissed me 226:378

My Ma Was Born in Texas 61:98

My Maid Mary 111:20

My maid Mary she minds her dairy 111:20

My mammy's in the cold, cold ground 226:30

My Man/Into Yam 163:50

My Mind to Me a Kingdom Is 189:83

My Mom gave me some pennies 166:18

My Mom Won't Allow 197:58, *see also:* 290:62

My Mom won't allow no pickin' and a-singin' 'round here 197:58, *see also:* 290:62

My Mother 207:117

My mother called me to her deathbed side 226:310

My mother draws water for me from the well 266:57

My mother, I am in trouble! 215:51

My Mother Said 68:24, *see also:* 63:97

My mother said that I never should play with the gypsies in the wood 63:97, 68:24

My Mother Sent Me Unto You 291:12

My mother's name was Mary 205:327, *see also:* 197:56

My Name 206:52

My Name Is _____ 204:13

My name is Frank Bolar 'nole bach'lor I am 61:58, 226:120, 277:91

My name is Henry Hollinder 24:845

My name is Juan Murray 159:158

My name is Queen Mary 227:30

My name is Sam, an' I don't give a damn 159:241

My name is Stamford Barnes, I come from Nobleville town 158:240, 159:283

My name is Tom Hight 158:238

My name is Yon Yonson 63:135

My name is Zacchaeus, I am but small 124:182

My name it is Hugh Reynolds 42:607

My name it is Joe Bowers and I've got a brother Ike 61:33, 159:375, 230:47

My name it is Nell, and quite candid I tell 290:179

My name's (David). That's a fine name 206:52

My Neighbor 155:18

My New Baby Kitten 207:14

My New Bicycle 207:116

My New Moccasins 207:39

My New Pet Mouse 245:39

My New Puppy 207:13

My New Snowsuit 207:63

My New Toy 177:73

My Nose Is Blue 290:139

My ol' mistiss promise me 158:90

My Old Bear 91:45

My Old Hammah 226:458

My Old Hen 234:44, 289:42, 292:156

My old hen's a good old hen 234:44, 289:42, 292:156

My Old Kentucky Home 21:134, 157:88, 205:135

My Old Top/Mon Vieux Moine 189:138

My Ole Man 46:206

My Paddle's Keen and Bright 62:19, 293:60

My Paisteen Fionn is my soul's delight 42:598

My Parakeet Talks 167:18

My Parents Raised Me Tenderly 61:173

My pigeon house I open wide 165:157

My Polite Panda 166:60

My Pretty Little Pink 226:166

My Pretty Maid 36:35, *see also:* Where Are You Going to, My Pretty Maid?

My Red Sled 207:70

My Roadside Stand 154:20

My Rolling Wagon 207:15

My Sabbath Home 66:144

My sad story should be told 49:42

My Sam is getting seedy now while holding down his claim 61:69

My Savior, Hear My Prayer 86:169

My ship sailed from China with a cargo of tea 68:16

My Sins Are Taken Away 83:472

My Sister She Works in a Laundry 226:381

My Son/Nuri 89:305 *(Oh, my son, thou art handsome as the hornbill)*

My Son 125:124 *(Rock-a-bye, oh my son)*

My Sovereign Jesus/Inkosi Jesus 209:87

My Spanish Guitar 197:90

My Sweetheart's the Mule in the Mines 24:864, 64:64

My tail it rattles 74:29

My Tambourine 41:23

My Tepee Home 207:40

My thoughts and all my memories belong to thee 22:114

My time it has expired all on the tenth of June 240:111

My true love is a soldier in the army now today 73:126

My Twenty Pennies 262:22

My uncle had an old mule 234:62, 292:34

My uncle he sells old clo' 71:102

My Uncle Roasted a Kangaroo 289:142, *see also:* 292:197

My Uncle Terwilliger Likes to Pat 237:unpaged

My Uncle Terwilliger Waltzes With Bears 237:unpaged

My wagon of red and white and blue 207:15

My wife and I lived all alone 21:198, 170:104, 205:172, *see also:* 20:61, 62:193, 126:50

My Wild Irish Rose 170:85, 205:263

My young love said to me, "My mother won't mind and my father . . ." 42:600

My youngest daughter, are you here? 74:33

Myan Myan 169:11, 269:17

Myan myan pay jah bah oh 169:11, 269:17

Myn Lyking 210:112

N

Na Bahia Tem/In Bahia 266:14

Na ka wai lukini wai anuhea oka rose 87:40

Na Lei O Hawaii/The Leis of Hawaii 87:60

Na Lei O Hawaii/Song of the Islands 87:81

Nací en la Cumbre/A Mountain High-Top 87:76

Nambu Ushiori Uta/Song of the Cattle Driver 49:28

Nan Sob-oy/We Pray 89:298

Nana, Thread Needle 109:83

Nancy Till 277:129

Nani Hawaii ka moku o Keawe, 87:81

Nani, Nani 125:128

Nanny goat, billy goat 176:78

Nantucket Lullaby 281:62

Nar Juldagsmorgon Glimmar/When Christmas Morn Is Dawning 54:194

Naranja Dulce/Sweet Orange 295:36

Naranjas y Limas/Oranges and Lemons 295:82

Natchez on the Hill 37:208

Nathan Hale 240:98, *see also:* 28:80

Natural History 17:133, *see also:* 18:31, 111:33, 175:102

Nature's Goodnight 125:50

Nature's Splendor/Varga Pavati 89:215

Nature's splendor fills the whole earth with its wonder 89:215

Navajo Happiness Song 277:99

Navajo Happy Song   69:26, 197:84, 262:107
    (Hi yo hi yo ip si ni yah)
Nay cong dan ai Quoc   100:143
Nda vi lizwi   163:36
Nden, nden, nden, nkumba nya meden
    100:52
Ndin umqokozo   163:78
Ne me him a a o a   89:225
Near Banbridge town in the County Down
    42:610
Near Breclav/Starej Breclavy   89:186
Near to My Fair One/Auprès de Ma Blonde
    21:340
Nearer, My God, To Thee   21:174
Nearly Missed   206:86
'Neath a tree by the margin of a woodland
    61:138
Neath the Crust of the Old Apple Pie
    118:10
'Neath the grand Sierra Madre   69:9
Nebraska Land   61:64, *see also:* 61:62,
    61:63, 159:410, 226:280
Needle Sing   130:36
The Needle's Eye   17:75, 68:31
*The needle's eye doth supply the thread that
    runs so true*   17:75, 68:31
Ne'er forget God's daily care   86:212
Negro Reel   226:134
A Negro Song   273:122
Neighbor, neighbor, well I met you   37:184,
    see also: 36:76
Neighbor, What Has You So Excited?/Quoi,
    Ma Voisine, Es-tu Fachée?   54:104
Nell Flaherty's Drake   290:179
Nelly Bly   21:137
Nelly Bly! Nelly Bly!   21:137
Nen nen Korori yo   286:63
Nesem Vám Noviny/Come All Ye Shep-
    herds   286:116, *see also:*   54:236,
    220:100
Nesem Vám Noviny/Come, Hear the Won-
    derful Tidings/Kommet, Ihr Hirten
    54:236, *see also:* 220:100, 279:116
Nesta Rua/On This Street   266:14
Never Forget the Dear Ones   73:238
Never Said a Mumblin' Word   158:356
Never Smile at a Crocodile   276:34
Never Weather-Beaten Saile   176:142
New Baby   91:44
New Baby Brother   166:56
The New-Born Baby   233:34
The New Dress   114:32
A New England Ballad   240:23
New England, New England   33:26
*New England, New England, my home by
    the sea*   33:26
A New Jerusalem   64:182
The New Moccasins   207:39
New Moon   77:49

New National Anthem   159:319
New-Plymouth   273:146
New River Shore   61:160, *see also:* 37:152,
    159:181
New River Train   62:126, 128:78, 148:250,
    230:74, *see also:* 88
New Shoes   207:12
A New Song, Written by a Soldier   240:111
A New Tory Ballad   240:177, *see also:*
    28:104
New Toys   207:56
A New Year Carol   209:56
New Year's Day in the Morning   188:168,
    see also: I Saw Three Ships
New York   157:102
The Newburgh Jail   35:64
Next to the fireplace, close to the wall
    207:51
Ngai I Tanga I   89:305
Ngaphaya kwezontaba   163:56
Ngarm Saeng Duen/Moonlight   267:54
Ngenyi mini eku se ni   163:100
Ngoma Kurila/A Lament   163:42
Nhim Ne Nhim/Lullaby   89:225
Nice Girls Don't Chase the Boys   262:88
*A nice young ma-wa-wan lived on a hi-wi-
    will*   159:194
*Nicht Jerusalem sondern Bethlehem hat
    bescheret was uns nahret*   277:109
Nick-Nack Paddy Wack   129:98, *see also:*
    This Old Man
Nick Spence   112:43
Nickety Nackety   37:122, 62:143, *see also:*
    36:36, 128:114
Nicky, roll the ball around   291:64
Nicodemus, the slave, was of African birth
    21:160, 73:96
Night   59:13
The night a Child was born   197:114
*The night before Thanksgiving when I had
    gone to bed*   162:44
Night Herding Song   59:49, 60:10, 61:224,
    69:23, 71:91, 89:44, 129:94, 146:27,
    159:60, 225:21, 239:30, 274:24
Night is come, owls are out   68:48
Night Is Coming   125:62
Night Noises   166:10
The Night Song   85:243
The Night Will Never Stay   59:68
The Nightingale   262:48
Nights are long since you went away
    170:20
Night's Dark Shadows/Walla Zala Mudduja
    89:245
Niña, Nana/Lullaby   89:161, 216:31, *see
    also:* 54:252, 279:108
Niña vamos al campo y cortaremos una flor
    89:77

Nine Hundred Miles   148:252, 158:254, *see also*: 72:17

Nine men slept in a boardinghouse bed 148:254, 290:34, *see also*: 26:23, 63:131, 147:32, 254:110

The Ninety and Nine   66:146

Ninety-Nine Bottles of Beer   147:30, *see also*: 82, 148:376, 290:32

Ninni, Baba/Hush, My Baby   169:30, 268:19

Njamb'et a Bolumbu, yak'en do   100:77

Nne N'eku Nwa/O Mary, Dear Mother 209:95

Nnoọnya Mwana Wange   236:8

Nnyonyi   236:27

No Bears Out Tonight   63:42

No Bread For the Poor   226:319

No, Child/Thanayi   163:112

No Hiding Place   31:49, 262:145

"No home, no home," cried an orphan girl 226:319

No Irish Need Apply   64:152

No keepsakes have we of days that are gone 198:268

The No Laugh Race   237:unpaged

No man in the West ever won such renown 61:266, *see also*: 61:268, 159:140

No Man Is an Island   72:116

No matter how young a prune may be 63:134

No mo' auction block for me   22:187, 64:173

No More Booze   226:208

No more moaning   64:164, *see also*: 21:167, 31:53, 157:138, 158:370

No more shall the sound of the war whoop be heard   157:64

No, Never Can I Go With You/No Puedo, Tengo Otro Dueño   89:77

The No, No, Yes, Yes Aria   197:72

No Other Love   218:278

No Puedo, Tengo Otro Dueño/No, Never Can I Go With You   89:77

No quiero que me cortejes   208:62

No Room In the Inn   241:24

No Sir   62:117, 83:478

No Use for the Women   61:177, *see also*: 159:300

Noah's Dove   157:100

The Noble Duke of York   39:10, 70:30, 126:103, 128:107, 130:63, 135:90, 289:184, *see also*: 26:25, 55:520, 63:37, 165:193

The Noble Lads of Canada   240:209

Nobody Knows de Trouble I See   22:302, 31:45, 71:92, 72:81, 148:256, 157:137

Nobody Likes Me   63:94, 290:190

Nobody likes me, everybody hates me! 63:94, 290:190

Nobody's eyes are quite the same as your eyes   206:112

Noche oscura, nada veo   89:96, 169:14, 216:24, 267:46

Nodle Kangbyon/Beside the Nodle River 49:38

Noel   209:123

Noel! A New Noel!   54:118, 220:78

Noël Alsacien/Dors, Ma Colombe/Sleep, My Little Dove   54:120, *see also*: 184:44

Noël des Ausels/Whence Comes This Rush of Wings Afar?   54:124, *see also*: Carol of the Birds

Noël Nouvelet/Christmas Comes Anew 54:118

Noel Sing We   264:108

Noel-Time   209:92

Nomeva/The Wasp   163:104

Nomthini/A Girl's Name   163:56

A North Country maid up to London had stray'd   71:54

The North Wind Doth Blow   17:129, 18:25, 135:116, 175:88, 188:106, 189:124, 227:31, 285:34, 292:139

Nos damos gracias, O Señor por nuestra pan de hoy   71:13, 72:175, 101:32

Nose, Nose   111:55

Nose, nose, jolly red nose   111:55

Not a thing on the river McCluskey did fear 24:849

Not Jerusalem, lowly Bethlehem   277:109

Not until my last breath   89:301

Nothin' From Nothin' Leaves You   84:52

Nothin' To Do   91:14

Nothing Else To Do   290:164, *see also*: 147:38, 231

Nothing Whatever To Grumble At 290:182

Nothing you attempt in the world is so hard to do   89:296

Nous N'Irons Plus au Bois/We Will Go No More to the Woods   217:40

Nova, Nova   220:50

Nova, nova; ave fix ex Eva   220:50

Now ain't it hard, hard, hard, to be a farmer 109:212

Now all the day long on the prairies I ride 60:90, *see also*: 146:132, 159:67

Now Brigham Young is a Mormon bold 159:400

Now by-low, baby, and slumber sweet and soundly   125:35

Now come all you young fellows that follow the sea   36:54, *see also*: Blow the Man Down

Now come, young men, and list to me 159:201

Now Comes the Hour   262:90

Now, don't you ever want to know some things concerning 33:106

Now, farewell, my Massa, my Missy, adieu 28:165

Now, go on, old 'gator, doggone your soul 234:74

Now heaven's gate has opened 245:116, *see also:* 244:187

Now heaven's gate is opened 244:187, *see also:* 245:116

Now, here comes Uncle Jessie 109:114

Now how I came to get this hat 205:219

Now I Lay Me Down to Sleep 17:30

Now I Wake 86:167

Now, if you want a merchant ship to sail the seas at large 98:45

Now, if you will listen, I'll sing you a song 290:68

Now I'm Going to Sing/Ahora Voy a Cantarles 216:43

Now I'm the king of the swingers 276:62

Now Is the Month of Maying 72:110, 85:19, 189:112, 197:53, 262:159

Now It Is Christmastime/Nu ar det Juligen 241:168, *see also:* 54:193, 89:170, 262:42, 279:112

Now it's one o'clock, one o'clock, one o'clock 291:36

Now I've got no use for women 61:177, 159:300

Now Let Every Tongue Adore Thee 55:253

Now Let Me Fly 22:300, *see also:* 148:222

Now Louis came home to the flat 205:296

Now, my wooden garment here was not always old and broken 67:14

Now 'neath the silver moon ocean is glowing 22:30

Now, now, soldier, won't you marry me? 21:186, *see also:* Soldier, Soldier, Won't You Marry Me?

Now, now that the sun hath veil'd his light 85:34

Now, O Lord, please lend Thine ear 61:338, 159:329

Now, Old Bill the Rolling Pin this morning 109:209

Now old Dan Tucker's a fine old man 230:52, *see also:* Old Dan Tucker

Now once again it's Noel-time 209:92

Now once I was happy but now I'm forlorn 205:167, *see also:* 21:191, 170:87, 198

Now put your hand on your hip and let your backbone slip 109:111, *see also:* Little Sally Water

Now Robin, Lend to Me Thy Bow 71:57, 72:121

Now singing we're bringing our praises before Him 21:338, *see also:* We Gather Together

Now some people say a man's made out of mud 64:52

Now tell me did you ever see 85:93

Now Thank We All Our God 86:130, 161:119

Now Thank We the Father 86:145

Now the Chesapeake so bold 240:196

Now the darkness creeps and my lambkin sleeps 245:98

Now the day is done; Boy Scouts one by one 25:62

Now the Day Is Over 45:64, 59:18, 71:124, 72:59, 125:39, 148:258, 161:74

Now the holly bears a berry as white as the milk 96:11

Now the little doves are stepping out 169:53

Now the moon is coming out! 286:62

Now the No-Laugh race is about to start 237:unpaged

Now the tribes are all departing 69:27

Now the Winter Is Past/Nu Er Vetur Ur Boe 89:171

Now there was an old soldier 62:91

Now (they) go the shepherds to (the) Estremadura 295:70

Now Walking John was a big rope boss 146:79

Now We'll Make the Rafters Ring 148:260, 290:195, 293:10

Now we'll play upon the drum and we'll make our voices hum 129:60

Now what do you think of Little Jack Jingle? 18:34, 100:67

Now Windy Bill was a Texas man 61:204, *see also:* 60:54, 146:69, 159:113

Now you can't expect a cowboy to agitate his shanks 61:284, *see also:* 159:251

Now, you get a line and I'll get a pole 129:30, *see also:* Crawdad

Now you lead right on down the valley 55:514, *see also:* Red River Valley

Now's the Time 85:202

Now's the time for fun and laughter 85:202

Nsangi 236:45

Ntuha Ntuha/Crested Crane 169:69, 265:56

Ntyilo-Ntyilo/Bird Song 163:36

Nu Ar Det Jul Igen 54:193, 89:170, 241:168, 262:42, 279:112

Nu Er Vetur Ur Boe/Now the Winter Is Past 89:171

Nu stiu satul ce voeste 208:60

Nun Danket Alle Gott/Now Thank We All Our God 86:130

Nuns in Frigid Cells   241:44
Nur Du/Thou Only   22:114
Nuri/My Son   89:305
The Nut Tree   59:24, 227:5, *see also:* I Had a Little Nut Tree
Nuts in May   14:367, 63:32, 128:102, 165:191, 175:78, 188:38, 189:36
Ny O L'on Nanacy/Song of the Orphan 89:267
Nyam'njenje w'enda kumba kwake   89:273
Nyo lon' nanary   89:267

O

O-Bar Cowboy   159:166
O duong banthea tis   89:222
O kau hana manu noia   87:73
O-Lu-We/Hen Fell Out of the Roost   265:57
O makala pua ulu ma hiehie   87:76
O Mane   266:25
O quante belle figlie, Madama Dore 188:86, *see also:* 265:23
O-saru-no Kagoya/The Monkey Palanquin 286:28
O-Tsuki-San Momo Iro   16:23
O-um anyu o-um aruonwu   215:16
O wie wohl ist mir am Abend   21:322
O-yama-no   O-saru/Mountain   Monkey 286:22
The Oak and the Ash   71:54
Oats and Beans   135:76, 165:83, *see also:* Oats, Peas, Beans
Oats and beans and barley grow   135:76, 165:83, *see also:* Oats, Peas, Beans
Oats, Peas, Beans   14:369, 17:60, 20:80, 63:14, 283:27, 289:181, *see also:* 135:76, 165:83
Oats, peas, beans and barley grow   14:369, 17:60, 20:80, 63:14, 283:27, 289:181, *see also:* 135:76, 165:83
Obedient Kitten   245:47
Ocean Go   130:98
Ocean go, ocean go, My boat makes the ocean go   130:98
Och, hush ye then, och hush ye,   281:59
Ockaya/Corn-Grinding Song   68:13, 89:38
October's Clouds   207:31
Odala me so nda   215:24
Ode for American Independence   273:64
Ode to Joy   71:27, 72:54
Oedo nihonbashi   89:237
Of All the Beast-ies   234:75
Of all the beast-ies in the world, I'd rather be a panther   234:75
Of All the Birds   85:21
Of all the birds that I do know   85:21
Of all the mighty nations   27:42, 66:87, 157:106

Of heroes and statesmen   240:134, *see also:* 35:16
Of the Father's Love Begotten/Corde Natus Ex Parentis   54:314
Of what use are you?   163:104
Off to the Garden Patch   207:103
Oft in the Stilly Night   66:26, 125:44
Oft times I get to thinking of the changes time has wrought   159:191
Ognuno ana Sabato notte   148:84
Oh, A-hunting we will go   47, 135:118, 136, *see also:* A-Hunting We Will Go
Oh, a life in the prairie shack when the rain begins to pour   61:108
Oh, a man there lives on the western plains 159:139
Oh a many a bird did wake and fly   183:22, *see also:* Carol of the Birds
Oh, a poor old man came a'riding by 128:22, *see also:* 37:157, 157:40
Oh! a private buffoon is a lighthearted loon 252:58
Oh, a-Rock-a My Soul   22:306, 72:80, *see also:* 55:278
Oh, a shanty man's life is a wearisome life 33:242, 226:390, *see also:* 35:11
O ah drove three mules foh Gawge McVane 226:400
O all you little blackey tops   188:164
Oh another man came to our town   111:46, *see also:* Aiken Drum
Oh as I was a comin' on down the road 20:72, 22:66, 126:48, 226:94
O Babe in the Manger   155:26
O Be Joyful   155:8
Oh be prepared prepared prepared   25:56
O Beautiful Banner   69:4, 71:6, 72:36
O beautiful banner all splendid with stars 69:4, 71:6, 72:36
O beautiful for spacious skies   25:46, 26:86, 45:34, 69:2, 71:5, 72:24, 127:184, 148:24, 157:216, 160:70, 161:35, 197:74, 205:351
O Belinda   39:32, *see also:* 126:105, 135:93, 178:52
Oh, Beloved/Aroi Toyong   89:295
O Bethlehem/Oi Betlehem   54:274
O Betsy B. was a lady fair   35:74
Oh, bird of song   163:54
Oh, Birthday Pal, we sing-a-ling-a-ling 197:124
Oh, blow the man down, bullies, blow the man down   22:152, 71:40, 72:77, 98:24, 230:39, *see also:* Blow the Man Down
Oh, blow the man down, laddies, blow the man down   25:105, *see also:* Blow the Man Down
Oh, Blue   234:30 *see also:* Old Blue
O boys, we're goin' for a fight, Yo-ho, yo-ho! 159:365

O brothers, you ought t' have been there 21:261, *see also:* 25:95, 31:37, 148:318, 290:96

Oh! Bubble, bubble, bubble, bubble, bubble, goes the pan 33:50

Oh, Buffalo gals won't you come out tonight 20:28, *see also:* Buffalo Gals

O Bury Me Beneath the Willow 226:314

Oh, Bury Me Not On the Lone Prairie 25:78, 61:314, 61:315, 61:316, 158:208, 159:48, 225:48, 226:20, *see also:* 60:20, 146:38

Oh, by and by, by and by 157:149

Oh, camels and bears and ponies are found 17:92

Oh, Can Ye Sew Cushions 71:82, 78:29, 125:68, *see also:* 27:110

Oh! Charlie is my darling, my darling, my darling! 71:42, *see also:* Charlie is My Darling

Oh, Charley he's a fine young man 66:76, *see also:* 24:813, 213:28, 226:161

O Chester! 25:25, 26:35

O Chester did you 'ear about Harry? 25:25, 26:35

Oh, childhood's joys are very great 66:60

Oh, Christmas comes but once a year 233:77

O Christmas Tree 54:138, 92:179, 129:51, 148:262, 197:118, 241:164, 279:68, *see also:* 21:196

O Christmas, You Season of Childlike Delight/O Jul Med Din Glede 54:200

O, clap, clap the hands 191:80

Oh, clap your hands and stamp your feet 177:76

O clear-running stream 188:62

O coffee grows on a white oak tree 39:42, *see also:* 158:100

O Columbia, the gem of the ocean 26:86, 157:116, 160:36

O Come All Ye Faithful/Adeste Fideles 22:244, 25:113, 45:20, 54:318, 66:94, 86:29, 92:171, 148:264, 210:48, 241:148, 262:162, 264:113, 279:18, 283:50, 284:35

Oh come along boys, and listen to my tale 60:4, 61:210, 146:20, 146:23, *see also:* Old Chisholm Trail

Oh, come and buy! says Farmer Small 154:20

O Come and Let Us Worship 86:191

Oh, come and rejoice with me 169:47, 265:36

O come and sing a song before we go our way 71:103

O Come Away, Ye Shepherds/Quittez, Pasteurs 54:98

Oh, come, cowboys, and listen to my song! 159:96

O Come, Let Us Worship 86:188

Oh, come let's go aplanting 100:64

O Come, Little Children/Ihr Kinderlein, Kommet 54:142, 86:42, 241:162, 279:72, 284:125

O Come, O Come, Emmanuel/Veni, Emmanuel 54:312, 86:27, 241:134

O Come Rejoicing/Dziasiaj w Betlejem 54:206

Oh, come with me to Fiddler's Fair 110:40

Oh cow, oh cow, what use are you 41:34, 291:35

O Dad O' Mine 25:7

O Dakota 61:63, *see also:* 61:62, 61:63, 61:64, 159:410, 226:280

O Dame get up and bake your pies 129:52, *see also:* 17:123, 138:unpaged, 188:150

O, Dance Like That!/Ozibane! Ozibane! Ozibane! 89:284

Oh! Dancer, little dancer 168:141, *see also:* 169:9, 266:13

O Dandelion, Yellow as Gold 245:24

Oh de boll weevil am a little black bug 24:916, 226:8, 239:40, 277:29, *see also:* The Boll Weevil

O, Dear Sixpence! 175:97, *see also:* 188:46

O dear the eye that softly looks 59:31

Oh, Dear! What Can the Matter Be? 17:88, 36:6, 62:126, 135:22, 148:271, 175:50, 188:80, 205:41, 262:101, 273:110, 283:44

Oh, Deat' he is a little man 24:915

Oh, Dem Golden Slippers! 21:205, 157:160, 205:189, *see also:* 126:63

Oh, dey whupped him up de hill 158:356

Oh, Dixie the land of King Cotton 73:20

O' do not cry, my little treasure 89:270, 169:51, *see also:* 208:47, 267:14

Oh, do not stand so long outside 66:94

Oh, do you know the muffin man 17:46, 129:99, 165:195, 283:53, 289:99, *see also:* 14:365, 135:27, 168:107, 175:42

Oh, do you remember sweet Alice, Ben Bolt 66:18

Oh, don't you remember sweet Betsy from Pike 24:861, 61:48, 157:38, 205:122, 224, 226:108, 239:66, *see also:* 22:62, 158:176, 159:388

O dove, O Holy Ghost, Upon their heads descending 124:251

O Du Fröhliche/O How Joyfully 54:136, 86:31

O Evergreen, O Evergreen 21:196, *see also:* O Christmas Tree

Oh, fairest of all maidens 89:222

O fare you well, sweet Ireland 240:147

Oh, farewell to you my Nancy 208:74

Oh, father, if you will agree 28:70

Oh, five fat turkeys are we 178:43

O flag of our America 207:42

O flamme monte que ta lumiere 72:174
Oh, for a ride o'er the prairies free 61:298
Oh, Freedom 21:167, 31:53, 64:164, 157:138, 158:370
Oh, Genevieve, I'd give the world 157:168, 158:42
Oh, give me a home where the buffalo roam 22:164, 25:75, 26:72, 60:42, 61:294, 61:295, 61:296, 71:90, 72:97, 146:166, 158:212, 159:425, 159:427, 170:101, 205:361, 230:26
Oh, give me land, lots of land under starry skies above 170:72
Oh, Give Thanks 71:13, 72:57, 101:31
Oh, give us a train or a boat or a plane 26:77
O Glorious Bells of Easter 197:41
O glorious star, how kindly you are 262:109
O God of Love, O King of Peace 86:94
O God, Our Help in Ages Past 21:334, 45:47, 161:23
O God, Who Art the Only Light 262:98
O God, whose love enfolds us all 86:142
O Grant Us Lord, Thy Peace 86:93
Oh Green Fields, Roxie 109:75
Oh, green grow the lilacs and so does the rue 148:132, *see also:* 22:174, 66:96, 157:70
O Gwiazdo Betlejemska/O Star O'er Bethlehem Shining 54:208
O Hangman, O Hangman 176:60, *see also:* 24:822, 226:72, 226:385
O Hanukkah, O Hanukkah, come light the menorah! 22:292, 197:110
Oh, happy is the miller boy who lives in the mill 20:34, *see also:* 17:118, 63:28, 135:82, 227:26
O Hark I Hear Those Pealing Bells 62:12, *see also:* 71:98, 72:166
O, have ye been in love, me boys 226:463
O have you heard de lates' 21:81, *see also:* Boll Weevil
Oh have you heard the news, my Johnny? 22:158
O, have you seen the Muffin Man 14:365, 168:107, 175:42, *see also:* Muffin Man
Oh, have you seen the Shah? 14:349, *see also:* A-Hunting We Will Go
Oh, haw, haw; Oh haw, haw Tweedle dee dee Um, paw paw 55:264
Oh he don't know what it's all about 87:84
Oh! He flew through the air with the greatest of ease 198, *see also:* 21:191, 170:87, 205:167
Oh, He Planted Ginger 114:54
Oh He sees all you do, He hears all you say 55:275
Oh, hear the sound of tinkling bells, Ding, ding, ding 162:67

Oh, here I come, a Spanish knight! 168:110
Oh, here sits a monkey in the chair, chair, chair 232:175
Oh! Hi-diddle diddle a rhyme and a riddle 288:3
O holy Infant, small and dear 241:174
O Holy Night 54:107, 92:173, 241:197, 264:79, 284:103
Oh home came the old man and home came he 37:118
O how glorious it will be 86:131
Oh! How I Hate to Get Up in the Morning 25:39
O How Joyfully/O Du Fröhliche 54:136, *see also:* 86:31
Oh, How Lovely Is the Evening 21:322, 62:11, 71:109, 72:173, 148:273, 241:232, 289:189, 293:22
O' how much wood could a woodchuck chuck if a woodchuck could chuck wood 97:unpaged
O Hush Thee, My Babie 262:94, *see also:* 125:66
O hush thee, my babie, thy sire was a knight 262:94, *see also:* 125:66
O Hush Thee, My Baby 125:66, *see also:* 262:94
Oh! Hush thee, my baby, the night is behind us 59:64
O hush thee, my baby, thy sire is a knight 125:66, *see also:* 262:94
O hush thee my dove, o hush thee my rowan 189:96
Oh, I am a lonely cowboy and I'm off of the Texas trail 61:307, *see also:* 60:102, 146:162, 159:19, 226:266
Oh, I am a poor girl, my fortune's been bad 36:64
Oh, I am a rusty cowboy 159:76
Oh, I am a Texas cowboy, far away from home 159:22, *see also:* 60:48, 61:91, 146:66
Oh, I don't want to be a gambler 226:465
Oh, I dreamt I shore in a shearin' shed 176:84
Oh, I had a horse and his name was Bill 226:340, 289:154, *see also:* 292:28
Oh I have a little mouth 204:19
Oh, I have eaten him. What did I eat? 62:75
O I know the Lord, I know the Lord 83:469
Oh, I look up and see a birdie flying 206:34
O I Lost Me Love 212:81
Oh! I love to travel far and near throughout my native land 226:52
Oh, I love trash 206:95
Oh, I stuck my head in the little skunk's hole 63:138
Oh, I took my gun out on my back 61:8

Oh, I was bo'n in Mobile town 22:148, *see also:* I've Been Workin' on the Railroad

Oh, I went down South for to see my Sal 66:70, 83:507, 205:139, 290:112, *see also:* 46:208

Oh, I went to Toledo and I walked around the block 63:132

Oh, I wonder at her 89:37

Oh, I wrote my love a letter 35:94

Oh, I'm a citizen in the Cub Scouts 26:64

O, I'm a Good Old Rebel 73:88

Oh, I'm a Texas cowboy and far away from home 60:48, 61:92, 146:66, *see also:* 159:22

Oh, I'm goin' for a ride 206:48

Oh, I'm goin' out West, down on the Rio Grande 226:28

Oh, I'm going down South for to see my gal 46:208, *see also:* 66:70, 83:507, 205:139, 290:112

Oh, I'm very special as you can see 204:29

Oh in eighteen hundred and forty-one 226:356, *see also:* Pat Works On the Railway

Oh, in my father's garden 21:340

Oh, it's clop, clop, clop, clop 69:37

Oh, it's old King Twine and he called for his wine 62:76

Oh, I've been to Winchester 39:2, *see also:* 20:56, 70:9, 129:120, 134:44

Oh, I've been workin' on the railroad 83:506, *see also:* I've Been Workin' On the Railroad

Oh, I've got five people in my family 206:18

Oh Jerus'lem in the Morning! 140:56, *see also:* 67:28, 190:142, 233:28

Oh! Jesse was the man, he traveled through the land 159:156, *see also:* Jesse James

O Jesu Most Kind 209:19

O Jesu parvule! 21:328, 210:32, *see also:* 220:98, 241:76

O Jesu So Kind 85:86

O Jesu so kind, o Jesu so mild 85:86

Oh, Jesus born in Galilee 37:166

O Jesus, Once a Nazareth Boy 86:122

Oh, John Henry was a new-born baby 274:16, *see also:* John Henry

Oh, John the Rabbit 232:100, 291:32

Oh, Johnny, Johnny, John, come along, come along 290:218

O Jul Med Din Glede/O Christmas, You Season of Childlike Delight 54:200

Oh, keep your hat upon your head 290:46

Oh! kind folks listen to my song 27:17, 73:102

Oh, kind friend you may ask me what makes me sad and still 146:120, *see also:* 61:217, 159:125

Oh! Ladies and gentleman, please to draw near 226:118

O, Land of Columbia how glorious the sight 73:12

O Ladybird, please won't you sit 85:162

O! Land of ours, to thee we raise our praises 262:155

O Laufet Ihr Hirten/Come Running, You Shepherds 54:154

Oh, lay still, dogies, since you have laid down 59:49, *see also:* Night Herding Song

O Leave Your Sheep 210:49

Oh, let me come and follow 67:50

Oh, Lily, Lily White 78:77, 125:10

Oh, listen, kind friends, I'll tell you a story you all know well 61:317, *see also:* Oh, Bury Me Not On the Lone Prairie

O, little bird husband found 236:34

O Little One 184:52

O little one sweet 184:52

O Little Town of Bethlehem 22:236, 45:18, 54:63, 65:98, 86:33, 92:177, 140:100, 148:268, 161:18, 184:24, 190:98, 210:52, 210:53, 210:114, 241:128, 242:unpaged, 264:106, 279:50, 284:27

Oh, look who is here, Punchinello little fellow 178:7, *see also:* 63:14, 109:106, 128:96, 135:113

O Lord, how doest Thou 124:31

Oh Lord, How Long? 37:169

Oh, Lord I Want 83:465

O Lord, I wonder, Bye and bye 233:54

Oh, Lord, I've never lived where churches grow 61:343

O, Lord, our fathers oft have told 273:146

O Lord, Turn Not Thy Face From Them 45:53

O Lord, Whose Mercies Are Numberless 85:62

Oh Lordy pick a bale of cotton 107:46, 230:54, *see also:* Pick a Bale of Cotton

O Love That Wilt Not Let Me Go 45:37

O, Lula! 158:272

Oh Lula, Oh Lord, gal 158:272

Oh, Mac Tavish is dead and his brother don't know it 134:49, 290:175

O madam, I have come to court 62:120

O maiden with the lovely golden tresses 208:39

O Mane 266:25

Oh, many a bird did wake and fly 140:96, *see also:* Carol of the Birds

Oh, Marguerite! go wash your feet 24:796

Oh, Mary and the Baby, Sweet Lamb 190:116, 233:35

O Mary, Dear Mother/Nne n'eku Nwa 209:95

Oh, Mary, Don't You Weep   148:274, 230:78, *see also:* 226:476

O Mary O Martha O Mary ring them bells 31:35

O Mary, Where Is Your Baby?   190:123, 233:56

O Master, Let Me Walk With Thee   45:25

O Master Workman of the Race   86:55

Oh, meet me when daylight is fading 66:103

O merry Christmas season   209:96

Oh, Missie Mouse, I come to see   35:88, *see also:* Frog Went A-Courtin'

Oh, Mister Moon   148:278

Oh, Mister Moon, you are very pink   16:23

Oh, Mister Rat took a notion one day 62:46, *see also:* Frog Went A-Courtin'

O Mollie, O Mollie, 'tis for your sake alone 159:253

O money is the meat in the cocoanut 226:112

O Mortal Man, Remember Well   210:54

Oh Mother! Oh Mother!   163:42

Oh, Music, Sweet Music   293:8

O my dear, I think of you only   87:34

O my deir hert, young Jesus sweit   210:88

Oh my donkey, my donkey   289:64

Oh, my golden slippers am laid away 21:205, 157:160, *see also:* 126:63, 205:189

Oh my golden slippers they are laid away 205:189, *see also:* 21:205, 126:63, 157:160

Oh, my grandma lived on yonder village green 62:131

O My Honey, Take Me Back   226:239

O my love, will you wear red?   135:62, *see also:* Jennie Jenkins

O   My   Loveliest   One/Chiquirriquitín 54:280

Oh my mother and my father, they went to the county fair   178:30, *see also:* 55:510, 83:495

Oh, my name it is Sam Hall, it is Sam Hall 159:422

Oh! My name was Robert Kidd   21:332

Oh, my son, thou art handsome as the horn-bill   89:305

Oh, No, John   148:282

Oh! oft at pleasant morning, sunshine all adorning   42:591

Oh! Oh! Oh! Cameroon   163:83

Oh, Oh, the Sunshine   232:64

Oh, once I was happy, but now I'm forlorn 21:191, 170:87, *see also:* 198, 205:167

Oh, once in my saddle I used to go dashing 157:157

Oh, once there was a maiden   245:47

Oh! Once there was a witch, in a castle she did dwell   145

O once upon a time in Arkansas   22:58

Oh, once was a horse and his name was Bill 292:28, *see also:* 226:340, 289:154

Oh, Paddy dear, and did you hear the news that's going round   21:286, 205:163

Oh Paddy O'Doyle lived in Killarney 37:150, *see also:* 134:76

O Perfect Love   45:50

O perfect Love, all human thought transcending   45:50

O pescator dell' onda   89:158

Oh please don't pet my gingerbread Duck 261:10

O Po' Little Jesus   54:86, *see also:* 140:60, 158:354, 190:90, 233:52

Oh! Potatoes they grow small, over there! 21:293

Oh, Promise Me   21:62, 205:223

Oh, promise me that some day you and I 21:62, 205:223

O Publish the Glad Story/Celebrons la Naissance   279:21, *see also:* 54:92

O quante belle figlie Madama Dore 188:86, 265:23

Oh, Rabbit, hopping high, looking at the starlit sky   16:25

Oh, ranky tank, ranky tank   109:130

Oh, Rejoice, Thou Frightful Grave/Bucura t'e Tintirim   89:192

Oh, Render Thanks   71:14

Oh, Robin Hood and Little John   262:132, *see also:* 164:10

O Sanctissima/O Thou Joyful Day   22:253, 241:120

O Santy Anna gained the day   21:288, 24:835, *see also:* 158:136, 262:105

O-saru-no Kagoya/The Monkey Palanquin 286:28

O say, can you see, by the dawn's early light 12, 21:272, 22:184, 25:48, 26:85, 27:151, 66:80, 69:2, 71:2, 72:26, 122, 127:39, 148:354, 160:14, 197:64, 240:207, 249, 283:67

Oh, say, John, won't you buy me   63:145

Oh say little dogies, why don't you lay down?   60:10, 89:44, 146:27, 274:24, *see also:* Night Herding Song

Oh say were you ever in Rio Grande 22:140, 78:9, 239:14, *see also:* 176:110

O see a young maid-mother lying   189:74

Oh! Set the campfire burning   25:121

Oh! Shall I Tell You, Mother/Ah! Vous Dirai-je, Maman   217:53

O Shanadoah, I love your daughter 157:40, *see also:* Shenandoah

Oh, Shanandar, I long to hear you   134:77, *see also:* Shenandoah

O Shanandoah, I long to hear you   22:136, 25:85, 69:35, 98:30, 148:326, 158:138, 205:82, 239:16, *see also:* Shenandoah

O Shannadore, I love your daughter 226:408, see also: Shenandoah

Oh, Shenandoah, I long to see you 176:113, 230:17, see also: Shenandoah

Oh Shenandoah, I want to hear you! 277:55, see also: Shenandoah

Oh, Sherman the brave, with his army array'd 73:75

Oh, She's Gone, Gone, Gone 128:113, see also: 20:64

O shipmates come gather and join in my ditty 35:20, 73:183

O Sing a Song of Bethlehem 86:48

Oh, sing for me tonight those merry songs we sang 73:288

O sinne' man how can you stan' 89:54

O sinner man, where are you going to run to? 134:82, 157:60, see also: 148:336

Oh sinner man, where you gonna run to? 148:336, see also: 134:82, 157:60

O sister Phoebe, how merry were we 27:88, 232:82

Oh, slow up, dogies, quit roaming around 69:23, 71:91, 129:94, 159:60, 225:21, see also: Night Herding Song

Oh, slow up, dogies, quit roving around 129:94, 239:30, see also: Night Herding Song

O slumber, slumber softly, dear Jesus 184:54

Oh, soldier, soldier, will you marry me 62:118, 142, 148:348, see also: Soldier, Soldier, Won't You Marry Me

Oh, soldier, won't you marry marry me 79:32, see also: Soldier, Soldier, Won't You Marry Me

O some tell me that a nigger won't steal 24:906

Oh! stand the storm, it won't be long 55:273

O Star O'er Bethlehem Shining/O Gwiazdo Betlejemska 54:208

Oh, Stormy's dead an' gone to rest 33:34, see also: 24:834

Oh Susanna 22:40, 25:107, 46:205, 55:505, 126:89, 157:94, 205:113, 227:35, 230:46, 283:38

Oh Susanna (parody) 66:46

O sweet sir, for your courtesie, when ye come by the Bass 182:21

O Tannenbaum 21:196, 54:138, 92:179, 129:51, 148:263, 197:118, 241:164, 279:68

O tell me, when was Jesus born? 190:119

O tell us, where are you going? 68:39

Oh, the bear went over the mountain 75:12, see also: 17:16, 147:14, 290:72, 292:110

O the big ship's asailing on the Allee Allee-o 135:54, 289:183, see also: 39:46, 63:37, 165:113, 291:16

O the big ship's a-sailing through the Allee Allee O 39:46, see also: Allee Allee-O

Oh the boll weevil is a little black bug 226:8, 274:38, see also: Boll Weevil

Oh, the Butterflies Are Flying 172:59, 174:45

Oh, the candidate's a dodger 64:150, see also: 24:875

O the cap'n told John Henry 158:260, see also: John Henry

Oh, the court of King Carraticus is just passing by 290:10

Oh, the cowboy's life is the life of the wind 61:236, see also: 60:36, 146:53, 159:15, 159:281

Oh, the cuckoo is a pretty bird 292:130, see also: 27:52, 59:23, 157:77, 217:60

Oh, the Devil in hell they say he was chained 159:317, see also: 61:80

Oh, the farmer comes to town with his wagon broken down 64:96, see also: 24:879, 226:282, 230:57, 239:42

O the fragrance of the flow'rs with their beauty all about 87:40

"Oh! the French are on the way" Says the Shan Van Vocht 42:592

Oh, the girls grow tall in Kansas 61:96, see also: 61:97

Oh, the grand old Duke of York 165:193, see also: Noble Duke of York

Oh, the hog-eye man is the man for me 24:836, see also: 226:410

O, the Hog-eye men are all the go 226:410, see also: 24:836

Oh, the Horse Went Around 290:30

Oh, the noble Duke of York 39:10, 55:520, 70:30, 126:103, 128:107, 130:63, 135:90, 289:184, see also: 26:25, 63:37, 165:193

O the old ark's a-movering, a-movering, a-movering 83:475, see also: 148:288

Oh, the old bell'd yoe 'n the little speckled wether 234:60

Oh, the old gray mare, she ain't what she used to be 226:102, see also: 292:22

O the organ grinder man 83:487

Oh, the prairie dogs are screaming 159:70

O the Rock Island Line, it's a mighty good road 130:64, see also: 35:52, 129:90, 148:314, 274:12

O the shamrock and the heather we love full dear 262:75

Oh, the shamrocks are green as the greenest I've seen 97:unpaged

O the slaves of Job were playing Kachanga 100:38

Oh, the smartest clipper you can find 239:18

O, the summer time is coming 134:100

Oh the times are hard and the wages low 226:412

Oh, the water is wide 148:406

Oh, the whole, long, weary night I lay awake and wept 67:4

Oh, the wind blow east (Whoo-oo) 130:95, 232:66

Oh the world is big and the world is small 107:32

O there came a man to our town 111:44, 162:36, 175:130, 188:104, 189:28, 289:96

Oh! There once was a swagman camped in a Billabong 186, see also: 22:216, 25:86, 72:154

Oh, there was a little girl, and she had a little curl 285:20

Oh, there was a man with a double chin 62:92

Oh, there was a moanish lady 226:11

O there was an old soldier 226:432

Oh, they built the ship Titanic to sail the ocean blue 290:153, see also: 226:254

Oh they call me hanging Johnny 98:24

Oh, those bones, oh, those bones 197:94, see also: 89:42, 226:470, 290:40

Oh, those West Virginia Hills 64:56

O Thou Joyful Day/O Sanctissima 22:253, 241:120

O thou joyful, O thou blessed 86:31, see also: 54:136

Oh, thou most adored 89:223

Oh Thou Zane/Al Ya Zane 89:207

Oh, Three Pega/O, Tres Pega 89:92

Oh times is hard and wages low 98:40

Oh, Tommy's gone! What shall I do? 157:41, see also: 37:157, 128:22

O, Tres Pega/Oh, Three Pega 89:92

O 'twas on a bright mornin' in summer 226:40

O two old men a-skating away 39:48, see also: 126:87

O', walk together children, don't you get weary 31:28

Oh, Watch the Stars 233:13

Oh, watch the stars see how they run 233:13

Oh, we are the men of the Steelworkers' Union 64:92

Oh, We Are Two Musicians 245:51

Oh, we came on the Sloop John B. 148:344, see also: 226:22

Oh, we can play on the big bass drum 165:184

Oh, we come on the sloop John B. 226:22, see also: 148:344

Oh, we don't have to march like the infantry 290:60

Oh, Weep Mine Eyes/Klahpsete 89:194

Oh, weep, oh, weep mine eyes 89:194

Oh, we'll all join hands and we'll walk around the ring 177:75

Oh, we'll all sing glory to the mountain 141:38

Oh we're comin' round the mountain one by one 178:40

Oh, we're up in the morning before break of day 225:24, see also: 61:208, 159:42, 262:64

Oh, we're up in the morning ere breaking of day 159:42, see also: 61:208, 225:24, 262:64

Oh, were you ever in Rio Grande? 176:110, see also: 22:140, 78:9, 239:14

O Wert Thou in the Cauld Blast 262:92

O What a Beautiful City 31:33, 230:81

Oh, What a Beautiful Mornin' 218:16

Oh, What a Charming City 157:102

Oh, what a dreary place this was when first the Mormons found it 61:78

Oh, what did Tenna-see, boys, what did Tenna-see? 26:79

Oh, what do you do at home, Papa Small 154:38

Oh, what has caused this great commotion 157:112

Oh, What Have You Got For Dinner, Mrs. Bond? 188:116, see also: 62:52, 175:72, 292:154

Oh, what have you got there for dinner, Mistress Bond? 175:72, 292:154, see also: 62:52, 188:116

Oh, what is that I see yonder coming 64:34

Oh what shall we have for dinner Mistress Bond 62:52, see also: 175:72, 188:116, 292:154

Oh, what was your name in the states? 21:307, 24:861, 226:106

O, what would you do if you married a sailor? 212:28

Oh, when I was a little boy, and so my mother told me 134:69, see also: Haul Away, Joe

Oh, when I was a little boy I lived by myself 129:38, see also: Swapping Song

O When, O When?/El Cuando 22:122

Oh, when the saints go marching in 25:104, 72:87, 148:416, 157:148, 205:377

O when will May be coming 85:107

Oh where, and oh where is your Highland laddie gone? 22:60, see also: 205:66

Oh! where are the merry, merry little men 191:12

Oh, where are you going, my pretty little maid? 36:35, *see also:* Where Are You Going to, My Pretty Maid?

"Oh, where are you going?" said Milder to Malder 64:175

Oh, where are you going? To Scarb'ro Fair 22:26, *see also:* 35:98, 37:112

Oh, where have you been, Billy Boy, Billy Boy 17:66, 36:28, 38, 66:56, 71:38, 135:42, 205:53, 283:52, *see also:* 27:22, 197:22

Oh, where have you been, little ghost, little ghost 197:95

O where have you been so long 89:169

Oh Where, Oh Where Has My Little Dog Gone? 17:43, *see also:* 26:18, 285:92, 292:70

Oh where, please tell me where is your highland laddie gone? 205:66, *see also:* 22:60

Oh, where were you last evening, my son 89:156, *see also:* 157:71, 232:140

Oh whisky is the life of man 98:25, *see also:* 21:246, 226:403

Oh, Whistle and I'll Come to You, My Lad! 182:53

Oh, who are the people in your neighborhood 206:43

O, who will drive the chariot when she comes? 226:373

O who will shoe my fair foot 226:99, *see also:* 110:24, 226:98, 230:65

Oh, who will shoe my little feet, feet, feet? 110:24, *see also:* 226:98, 226:99, 230:65

O, who will shoe your pretty little foot 226:98, *see also:* 110:24, 226:99, 230:65

Oh, why don't I work like other men do? 22:102, 24:882, *see also:* 64:126, 226:184, 239:54

Oh, why don' you work like other men do? 226:184, 239:54, *see also:* 22:102, 24:882, 64:126

O Wie Wohl Ist's Mir Am Abend/O, How Lovely Is the Evening 241:232

Oh, will you wear white, oh my dear, oh my dear 20:40, 257, *see also:* Jennie Jenkins

O Willie Dear 212:33

Oh, Windy Bill was a Texas boy 60:55, *see also:* 61:204, 146:69, 159:113

Oh, wolves are howling, howling, howling 234:79

O woman passing by 236:11

Oh won't you come a waltzing with me? 296:32

Oh, won't you come with me to my father's house 25:119

Oh, Won't You Sit Down? 262:71, 290:84, *see also:* Set Down, Servant

Oh, won't you sit down? Lawd, I can't sit down 22:312, 148:284, 262:71, 290:84, *see also:* 83:465, 128:26, 158:362

Oh, won't you sit down, Sister? 128:26, *see also:* Set Down, Servant

O Worship the King 25:115, 86:16

O Worship the Lord 86:189

Oh, yes I am a Southern girl, and glory in the name 73:248

Oh yesterday at morning 114:72

Oh, You Can't Get to Heaven 147:46, 290:93

Oh, you can't get to heaven in a rocking chair 147:46, 290:93

Oh, you know Joe Silovatsky 24:865

Oh, you must answer my questions nine 27:214, 37:110, 134:85

Oh, you push the damper in 26:34, 253:90

Ohlee ahgahpoon to Sahvahtoh 148:84

Oi Betlehem/O Bethlehem 54:274

Oi no noi nong oeui 89:223

Oj Pastiri/Hear, O Shepherds 241:70

Oki no kamomeini 49:27

Okino Kamomeini/To the Sea Gull Offshore 49:27

Oklahoma 218:54

Ol' Dan Tucker 137, *see also:* Old Dan Tucker

Ol' Rattler 130:32

Ol' Texas 21:108, *see also:* 61:182, 69:21, 159:57, 277:35

Old Abe Lincoln 21:140, 27:12, 226:168

Old Abe Lincoln came out of the wilderness 21:140, 226:168, *see also:* 27:12

Old Abe Lincoln, he came out of the wilderness 27:12, *see also:* 21:140, 226:168

Old Adam 62:102, 129:20, 226:339

Old Akela Had a Pack 26:48

The Old Ark's A-Moverin' 83:475, 148:288

Old Aunt Dinah went to town 234:47

Old Aunt Kate 232:139

Old Aunt Kate she bake a cake 232:139

Old Bald Eagle 135:72

Old bald eagle sail around 135:72

Old Bangum and the Bear 37:126

Old Bell'd Yoe 234:60

Old Bill the Rolling Pin 109:209

Old Blue 158:24, 258, 261:58, 277:147, 289:55, 292:72, *see also:* 234:30

Old Brass Wagon 33:98, 55:506, 226:159

Old Chairs To Mend! 111:58, *see also:* Chairs to Mend

The Old Chariot 66:148, *see also:* 226:196

The Old Chisholm Trail 21:219, 24:851, 25:72, 60:4, 61:210, 61:211, 64:122, 146:20, 146:23, 158:200, 158:202, 225:14, *see also:* 159:37

Old Christmas 233:80

Old Colony Times 21:252, 157:30

The Old Cow Died   234:56, 292:44, *see also:* 107:18, 232:112, 292:20
The Old Cowboy   61:299, 159:93
Old Cromwell   71:93, *see also:* Old Grumbler
Old Cromwell was an angry man   71:93, *see also:* Old Grumbler
Old Dan Tucker   21:304, 33:82, 66:66, 137, 157:84, 158:92, 230:52, *see also:* 137
Old Danish Toast   83:468
Old Diamond Joe was a rich old jay   159:65
Old Doctor Wango Tango   111:68
Old Dog Tray   292:67
Old England Forty Years Ago   240:214
The Old Family Toothbrush   290:145
Old Farmer Grumble   110:28, *see also:* Old Grumbler
Old Farmer John came walking home one summer afternoon   71:94
Old Folks At Home   22:86, 127:99, *see also:* 230:83
Old Fox   234:32, *see also:* Fox Went Out On a Chilly Night
Old fox walked out one moonshiny night   234:32, *see also:* Fox Went Out On a Chilly Night
Old Gray Goose   37:176, 135:61, *see also:* Go Tell Aunt Rhody
The Old Gray Mare   226:102, 292:22
Old Grey Goose   188:176, *see also:* Go Tell Aunt Rhody
The old Grey Hearse goes rolling by   226:44, *see also:* 62:109, 290:178
The Old Grey Hen/La Poulette Grise   289:30
Old Grimes   66:68
Old Ground Hog   234:22
Old Grumbler   27:115, *see also:* 62:138, 71:93, 79:57, 110:28, 128:120, 213:56
Old Grumbler swore by the shirt he wore   27:115, *see also:* Old Grumbler
The Old Hen Cackled and the Rooster Laid the Egg   234:42
The old hen she cackled, she cackled in the loft   234:42
Old Highland Cradle Song/Oh, Can Ye Sew Cushions?   71:82, 78:29, *see also:* 27:110, 125:68
The Old Home Guard   275:79, 276:66
Old Horse   290:220
Old Howard   274:44, *see also:* 232:132
Old Hundredth   21:312, 22:287, 45:7, 86:213, 148:74, 157:12, 161:11
Old Hungarian Round   71:111, 72:171
Old Joe Clark   20:78, 24:814, 134:46, 158:86, 230:35, 232:84, 261:60
Old Joe Clark, the preacher's son   24:893, *see also:* Old Joe Clark

Old Joe Clarke he had a dog   232:85, *see also:* Old Joe Clark
Old Joe Clarke he had a house   261:60, *see also:* Old Joe Clark
Old Joe Digger, Sam and David   24:893, 158:26, *see also:* 213:68, 289:46, 292:98
Old King Cole (version I)   17:28, 55:261, 71:96, 162:87, 175:142, 188:114, 283:34, 285:53
Old King Cole (version II)   27:122
Old King Cole was a merry old soul   17:28, 55:261, 71:96, 162:87, 175:142, 188:114, 283:34, 285:53
Old King Twine   62:76
Old Lady Goose   234:40
Old lady goose, done turned her loose   234:40
Old Lady Mac   141:80
Old Lady Mitchell/La Mère Michel   217:57
Old lady Mitchell has lost her cat   217:57
Old Ma Bell   64:42
Old MacDonald Had a Farm   4, 17:148, 26:20, 55:262, 75:56, 81, 199, 283:12, 291:30
The Old Maid and the Burglar Bold   84:12
The Old Maid's Lament   36:96
The Old Man Clothed in Leather   188:64, *see also:* 17:15, 18:42, 111:73, 177:89, 289:104
The Old Man in Leather   289:104, *see also:* Old Man Clothed in Leather
The Old Man in the Woods   62:138, 128:120, 213:56, *see also:* 27:115, 71:93, 79:57, 110:28
Old man Sargent, sitting at the desk   64:74
Old man went out to plow, Rigby Johnson Chandler   61:26
Old Mister Rabbit   232:98
Old Mister Rabbit, you've got a mighty habit   232:98
Old Molly Hare   232:99, 289:44, 292:91
Old Molly Hare, What you doing there?   232:99, 289:44, *see also:* 292:91
Old Mother Goose   17:44
Old Mother Goose, when she wanted to wander   17:44
Old Mother Hubbard   175:22, 285:95
Old Mother Hubbard went to the cupboard (parody)   25:24, 26:38, 175:22, 290:102
An old mother piggie had three little pigs   62:40, *see also:* 130:110, 289:50, 292:57
The Old Navy   290:60
Old Noah, he built himself an ark   148:296, 292:206, *see also:* 22:308, 57, 290:42
Old Noah built himself an ark   57, 290:42, *see also:* 22:308, 148:296, 292:206
Old Noah once he built the ark   22:308, *see also:* 57, 148:296, 290:42, 292:206

The Old Oaken Bucket   21:178
The Old Old Man   91:43
Old Paint (version I)   61:227, *see also:* Goodbye, Old Paint
Old Paint (version II)   158:216, *see also:* I Ride an Old Paint
Old Provençal Christmas Song   209:125
Old Roger   39:54, 63:27, 129:112, 135:86, 165:185, 168:154, 213:32, *see also:* 176:12
Old Roger is dead and he lies in his grave 63:27, *see also:* Old Roger
Old Roger is dead and lies in his grave 39:54, 129:112, 135:86, 165:185, 168:154, 213:32, *see also:* 63:27, 176:12
Old Rosin the Beau   61:10, 157:50, 159:278
The Old Rugged Cross   45:46
Old Salt River   37:207
The Old Scout's Lament   159:354
Old Seth Coon   62:92
The Old Settler's Song   158:184
The Old Shepherd   67:53
Old Ship of Zion   21:262, *see also:* 35:58
Old Smokie   33:146, *see also:* On Top of Old Smoky
Old Smoky   158:60, *see also:* On Top of Old Smoky
The Old Soap-Gourd   213:48
The Old Soldier   62:91
The Old Soldiers of the King   27:166, 28:89, *see also:* 240:89
The Old Sow   234:52
The Old Sow Song   84:56
The Old Spotted Cow   35:78
Old Stewball, uh huh, was a red horse, uh huh 234:68, *see also:* 61:18, 61:20
Old Stormy was a fine old man 24:834, *see also:* 33:34
Old Thompson had a big gray mule 84:33
Old Thompson's Mule   84:33
The Old-Time Cowboy   159:191
Old-Time Religion   157:165
The Old Woman   85:105 *(In my young days)*
Old Woman   20:26, 46:223, 83:470, *see also:* Deaf Woman's Courtship *(Old woman, old woman, will you do my carding?)*
The Old Woman All Skin and Bones 37:186, 134:86, *see also:* 213:76, 290:171
The Old Woman and Her Pig   129:27, 178:16, 292:60, *see also:* 79:23, 110:42, 135:56, 213:52, 232:102, 234:50
The Old Woman and the Pedlar   68:14, 79:41, 188:132, *see also:* 17:64, 27:58, 259
Old Woman and the Pig   213:52, *see also:* Old Woman and Her Pig
The Old Woman of Norwich   175:164
Old woman, old woman, are you fond of smoking? 69:19, 129:100, 262:119, *see also:* Deaf Woman's Courtship

Old woman, old woman, are you fond of walking? 20:26, *see also:* Deaf Woman's Courtship
Old woman, old woman will you do my carding? 46:223, *see also:* Deaf Woman's Courtship
Old woman, old woman, will you do my washing? 69:19, 290:75, *see also:* Deaf Woman's Courtship
Old woman, old woman, will you go a-shearing? 37:136, 213:72, *see also:* Deaf Woman's Courtship
Old woman, old woman, won't you card my wool for me? 83:470, *see also:* Deaf Woman's Courtship
The Old Woman Taught Wisdom   240:40, *see also:* 28:15, 273:58, 289:133
Old Woman Tossed Up In a Basket 175:154, *see also:* 17:142, 18:20, 188:166, 285:30, 289:78
The Old Woman Tossed Up In a Blanket 188:166, *see also:* Old Woman Tossed Up In a Basket
The old year now away is fled   128:68, 210:68, 220:42
The old year now does pass away   27:4
Old Zip Coon   157:80
Ole Clo'   71:102
The Ole Grey Goose   21:294, 157:96
Olilili/Lullaby   163:100
Oliver Cromwell   176:12, *see also:* Old Roger
Oliver Cromwell lay buried and dead 176:12, *see also:* Old Roger
Omega   273:158, *see also:* 45:31, 86:15, 161:85
On a bright and summer's morning 234:34, 292:80
On a bright summer's evening I rambled 35:86
On a bright summer's morning the day was a-dawning 35:92
On a brightly lighted stage, Magicians stand and bow 166:58
On a Dog Sled   207:71
On a hill far away stood an old rugged cross 45:46
On a Monday mornin' it began to rain 226:364
On a Monday morning, sunny Monday morning 168:59, 268:61
On a Mountain   63:66, *see also:* 24:804, 39:20, 135:70
On a mountain stands a lady   63:66, *see also:* 24:804, 39:20, 135:70
On a Rainy Day   162:31
On a Summer Day   154:6
On a summer's day while the waves were rippling 226:146

On a Sunday morn, sat a maid forlorn
157:209, 205:322

On a Sunday mornin' it begins to rain
158:264, *see also:* Casey Jones

On a Suskehanna raft I come down the bay
157:83

On a tree by a river a little tomtit sang
252:48

On a Winter Morning 86:40

On Breaking the Piñata/Al Quebrar La
Piñata 295:79

On business to market 36:62

On Calvert's plains new faction reigns
28:33

On Children's Day We Sweetly Sing
86:185

On Christmas Day in seventy-six 28:86,
240:121

On Christmas Day in the Morning
138:unpaged, 197:121, *see also:* 220:64

On Christmas Night 54:40, *see also:* 210:56

On Christmas Night All Christians Sing
210:56, *see also:* 54:40

On Christmas night, true Christians sing
54:40, *see also:* 210:56

On December five and twenty 54:258, *see
also:* Fum, Fum, Fum

*On December twenty-fifth, sing foom,
foom, foom!* 241:80, *see also:* Fum, Fum,
Fum

*On December twenty-fifth, sing fum, fum,
fum* 241:80, *see also:* Fum, Fum, Fum

On foot I gaily take my way 71:45, *see also:*
72:135

On His Bronco the Gay Caballero 262:87

On homeward pinion the bird flies forth
89:273

On Ilkla Moor Baht Hat 134:107

On Independence 240:84, *see also:* 28:68

On Jordan's Bank the Baptist's Cry 86:28

On Jordan's stormy banks I stand 21:256,
157:58, 158:350

On Memorial Day 207:118

On Monday, on Monday 89:147

On Monday, when the sun is hot 172:31

On mules we find two legs behind 26:19,
289:148, 292:36

On My Honor 25:63

*On my honor I'll do my best to do my duty
to God* 25:63

On New Year's Day, Sz Bbei has to work
49:16

On one summer's day sun was shinin' fine
205:272, *see also:* 21:88, 148:42, 170:44

On our honor we've been true 26:67

On Parade 207:80

On passing the stream of Santa Clara
295:68

On Red River Shore 61:161, *see also:*
37:152, 159:181

On, Roll On 128:74, *see also:* 89:34

On, roll on, my ball, roll on 89:34, 128:74

On Shiloh's dark and bloody ground
73:200

On Springfield Mountain 24:828, *see also:*
21:254, 72:91, 157:49, 158:28, 290:51,
292:114

On Springfield mountain, there did dwell
21:254, 24:828, 72:91, 157:49, 158:28,
290:51, 292:114

On That Christmas Day Morn 210:116

On the Banks of the Wabash 205:254, *see
also:* 157:197

On the Banks of the Wabash, Far Away
157:197, *see also:* 205:254

On the Beach 207:127

On the Bridge at Avignon/Sur le Pont d'A-
vignon 78:39, 148:364, 165:199, 189:44,
217:57, *see also:* 14:372, 168:162, 188:76

On the Bridge of Avignon/Sur le Pont D'A-
vignon 14:372, 168:162, 188:76 *see also:*
On the Bridge at Avignon

On the bridge, on the bridge 188:76,
189:44, *see also:* On the Bridge at
Avignon

On the bridge one day a rook 85:235

On the Charlie So Long 226:365

On the Corner 241:228

*On the Double Circle Range where the grass
grows green* 61:32, *see also:* 61:30

On the Farm 207:106

On the first day of Christmas 22:248,
54:36, 87:91, 92:183, 113, 121, 148:400,
233:72, 241:30, 264:66, 290:26, 292:160,
see also: Twelve Days of Christmas

On the First Thanksgiving Day 148:290,
197:108

On the green bank stands a little birch tree
78:69

On the Hill 20:94

On the hill above is my father's house
262:48

On the hill there stands a lady 20:94

On the hill there stands an oak tree 262:72

On the Lake of the Poncho Plains 146:46

On the Line 64:30

On the mountain where breezes sigh
241:86, *see also:* 279:74

On the mountain wind bloweth wild
279:74, *see also:* 221:86

On the nights of (Christmas) parties
295:79

*On the ninth day of November at the dawn-
ing in the sky* 27:168, 28:17

On the plain the tepees stand 166:14

On the Road/Kouh Beh Kouh 89:201

On the road the mountainside 89:201
On the Road to California 61:22
On the roadway to the city 54:293
On the swaying limb of a rubber tree 84:19
On the Trail to Idaho 159:24
On the Train 227:21
On the twenty-fifth of December, Fum, fum, fum 125:121, see also: Fum, Fum, Fum
On this bright and happy day a morning song we sing to you 162:56
On this day, we do remember 207:118
On This Street/Nesta Rua 266:14
On To the Morgue 226:199, 290:185
On to War/Anio 89:32
On Tombigbee River so bright I was born 66:117
On Top of Old Smoky 22:42, 148:292, 205:92, 230:60, see also: 33:146, 158:60
On Top of Spaghetti 75:58, 76, 118:23, 147:29
On twenty-fifth of December—fum, fum, fum 295:84, see also: Fum, Fum, Fum
On yonder hill there stands a creature 148:282
Once/Pa'am Akhat 70:16, 266:35
Once a boy beheld a rose 85:141
Once a jolly swagman sat beside the billabong 22:216, 25:86, 72:154, see also: 186
Once a lad went walking 70:16, 266:35
Once a lady loved a pig, "Honey," said she 46:226, see also: 175:76
Once a little titmouse lived far beyond the sea 79:83
Once a rat who loved the city 17:96
Once Again Has Come My Birthday 86:153
Once an Austrian Went Yodeling 290:22
Once I had a pretty little girl 292:124
Once I had a sniffly cold and got a little hoarse 97:unpaged
Once I had an old gray mule 110:32, see also: 208:80
Once I Saw A Little Bird 111:49, 285:99, see also: 18:32
Once I thought this sailor boy ought to have a wife 205:371
Once I Wandered in a Golden Meadow 261:14
Once in Royal David's City 65:101, 86:32, 189:72, 210:55, 241:186, 242:unpaged, 284:111
Once in the dear dead days beyond recall 66:30, 205:216
Once More a Lumb'ring Go 158:166
Once on a time there lived a man 22:56
Once on a time there were four little birds 41:12

Once There Was/Era una Vez 89:62, 216:50, see also: 217:14
Once there was a little kitty 17:146, 62:47, 129:26, see also: 130:108
Once there was a tiny little sailboat 89:62, see also: 216:50, 217:14
Once there was an elephant who tried to use the telephant 44:64
Once there were some children in the kitchen 41:9
Once There Were Three Fishermen 148:294, see also: 26:13, 63:98, 290:50
Once three little kittens they lost their mittens 17:12, see also: 188:90, 283:18, 285:29, 292:64
Once to Bethl'hem shepherds came 86:40
Once to Every Man and Nation 45:63, 262:161
Once Upon a Dream 275:64, 276:41
Once Upon a Hillside 86:53
Once upon a time there was a dragon bold 166:12
Once upon a time there were three little foxes 172:132
Once was a sow who had three little piggies 292:57, see also: 130:110, 289:50
Once when the sheriff of Nottingham was plagued sore with grief 164:76
Once You Git the Habit 159:289
One and one are two 167:46
One and two and three and four 16:55
1 & 2 & 3 Clap, clap 178:45
One battle is won, but the fight's just begun 64:78
One Bottle of Pop 290:202
One cannot walk to the horizon 49:13
One Cold and Frosty Morning 232:70
One dark night when we were all in bed 203, see also: 21:30, 126:57, 157:191
One day as I rambled down by the seashore 230:29
One day as I wandered 64:136
One day down in some lonesome grove 157:78
One day I thought I'd have some fun 159:119, 226:274, see also: 61:198, 277:67
One day I was sitting in my father's hall 232:87
One Day I Went A-Walking/Ich Ging Emol Spaziere 89:144
One day Joseph, resting, the Child by his side 54:264
One day, one day Congo tay, I went away, Congo tay 130:82
One day one day I was a-walkin' along 107:52
One day when I was sailing 290:168
One day when I went visiting, a little lamb was there 245:40

One dream in my heart, one love to be living for 218:147

One duck on a pond 290:197

One Elephant Went Out to Play 178:14

One evening, as I roamed ashore from my gallant brigantine 36:46

One evening, as the sun went down 21:112, 24:884, 158:278, 230:66

One evening last June as I rambled 157:42

One-Eyed Riley 24:838

One Fine October Morning 112:34

One Finger Keep Moving 253:104, *see also:* 14:352, 26:37

One Finger, One Thumb 26:37, *see also:* 14:352, 253:104

One finger, one thumb keep moving 14:352, *see also:* 26:37, 253:104

One finger, one thumb, one hand, keep moving 26:37, *see also:* 14:352, 253:104

One Friday morn when we set sail 117:unpaged, *see also:* 71:78, 72:72, 290:160

One goblin, two goblins, three little goblins 197:96

One grasshopper jumped right over the other grasshopper's back 46:222

One Happy Swede 64:110

100 Psalm Tune New 273:132

148th Psalm 273:126

One is for the one night 286:86

One Is God 192

One it's stricking, two it's striking 288:22

One lantern, two lanterns, three jack-o-lanterns 197:96

One little bell said "do, do" 162:67

One Little Brown Bird 68:17

One little brown bird, up and up he flew 68:17

One Little Elephant Balancing 63:42

One little kitty drinks her milk 162:86

One little owl said, "Whoo, whoo" 162:10

One little raindrop riding on a cloud 162:29

One little, two little, three little Indians 17:144, 75:74

One Man Shall Mow My Meadow 132:unpaged

One misty, moisty morning 17:15, 18:42, 111:73, 177:89, 188:64, 289:104

One More Day 22:158

One More River 22:308, 148:296, 290:42, 292:206, *see also:* 57

One Morning I Rose/Ka Tam Ma Wui 89:264

One Morning in May 226:136

One morning, one morning, one morning in May 226:136

One night when we were getting dry 74:11

One of these mornings bright and fair 64:40

One of These Things 206:40

One of these things is not like the others 206:40

One of us has gone away 168:56

One, One, One 296:12

One, one, one, my lady's having fun 296:12

One plus one minus one is one 217:unpaged

One Saw, Two Saw 109:30

One snowy day "Look!" said John 7:12

One song my comrades, ere we go 262:121

One springtime I thought just fer fun 277:67, *see also:* 61:198, 159:121, 226:274

One Star Above All Stars 244:146

One star above all stars shone down from heav'n afar 244:146

One Starlit Night/Sarong Bangui 208:55

One Sunday mornin', Lawd, Lawd, Lawd 134:89, *see also:* Grey Goose

One time I wished that a lion would come 219:14

One, Two, Buckle My Shoe 175:38

One Two Three 162:40

One, Two, Three Alairy 24:796, *see also:* 63:74

One, Two, Three, Alary 63:74, *see also:* 24:796

One, Two, Three, and Around We Go! 204:27

One, Two, Three, Four, Five 107:22, 175:114

One, two, three, four, five 206:31

1 2 3 4 5 6 7 8 9, Time to be in school 41:18

One, two, three, owls in a tree 162:40

One Was Johnny 235:35

One Wide River 57, *see also:* 22:308, 148:296, 290:42, 292:206

One-ry, Two-ry 109:28

Onery, twory, dickery seven 109:28

One's a One and all alone and that shall never be-uh 233:66, *see also:* Green Grow the Rushes, Ho!

Onkel Jakob, Onkel Jakob 148:102, 293:43

Only a Cowboy 159:116

Only a Manger Bed/Mizerna Cicha 54:214

Only One More Day 290:222

Ons Is Geboren Een Kindekin/Today We Welcome a Tiny Child 54:184

Onward, Christian Soldiers 25:110, 161:113

Oo-De-Lally 276:76

Oo-oo-oh, lil' man, go get yo' pan 226:459

Oo oo oo oo oo 74:21

Ooh, wah doo, ooh wah doo bee yoo 206:60

Ooo Ooo the wind is singing a song to you 162:33

Open, Open/Hiraita, Hiraita 16:47, 286:36

Open the Gates As High As the Sky 283:31

Open the Window 212:18

Open up the manger shutters 67:18

Ora No Omboko 16:37

Oranges and Lemons/Naranjas y Limas 295:82

Oranges and Lemons 17:58, 63:31, 165:198, 175:94, 188:78, 189:38, 227:17, see also: 295:82

Oranges and lemons, say the bells of St. Clements 17:58, 63:31, 165:198, 175:94, 188:78, 189:38, 227:17, see also: 295:82

Oranges Sweet 114:81

Oranges sweet and some lemon slices 114:81

The ore is waiting in the tubs 64:134, see also: 117:unpaged

The Organ Grinder Man 83:487

Oriole's nest is a hush-a-by swing 207:91

Orleans, Beaugency, Notre Dame de Clery 71:101, 72:165, 293:38

Oro, My Little Boat 245:76

Oro, my little boat that rests in the bay 245:76

The Orphan Girl 226:319

Otete tsunaide nomichio yukeba 286:60

The other day by sleep oppressed as I a mossy hillock pressed 273:116

Others Are Special 204:29

Ou vas tu donc, mon ami Colin? 262:147

Ouliastai/The Waters of Ouliastai 89:230

Ouma/Mother Horse and Colt 286:16

Our Beautiful Earth 86:149

Our Blessed Lady's Lullaby 220:44

Our boys will shine tonite, our boys will shine 25:122

Our Cabana Song 69:9

Our camp fires shone bright on the mountain 73:216

Our Chalet Song 69:8, 71:15, 72:38

Our Comrade Has Fallen 73:206

Our Cookie Jar 207:11

Our Dog 149:12

Our Father 155:14

Our Father in Heaven above us 25:55

Our Father who art in heav'n 155:14

Our Father, You Have Given Me 86:148

Our fathers dear fought for our liberty 24:881

Our Flag 207:42

Our flag is proudly floating 73:38

Our flag is unfurl'd and our arms flash bright 73:109

Our Gallant Ship 135:79, see also: 62:98, 291:73

Our garden grows along the wall 207:99

Our Great Leader/Shellila Shek 89:280

Our hands are ears of corn 245:64

Our honored guests are here 26:11

Our horse fell down the well around behind the stable 128:124, 226:51

Our House 149:4

Our house has a chimney 149:4

Our Israel may say and that truly 21:313

Our Jimmy has gone to live in a tent 73:133

Our knapsacks sling, and blithely sing 73:220

Our Legs 204:23

Our little (Peter) is (six) today 245:107

Our little yellow bird has a very sweet song 41:20

Our oats they are hoed, and our barley's reap'd 189:122

Our paddles keen and bright 25:28

Our school has a new band 177:79

Our Village Deacon/Milínkej Pan Děkan 89:184

Our Yard 149:8

Out from the lands of Orient was the donkey divinely sent 292:31

Out in Our Meadow/Uti Var Hage 262:39

Out in our meadow grow blueberries sweet 262:39

Out in the Country 154:16

Out in the lonely forest 207:30

Out in the meadow I walked one day 207:29

Out in the Open Air 85:165

Out in the West you have oft heard it said 61:192

Out of My Dreams 218:50

Out of my dreams and into your arms I long to fly 218:50

Out of my window looking in the night 72:96

Out of Work 157:172

Out of work without a penny 157:172

Out on a ranch way out West 159:287

Out, Out, Out 78:55

Ovai e? 89:300

Over and Under 296:36

Over and under and over and under 296:36

Over hill, over dale, we have hit the dusty trail 197:103

Over hill, over dale, we will hit the greenwood trail 25:57

Over in the Meadow 17:21, 116, 139, 178:32, 289:70, see also: 129:14

Over the Hills and Far Away 17:45, 175:62, 188:36, 189:54, see also: 111:38

Over the hills I went one morn 35:34

Over the River and Through the Woods 17:56, 40, 148:298, 197:106

Over the River to Feed My Sheep 213:28, see also: 24:813, 66:76, 226:161
Over the Sea in My Boat With Me 227:16
Over the Sea Sails He 154:25
Over the Wall 288:14
Over There 21:293
Over Yonders Ocean 37:170
Overflowing Torrent/Río de Avenida 89:99
The Overlander 89:310
The Owl 18:10
The Owl and the Pussy Cat 112:26
The owl and the pussy cat went to sea 112:26
The Owl Sings 74:21
The owl wide winging through the sky 85:243
The Ox and the Ass 67:34
Ox Driving Song 61:35
Oxen and Sheep/Entre le Boeuf et l'Ane Gris 241:82, see also: 54:100
Oxen and sheep Thy guardian mild 241:82, see also: 54:100
The Oxen Song 21:250
Oxford 240:17
Oye, oye 278:40
The Oyster Fishers' Song 262:140
Ozibane! Ozibane! Ozibane!/O, Dance Like That! 89:284

P

Pa ra poo reh see ta kal leh 169:13, 271:50
Paa Vossevangen 83:490
Pa'am Akhat/Once 70:16, 266:35
Pacific Northwest Girl Scout Regional Song 69:47
The Pack Meet 26:51
Pack up all my care and woe 170:17
Pack Up Your Troubles 25:59
Packages come, Packages go 207:47
The Paddle Song 25:28
Paddle Your Own Canoe 66:40
Paddy Doyle 134:76, see also: 37:150
Paddy O'Doyle 37:150, see also: 134:76
Paddy Works on the Erie 22:150, 158:270, see also: Pat Works on the Railway
Pagtatanim ng Palay/Planting Rice 70:12, see also: Planting Rice
Pahupahu/Who Is Knocking? 87:19
The Painter Elves 7:32
A pair of cowboy boots 207:121
Paisteen Fionn 42:598
Panhandle Cob 159:105
Papa, les Petits Bateaux/Papa, the Little Boats 217:45

Papa Quelele has died 262:118
Papa, the Little Boats/Papa, les Petits Bateaux 217:63
A papalas pteechka 289:62
Papa's Going to Buy Me a Mockingbird 93, see also: Hush Little Baby
Paper of Pins 20:42, 62:114, 80, 134:18, 148:300, 290:78, see also: 17:93, 68:22
Para Subir al Cielo/To Get to Heaven 194:26
Parangsai/Blue Bird 49:34
Pardon, I'm the linden tree above the roof I'm talking through 67:21
Parents Are People 260:48
A Parody of the Banks of the Dee 28:77, see also: 240:62, 273:32
Parody Upon a Well-Known Liberty Song 240:45
Parting Song 26:92
Partridge in the pea patch, picking up the peas 128:40
Party Parting 237:unpaged
Pásli Ovce Valaši/Shepherds Watched their Flocks by Night 241:179
Pass the Ball 178:68
Pass the Shoe 20:90, 289:173, see also: 55:250, 70:18, 83:491
Pass Through This Gate/Toryanse 16:61, 286:46
A passing policeman found a little child 21:48
Passing Through 230:31
Passing thro' a cool, green woodland 227:11
Passing Through Lorraine/En Passant par la Lorraine 208:23, see also: 176:66, 217:60
Past Three A Clock 210:58
Pastime With Good Company 189:12
Pastoral Symphony from "Messiah" 210:145
Pastorale from the Christmas Concerto 210:141
Pastores A Belén/Shepherds in Bethlehem 54:290
Pastures Green 276:78
Pat-A-Cake 17:127, 75:60, 175:80, 188:162
Pat-a-cake, pat-a-cake, baker's man 17:127, 75:60, 175:80, 188:162
Pat-A-Pan 54:112, 129:60, see also: 210:80, 220:90, 241:176, 262:50
Pat Works on the Railway 27:40, 64:84, 239:72, 277:115, see also: 22:150, 62:90, 158:270, 226:356, 230:43
Patapan 220:90, 241:176, see also: 54:112, 129:60, 210:80, 262:50
The Patio of My House/El Patio de Mi Casa 295:40

The Patriotic Diggers 27:172, *see also:* 240:205

Patriotic Medley 162:108

Patsy on the Railroad 62:90, *see also:* Pat Works on the Railway

Pattonio 61:184, 159:356, *see also:* 60:82, 128:46, 146:116

Paul and Silas, bound in jail 66:136, 226:448

Paul Jones 35:16, *see also:* 240:132 *(An American frigate from Baltimore came)*

Paul Jones 240:134 *(Of heroes and statesmen)*

Paul Jones' Victory 240:132, *see also:* 35:16

Paul let his chickens run out on the hillside 79:76

Paul On the Hillside 79:76

Paul's Steeple 175:46, *see also:* 17:126, 188:154

Pauvre cigale, le beau temps passe 79:63, *see also:* 243:34

Pauve piti Lolotte a mouin 157:150

The pawkie auld carle came o'er the lea 182:9

The Pawpaw Patch 20:52, 25:20, 39:40, 46:212, 129:116, 189:48, 291:80 *see also:* 33:138, 178:38, 232:172

Peace 69:7, *see also:* 55:255, 262:91

Peace I ask of thee, O River 55:255, 69:7, 262:91

Peace of the River 262:91, *see also:* 55:255, 69:7

The Pealing Bells 71:98, 72:166, *see also:* 62:12

The Peanut Stand 27:211

Peasant Chorus from "Faust" 262:97

Pease Porridge Hot 17:74, 162:89, 285:90, 291:58, *see also:* 175:90

Pease Pudding Hot 175:90, *see also:* 17:74, 162:89, 285:90, 291:58

The Peat-Bog Soldiers 22:212, 64:192

The Pecos Puncher 61:303, 159:95

The Peddler 72:150

Peek-a-Boo 165:20, 291:62

The Peeler's Lament 159:189

"Peep! Peep! Peep!" says the little bird 125:48

Peep Squirrel 109:216, 234:18

Peep, squirrel, dah dah diddle-um 234:18, *see also:* 109:216

Peeping through the knothole 197:33, 226:332, 289:150

Pele now has come to Hawaii, oh! 87:14

Pele Is at Hawaii/Aia O Pele I Hawaii 87:14

Pendant l'été, chante et bondit la sauterelle 243:34, *see also:* 79:65

A penny for a spool of thread 21:302, 55:508, 66:72, *see also:* Pop! Goes the Weasel

A Penny in My Pocket 288:20

A penny in my pocket and I'm going to the store 288:20

The people in the bus go up and down 75:16, *see also:* 147:6, 165:73, 291:46

The People in Your Neighborhood 206:43

The People That in Darkness Walked 123:278

People who play hide and seek must toss for "It" 286:41

People Will Say We're in Love 218:40

The people's flag is deepest red 64:190

Pepito 194:22

Per Spelemann/Pete Fiddler 208:52

Per Spelemann han hadde ei einaste ku 208:52

Perfect Posture 26:43

Perfect posture, perfect posture 26:43

Perhaps I had a wicked childhood 218:249

Perica 262:18

Perry's Victory 240:197

Personent Hodie/The Boys' Carol 220:104

Pesah, Season of Cheer 77:57

Pescator dell'Onda/The Gallant Fisherman 89:158

The Pesky Sarpent 21:254, 157:49, 292:114, *see also:* 24:828, 72:91, 158:28, 290:51

Pete Fiddler/Per Spelemann 208:52

Pete Fiddler, he once owned a very fine cow 208:52

Peter Gray 22:56

Peter Hammers 75:61, 165:166, *see also:* 178:28

Peter hammers with one hammer, one hammer 75:61, 165:166, *see also:* 178:28

Peter Parker 28:66, *see also:* 240:91

Peter Piper 112:61

Petticoat Lane 35:98, *see also:* 22:26, 37:112

Pharaoh's Army Got Drownded 226:476, *see also:* 148:274, 230:78

Philippine Carol 209:96

Philmont Grace 25:57

Philmont Hymn 25:58

A Philosophical Cowboy 61:32, *see also:* 61:30

Phoebe in Her Petticoat 135:57

Phoebe in her petticoat, Phoebe in her gown 135:57

Piango, piango, piango, aye 215:34

Pick a Bale of Cotton 20:38, 21:128, 25:21, 75:62, 107:46, 130:80, 135:106, 148:302, 158:234, 230:54, 232:148, 277:51

Pick It Up 130:18

Picnic Time 207:129

111

Pico Serenico   189:156
Picture a World   206:90
Picture a world where the rivers are clear 206:90
Pie in the Sky   24:886, *see also:* 64:155, 226:222
Pierre   235:43
The Pig in the Parlour   20:50, 63:28, 291:66
Pigeons/Hato Popo   286:17
Piggie Wig and Piggie Wee, hungry pigs as pigs could be 191:28
The Pigs   191:28
Pilgrims   207:44
Pilgrims' Melody   21:313
The Pinery Boy   239:34
A pinery boy's life is a wearisome one 239:34
Pinewood Derby Song   26:75, 26:76
Pink Pajamas   25:41
Pinnal Kolattam/Weaving Dance   89:217
Pinto   159:73
Pio, Pio, Pio   114:38
The Piper Came to Our Town   182:59
Pippen Hill   18:14
Pit, Pat, Pat   245:67
Pit, pat, pat, go the little wet feet 245:67
Pitter, patter, pitter, pat, See the rainbows come 162:27
"Pitter, patter," says the rain 97:unpaged
Pitty Patty Polt   188:158, 189:33
Pity the cowboy all bloody and dead 61:113 *see also:* 61:112, 159:288, 290:170
Pizza, Pizza, Mighty Moe   109:64
The Plains of Illinois   35:62, *see also:* 21:298, 226:162
Planting Cabbage/Savez-vous Planter des Choux?   168:164, 217:53, *see also:* 165:85
Planting Rice/Magtanim   55:262, 64:102, 70:12, 87:54, 169:57, 271:23, *see also:* 286:78
Planting rice is never fun   55:262, 64:102, 70:12, 87:54, 169:57, 271:23, *see also:* 286:78
Plantonio, The Pride of the Plain   60:82, 128:46, 146:116, *see also:* 61:184, 159:356
Play Ball   166:32
Play in the snow   207:77
Play, play on a summer day   154:6
Playing in the Sand   162:77
Playing in the water   207:127
Playing Teacher   207:18
Playmates   162:73
Please call me on the telephone   166:36
Please Don't Think It's Funny   219:32
Please leave us alone   236:23
Please let me pass   114:18
Please pass on through, Please pass on through 16:61

Please skip down to the market, oh   162:63
Please tell me why the stars do shine 148:372
Pledge of Allegiance to the Flag   32:28
Plinker, Plunker   237:unpaged
Pliot Mola Lule/The Apple Tree   89:193
The Ploughboy   262:131
A plumber sallied forth to plumb   84:36
A plump little pig hangs over your bed 19:23
Po' Boy   226:30
Po' Laz'us   24:909, 158:308
Po' Lil Jesus   158:354, 233:52, *see also:* 54:86, 140:60, 190:90
Pochvalen Bud', Jezis Kristus/Praise to Jesus, Our Salvation   54:222
Počtovsky Panáček/The Mailman   289:80
Podkóweczki Dajcie Ognia/Click your Heels   89:182
The Poet   67:45
Poets may sing of their Helicon streams 273:62
The Poisoned Lover/L'Avvelenato   89:156, *see also:* 157:71, 232:140
A Policeman's Lot Is Not a Happy One 252:22
Polish Lullaby/Lulajze Jezuniu   54:220, 241:74, *see also:* 279:122
A Polish Tune   220:85
Politeness   172:135, 173:21
Polly Perkin   135:109
Polly Perkin, hold on to my jerkin   135:109
Polly Put the Kettle On   17:54, 135:40, 175:12, 188:74, 283:59, 285:76
Polly-Wolly-Doodle   46:208, 66:70, 83:507, 205:139, 290:112
Pomme de reinette, pomme d'api   227:9
Pondo Man/Amampondo   163:65
Ponies   162:83
Ponies grazing in the meadow   162:83
The Pony   177:83
Pony Song   41:42, 162:82
Ponycart Driver/Song of the Delhi Tongawallah   262:150
Poor Algy   144:19
A Poor and Carefree Stranger   69:53
Poor and Foreign Stranger   22:34, 35:68, 148:304, *see also:* Wayfaring Stranger
Poor Butterfly   170:35
Poor Howard's dead and gone   274:44, *see also:* 232:132
Poor Jenny   212:42, *see also:* 165:196, 175:134
Poor Jenny sat aweeping   212:42, *see also:* 165:196, 175:134
Poor Jenny Sits A-Weeping   165:196, 175:134, *see also:* 212:42
Poor Kitty Popcorn   226:431
Poor Lazarus   24:909, 158:308

Poor Little Jesus 190:90, 233:52, *see also:* 54:86, 140:60, 158:354
Poor little turtle dove, sitting in a pine 232:179, 277:27, *see also:* 292:124
Poor Lonesome Cowboy 60:76, 61:229, 61:230, 146:112, 159:290, 226:273, *see also:* 225:46
Poor Mister Wind 162:33
Poor Old Crow 232:121, *see also:* Three Ravens
Poor old Howard's dead and gone 232:132, *see also:* 274:44
Poor Paddy Works On the Railway 226:356, *see also:* Pat Works on the Railway
Poor Sz Bbei/Sz Bbei Shang Gung 49:16
Poor Wandering One 252:24
A Poor Wayfaring Stranger 35:68, 148:304, *see also:* I Am a Wayfaring Stranger
The Poor Working Girl 226:195
The poor working girl, may heaven protect her 226:195
Pop! Goes the Weasel 17:136, 20:48, 21:302, 46:209, 55:508, 66:72, 75:64, 135:115, 157:45, 175:36, 200, 205:132, 283:33, 289:100, 292:88
Popcorn Balls 207:69
Popcorn balls are fun to make 207:69
The Popcorn Man 207:90
Popopo! Hato popo! 286:17
Por aquí paso' una pava 89:79, 216:36
Por az mehre Shah asto mara ravan 169:36, 268:51
Por un Beso de Tu Boca/For a Tender Kiss 89:94
Pore Jud 218:44
Pore Jud is daid, Pore Jud Fry is daid 218:44
Portland County Jail 226:214
A portly Roman Senator was sipping 226:438
Portobello Road 275:84, 276:70
Possum up-a that 'simmon tree 109:128
Possum-la 109:128
Post-Rail Song 226:138
The Postman 41:24 *(Ho, there you are, Mister Postman)*
The Postman 207:81 *(Good morning, Mister Postman)*
Postman, Postman 178:5
Postman, postman, did you bring a letter? 178:5
Pour ce repas pour toute joie 71:13, 72:175, 101:32
Poverty Carol 244:96, *see also:* 96:1
Powder River 61:167
Powderhorn 61:192
Poymanaya Pteechka/The Captured Bird 289:62

The Prairie 91:18
Prairie Music 207:122
Praise and Thanksgiving Let Everyone Bring 86:210
Praise God, from whom all blessings flow 21:312, 22:287, 45:7, 86:213, 148:74, 157:12, 161:11
Praise Him, Praise Him 86:133
The Praise of Christmas 184:32
Praise, O Praise 72:55
Praise, o praise our God and King 72:55
Praise the Lord 86:156
Praise to God for Things We See 86:5
Praise to God, Immortal Praise 86:175, 262:106
Praise to God in the Highest 210:59
Praise to Jesus, Our Salvation/Pochvalen Bud', Jezis Kristus 54:222
Praise We the Father 86:210
Praise we the Lord, who made all beauty 184:64
Pray Give Us Lodging/En Nombre del Cielo 54:306
Pray God Bless 262:68
Pray, Maiden, Pray 73:262
Pray open your umbrella 165:62
Prayer for Each Day 86:163
Prayer for Peace 155:32
Prayer of Thanksgiving 21:338
A Prayer to Jesus 86:113
Prayer to the Child Jesus/Gebet an den Heiligen Christ 241:174
The Preacher and the Slave 64:155, 226:222, *see also:* 24:886
Prelude 67:1
Preparing for Seder 197:44
The Presbyterian Cat 62:43
The Presidents 27:222
Pretending 91:6
Pretending, pretending that I'm not me at all 91:6
The prettiest girl I ever saw 148:338, *see also:* 226:329, 290:38
The prettiest girl that ever I saw 226:329, 290:38, *see also:* 148:338
Pretty and Shiny-O 130:22
Pretty baby, sleep well 114:60
Pretty bird, I've got you now 289:62
Pretty Bracelet/Hos Bilezik 70:20
Pretty Dolly Madison 166:46
A Pretty Fair Maid 226:68, *see also:* 35:32, 213:60
A pretty fair maid all in a garden 226:68, *see also:* 35:32, 213:60
Pretty Fair Miss 213:60, *see also:* 35:32, 226:68
A pretty fair miss a-working in the garden 213:60, *see also:* 35:32, 226:68

Pretty Little Girl with the Red Dress On 232:132, *see also:* 274:44
Pretty Girls and the Shoemaker 68:44
Pretty Little Horses 188:136, *see also:* All The Pretty Little Horses
Pretty little pussy cat 165:158
Pretty little rainy day lady 296:30
The pretty little snowflakes falling down 177:88
Pretty Pear Tree 109:197, *see also:* Green Grass Grows All Around
Pretty Polly 158:304, 226:60
Pretty Poppies/Gentil Coquelicot 217:56
Pretty rabbit of Hope 194:20
Pretty Saro 21:278, 157:75, 213:92
Pretty Skies Above/Cielito Lindo 216:48, 226:298, 230:23, *see also:* 197:36
Pretty Valentines 207:79
Primroses 273:112
The Princess Was a Lovely Child 245:53
A princess was I in a castle high 62:31
The Princess Wed to an Englishman/La Princesse Mariée à un Anglais 89:150
A Prisoner For Life 159:88
The Prisoners' Hope 73:172, *see also:* 21:147
Prithee, Pretty Maiden 230:31
A Private Buffoon 252:58
Prom Kut/Love Song 89:222
The Promise and Law 26:62
A Promise to Our Country 32
Proudly riding the crest of waves in the moonlight 87:36
Proudly sweeps the rain cloud o'er the pali 87:99
Przybieżeli do Betleem Pasterze/Shepherds, Come A-Running 245:119, 279:120, *see also:* 54:212
Przybiezeli do Betlejem/Shepherds Came to Bethlehem 54:212, *see also:* 245:119, 279:120
Psallite Unigenito/Sing, O Sing! 279:23
Psalm of Sion 184:72
Puer Natus 220:111, *see also:* 54:316, 279:12
Puer Natus in Bethlehem/A Child Is Born in Bethlehem 54:316, 220:111, 279:12
Puff, puff, puff! Jeremiah blow the fire 291:34, *see also:* 135:119
Puffer train, puffer train 165:109
Pujdem Spolu Do Bethlema/We Are Going to the Stable 54:224
Puka kini kini 87:16
Pull For the Shore 66:152
A Pumpkin Man 162:42
Pumpkins are gay on Halloween day 41:46
Puna Paia Aala/Puna's Bow'ry Walls 87:43
Puna's Bow'ry Walls/Puna Paia Aala 87:43
Punchin' Dough 61:110

Punchinello 63:14, 109:106, 128:96, 135:113, 178:7
Pupu Hinu Hinu/Shiny Shells 87:68
Purer light flows from my heart 89:221
Purim Time Is Fun 77:55
Purple Bamboo Flute/Dze(r) dzoo diow 208:12
Purple Tulip Morning 261:30
Purrrrr Ce! 236:34
Push the Business On 70:13
Pussy Cat 175:166, 188:28
Pussy Cat High, Pussy Cat Low 175:166, 188:28
Pussy-Cat Pussy-Cat 17:108, 144:15, 175:110, 188:112, 285:70, 292:66
Pussy-Cat, Pussy-Cat, where have you been? 17:108, 144:15, 175:110, 188:112, 285:70, 292:66
Pussycat Mole 111:14
Pussycat Mole jump'd over a coal 111:14
Pussycat Wussycat 111:65
Pussycat, Wussycat, with a white foot 111:65
Put 'em up solid 226:138
Put On Your Wooden Shoes 167:57
Put Your Finger In the Air 75:66, 130:12, 253:108, 289:164
Putting On the Style 35:60, 148:306, 230:68
Pyom, Pyom, Pyom, Rabbits jump 286:18, *see also:* 16:25
Python, Python, Python! 236:63

Q

Qhude/The Cock 163:76
Qongqothwane/The Click Song 163:28
"Quack, quack, quack," said the old mother duck 288:4
The Quail 262:54
The Quaker's Wife 17:20
The Quaker's wife sat down to bake 17:20
The Quaker's Wooing 226:71
Quan' Patate La Cuite/When Your Potato's Done 285:99, *see also:* 79:38
Quand J'étais Chez Mon Père 176:64
Quanno nascette Ninno a Bettelemme 54:242, 241:100, 279:100
Quante me morta moria 169:41, 265:24
Quantrell 159:142, 159:144
The Quartermaster's Store 25:36
Que Bonita Bandera 230:14
Que' li darem a nel Noi de la Mare? 54:260
Que grande que viene el rio 208:7
Que Pase el Rey/The King May Pass 168:149

Queen Mary 227:30

Queen of the Desperadoes 61:269, 61:270

Quelle Est Cette Odeur Agréable?/Whence Is That Goodly Fragrance? 54:102, 210:76

Quem Pastores Laudavere/He, Whom Joyous Shepherds Praised 54:317, 220:58, 279:14

The Quest 71:53

Qui ne part au point certain 243:24

Qui vent tromper, souvent s'abuse 243:30

Quieres que te quite mi bien de las pajas 54:256

Quietly tiptoe, tiptoe, tiptoe 162:65

The Quilting Party 21:180, 157:48

Quisiera Ser Tan Alta Como la Luna/I Would Like To Be As Tall As the Moon 295:47

Quite Different 68:26

Quite Young and Carefree Was I/Kol Jauns Nevedes Buvau 89:175

Quittez, Pasteurs/O Come Away, Ye Shepherds 54:98

Quoc Ca Viet Nam 100:143

Quodlibet (What You Will) 262:82

Quoi, Ma Voisine, Es-Tu Fachée?/Neighbor, What Has You So Excited? 54:104

Quoique Soyez Petit Encore/Although You Still Are Weak and Helpless 54:116

R

Rabbit 162:16

Rabbit Ain't Got 292:96

Rabbit ain't got no tail at all 292:96

Rabbit and the Possum 109:212

Rabbit and the possum going up the hill 109:212

The rabbit is the kind of thing 128:36

The Rabbit of Hope/El Conejo de Esperanza 194:20

Rabbits/Usagi 16:25, 286:18

Rabble Soldier 159:253, 226:284

Raccoon and Possum 234:15

Raccoon's got a ring-round tail 234:15

Race You Down the Mountain 130:56

Radiant moonbeams brighten the heavens tonight 49:20

Raftsman Jim 24:840

Raging Canawl 226:178

The Ragman and the Bagman 62:68

Ragtime Cowboy Joe 61:290

Railroad Bill 226:384

The Railroad Cars Are Coming 226:358

The Railroad Corral 61:208, 159:42, 225:24, 262:64

A Railroad Man For Me 66:119

Rain 11:28 *(Little drops of rain)*

Rain 117 *(The rain is raining all around)*

Rain/Yagmur 266:57

Rain, Come Wet Me 232:67

Rain Dance (music only) 178:62

Rain Dance 197:86 *(Rain now is here with us)*

The rain is raining all around 17:117

Rain Falls 206:102

Rain falls softly on the ground 206:102

Rain in the Night 245:70

Rain is falling down 41:38

Rain now is here with us 197:86

Rain, Oh Rain 296:18

Rain or Shine 232:69, *see also:* 61:232, 61:233, 159:8

Rain, Rain, Go Away 17:48, 262:18

Rain, rain, you rain 266:57

The rain sings a lullaby, quietly, softly 162:31

Rain Song 41:38

The Rainbow 207:125 *(A shower on a summer day)*

The "Rainbow" 35:36 *(The last I was in London, I heard the happy news)*

Rainbow Round My Shoulder 158:323

Raindrop Round 72:161

Raindrops 162:29 *(One little raindrop riding on a cloud)*

Raindrops/Hej Pada Pada 289:36

Raindrops afalling from the skies 289:36

Raindrops on roses and whiskers on kittens 218:226

Rainy Day in Utica, N.Y. 237:unpaged

Rainy Day Lady 296:30

Rainy Day Round 71:114

Raise a Rukus 158:90

Raise me in your arms my brother 73:242

Raise your hands above your head 165:124

Raised on six-shooters till I get big enough to eat ground shot-guns 159:135

Raisins and Almonds 59:67, 128:24

Rally Song 262:144

Ram of Darby 234:58, *see also:* Darby Ram

The Rambling Cowboy 159:192

Rambling Gambler 159:266

Rana Djinak/We Have Come Here 89:243

The Range Riders 159:185, 159:280

Ranky Tank 109:130

Rap! Tap, tap, tap. Rap! Tap, tap, tap 237:unpaged

The Rat and the Elephant/Le Rat et l'Eléphant 243:13

Rat In the Rice Sack/Zui, Zui, Zukorobashi 16:51, 286:42

Rätsel/A Riddle 79:71

Rattle on the Stovepipe 62:128

The Rattlesnake 159:194

Ravioli 26:25
Ravioli, I like ravioli 26:25
The Raw Recruit 27:17, 73:102
Read in the gospel of Mathayew 190:123, *see also:* 233:56
A Real Cowboy 207:121
A Real Nice Clambake 218:106
Really Rosie 235:33
Reared midst the war empurpled plain 273:108
The Rebel horde is on thy shore 73:24
Recognition Song 26:11
Red Beans/Butsu Butsu Mame 286:39
Red candy hearts, cards with white lace 7:16
The Red Flag 64:190
The Red Herring 262:27
Red Iron Ore 226:176
Red leaves falling down 41:44
Red Riding Hood's Hood 166:72
Red River Gal 61:279
Red River Shore 159:181, *see also:* 37:152, 61:161
Red River Valley 22:146, 25:73, 55:514, 61:157, 126:55, 158:220, 159:298, 205:380, 226:130
The red sun will be setting soon 67:53
The red, the white, the blue 207:80
The Red, White, and Blue 197:65, *see also:* 26:86, 157:116, 160:36
Red Wing 61:142
Redbird 130:104
Redbird, soon in the mornin' 130:104
The Redbird Sings 74:19
Reel 107:50
A reg'ment of soldiers came down from Yorkshire 35:76
Rejoice All the Heavens 244:232
Rejoice and Be Merry 209:21
Rejoice My Friends 233:65
Rejoice my friends, the Lord is King! 233:65
Remember All God's Children 86:95
Remember us poor Mayers all! 208:70
Remember what I promised you 146:87, 159:265, *see also:* 61:304
Remembrance/Like No A Like 89:299
Ren ren si huan li pai lu 148:84
Rented 207:92
Reply to "The Little Old Sod Shanty on the Claim" 61:69
Restore Africa to Its Owners/Mayibuye 163:91
The Resurrection 35:70
Retocemos en el bosque mientras el lobo no esta' 70:27
Reuben James 230:84
Reveille 197:104
The Revolutionary Alphabet 28:36

Revolutionary Tea 157:18, 240:55
Rheumatism 26:42, 62:16
Rheumatism, rheumatism 26:42, 62:16
A Rhyme and a Riddle 288:3
Rice Planting/Taue 286:78, *see also:* Planting Rice
Rice Pudding/Arroz Con Leche 168:136, *see also:* 216:43, 295:28
The rice sprouts now are ready 286:78, *see also:* Planting Rice
Rice with Milk/Arroz Con Leche 216:43, *see also:* 168:136, 295:28
De rich folks 'cided to take a trip 226:254, *see also:* 290:153
The Rich Man and the Poor Man 62:101, 64:148, *see also:* 36:70
The rich man lay on his velvet couch 226:316
Rich Mongolia/Bahyahn Mongol 208:45
The Rich Old Lady 37:130
A rich old lady in outer town 37:130
Rickety Tickety Tin 290:186
A Riddle/Rätsel 79:71
The Riddle 22:25, 205:39, *see also:* Riddle Song
The Riddle Song 37:156, 69:21, 135:46, 148:310, 205:39, 230:72, 262:152, 277:105, *see also:* 17:22, 22:25, 2:28, 188:24, 189:26, 205:39
Ride A Cock-Horse 17:79, 175:26, 188:70, 283:37, 285:50
Ride a cock-horse, to Banbury Cross 17:79, 175:26, 188:70, 283:37, 285:50
Ride a Red Auto 154:10
Ride away on your horses, your horses 129:74
Ride, Charley, Ride 109:11
Ride Cowboy, Ride 162:80
Ride West to the mesas and the mountains 69:42
Riding a Raid 73:90
Riding in My Car 130:66, *see also:* 274:8
Riding in the Buggy, Miss Mary Jane 232:78
Riding Round the Cattle 234:70, *see also:* 159:37
Riflemen of Bennington 20:14, 240:102
Rig a Jig Jig 63:12, 128:80, 283:41, *see also:* Buffalo Gals
Rigby Johnson Chandler 61:26
Right hand across and you don't get lost 61:273, *see also:* 61:272, 61:274, 158:103
Right in the Middle of My Face 206:28
Ring-A-Ring-A Round-O/Gira, Gira Tondo 188:48, 189:25
Ring-A-Ring O' Roses 175:41, 188:108, 189:24, 227:23, *see also:* Ring Around a Rosy

Ring Around a Rosy 17:139, 63:11, 277:19, 283:31, 291:63, *see also:* 100:32, 175:41, 188:108, 189:24, 227:23

Ring around a rosy, A pocket full of posies 17:139, 63:11, 283:31, 291:63, *see also:* Ring Around a Rosy

Ring Around the Rosie 100:32, *see also:* Ring Around a Rosy

Ring Around the Rosy 277:19, *see also:* Ring Around a Rosy

Ring, Little Bells/Kling, Glöckchen 54:140

Ring On A String 20:11, *see also:* 232:80, 274:18

Ring Out, Wild Bells 210:118

Ring the Christmas Bells 167:54

Ringel, Ringel 100:33, 168:95

Ringeltanz/Round Dance 188:144

Ringo, Ringo, Ringo Starr 141:16

Río de Avenida/Overflowing Torrent 89:99

The Rio Grande 22:140, 176:110, 239:14, *see also:* 78:9

Río, Río/Flowing River 208:7

A Ripping Trip 61:36, 159:387

Riqui Ran 262:17, *see also:* 295:45

Riquirran 295:45, *see also:* 262:17

Rise and Shine 148:312

Rise and shine, and give God the glory, glory 148:312

Rise, arise, arise 69:26, 262:136

Rise, O sleepy maiden, wherefore dreaming still 262:97

Rise, Sally, Rise 63:26

Rise Up, O Flame 69:7, 71:11, 72:174

Rise Up, Shepherd, an' Foller 22:266, 190:55, 209:22, *see also:* Rise Up, Shepherd, and·Follow

Rise Up, Shepherd, and Follow 54:80, 129:66, 140:49, 233:16, 241:54, *see also:* 22:266, 190:55, 209:22

Rise ye up, my dearest dear, and present to me your hand 61:274, *see also:* 61:272, 61:273, 158:103

The Rising of the Lark 262:81

Risseldy, Rosseldy 128:114, *see also:* 36:36, 37:122, 62:143

Ritka Búza/Thrifty Miss 208:33

The River 114:84

The river is deep, and the channel is wide 197:82, *see also:* 20:72, 27:176

The river is up and the channel is deep 20:74, *see also:* 27:156, 197:82

River, overflowing torrent 89:99

Rivers and valleys and oceans beyond 69:36

Rivington's Reflections 28:163

The Road to Cook's Peak 159:384

The roads are very dirty, my boots are very clean 220:116

The Roaring Crocodile 62:50

The Robbers Coming Through 63:31

The Robin 41:22

Robin A Thrush 78:15

Robin Adair 21:342

Robin he married a wife in the west 78:15

Robin Hood and Allen A Dale 164:42

Robin Hood and Guy of Gisborne 164:68

Robin Hood and Little John 164:10, 262:132

Robin Hood and Little John walkin' thru the forest 276:76

Robin Hood and Maid Marian 164:48

Robin Hood and the Bishop 164:52

Robin Hood and the Bishop of Hereford 164:94

Robin Hood and the Bold Pedlar 164:64

Robin Hood and the Butcher 164:58

Robin Hood and the Curtal Friar 164:36

Robin Hood and the Golden Arrow 164:76

Robin Hood and the Prince of Aragon 164:28

Robin Hood and the Ranger 164:82

Robin Hood and the Stranger 164:16

Robin Hood and the Tanner 164:22

Robin Hood Rescuing Three Squires 164:104

Robin Hood Rescuing Will Stutly 164:88

Robin Hood, Scarlet, and Little John were walking over the plain 164:28

Robin Hood's Death 164:110

Robin Hood's Golden Prize 164:98

Robin Loves Me/Robin M'Aime 22:125, 189:94

Robin M'Aime/Robin Loves Me 22:125

Robin the Bobbin 111:74

The Robin's Last Will 262:45

Rock-A-Bye 125:25

Rock-A-Bye Baby 59:36, 283:56, 289:20, *see also:* 17:68, 125:142

Rock-a-bye, baby, on the tree top 17:68, 125:142, 289:20, *see also:* 59:36, 283:56

Rock-a-Bye, Boy 125:123

Rock-a-bye, my little owlet 245:84

Rock-a-bye oh my son 125:124

Rock-a-bye, rock-a-bye, croon a sweet song 125:25

Rock-a-bye, yon boy 125:123

Rock-a My Soul 55:278, *see also:* 22:306, 72:80

Rock-a my soul in the bosom of Abraham 55:278, *see also:* 22:306, 72:80

Rock-a-rock, old Joe Clarke 232:84, *see also:* Old Joe Clark

Rock About My Saro Jane 158:151

The Rock Island Line 35:52, 129:90, 130:64, 148:314, 274:12

Rock Me to Sleep 66:28

Rock of Ages   22:296, 45:13, *(Rock of Ages, cleft for me)*
Rock of Ages   72:44, *(Rock of Ages, God above) see also:* 197:112
Rock of Ages, cleft for me   22:296, 45:13
Rock of Ages, God above   72:44, *see also:* 197:112
Rock of Ages, let our song   197:112, *see also:* 72:44
Rock the Cradle   125:54
Rockaby   17:141
Rockaby, baby, the moon is a cradle   17:141
Rockabye, Baby   17:68, 125:142, *see also:* 59:36, 283:56, 289:20
Rockabye Jesus/Lulajze Jezuniu   279:122, *see also:* 54:220, 241:74
The rocket is ready to lift off   166:68
Rocking   68:45, 184:66, 220:28, 241:64, *see also:* 54:226, 210:45, 279:118
Rocking Carol/Hajej, Nynej, Ježišku   54:226, *see also:* Rocking
Rocking Jerusalem   31:35
The Rocking of the Child/El Rorro   279:106, *see also:* 54:308, 100:154
Rocking Song/Hajej, Nynej, Ježišku   279:118, *see also:* Rocking
Rocking the Cradle   111:26
Roll, Jordan, Roll   21:261, 25:95, 31:37, 148:318, 290:96
Roll Out, Heave Dat Cotton   277:101
Roll Over   63:131, 254:110, *see also* 26:23, 147:32, 148:254, 290:34
Roll Over, Roll Over   290:34, *see also:* Ten in the Bed
Roll That Brown Jug Down to Town   232:88
Roll the Ball   291:64
Roll the Chariot   226:196, *see also:* 66:148
Roll the R   290:195
Roll the Union On   64:44
Rolling Home   69:44
The Rolling Stone   35:56
The Roman Soldiers   39:26, 129:114, 135:88
Romance(Mozart)   85:103
Romance(Schubert)   85:151
The romance that you have waited for will come when it comes   218:286
The Rommelpot/De Rommelpot   89:140
Rondo   273:100
The Roof Above the Manger   67:9
The Rook   85:235
The Rooster's Our Watchman   245:6
Root Hog or Die   61:30, *see also:* 61:32
Rory O'More   167:10
Rory O'More is dancing a jig   167:10
Rosa, Let Us Be Dancing   100:116
The Rosary   205:344

The Rose Bush   67:18
Rose Red   46:229
Rose, Rose   262:159, 293:24
Rose, Rose, and Up She Rises   232:145, 289:14
Roselil   20:46
Roselil and her mother sat over their tea   20:46
Rosen Fra Fuhn   69:52
Rosie Nell   226:114
Rosy Apple, Lemon, and Pear   63:68
Round-About Round   68:19
Round and Round   296:7
Round and round and round about   68:19
Round and Round Hitler's Grave   158:88
Round and round my wheel is whirling   85:920
Round and round, old Joe Clarke   232:84, *see also:* Old Joe Clark
Round and Round the Village   14:375, 17:140, 165:189, 283:25, *see also:* 37:191, 39:14, 63:22, 75:27, 83:504, 109:77, 110:52
Round Dance/Ringeltanz   188:144
Round Her Neck She Wore a Yellow Ribbon   205:384, *see also:* 170:22
A round little pumpkin grew in the sun   162:40
Round my Indiana homestead wave the cornfields   162:197, 205:254
Round, round! We made a ball of yarn   207:64
Round the house we go   149:42
Round the Mountain   63:17, 70:11, *see also:* 168:183
Round the Mulberry Bush   283:17, *see also:* Here We Go Round the Mulberry Bush
Round the ring of roses   100:32, *see also:* Ring Around A Rosy
Round the Village   283:25, *see also:* Round and Round the Village
Rounded Up in Glory   159:330
The roundhouse in Cheyenne is filled ev'ry night   226:264, *see also:* 61:65, 146:95, 159:372, 277:125
Rouse, Britons   28:104, *see also:* 240:177
Roving Cowboy   61:163
The Roving Gambler   24:889, 226:312, *see also:* 226:313
The Roving Pedlar   36:98
The Row Boat   41:30
Row, Row, Row Your Boat   17:117, 25:30, 26:44, 62:10, 148:320, 165:116, 283:10, 289:185, 293:56
Row together, row together, row, row, row   162:94
Row your boat, boys, row your boat   41:30
Rowan County Troubles   24:891
Rowing in my little boat   288:18
Rowing Song   288:18

Rowing Toward the Sunlight/Bogando a la Luz del Sol   89:103
Roy Bean   159:147
Rub-a-dub-dub   175:138
Rub Your Tummy   206:54
Rub your tummy, just like this   206:54
Rubber Duckie   206:121
Rubber duckie, you're the one   206:121
Rudolph the Red-Nosed Reindeer   127:232
Rules   290:142
Run, Children, Run   291:70, *see also:* 232:92
Run, Chillen, Run   232:92, *see also:* 291:70
Run, Nigger, Run   24:906
Run, Run/Kattan, Kattan   89:257
The Runaway Train   26:80
The runaway train came down the track 26:80
Russian Slumber Song   78:71
The Rustler   159:105
Rusty Jiggs and Sandy Sam   146:76, *see also:* 61:202, 225:52
Rwiyo Rwedande   278:40
Rye Whisky   24:855, 158:218, 159:163, 230:69, *see also:* 37:142, 159:166, 226:307
Rye whisky, rye whisky, you're no friend of mine   159:166, *see also:* Rye Whisky

S

Sa gah, sa gah nahrahdundah   208:41
Sa Tah Ryung/Song of Birds   208:41
Sabbath Song   77:39
Sacramento   21:306, 158:140, 262:38
Sad I sit on Butternut Hill   158:117, *see also:* Johnny Has Gone for a Soldier
Saddle your pony, here we go   119:104
Sadie   226:86, *see also:* Frankie and Johnny
Sadie went into the barroom   226:86, *see also:* Frankie and Johnny
Saeyasaeya, parangsaeya   49:34
Safety First   207:114
Safety Song   177:90
Sag Meiteli   208:67
Said Beauregard, to Lee, and Jeff   73:53
Said the Duck to the Kangaroo   112:53
Said the lord to his lady   176:153
The Sail Boat   41:32
Sail! home as straight as an arrow   21:227
Sailing At High Tide   24:812, 75:68, *see also:* 232:160
Sailing in the Boat   232:160, *see also:* 24:812, 75:68
Sailing in the boat when the tide runs high 75:68, 232:160, *see also:* 24:812

Sailing on the Sea   27:202
Sailing, sailing, little white sail boat sailing 41:32
A Sailor Went to Sea   63:79
The Sailor's Address   240:164
The Sailor's Return   262:78
The Sailor's Song   85:109
St. George and the Drag-On   61:78
St. James Hospital   157:157
St. Joseph's Carol   189:74
St. Louis Blues   21:120
Saint Patrick Was a Gentleman   197:28
St. Patrick's Day   162:55 *(We're wearing green for the Irish)*
Saint Patrick's Day   205:154 *(Though dark are our sorrows)*
Saint Patrick's Day Jig   97:unpaged
St. Paul's Steeple   17:126, 188:154, *see also:* 175:46
Saint Sereni of the Mountain/San Sereni del Monte   188:138
Saint Stephen and Herod   190:140
Saint Stephen Was Riding/Staffansvisa 279:114
Saint Stephen was a serving man   190:140
St. Stephen's Day   212:12
Sakura/Cherry Trees   72:141, 286:73
Sakura! sakura! Yayoi no sora wa   72:141, 286:73
Salagadoola menchicka boola bibbidibob-diboo   275:39
Sally Ann   230:53
Sally Down Our Alley   110:50, *see also:* 55:507
Sally Down the Alley   55:507, *see also:* 110:50
Sally Go Round the Moon   135:73, *see also:* 63:11, 130:90, 232:164
Sally Go Round the Sun   63:11, *see also:* 130:90, 135:73, 232:164
Sally Go Round the Sunshine   130:90, 232:164, *see also:* 63:11, 135:73
Salomey was a dancer   178:70, *see also:* 36:109, 290:156
Salty Dogs   159:110
Salute to Freedom/Freiheit   22:210
Salve, O Jesus   124:29
Sam Bass   61:263, 146:159, 158:298, 159:150, 226:422
Sam Bass was born in Indiana   61:263, 146:159, 158:298, 159:150, 226:422
Sam Hall   159:422
Sam, Sam, the butcher man   112:24
Sam, Sam, Tommy Trot, and Barber, Barber 112:24
Samba-le-le   114:69
Samson   123:178
San Jose y María van para Belén   140:28
San Sereni   20:83, 262:16

San Sereni del Monte/Saint Sereni of the Mountain 188:138
San Wu Yao/Song of the Three "Nots" 49:19
Sand Castle 91:27
Sand castle, sand castle 91:27
The Sandman 91:47
The Sandman Comes 17:78
The sandman sprinkles dreams in the air 91:47
Sandman Will Come 125:28
Sandpiper 69:24
Sandy Dow 63:91
Sandy Dow, Sandy Dow, Sandy deedleum deedleum Dow 63:91
Sandy Land 46:211, 70:25, 135:75
Sandy lent the man the mill 62:68, *see also:* 262:32
Sandy McNab 290:193, 293:54
Sandy Ree 109:136
Sandy's Mill 62:68, 262:32
Sankt Staffan han rider sina hastar till vanns 279:114
Sans Day Carol 96:11
Sant Josep i la Mare de Deu/Holy Joseph and Mary the Maid 54:262
Santa Claus 41:4 *(Santa Claus will soon be here)*
Santa Claus 191:80 *(O, clap, clap the hands)*
Santa Claus will soon be here 41:4
The Santa Fe Trail 159:308
Santa Lucía 22:30
Santa's Coming 26:43
Santa's coming in his sleigh 162:52
Santa's coming, Santa's coming 26:43
Santy Anna 21:288, 24:835, 262:105, *see also:* 158:136
Santy Anno 158:136, *see also:* 21:288, 24:835, 262:105
Santy Maloney 135:123
Sarasponda 290:200
Sarong Banqui/One Starlit Night 208:55
Sasano ha sarasara 286:81
Satan's A Liah 226:250
Saurais-tu passer de ri 70:18, *see also:* 55:250
The Savannah Song 28:129
Savez-vous Planter les Choux?/Do You Know How to Plant Cabbages? 168:164, 217:10, *see also:* 165:85
Saviour, Again to Thy Dear Name 45:23, 86:207
Savior, Hear Us, We Pray/Wiegenlied 86:139
Saviour, Like a Shepherd Lead Us 45:62, 87:97
Savior, While My Heart Is Tender 86:115
The Saviour's Work 220:54, 241:28

Saw-a crow a-flying low 289:28
Saw a flea kick a tree 289:136
Say Christmas comes but once a year 190:112, *see also:* 233:77
Say, darkeys, hab you seen de massa 73:93
Say, it's only a paper moon 170:52
Say, Kwezelken, will you go dancing? 21:320
Say, man, say, the sun has set 163:115
Say, my love, will you go to Boston? 63:39, *see also:* Going to Boston
Say, pard, have you sighted a schooner 159:308
Say, Uncle, have you seen the master 27:134
Say, where have you been, Billy Boy, Billy Boy 197:22, *see also:* Billy Boy
The Scabs Crawl In 64:46
Scarborough Fair 22:26, *see also:* 35:98, 37:112
The Scarecrow 188:164
The Scary Song 290:171, *see also:* 37:186, 134:86, 213:76
Scattered with a sparing hand are wheat and rye 208:33
Schäferin und Kuckuck/The Shepherdess and the Cuckoo 78:59
Schlaf, Kindlein, Schlaf/Sleep, Baby, Sleep 188:96, 289:16
Schlaf mein kindelein, schlaf 54:322
Schlaf wohl, du Himmelsknabe du 54:156
Schlafe, mein Prinz-chen, Schlafein 289:34
Schneiderlied/Song of the Tailor 208:2
Schöne Rosa/Lovely Rosa 189:144
Schönster Herr Jesu/Fairest Lord Jesus 86:116
The School Band 177:79
Scintillate 290:122
Scintillate, scintillate, globule aurific! 290:122
Scissors and String 175:156
Scotland's Burning 46:227, 62:13, 148:321, 283:35, 289:188, 293:36, *see also:* 25:30, 175:20
Scottish Grace 71:14, 101:33
Scout Benediction 26:94
Scout Chant 71:30, 72:40
Scout Hearted Men 25:68
A Scout is trustworthy, Lord, Kum ba yah! 25:109
Scout Law Version of Kum Ba Yah 25:109
Scout Leader's Prayer 25:55
Scout Vesper 25:125, 26:94
Scout Vesper Song 25:125, 26:94
Scouting We Go 26:68
Scout's Good-Night Song 25:61, 26:93
Scraping Up Sand in the Bottom of the Sea 232:96

Screaming and Yelling 235:53

Sea Lion 100:54, 168:161

Seal Lullaby 59:64

The Season for Singing 140:95

The season for singing a joyous refrain
140:95

Seasons' Birthday Song 245:106

*Seated on chair of gold was the mister Sir
Cat* 295:4, *see also:* 216:41

Seba Alaso Trodje/The Dew Is Dry at Midday 89:234

Sebakazi abatalima 236:42

Secession is our watchword 73:46, 73:48

Second Star to the Right 276:33

*The Second Star to the Right shines in the
night for you* 276:33

See, a cloud of dust is rising 22:214

See, Amid the Winter's Snow 210:60

*See colors flashing everywhere, upon a Sum-
mer's day* 261:34

See each India rubber ball 165:55

See here comes the big procession 41:7

*See how each little hand turns to your bed
and prays!* 67:37

See How I'm Jumping 135:107

See how I'm jumping, jumping, jumping!
135:107

*See, I am the bed of hay from the Blessed
Night* 67:64

See my new snowsuit 207:63

See my pack, it's filled to overflowing
178:60

See My Wagon, It's Full-Laden 21:318

See-Saw 17:103, 175:172, 188:68, 283:14,
285:40 *(See-Saw, Margery Daw)*

See-Saw 177:91 *(See saw, see saw)*

See-Saw, Margery Daw 17:103, 175:172,
188:68, 283:14, 285:40

See-Saw, Sacra-down 111:24, 135:124,
162:89

See saw, see saw 177:91

See the clock up on the wall 11:17

See the clouds are gath'ring up in the sky
89:38, *see also:* 68:13

See the fairies dancing 207:94

See the little bunny sleeping 165:154

See the lovely sunset 207:27

See the people turning out 73:56

*See the pony galloping, galloping down the
country road* 162:82, *see also:* 41:42

See the pretty moon above 267:54

See the raindrops now are gently falling
71:114

See the Star of Bethlehem 140:119

See the sun up in the sky? 206:14

See what Santa brought me 207:56

Seeing Nellie Home 21:180, 157:48

Sein Kyu Kya Nyaung/Song of the Princess
89:221

Sel Bych Rád K Betlému/I Go to Bethlehem
54:232, 241:184

Sel Bych Rád K Betlém/To Bethl'em I
Would Go 54:232, 241:184

Sempuku-Yama 16:44

Sen chain, sen chain, sen chain 215:8

Send My Brown Jug Down to Town 20:64,
see also: 128:113

Sengdzinga nemho 163:39

Señor Caracol/Mr. Snail 168:129

Señora Santa Ana/Lady Saint Anne 216:16

Señores, vengo a contarles 89:78

Sent my brown jug downtown 128:113, *see
also:* 20:64

*Sentado en silla de oro estaba el señor Don
Gato* 295:4, *see also:* 216:3

September Days 97:unpaged

September Days are warm and sweet
97:unpaged

Sera jette, sera jette a la marina 21:200

Serenade/Lulay 89:296

Sergeant Champe 240:107, 273:52, *see
also:* 28:150

The Sergeant, He Is the Worst of All
226:435

*The sergeant, the sergeant he is the worst of
all* 226:435

Sesame Street 206:7

Set Down, Servant 148:284, 158:362, *see
also:* 22:312, 83:465, 128:26, 262:71,
290:84

Set down, servant, I cain' set down
158:362, *see also:* Set Down, Servant

Settin' on a Rail 78:91

Seven-Cent Cotton and Forty-Cent Meat
24:877

Seven Great Towns of Greece 293:34

The Seven Joys of Christmas 241:192

The Seven Joys of Mary 22:262, 54:14,
140:14, 140:116, 148:322, 210:65, 220:30,
241:193, 279:46, *see also:* 190:61, 233:58

Seven Long Years in State Prison 226:218

Seventeen Come Sunday 27:106, 36:42

Sev'n great towns of Greece, 'tis said
293:34

Sh-Ta-Ra-Dah-Dey (Irish Lullaby) 226:35,
see also: 64:154

The shades of night were falling fast
73:154

A shadow is floating through the moonlight
44:44

Shadows 207:128

Shadows on a sunny day 207:128

Shady Grove 134:50, 157:74, 213:44

*Shake, shake, knock, knock, shake, shake,
knock, knock* 41:23

Shake, shake, Shaker life 293:108

Shake That Little Foot, Dinah-O 234:47

Shaker Life 293:108

Shall We Dance? 198:212

Shall We Gather at the River? 22:297, 157:164

Shalom Chaverim 55:255, 293:110

The Shamrock and the Heather 262:75

The Shan Van Vocht 42:592

Shanadoah 157:40, *see also:* Shenandoah

Shanandar 134:77, *see also:* Shenandoah

Shanghai Chicken 135:21

Shango 208:30, 208:31

Shango. A-go oh, ah mayan va 208:30, *see also:* 208:31

Shango! Shango! Shango! 208:31, *see also:* 208:30

The *Shannon* and the *Chesapeake* 240:196

The Shanty-Boy and the Pine 239:36

A shanty lad, he leads a dreadful dreary life 35:11, *see also:* 33:242, 226:390

The Shantyman's Life 33:242, 35:11, 226:390

Shao Hua Tang Shui/Gently Flowing Stream 49:20

Sharp Den Song 26:54

Shawnee Town 33:90

She had no business doin' it, but she come out o' the East 159:189

She Moved Through the Fair 42:600

She Perished In the Snow 35:50, *see also:* 24:825, 27:244, 159:231, 226:58

She Promised She'd Meet Me 226:207

She Said the Same to Me 226:38

She sailed away on a bright and sunny day 26:36, *see also:* 62:48

She sailed away on a lovely day 62:48, *see also:* 26:36

She Sells Sea Shells 112:37

She was a two-gun woman, Belle Shirley was her name 61:269, *see also:* 61:270

She was a two-gun woman: Miss Belle Shirley was her name 61:270, *see also:* 61:269

She Was Bred in Old Kentucky 21:52

She Was Happy Till She Met You 157:206

She Wore a Yellow Ribbon 170:22, *see also:* 205:383

The Shearer's Dream 176:84

Sheena sha, sheena sha 277:99

Sheep May Always Graze 85:76

Sheep may always graze in safety 85:76

Sheep nor shepherds, none are here 210:90

Sheep Shearing 129:36, 134:102, 292:54

The sheep's in the meadow, the cow's in the corn 292:146

She'll Be Comin' 'Round the Mountain 20:36, 22:156, 25:14, 62:70, 148:324, 165:197, 170:33, 201, 205:175, 226:372, 232:90, 283:30, 290:24

Shellila Shek/Our Great Leader 89:280

Shelter Where Ox and Ass Are One 209:24

Shenandoah 22:136, 25:85, 61:2, 69:35, 98:30, 148:326, 158:138, 176:113, 205:82, 230:17, 239:16, 277:55, *see also:* 134:77, 157:40, 226:408

The Shepherd Boy's Song 112:62

Shepherd, Lonely Shepherd 155:23

The Shepherd Maid 227:6

The Shepherd Maiden 245:56

The shepherd maiden one fine day 78:61

The Shepherd Moon 125:78

Shepherd, Shake Off Your Drowsy Sleep/ Berger, Secoue Ton Sommeil Profond 54:122, 220:88, 284:59

Shepherd, Shepherd 233:18

Shepherd, Shepherd, Leave Decoying 85:45

Shepherd, shepherd, where'd you leave your lambs 233:18

A shepherd walked among the hills 155:17

The Shepherd Wolf/Le Loup Berger 243:30

The Shepherdess and the Cuckoo/Schäferin und Kuckuck 78:61

The Shepherds/Los Pastores 295:70

Shepherds Awake 124:27

Shepherds Came to Bethlehem/Przybieželi do Betlejem 54:212, *see also:* 245:119, 279:120

Shepherds Come A-Running/Przybieželi do Betleem Pasterze 245:119, 279:120, *see also:* 54:212

Shepherds come a-running into Bethlehem 245:119, 279:120, *see also:* 54:212

Shepherds' Cradle Song/Wiegenlied Der Hirten 54:156

The Shepherds' Farewell to the Holy Family 210:126

Shepherds In Bethlehem/Pastores A Belén 54:290

Shepherds In Judea 140:92, 190:108, 233:32

Shepherds Leave the Hillside 86:39

Shepherds, Rejoice 190:47, 233:30

Shepherds, rejoice, lift up your eyes 190:47, 233:30

Shepherds! Shake Off Your Drowsy Sleep 54:122, 220:88, 284:59

The Shepherd's Song 67:80

Shepherds, Up!/Hirten, auf um Mitternacht! 279:80

Shepherds, up, your watch to take! 279:80

Shepherds Watched Their Flocks By Night/ Pásli Ovce Valaši 241:179

The Shepherds Went Their Hasty Way 220:52

Sherman the Brave 73:75

Shiao Bao-Bao/A Chinese Christmas Cradle Song 209:68

Shiloh 232:96

Shimmy, Shimmy, Coke-Ca-Pop! 141:78

Shine Like a Star In the Morning 233:14

Shinin' adobe fireplace, shadows on the wall 61:282

Shiny Shells/Pupu Hinu Hinu 87:68

A Ship A-Sailing 33:66, 130:97, 188:58, *see also:* 14:346, 17:61, 18:6, 52, 68:25

A ship, a ship a-sailing 68:25, 188:58, *see also:* A Ship A-Sailing

The ship came sailing down the bay 162:92, *see also:* 290:214

The ship is sailing down the bay 290:214, *see also:* 162:92

The Ship of Zion 35:58, *see also:* 21:262

The Ship That Never Returned 226:147

The Ship Titanic 290:153, *see also:* 226:254

The Ship's Carpenter 35:82, *see also:* 226:66

Shock Along, John 24:906

Shoe Game 55:250, 70:18, *see also:* 20:90, 83:491, 289:173

The Shoemaker/El Zapatero 78:89 *(I spoke to a shoemaker)*

The Shoemaker 239:52 *(I am a shoemaker by my trade)*

Shoemaker, Shoemaker 75:69

Shoemaker, shoemaker, mend my shoe 75:69

Shoes Squeak/Kutsu-ga Narn 286:60

Sholom A'leychem 25:112

Shoo, Fly Don't Bother Me 21:159, 46:208, 70:24, 126:85, 129:108, 178:20, 292:198

Shoo, Turkey 109:54

Shoot/Dubula 163:54

Shoot an Arrow 166:8

Shoot the Buffalo 61:272, 61:273, 61:274, 158:103

Shootin' with Rasputin 290:150

Short Rations to the Corn-Fed Army of Tennessee 73:163

Shorty George 158:70

Should auld acquaintance be forgot 22:76, 25:89, 27:2, 46:207, 148:32, 170:62, 197:10, 205:50, 290:216

Shout, Josephine! Shout, shout! 109:60

Shout the Glad Tidings 241:140

Shout to Jehovah, all the earth 21:312, *see also:* Old Hundredth

Shovellin' Iron Ore 226:183

Show Ha Mo/Frogs 49:14

A shower on a summer day 207:125

Showt to Jehovah, al the earth 157:12, *see also:* Old Hundredth

Shtet a bocher und er tracht 148:398

Shuckin' of the Corn 21:296, 27:196

Shule Agra 21:344, *see also:* 89:136

Shule Aroon/Come, Oh Love 89:136, *see also:* 21:344

Shusti-Fidli 71:56, 72:138, *see also:* Musicians

Shut your eyes, put your heads down 74:48

Si Hubbard 226:350

The Siamese Cat Song 276:50

Sich a Gitting Up Stairs 157:83

Sicilian Circle 126:101

The Sidewalks of New York 148:328, 157:188, 205:240

Sifting in the Sand 107:60

Sighing, Lamenting 85:72

Silent Night 22:267, 54:176, 65:97, 86:45, 92:181, 148:332, 148:333, 161:61, 184:26, 187, 210:61, 241:58, 242:unpaged, 264:90, 279:86, 282, 283:48, 284:71

Silently I adore you, beloved 89:55

Silver flow'ret 208:37

Silver Jack 159:234

The Silver Moon is Shining 55:259, 72:133

Silver on the sage, starlit skies above 25:58

Silver sage asettin' in the pale twilight 277:135

Silver Threads Among the Gold 21:231, 170:27

Simon's Song 58, *see also:* 17:31, 175:16, 285:33

The Simple Birth/De Nederige Geboorte 54:182

Simple Gifts 157:62, 176:92

Simple Little Nancy Brown 36:86

Simple Simon 17:31, 175:16, 285:33, *see also:* 58

Simple Simon Call'd on Little Mother Goose 167:34

Since First I Saw Your Face 189:92

Since the times have grown harder 35:56

Since you all must have singing and won't be said, "Nay" 27:166, 28:89, *see also:* 240:89

Since you all will have singing and won't be said nay 240:89, *see also:* 27:166, 28:89

Sing 206:104

Sing a Christmas lullaby 207:50

Sing a Little Hoe-Down Jordan 110:20

Sing a pretty song, little birdie 162:10

Sing a Song About the Flag 162:111

Sing a Song of Sixpence 17:24, 135:114, 175:122, 188:26, 189:16, 283:22, 285:47

Sing a song of six pence, a pocket full of rye 17:24, 135:114, 175:122, 188:26, 189:16, 283:22, 285:47

Sing aloud on this day! 220:104

Sing for the wide, wide fields 55:257

Sing Hallelu 233:46

Sing Ho! For the Life of a Bear 172:35, 174:21

Sing I for a brave and gallant barque 226:100

Sing Little Birdie 162:10

Sing Lullaby! Lullaby Baby 209:25

Sing O Sing 41:11 *(Sing, o, sing for it is Spring)*

Sing, O Sing!/Psallite Unigenito 256:23 *(Sing, O, sing! Hail the Holy One!)*

"Sing" Said the Mother 129:14, see also: Over in the Meadow

Sing! Sing a song 206:104

Sing, sing together, merrily merrily sing 71:99, 72:41

Sing, Sing, What Shall I Sing? 111:17

Sing Song Merry Go Round 112:70

Sing to God in Joyful Voice 86:1

Sing to the Lord of Harvest 86:174

Sing Together 71:99, 72:41

Sing We Christmas 209:61

Sing We the Virgin Mary 140:20, 140:108

Sing Your Way Home 46:217, 148:334

Sing your way home at the close of the day 46:217, 148:334

The Singing Bird 110:36

Singing ever, weary never 169:21, 267:27

Singing In the Land 233:64

The Singing School 66:60

Singing Time 245:15

Singing too-ral li-oo-ra li-addity 176:88

Singing, we are singing! 54:296

The Single Girl 157:67, see also: 36:87, 158:48

Sinhalese Carol 209:98

Sinner Man 134:82, 148:336, 157:60

Sioux Indians 61:123, 159:344, 277:119

Sioux Night Song 197:84

Sippin' Cider Through a Straw 148:338, 290:38, see also: 226:329

Sir Cat/Don Gato 216:41, 295:4

Sir Donkey 292:31

Sir Eglamore That Valiant Knight 71:72

Sir, I see you coming again 37:146

Sir Mister Brown 109:99

Sir Peter Parker 240:91, see also: 28:66

Sir Tomcat/El Señor Don Gato 216:41, 295:4

Sisken 83:499

Sissie in the Barn 178:59

Sister Carrie or the Compromise Song 73:60

Sister Carrie my dear, I am sorry to hear 73:60

Sister Mary Had But One Child 140:66, 190:134, 209:26, see also: 140:69, 190:114, 233:44

Sisters and Brothers 260:68

Sisters and brothers, brothers and sisters 260:68

Sister's Lullaby 207:20

Sit Down, Sister 128:26, see also: Set Down, Servant

Sittin' on the ice till my feet got cold, sugar babe 24:896, see also: Crawdad

Sitting by the roadside on a summer day 27:132, 73:166, 157:128, 277:85, see also: 99:48

Sitting in the apple tree 207:87

Six ladies in the center with the right hand crossed 83:500

Six Little Ducks 43, 55:271, 63:104, 148:342, 289:106

Six little ducks that I once knew 43, 55:271, 63:104, 148:342, 289:106

Six Little Girls A-sliding Went 83:502, see also: 17:40, 68:5, 188:16, 197:52

Six Little Mice Sat Down to Spin 111:12, see also: 175:144

Six Little Snails 17:62, 165:48

Six little snails lived in a tree 17:62, 165:48

Sixteen Tons 64:52

Skate With Me 167:52

The Skaters' Song 207:72

Skating 7:14

Skating Away 39:48, 126:87

Skeeters are a-humming on the honeysuckle vine 125:139

Skeleton Bones 197:94, see also: 89:42, 226:470, 290:40

The Skew-Ball Black 159:14

Skim, skim, skim 191:76

Skin 91:16

Skin and Bones 213:76, see also: 37:186, 134:86, 290:171

Skinamarink 290:114

Skip lively now, skip lively now 168:114, see also: 194:24

Skip one window, Tideo 232:173

Skip, Skip, Skip to my Lou 107:48, see also: Skip to My Lou

Skip to Market 162:63

Skip to My Lou 17:128, 20:55, 37:193, 61:275, 70:32, 107:48, 129:104, 158:98, 188:94, 189:46, 202, 205:76, 230:90, 232:166, 289:178

Skip to the Barbershop 109:50

Skip-a to My Lou 232:166, see also: Skip to My Lou

Skipping Music 11:33

The Sky-Blue Dove/La Paloma Azul 89:72

The sky is a-glow in the morning 89:100

Sky is his ceiling, grass is his bed 159:315

Skye Boat Song 22:18, 71:58, 72:115

Slack your rope, hangsman 24:822, 226:72, see also: 176:60, 226:385

Sleep, ah, sleep, my darling baby 125:18, 262:93

Sleep, baby, night has fallen 16:37

Sleep, Baby, Sleep 59:48, 285:62

Sleep, Baby, Sleep/Schlaf, Kindlein, Schlaf 17:84, 125:105, 185, 188:96, 289:16

Sleep, baby, sleep, and good night 289:34

Sleep, baby, sleep, our cottage vale is deep 59:48, 285:62

Sleep, baby, sleep, Thy father guards the sheep 17:84, *see also:* 125:105, 185, 188:96, 289:16

Sleep, baby, sleep, thy father watches his sheep 125:105, 185, *see also:* 17:84, 188:96, 289:16

Sleep, baby, sleep! Your father keeps the sheep 188:96, *see also:* 17:84, 125:105, 185, 289:16

Sleep Is a Pillow 91:48

Sleep, little boy, go to sleep 125:92, *see also:* 71:123, 85:101, 125:96

Sleep, Little Daughter 19:17

Sleep, Little Dove 54:120, 184:44

Sleep, little Dove of mine 54:120, 184:44

Sleep, little Dove, the sky's dark above 54:120, 184:44

Sleep, little Jesus, my treasure, my blessing 241:74, *see also:* 54:220, 279:122

Sleep, little one, sleep! Out the doors there runs a sheep! 33:74

Sleep, little princeling, oh sleep! 71:123, *see also:* 85:101, 125:92, 125:96

Sleep, my babe, the hum of bees foretells that night is coming 125:62

Sleep, my baby, sleep now and rest 125:17

Sleep, my baby, slumber deep 177:92

Sleep my beauty, close to mother 78:71

Sleep, My Child 125:118, 194:16

Sleep, my child and peace attend thee 21:337, 125:72, 289:26, *see also:* 59:20, 205:60

Sleep, my child, my princeling, rest 125:118, *see also:* 194:16

Sleep, My Darling/Dormi, Dormi, O Bel Bambin 209:30, *see also:* 54:248, 241:94

Sleep, My Duckling 245:87

Sleep, my duckling in the rushes 245:87

Sleep, My Little Jesus 241:182

Sleep, my little one, my loved one 125:130

Sleep, my love and peace attend thee 59:20, 205:69, *see also:* 21:337, 125:72, 289:26

Sleep, My Saviour, Sleep 220:107, 241:194

Sleep, My Son 123:56

Sleep my son, oh slumber softly 123:56

Sleep Now and Rest 125:17

Sleep now, my little baby 125:122

The Sleep of the Infant Jesus/Le Sommeil de l' Enfant Jésus 54:100, 241:82

Sleep, O Holy Child of Mine/Dormi, Dormi, O Bel Bambin 241:94, *see also:* 54:248, 209:30

Sleep, O Sleep, My Lovely Child/Dormi, Dormi, O Bel Bambin 54:248, *see also:* 209:30, 241:94

Sleep oh, sleep oh, sleep oh 79:17

Sleep On, Little One 125:90, *see also:* 71:52

Sleep, sleep, beauty bright 59:41

Sleep, sleep, come to my darling 208:25

Sleep, sleep, little child, the bed of moss is warm 125:29

Sleep, sleep, my little baby 125:28

Sleep, sleep, to dreamland fly 125:107

Sleep, Sweet Babe 125:132, *see also:* 210:124

Sleep, sweet babe, my cares beguiling 125:132, 210:124

Sleep well, Thou lovely heav'nly Babe 54:156

Sleepers, Arise! 71:60

The Sleepy Bear 207:30

Sleepy Dolly 167:40

Sleepy, sleepy, dolly, nestle here on my arm 167:40

Sleepy, sleepy the cow went to bed for the night 41:14

Sleepytime 125:110

Sleepytime has come for my baby 125:110

Sliczna Panienka/Carol of the Hay 54:216

A Sliding Song 207:74

Slip one and two 165:183

The Sloop John B. 148:344, *see also:* 226:22

Slovak Polka 100:111

Slow down, dogies, quit your roving around 61:224, *see also:* Night-Herding Song

Slowly, slowly walks my Granddad 165:172

Slowly winding thro' the desert in stately motion 89:244

Slumber, Dear Jesus 184:54

Slumber, my little one, slumber, my pretty one 71:121, 72:60

Slumber, Slumber 71:121, 72:60

Slumber Song 77:34

Slumber Soundly 125:35

The sly fox, passed, passed 269:62

A sly young fox one day did spy 62:43

Slysèli Jsme V Betlemě/We Have Heard in Bethlehem 54:228

Smack Aunt Julie Down 83:489

A Small Bird Swings 7:22

Small shells, shining brightly 87:68

The Smallest Man in Jericho 124:182

A Smile Is Quite a Funny Thing 26:20

Smile Song (S–M–I–L–E) 25:39, 26:12

Smile the while you kiss me sad adieu 170:109

Smiles 170:37

Smoke Goes Up the Chimney 253:90, *see also:* 26:34

Smokey the Bear 26:81

Smoo 261:10

Smoothly we go like a bird on the wing 7:14

Snagtooth Sal 61:289

Snail 14:378, 100:96 *(Hand in hand you see us well)*

The Snail/Dendenmushi 286:21 *(Here comes the snail)*

Snail Snail 162:26

Snail, snail, come out and be fed 17:134, 59:27

The Snake 144:7

The Snake Baked a Hoecake 234:24, 292:115

The snake in sleepy sunlight lies 144:7

The Snappy Turtle Says 166:40

Snow 162:35 *(The snow is piled so high)*

Snow 11:30 *(Snow is falling on the ground)*

Snow Boy 207:75

Snow Feathers 7:11

Snow Flakes 41:3

Snow flakes and winter winds all have gone away 41:10

Snow is falling on the ground 11:31

The snow is piled so high 162:35

The Snow Lay On the Ground 54:54

Snow, snow from the sky! 207:74

Snowfall, snowfall 91:30

The Snowflakes 177:88

Snowflakes gently falling down 41:3

The Snowman 41:5

Snows 261:42

Snows are fallin' on Douglas Mountain 59:70

Snows descend sugar softly 261:42

The Snowy Breasted Pearl 42:597

Snuff Is Very Guilty/Fhola Li Na Mulanda 89:275

So cheer up my lads, 'tis to glory we steer 98:51

So Far 218:268

So gaily I was riding 85:179

So her pop sez "Nay" 24:840

So Long, It's Been Good to know Yuh! 64:107, 130:59, 230:92

So many, many things to wear 91:5

So This Is Love 276:39

So we tap, tap, tap, tap the feet of dancing dollies 128:98

A Soft Answer 155:11

Soft cool breezes help us sing 49:18

Soft Falls the Dew 262:53

Soft o'er the fountain, ling'ring falls the southern moon 21:259, 170:25, see also: 61:144

Soft the night is falling 125:33

Softly falls the light of day 25:125, 26:94

Softly Now the Light of Day 125:83

Softly, Silently 7:30

Softly silently kittens and cats 7:30

Softly, so softly it came 162:30

Softly the evening, softly the night 155:29

Softly the Night is Sleeping 251

Solas Market 130:85

Soldier Boy 134:96

Soldier, Soldier 17:55, 290:80, see also: Soldier, Soldier, Won't You Marry Me

Soldier, Soldier, Will You Marry Me? 17:55, 62:118, 148:348, 290:80, see also: Soldier, Soldier, Won't You Marry Me

Soldier, Soldier, Won't You Marry Me 21:186, 142, 157:72, 227:24, see also: 17:55, 62:118, 80:32, 148:348, 290:80

Soldier, Won't You Marry Me? 79:32, see also: Soldier, Soldier, Won't You Marry Me

The soldiers from town to the foot of the hill 240:114

Soldier's Joy 126:49

The Soldier's Lamentation 240:116

The Soldier's Life 27:130

Soldier's Song 85:167

Solidarity Forever 64:12, 230:91

Soliloquy 218:91

Solo River/Bengawan Solo 265:14

Solomon Grundy 112:49

Some are fancy on the outside 219:11

Some corn for this baby? 236:77

Some Day My Prince Will Come 275:14, 276:2

Some Enchanted Evening 218:129

Some enchanted evening you may see a stranger 218:129

Some hae meat and canna eat 71:14, 101:33

Some homes are on the mountainside 86:152

Some Love Coffee, Some Love Tea 110:38

Some people say a teacher's made out of steel 64:141

Some Say the Devil's Dead 134:43

Some talk of Alexander, and some of Hercules 22:198, 240:142

Some they will talk of bold Robin Hood 164:94

Some think the world is made for fun and frolic 22:43

Some time ago—two weeks or more 159:272

Somebody 226:464

Somebody Come and Play 206:124

Somebody come and play 206:124

Somebody, Nobody, Walks Down the Aisle 63:70

Somebody Stole 110:34

Somebody Stole My Hoo-to Foo-to Boo-to Bah! 237:unpaged

Somebody stole my old coon dog 110:34

Somebody's Coming! 149:30

Somebody's Darling 73:228

Somebody's tall and handsome 226:464

Someday Little Children 206:108

Someday, little children, someday soon 206:108

Someday Very Soon 162:71

Someone is hiding, hiding, hiding 291:62, *see also:* 165:20

Someone Nice 206:74

Someone's Opinion of Arizona 61:82

Something Good 218:249

Something happened the other day, that never happened before 226:183

Something Kind 86:101

Something to Share 77:25

Something Wonderful 218:208

Sometimes I Feel Like a Motherless Child 158:368, 230:49, 277:95

Sometimes I plow my old grey horse 158:232

Sometimes I'm very, very small 165:187

Sometimes People Are Good 219:24

Sometimes you feel like holding your pillow all night long 219:32

The Son of a Gambolier 226:44

Son of a Gun 159:287

The Son of Mary/El Noi de la Mare 54:260

Song for a Boy 156:4

Song for a Girl 156:26

Song for a New Baby 244:290

Song For New Things 77:23

Song for Returned Pawnee Soldiers 74:54

A Song Made Upon the Election of New Magistrates for This City 240:27

A Song Made Upon the Foregoing Occasion 240:28

Song of a Boy Growing Up 19:39

Song of Baptism 124:89

Song of Birds/Sa Tah Ryung 208:41

Song of Departure 69:27

Song of Dixie 69:40

Song of Five 206:31

Song of Greeting 79:8

Song of Love/I ga'ma Lo Tando 89:274

Song of Pentecost 124:251

Song of Praise 155:7 *(Let us now our voices raise)*

Song of Praise 207:43 *(Heav'nly Father, we sing praises)*

Song of Praise/Um Home 163:39 *(I praise my fathers who came from Ngoni)*

Song of Praise 85:81 *(Thou, Thou, Jehova, hear my singing)*

Song of the Big Tree Region 69:42

Song of the Blackbirds 74:17

Song of the Border 61:81

Song of the Bunnies 245:45

Song of the Buzzards 74:18

Song of the Cactus Region 69:37

Song of the Captive Goose Woman 74:33

Song of the Cattle Driver/Nambu Ushiori Uta 49:28

Song of the Children 124:31

Song of the Coyote 74:48

Song of the Crib 184:42, *see also:* Joseph, Dearest Joseph

Song of the Deer Dancing 19:13

Song of the Delhi Tongawallah/Ponycart Driver 262:150

Song of the Emigrant Trail 61:124

Song of the Fig Vendors/Mahiya Illa Zalab 89:246

Song of the Fishes 289:72, *see also:* 292:168

Song of the Flute 74:27

Song of the Followers 124:99

Song of the Frog Waiting for Spring 19:29

Song of the Great Lakes Region 69:46

Song of the Great Wall 22:204

Song of the Guaranteed Wage 64:162

Song of the Heads 28:82, 240:165

Song of the Honduran Sailor/Canción del Marinero Hondureño 89:74

Song of the Hummingbird 74:20

Song of the Islands/Na Lei Hawaii 87:81

Song of the Kansas Emigrant 157:36

Song of the Land Shell/He Mele O Ke Kahuli 87:15

Song of the Maremma 262:47

Song of the Minute Man 240:86

Song of the Moccasin Game 74:45

Song of the Nighthawk 74:22

Song of the Old Wolf 74:44

A Song of the Open Air 262:84

Song of the Orphan/Ny O L'on Nanacy 89:267

Song of the Plumber 84:36

Song of the Princess/Sein Kyu Kya Nyaung 89:221

Song of the Sacred Stones 74:37

The Song of the Salvation Army 290:134

Song of the Sea 72:129

Song of the Seasons 86:184

The Song of the Ship-Builders 262:133

Song of the Six Hundred Thousand 73:130

Song of the Southland 69:45

Song of the Sun 79:9

Song of the Tailor/Schneiderlied 208:2

Song of the Three "Nots"/San Wu Yao 49:19

The Song of the Three Wise Men 241:66, 284:93

Song of the Watchers 74:59

Song of the Wind 162:33

Song of the Wise Men/De Tierra Lejana Venimos 54:288, *see also:* 140:22

Song of the Wise Men/Los Reyes Oriente 140:22, *see also:* 54:288

Song of the Young Wolves 74:43
Song of Wind and Water 124:126
A Song On the Brave General Montgomery 240:118
Song to Make a Baby Laugh 19:23
Song to the Moon/Cancao a Lua 89:164
Songs of Praise the Angels Sang 65:93
The Songs We Sang Upon the Old Camp Ground 73:288
Sons of freedom, listen to me 240:200
The Sons of Liberty 240:147
The sons of the Prophet are hardy and bold 226:344, *see also:* 25:34
The sons of the prophet were hardy and bold 25:34, *see also:* 226:344
Soon as we all cook sweet potatoes 290:198
Soon One Mornin' 158:358
Soplan la brisas de la mañana 89:103
Soroud-e-daneshkade Afsari 169:36
A soul! A soul! A soul cake 134:26, 210:26, *see also:* 293:72
Soul Cakes 293:72, *see also:* 134:26, 210:26
Soul, soul, soul cake 293:72, *see also:* 134:26, 210:26
The Souling Song 134:26, 210:26, *see also:* 293:72
Soum, Soum/Lullaby 208:25
The Sound of Music 218:220
Sounds Are Fun 91:26
Soup Song 64:130
Soup, Soup 109:103
Sourwood Mountain 37:148, 46:214, 134:38, 158:84, 226:125, *see also:* 24:897, 226:320
The Southern Girl 73:248
The Southern Soldier Boy 73:252
Southrons, hear your country call you! 73:11
Southwel New 273:130
Sovu Dance 89:262
Sow Got the Measles 292:62, *see also:* 277:63
The Sow Took the Measles 277:63, *see also:* 292:62
Sow your oats and reap your corn 83:489
The Sower 155:16
Sowing in the morning, sowing seeds of kindness 157:166
Soy Pobre Vaquero 61:230
Space Bug 97:unpaged
Space Derby Song 26:76
Space Rocket Rick 167:16
The Spacious Firmament on High 262:100
Spanish heavens spread their brilliant starlight 22:210
Spanish is the lovin' tongue 61:146
The Spanish Knight 168:110
Spanish Ladies 21:330, 27:204, 262:65
Spanish Lullaby 125:122

Sparkling in the windows 207:61
Sparrow School/Su zu me No Gakko 266:47, *see also:* 286:14
The Sparrows 191:52
Sparrows' Music School/Suzume-no Gakko 286:14, *see also:* 266:47
Speak/Khuluma 163:115
Speak very softly 91:44
Speaking of Cowboy's Home 159:315
Special 206:112
The Speckled Bird 114:76
The speckled duck plays the bagpipes 51
Speed, bonnie boat, like bird on the wing 22:18, 71:58, 72:115
Speed Your Journey 85:191
The Speller's Fate 84:30
The Spider 46:216, *see also:* Eency Weency Spider
The Spider and the Fly 175:168
A Spider for Miss Muffet 166:24
The Spider in the Corner 67:71
The spider made a road 74:16
The Spider Makes a Road 74:16
Spin, Little Dreidel 207:62
Spin, Spin 262:135
Spin, spin, O my darling daughter 262:135
Spinning Chorus 85:209
Spirit of the Living God 85:205
Spirit Song/Manthi'ki 89:273
The Spirit Will Appear 19:41
Spirits! You press me under! 19:29
Sponge Fishing 114:56
Spoon 100:38
A Spoonful of Sugar 276:54
The Sporting Bachelors 158:52
A Spotless Rose 210:82
A spotless rose is blowing 210:82
The Spotted Bird/La Pájara Pinta 168:127
The Spotted Bull/El Toro Pinto 216:41
Spring 91:32
Spring Carol 27:54, 189:68
Spring has now unwrapped the flowers 184:58
Spring Is Coming 112:50
Spring is coming, spring is coming, birdies, build your nest 112:50
Spring is here with all her joys 27:54, *see also:* 189:68
Spring Puddles 207:88
Spring Rain 261:28
Spring Song 41:10 (*Snowflakes and winter winds*)
Spring Song 97:unpaged (*Hello, Mister Robin in the tree*)
Spring Song/Haru-ga Kita 286:69, *see also:* 100:15 (*Springtime has come*)

Springfield Mountain 72:91, 158:28, 290:51, *see also:* 21:254, 24:828, 157:49, 292:114

Springtime 91:33 *(Eggs in nests turn into birds)*

Springtime 207:94 *(Apple blossoms pink and white)*

Springtime/Yangsando 49:43 *(Springtime, springtime, beautiful springtime)*

Springtime Has Come 100:15, *see also:* 286:69

Springtime in the Rockies 290:132

Springtime, springtime, beautiful springtime is here with us again 49:43

Square Dance 178:46

Squeball 61:18, 61:20, *see also:* 234:68

The Squirrel 79:43, 128:38, 292:100, *see also:* 234:19 *(The squirrel is a pretty thing)*

The Squirrel 191:48 *(Little Squirrel, living there in the hollow tree)*

The squirrel is a pretty thing 79:34, 128:38, 234:19, 292:100

Squirrel Nutkin 245:44

Squirrel Nutkin has a coat of brown 245:44

Ssemukazi agenda 236:11

Ssemusota/Giant Snake 89:265

The Stable 67:4

Staffan 238

Staffan looked out and there in the sky 238

Staffansvisa/Saint Stephen Was Riding 279:114

Stagolee 230:51

Stagolee was a bad man 230:51

Stamp and dance, be nimble and merry 69:17, 71:76, 72:140

The Stampede 159:99

Stand the Storm 55:273

Stand Up, Stand Up, for Jesus 22:290

Standin' On the Walls of Zion 226:484

Standing in a stream 74:14

Standing in the Need of Prayer 148:350

Standing stiff and straight and tall 166:54

Star Bright 59:58, 162:37, *see also:* 68:8

Star bright, star light, First star I see tonight 162:37, *see also:* 59:58, 68:8

Star Festival/Tanabata 286:81

Star in the East 140:78, 233:36, *see also:* 54:88, 210:20

Star light, star bright, first star I see tonight 59:58, 68:8, *see also:* 162:37

Star of Bethlehem 140:119 *(See the Star of Bethlehem)*

Star of Bethlehem 197:114 *(The night a Child was born)*

The Star of the County Down 42:610

Star of the East 54:88, *see also:* 140:78, 210:20, 233:36

Star Promenade 83:500

The Star-Spangled Banner 12, 21:272, 22:184, 25:48, 26:85, 27:151, 66:80, 69:2, 71:2, 72:26, 122, 127:39, 148:354, 160:14, 197:64, 240:207, 249, 283:67

Star Wish 59:58, *see also:* 68:8, 162:37

Starej Breclavy/Near Breclave 89:186

Starlight, Starlight 68:8, *see also:* 59:58, 162:37

The Starlighter 59:16

The Stars and Stripes Forever 25:42

The Stars and the Moon 67:26

The stars are burning cheerily, cheerily 71:64, 72:122, *see also:* 208:76

The stars are shining cheerily, cheerily 208:76, *see also:* 71:64, 72:122

Stars in the Heaven 233:12

Stars in the Sky 125:23

Stars of Glory 209:32

Stars of glory shine more brightly 209:32

Stars of the Summer Night 71:124, 72:61

Start not as the sparkling light 59:61

Starving to Death on a Government Claim 158:238

The State of Arkansas 158:240, 159:283

The State Song 26:79

A Stately Song 290:136

Statistics prove, prove that you've one birthday 275:44, 276:45

Stay Awake 275:53

Stay, mighty love, and teach my song 273:150

Steal Away 22:298, 148:358, 277:21

Steal away, steal away, steal away to Jesus 22:298, 148:358, 277:21

Steal Up, Young Lady 109:119

Steamboat Bill 61:42

Stepping On the Dog/Guan Pazek 168:75

Stepping Tigers 207:110

Steve is the engine, oh yes 232:151, *see also:* 232:150

Stewball 234:68, *see also:* 61:18, 61:20

Stick Dance/Kolattam 70:10, 100:126, 168:57

Still and dark the night about the sheiling 210:92

Still, Still, Still 54:180

Stille Nacht/Silent Night 54:176, 86:45, 148:332, 148:333, 241:58, 279:86, 282, 283:48

Stilly Night, Starry and Bright 125:76

Stodola Pumpa 148:360, *see also:* 25:88, 262:23

Stodole Pumpa 262:23, *see also:* 25:88, 148:360

Stonewall Jackson's Way 73:84

Stonewall's Requiem 73:203

Stop Your Groaning 289:52, *see also:* 292:213

Store ure siger tick, tock, tick, tock 262:33, see also: 68:48

Stork Lange Bein/Stork Long-O'-Leg 189:146

Stork Long-O'-Leg/Stork Lange Bein 189:146

Stork, stork, long-o'-leg 189:146

Stormalong 24:834, 33:34

Stornello Toscano/Tuscan Serenade 208:37

A story, a story to you I will tell 35:100

A story has come down from old Mathusem 35:80

A Story of Four Little Birds 41:12

The Story of Twelve 129:62, see also: Green Grow the Rushes, Ho!

The Story the Crow Told Me 290:68

Strangest Dream 230:32

The Strawberry Roan 223, 225:32, see also: 61:187, 61:189

Streets of Cairo 157:186

The Streets of Forbes 176:80

The Streets of Laredo 21:212, 61:321, 148:262, 158:206, 225:56, 230:41, 272:18, 277:61, see also: 24:859, 60:16, 146:30, 159:417, 226:263

Stretch Your Arms 204:21

Stretch your arms away up high 204:21

The Strife Is O'er 161:47

The strife is o'er, the battle done 161:47

Strike for the South 73:32

Striking a Tune/Kabak da Boynuma 89:180

A String of Beads/Umqokozo 163:78

A Strutting Rooster/He Moa Kane 87:17

Study War No More 230:50, see also: Down By the Riverside

Su Zu Me No Gakko/Sparrow School 266:47, see also: 286:14

Suantree (Hush Song) 125:60, see also: 42:613

Such a Getting Upstairs 232:53

Such a very big girl 49:17

Sucking Cider Through a Straw 226:329, see also: 148:338, 290:38

Sugar Babe 158:108

Sugar-Lump 24:810

Suitors 72:104

Sumer Is a-Cumen In 71:108, see also: 27:154, 176:144, 189:110, 293:80

Summer Bouquet 97:unpaged

Summer Is a-Coming In 27:154, 71:108, 176:144, 293:80, see also: 189:110

Summer Is I-cumen In 189:110, see also: 27:154, 71:108, 176:144, 293:80

Summer Puddles 261:36

Summer Sweet 275:76, 276:72

The Sun 245:14

The Sun and the Moon/El Sol y la Luna 216:44

The Sun Be Warm 55:259

The sun calls himself Lorenzo 216:44

Sun Is Down 125:112

The Sun is Rising Out of Bed 245:2, see also: 71:48

The Sun It Rises 293:102

Sun of My Soul 45:17

The sun sets at night 61:116, 273:114

The sun shines bright on the old Kentucky home 21:134, 157:88, 205:135

The sun shines down on the cornfield 27:196, see also: 21:296

The sun was sinking in the west 159:366

The sun, whose rays are all a-blaze with ever living glory 252:52

The Sun Worshippers 69:26, 262:136

Sunday 85:173

Sunday Morning Song 86:157

Sunny Bank 190:128, see also: I Saw Three Ships

Sunny Day 11:22

Sunny day, sweepin' the clouds away 206:7

Sunny Morning 7:24

The sun's so hot that eggs will hatch 61:97, see also: 61:96

Sunset 125:32

Sunsets of Smiles 261:24

Sunshine and Rain 245:78

Sunshine and rain, yes, both these must be 245:78

The Sunshine Special comin' around de bend 226:246

Suo-Gan 220:80

Suo-gan, do not weep 220:80

Suomen Salossa/The Finnish Forest 89:172

The Super-Supper March 237:unpaged

Supercalifragilisticexpialidocious 275:50, 276:52

Sur le Pont d'Avignon/On the Bridge 78:39, 148:364, 188:76, 189:44, 217:24, see also: 14:372

Sure I love the dear silver 170:40

Sure never was picture drawn more to the life 240:42

Suriram 114:24

Surprise! 206:60

The Surrender of Cornwallis 240:139

The Surrey with the Fringe on Top 218:19

Sus In Poarta Raiului/At the Gates of Heaven Above 54:238

Susan, Billy everyone 11:23

Susani 54:152

Süse, Liebe Süse/Susy, Lovely Susy 79:74

Susie's Sitting Sewing 178:10

Suspira, Coracao Triste/My Heart Is Heavy With Sadness 89:91
Sussex Carol 54:40, *see also:* 210:56
Sussex Mummers' Carol 210:54
Susy, Lovely Susy/Süse, Liebe Süse 79:74
Susy, lovely Susy, pray what is the news? 79:74
Suzume-no Gakko/Sparrows' Music School 286:14, *see also:* 266:47
Svensk Masquerade 83:498
The Swan Sings 262:35
Swan Swum 112:63
Swan swum over the sea 112:63
Swanee River 230:83, *see also:* 22:86, 127:99
Swans sing before they die 176:141
Swansea Town 208:74
The Swapping Boy 143, *see also:* Swapping Song
The Swapping Song 37:174, 129:38, 213:10, *see also:* 18:36, 111:63, 143, 188:44
Sway away away to sleep 19:17
Sway, sway, sway, the dead tree nearly totters 100:52
Sweep, Sweep and Cleanse Your Floor 190:138
Sweet Adeline 157:200
Sweet and Low 125:52
Sweet are the girls from my country 89:71
Sweet babe, a golden cradle holds thee 42:613, 125:60
Sweet Baby, Sleep 184:70
Sweet Be Your Sleep 125:34, 262:86
Sweet Betsy From Pike 1, 22:62, 24:861, 61:48, 157:38, 158:176, 159:388, 205:122, 224, 226:107, 239:66
Sweet By and By 66:150, *see also:* 21:176
Sweet camellia flower, oh! 49:41
Sweet Genevieve 157:168, 170:42
Sweet Kate 85:13
Sweet Lei Lehua 87:42
Sweet Lily 61:228
Sweet Mary Sings Her Babe to Sleep/Chtic, Aby Spal, Tak Zpívala 54:234
Sweet Music Enchanting 262:148
Sweet nightingale awake 279:62
Sweet Orange/Naranja Dulce 295:36
Sweet Potatoes 290:198
The Sweet Rosy Morn 245:11
The sweet rosy morn peeps over the hills 245:11
Sweet Sabbath school more dear to me 66:144
Sweet Sixteen/I-pal Chyongchyun Ka 49:42
Sweet the evening air of May 71:111, 72:171
Sweet Thing 158:106

A sweet Tuxedo girl you see 21:23
Sweet Was the Song the Virgin Sang 210:62
Sweet Water Rolling 232:65
Sweeter figs you will find nowhere 89:246
Sweetest Little Baby 63:102
Sweetest little fellow, eve'rybody knows 125:136, 205:268
Sweetheart, Good Night/Dobrou Noc 208:13
Sweetly Sings the Donkey 26:45, 62:17, 143:3, 148:366, 176:129, 254:116, 289:187, 292:32, 293:94
Swiftly Flowing Labe 262:63
Swim, Little Duck 162:15
Swim, little fish, in water clear 165:112
Swimmin' Fun 166:74
Swine-Herders 24:810, *see also:* 27:24
The Swing 245:20
Swing into line, my boys, send the chorus 'round 197:99
Swing high a low gently down 19:37
Swing Low Sweet Chariot 22:310, 25:106, 31:43, 69:30, 83:474, 148:368, 157:144, 205:354, 230:16
Swing on the Corner 55:509
Swing Song 41:37
Swing, swing, swing, the swing goes up and down 100:52
A swing to swing 149:8
Swinging 288:16
Swinging Along 69:55
Swinging along the open road 69:55
Swinging Game 100:52
Swinging in the Swing 227:44
Swinging, swinging, now we go up 41:37
Swinging, swinging, on a high trapeze 288:16
The Sword of Robert E. Lee 73:78
Sycamore Tree 288:4
Sylvie 72:74, *see also:* 130:79
Symphony from the Christmas Oratorio 210:147
Sz Bbei Shang Gung/Poor Sz Bbei 49:16

T

Ta Av Na Legba 278:43
Ta-Ra-Ra Boom-De-Ay (parody) 147:23
Ta-ra-ra-boom-dee-ay, ta-ra-ra-boom-dee-ay 170:90
Ta-ra-ra boom-de-ay, we had no school today 147:23
Ta-Ra-Ra-Boom-Der-E 21:23
Table Graces 86:213
Tachanka 22:214

Taddle-o-Day 274:32, *see also:* 234:28

Taffy Was a Welshman 17:135

Tahleeng Tahvahng Toalgoy/Five Hills 208:43

The Tailor and the Mouse 75:70, 117:unpaged, 292:194

Take a common little bronco 159:296

Take a Whiff on Me 158:314

Take Back Your Gold 21:58

Take from purple tree bamboo straight and true 208:12

Take heart, the journey's ended 241:90

Take me out to the hospital 63:97

Take me riding in the car-car 274:8, *see also:* 130:66

Take my brush, take my broom 130:22

Take My Life and Let It Be 86:123

Take my little hoe 130:92

Take these stripes from, stripes from around my shoulder 129:324

Take This Hammer 21:210, 24:913, 64:80, 158:322, 239:48, 277:87

Take you riding in my car 130:66, *see also:* 274:8

Take Your Gun and Go, John 73:112

Take your partner by the hand 207:72

Take Your Time, Miss Lucy 128:16

Tale of a Pig 110:42, *see also:* The Old Woman and Her Pig

Talent Roundup 119:104

Talk It Out 91:12

Talk it out, talk it over 91:12

Talking Union 64:22

Tall shop in the town 165:66

A tall thin man walking along, walking along 165:168

Tallis's Canon 71:106, 72:51, 86:170, 176:104, 189:60

Tanabata/Star Festival 286:81

Tancuj 69:17, 71:76, 72:140

Tandis que tout sommeille 89:141

Tangishaka 89:258

Tant Hessie Se Witperd/Aunt Hessie's White Horse 189:140

Tap Tap i yi langa more 163:108

Tap, tap, oh, more sun 163:108

Tap Your Foot 130:14

Taps 25:126, 26:92, 69:10, 71:12, 72:53, 148:370, 197:62, 277:45

Tarancuta/Happy Bride 208:60

Tarantella of Posilipo/Cicerenella 78:47

Taticek/Father 189:148

Taue/Rice Planting 286:78, *see also:* Planting Rice

Taw Nye Vyetyer/'Tis No Wind 208:78

Te Kieldrecht/In Kieldrecht 89:139

A Tea Party 162:76 *(Come and have a cup of tea)*

The Tea Party 28:26, *see also:* 240:53 *(I snum I am a Yankee man)*

Teach Us, Dear Lord, to Pray 86:22

Teach Us to Pray 86:142

The Teacher's Lament 64:141

Teče Voda Teče/Flow, Oh Water, Flow On 208:15

Tecolote 27:70

Tee-bee-wenda-bah-no-gwen 19:13

Teen, Teen, Teeny Weeny Lady/Tin Tin Tini Mini Hanim 169:72, 266:58

The Teensy Weensy Spider 292:202, *see also:* Eency Weency Spider

The Telephone 227:14

The Telephone Book Lullaby 59:62

Telephones 162:74

Tell me a tale of kings and queens 125:42

Tell Me, Fair Ladies 85:96

Tell Me, Is My Father Coming Home? 73:282

Tell me lovely Shepherd, where thou feeds't at noon thy fleecy care? 189:86

Tell me one thing, tell me truly 62:117, 83:478

Tell Me, Rain/Dime, Lluvia 216:45

Tell me, tell me, tell me true 204:25

Tell me . . . tell me . . . where is Fancie bred(Britten) 85:251

Tell Me the Stories of Jesus 86:121

Tell me the tales that to me were so dear 205:99

Tell me where have you been, Billy boy 38, *see also:* Billy Boy

Tell me where is fancy bred(Kodaly) 85:257

Tell me where is fancy bred(Poulenc) 85:255

Tell me where you're going now 16:16

Tell me who? 89:300

Tell Me Why 25:122, 26:63, 148:372

Tell me why the sky is filled with music 218:134

Tell old Bill, when he leaves home dis mornin' 226:18

Tell once more the ancient story 209:56

Tell Tale, Tit 17:78

Tell us, where do you come from? 286:50

Telling Time 41:18

Ten Fingers 75:72

Ten Green Bottles 82, 148:376, *see also:* 147:30, 290:32

Ten in the Bed 147:32, *see also:* 26:23, 63:131, 148:254, 254:110, 290:34

Ten Little Goblins 197:96

Ten Little Indians 17:144, 75:74

The Ten Puppies/Los Diez Perritos 295:17

Ten Thousand Cattle 146:152, 159:128

Ten thousand cattle, gone astray 146:152, 159:128

Ten Thousand God-Damn Cattle 159:130

Ten Thousand Men Were Going On Manoeuvres 262:137

Ten Thousand Miles Away 226:100

Ten Thousand Miles Away From Home 226:456

The Tenderfoot 61:198, 226:274, 277:67, *see also:* 159:121

Tenting on the Old Camp Ground 73:152, 197:60, *see also:* 21:150, 127:157

Tenting Tonight 21:150, *see also:* 73:152, 127:157, 197:60

A tepee is my home 207:40

Teru, Terubozu/Wishing Dolls 286:56

The Texas Cowboy 61:107 *(With a sort of careless swagger)*

The Texas Cowboy 60:48, 61:91, 61:93, 146:66, 159:22 *(Oh, I'm a Texas cowboy, far away from home)*

A Texas cowboy lay down on a bar room floor 61:336, 159:236

The Texas Cowboys 159:291, *see also:* 159:342

The Texas Idol 61:104, *see also:* 159:138

Texas Jack 61:125

Texas Rangers 33:234, 159:359, 159:361

The Texas Song 159:57, *see also:* 21:108, 61:182, 69:21, 277:35

The Texian Boys 158:44, 159:338

Thanayi/No, Child 163:112

Thank Him for work and play 86:201

Thank Thee, Heav'nly Father 86:144

Thank You 11:26

Thank You for the sun, big and round and bright 77:12

Thank You for the World So Sweet 55:253

Thank You for This Lovely Day 55:253

Thank You, Loving Father 86:206

"Thank You, Ma'am," Says Dan 42:603

Thank you mother! I'm near you! 89:59

Thank You, our dear Father 77:16

Thank you, pretty cow that made 17:115

Thank you, thank you, thank you, Wati 89:261

Thank You, Wati/Tole Ya Wati 89:261

Thanking God 86:201

Thanks and praise for our days 'neath the sun 71:12

Thanks for Thanksgiving 167:50

Thanks to God 86:164

Thanksgiving Canon 72:63

Thanksgiving Day 17:56, *see also:* 40, 133:298, 197:106 *(Over the river and through the woods)*

Thanksgiving Day 97:unpaged *(We have Thanksgiving Day as did the Pilgrims long ago)*

Thanksgiving Prayer 205:24, *see also:* 21:338, 27:234, 45:56

Thanksgiving Time Has Come 86:176

That big husky brute from the cattle chute 128:84, *see also:* 239:26

That chuck wagon brute from the cattle chute 239:26, *see also:* 128:84

That Great Getting-Up Morning 27:74

That Is Even So 61:44

That my wishing might be smaller here I kneel, dear Child, at Thy feet 67:40

That New River Train 88, *see also:* New River Train

That old jackfish swimming up the stream 135:45

That seat of science, Athens 240:57, *see also* 27:120, 28:43, 273:28

That Sunshine Special comin' around de bend 226:246, *see also:* 158:68, 226:247

That's All About Mr. Small 154:40

That's what I should like the best 67:75

Then God sent an angel from heaven so high 233:32

Then it's a hooraw, and a hooraw 226:484

Then it's allemande left on the corner 61:279

Then we'll sing of Lydia Pinkham 226:210

There ain't no liars there in my Father's house 226:483

There aloft in a soft and friendly breeze 25:42

There are bonds of all sorts in this world of ours 73:276

There Are Boys 26:15

There Are Cubs 26:52

There Are Dads(Boys) 26:15

There are smiles that make us happy 170:37

There are snakes, snakes, snakes big as garden rakes 25:36

There are suitors at my door 72:104

There are ten green bottles a-standing on the wall 290:32, *see also:* 147:30, 148:376

There are twelve months in all the year 164:104

There Came a Girl from France 63:52

There came to my window one morning in spring 245:10

There chanced to be a pedlar bold 164:64

There I sat on Buttermilk Hill 22:69, 157:24, 262:25, *see also:* Johnny Has Gone for a Soldier

There is a charm I can't explain 21:202, 66:114

There is a flower within my heart 21:19, 205:234, *see also:* 26:19, 83:493, 148:40

There Is a Green Hill Far Away 45:15, 86:58, 161:41

There Is a Happy Land 66:155
There is a house in New Orleans 230:18
There Is a Lady in This Town 62:144
There is a Lady Sweet and Kind 85:12
There is a little town in Switzerland 107:34
There Is a Tavern in the Town 205:205
There is fire up aloft 129:84
There Is No Rose 85:237, 220:48
There is no rose of such vertu 85:237, *see also:* 220:48
There is no rose of such virtue 220:48, *see also:* 85:237
There Is Nothin' Like a Dame 218:173
There is someone in our house 207:117
There is the moon 89:256
There once was a boy named Pierre 235:43
There once was a certain yellow fox 261:18
There once was a frog who lived in a bog 63:134
There Once Was a Maiden 62:96
There once was a man named Michael Finnigin 36:80, *see also:* 25:41, 62:67, 197:30, 289:138
There once was a noble ranger 159:363, *see also:* 61:140
There once was a sailor named Crumpit 91:42
There once was a sow who had three little piggies 130:111, 289:50, *see also:* 292:57
There once was an Indian maid 61:142
There once was a union maid 64:17
There She Stands, A Lovely Creature 24:804, *see also:* 39:20, 63:66, 135:70
There Stands a Lady on a Mountain 135:70, *see also:* 24:804, 39:20, 63:66
There stands a lady on a mountain, who she is I do not know 39:20, 135:70, *see also:* 24:804, 63:66
There walked on Plover's shady banks 226:396
There was a bee sat on a wall 162:23
There was a big ranch 216:47
There was a bold fisherman who sailed out from Pimbeco 27:208, 128:116, 239:21, 256
There was a bold soldier that lately came from war 35:42
There was a captive maiden 85:103
There was a charro a-sitting 262:14
There was a crane sat on a stone 189:52, *see also:* 27:104
There Was a Crooked Man 17:19, 62:88, 111:67, 175:28, 285:37, 289:82
There was a crow sat on a stone 27:104, *see also:* 189:52
There Was a Donkey Standing By 197:119
There was a fair lady who lived on the plains 61:121, 146:48
There was a fair maiden I dearly adored 36:8
There was a farmer had a dog and Bingo was his name-o 289:54, *see also:* Bingo
There was a field that waiting lay 191:64
There was a frog lived in a well 62:44, 129:32, *see also:* Frog Went A ·Courtin'
There was a frog lived in the spring 292:118
There was a gallant ship, and a gallant ship was she 133, *see also:* 22:172, 35:46, 35:48, 89:128
There was a gallant ship from the North 133, *see also:* 22:172, 35:46, 35:48, 89:128
There was a jolly blade, that married a country maid 78:23
There was a jolly miller and he lived by himself 110:51, 165:200
There was a jolly miller once lived on the River Dee 17:76, 283:26
There was a lady, a lady gay 37:116
There was a lady loved a swine 175:76, *see also:* 46:226
There Was a Li'l Woman Who Took a Stroll 197:92
There was a lark hanging from a balcony 295:7
There was a little boy nam'd Gus 112:14
There was a little Dutchman, his name was Johnnie Verbeck 25:18
There was a little family who lived in Bethany 37:183
There Was a Little Girl 285:20
There was a little maiden 227:6
There Was a Little Man 17:119
There was a little man and he had a little can 226:208
There was a little man, and he had a little gun 175:112
There was a little man and he wooed a little maid 17:119
There was a little man with a stick for a horse 217:55
There was a little ship 217:54, *see also:* 89:62, 216:50
There was a little ship and she sailed on the sea 37:120
There was a little tree in yonder field 132:unpaged, *see also:* Green Grass Grows All Around
There Was a Little Turtle 75:76
There Was a Little Woman 17:64, *see also:* Old Woman and the Pedlar
There was a little woman as I've heard tell 17:64, 188:132, *see also:* 27:58, 68:14, 79:41, 259
There Was a Man and He Had Nought 111:62

There Was a Man and He Was Mad   232:76, 266:120

There Was a Man in Our Town   17:82, 111:36

There was a man in our town and he was wondrous wise   17:82, 111:36

There was a man lived in the moon   111:44, 162:36, 175:130, 188:104, 189:28, 289:96

There was a man named Dunderbeck invented a machine   290:158

There was a man nam'd Jackson Scott   112:56

There was a man, now please take note   62:38, 171

There Was a Naughty Boy   112:32

There was a pig went out to dig   138:unpaged, 197:121, 220:64

There Was a Piper Had a Cow   111:37

There was a poor young man, and he came to New York   290:166

There was a Presbyterian cat   62:43

There was a princess long ago   165:188

There was a rich man and he lived in Jerusalem   36:70, 62:101, 64:148

There was a rich old rancher who lived in the country by   159:192

There Was a Shepherdess/Il Etait une Bergère   217:59

There was a ship came from the north country   22:172, 35:46, *see also:* 35:48, 89:128, 133

There was a ship in the North Counteree   35:46, *see also:* 22:172, 35:48, 89:128, 133

There was a silk merchant   213:64

There was a star in David's land   96:9

There was a tailor had a mouse   75:70, 117:unpaged, 292:194

There was a tree and a very fine tree   213:20, *see also:* Green Grass Grows All Around

There was a tree (There was a tree) all in the wood (all in the wood)   290:19, *see also:* Green Grass Grows All Around

There was a wee cooper who lived in Fife   20:24, 59:44, 71:66, 72:120, 78:33, 176:24

There was a wee house in the heather   179

There was a wee lambie fell over a rock   62:37

There was a wild boar in these woods   37:126

There was a wild Montana boy, Jack Nolan was his name   159:167

There was a young man named Michael Finnegan   197:30, *see also:* 25:41, 36:80, 62:67, 289:138

There was a youth, and a well-beloved youth   71:37

There was an auld laird in Kellyburn Braes   180

There was an old coddle so molly   59:19

There was an old fellow named Sandy McNab   290:193, 293:54

There Was an Old Fish   128:48

There Was an Old Frog   234:48, *see also:* 290:108

There was an old frog and he lived in a spring   234:48, 290:108

There Was an Old Lady   27:58, *see also:* The Old Woman and the Pedlar

There was an old lady, as I've heard tell   27:58, *see also:* Old Woman and the Pedlar

There was an old lady lived over the sea   157:18, 240:55

There Was an Old Lady Who Swallowed a Fly   5, *see also:* I Know an Old Lady Who Swallowed a Fly

There was an old man and he had an old sow   84:56

There was an old man, he owned a small farm   36:74, *see also:* 230:58

There was an old man, lived over the hill   230:58, *see also:* 36:74

There was an old man named Michael Finnegan   25:41, 62:67, 289:138, *see also:* 36:80, 197:30

There was an old man that lived in the wood   62:138, 110:28, 128:120, 213:56, *see also:* 27:115, 71:93, 79:57

There was an old miller so I've heard told   37:144

There was an old rabbit lived under a hill   162:17

There Was an Old Soldier   226:432

There was an old sow   130:110, *see also:* 289:50, 292:57

There Was an Old Woman   175:120 (*There was an old woman who lived in a shoe*)

There Was an Old Woman   177:87 (*There was an old woman who lived under a hill*)

There Was an Old Woman   17:142, 18:20, 285:30, 289:78, *see also:* 111:56, 175:154, 188:166 (*There was an old woman tossed up in a basket*)

There Was an Old Woman   120, 148:378, *see also:* I Know an Old Lady Who Swallowed a Fly

There was an old woman all skin and bones   37:186, 134:80, 213:76, 290:171

There was an old woman and she had a little pig   129:27, 178:16, 213:52, 232:102, 292:60, *see also:* 79:23, 110:42, 135:56, 234:50

There was an old woman, and what do you think?   175:164

There was an old woman as I've heard tell   68:14, 79:41, 259, *see also:* 17:64, 27:58, 188:132

There was an old woman call'd Nothing At All 112:5

There was an old woman lived in Athlone 176:57

There was an old woman lived under a hill 177:87

There was an old woman tossed up in a basket 17:142, 18:20, 111:56, 175:154, 285:30, 289:78, *see also:* 188:166

There was an old woman tossed up in a blanket 188:166, *see also:* Old Woman Tossed Up in a Basket

There was an old woman who had a little pig 79:23, 110:42, 135:56, *see also:* Old Woman and Her Pig

There was an old woman who lived in a shoe 175:120

There was an old woman who swallowed a fly 148:378, *see also:* I Know an Old Lady Who Swallowed a Fly

There was an old yellow cat had troubles all her own 102

There was blood on the saddle 159:288, 290:170, *see also:* 61:112, 61:113

There Was Once/Era una Vez 89:62, 216:50

There was once a Filipino hombre 226:434

There Was Once a Little Ship 262:62

There was once a noble ranger 61:140, *see also:* 159:362

There was once a tiny little boat 216:50, *see also:* 89:62

There was one, there was two, there was three little angels 129:54, 233:74

There was Sir Tomcat, hooray! 216:41, *see also:* 295:4

There was some wheels on the ground 118:16

There We Would Be 69:51

There were four jolly blacksmiths so merry and free 72:90

There were four little white doves 33:202

There were nine to guard the British ranks 240:25

There were ninety and nine that safely lay 66:146

There were seven sons, and two of them twins 35:40

There were ten green bottles hanging on the wall, 82, *see also:* 147:30, 148:376, 290:32

There were ten in the bed and the little one said 26:23, 147:32, *see also:* 63:131, 148:254, 254:110, 290:34

There were three craws sat upon a wa' 62:55, 292:144, *see also:* 128:32, 134:17, 290:144

There were three crows sat on a tree 62:54, 290:70, *see also:* Three Ravens

There were three crows sat on one tree 292:142, *see also:* Three Ravens

There were three gypsies a-come to my door 22:70, 227:12, *see also:* 148:144, 211, 226:311

There were three jolly fishermen 26:13, 63:98, 148:294, 290:50

There were three jolly hunters 27:62, *see also:* 106, 128:122, 234:36, 292:190

There were three jovial huntsmen 106, *see also:* 27:62, 128:122, 234:36, 292:190

There were three little kittens put on their mittens 188:90, *see also:* 17:12, 283:18, 285:29, 292:64

There were three ravens sat on a tree 22:94, 189:88, 292:140, *see also:* 37:115, 232:121, 290:70, 292:140

There were two birds sat on a stone 18:38, 112:66

There were two ravens who sat on a tree 37:115, *see also:* Three Ravens

There'll Be a Hot Time 203, *see also:* 126:57, 157:191 *(There'll be a hot time in the old town)*

There'll Be a Hot Time 21:30 *(Come along, get you ready)*

There'll be a hot time in the old town 21, 203, *see also:* 126:57, 157:191

There'll be a new world beginnin' from t'night! 210:96

There's a bear in yon hill 292:106

There's a big old bullfrog down in the meadow 97:unpaged

There's a big ship sailing on the illiallioh 291:16, *see also:* Allee Allee-o

There's a bower of roses by Bendemeer's stream 22:20

There's a bright golden haze on the meadow 218:16

There's a castle in my city 296:8

There's a church in the valley 21:164, 25:117

There's a colleen fair as May 42:597

There's a crazy carrousel 166:66

There's a feeling comes astealing and it sets my brain reeling 205:331, *see also:* 72:28, 197:66

There's a fire in the galley 98:34, 129:84, 134:64, 232:162

There's a Flea in Lizzie's Ear 197:33, *see also:* 226:332, 289:150

There's a girl named Dinah over there 109:202

There's a Hole in Our Bucket 197:32, *see also:* 290:74

There's a Hole in the Bottom of the Sea 75:78, *see also:* 290:14

There's a hole in the bucket, dear Liza 290:74, *see also:* 197:32

There's a hole in the middle of the sea 290:14, *see also:* 75:78
There's a jolly old miller and he lives by himself 63:28, *see also:* 17:118, 20:35, 135:82, 227:26
There's a land that I see 260:16
There's a land that is fairer than day 21:176, 66:150
There's a little ball, such a tiny little ball 165:186
There's a little black train a-coming 232:152, *see also:* 24:914, 148:228
There's a Little Wheel A-Turnin' in My Heart 129:10, *see also:* 157:146, 227:27
There's a little white duck sitting in the water 75:46, 289:56
There's a long, long nail a-grinding 118:26
There's a Long Long Trail 25:121, 170:82
There's a long, long trail a-winding 25:121, 170:82
There's a low green valley 21:132, *see also:* 126:59
There's a man goin' roun' takin' names 226:447
There's a red light on the track for Bolsum Brown 226:355
There's a Song in My Heart 155:9
There's a Song in the Air 50:61, 148:384
There's a spot that the soldiers all love 73:168, 99:47
There's a springtime fallin' down rain 261:28
There's a star in the East on Christmas morn 22:266, 129:66, 140:49, 190:55, 241:54, *see also:* 54:80, 209:22, 233:16
There's a Sun for the Morning 245:16
There's a time in each year 21:76, 205:277, *see also:* 25:98
There's a Train 296:38
There's a train a chuggin' 'round the mountain boys 296:38
There's a yellow rose in Texas 73:245, 205:392
There's blood on the saddle and blood on the ground 61:112, *see also:* 61:113, 128:288, 290:170
There's fire in the lower deck 232:162, *see also:* 98:34, 129:84, 134:64
There's Many a Man Killed on the Railroad 226:371
There's Nae Luck About the House 176:38, *see also:* 262:138
There's no hiding place down there 31:49
There's no respect for youth or age 159:393
There's none can smash the wagon 73:46
There's snakes on the mountain 226:189
There's Something About a Boy Scout 25:52
There's Yes! Yes! in Your Eyes 170:67

These Bones Gonna Rise Again 290:40, *see also:* 89:42, 226:470, 197:94
These Things Shall Be! 64:174, 71:28
They All Went Off to Discover the Pole 172:39, 157:25
They called her frivolous Sal 148:246
They do, do, do like this 217:56
They Do Like This/Ainsi Font, Font, Font 217:56
They dug him a grave at the set of the sun 146:164
They saw the light shine out afar 184:48
They say, old man, your horse will die 226:406, *see also:* 98:39
They say that a turtle just wobbles and wobbles 166:40
They say that in the army the drinks are mighty fine 63:140
They say there is a land 61:304, *see also:* 146:87, 159:265
They say you "make the world go 'round" 218:304
They tell you in the Army 27:226, *see also:* 158:124
They took away my brogues 240:32
They took John Henry to the steep hillside 226:362
They were here, the Pondos 163:65
They'll Be a Hot Time in the Old Town Tonight 203, *see also:* 21:30, 126:57, 157:191
They're changing guard at Buckingham Palace 172:128
They're Moving Grandpa's Grave 290:172
They're sailing on England, oh; what a shame 275:79, 276:66
The Thief 55:504
Thief, yes, thief, that is your name 55:504
Things I Used to Do 226:482
The things I used to like I don't like anymore 218:260
Think of the presents you've brought 275:58, 276:30
Think of Your Head in the Morning 73:156
The Thirteen Days of Yule 95
This beauty doth all things excel 189:58
This cotton want a-pickin' 239:45
This day to you is born a Child 54:56, 241:14, *see also:* 125:64
This Endris Night 54:16
This first day of Christmas, my true love sent to me 197:120, *see also:* Twelve Days of Christmas
This great day I met upon the way 54:126, *see also:* 241:105
This house is haunted this house is haunted 226:349
This is a lullaby 216:49, *see also:* 54:252, 89:161, 279:108

This is a man who thinks with his heart 218:208

This Is God's House 86:160

This is how the big tall Indian beats upon his drum 41:26, 162:43

This is in honor of (name), hurrah! 83:468

This is just the kind of day that you dream about 275:33

This is my air, the wonderful air 74:19

This is my little house 165:29

This Is My Father's World 86:2

This is our native land 266:25

This Is the Day 245:103

This Is the Day the Lord Hath Made 86:155

This is the day, this is the day! 245:103

This is the man that stole Mister Railroad's taters 109:207

This is the meadow where all the long day 191:16

This is the night, it's a beautiful night 275:62, 276:49

This is the relieving guard 85:196

This Is the Truth Sent from Above 210:69

This Is the Way the Ladies Ride 17:91, 130:61, 175:158

This is the way the ploughboy goes 262:131

This is the way we wash our clothes 104:52, see also: Here We Go Round the Mulberry Bush

This is the way the witches fly 162:41

This Is the Way We Wash Our Hands 291:2, see also: Here We Go Round the Mulberry Bush

This Is What I Can Do 291:10

This Lady She Wears a Dark Green Shawl 232:133

This Land Is Your Land 25:81, 26:90, 72:4, 130:116, 230:30

This land is your land—this land is my land 25:81, 26:90, 72:4, 130:116, 230:30

This life is a difficult riddle 66:52

This Little Cubbing Light 26:49

This Little Light o' Mine 135:20, see also: 148:224

This little light o' mine, I'm goin' to let it shine 135:20, 148:224

This Little Pig 17:71, 75:80, 285:14, see also: 175:48

This little pig went to market 17:71, 75:80, 285:14, see also: 175:48

This morning is the month of May 27:102, see also: 128:70, 134:31, 213:80

This Morning, This Evening, So Soon 226:18

This Nearly Was Mine 218:47

This Ol' Hammah 55:265, see also: 232:149

This ol' hammah killed John Henry 55:265, see also: 232:149

This ol' man, he goes one 197:34, see also: This Old Man

This Old Hammer 149, see also: 49:265

This old hammer shine like silver 232:149, see also: 55:265

This Old Man 6, 17:94, 75:82, 129:98, 135:104, 147:42, 148:386, 175:70, 197:34, 232:165, 289:85, see also: 20:44

This old man, he played one 17:94, 20:44, 75:82, 129:98, 135:104, 147:42, 148:386, 175:70, 232:165, 289:85, see also: 6, 197:34

This old road is hard and bumpy 289:86

This one, yes! It is Christmas Eve 295:78

This Pig Went to Market 175:48, see also: 17:71, 75:80, 285:14

This, This My Lad's the Soldier's Life 99:47

This time another year we may be dead and gone 37:169

This Train 72:86, 75:84, 148:388

This train is bound for glory, this train 72:86, 75:84, 148:388

This Warm and Sunny Spot 172:67, 174:53

This was a real nice clambake 218:106

This Way, That-a Way 189:50, see also: Ha-Ha, This-A-Way

This way, you willowbee, you willowbee, you willowbee 129:106

Those Gambler's Blues 226:228

Thou art ever extending welcome 87:73

Thou Art Well Content/Las Posadas 54:256

Thou Must Leave Thy Lowly Dwelling 210:126

Thou Only/Nur Du 22:114

Thou Poor Bird 292:129, 293:88

Thou poor bird, mournst the tree 292:129, 293:88

Thou, thou, Jehovah, hear my singing 85:81

Thou who art near 85:132

Thou Who Once on Mother's Knee 86:168

Thou wilt come no more 157:110

Thou Wilt Keep Him in Perfect Peace 86:79

Though dark are our sorrows 205:154

Though full the flowing river 208:7

Thoum/Most Adored 89:223

Thul Tahryung 89:235

Three Black Cats 162:39

Three Blind Mice 17:25, 25:29, 26:41, 62:10, 92, 148:391, 175:52, 188:82, 189:14, 283:66, 292:192, 293:98

Three Cheers for Pooh 172:43, 174:29

Three Children Sliding on the Ice 17:40, 188:16, see also: 68:5, 197:52

Three Craws 62:55, 128:32, 134:17, 290:144, 292:144

Three craws sat upon a wall 128:32, 134:17, 290:144, *see also:* 62:55, 292:144

Three Crows 62:54, *see also:* Three Ravens

Three Days/Tri Dni 89:189

Three days after war was over homeward bound 89:189

Three Doves 72:145

Three Drummer Boys/Trois Jeunes Tambours 217:58

Three Dukes 39:16, 100:92, 227:18, *see also:* 110:46, 135:84, 213:40

Three eastern kings toiled many miles 209:110

Three fair maids went out for a walk 134:52

Three Foxes 172:132, 173:18

Three jelly fish, three jelly fish 165:110

Three Jolly Fishermen 63:98, 290:50, *see also:* 26:13, 148:294

Three jolly gentlemen in coats of red 59:54

Three Jolly Hunters 27:62, *see also:* 106, 128:122, 234:36, 292:190

Three Jovial Huntsmen 106, *see also:* 27:62, 128:122, 234:36, 292:190

The Three Kings 210:121, *see also:* 241:215 *(Three kings from Persian lands afar)*

Three Kings 245:124 *(Three kings traveled long from lands far away)*

Three Kings A-Riding 63:36

Three kings from Persian lands afar 210:121, 241:215

Three Kings of Orient 190:75, *see also:* We Three Kings

Three kings traveled long from lands far away 245:124

Three little angels all dressed in white 141:94

Three Little Girls 68:5, 197:52, *see also:* 17:40, 83:502, 188:16

Three little girls went sliding on the ice 68:5, *see also:* 17:40, 83:502, 188:16, 197:52

Three Little Kittens 17:12, 188:90, 283:18, 285:29, 292:64

The three little kittens, they lost their mittens 188:90, 283:18, 285:29, 292:64, *see also:* 17:12

Three Little Maids from School 252:50

Three Little Old Men/Trois Petits Bonshommes 217:58

Three Little Pigeons 46:215

Three little pigeons sitting on a fence 46:215

Three Little Piggies 62:40, 289:50, 292:57, *see also:* 130:110

Three Little Witches 68:46

Three Mice Went into a Hole to Spin 175:144, *see also:* 111:12

Three Myopic Rodents 290:126

Three old crows sat on a tree 232:121, *see also:* Three Ravens

Three old witches in big green hats 162:39

Three Owls 162:10

Three Pigs 130:110, *see also:* 62:40, 289:50, 292:57

Three Pirates Came to London Town 128:90, 262:76

Three rascals were gathered and thinking up a way 208:19

The Three Ravens 22:94, 189:88, 290:70, 292:140, 292:142, *see also:* 37:115, 62:54, 232:121, 290:70, 292:142

The Three Ships 241:52

Three times around went our gallant ship 135:79, 291:73, *see also:* 62:98

Three times round the cuckoo waltz 226:160

Three Turkeys 162:44

Three Wise Men of Gotham 112:57, 285:57

Three Wise Old Women 62:95

Three Wood Pigeons 25:9

Threshing Song/Canco de's Batre 89:163

Thrifty Miss/Ritka Búza 208:33

Through My Window/Ablakomba 89:188

Through rocky arroyos so dark and so deep 61:191

Throughout the world, who is there like little me? 79:12

Throw It Out the Window 25:24, 26:38, 290:102, *see also:* 175:22

Thul Tahryung 89:235

Thumbkin make a bow 104:50

Thus said Robin Hood to Little John in Greenwood where they lay 164:68

Thus Saith the High, the Lofty One 273:138

Thy Little Ones, Dear Lord, Are We/Her Kommer Dine Arme Smaa 54:196

Thy Word Is Hid 86:84

Thy Work, O God, Needs Many Hands 86:196

Thy Works of Love 86:50

Tick Tock 11:16

The Tick-Tock Man 91:38

Tick tock! Tick tock! Tick tock! Tick tock! 175:68, *see also:* Hickory, Dickory, Dock

Tideo 232:173

Tiene la Tarara un jardin de flores y me da 295:61

Tigers on their cushion paws 207:110

Till We Meet Again 170:109

Tim Finnegan liv'd in Walkin Street 42:611

Timber 226:386

Time for Bed 125:58

Time Sends a Warning Call   125:55
Time to twist our mousekadial   119:109
The times are hard and the wages low
   134:73, *see also:* 64:114, 98:40
Times Are Sadly Out of Joint   197:99
Times Gettin' Hard, Boys   226:242
Times Is Mighty Hard   64:154, *see also:*
   226:35
Tin Tin Tini Mini Hanim/Teen, Teen,
   Teeny Weeny Lady   169:72, 266:58
Tinga Layo   290:54
Tinga Layo! Come, little donkey come
   290:54
The Tinker   71:102
Tinker likes to jump up   154:36
Tinker—Mr. Small's Dog   154:36
The Tinker's Daughter   117:unpaged
The Tinker's Song   239:83, *see also:* 262:60
Tinkling Bells   162:67
Tiny precious Christ Child   7:6
The Tip and Heel Dance/La Punta y el Ta-
   cón   194:32
Tip-Toe Song   162:65
Tip-Toe Thru the Tulips with Me   170:79
Tip-toe to the window   170:79
Tippecanoe and Tyler Too   157:112
Tiptoe   291:60
Tiptoe Night   59:76
Tiptoe night comes down the lane   59:76
Tiptoe, tiptoe, tippy toe   292:60
Tiritomba   21:200
'Tis advertised in Boston, New York and
   Buffalo   24:829, 64:112, 71:84, 72:71,
   158:144
'Tis done, the edict passed   273:64
'Tis life in a half-breed shack   159:409
'Tis money makes the member vote   240:66
'Tis No Wind/Taw Nye Vyetyer   208:78
'Tis of a gallant Yankee ship that flew the
   stripes and stars   240:130
'Tis old Stonewall the Rebel that leans on
   his sword   73:90
'Tis pretty to be in Ballinderry   42:596,
   134:66
'Tis the gift to be simple, 'tis the gift to be
   free   157:62, 176:92
'Tis the ilima my heart doth long for   87:62
'Tis the Voice of the Lobster   112:40
'Tis Vossevangen that I will choose   83:490
'Tis Washington's health, fill a bumper all
   round   157:22, 240:96, 273:48
'Tis Women Make Us Love   290:194
De Titanic   226:254, *see also:* 290:153
Titwillow   252:48
To Anacreon in heaven   273:88
To and fro, to and fro   165:42
To Babyland   17:18
To be a clown, to be a clown   167:12
To Bed, To Bed   17:50, 112:54, 285:101

"To bed, to bed," says Sleepyhead   17:50,
   112:54, 285:101
To Bethlehem I Would Go   54:232,
   241:184, 245:120
To Canaan   73:130
To drive the kine one summer's morn the
   tanner took his way   28:134
To France there journeyed two grenadiers
   85:155
To Get to Heaven/Para Subir al Cielo
   194:26
To God's Most Holy House   86:82
To His Lute   85:143
To Honor Lincoln   207:82
To look sharp (clap) be a C-U-B   26:54
To Market, To Market   17:112, 285:74
To Midnight   159:327
To Music   85:224
To my little one's cradle in the night   59:67,
   128:24
To my way-ay-ay!   134:76, *see also:* 37:150
To Ope Their Trunks   62:15
To People Who Have Gardens   135:30
To Portsmouth   85:15, 176:103
To Portsmouth! To Portsmouth!   85:15,
   176:103
To pray to Buddha   89:236
To Push the Business On   17:95, *see also:*
   70:13
To see how crude the baby's bed would
   grieve most anyone   67:42
To Teach a Young Girl to Sing/A Cantar a
   una Niña   216:44
To the Commons   240:161
To the Cub Scouts, the hope of America
   26:63
To the Garden Annie Went   262:26, *see*
   also: 78:51
To the Ladies   240:38
To the olive tree   216:47
To the Sea Gull Offshore/Okino Kamomeini
   49:27
To the Serpent/A la Víbora   295:24
To the Town of Bethlehem   220:112
To the Troops in Boston   28:53, *see also:*
   240:64
To Thee the tuneful anthem soars   240:48
To thine almighty arm we owe the triumphs
   of the day   273:148
To Thy Father and Thy Mother   86:154
To Tragothi to Gamo/The Wedding Song
   89:195
To travel is to miss the way   85:130
To us in Bethlem city   241:207
To Wander   85:153
To wander is my one delight   85:153
To you good lads that dare oppose   240:27
The Toad/El Sapo   216:46
The toad is an animal   216:46

The Toast 157:22, 240:96, 273:48
A toast we pledge to Gustaf 46:204, 70:29
Today 72:14
Today is a day that is filled with surprises
  119:100
Today Is Monday 84:28, 253:92
Today Is Tuesday 119:98
*Today is Tuesday; you know what that
  means!* 119:98
Today our dear friend Chicken Soup
  235:56
Today We Welcome a Tiny Child/Ons Is
  Geboren Een Kindekin 54:184
*Today while the blossoms still cling to the
  vine* 72:14
Today's the First of May 197:54
Tokens and treasures, yesterday's pleasures
  275:84
Toko dia youmina 89:272
Tole Ya Wati/Thank You, Wati 89:261
Tom Dooley 392, 158:300, 205:402
Tom he was a piper's son 17:45, 111:38,
  188:36, 189:54, *see also:* 175:62
*Tom Hight is my name, an old bachelor I
  am* 159:407
*Tom Jennings who never could drinking
  avoid* 73:156
Tom Pearce 292:24, *see also:* 22:50, 71:68,
  193
*Tom Pearse, Tom Pearse, lend me your grey
  mare* 22:50, 71:68, 193, 292:24
Tom the Cat 85:234
Tom the cat, the cat 85:234
Tom, the Piper's Son 188:130, *see also:*
  17:6, 175:100, 285:85
Tom, Tom Greedy-Gut 109:15
Tom, Tom, the Piper's Son 17:6, 175:100,
  285:85, *see also:* 188:130, 285:85
Tommy and the Apples 62:89
Tommy Snooks and Bessie Brooks 111:77
*Tommy Thumb, Tommy Thumb, where are
  you?* 165:169
Tommy Tucker 175:24, *see also:* 17:99,
  285:88
Tommy Was a Soldier 291:11
Tommy's Gone to Hilo 157:40, *see also:*
  37:157, 128:22
Tomorrow Shall Be My Dancing Day
  220:94, *see also:* 189:78
Tonari-no Obasan/Auntie Nextdoor
  286:48
Tongue Twister 97:unpaged
Too Old to Work 64:143
Toodala 232:54, 291:14
Too-Ra-Loo-Ra-Loo-Ral 170:39
Toompa toompa rain upon the tent top
  72:161
Torah, torah-torah 55:256
Toraji Taryong/Bellflower Taryong 55:36

Toraji, toraji, paektoraji 55:36
The Torch of Scouting 25:60
Torches here, Jeannette, Isabella! 22:242,
  see also: Bring a Torch, Jeannette,
  Isabella
Torn from a world of tyrants 27:120,
  28:43, 240:57, 273:28
The Tortilla-Seller/El Tortillero 216:47,
  see also: 89:96, 169:14, 267:46
The Tortilla Vender 267:46, *see also:*
  89:96, 169:14, 216:47
The Tortoise and the Two Ducks/La Tortue
  et les Deux Canards 243:22
Toryanse 16:61, 286:46
The Tottenham Toad 135:49
*The Tottenham toad came trotting up the
  road* 135:49
Tou Oua 89:272
Tough Mister Buff 91:36
Touro-Louro-Louro 54:130
Tout le monde Samedi soir 148:84
Tout doit sur terre 69:50
The Tower of Alicante/La Torre de Ali-
  cante 216:43
The Toy Shop 207:53
Toy Soldier Sam 166:54
Tra, La, La 25:15
Tra, la, la Ja sas 83:501
Tra-la-la-la guess what I'm making 77:54
Tra la la la la la la la la 25:15
Tra la la la la, my zither I'm strumming
  262:145
Tra-la-la, tra-la-la 168:33
Track-Lining Chant 239:74
The Tractor's Song 288:12
Trail End 159:288, *see also:* 61:112, 61:113,
  290:170
Trail the Eagle 25:59
The Trail to Mexico 24:858, 61:179,
  146:62, 159:52, 225:64, 226:285, 239:32
The Train 41:29 *(Choo, choo, choo, the
  train will soon be going)*
The Train/Kisha 286:58 *(When we think
  the train is running)*
The Train Is A-Coming 68:33, 232:150, *see
  also:* 232:151
The train is carrying coal 165:69
Train Song 26:77
Tramp! Tramp! Tramp! 21:147, 73:172,
  197:62
Tramp, Tramp, Tramp, Keep on A-Tramp-
  ing 226:185
*Tramp, tramp, tramp, tramp, tramp, tramp,
  tramp, tramp* 25:65, 26:65, *see also:*
  227:34
Trampin' 83:464, 148:394
Trapeze Artists 207:108
The Trappan'd Maiden 240:20
Traveler's Grace 69:11, 101:34

Traveling up the Lonesome Trail 61:233, *see also:* 61:232, 159:8, 232:69

The trav'ler benighted and lost 273:104

Treasure Hunt 167:36

The Treasure of the Santa Clara/El Tesoro de Santa Clara 295:68

Treasury Rats 73:68

Treasury rats are swarming around 73:68

The Tree in the Forest 176:130, *see also:* Green Grass Grows All Around

The Tree in the Valley-o 213:20, *see also:* Green Grass Grows All Around

The Tree in the Wood 27:90, *see also:* Green Grass Grows All Around

A Tree in Yonder Field 132:unpaged, *see also:* Green Grass Grows All Around

The tree of life my soul hath seen 190:93

Tree Song 71:25, 72:62

Tree Tree Tree 219:57

The Trees Have Put Their Nightgowns On 7:12

Tri Dni/Three Days 89:189

Tried to catch an old black mule 208:80, *see also:* 110:32

Trip a Trop a Tronjes 128:41

The Trip to Cambridge 28:49, *see also:* 240:79

The Triple "R" Song 119:106

Troika 55:515

Trois Jeunes Tambours/Three Drummer Boys 217:30

Trois Petits Bonshommes/Three Little Old Men 217:29

Trot Old Joe 162:82

Trot, trot, trot, go and never stop 165:17

Trot, trot, trot, through the pasture lot 291:53

The Troubled Soldier 226:137

Troy, the Drummer Boy 167:30

True love, true love, don't lie to me 148:186

The True Lover's Farewell 226:98, *see also:* 110:24, 226:99, 230:65

Truly True 290:140

Try a Spanish Dance 166:62

Tso shon lo 89:232

Tsubodono 16:27

Tsukiyono tambode 286:32

Ttimba 236:63

Tu Scendi Dalle Stélle/From Starry Skies Descending 54:244, 279:98

Tucker's Waltz 126:71

Tuleeke tulye 236:23

Tumbalalaika 148:298

The Tune the Old Cow Died On 62:34, 71:94

The Turkey/Debreczenbe K'éne Menni 289:86

The Turkey Game/Juego de los Pavos 194:34

Turkey in the Straw 20:72, 22:66, 126:48, 197:107, 226:94

Turkey on the platter 207:41

Turkey Song 234:46

Turn Again, Whittington 62:16, 175:11, 176:83, 262:69, 293:40

Turn on the tap and out with a dash 149:28

Turn the Glasses Over 20:56, 39:2, 70:9, 129:120, *see also:* 134:44

Turn Ye to Me 71:64, 72:122, 208:76

Turning, turning! See how the windmill is 207:104

The Turtle 177:85

Turtle Dove 232:179, 277:27, *see also:* 292:124

Tuscan Serenade/Stornello Toscano 208:37

Tutu Maramba 262:15

Tuvaeno 236:3

Twankydillo 262:24

'Twas a bright and sunny day when a young wife went away 157:206

'Twas a calm and peaceful evening in a camp called Arapahoe 159:170

'Twas a calm, still night 66:128, 157:108

'Twas a cold winter's night and the wind it was brawlin' 89:137

'Twas a sunny day in June and the birds were all in tune 205:292

'Twas a Wonder in Heaven 233:54

'Twas at the Siege of Vicksburg 73:208

'Twas break of day, the seventeenth 28:46

'Twas down on the Lone Star Trail in eighteen seventy-three 61:308, *see also:* 60:102, 146:162, 159:19, 226:266

'Twas Friday morn when we set sail 71:78, 72:72, 290:160, *see also:* 117:unpaged

'Twas good to live when all the range 159:333

'Twas in eighteen hundred and fifty-three and of June the thirteenth day 24:832, *see also:* 292:170

'Twas in the merry month of May 157:69, *see also:* Barbara Allen

'Twas in the month of August or the middle of July 226:38

'Twas in the Moon of Winter Time 2, 54:76, 161:79, *see also:* 140:38

'Twas in the town of Jacksboro in the spring of seventy-three 64:120, 146:92, 158:174, 226:270, 277:137, *see also:* 24:854, 159:41, 159:335, 230:63

'Twas Jolly Old Roger, the tinmaker man 239:83, 262:60

'Twas May Day in the Morning 27:104, *see also:* 189:52

'Twas midnight on the ocean 290:138

'Twas on a merry time 188:148

'Twas on a Monday morning, the first I saw my darling 226:117, 232:137, see also: 71:42, 134:14, 176:30, 205:72

'Twas on a Monday morning when I beheld my darling 134:14, see also: Charlie Is My Darling

'Twas on a pleasant morning all in bloom of spring 35:26, see also: 35:28

'Twas on the eight of January 240:213

'Twas once in my saddle I used to be happy 61:321, see also: Streets of Laredo

'Twas one October mornin' that I seen a wond'rous sight 226:174, see also: 24:843, 158:149

'Twas summer and softly the breezes were blowing 28:74, 240:61, 273:30

'Twas Summer and 'Twas Evening/Kesailta 208:21

'Twas the end of round-up, the last day of June 159:117

'Twas way down in Missouri, there lived a shootin' man 61:258, see also: Jesse James

'Twas winter and blue Tory noses were freezing 28:77, 240:62, 273:32

Tweedle-dum and Tweedle-dee 111:70, 285:26

The Twelve Apostles 129:62, 176:146, 233:66, see also: Green Grow the Rushes, Ho

The Twelve Days of Christmas 22:248, 30, 50, 54:36, 87:91, 92:183, 113, 121, 148:400, 190:148, 197:120, 210:64, 233:72, 241:30, 264:66, 287, 290:26, 292:160

Twelve Gates to the City 230:81, see also: 31:33

Tweriire 236:23

Twilight 114:34

The Twilight Is Falling/Es Wird Scho Glei Dumpa 54:172, 279:82

Twilight Song 125:33

Twinkle, Twinkle, Little Bat (parody) 289:84

Twinkle, Twinkle, Little Star 17:41, 130:91, 175:108, 205:193, 283:69, 289:84

Twirl, dreidel, turn spin! 68:30

Two and Two Are Four 167:46 (One and one are two)

Two and Two Are Four/Dos y Dos Son Cuatro 194:36 (Two and two are four, four and two are six)

Two Birds Sat on a Stone 18:38, 112:66

Two blue pigeons, one was black and white, Pom! 262:32, see also: 62:68

Two cowboys left their camp one day 61:199

Two drummers sat at dinner 21:26

The Two Dogs/Les Deux Chiens 243:46

The Two Dogs and Their Master /Les Deux Chiens et Leur Maître 243:8

Two Ducks on a Pond 262:86

Two Dukes A'Riding 213:40, see also: Three Dukes

Two German officers crossed the Rhine 226:440, see also: 126:61, 158:122, 170:61, 205:348

The Two Goats/Les Deux Chèvres 243:23

The Two Grenadiers 85:155

Two in a Boat 135:92

Two in a boat and the tide rolls high 135:92

Two in the Middle 128:97, see also: 135:94

Two in the middle and you can't jump, Josie 128:97, see also: 135:94

Two legs, four legs, six legs, eight 237:unpaged

Two Little Blackbirds 162:9, 178:18, 290:104, 291:40, see also: 75:20, 111:32

Two Little Blackbirds (parody) 290:104

Two Little Boats/Diw Laiwinas 89:174

Two little boats are on the sea 165:115

Two Little Children 277:145

Two little children, a boy and a girl 277:145

Two Little Dicky Birds 111:32, see also: Two Little Blackbirds

Two little dickey-birds sat upon a hill 75:20, see also: Two Little Blackbirds

Two Little Hands 86:120

The Two Magicians 145

The Two Mules/Les Deux Mulets 243:20

The two of us will make a new lemonade stand 166:44

The Two Ravens 37:115, see also: Three Ravens

Two soldiers lying as they fell 73:264

Two Valentines for You 167:14

Two wheels 'round a corner 148:306

Two White Horses 226:472

Two Wings 262:36

Two wings to veil my face 262:36

Tying Apples on a Lilac Tree 62:133

Tying Knots in the Devil's Tail 61:202, 225:52, see also: 146:76

Tyini Suku ndi jonga 163:72

Tzena 72:151

U

U.A.W.—C.I.O. 64:90

U-li li-e sings the sandpiper 69:24

The U–S–U Range 159:96

U starej Breclavy na hrazi 89:186

U vorot, vorot, vorot 89:176

Ua like no a like 89:299
Ud av alle som gaar i ringen 83:501
Udali usele matshon 89:274
Uga, Uga, Uga 266:36
Ula o luna, ula o lao 87:17
Ular Naga 169:32, 265:12
Ular naga pandjangnja bukah kepalang
 169:32, 265:12
Um Home/Song of Praise 163:39
Umqokozo/A String of Beads 163:78
Un coq en sentinelle, veillait avant le jour
 243:36
Un corbeau tenant un fromage 243:2
Un Flambeau, Jeannette, Isabelle 217:50
Un personnage de renom 243:8
Un rat auprès d'un éléphant 243:13
Un rat se trouva, diton 243:6
Un renard dont la genie 243:42
The Unbirthday Song 275:44, 276:45
Uncle Jessie 109:114
Uncle John 66:74
Uncle John is sick abed 66:74
Uncle John Is Very Sick 17:101
Uncle Sam, wake up! wake up! 73:62
Uncle Sam, What Ails You? 73:62
Uncle Sam's Farm 27:42, 66:87, 157:106
Under the Bamboo Tree 21:68
Under the Chestnut Tree 26:31, 254:122
Under the spreading chestnut tree 26:31,
 254:122
Under this sod lies a great bucking hoss
 159:327
Under Yonder Oaken Tree 78:19
Under Your Shade 85:68
Underneath the lantern by the barrack gate
 22:202
Une chèvre altiere sur un petit pont 243:23
Une poule qui pondait 243:14
Une tortue, a la tête légère 243:22
Unhappy Boston, see thy sons deplore
 28:20
Unhappy Times 28:161
Unhappy times of late we've seen 28:161
*The union is behind us; we shall not be
 moved* 64:38, *see also:* 230:38
The union is the place for me 64:30
Union Maid 64:17
Union Man 64:62
Union Train 64:34
The Union Wagon Couldn't Be Split 73:46
Unite and Unite 130:28
Unite and unite, now let us unite 130:28
United Nations make a chain 158:376, *see
 also:* 157:147, 226:474
United Steelworkers Are We 64:92
Unto Us a Boy Is Born 210:71, 220:74
Unto Us a Boy Was Born 241:60
Unto you, hail, O Mary, for blessed are you!
 124:26

Up above the roofs a sea of waving tiles
 87:52, 286:74
Up and Down 206:34
Up and Down Jamaica Plain 141:58
Up and down the City Road 175:36, *see
 also:* Pop! Goes the Weasel
Up and Down the Railroad Track 61:276
Up I stretch on tippy toe 165:142
Up in a Balloon 157:182
Up in the sky a big bird flies 154:26
Up, Little Hans 245:13
Up, little Hans! Up, little Hans! 245:13
Up, my neighbor, come away 184:68
Up on the House Top 54:72
Up on the Mountain 129:110
Up the airy mountain 227:40
Up the Ladder 26:47
Up Up in the Sky 162:8
The Upidee Song 73:154
Upon a slender branch of larch 7:22
Upon a tree a cuckoo 20:86
Upon my lap my Sov'reign sits 220:44
Upon Paul's steeple stands a tree 17:126,
 175:46, 188:154
Upon the bridge it's raining 188:144
Upon the water swam a duck 17:73
Upon this holy night 54:268, *see also:*
 Carol of the Birds
Upstairs and Down 149:20
Usagi, Usagi/Rabbits 16:25, 286:18
Uskudar 89:209
Usted qué le da al pollo? 295:15
Ut kommer Staffan pa himmelen var 238
Utah Carl 61:217, *see also:* 146:120,
 159:125
Utah Carroll 146:120, 159:125, *see also:*
 61:217
Uti Var Hage/Out in Our Meadow 262:39
Uyadela/You Are Arrogant 163:88
Uyinto kwenza ni u mbika ngaka 163:104

V

The Vacant Chair 73:286
Vacation's Here 167:24
The Vagabond's Song/Lio Lang Jr Ge
 49:13
Vai alta a noite vem ver a lua 89:164
*Vain Britons, boast no longer, with proud
 indignity* 240:97
Vaj, Gulum Gitti?/Where Is My Red Rose?
 89:213
Valentine Dance 162:54
A Valentine from Grandma 207:78
Valentine's Day 7:16
V'alkulam Eloah s'lihot 77:42

Valleys Green, You Are My Joy 72:132
Vamos a Belén/Going to Bethlehem 54:303
Vamos a la Mar/Let's Go to the Sea 216:30
Vamos al baile y veras que bonito 295:66, *see also:* 22:78, 72:106
Vamos, Pastorcitos/Hasten Now, O Shepherds 54:310
Vandura 169:13, 271:50
Varga Pavati/Nature's Splendor 89:215
Varsang 20:92
Varvindar friska leka 20:92
Veinti-cinco de december, fum, fum, fum 54:258, 241:80, 279:104, *see also:* 197:115
Velkomin Vertu/We Welcome Thee Tonight 209:36
Vengan a ver mi chacra que es hermosa 262:19
Veni, Emmanuel/O Come, O Come, Emmanuel 54:312, 241:134, *see also:* 86:27
Veni, veni, Emmanuel 241:134, *see also:* 54:312, 86:27
The 'vention did in Boston meet 240:181
Versos de Montalgo 226:303
The very first blessing Mary had 190:61, 233:58, *see also:* The Seven Joys of Mary
Very Good Advice 276:44
Very Much Afraid 19:33
Very softly I will walk 86:76
A very tiny fairy 207:65
Vesper Hymn 262:171
Vespers 172:145, 173:31
Victory 273:148
Vie dans nos, vie dans 89:61
Viente-cinco de diciembre, fum, fum, fum 197:115, *see also:* 54:258, 241:80, 279:104
Vigndig A Fremd Kind/Baby Sitter's Lullaby 289:32
Village Festival/Mura Matsuri 286:82
The violin's ringing like lovely singing 262:82
The Virgin Mary 274:14
The Virgin Mary Had a Baby Boy 209:34
Virgin Mary had a little baby 274:12
The Virgin Mary had-a one Son 233:44
Virgin Mary, Meek and Mild 190:126
A Virgin Most Pure 190:34, 210:14, 220:38, 220:40, 233:26, *see also:* 48:47, 140:88
A Virgin most pure, as the prophet foretold 190:34, 233:26, *see also:* A Virgin Most Pure
A Virgin most pure as the prophets do tell 210:14, 220:38, 220:40, *see also:* 54:42, 140:88, 190:34, 233:26
A Virgin Unspotted 54:42, 140:88, *see also:* 190:34, 210:14, 220:38, 220:40, 233:26
Virginia hears the dreadful summons 73:39
Virginia Marseillaise 73:39

The Virgin's Cradle Hymn 210:124, *see also:* 125:132
The Virgin's Slumber Song 209:59
Viva la Música 71:98, 72:170, 293:14
Viva viva la música 71:98, 72:170, 293:14
Viva l'Amour 25:124, 290:208, *see also:* 205:103
Vive la Canadienne/Long Live the Girls of Canada 208:5
Vive la Compagnie 205:103, *see also:* 25:124, 290:208
The Voice of God 123:273
The voice of God called Jonah out 123:273
Voices of the autumn winds 72:136
Voici l'hiver arrive 176:62
Vom Himmel Hoch/From Heaven High 54:152, 241:150, 279:64
Vom Himmel Hoch, Da Komm' Ich Her 54:161, 241:150, 279:64
Vorira 89:179
Voyez ce mulet la, Musieu Bainjo 157:152
Vreneli 208:67
Vu-gu vu-gu vu-gu 215:17
Vuka makoti sebusi 163:76

W

W Zlobie Lezy/Jesus Holy, Born So Lowly 54:204
The Wabash Cannon Ball 21:208, 157:163, 205:368, 230:85
Wachet auf/Wake, Awake for Night Is Flying 241:118
Wading 207:126
The Wagoner's Lad 36:64, 37:181, 61:13, *see also:* 230:21, 232:110
Wah-hoo! Wah-hoo! 207:44
Wai-Kun 79:12
Wai O Punalau/Waters of Punalau 87:71
Waiata Aroha/Love Song 89:301
Waillie, Waillie! 226:16
Waipio 87:73
Wait for the Wagon 66:108, 73:44, 83:513, 205:129
Wait for the Wagon—A Northern Parody 73:46
Wait for the Wagon—A Southern Parody 73:46, 73:48
Wait Till the Sun Shines, Nellie 157:209, 205:322
Wakan'tanka Hears Me 74:36
Wake, Awake, for Night Is Flying 45:58, 241:118
Wake Ev'ry Breath 140:109
Wake Nicodemus 21:160, 73:96
Wake Up 130:10

Wake up darlin', dont sleep so late 129:21, see also: 262:35

Wake up, darling, don't sleep too late 262:35, see also: 129:21

Wake up, daughter-in-law 163:76

Wake Up, Jacob! 289:24, see also: 159:3

Wake Up Little Sparrow 107:66

Wake up, old man, you slept too late 158:107, see also: Crawdad

Wake up, wake up, darlin' Corey 21:274, 158:310, 230:73

Wake up, wake up little sparrow 107:66

Wake up, wake up, wake up, wake up 130:10

Wake Up, You Lazy Bones 291:74

Walk Along, John 178:13, 232:134

Walk, believer, walk, Daniel 109:146

Walk Down the Street 206:98

Walk in the sunshine, play on the sand 69:45

Walk jim along 232:73, see also: 63:38, 135:108

Walk Together Children 31:28

Walked up Ellum and I come down Main 158:314

Walkin' down the road 130:50

Walking at Night 25:88, 262:23, see also: 148:360

Walking John 146:79

Walking Music 11:32

Walking on the Green Grass 24:807 *(Walking on the green grass, walking side by side)*

Walking on the Green Grass 134:96 *(We go walking on the green grass)*

Walky-Talky Jenny 226:48

Walla Zala Mudduja/Night's Dark Shadows 89:245

The Walloping Window Blind 48, see also: 34, 289:126

Walrus Hunt Song 26:33

Waltzing Bear 296:32

Waltzing Matilda 22:216, 25:86, 72:154, 186

Wander Here with Me/Hua-Hua'i 87:34

The Wanderer/Mengedagnan 169:21, 267:27

Wanderin' 148:404, 226:188

The Wandering Cowboy 146:144, 159:305

A Wandering Minstrel 252:44

A wandring minstrel I 252:44

War and Washington 240:97

A War Bird's Burlesque 226:438

War Department 157:64

War Is Declared/La Gue Declarée 89:61

War Song/Yaya 89:282

Warm Mittens 207:64

Was an old fish and his name was Whale 128:48

Was I Not a Flower in the Meadow?/Chi Ya V'luzi Ne Kalina Bula? 89:177

Was in the merry month of May 272:11, see also: Barbara Allen

Washchingge, hinkhu lushka le! 79:10

Washchingge, let me loose I cry! 79:10

The Washington Badge 157:51

Washington the Great 197:26

Wasn't That a Mighty Day 140:53, 190:145, 233:49

The Wasp/Nomeva 163:104

Wassail 89:130, see also: Wassail Wassail All Over the Town

Wassail Song 22:270, 27:6, 54:35, 92:186, 96:6, 128:66, 148:154, 184:8, 189:130, 197:8, 209:12, 220:42, 262:112, 279:36, 284:47, see also: 264:82

Wassail Wassail All Over the Town 184:12, 210:74, 220:96, see also: 54:32, 89:130, 241:22

Watashiga onemuni natatoki 286:54

Watch the little turkey running 89:79, see also: 216:51

Watching for Pa 197:69

Watching in the meadows o'er their flocks by night 65:92

Watchman, Tell Us of the Night 241:138

The Water Bug Stands Upon a Fish 74:14

Water Come a Me Eye 72:107

The water in the river 114:15

The water is bright and shining like gold 27:156, see also: 20:75, 197:82

Water is the thing I sprinkle flowers with 91:24

The Water Is Wide 148:406, 230:77

The Water Pipes 149:28

Water Song 91:24

Watermelons 63:124, see also: 25:40 *(Just plant a watermelon on my grave)*

Watermelons 239:87 *(Watermelons off de vine)*

Watermelons off de vine 239:87

Watermelons will be growing 270:63

The Waters of Ouliastai/Ouliastai 89:230

Waters of Punalau/Wai O Punalau 87:71

Watts' Cradle Song 190:43, 190:45, see also: Hush My Babe

Wave the spear and raise the rifle 28:118

The Waves and Wacs will win the war 158:123, see also: 126:61, 170:61, 205:348, 226:440

Wavvuuvuumira 236:18

'Way back in the days of depression 64:130

Way Down in Mexico 159:365

Way down in old Varginni, I suppose you all do know 73:123

Way Down in the Paw-Paw Patch 33:138, see also: Pawpaw Patch

'Way down on de old plantation 157:92
Way Down on the Bingo Farm 109:202
'Way Down South 112:51
Way down South in the land of cotton, I wrote this song and wrote it rotten 226:342
Way down south in the Yankety-yank 147:38, 231, 290:164
'Way down South where bananas grow 112:51
Way down upon the Swanee river 22:86, 127:99, 230:83
Way down upon the Wabash 21:298, 226:162, see also: 35:62
Way down yonder, Hey 109:97
Way Down Yonder in the Brickyard 109:116
Way down yonder in the middle of the field 22:300, 148:222
Way Down Yonder in the Pawpaw Patch 178:38, see also: Pawpaw Patch
Way down yonder, Sandy ree 109:136
Way Down Yonder, Sometimes 109:101
Way down yonder, soup, soup 109:103
Way Go, Lily 109:118
Way, haul away, oh haul and sing together 128:87, see also: Haul Away, Joe
Way, haul away, we'll haul away the bowlin' 22:145, see also: Haul Away, Joe
Way high up the Mogollons 61:335
Way Out in Idaho 61:304, 146:87, 159:265
Way out in western Texas 159:246
Way out there on the Triple "R" Yippi-a 119:106
Way Out West 159:333
Way Out West in Kansas 61:97, see also: 61:96
Way out West on the lonesome trail 61:232, see also: 61:233, 159:8, 232:69
Way Over in the New Buryin' Ground 226:473
Way Up in the Holler 20:76
Way Up on Clinch Mountain 226:307, see also: Clinch Mountain
Way up on the Osage mountain where the wind blows chilly and cold 61:252
Way up yonder above the moon 21:277, 277:83, see also: 158:12
'Way up yonder above the sky 158:12, see also: 21:277, 277:83
Way up yonder in the Sierra peaks, where the yellow jack pines grow tall 225:52, see also: 61:202, 146:76
Way way way 19:11
The Wayfarer's Grace 262:173
Wayfaring Stranger 24:880, 27:45, 37:162, 158:346, 205:56, 230:15, 262:47, 277:41, see also: 22:34, 35:68, 148:304 (I am a poor wayfaring stranger)

Wayfaring Stranger 24:881 (Our fathers dear fought for our liberty)
We all clap hands together 165:181
We all went down to New Orleans 73:192
We are a band of brothers 21:142, 73:16, 127:141, 157:124
We Are All Nodding 291:18
We Are Building a Strong Union 64:72
We are climbing Jacob's ladder 21:130, 25:97, 31:11, 69:29, 86:110, 148:198
We Are Coming, Father Abra'am 73:120
We Are Cub Den Number One 26:54
We are dancing in the forest while the bad wolf is far away 70:27
We Are Four Bums 226:192
We Are Going to the Stable/Pujdem Spolu Do Betlema 54:224
We Are Happy and Merry/Mir Senne Heil's Lustig 89:154
We are little Dixie girls standing in a row 141:90
We Are Marching on to Richmond 73:220
We Are Marching on to Victory 64:165
We are Siameeiz if you pleeiz 276:50
We Are Singing/Cantemos 54:296
We are soldiers marching along 165:140
We Are Thankful 162:46
We are the Cub Scouts, the blue 'n gold Scouts 26:61
We are the happy Brownies 68:28
We are the Merry Mouseketeers! 119:94
We Are Thy Children 155:1
We are trying to carry this timber to the building 226:386
We are up in the morning ere dawning of day 61:208, see also: 159:42, 225:24, 262:64
We are woodmen sawing trees 165:92
We ask not that the slave should lie 64:167
We bid Thee welcome, Thou Savior of all 279:84
We bless you, Lord, our God 77:14
We Bring You Flowers 245:105
We bring you flowers for love and joy 245:105
We Brownies work around the house 68:10
We Can Overcome 197:12, see also: 64:33, 72:79
We can travel in the country 207:16
We can travel only eight ri of the road 49:30
We Come to Greet You in Peace/Hevenu Sholom Aleichem 72:149, 169:39, 208:36, 266:36
We come to see Miss Jennie Jones 100:90, see also: 17:39, 63:32, 68:12
We come, we come! 168:27
We cook in a pot on a stove so hot 149:14
We country clodhoppers are 262:78

We crave your condescension 157:177

We cross the prairie as of old 157:36

We followed where the Swamp Fox guides 28:144

We Gather Together 45:56, 205:24, *see also:* 21:338, 27:234

We gather together to ask the Lord's blessing 21:338, 27:234, 45:56, 205:24

We Give Thee But Thine Own 86:195

We go walking on the green grass 134:96

We Got a Lot for Christmas 241:221

We got sunlight on the sand, we got moonlight on the sea 218:173

We got to get up, we got to get up 197:104

We Have a Car 149:44

We have a car at our house 149:44

We have a dear ol' daddy 197:70, 197:71

We have a dog at our house 149:12

We have a pig in the parlour 63:28, *see also:* 20:50, 291:66

We have a stairs at our house 149:20

We Have Come Here/Rana Djinak 89:243

We have fun at our house 149:6

We Have Heard in Bethlehem/Slysèli Jsme V Betlemě 54:228

We have mothers over yonder 37:170

We have no cake to celebrate 97:unpaged

We have not come like eastern kings 244:28

We have nothing to remember so far, so far 218:268

We have Thanksgiving day as did the Pilgrims long ago 97:unpaged

We have travelled far 140:22, *see also:* 54:288

We hear the night owl calling 144:13

We Hunted and We Hunted 292:190, *see also:* 27:62, 106, 128:122, 234:36

We journey along quite contented with life 66:21

We Kiss in a Shadow 218:204

We Love Our Church, O God 86:75

We mean to make things over 21:215

We meet today in freedom's cause and raise our voices high 64:36, 230:20, *see also:* 73:214

We Must Run 74:58

We Pray/Nan Sob-oy 89:298

We Pray for Children O'er the Sea 86:89

We rub and we scrub in the big bathtub 149:22

We Sail the Ocean Blue 252:6

We shall meet, but we shall miss him 73:286

We Shall Not Be Moved 64:38, 230:38

We Shall Overcome 72:79, *see also:* 64:33, 197:12

We Sing in Celebration/Celebrons la Naissance 54:92, *see also:* 279:21

We sit up straight and eat from our plate 149:16

We stand before the Christmas tree 241:164, *see also:* O Tannenbaum

We thank Thee for all our daily bread 69:11, 101:34

We Thank Thee, Lord 155:6

We thank Thee, Lord, for happy hearts 86:211

We thank Thee, loving Father 86:202

We Thank Thee, O Our Father 86:135

We thank Thee, O our Father, for all Thy loving care 86:135

We thank Thee, O our Father, for stories fine and true 86:83

We thank You God for all the leaves 7:8

We Three Kings 21:169, 54:66, 65:99, 86:46, 96:13, 140:98, 148:408, 241:188, 264:124, 279:52, 284:87, *see also:* 92:168, 184:34, 190:75

We three kings of Orient are 21:169, 54:66, 65:99, 86:46, 92:168, 96:13, 140:98, 148:408, 184:34, 190:75, 241:188, 264:124, 279:52, 284:87

We three kings of Orient are, tried to smoke a rubber cigar 63:145

We true South Africans have suffered for a long time 163:91

We was boomin' down the ole Miss'ip 24:839

We was camped on the plains at the head of the Cimarron 60:30, 146:50, *see also:* Zebra Dun

We was laying on the prairie at French Ranch one night 146:144, *see also:* 159:305

We Welcome Glad Easter 86:60

We Welcome Thee Tonight/Velkomin Vertu 209:36

We were camped on the plains at the head of Cimaron 159:78, 159:81, 225:38, *see also:* 60:30, 61:194, 61:195, 146:50

We were comrades close together when the boys march'd away 73:274

We Were Comrades Together in the Days of War 73:274

We were forty miles from Albany 21:282, 158:146, 226:180, 230:87, 277:39, 290:44

We were lying on the prairie at Frank Slaughter's ranch one night 61:243

We were sailing along 170:65

We Were Ten Maidens 227:38

We Whooped And We Hollered 128:22, *see also:* 27:62, 106, 234:36, 292:190

We Will Go No More to the Woods/Nous N'Irons Plus au Bois 217:61

We Will Overcome 64:33, *see also:* 72:79, 197:12

We Wish You a Merry Christmas 27:254, 54:10, 128:57, 148:410, 209:37, 220:26, 241:220, 264:74, *see also:* 227:32

We Won't Go Home Until Morning 290:210

We Would See Jesus 86:49

Wearin' of the Green 21:286, *see also:* 205:163

Wearing of the Green 205:163, *see also:* 21:286

Wearing of the Grey 73:292

Wears the miller's wife rich necklaces 295:59

Weary, Now I Close Mine Eyes/Müde Bin Ich, Geh Zur Ruh 86:173

The Weasel from the Lovely Woods/Le Furet du Bois Joli 217:64

The weasel is running, running 217:64

Weasel's Nest 46:210

The Weaver 226:460, *see also:* 22:32, 205:388, 226:14

The Weaver of Nanduti/La Tejedora de Nanduti 89:98

Weaving Cloth 70:26

Weaving Dance/Pinnal Kolattam 89:217

Weaving the Kanti Cloth 266:25

Web-Footed Friends 118:32, *see also:* 26:12, 292:158

Weblos on Parade 26:66

We'd camped out on the plains at the head of the Cimarron 61:194, *see also:* Zebra Dun

Wedding Chorus 85:207

The Wedding Song/To Tragothi to Gamo 89:195 *(May your life be filled with joy)*

Wedding Song/Ye Hahmoomee Sit Besahzum 208:35 *(For you I will build)*

Wee Cooper of Fife 59:44, 71:66, 72:120, 78:33, 176:24, *see also:* 20:25

Wee Lambie 62:37

Wee Little Piute 61:237

Wee Willie Winkie 59:73, 112:60, 162:91, 175:146

A Week of Birthdays 18:44

Weep not my love 89:225

Weeping, Sad and Lonely 73:267

Weeping willow tree, Hung! Hung! 49:35

Weeping willow trees line the river bank 49:38

Weevily Wheat 24:813, 66:76, 226:161, *see also:* 213:28

Wei Sha Bu Hwei Ja/Why Don't You Come Home? 49:12

Weihnachtslied/Silent Night 279:86, *see also:* Silent Night

Weisst du, wieviel Sternlein stehen an dem blauen Himmelszelt? 86:3, *see also:* 125:80

Welcome, Happy Morning! 45:41

Welcome Here! 140:41, 233:78

Welcome, here, welcome here 140:41, 233:78

Welome, here's to you! 262:27

Welcome Song 68:4 *(Come in! Come in! Come in!)*

Welcome Song 77:19 *(Your bright face makes us glad today)*

Welcome Spring/Yin Chuin Wha Ur Kai 49:15

Welcome, welcome! Pupils of the Music School 286:14, *see also:* 266:47

Welcome, welcome, welcome to you 79:8

Welcome, welcome, you are welcome 83:497

We'll All Go Down the Meadow 262:46

We'll all sing together for Grace is five years old 41:25

We'll All Work Together 27:178

We'll Be Loyal Scouts 26:67

Well, come along boys, and listen to my tale 25:72, 159:37, 225:14, *see also:* Old Chisholm Trail

Well, ev'ry Monday morning, when the bluebirds begin to sing 158:262, 232:156, *see also:* John Henry

We'll Fight for Uncle Abe 73:123

We'll haul the bowlin' so early in the morning 98:12, *see also:* 227:12, 239:13, 274:34

Well, I landed in old Santa Fe in nineteen hundred and three 61:89

Well, I'm a wild cowboy, I've roved the West o'er 159:85

Well, I'm walking down this track 148:252

Well, it's where do you come from, and where do you go? 274:6

We'll Land on the Moon 166:68

Well, las' Monday mornin', Lawd, Lawd, Lawd 24:907, 158:20, *see also:* Grey Goose

Well, mates, I don't like stories 146:136, 159:346

Well, me and my partner can pick a bale of cotton 232:148, *see also:* Pick a Bale of Cotton

Well, one Sunday morning, Lord, Lord, Lord 274:28

We'll roll the old chariot along 66:148, *see also:* 226:196

We'll roll, we'll roll the chariot along 226:196, *see also:* 66:148

We'll Speak Very Softly/Falade Ben Baixo 54:271

Well, the Rock Island Line is a mighty good road 274:12, *see also:* 35:52, 129:90, 130:64, 148:314

Well, there are lots of worms way under the ground 296:26

(Well) you can play with me   130:54

Well, you wake up in the morning   21:90, 24:908, 158:318, 230:55, see also: 226:26, 226:217

Well-a, Shorty George, he ain't no friend of mine   158:70

The Wells and Fargo Line   61:46

Went out to milk and I didn't know how 197:107, see also: 20:72, 22:66, 226:94

Wer Klopfet an?/Who's Knocking There? 279:77

We're All Gonna Shine Tonight   290:206

We're All Here: The Song of the Freed Men 66:136, see also: 226:448

We're All Together Again   25:7, 26:9, 71:12, 72:39

We're alone, Dona Gal, in the rain and hail 61:232, see also: 61:233, 159:8, 232:69

We're alone, Doney Gal, in the rain and hail   61:231, 159:8, see also: 61:233, 232:69

We're Bound for Rio   71:70, 72:76

We're brave and gallant miner boys who work down underground   64:26

We're coming, we're coming, our brave little band   290:134

We're fighting for our Union, we're fighting for our trust   73:19

We're floating down the river   135:94, see also: 128:97

We're girls and boys together   204:13

We're Glad to See You Here   26:11

We're going to Chicago, we're going to the fair   63:26

We're gonna roll, we're gonna roll, we're gonna roll the union on!   64:44

We're Here Because We're Here   290:217

We're Here for Fun   25:6, 26:9

We're leaving here, and we're going there 33:226

We're marching'round the levee   37:191, 39:14, 83:504, see also: Round and Round the Village

We're on the Upward Trail   25:56, 26:69

We're sailing down the river from Liverpool 158:136, see also: 21:288, 24:835, 262:105

We're Singing Our Praises/Wilt Heden Nu Treden   21:338, see also: 27:234, 45:56, 205:24

We're Tenting To-night   127:157, see also: 21:150, 73:152, 197:60

We're tenting tonight on the old camp ground   21:150, 73:152, 127:157, 197:60

We're the Boy Scouts of America   25:50

We're up in the morning ere breaking of day   262:64, see also: 61:208, 159:42, 225:24

We're wearing green for the Irish   162:55

Were you ever in Quebeck stowing timber on the deck   71:81, 72:117, 78:11, 128:89

Were You There?   21:264, 31:39

Were you there when they crucified my Lord?   21:264, 31:39

West Texas   159:413

The West Virginia Boys   36:66

West Virginia Hills   64:56

Western Cowboy   61:87

Western Home   61:295

Western Lullaby   166:30

Westward Ho   159:415

We've been to   236:3

We've Been Told a Joyful Thing   86:36

We've Come from Spain   63:34

We've come from Spain, we've come from Spain   63:34

We've come to see Miss Jenny Jones, Miss Jenny Jones, Miss Jenny Jones   17:39, 68:12, see also: 63:32, 100:90

We've completed the harvesting   49:23

We've Drunk from the Same Canteen 73:276

We've formed our band and we are well manned   239:64

We've got a pig in the parlor   291:66, see also: 20:50, 63:28

We've got an old grey hen in our chicken pen   289:30

We've just been introduced. I do not know you well   218:212

We've reached the land of desert sweet 159:410, 226:280, see also: 61:62, 61:63, 61:64

Whai Lyang Shin/Bad Faith   49:17

The Whale   62:49

A Whale of a Tale   276:79

Wha'll dreg a buckie, O?   262:140

What a Court   28:51, see also: 27:164, 240:67, 273:36

What a court hath old England of folly and sin   27:164, 28:51, 240:67, 273:36

What a lovely sunny morning   7:24

What Are Little Boys Made Of?   18:31, 111:33, 175:102, see also: 17:133

What Are Little Girls Made Of?   18:30, 111:33, 175:102, see also: 17:133

What are Summer Puddles good for? 261:36

What brought you into my room   42:603

What Can I Do?   206:58

What can I do when I'm alone?   206:70

What Can the Matter Be?   36:6, see also: Oh, Dear! What Can the Matter Be

What can the matter be, Nomalizo, ohmn? 163:112

What can we do with a drunken sailor 205:33, see also: Drunken Sailor

What can you do, Punchinello, funny fellow? 135:113, *see also:* 63:14, 109:106, 128:96, 178:7

What Child Is This? 21:238, 54:30, 92:188, 125:46, 148:412, 241:50, 243:unpaged, 261:52, 264:123, 279:40, 284:99

What Did I See? 68:20

What Did You Have for Your Supper 232:140, *see also:* 89:156, 157:71

What Do I Do When I'm Alone? 206:70

What Do You Do? 219:27

What Do You Do, Papa Small 154:38

What do you do with the big black coal? 289:94

What do you do with the mad that you feel 219:27

What does the clock in the hall say? 165:38

What d'ye think I have made with my red herring's head? 262:27

What hue shall my apples be? 227:10

What Is Big?/Chinene Nye? 168:18

What is that thing? What is that thing over there 74:53

What Is the Rhyme for Porringer? 112:70

What Is This Fragrance 54:102, 220:32, *see also:* 210:76

What is this fragrance softly stealing? 220:32, *see also:* 54:102, 210:76

What Is This I Promise You? 19:27

What Kin' O' Pants Does the Gambler Wear 226:240

What Makes Music 206:36

What makes music? Anything makes music! 206:36

What means this omen so strangely appearing? 262:103

What month was my Jesus borned in? 233:50

What shall I call my dear little dormouse 172:138

What Shall I Do to Show 85:43

What shall I do to show how much I love her 85:43

What Shall We Do? 291:48, *see also:* 164:179, 232:59

What Shall We Do About Poor Little Tigger 172:51, 174:37

What Shall We Do When We All Go Out? 165:179, 232:59, 291:48

What shall we do with the drunken sailor 22:176, 39:35, 98:25, 176:108, 205:33, 239:10

What shall we give to the Son of the Virgin 54:260

What ship is this that will take us all home? 21:262, *see also:* 35:58

What ship is this that you're going on board 35:58, *see also:* 21:262

What solemn sounds the ear invade 273:76

What Sweeter Music 241:20

What though America doth pour 240:168

What Use Are You 41:34, 291:35

What Was Your Name in the States? 21:307, 24:861, 226:106

What Will We Do with the Baby-O? 75:86, *see also:* 110:26, 232:146

What will we do with the old sow's hide? 234:52

What wondrous love is this 21:351, 37:160, 134:108, 140:76, 157:57, 158:348

What Would You Do? 212:28

What You Gonna Call Yo' Pretty Little Baby? 140:69, 190:114, *see also:* 140:66, 190:134, 209:26, 233:44

What you gonna do when the liquor gives out, sweet thing? 158:106

What you gwain to do when the meat gives out, my Baby? 226:240

Whatever you wish that men would do to you 86:87

What'll We Do With the Baby? 232:146, *see also:* 75:86, 110:26

What'll We Do With the Baby-O? 110:26, *see also:* 75:86, 232:146

What'll you have for supper, my good old man? 71:89

What's the Matter? 73:56

What's the Use of Wond'rin' 218:115

What's the use of wond'rin' if he's good or if he's bad 218:115

What's this dull town to me? 21:342

The Wheat 46:203, 55:521

Wheels 91:23

The Wheels of the Bus Go Round and Round 147:6, 165:73, 291:46, *see also:* 75:16

Wheels on a wagon, wheels on a bike 91:23

When a Baby Comes 219:37

When a baby comes to your house 219:37

When a fellow loves a maiden 21:110, 226:290, *see also:* 197:38

When a felon or not engaged in his employment 252:22

When a lad, I stood one day 21:52

When a Merry Maiden Marries 252:64

When a Woman Blue 226:236

When Akela holds his council 26:64

When all the cows are sleeping 165:86

When all the snow was on the ground 41:5

When all the winds were mild 67:94

When are we gonna get married, married, married? 290:88

When at night I fall asleep 262:149, *see also:* 125:98

When at night I go to sleep 125:98, *see also:* 262:149

When Barnacle Bill was one he learned to play a drum 162:62

When British troops first landed here 240:137, 273:56

When Britons first, by Heav'n command 240:58

When Buster Brown Was One 63:86

When but a child I used to go to bed at eight each night 84:26

When Caesar Augustus had raised a taxation 241:24

When Captain Jinks come home at night 135:96, *see also:* 66:63, 70:28, 126:65

When Christ our Lord was born at Bethlehem afar 279:100, *see also:* 54:242, 241:100

When Christ Was Born of Mary Free 54:20, 209:45, 210:134

When Christmas Morn Is Dawning/Nar Juldagsmorgon Glimmar 54:194

When cockle shells turn silver bells 226:16

When company's there 149:18

When Congress sent great Washington 28:49, 220:79

When Daisies Pied 85:53, 189:114

When did the world begin and how? 59:38

When Discord did rear her black standard on high 273:44

When Ducks Get Up in the Morning 291:26

When early morning's ruddy light 83:471

When evening comes and my play is done 207:21

When everybody screams and yells 235:53

When first I heard the people tell 61:44

When first I started out cow-driving 159:105

When formed our band 226:110

When fortune's blind goddess had fled my abode 61:15, 61:16, 159:217

When Frederic Was a Little Lad 252:20

When gold was found in Forty-nine the people thought 'twas gas 159:381

When Gombei sows the seed 78:83

When good King Arthur rul'd the land 17:100, 18:28, 112:7, 188:142

When he cometh, when he cometh 189:66

When I am far away, Eileen Aroon 42:599

When I am older I'll fly to the moon 162:71

When I Can Read My Title Clear 66:139

When I enter the village 89:160, *see also:* 216:45

When I First Came to This Land 27:138, 29, 230:13

When I first came to town 36:60, 157:14, *see also:* 37:154, 62:142, 230:70

When I First Put This Uniform On 252:29

When I Go Out of Doors 252:34

When I Go to Bed 124:148

When I grow up, I'd like to be a captain brave who sails the sea 156:4

When I grow up, I'd like to be a dancer dancing merrily 156:26

When I Say My Prayer 86:172

When I See an Elephant Fly 275:23, 276:10

When I take you out, tonight, with me 218:19

When I think of the last great roundup 61:330, 159:327

When I think of Tom, I think about a night 218:189

When I Was a Baby 63:22

When I was a baby, a baby, a baby 63:22

When I Was a Bachelor 18:36, *see also:* Swapping Song

When I was a bach'lor 22:32, 205:388, 226:14, *see also:* 226:460

When I was a boy and a farmer's boy 212:48

When I Was a Brave Cowboy 159:228

When I Was a Cowboy 61:86, 159:39

When I was a cowboy out on the Western plains 61:87

When I was a cowboy way out on de western plains 61:86, 159:39

When I Was a Little Boy 111:63, *see also:* Swapping Song

When I was a little boy 27:192, 128:11, 189:50, *see also:* Ha, Ha, This-a-way

When I was a little boy I lived by myself 111:63, 129:38, 143, 213:12, *see also:* 18:36, 37:174, 188:44

When I was a little lad, and so my mother told me 272:13, 290:48, *see also:* 22:145, 98:18, 128:87, 134:69

When I was a sailor in Palos 197:90

When I was a seeker 92:156, 241:34, *see also:* Go Tell It on the Mountain

When I Was a Shoemaker 75:87, *see also:* Ha, Ha, This-a-way

When I Was a Young Girl 17:110, 135:74, 289:166, *see also:* Ha, Ha, This-a-way

When I Was a Young Maid 232:168, *see also:* Ha, Ha, This-a-way

When I was a young man and never been kissed 230:93

When I was a young man growin' up 37:154, *see also:* 36:60, 62:142, 157:14, 230:70

When I was a young man I lived upon the square 159:161

When I was bound apprentice 117:unpaged, 176:44

When I Was But a Small Young Laddie/Kui Mina Alles Noor Veel Olin 89:173

When I was one, I ate a bun 63:84

When I was shipwrecked 89:33, 234:72, *see also:* 26:36

When I Was Single (Woman's Story) 62:141, 158:48, *see also:* 36:87, 157:67

When I Was Single (Man's Complaint) 20:30, 158:50, *see also:* 36:102, 62:140, 226:47,

When I was single, living at my ease 62:141, *see also:* 36:87, 157:67, 158:48

When I was single, marrying was my crave 36:87, *see also:* 62:141, 157:67, 158:48

When I was single, o then, o then 20:30, 62:140, 157:67, 158:50, 226:47

When I was single, went dressed all so fine 157:67, 158:48, *see also:* 36:87, 62:140

When I Was Young and Foolish 226:219

When I was young and in my prime 62:142, *see also:* 36:60, 37:154, 157:14, 230:70

When I was young I use' to wait 22:72, 205:110, 230:12, *see also:* 27:10, 129:42, 178:26, 232:124

When I was young I used to wait 27:10, 178:26, 205:110, *see also:* 22:72, 129:42, 230:12, 232:124

When I Went A-Courtin' 61:24

When I went out exploring 89:310

When I Went to the Bar 252:38

When I went to town today 166:26

When I worked in the mill, weavin' at the loom 218:80

When Irish Eyes Are Smiling 170:84

When Is the Day? 162:72

When Israel was in Egypt land 22:316, 158:372, 197:45, *see also:* 31:13, 64:168, 148:106, 205:178

When Israel was in Egypt's land 31:13, 64:168, 148:108, 205:178, *see also:* 22:316, 158:372, 197:45

When Jack the King's commander bold 240:127

When Jacky is a good boy 18:48

When Jesus was a baby boy 86:100

When Jesus was a child 86:151

When Jesus Was a Little Boy 154:4

When Jesus Wept 140:112, 157:13, 273:136

When John Henry was a little baby 64:82, 89:40, 230:81, 272:15, *see also:* John Henry

When John Henry was about three days old 232:154, *see also:* John Henry

When Johnny Comes Marching Home 22:196, 27:228, 66:82, 73:284, 117:unpaged, 128:92, 148:414, 157:134, 197:61, 205:251

When Joseph was an old man 140:26, *see also:* Cherry Tree Carol

When lights are on they shine so bright 11:15

When Little Children Go to Sleep 125:100

When Morning Gilds the Skies 86:162

When Moses was a baby, then he was in the water laid 124:89

When my baby's birthday comes 125:12

When My Blood Runs Chilly an' Col' 158:360

When my father and my mother 55:510, *see also:* 83:495, 178:30

When my friend William was five years old 260:78

When my poor wife died 169:40

When others hate, may I speak peace 155:12

When Paul and Silas were bound in jail 66:136, *see also:* 226:448

When Phoebus had melted the sickles of ice 164:82

When Poor Mary Came Wandering Home 226:466

When Robin Hood and Little John went o'er yon bank of broom 164:110

When Robin Hood in the greenwood lived 164:88

When Robin Hood was about twenty years old 164:10, *see also:* 262:132

When Royal George ruled o'er this land 240:157

When San Juan folk from mountains come down for water 89:88

When Sherman Marched Down to the Sea 73:216

When slumbering in my convict cell my childhood days I see 159:90

When springtime does come 24:883

When That I Was and a Little Tiny Boy 71:71

When the bats on the wing 59:16

When the Blackbird in the Spring 73:234, *see also:* 205:396

When the Corn Is Planted 86:177

When the Cruel War Is Over 73:267

When the Cruel War Is Over—Answer 73:270

When the Curtains of Night Are Pinned Back 61:244, 83:468, 226:259

When the farmer comes to town 24:879, 226:282, 230:57, 239:42, *see also:* 64:96

When the hot sun smiles on the endless miles 159:99

When the Kye Comes Home 182:43

When the lumberman comes down 158:172

When the Master Calls Me Home 86:131

When the mother and the father take the children to the fair 83:495, *see also:* 55:510, 178:30

When the Navy floats its battle boats to rule the rolling sea 27:126

When the night falls silently 21:72

When the rain on leaves falls gently 89:299

When the Saints Go Marching In 25:104, 72:87, 148:416, 157:148, 205:377

When the shades of night are falling 85:188

When the snow is crisp and crunchy on the ground 167:54

When the starry dew lies 87:66

When the stars are brightly beaming 66:12

When the sun comes back, when the first quail calls 33:162

When the sun sets in the West 286:64

When the Train Comes Along 232:153

When the umpire stands and yells, "Play Ball!" 166:32

When the union's inspiration through the workers' blood shall run 64:12, *see also:* 230:91

When the waters are calm 19:41

When the wind is in the east 18:26, 281:58

When the Work's All Done This Fall 27:112, 61:220, 126:79, 159:74, 226:260

When to Church I Go 86:76

When Upon the Field of Glory 73:270

When We Grow Up 260:32

When we grow up will I be pretty? 260:32

When we think the train is running on the mountain ridge 286:58

When will come the happy morning 22:122

When Wilt Thou Save the People? 64:180

When You and I Were Young, Maggie 21:183, 205:158

When You awakened us from dreams 124:243

When you come to the end of a lollypop 26:16

When you get in trouble and you don't know right from wrong 275:19, 253:16

When You Go A-Courtin' 158:42

When you go to Mount Holly, it's there where you're set 24:887

When you rush around in hopeless circles 276:65

When You Sing 162:106

When you think you're looking wide 69:12

When you walk through a storm, hold your head up high 218:118

When You Wish Upon a Star 275:16, 276:14

When Your Potato's Done 79:38, 262:99

When-a my blood runs chilly an' col' 158:360

Whence Art Thou, My Maiden?/D'où Viens-Tu, Bergère? 54:133, *see also:* 279:96

Whence Comes This Rush of Wings 209:119, 241:62, 284:61, *see also:* Carol of the Birds

Whence Is That Goodly Fragrance?/Quelle Est Cette Odeur Agréable? 54:102, 210:76, *see also:* 220:32

Whence, O Shepherd Maiden?/D'où Viens-Tu, Bergère? 279:96, *see also:* 54:133

Whene'er I poke sarcastic joke 290:182

Whene'er You Make a Promise 68:38, 69:6, 71:30, 72:25

Whenever I feel afraid I hold my head erect 218:184

Whenever I go up to sleep 124:148

Whenever I walk in a London street 172:142

Whenever the moon and stars are set 59:47

Where a campfire's brightly burning 69:51

Where Are the Keys of the Castle?/Donde Están las Llaves? 188:54, *see also:* 189:154

Where Are You Going? (round) 293:62

Where Are You Going, Abe Lincoln? 73:64

Where Are You Going Grandmama? 68:39

Where are you going, my good old man? 20:68, 129:24, 274:40

Where Are You Going, My Pretty Maid? 62:116, 290:79, 293:62, *see also:* Where Are You Going to, My Pretty Maid?

Where are you going, pretty maids today? 68:44

Where are you going soldiers 73:130

Where Are You Going to, My Pretty Maid? 17:114, 128:110, 175:118, 188:140, 262:53, *see also:* 36:3, 36:35, 62:116, 290:79, 293:62

Where are you goin'? Where are you bound? 296:14

Where Are You Going, You Little Pig? 112:19

Where did you come from, where did you go? 128:20, *see also:* 274:6, 289:25

Where Did You Get That Hat 205:219

Where Do You Come From?/Antagata Dokosa? 286:50

Where Do You Sleep? 59:26

Where Does This River Go? 91:17

Where Go the Boats? 69:43

Where God Hath Walked 71:32, 72:52

Where Has My Little Boy Gone 26:54

Where Has My Little Dog Gone? 26:18, *see also:* 17:43, 285:92, 292:70

Where hast thou been since I saw thee 134:107

Where Have All the Flowers Gone? 72:5

Where have ye been a-day, my boy Tammie?
182:56

Where have you been all day, Henery, Henery, my boy 62:113, *see also:* 89:39

Where have you been all day, Henry, my son 89:39, *see also:* 62:113

Where have you been all the day, Billy Boy, Billy Boy? 71:38, *see also:* Billy Boy

Where have you been all the day, my boy Billy? 27:22, *see also:* Billy Boy

Where have you been all the day, my boy Willie 62:112, *see also:* Billy Boy

Where have you been a-roving, Jimmy Randal, my son? 157:71, *see also:* 89:156, 232:140

Where have you been, Billy Boy, Billy Boy 62:111, *see also:* Billy Boy

Where Have You Been Walking, Shepherdess? 262:170

Where Is John? 144:5, 262:67, 293:44

Where is Ma' Teodora? 216:46

Where Is My Boy Tonight? 21:171

Where Is My Red Rose?/Vaj, Gulum Gitti? 89:213

Where is my wand'ring boy tonight 21:171

Where Is Our Rose? 85:218

Where is the girl who will go out west with me? 35:54

Where is the goat? 292:56

Where Is Thumbkin? 75:88, *see also:* 289:110

Where, Oh, Where 75:89

Where oh where are the three pretty girls? 178:38, *see also:* Pawpaw Patch

Where, oh, where has my little boy gone 26:54

Where, oh, Where Has My Little Dog Gone? 26:18, 285:92, 292:70, *see also:* 17:43

Where, oh, where, is dear little Nelly? 129:116, 291:81, *see also:* Pawpaw Patch

Where, oh where is my little ring? 75:89

Where O Where Is Old Elijah? 226:92

Where oh where is pretty little Sally? 20:52, *see also:* Pawpaw Patch

Where oh Where Is Pretty Little Susie? 232:172, *see also:* Pawpaw Patch

Where, oh where is sweet little Betty? 33:138, *see also:* Pawpaw Patch

Where, o where is sweet little Mary? 39:40, *see also:* Pawpaw Patch

Where, oh where, oh where is Susie? 25:20, *see also:* Pawpaw Patch

Where Shall I Be? 31:47

Where shall I be when the first trumpet sounds 31:47

Where the Bee Sucks 71:125, 85:56, 189:108

Where the Bravest Cowboys Lie 61:155

Where the cowboys roost on the green rolling prairie 159:103

Where There's a Will There's a Way 66:52

Where They Were 226:442

Where Was Moses When the Lights Went Out? 84:26

Where you can go farther and see less 159:413

Where you going, buzzard? 109:57

Where'er You Walk 71:31

Where's Mister Thumbkin? 289:110, *see also:* 75:88

Whet up your knife and whistle up your dog 213:68, 289:46, *see also:* 24:893, 158:26, 292:98

Which is the Way the Wind Blows? 245:95

Which Side Are You On? 64:54, 230:94, 239:90

While By My Sheep I Watch at Night/Als Ich Bei Meinen Schafen Wacht 54:146, 241:136

While Eastern shepherds watched their flocks by night 209:98

While going the road to sweet Athy, Hurroo! 42:605, *see also:* 148:204

While I relate my story, Americans give ear 28:4, 240:36

While I Was Dancing the Other Day/ L'Autre Jour en Voulant Danser 89:152

While Jesus Sleeps/L'Enfant Jésus S'endort 241:107

While lookin' at my feet at a crack in the sidewalk 206:86

While Mary washed linen 188:156, *see also:* 189:76

While passing near a little wood 217:61

While Passing Through Lorraine/En Passant par la Lorraine 176:66, 217:60, *see also:* 208:23

While shepherds washed their socks by night 63:146

While Shepherds Watched Their Flocks by Night 54:31, 134:105, 140:80, 184:28, 210:79, 241:154, 264:104, 284:95

While some on rights and some on wrongs 27:218

While Strolling Through the Park 205:209

While the shot and shell were screaming upon the battlefield 21:41

Whilst Through the Sharp Hawthorn 273:104

Whip-Poor-Will 262:35

Whip-Poor-Will's Song 66:103

Whippily, Whoppily, Whoop 197:93

Whirling Maiden 262:142

Whirling, turning, whirling, turning 262:142

Whisky Frisky 112:55

Whisky, frisky, hippety hop 112:55

Whisky is the life of man 21:246, *see also:* 98:24, 226:403

Whisky Johnnie 21:246, *see also:* 98:24, 226:403

Whisky Johnny 98:24, 226:403, *see also:* 21:246

Whistle, Mary, Whistle 72:95

The Whistle of the Train 114:38

The Whistle Pig Song 110:19

Whistle While You Work 275:12, 276:6

The White Army Bean 99:47, *see also:* 73:168

White Coral Bells 46:227, 62:13, 72:160, 148:416, 262:32, 293:18

White Fields 44:26

The White Hawk/El Quele'le 262:118

White Mornings 207:32

White Rose of My Heart/Lliw Gwyn Rhosyn Yr Haf 89:134

White Sand and Gray Sand 62:18, 71:113, 293:68

White Sheep 245:79

White sheep, white sheep, on a blue hill 245:79

The White Ship Sails 63:37, *see also:* Allee Allee-o

The white ship sails through the Alley Alley O 63:37, *see also:* Allee Allee-o

The White Steed of the Prairies 159:227

White Violets 227:8

White Wings 21:227

The Whizz-Fish Song 84:19

Who All Is Here? 107:58

Who Built the Ark 141:24, 232:128

Who built the ark? Noah, Noah 135:24, 232:128

Who can crawl under a table 219:45

Who Can Retell? 22:280

Who can retell the things that befell us? 22:280

Who Comes Here? 18:11, 111:61

Who comes here? A grenadier 18:11, 111:61

Who Comes Laughing? 262:143

Who Did? 129:102, 289:102

Who Has a Nose? 178:9

Who Has Seen the Wind? 112:25

Who has the whitest lambkins? 125:78

Who Is It? 168:56

Who is it up there on top of the lodge? 19:31

Who Is Knocking?/Pahupahu 87:19

Who Is the Man? 22:295, 262:110

Who is the man, that life doth will 22:295, 262:110

Who Killed Cock Robin? 62:56, 134:58, 292:138, *see also:* 37:177, 135:32, 289:74

Who Killed Cocky Robin? 289:74, *see also:* Who Killed Cock Robin?

Who Knows One? 192

Who Loves the Rain 69:49

Who Loves the Wind on a Stormy Night 245:68

Who made ocean, earth and sky? 71:24, 72:46, 135:31

Who Made the Sky So Bright and Blue 86:4

Who Made the Stars 86:7

Who Stole My Chickens and My Hens? 63:93

Who Will Care for Mother Now? 73:259

Who will go in must softly go 244:290

Who Will Shoe My Little Feet? 110:24, *see also:* 226:98, 226:99, 230:65

Who Will Shoe Your Pretty Little Foot? 226:98, *see also:* 110:24, 226:99, 230:65

Who wouldna be in love wi' bonnie Maggie Lauder? 182:15

Whoa Buck 158:232

Whoa! Ha! Buck and Jerry Boy 61:54

Whoa, Mule! Can't Get the Saddle On 234:64

Whoa, Mule, Whoa! 110:32, 208:80

Whoever Shall Have Peanuts 128:118

Whoever shall have some good peanuts 128:118

The Whole Dam Family 84:54

Who'll buy caller herrin'? 292:174

Who'll buy my posies, who'll buy my roses 71:102

Whom of Old the Shepherds Praised/Quem Pastores Laudavere 54:317, 279:14

Whoopee, Ti Yi Yo [Git Along, Little Dogies] 22:162, 129:92, 159:4, 226:268 *see also:* Git Along Little Dogies

Whoopin' up cattle, I'm settin' up straddle 159:37 234:70

Who's Afraid of the Big Bad Wolf? 275:28, 276:20

Who's Gonna Shoe Your Pretty Foot? 230:65, *see also:* 110:24, 226:98, 226:99

Who's In 44:68

Who's Knocking There?/Wer Klopfet an? 279:77

Who's That Knocking At My Door? 291:84, *see also:* 232:52

Who's That Tapping At the Window? 232:52, *see also:* 291:84

Who's that yonder dressed in red? 83:466, *see also:* Set Down, Servant

Who's the Hero? 77:53

Who's the hero of the story! 77:52

Who's the leader of the club that's made for you and me? 275:92, 276:85, *see also:* 119:92

Who's the Pretty Girl Milkin' the Cow? 226:40

Whose Bag Is My Gold Ring? 109:165

Whose Birthday? 97:unpaged

Whose Old Cow? 159:117

Why am I so weak and weary 73:259

Why are you standing outside, young man? 71:53

Why come ye hither red coats 20:14, 240:102

Why do they think up stories that link my name with yours? 218:40

Why does the crow sing with so much joy? 286:26

Why does your brand sae drop wi' blude? 85:137

Why doesn't Mommy like worms in my pocket? 245:42

Why doesn't my goose sing as well as thy goose 144:21, *see also:* Why Shouldn't My Goose

Why Don't You Come Home?/Wei Sha Bu Hwei Ja 49:12

Why don't you try a Spanish dance? 166:62

Why don't you work like other men do? 57:126, *see also:* 22:102, 24:882, 226:184, 239:54

Why in forest deep, grieves, vidalita 22:108

Why should vain mortals tremble at the sight of Death 240:115, 273:40

Why should we mourn departing friends 273:152

Why Shouldn't My Goose 148:420, 262:91, 289:189, 292:149, 293:90, *see also:* 128:101, 144:21, 176:91

Wi' a Hundred Pipers 71:61

The Wicked Rebels 27:168, 28:17

The Wicky Wacky Wocky Bird 97:unpaged

Widdicome Fair 22:50, 71:68, 193, *see also:* 292:24

The Wide Mizzoura 226:408, *see also:* Shenandoah

Widewidewenne/Biddy Biddy Burkey 188:126

Widewidewenne heisst meine Trut-henne 188:126

The Widow of Count Laurel/La Viudita del Conde Laurel 295:43

Wie Schön Leuchtet der Morgenstern/How Brightly Shines the Morning Star 54:164, 241:132

Wie Soll Ich Dich Empfangen?/How Shall I Fitly Meet Thee? 241:152

Wiegenlied/Savior, Hear Us, We Pray 86:139

Wiegenlied Der Hirten/Shepherds' Cradle Song 54:156

The Wife Who Was Dumb 36:72

Wiggle the Wool 290:12

Wild Americay 35:44

Wild Animals 112:20

Wild Bronc Peeler 159:85

Wild Buckaroo 61:106

Wild Geese/Kari 286:20

The Wild Man of Borneo 62:74

The Wild Montana Boy 159:167

Wild Mountain Thyme 134:100

A Wild Rattling Cowboy 159:221

The Wild Rippling Water 61:6, 159:183

Wild roved an Indian maid 66:92

Will I Get a Christmas Present? 241:226

Will the Weaver 37:184, *see also:* 36:76

Will Ye No Come Back Again? 176:32, 262:144

Will You Come to the Bow'r? 277:77

Will you come to the bow'r I have shaded for you? 277:77

Will you come with me, my Phillis dear 66:108, 73:44, 205:129, *see also:* 83:513

Will you give us bread and wine? 63:34

Will You Go Out West? 35:54

Will you please to give ear a while unto me 240:23

Will You Walk a Little Faster? 112:22

"Will you walk a Little Faster?" said a whiting to a snail 112:22

"Will you walk into my parlour?" said the Spider to a Fly 175:168

Will you wear blue, oh my dear, oh my dear 291:28, *see also:* Jennie Jenkins

Will You Wear Red? 135:62, *see also:* Jennie Jenkins

Will you wear red, my dear, O dear? 69:20, 262:37, *see also:* Jennie Jenkins

Will you wear white, oh my dear, oh my dear? 75:42, 129:22, 158:54, *see also:* Jennie Jenkins

William's Doll 260:78

Willie 91:37

Willie Foster 135:67

Willie Foster had a coo 135:67

Willie, get your little drum 54:112, *see also:* Patapan

Willie is a walrus 91:37

Willie, take your little drum 210:80, 220:90, 241:176, 262:50, *see also:* 54:112, 129:60

Willie the Weaver 36:76, *see also:* 37:184

Willie, Willie, Will 262:141

Willie Wood 111:46, *see also:* Aiken Drum

Willowbee 129:106

Willum he had seven sons 165:167

Willy the Weeper 22:54, 226:204

Wilt Heden Nu Treden/We're Singing Our Praises 21:338

Wilt heden nu treden voor God den Heere 21:338

The Wind 177:86 (*The wind is crying: "ooh-ooh o-o-h"*)

The Wind 44:4 *(I saw you toss the kites on high)*
The Wind and I 207:29
The Wind and I Went Dancing 7:34
The Wind Blow East 130:95, 232:66
The wind blows off yon rocky shore 73:186
Wind In the Willows 125:14 *(Lie down, baby, on your pillow)*
The Wind In the Willows 71:113, 72:170 *(The wind in the willows sighing)*
The wind is crying: "ooh-ooh o-o-h" 177:86
The Wind It Blew Up the Railroad Track 226:379
The Wind Mill 262:85
Wind the bobbin up 165:122
The Wind, the Wind 63:65
The wind, the wind, the wind blows high 63:65
Wind Up the Apple Tree 39:30, 100:114
Wind, wind, wind the bobbin 245:58
Winding lanes, peaceful land 49:28
Winds through the olive trees softly did blow 220:86
Windsor 21:315
Windy Bill 60:54, 61:204, 146:69, 159:113
Windy Bill was a Texas man 146:69, 159:113, see also: 60:54, 61:204
Windy Day 296:19
Windy Nights 59:47
A windy, windy, windy day 296:19
Winkum, Winkum 17:26
Winkum, Winkum, shut your eye 17:26
Winnie the Pooh 275:66, 276:82
The Winnsboro Cotton Mill Blues 64:74
Winter 91:30
Winter baked a birthday cake 207:68
Winter Has Come 27:240
Winter has come upon our loved ones 27:240
The winter has gone 86:184
Winter Holiday 162:47
The Winter Season 27:250
The winter season of the year 27:250
Winter Song 86:180
Winter Walks 207:67
Winter's Birthday Cake 207:68
The Wise Men Were But Seven 293:32
A wise old owl sat in an oak 18:10
The Wisemen 67:57
Wish I had a bushel, wish I had a peck 158:88
Wishes 261:14
Wishes Don't Make Things Come True 219:14
Wishing Dolls/Teru, Terubozu 286:56
Wishing Song 110:23
The Wisp of Straw 67:67
The Witches 162:41

The witches are coming tonight 162:41
Witches, goblins, owls and cats 7:38
With a hop and a skip and a jump, ho-ho! 167:24
With a merry little jog and a gay little song 61:54
With a morning song we greet you 169:48, 262:21, 268:41
With a ranger's hat and shovel and a pair of dungarees 26:81
With a Smile and a Song 275:10, 276:4
With a sort of careless swagger 61:107
With a spade and a rake 207:103
With Cat-Like Tread 252:25
With cat-like tread upon our prey we steal 252:25
With heavy tread goes the elephant so strong 169:12
With Kitty I'll Go 212:58
With my hands and my fingers, oh 290:12
With My Hands I Clap Clap Clap 178:29
With my little broom I sweep, sweep, sweep 165:33
With new cloth my mama sews 114:32
With one consent let all the earth 273:132
With one round eye I'm a pumpkin man 162:42
With someone like you 170:94
With the gentle breeze that wafts t'ward me 87:47
With the walls o'er flowing with blossoms 87:43
With tuppence for paper and strings 275:55
With twenty pennies, with twenty pennies 262:22
With words of peace now we greet you 266:36
With your guns and drums and drums and guns, hoo-roo, hoo-roo 148:204
With your kind attention a song I will trill 24:869, 158:188
Within a Humble Stable 220:108
Wizard Oil 226:52
Wlui nado loo 89:262
Wo Seywa De 169:28, 268:30
Wo seywa de, Wo seywa de 169:28, 268:30
Wo! Wo! Wo! Cameroon 163:83
The Wolf/El Lobo 70:27
The Wolf and the Stork/Le Loup et la Cicogne 243:30
The (Wolf) (Bear) (Web'lo) Went Over the Mountain 26:60
The Wolf went over the mountain 26:60
Wolves A-Howling 234:79
Women who never have to hoe 236:42
The Wonder Ball 141:24
The wonder ball goes round and round 141:24

A Wonderful Guy 218:153
Wondrous Love 21:351, 37:160, 134:108, 140:76, 157:57, 158:348
Won't You Be My Neighbor? 219:3
Won't you be my valentine, my valentine, please do 162:54
Won't you bring back won't you bring back Missus Murphy's chowder? 290:16
Won't you come home, Bill Bailey? 21:88, 148:42, 170:44, *see also:* 205:272
Won't You Go My Way? 134:68
Won't You Let the Birdie Out? 109:177
Won't You Sit Down? 83:465, *see also:* Set Down, Servant
The Wood Bird's Lullaby 125:29
The Woodchuck 144:9
Woodman, Spare That Tree 157:104
The Woodmen's Alphabet 35:12
The Wooing of the Titmouse 79:80
Woowooto 236:71
The Word of God 124:17
Work All de Summer 239:50
Work For the Night Is Coming 25:116
The Work Song 276:36
Workers' Carol 210:139
The workers on the S. P. Line to strike sent out a call 64:43
Working on the railroad, working in the mine 27:178
The World Is Big, The World Is Small 107:32
A World of Snow 162:34
The world today is mourning the death of Mother Jones 64:58
The World Turned Upside Down 28:159, 273:58, 289:133, *see also:* 240:40
The World's Desire 184:47, 209:117, *see also:* 244:64
The world's so wide I cannot cross it 226:323
The Worm Song 290:178, *see also:* 62:109, 226:444
Worms 245:42
Worried Man Blues 24:890, 148:422, *see also:* 147:40
Wou Liang/Hymn to Buddha 89:231
Wounded and sorrowful, far from my home 73:256
Woza/Come 163:68
Woza sithandwa 163:68
The Wraggle-Taggle Gypsies, O! 22:70, 227:12, *see also:* 148:144, 211, 226:311
Wrap Me Up In My Tarpaulin Jacket 226:436
The Wren Song 134:32
The wren, the wren, the king of all birds 134:32
Write a Letter To My Mother 73:242

Wsrod Nocnej Ciszy/In Midnight's Silence 54:218
Wynken, Blynken and Nod 112:68, 245:92

Y

Ya Ghizayyel 169:46, 265:36
Ya ghizayyel ya bulhiba 169:46, 265:36
Ya mama ku theni nomalizoo 163:112
Ya salen las palomitas 169:53, 265:45
Ya se van los pastores a la Extremadura 295:70
Ya Tsa Tsa, Via La La 178:51
Ya viene la burriquita 216:6
Ya Viene La Vieja/Come, My Dear Old Lady 54:254
Yag, yag, yagmur 266:57
Yagmur/Rain 266:57
Yammil Abaya/Lovely Maiden 89:202
Yangsando/Springtime 49:43
Yankee Doodle 17:80, 21:240, 26:14, 46:225, 127:14, 157:21, 160:20, 162:108, 188:22, 197:24, 199, 205:36, 228, 230:71, 240:71, 240:74, 240:76, 273:42, 277:15, 283:40, *see also:* 15, 28:61
The Yankee Doodle Boy 157:212, 197:75, *see also:* 205:301
Yankee Doodle Dandy 205:301, *see also:* 157:212, 197:75
Yankee Doodle Doodle Doo 28:61, *see also:* Yankee Doodle
Yankee Doodle went to town, a riding on a pony 17:80, 162:108, 188:22, 197:24, 228, 230:71, *see also:* Yankee Doodle
Yankee Doodle went to town upon a little pony 21:240, 157:21, 283:40, *see also:* Yankee Doodle
Yankee Doodle's Expedition to Rhode Island 28:114, 240:155
A Yankee Federal Song 240:181
The Yankee Man-of-War 240:130
The Yankee Privateer 28:120
A yankee ship came down the river 232:161, *see also:* 33:42
The Yankee's Return from Camp 240:76, *see also:* Yankee Doodle
Yasashii Okasan/Gentle Mother 286:54
Yawn Song 237:unpaged
Yaya/War Song 89:282
Ye Banks and Braes 21:284, *see also:* 66:124
Ye banks and braes and streams around 66:126
Ye banks and braes o' bonnie Doon 21:284, *see also:* 66:124

Ye banks and braes of Bonny Doon 66:124, see also: 21:284

Ye gentlemen and ladies fair who grace this famous city 157:34, 226:427

Ye Hahmoomee Sit Besahzum/Wedding Song 208:35

Ye Highlands and Ye Lowlands 134:54

Ye Ke, Omo Mi/Hush Now, My Children 208:47, see also: 89:270, 169:50, 267:14

Ye men of earth in God rejoice 21:314

Ye muses mine, with me combine 89:36

Ye nations all, on you I call 140:74, 190:37, 233:38

Ye Parliament of England 21:270, 240:203

Ye Saints who dwell on Europe's shore 277:107

Ye sons of Columbia, who bravely have fought 157:28

Ye sons of Columbia, your attention I do crave 146:127, 159:205

Ye sons of France, awake to glory! 22:223, see also: 64:183

Ye Sons of North Britain 28:91

Ye tars of Columbia, give ear to my story 240:197

Ye Tories all rejoice and sing success to George our gracious king 240:150

Ye wrong heads, ye strong heads, attend to my strains 28:82, 240:165

Ye Yankees who, mole-like, still throw up the earth 28:63, 240:152

Yeab'o, yeab'o! 168:27

Year of Jubilo 73:93

The years creep slowly by, Lorena 73:231

Yehrgeenkun Ahmbel Eh/Gray Clouds Engulf the Sky 73:181

Yeke Omo Mi/Do Not Cry, My Child 89:270, 169:50, 267:14, see also: 208:47

Yellow Fox 261:18

The Yellow-Haired Laddie 182:18

The Yellow Rose of Texas 73:245, 205:392

Yenelal ya sa frini 266:25

Yeo, Heave Ho! 22:134

Yes, I Love You/Yo Te Amo, Idalatro 89:75

Yes! It Is Christmas Eve/Esta sí Que Es Nochebuena 295:78

Yes, muster them out, the valiant band 159:368

Yes, the candidate's a dodger 24:875, see also: 64:150

Yes, we'll rally round the flag, boys 73:36, 157:122, 160:56

Yesterday Morning 114:72

Yesterday my sweater was inside out 91:8

Yi ji ha mo yi jang zwei 49:14

Yin Chuin Wha Ur Kai/Welcome Spring 49:15

Yippee-yay, get along little dogie, get along 61:341

Yismah Moshe b'matnat 77:38

Yo no quiero que me miren 295:26

Yo no tengo dinero 61:230

Yo soy guajira Nacien Melena 89:58

Yo Te Amo, Idalatro/Yes, I Love You 89:75

Yo Tengo un Castillo/I've A Fine Bonny Castle 189:154, see also: 188:54

Yo tengo un castillo, matarile-rile-rile 188:54, 189:154

Yo Tengo una Muñeca/I Have a Little Doll 194:28

Yo tenía diez perritos 295:17

Yodeling Song 25:92

Yoki and the Kaiser 63:72

Yoki and the kaiser, Yoki addy ay 63:72

Yom Kippur Day 77:43

Yon Yonson 63:135

Yonder come Roberta! 226:26, see also: Midnight Special

Yonder comes dat ole Joe Brown 226:48

Yonder Comes My Pretty Little Girl 226:313, see also: 24:889, 226:312

Yonder Comes Sister Mary 233:57

Yonder Comes the High Sheriff 226:213

Yonder Lies the World Before Us 71:16, 72:42

Yonder She Comes 232:50

Yonder she comes and it's howdy howdy do 232:50

Yonder Tree 27:96, see also: Barnyard Song

Yonlyem Jinku 89:236

York 21:314

You Are Arrogant/Uyadela 163:88

You Are Beautiful 218:314

You are coming home, you are coming home 74:54

You Are Dumber Than a Horse 84:50

You are gazing now on old Tom Moore 159:378, see also: 158:180

You Are Going To the Wars, Willie Boy! 73:106

You are my friend, you are special 219:7

You Are Never Away 218:272

You Are Special 219:7

You ask what causes me to weep 66:132

You ask what place I like the best 159:412, 226:278

You Can Dig My Grave 25:96

You can dig my grave with a silver spade 25:96

You Can Fly! You Can Fly! You Can Fly! 275:58, 276:30

You can make believe it happens 219:53

You Can Tell a Scout 25:68

You can tell today that spring is on its way 91:32

You can't expect a cowboy to agitate his shanks 159:250, see also: 61:284

You Cowards/Magwalandini 163:62
You Fight On 226:248
You gentle birds of Erin's Isle who crossed the Atlantic Sea 35:44
You get a hammer an I'll get a nail 130:74
You get a line and I'll get a pole, honey 27:160, 129:30, 148:58, 230:86, 292:182, see also: Crawdad
You go aboard a leaky boat and sail for San Francisco 159:387, see also: 61:36
You go aboard of a leaky boat and sail for San Francisco 61:36, see also: 159:387
You Got To Cross It Foh Yohself 226:486, see also: 86:54, 148:238, 158:352
You got to cross that River Jordan 226:486, see also: 86:54, 148:238, 158:352
You got to jump down, turn around, pick a bale of cotton 21:128, 135:106, 148:302, 158:234, 277:51, see also: Pick a Bale of Cotton
You got to walk that lonesome valley 158:352, see also: 86:54, 148:238, 226:486
You gotta jump down, turn aroun' 130:80, see also: Pick a Bale of Cotton
You Green and Glittering Tree, Good Day/ Du Gronne, Glitrende Tre, God-Dag 54:198
You had a dream, dear 170:99
You have loved lots of girls 21:102
You may call the cowboy horned and think him hard to tame 159:83
You may have seen some wonders 84:39
You may sing about the little old log cabin in the lane 61:72, see also: 61:68, 159:405, 226:89
You may talk about your man of Gideon 158:374, see also: 22:304, 107:28, 148:208, 230:37
You must answer my questions nine 20:66
You must pass this shoe from me to you 55:250, 70:18, see also: 20:90, 83:491, 289:173
You Must Pass This Spoon 83:491, see also: 20:90, 55:250, 70:18, 289:173
You Naughty, Naughty Men 157:180
You Need Not Fear the Horse 74:53
You never told me how you felt then 275:76, 276:72
You ought to see my Cindy 158:94, 176:122, 205:146, 230:61, see also: 24:899
You put your right foot in 148:164, 289:168, see also: 178:34
You put your hand in 178:34, see also: 148:164, 289:168
You ride dat horse, you call him Macaroni 226:469
You Simple Bostonians 28:22, see also: 273:26
You Simple Bostonians, I'd have you beware 28:22, 273:26
You stick out your heart and hand 274:30
You take a little fruitgum wrapper 206:116
You Tell Me Your Dream, I'll Tell You Mine 170:99
You that in merriment delight 36:90
You used to creep and crawl real well 219:21
You walk like nothin' 84:52
You what give to the chicken? 295:15
You who sit in the room 89:283
You work in the factory all of your life 64:143
You, You, You 78:51, see also: 262:26
You'll Never Walk Alone 218:118
You'll Sing a Song And I'll Sing a Song 107:12
Young and old are singing 197:49
Young Charlotte lived on a mountain top 27:244, see also: 24:825, 35:50, 159:231, 226:58
Young Charlottie 24:825, 159:231, see also: 27:244, 35:50, 226:58
Young Charlottie lived by a mountain side in a wild and lonely spot 24:825, 27:244, 159:231, see also: 35:50, 226:58
Young Companions 146:109, 159:212
Young Folks, Old Folks 178:70, see also: 36:109, 290:156
Young folks, old folks, ev'rybody come 36:109, 178:70, 290:156
Young girls they dance and they flirt 289:32
Young Johnnie Steele has an Oldsmobile 157:203, 205:317
Young ladies in town, and those that live round 240:38
Young Lambs To Sell 135:48
Young maid, young maid, young maid, young maid dear 70:22
Young man in a carriage driving like he's mad 35:60, 230:68, see also: 148:306
The Young Man Who Wouldn't Hoe Corn 24:874, 158:230, 230:42
Young Roger was a butcher 62:136
The Young Volunteer 73:109
The Young Voyageur 22:36
Young women they run like hares on the mountain 292:92
Younger Than Springtime 218:159
Your Brownie hand in my Brownie hand 68:32
Your gift, your gift, your gift 89:295
Your lips tell me no! no! 170:67
Your Mother and Mine 276:31
You're a Grand Old Flag 72:28, 197:66, 205:331
You're Growing 219:21

You're in the Army Now   197:104
You've changed, bub, you've changed a lot
   218:282
You've got to be taught to hate and fear
   218:169
You've Got To Do It   219:53
You've Got To Go Down   64:25
You've got to go down and join the union
   64:25
You've heard of heroes brave in all their
   glory   61:260, *see also:* Jesse James
Yu-Yake Koyake/Evening Glow   286:64
Yuko ka   89:236
Yuletide Is Here Again   54:193, 279:112, *see*
   also: 89:170, 241:168, 262:42
Ywe ur le shi shia sze shung shao yuen ja
   49:12

Z

Ze hahm hahrah mahstah Lailaw yum
   208:1
The Zebra Dun   60:30, 61:194, 146:50,
   159:78, 159:81, 225:38
Zeg, kwezelken, wilde gy dansen?   21:320
Zek'l Weep   226:449
Zenizenabo/Bring Them With You   163:31
Zezulka Z Lesa Vylítla/From Out the For-
   est a Cuckoo Flew   54:230
Zip-a-Dee Doo-Dah   275:33
Zither and I   262:145
Zizzy, Ze Zum, Zum!   84:42
Zo bbu ddao de tien pien yo   49:13
Zolst azoy lebn un zayn gezint   289:32
Zu Bethlehem Geboren/In Bethlehem So
   Lowly   54:144
Zu Weihnachten/Christmas Song   279:66
Zudie-O   109:139
Zui, Zui, Zukorobashi/Rat in the Rice Sack
   16:51, 286:42
Zulu Warrior   72:146
Zum Gali Gali   25:90, 64:106, 69:49,
   148:424, 290:196

Broad Topic Guide To Subject Index

The Subject Index, which begins on page 169, organizes all the song titles found in Part I under more than 1,000 subject headings, most of them very specific—ANIMAL SOUNDS, COWBOYS, STREET CRIES, TELLING TIME, and YUCATAN, for instance. Many users will have broader, less specific subjects in mind as they begin a search for songs. For them, this Broad Topic Guide contains forty-five more general categories—such as *Animals, Occupations, Music, North America,* and *Time.* Under each broad topic are listed the headings in the Subject Index to which a user can turn to locate song titles.

Africa
ALGERIA
ANGOLA
BOTSWANA
BULULAND
CHAD
CONGO
EGYPT
ETHIOPIA
GABON
GHANA
KENYA
LESOTHO
LIBERIA
LIBYA
MADAGASCAR
MARRAKESH
MOZAMBIQUE
NIGERIA
NYASALAND
RHODESIA
RWANDA
SIERRA LEONE
SOMALIA
SOUTH AFRICA,
  REPUBLIC OF
SUDAN
TANZANIA
TUNISIA
UGANDA
ZAMBIA

Asia
AFGHANISTAN
BURMA
CAMBODIA

CEYLON
CHINA
INDIA
INDONESIA
IRAN
IRAQ
ISRAEL
JAPAN
KOREA
LAOS
LEBANON
MALAYSIA
MONGOLIA
NEPAL
PAKISTAN
PALESTINE
SAUDI ARABIA
SINGAPORE
SYRIA
THAILAND
TIBET
VIET NAM

Astronomy
ASTRONAUTS
MOON
SPACE (OUTER)
STARS
SUN

Birds
ANIMAL SOUNDS
BLACKBIRDS
BLUEBIRDS
BUZZARDS
CANARIES

CHICKENS
CRANES
CROWS
CUCKOOS
DOVES
DUCKS
EAGLES
GEESE
HAWKS
HUMMING BIRDS
KOOKABURRA
LARKS
LOONS
MOCKINGBIRDS
NIGHTINGALES
OWLS
PARAKEETS
PARTRIDGES
PETS
PIGEONS
QUAIL
RAVENS
ROBINS
SANDPIPERS
SPARROWS
STORKS
SWANS
TURKEYS
WHIP-POOR-WILLS
WOODPECKERS
WRENS
ZOOS

Body, Human
EARS
FACES

163

Body, Human—Cont.
HAIR
HANDS
LEGS
NOSES
SELF-CONCEPT
SKIN
SNEEZING
TEETH

Clothing and Dress
COTTON
HATS
MOCCASINS
SHOES
WOOL

Communications
MOVING PICTURES
TELEPHONES
TELEVISION SHOWS

Concepts
ALPHABETS
COLOR
COUNTING
NUMBERS
SIZE AND SHAPE

Countries
(See Subject headings for names of countries, continents and **Islands**)

Ecology
EARTH DAY
LITTER AND LITTERING
POLLUTION

Emotions
CRYING
FEAR
FRIENDSHIP
JOY
KINDNESS
SELF-CONCEPT
SHARING
SMILES

Europe
ALBANIA
ARMENIA
AUSTRIA
BELGIUM
BOHEMIA
BULGARIA
CYPRUS
CZECHOSLOVAKIA
DENMARK
ENGLAND

FINLAND
FLANDERS
FRANCE
GERMANY
GREECE
HUNGARY
ICELAND
IRELAND
ITALY
LUXEMBOURG
NETHERLANDS
NORWAY
POLAND
PORTUGAL
RUMANIA
RUSSIA
SCOTLAND
SICILY
SPAIN
SWEDEN
SWITZERLAND
TURKEY
WALES
YUGOSLAVIA

Farms
ANIMAL SOUNDS
CHICKENS
COWS
DONKEYS
DUCKS
FARM LIFE
FARMERS
4-H CLUBS
GEESE
GOATS
HARVEST
HERDING
HORSES
MULES
PIGS
RANCH LIFE
SCARECROWS
SHEEP
SHEPHERDS AND SHEPHERD LIFE
TURKEYS

Fish and Sea Life
CLAMS
COCKLES
CRABS
FISH
HERRING
MUSSELS
SEASHORE
SHARKS
SHELLS (MOLLUSKS)
WHALES AND WHALING

Flowers
BLUEBELLS
BUTTERCUPS
DAISIES
DANDELIONS
HOLLYHOCKS
LILACS
POPPIES
ROSES
TULIPS
VIOLETS

Folklore
ALLAN-A-DALE
ARTHUR, KING
CASEY JONES
FABLES
JOHN HENRY
LITTLE JOHN
ROBIN HOOD
STORIES
STORMALONG
TALL TALES

Food and Eating
BAKERS AND BAKING
BARLEY
BREAD
BREAKFAST
BUTTER
CAKES AND COOKIES
CANDY
CLAMS
COOKS AND COOKERY
DOUGHNUTS
FRUIT
HARVEST
LEMONADE
PICNICS
PIES
RAVIOLI
RICE
SOUP
SPAGHETTI
SUPPER
TEA
VEGETABLES

Fruit
APPLES
CHERRIES
GRAPES
WATERMELONS

Games
ACTION SONGS
BALL BOUNCING
BALL ROLLING
BASEBALL
CIRCLE GAMES

Games—Cont.
CLAPPING GAMES
EXERCISE GAMES
FINGER AND HAND
   PLAY
GUESSING GAMES
RHYTHMS
RIDDLES
SINGING GAMES
SKIPPING ROPE
TONGUE TWISTERS
TOYS

Government
CIVIL RIGHTS
DEMOCRACY
ELECTIONS
FREEDOM
POLITICAL SONGS
WOMEN—EQUAL
   RIGHTS

Health
BEDTIME
CLEANLINESS
GROOMING,
   PERSONAL
SAFETY
SLEEP

Holidays
ALL SOUL'S DAY
ARBOR DAY
BIRTHDAYS
CHILDREN'S DAY
CHRISTMAS CAROLS
CHRISTMAS SONGS
EARTH DAY
EASTER
FOURTH OF JULY
HALLOWEEN
HANUKKAH (FEAST OF
   LIGHTS)
MAY DAY
MEMORIAL DAY
MOTHER'S DAY
NEW YEAR
PINATAS
ST. PATRICK'S DAY
ST. STEPHEN'S DAY
THANKSGIVING DAY
VALENTINE'S DAY

Indians of North America
CHEROKEE
ESKIMOS
HOPI
HURON
KWAKIUTL
MANDAN

NAVAJO
OJIBWAY
PAIUTE
PAPAGO
PAWNEE
PENOBSCOT
SIOUAN
WINNEBAGO
YUMA
ZUNI

Insects
ANTS
BEES
BEETLES
BOLL WEEVILS
BUTTERFLIES
CATERPILLARS
COCKROACHES
CRICKETS
FIREFLIES
FLEAS
FLIES
GRASSHOPPERS
LADYBUGS
LICE
LOCUSTS
MOSQUITOES
SPIDERS
TICKS

Islands
CAROLINE ISLANDS
CUBA
DOMINICAN REPUBLIC
GREENLAND
HAITI
ISLANDS OF THE
   PACIFIC
JAMAICA
NEW GUINEA
NEW ZEALAND
PHILIPPINES
PUERTO RICO
SOLOMON ISLANDS
TRINIDAD
TROBRIAND SUNSET
   ISLES
VIRGIN ISLANDS

Landforms
DESERTS
GLACIERS
MOUNTAINS

Mammals
ANIMAL SOUNDS
ANTELOPES
BABOONS
BATS

BEARS
BISON
CATS
CHIPMUNKS
COWS
DEER
DOGS
DONKEYS
ELEPHANTS
FOXES
GOATS
GOPHERS
HORSES
KANGAROOS
LIONS
MICE
MOLES
MONKEYS
MULES
MUSKRATS
OPOSSUMS
OXEN
PANTHERS
PETS
PIGS
PRAIRIE DOGS
RABBITS
RACCOONS
RATS
SEALS
SHEEP
SKUNKS
SQUIRRELS
TIGERS
WEASELS
WHALES AND
   WHALING
WOODCHUCKS
ZOOS

Months
APRIL
FEBRUARY
JANUARY
JUNE
MAY
SEPTEMBER

Music
BELLS
BLUES (MUSIC)
CANONS
CHRISTMAS CAROLS
CHRISTMAS SONGS
CONTEMPORARY
   FOLK SONGS
DANCES
DRUMS
FLUTES
GUITARS

Music—Cont.
HULA
MARCHING
MUSIC AND
MUSICIANS
MUSICAL
INSTRUMENTS
OPERAS AND
OPERETTAS
RAGTIME
RHYTHMS
ROUNDS
SINGING
SINGING GAMES
SKIPPING MUSIC
SPIRITUALS
SQUARE DANCING
TAMBOURINES
VIOLINS
WHISTLES AND
WHISTLING
YODELS
ZITHER

North America
CANADA
COSTA RICA
EL SALVADOR
GUATEMALA
HONDURAS
LATIN AMERICA
MEXICO
NICARAGUA
PANAMA
UNITED STATES
YUCATAN

Occupations
ART AND ARTISTS
ASTRONAUTS
BABY SITTERS
BAKERS AND
BAKERIES
BLACKSMITHING
BUILDERS AND
BUILDING
BUYING AND SELLING
CARPENTERS AND
CARPENTRY
CHIMNEY SWEEPS
COMMUNITY HELPERS
COOKS AND COOKERY
COWBOYS
DANCERS AND
DANCING
DRILLING
ENGINEERS
FARMERS
FIREFIGHTERS

FISHERMEN AND
FISHING
GARDENS AND
GARDENERS
LABOR AND
LABORERS
LAWYERS
LUMBERING AND
LUMBERJACKS
MILKMEN
MILLERS
MINERS AND MINING
MUSIC AND
MUSICIANS
PLUMBERS AND
PLUMBING
POLICE
POSTAL SERVICE
SEAMEN
SERVICE STATIONS
SHEPHERDS AND
SHEPHERD LIFE
SHOEMAKERS
SOLDIERS
STREET CRIES
TAILORS
TEACHERS AND
TEACHING
TINKERS
WHALES AND
WHALING
WORK
WORK SONGS

People
(see Subject Index under
names of specific
persons and the
heading BIOGRAPHY)

Pioneers and Pioneer Life
CHAPMAN, JOHN
(JOHNNY
APPLESEED)
COWBOYS
HERDING
RANCH LIFE

Plants
APPLE TREES
ARBOR DAY
COTTON
FLOWERS
FORESTS AND WOODS
FRUIT
GARDENS AND
GARDENERS
GRASS
HARVEST
LEAVES

TREES
VEGETABLES

Religion
ABRAHAM
ALL SOUL'S DAY
ANGELS
APOSTLES
BUDDHISM
CANONS
CHRISTMAS CAROLS
DANIEL
EASTER
EZEKIEL
HANUKKAH (FEAST OF
LIGHTS)
HYMNS
JONAH
JOSHUA
JUDAISM
MORMONS AND
MORMONISM
MOSES
NOAH
PRAYER
ST. PATRICK'S DAY
ST. STEPHEN'S DAY
SAINTS
SAMSON
SPIRITUALS

Reptiles (and Amphibians)
ALLIGATORS
CROCODILES
FROGS
LIZARDS
PETS
SNAKES
SNAILS
TOADS
TURTLES
WORMS

Seasons
AUTUMN
MONTHS
SPRING
SUMMER
WEATHER
WINTER

South America
ARGENTINA
BOLIVIA
BRAZIL
CHILE
COLOMBIA
ECUADOR
PARAGUAY
PERU

SUBJECT GUIDE

So. America—Cont.
SURINAM
URUGUAY
VENEZUELA

Sports
BASEBALL
BICYCLES AND
  BICYCLING
BOATS AND BOATING
BOWS AND ARROWS
CAMPING
CANOES AND
  CANOEING
CHEERS AND
  CHEERLEADING
GAMES
HORSE RACING
HUNTING
SAILING
SKATING
SKIING
SKIN DIVING AND
  SCUBA DIVING
SURFING
SWIMMING AND
  DIVING
WALKING

Supernatural
BROWNIES
DEVILS
DRAGONS
DWARFS
ELVES
FAIRIES
GHOSTS
LEPRECHAUNS
MERMAIDS AND
  MERMEN
SANDMAN
WITCHES AND
  WITCHCRAFT

Time
AUTUMN
CALENDARS
CLOCKS AND
  WATCHES
DAWN
DAY
DAYS
EVENING
MORNING
NIGHT
SPRING
SUMMER
TELLING TIME
TIME
WINTER

Toys
BALLOONS
BALLS
BICYCLES AND
  BICYCLING
DOLLS
HOBBY HORSES
KITES
MERRY-GO-ROUNDS
PINATAS
PUPPETS
SEESAWS
SKIPPING ROPE
SLED AND SLEIGHS
SWINGS AND
  SWINGING
TOPS

Transportation
AIRPLANES
AUTOMOBILES
BALLOONS (AIRSHIPS)
BICYCLES AND
  BICYCLING
BOATS AND BOATING
BUSES
CANOES AND
  CANOEING
DOG SLEDS
ERIE CANAL
FERRIES
FLIGHT
RAILROADS
SAILING
SHIPS
STAGECOACHES

Trees
APPLE TREES
ARBOR DAY
CHAPMAN, JOHN
  (JOHNNY
  APPLESEED)
FORESTS AND WOODS

United States
ALABAMA
ALASKA
ARIZONA
ARKANSAS
CALIFORNIA
HAWAII
IDAHO
ILLINOIS
INDIANA
KANSAS
KENTUCKY
MARYLAND
MISSISSIPPI
MISSOURI

NEBRASKA
NEW YORK
OKLAHOMA
TEXAS
VIRGINIA

United States History
ALLEN, ETHAN
ARNOLD, BENEDICT
BEAUREGARD, GEN.
  PIERRE
BONNEY, WILLIAM
  (BILLY THE KID)
BOONE, DANIEL
BROWN, JOHN
CIVIL RIGHTS
CIVIL WAR—U.S.
  (1861-1865)
COLONIAL PERIOD IN
  AMERICA
COLUMBUS,
  CHRISTOPHER
CROCKETT, DAVID
  (DAVY)
CUSTER, GEORGE
  ARMSTRONG
DAVIS, JEFFERSON
DEPRESSION YEARS
EMANCIPATION
  PROCLAMATION
FRENCH AND INDIAN
  WAR (1754-1763)
HALE, NATHAN
JACKSON, ANDREW
JACKSON, THOMAS J.
  "STONEWALL"
JAMES, JESSE
  WOODSON
JEFFERSON, THOMAS
JONES, JOHN PAUL
LEE, ROBERT
  EDWARD
LINCOLN, ABRAHAM
MADISON, DOLLEY
MARION, FRANCIS
  (SWAMP FOX)
MEXICAN WAR
  (1846-1848)
MONTGOMERY,
  RICHARD
NAVAL BATTLES
PILGRIMS
PIONEERS AND
  PIONEER LIFE
PRESIDENTS—UNITED
  STATES
REVOLUTIONARY WAR
  IN AMERICA
  (1776-1781)
SHERMAN, WILLIAM T.

167

Subject Index

ABRAHAM
  Abraham the Faithful   123:51
ACTION SONGS: *see also* BALL BOUNCING;
  BALL ROLLING; CIRCLE GAMES; CLAP-
  PING GAMES; FINGER AND HAND PLAY;
  RHYTHMS; SINGING GAMES; SKIPPING
  MUSIC; SKIPPING ROPE
  At Halloween   207:24
  Bedtime Stories   207:21
  The Big Procession   135:103
  The Birthday Cake   207:10
  The Bus Song   75:16, *see also:* 147:6,
    165:73, 291:46
  Clapping Game   68:9
  Creep, Mouse, Creep   135:111
  A Day to Ski   207:73
  El Juego del Pañuelo/The Handkerchief
    Game   194:18
  The Farm Windmill   207:104
  Girls Clap, Boys Clap   204:11
  Grandpa and I   207:17
  Grasshopper   177:84
  Hand Shadow Song   114:16
  The Handkerchief Game/El Juego del
    Pañuelo   194:18
  Head and Shoulders   26:35, 63:46, *see
    also:* 55:266, 165:125
  Head, Shoulders   55:266, *see also:* 26:35,
    63:46, 165:125
  Heads and Shoulders, Knees and Toes
    165:125, *see also:* 26:35 55:266, 63:46
  Here We Come on Our Ponies   135:102
  Hey Dee Roon   72:105, *see also:* 291:8
  Hi-Dee-Roon   291:8, *see also:* 72:105
  Hot Cross Buns   17:122, 135:105, 175:64,
    188:100, 296:54
  Hush-a-bye, Baby   175:85, 188:88
  I Have a Little Doll/Yo Tengo una Muñe-
    ca   194:28
  I Points to Mineself   25:12
  If You're Happy and You Know It   25:16,
    26:39, 63:44, 147:20, 253:91
  I'm a Person   204:9
  In Father's Car   207:16
  John Brown Had a Little Indian   135:112,
    165:135, *see also:* 107:24
  John Brown Knew a Little Indian
    107:24, *see also:* 135:112, 165:135
  Knick Knack   20:44, *see also:* This Old
    Man

Mammy Don't 'Low   290:62, *see also:*
    197:58
  Mary Ann McCarthy   290:58
  Mother's Washing   165:34
  My Pigeon House I Open Wide   165:157
  O Chester   25:25, 26:35
  Oh, We Can Play on the Big Bass Drum
    165:184
  Once an Austrian Went Yodeling   290:22
  One Finger Keep Moving   253:104, *see
    also:* 14:352, 26:37
  One Finger, One Thumb   26:37, *see also:*
    14:352, 253:104
  One, Two, Three, and Around We Go!
    204:27
  Our Legs   204:23
  The Pony   177:83
  Ponycart Driver/Song of the Delhi Ton-
    gawallah   262:150
  Pray Open Your Umbrella   165:62
  Pretty Little Pussy Cat   165:158
  Puffer Train, Puffer Train   165:109
  Raise Your Hands Above Your Head
    165:124
  Ravioli   26:25
  The School Band   177:79
  See the Little Bunny Sleeping   165:154
  She'll Be Comin' 'Round the Mountain
    20:36, 25:14, 148:324, 165:197, 290:24
  Slip One and Two   165:183
  Slowly, Slowly Walks My Granddad
    165:172
  Song of the Delhi Tongawallah/Ponycart
    Driver   262:150
  Swim, Little Fish, in Water Clear
    165:112
  Tall Shop in the Town   165:66
  A Tall Thin Man Walking Along Walking
    Along   165:168
  Three Jelly Fish, Three Jelly Fish
    165:110
  Three Wood Pigeons   25:9
  To and Fro, To and Fro   165:42
  Tra, La, La   25:15
  The Train Is Carrying Coal   165:69
  Trot, Trot, Trot, Go and Never Stop
    165:17
  The Turtle   177:85
  Two Little Boats Are on the Sea   165:115
  Under the Chestnut Tree   26:31, 254:122
  Walrus Hunt Song   26:33

ACTION SONGS—*Continued*

We All Clap Hands Together 165:181

We Are Soldiers Marching Along 165:140

We Are Woodmen Sawing Trees 165:92

What Did I See? 68:20

The Wheels on the Bus Go Round and Round 147:6, 165:73, 291:46, *see also:* 75:16

When All the Cows Are Sleeping 165:86

Wiggle the Wool 290:12

Willum He Had Seven Sons 165:167

Wind the Bobbin Up 165:122

Yo Tengo una Muñeca/I Have a Little Doll 194:28

Zulu Warrior 72:146

AFGHANISTAN

Lailaw/Lament for an Absent Lover 208:1

Lament for an Absent Lover/Lailaw 208:1

*Vaj, Gulum Gitti?/Where Is My Red Rose? 89:213

*Where Is My Red Rose?/Vaj, Gulum Gitti? 89:213

AFRICA: *see also* names of countries, e.g., EGYPT

*Amampondo/Pondo Man 163:65

*Ar Go Eat You Wan 215:50

As the Sun Goes Down 72:144

Aunt Hessie's White Horse/Tant Hessie Se Witperd 189:140

*Bajabula Bonke/I Became Ill 163:95

*Bird Song/Ntyilo 163:36

*Bring Them With You or Be Victorious/ Zenizenabo 163:31

*Cameroon 163:83

*The Click Song/Qongqothwane 163:28

*The Cock/Qhude 163:76

*Come/Woza 163:68

*Davi Ayele No Bu Lo 215:44

*Dubula/Shoot 163:54

*A Girl's Name/Nomthini 163:56

*Go Round to the Rocks/Jikele' Maweni 163:45

*I Became Ill/Bajabula Bonke 163:95

*Ibo of Nigeria 215:17

*Into Yam/My Man 163:50

*Jikele' Maweni/Go Round to the Rocks 163:45

*Kattan, Kattan/Run, Run 89:257

'Keenene 236:3

*Khuluma/Speak 163:115

*A Lament/Ngoma Kurila 163:42

*Langa More/More Sun 163:108

*Lullaby/Olilili 163:100

*Lullaby (Zulu) 262:127

*Maduna/Maduna Clan (Xhosa) 163:72

*Maduna Clan/Maduna (Xhosa) 163:72

*Magwalandini/You Cowards 163:62

*Mayibuye/Restore Africa to Its Owner (Xhosa) 163:91

*More Sun/Langa More 163:108

*My Man/Into Yam (Xhosa) 163:50

*Ngoma Kurila/A Lament 163:42

*No, Child/Thanayi (Xhosa) 163:112

*Nomeva/The Wasp (Xhosa) 163:104

*Nomthini/A Girl's Name 163:56

*Ntyilo-Ntyilo/Bird Song 163:36

*Odala Me So Nda 215:24

*Olilili/Lullaby 163:100

*Pondo Man/Amampondo 163:65

*Qhude/The Cock 163:76

*Qongqothwane/The Click Song 163:28

*Restore Africa to Its Owners/Mayibuye (Xhosa) 163:91

*Run, Run/Kattan, Kattan 89:257

Rwiyo Rwedande 278:40

*Sen Chain, Sen Chain, Sen Chain 215:8

*Shoot/Dubula 163:54 (Xhosa)

*Song of Praise/Um Home (Xhosa) 163:39

*Speak/Khuluma 163:115

*A String of Beads/Umqokozo (Xhosa) 163:78

Ta Avo Na Legba 278:43

*Tangishaka (Burundi) 89:258

Tant Hessie Se Witperd/Aunt Hessie's White Horse 189:140

*Thanayi/No, Child (Xhosa) 163:112

*Um Home/Song of Praise (Xhosa) 163:39

*Umqokozo/A String of Beads (Xhosa) 163:78

*Uyadela/You Are Arrogant (Zulu) 163:88

*The Wasp/Nomeva (Xhosa) 163:104

*Woza/Come (Zulu) 163:68

*You Are Arrogant/Uyadela (Zulu) 163:88

*You Cowards/Magwalandini 163:62

*Zenizenabo/Bring Them With You or Be Victorious (Xhosa) 163:31

*Zulu Warrior 72:146

AFRO-AMERICAN

Ain't It Hard to Be a Farmer 109:212

All Hid 109:185

Bob-a-Needle 109:164

Brother Rabbit and Mister Railroad's Taters 109:207

Coonshine 109:132

Daniel 109:146

Draw a Bucket of Water 14:345, 39:24, 109:80, 135:78

East Coast Line 109:97

Elephant Fair 109:62

Go to Sleepy, Little Baby 109:8

Green, Green, the Crab Apple Tree 109:70

Green Sally Up 109:26

Hambone 109:36, 274:36

Have Courage to Say No 109:204

Head and Shoulder, Baby 109:33

Horse and the Buggy 109:175

I Had an Old Rooster 109:193

I'm Going Away to See Aunt Dinah 109:142

Johnny Cuckoo 109:73

Josephine 109:60

Jump That Jody 109:10

Knock Jim Crow 109:57

Little Johnny Brown 109:94

Little Sally Walker 109:109, 109:110, 109:111, 291:68, see also: Little Sally Water

Miss Lucy 109:173

Nana, Thread Needle 109:83

Oh Green Fields, Roxie 109:75

Old Bill the Rolling Pin 109:209

One Saw, Two Saw 109:30

One-ry, Two-ry 109:28

Peep Squirrel 109:216, 234:18

Pizza, Pizza, Mighty Moe 109:64

Possum-la 109:128

Pretty Pear Tree 109:197, see also: Green Grass Grows All Around

Rabbit and the Possum 109:212

Ranky Tank 109:130

Sandy Ree 109:136

Settin' on a Rail 78:91

Shock Along, John 24:906

Shoo, Turkey 109:54

Sir Mister Brown 109:99

Skip to the Barbershop 109:50

Soup, Soup 109:103

Steal Up, Young Lady 109:119

Uncle Jessie 109:114

Way Down on the Bingo Farm 109:202

Way Down Yonder in the Brickyard 109:116

Way Down Yonder, Sometimes 109:101

Way Go, Lily 109:118

Whose Bag Is My Gold Ring? 109:165

Won't You Let the Birdie Out? 109:177

Zudie-O 109:139

AGRICULTURE: see FARM LIFE; FARMERS; HARVEST; PLANTS; PLANTING

AIRPLANES

Airplane, Airplane 154:28

Airplanes, Airplanes All in a Row 165:72

Bird With Silver Wings 154:26

In My Plane 162:100

ALABAMA

Alabama Bound 230:44

THE ALAMO: see MEXICAN WAR (1846-1848)

ALASKA

Alaska, or Hell of the Yukon 61:83

ALBANIA

*The Apple Tree/Pliot Mola Lule 89:193

Luli, Deck the Crib 125:126

My Son 125:124

*Pliot Mola Lule/The Apple Tree 89:193

Rock-A-Bye, Boy 125:123

ALGERIA

*Rana Djinak/We Have Come Here 89:243

*We Have Come Here/Rana Djinak 89:243

ALL SOULS' DAY

Soul Cakes 293:72, see also: 134:26, 210:26

The Souling Song 134:26, 210:26, see also: 293:72

ALLAN-A-DALE

Robin Hood and Allen-A-Dale 164:42

ALLEN, ETHAN

The Green Mountaineer 28:40

ALLIGATORS

Alligators All Around 235:39

Go On, Old 'Gator 234:74

Joseph Henry Alligator 166:70

ALPHABETS

AB-C-DEF-GHI 206:10

Alligators All Around 235:39

Alphabet in the Air 112:35

Alphabet Song 17:41

J Jump 187:20

The Revolutionary Alphabet 28:36

The Woodmen's Alphabet 35:12

AMERICAN INDIANS: see INDIANS OF NORTH AMERICA

AMERICAN REVOLUTION: see REVOLUTIONARY WAR IN AMERICA (1776-1781)

ANATOMY: see BODY, HUMAN

ANGELS: see also CHRISTMAS CAROLS; SPIRITUALS

The Angel Band 233:74

Go Away, Little Fairies 125:74

Heaven's Gate Has Opened 244:187, 245:116

Three Little Angels All Dressed in White 141:94

ANGOLA

*Chinene Nye?/What is Big? 168:18

*What Is Big?/Chinene Nye? 168:18

ANIMAL SOUNDS

And I Ran Away/Et Moi de M'Encourir 217:61

The Animals Wake Up 41:15

Bow Wow, Says the Dog 18:24, 112:2

The Children's Zoo 162:19

Come to the Farm 162:15

ANIMAL SOUNDS—*Continued*
Et Moi de M'Encourir/And I Ran Away 217:38
Old MacDonald Had a Farm   4, 17:148, 26:20, 55:262, 75:56, 81, 199, 283:12, 291:30
Wild Animals   112:20
ANIMALS: *see also* ANIMAL SOUNDS; names of animals, e.g., DOGS
The Animal Fair   25:38, 26:17, 62:33, 226:348, 289:152, 292:188, *see also:* 254:121
The Animal Song   234:80, 289:41
The Animals Wake Up   41:15
Bahyahn Mongol/Rich Mongolia   208:45
The Barnyard Song   68:27, 75:10, 128:34, 129:76, *see also:* 27:96, 37:171, 55:265, 109:193, 118:unpaged, 232:104, 254:108, 289:47, 292:13, 292:18
Biddy Biddy Burkey/Widewideween   188:126
Bossy Cow   112:30
Bought Me a Cat   232:104, *see also:* Barnyard Song
Bumblebees Are Humming   245:37
Doña María   295:55
El Lobo/The Wolf   70:27
Farmer's Boy   212:48
Fiddle-I-Fee   37:171, 292:18, *see also:* The Barnyard Song
God Made the Sky, the Wild Ones   245:34
Had a Little Rooster   128:34, *see also:* Barnyard Song
Hand Shadow Song   114:16
Have a Little Dog   232:114
Here Sits a Monkey   232:175
How Creatures Move   18:8
How Does a Caterpillar Go   165:44
I Bought Me a Rooster   289:47, *see also:* Barnyard Song
I Had a Little Cat   132:unpaged, *see also:* Barnyard Song
I Had a Little Rooster   292:13, *see also:* Barnyard Song
I Had an Old Rooster   109:193, *see also:* Barnyard Song
I Know an Old Lady Who Swallowed a Fly   23, 75:34, 289:116, 292:216, *see also:* 5, 120, 148:378
I Sing for the Animals   74:40
I Went to Visit a Farm One Day   165:77
I'd Rather Be a Panther   234:75
If I Were a Little Bird   165:153
In the Fashion   172:120, 173:6
Kids   206:25
Let's Go to the Zoo   128:42
Little Boy Blue   17:10, 175:56, 188:32, 283:23, 285:38

Little White Duck   75:46, 289:56
Over in the Meadow   17:21, 116, 139, 178:32, 289:70, *see also:* 129:14
Rich Mongolia/Bahyahn Mongol   208:45
"Sing," Said the Mother   129:14, *see also:* 17:21, 116, 139, 178:32, 289:70
Somebody Stole   110:34
Song of the Young Wolves   74:43
What Use Are You   41:34, 291:35
When Ducks Get Up in the Morning   291:26
Who's Afraid of the Big Bad Wolf?   275:28, 276:20
Who's In   44:68
Widewideween/Biddy Biddy Burkey   188:126
Willie (Walrus)   91:37
The Wolf/El Lobo   70:27
Wolves A-Howling   234:79
The Woodchuck   144:9
Yonder Tree   27:96, *see also:* Barnyard Song
ANNIVERSARIES: *see* HOLIDAYS
ANTELOPES
The Gazelle/Gbodi   89:281
Gbodi/The Gazelle   89:281
ANTS
The Ant and the Grasshopper/La Fourmi et la Sauterelle   243:34, *see also:* 79:65
The Ants Came Marching   63:82, 118:24, *see also:* 147:10
The Ants Go Marching   147:10, *see also:* 63:82, 118:24
The Counting Lesson   191:56, *see also:* 162:23
The Fly and the Ant/La Mouche et la Fourmi   243:10
The Grasshopper and the Ant/La Cigale et la Fourmi   79:65, *see also:* 243:34
Honey-Ant Song of Ljabe/Makerenben   89:309
La Cigale et la Fourmi/The Grasshopper and the Ant   79:65, *see also:* 243:34
La Fourmi et la Sauterelle   243:34, *see also:* 79:65
La Mouche et la Fourmi/The Fly and the Ant   79:65, *see also:* 243:34
Makerenben/Honey-Ant Song of Ljaba   89:309
APOSTLES
Green Grow the Rushes Ho!   22:116, 25:100, 27:76, 71:50, 72:112, 148:134, 190:64, *see also:* 129:63, 176:146, 233:66
The Song of Twelve   129:63, *see also:* Green Grow the Rushes Ho!
The Twelve Apostles   176:146, 233:66, *see also:* Green Grow the Rushes Ho!

APPLE TREES
 Apple Tree 41:17
 The Apple Tree/Pliot Mola Lule 89:193
 Derrière de Chez Mon Père/My Father's
  Apple Tree 188:110
 In the Orchard 41:43
 My Father's Apple Tree/Derrière de
  Chez Mon Père 188:110
 Pliot Mola Lule/The Apple Tree 89:193
APPLES
 Apple Dumplings 166:22
 Apple Tree 41:17
 The Apples 227:10
 Baking Apples 41:9
 Derrière de Chez Mon Père/My Father's
  Apple Tree 188:110
 In the Orchard 41:43
 My Father's Apple Tree/Derrière de
  Chez Mon Père 188:110
 Tommy and the Apples 62:89
APPLESEED, JOHNNY: see CHAPMAN,
 JOHN (JOHNNY APPLESEED)
APRIL
 Little April Shower 276:26
AQUARIUMS
 In Our Aquarium 162:85
ARBOR DAY
 Arbor Day Song 197:49
ARCHERY: see BOWS AND ARROWS
ARGENTINA
 *Ahora Voy a Cantarles/Now I'm Going
  to Sing 216:8
 *Arroz Con Leche 168:136, see also:
  216:10, 295:28
 *Bailando el Gato/Dancing the Gato
  89:88
 Dancing the Gato/Bailando el Gato
  89:88
 El Cuando/O When, O When? 22:122
 *La Chacarera/The Little Farm Girl
  70:17, 197:37
 The Little Farm Girl/La Chacarera
  70:17, 197:37
 *Mi Chacra/My Farm 262:19
 My Farm/Mi Chacra 262:19
 Now I'm Going to Sing/Ahora Voy a Can-
  tarles 216:43
 O When, O When?/El Cuando 22:122
 Rice Pudding/Arroz Con Leche
  168:136, see also: 216:43, 295:28
 Rice With Milk/Arroz Con Leche
  216:43, see also: 168:136, 295:28
ARITHMETIC: see COUNTING; MATH-
 EMATICS; NUMBERS
ARIZONA
 Someone's Opinion of Arizona 61:82
ARK: see NOAH

ARKANSAS
 The State of Arkansas 158:240, 159:283
ARMENIA
 Armenian Lullaby 125:130
 The Quail 262:54
ARMY LIFE: see SOLDIERS
ARNOLD, BENEDICT
 Arnold Is as Brave a Man 28:55
ART AND ARTISTS
 Imag-inat-ion 261:12
ARTISTS: see ART AND ARTISTS
ARTHUR, KING
 Fairest Isle 85:41, 189:102
 Good King Arthur 18:28, 112:7, 188:142,
  see also: 17:100
 King Arthur 17:100, see also: 18:28,
  112:7
ASSES: see DONKEYS; MULES
ASTRONAUTS
 Jackson Scott, the Astronaut 112:56
ASTRONOMY: see MOON; SPACE (OUTER);
 STARS; SUN
AUSTRALIA
 Australia 71:34
 Botany Bay 21:247, 176:88
 *Honey-Ant Song of Ljaba/Makerenben
  89:309
 Kookaburra 128:108, 148:218, 176:23,
  178:55, 189:136, 262:148, 289:188,
  293:86
 *Makerenben/Honey-Ant Song of Ljaba
  89:309
 The Overlander 89:310
 The Shearer's Dream 176:84
 The Street of Forbes 176:80
 Waltzing Matilda 22:216, 25:86, 72:154,
  186
AUSTRIA
 *Above, on the Mountain/Da Droben
  Vom Berge 54:174
 *As Lately We Watched/Die Hirten auf
  dem Felde 54:170
 *The Binschgauer Pilgrimage/Die
  Binschgauer Wallfahrt 89:149
 *Blue Monday/Der Blaue Montag
  89:147
 *Carol of the Children of Bethlehem/
  Lied der Kinder zu Bethlehem 279:84
 *Da Droben Vom Berge/Above, On the
  Mountain 54:174
 *The Darkness Is Falling/Es Wird Scho
  Glei Dumpa 279:82, see also: 54:172
 *Der Blaue Montag/Blue Monday
  89:147
 *Die Binschgauer Wallfahrt/The Binsc-
  hgauer Pilgrimage 89:149
 *Die Hirten auf dem Felde/As Lately We
  Watched 54:170

AUSTRIA—*Continued*
  *Es Wird Scho Glei Dumpa   54:172, 279:82
  *Gloria   54:181
  *Hirten, auf um Mitternacht/Shepherds, Up!   279:80
  *Lied der Kinder zu Bethlehem/Carol of the Children of Bethlehem   279:84
  *Schneiderlied/Song of the Tailor   208:2
  *Shepherds, Up!/Hirten, auf um Mitternacht!   279:80
  *Song of the Tailor/Schneiderlied   208:2
  *Still, Still, Still   54:180
  *The Twilight Is Falling/Es Wird Scho Glei Dumpa   54:172, 279:82
  *Weihnachtslied/Silent Night   279:86, *see also:* Silent Night
  *Wer Klopfet An?/Who's Knocking There?   279:77
  *Who's Knocking There?/Wer Klopfet An?   279:77
AUTOMATION
  Automation   64:146
AUTOMOBILES
  The Car Song   274:8
  Ford Song   118:16
  The Gas Station   154:12
  Goin' for a Ride   206:48
  In Father's Car   207:16
  In My Merry Oldsmobile   157:203, 205:317
  John Brown's Ford   26:31
  Playing in the Sand   162:77
  Ride a Red Auto   154:10
  Riding in My Car   130:66, *see also:* 274:8
  We Have a Car   149:44
AUTUMN: *see also* HARVEST; MONTHS; names of months, e.g., SEPTEMBER
  Autumn   86:183
  Autumn Dance   162:42
  Autumn Is Here   245:109
  The Autumn Leaves Have Fallen Down   165:61
  Autumn Nights By the River   261:40
  Autumn Song   77:50 (*Autumn leaves are falling down*)
  Autumn Song   227:22 (*From the boughs o'er head the leaves are floating down*)
  Autumn Voices   72:136
  Autumn's Message   207:27
  Busy Little Bushytail   207:28
  Falling Leaves   41:44
  Flowers Are Dying   71:113
  Gone Is Autumn   71:113, 72:175
  Good Night Flowers   97:unpaged
  In the Woods   207:35
  The Painter Elves   7:32
  September Days   97:unpaged
  White Mornings   207:32

AVIATION: *see* AIRPLANES
AWAKENING: *see* WAKE UP SONGS

B

BABIES: *see also* FAMILIY AND FAMILY LIFE; LULLABIES
  All for Baby   191:40
  Cheeks of Rose   17:139
  Kids   206:25
  New Baby   91:40
  New Baby Brother   166:56
  To Babyland   17:18
  What Will We Do With the Baby-O?   75:86, *see also:* 110:26, 232:146
  What'll We Do With the Baby?   232:146, *see also:* 75:86, 110:26
  What'll We Do With the Baby-O?   110:26, *see also:* 75:86, 232:146
  When a Baby Comes   219:37
BABOONS
  The Baboon Climbs the Hill   292:213, *see also:* 289:52
  Stop Your Groaning   289:52, *see also:* 292:213
BABY SITTERS
  Baby-Sitter Sense   166:50
  Baby Sitter's Lullaby/Vigndig A Fremd Kind   289:32
  Vigndig A Fremd Kind/Baby Sitter's Lullaby   289:32
BAKERS AND BAKERIES: *see also* BREAD; CAKES AND COOKIES; PIES
  The Baker-Girl/La Panaderita   89:160, 216:18
  La Panaderita/The Baker-Girl   89:160, 216:18
BALL BOUNCING
  Barnacle Bill   162:62
  Down By the River   141:22
  Elephants Marching   63:80
  Oh, Marguerite! Go Wash Your Feet   24:796
  One, Two Three Alairy   24:796, *see also:* 63:74
  One, Two Three Alary   63:74, *see also:* 24:796
  A Sailor Went to Sea   63:79
  The Wonder Ball   141:24
BALL ROLLING
  As I Roll My Rolling Ball   262:49
  Down By the Greenwood Sidey-O   232:87
  En Roulant Ma Boule Roulant   89:34
  On, Roll On   128:74, *see also:* 89:34
  Over the Wall   288:14

Pass the Ball 178:68
Roll That Brown Jug Down to Town 232:88
Roll the Ball 291:64
Tsubodono 16:27
BALLOONS (AIRSHIPS)
Up in a Balloon 157:182
BALLOONS (TOYS)
Balloons for Sale 162:68
Blow Up a Balloon 162:68
BALLS (TOYS)
See Each India Rubber Ball 165:55
BANDITS: *see* OUTLAWS
BANDS (MUSIC): *see* MUSICAL INSTRU-MENTS
BARGES: *see* BOATS AND BOATING
BARLEY
Barley Harvesting/Mugi Kari 286:76
Mugi Kari/Barley Harvesting 286:76
BASEBALL
Play Ball 166:32
BATS (ANIMALS)
Leatherwing Bat 36:56, 158:18
Twinkle Twinkle Little Bat 247:84
BEACHES: *see* SEASHORE
BEAN, ROY
Roy Bean 159:147
BEANS
The Army Bean 73:168, *see also:* 99:47
Butzu Butzu Mame/Red Beans 286:39
Buy My Dainty Fine Beans 293:70
Red Beans/Butzu Butzu Mame 286:39
The White Army Bean 99:47, *see also:* 73:168
BEARS
The Bear and the Two Gascons/L'Ours et les Deux Gascons 243:26
The Bear in the Hill 292:106
The Bear is Pointing at the Sun 74:49
Bear Went Over the Mountain 17:16, 75:12, 147:14, 290:72, 292:110
Bears Are Sleeping 294
Grizzly Bear 274:10, 292:108
Isn't It Funny 172:17, 174:3
Lines and Squares 172:142, 173:28
L'Ours et les Deux Gascons/The Bear and the Two Gascons 243:26
My Uncle Terwilliger Waltzes With Bears 237:unpaged
No Bears Out Tonight 63:42
The Sleepy Bear 207:30
Smokey the Bear 26:81
Waltzing Bear 296:32
BEAUREGARD, GENERAL PIERRE GUS-TAVE TOUTANT
Beauregard 73:86
BEDTIME: *see also* LULLABIES; NIGHT; SLEEP
Bedtime Song 125:42

Bedtime Stories 207:21
Such a Getting Upstairs 232:53
To Bed, To Bed 17:50, 112:54, 285:101
BEES
A Baby Bumblebee 63:135
The Bee 162:23
Bees 7:27
The Counting Lesson 191:56, *see also:* 162:23
Here Is the Beehive 162:23, *see also:* 191:56
I'm Little White Clover 245:36
Isn't It Funny 172:17, 174:3
BEETLES: *see also* BOLL WEEVILS; LADY-BUGS
Koganemushi/Mister Golden Beetle 286:23
Mister Golden Beetle/Koganemushi 286:23
BELGIUM
*De Rommelpot/The Rommelpot 89:140
*Donkeys and Carrots 293:92
Leonore 89:141
*The Rommelpot/De Rommelpot 89:140
Rosa, Let Us Be Dancing 100:116
St. Joseph's Carol 189:74
BELLS
The Bell 67:88
The Bell Doth Toll 71:105, 72:172, 293:16
Bells 162:67
Din Don 188:170
Great Tom Is Cast 71:103, 176:29, 293:21
I Heard the Bells on Christmas Day 54:58, 148:172, 190:86, 241:126
Jingle at the Windows 232:173
Jingle Bells 17:63, 54:70, 92:163, 127:220, 148:200, 241:171, 264:114, 283:64
List to the Bells 46:228
Listen to the Bells 27:238
The Little Bells 71:101, 72:164, 293:20
Little Bells of Westminster 71:101, 72:164, 293:20
Longfellow's Carol 54:58, 148:172, 190:86, 241:126
Lovely Evening 71:109, 72:173
Merry Are the Bells 111:40
O Glorious Bells of Easter 197:41
O Hark I Hear Those Pealing Bells 62:12, *see also:* 71:98, 72:166
The Pealing Bells 71:98, 72:166, *see also:* 62:12
Tideo 232:173
Tinkling Bells 162:67
BENEDICTION: *see* PRAYERS

BIBLE STORIES: *see* RELIGION; names of biblical characters, e.g., MOSES
BICYCLES AND BICYCLING
  The Bicycle 245:26
  Bicycle Built for Two 21:19, 148:40, *see also:* 26:19, 83:493, 205:234
  Daisy Bell 21:19, 205:234, *see also:* 26:19, 83:493, 148:40
  Daisy, Daisy 26:19, 83:493, 148:40, *see also:* 21:19, 205:234
  The Gol-Darned Wheel 159:269
  Here Comes a Policeman, Riding a Bicycle 165:71
  I'm No Fool 119:108
  My New Bicycle 207:116
BIOGRAPHY
  The Abe-iad 73:50 (Abraham Lincoln)
  Anthony Wayne 28:126, *see also:* 240:100 (Anthony Wayne)
  Arnold Is As Brave a Man 28:55 (Benedict Arnold)
  The Ballad of Billy the Kid 61:266, 61:268, 159:140 (William Bonney)
  The Ballad of Davy Crockett 275:90, 276:86 (Davy Crockett)
  Beauregard 73:86 (General Pierre Beauregard)
  Billy the Kid 61:266, 61:268, 159:140 (William Bonney)
  Brave Wolfe 158:118, 240:33, 273:16 (General James Wolfe)
  Call 'em Names, Jeff 73:53 (Jefferson Davis)
  Captain Kidd 21:332 (Captain William Kidd)
  Christopher Columbo 27:200, *see also:* 197:88 (Christopher Columbus)
  Cole Younger 61:262 (Cole Younger)
  Cumberland Gap 33:154, 230:67, 277:79 (Daniel Boone)
  Custer's Last Charge 61:127 (General George Custer)
  Davy Crockett 33:106 (Davy Crockett)
  Death of General Wolfe 273:18 (General James Wolfe)
  The Death of Jesse James 61:258, *see also:* Jesse James
  Ever Since Uncle John Henry Been Dead 226:376 (John Henry)
  Every Monday Morning 232:156, *see also:* John Henry (John Henry)
  Farewell Father, Friend and Guardian 73:72 (Abraham Lincoln)
  Follow Washington 27:32, 28:84 (George Washington)
  A Funeral Dirge on the Death of General George Washington 273:74 (George Washington)

Great Americans 207:80 (Abraham Lincoln, George Washington)
The Green Mountaineer 28:40 (Ethan Allen)
Hale in the Bush 28:80, *see also:* 240:98 (Nathan Hale)
He Knew the Earth Was Round-o 197:88, *see also:* 27:200 (Christopher Columbus)
The Hunters of Kentucky 157:34, 226:427 (Andrew Jackson)
I Went Down to the Depot 226:374 (Jesse James)
It's All Wrong 197:89 (Christopher Columbus)
Jeff Davis' Dream 73:66 (Jefferson Davis)
Jesse James 21:224, 60:96, 61:255, 61:257, 61:259, 61:260, 146:154, 157:158, 158:296, 159:152, 159:155, 159:156, 159:157, 226:420, 230:36, *see also:* 61:256, 61:258 (Jesse James)
Jesse James and His Boys 61:256, *see also:* Jesse James
John Brown's Body 22:222, 64:170, 73:7, 158:120, 230:62, 277:57 (John Brown)
John Henry 22:170, 33:178, 64:82, 89:40, 158:258, 158:260, 158:262, 226:24, 230:82, 232:154, 239:68, 272:15, 274:16, *see also:* 232:156 (John Henry)
Lincoln and Liberty 27:14, 157:51, 226:167 (Abraham Lincoln)
Mad Anthony Wayne 240:100, *see also:* 28:126 (Anthony Wayne)
Marion's Men 28:144 (Francis Marion)
Mount Vernon 273:76 (George Washington)
Nathan Hale 240:98, *see also:* 28:80 (Nathan Hale)
Old Abe Lincoln 21:140, 27:12, 226:168 (Abraham Lincoln)
Paul Jones 35:16, *see also:* 240:132 (John Paul Jones)
Paul Jones 240:134 (John Paul Jones)
Paul Jones' Victory 240:132, *see also:* 35:16 (John Paul Jones)
Perry's Victory 240:197 (Oliver Hazard Perry)
Pretty Dolly Madison 166:46 (Dolley Madison)
Quantrell 159:142, 159:144 (William Clarke Quantrell)
Riding a Raid 73:90 (J. E. B. Stuart)
Ringo, Ringo, Ringo Starr 141:16 (Ringo Starr)
Round and Round Hitler's Grave 158:88 (Adolf Hitler)
Roy Bean 159:147 (Roy Bean)
Sailing on the Sea 27:202 (Christopher Columbus)

Santy Anna   21:288, 24:835, 262:105, *see also:* 158:136 (Santa Anna)

Santy Anno   158:136, *see also:* 21:288, 24:835, 262:105 (Santa Anna)

Sherman the Brave   73:75 (General William Sherman)

Stonewall Jackson's Way   73:84 (Stonewall Jackson)

Stonewall's Requiem   73:203 (Stonewall Jackson)

The Surrender of Cornwallis   240:139 (Marquis Charles Cornwallis)

The Sword of Robert E. Lee   73:78 (Robert E. Lee)

To Honor Lincoln   207:82 (Abraham Lincoln)

Versos de Montalgo   226:30 (Montalgo)

Way Down in Mexico   159:365 (Santa Anna)

When Sherman Marched Down to the Sea   73:216 (General William Sherman)

The Yankee Man-of-War   240:130 (John Paul Jones)

BIRDS: *see also* names of birds, e.g., ROBINS

Bam Chi, Chi, Bam   130:102

Bendemeer's Stream   22:20

The Bird/El Pájaro   295:10

The Bird of Night   44:44

The Bird Song   69:18, 157:76, 262:44, *see also:* 36:56, 129:40, 158:18, 289:68, 292:122

The Birds   184:18, *see also:* Carol of the Birds

Birds' Courting Song   129:40, 289:68, *see also:* Bird Song

Birds Have Wings   7:28

Birds' Song   292:122, *see also:* Bird Song

The Captured Bird/Poymanaya Pteechka   289:62,

Carol of the Birds   54:124, 54:268, 128:60, 140:96, 183:22, 184:18, 209:119, 241:61, 264:94, 284:61, 292:126

The Dickey-Bird Song   75:20, *see also:* Two Little Blackbirds

El Cant dels Ocells   54:268, *see also:* Carol of the Birds

El Pájaro/The Bird   295:10

Fare You Well   35:49

Feed the Birds   97:unpaged

Hey, Pretty Little Bird   292:124, *see also:* 232:179, 277:27

Hi! Ho! The Rattlin' Bog   134:11, *see also:* Green Grass Grows All Around

Hushabye Swing   207:91

I Have Made a Pretty Nest   165:155

La Pájara Pinta/The Spotted Bird   168:127

Lata Ptaszek Po Uticy/The Little Bird   189:150

Leatherwing Bat   36:56, 158:18, *see also:* Bird Song

The Little Bird/Lata Ptaszek Po Uticy   189:150

The Little Bird   18:32, *see also:* 111:49, 285:99

Little Bird, Little Bird   232:118, *see also:* Blue Bird

Little Birdie   292:128

Little Red Bird   176:52, 245:86

Little Trotty Wagtail   44:10

The Lonesome Grove   157:78

The Night Song   85:243

Oh, Three Pega/O, Tres Pega   89:92

O, Tres Pega/Oh, Three Pega   89:92

Once I Saw a Little Bird   111:49, 285:99, *see also:* 18:32

Poymanaya Pteechka/The Captured Bird   289:62

Redbird   130:104

The Redbird Sings   74:19

Rented   207:92

Sa Tah Ryung/Song of Birds   208:41

Sing Little Birdie   161:10

The Singing Bird   110:36

A Small Bird Swings   7:22

Song of Birds/Sa Tah Ryung   208:41

A Story of Four Little Birds   41:12

Thou Poor Bird   292:129, 293:88

Titwillow   252:48

Two Birds Sat on a Stone   18:38, 112:66

Two Little Dicky Birds   111:32, *see also:* Two Little Blackbirds

Up Up in the Sky   162:8

Who Killed Cock Robin?   62:56, 134:58, 292:138, *see also:* 37:177, 135:32, 289:74

Who Killed Cocky Robin?   289:74, *see also:* Who Killed Cock Robin?

BIRTHDAYS

Baby's Birthday   125:12

The Birthday Cake   207:10

Birthday Presents   245:121

Birthday Roundelay   245:107

Birthday Song   11:18 (*Billy has a birthday*)

Birthday Song   77:61 (*I'm five years old today*)

Birthday Song   130:24 (*How do you feel one year older*)

Birthday Song   162:56 (*On this bright and happy day*)

Birthday Song   197:124 (*Oh, Birthday Pal, we sing-a-ling-a-ling*)

A Birthday Song   41:25 (*We'll all sing together*)

Happy Happy Birthday   204:15

BIRTHDAYS—*Continued*
How Old Are You? 128:21, 232:56
Joyful Greetings 245:107
Once Again Has Come My Birthday 86:153
Season's Birthday Song 245:106
The Unbirthday Song 275:44, 276:45
We Bring You Flowers 245:105
BISON
Boggy Creek 159:41, *see also:* Buffalo Skinners
The Buffalo Skinner 24:854, 64:120, 146:92, 158:174, 159:335, 226:270, 230:63, 277:137, *see also:* 159:41
Shoot the Buffalo 61:272, 61:273, 61:274, 158:103
BLACKBIRDS
Song of the Blackbirds 74:17
Two Little Blackbirds 162:9, 178:18, 290:104, 291:40, *see also:* 75:20, 111:32
BLACKS: *see* AFRO-AMERICAN
BLACKSMITHING
The Blacksmith 85:171
The Forge 262:31
Twankydillo 262:24
BLESSINGS: *see* PRAYERS
BLOSSOMS: *see* FLOWERS; names of flowers, e.g., VIOLETS
BLUEBELLS
In and Out the Bonnie Bluebells 245:54
BLUEBIRDS
Blue Bird/Parangsai 49:34
Parangsai/Blue Bird 49:34
BLUES (MUSIC)
De Blues Ain' Nothin' 226:234
Got Dem Blues 226:232
Joe Turner 226:241
Meet Me in St. Louis, Louis 205:296
St. Louis Blues 21:120
Shorty George 158:70
Wanderin' 148:404, 226:188
When a Woman Blue 226:236
BOATS AND BOATING: *see also* CANOES AND CANOEING; FERRIES; SAILING; SEAMEN; SHIPS
A Canoa Virou/My Little Boat 168:139
All the Ducks 135:25, *see also:* 227:37
All the Fish Are Swimming in the Water 128:30, 130:100
Banks of the Little Eau Pleine 157:42
Barges 72:96
Bigerlow 226:174, *see also:* 24:843, 158:149
The Bigler 158:149, *see also:* 24:843, 226:174
The Bigler's Crew 24:843, *see also:* 158:149, 226:174
A Boat, a Boat 290:192, 293:58
The Boatman Dance 33:114

The Boatmen's Song 239:58
Boats Sail on the River 245:75
The Bold Fisherman 27:208, 128:116, 239:20, 256
Down the River 20:75, 27:156, 197:82
The Ducks 227:37, *see also:* 135:25
The E-RI-E 21:282, 158:146, 226:180, 290:44, *see also:* 230:87, 277:39
En Roulant Ma Boule Roulant 89:34
Era una Vez/There Was Once 89:62, 216:34
Erie Canal 230:87 277:39, *see also:* 21:282, 158:146, 226:180, 290:44 (E-RI-E)
Erie Canal 22:37, 69:34, 197:78, 226:171, 239:60, 246, 262:74, 292:38, *see also:* 33:58 (*Low bridge everybody down*)
Four in a Boat 20:23, 71:31
Goin' for a Ride 206:48
I Love to Row in My Big Blue Boat 165:111
If I Had a Boat 154:24
In Our Rowboat 162:94
Low Bridge Every Body Down 33:58, *see also:* Erie Canal
My Little Boat/A Canoa Virou 168:139
Nancy Till 277:129
Ocean Go 130:98
Once There Was/Era una Vez 89:62, 216:50, *see also:* 217:14
Oro, My Little Boat 245:76
Over the Sea in My Boat With Me 227:16
Over the Sea Sails He 154:25
Papa, les Petits Bateaux/Papa, the Little Boats 217:45
Papa, the Little Boats/Papa, les Petits Bateaux 217:63
The Row Boat 41:30
Row, Row, Row Your Boat 17:117, 25:30, 26:44, 62:10, 148:320, 165:116, 283:10, 289:185, 293:56
Rowing Song 288:18
The Sail Boat 41:32
Sailing at High Tide 24:812, 75:68, *see also:* 232:160
Sailing in the Boat 232:160, *see also:* 24:812, 75:68
Santa Lucía 22:30
Shawnee Town 33:90
Skye Boat Song 22:18, 71:58, 72:115
Steamboat Bill 61:42
There Was Once/Era una Vez 89:62, 216:50
Two in a Boat 135:92
Two Little Boats Are on the Sea 165:115
Where Go the Boats? 69:43

BODY, HUMAN: *see also* names of parts of the body, e.g., EARS
Anatomical Song   129:118
Dese Bones Gwine to Rise Again   89:42, 197:94, 226:470, *see also:* 290:40
Everything Grows Together   219:12
Eye Winker   75:24
I'm Gonna Pat My Little Old Head   204:17
In My Bureau Drawer   237:unpaged
It's Fun to Be a Person, Yes-Sir-ee!   204:31
I've Got Two   206:22
Mouth and Eyes   204:19
Others Are Special   204:29
Our Legs   204:23
Right in the Middle of My Face   206:28
Skeleton Bones   197:94, *see also:* 89:42, 226:470, 290:40
Skin   91:16
Tap Your Foot   130:14
These Bones Gonna Rise Again   290:40, *see also:* 89:42, 197:94, 226:470
Wake Up   130:10
Who Has a Nose?   178:9
Wiggle the Wool   290:12
With My Hands I Clap Clap Clap   178:29
BOHEMIA
Autumn Song   227:22
To the Garden Annie Went   262:26, *see also:* 78:51
BOLIVIA
*De Blanca Tierra/From Lands Far Away   89:90, *see also:* 262:19
*De Blanca Tierra/From the White Earth   262:19, *see also:* 89:90
*El Cuando/O When, O When?   22:122
*From Lands Far Away/De Blanca Tierra   89:90, *see also:* 239:19
*From the White Earth/De Blanca Tierra   262:19, *see also:* 89:90
La Imilla   114:66
*O When, O When?/El Cuando   22:122
BOLL WEEVILS
Ballet of the Boll Weevil   21:81, 226:252, *see also:* Boll Weevil
The Boll Weevil   24:916, 33:170, 64:98, 158:236, 221, 226:8, 239:40, 274:38, 277:29, 292:204, *see also:* 21:81, 226:252
BONNEY, WILLIAM H. (BILLY THE KID)
The Ballad of Billy the Kid   61:266, 61:268, 159:140
Billy the Kid   61:266, 61:268, 159:140
BOONE, DANIEL
Cumberland Gap   33:145, 230:67, 277:79
BOTSWANA
*Kattan, Kattan/Run, Run   89:257
*Run, Run/Kattan, Kattan   89:257

BOWS AND ARROWS
Shoot an Arrow   166:8
BOY SCOUTS: *see* SCOUTS AND SCOUTING
BRAZIL
*A Canoa Virou/My little Boat   168:139
*Ciranda Cirandenha/Dancer, Little Dancer   168:141, 169:9, 266:13
*Dancer, Little Dancer/Ciranda Cirandenha   168:141, *see also:* 169:9, 266:13
*In Bahia/Na Bahia Tem   266:14
*My Heart Is Heavy With Sadness/Suspira, Coracao Triste   89:91
*My Little Boat/A Canoa Virou   168:139
*Na Bahia Tem/In Bahia   266:14
*Nesta Rua/On This Street   266:14
*Oh, Three Pega/O, Tres Pega   89:92
*O, Tres Pega/Oh, Three Pega   89:92
*On This Street/Nesta Rua   266:14
Samba-le-le   114:69
Spoon   100:38
Suitors   72:104
*Suspira, Coracao Triste/My Heart Is Heavy With Sadness   89:91
Thanks to God   86:164
Tutu Maranba   262:15
BREAD
Dame, Lend Me a Loaf   293:74
Five Currant Buns in a Baker's Shop   165:30
Hot Cross Buns   17:122, 135:105, 175:64, 188:100, 285:54
Little Red Hen   245:60
Little Tommy Tucker   17:99, 285:88, *see also:* 175:24
Mama Bake the Johnny Cake, Christmas Comin'   130:42
The Muffin Man   15:365, 17:46, 129:99, 135:27, 165:195, 168:107, 175:42, 283:53, 289:99
Punchin' Dough   61:110
Tommy Tucker   175:24, *see also:* 17:99, 285:88
BREAKFAST
The King's Breakfast   172:93
BRITISH ISLES: *see* ENGLAND; IRELAND; SCOTLAND; WALES
BROOKS
Arroyo Claro   188:62
Down By the Old Mill Stream   290:66
BROTHERHOOD
All Men Are Brothers   77:20
Brethren in Peace Together   72:147
The Hammer Song   230:19
It Could Be a Wonderful World   64:198
It's a Small World   275:88
Sisters and Brothers   260:68
There's a Song in My Heart   155:9

BROWN, JOHN
  John Brown's Body 22:222, 64:170, 73:7,
    158:120, 230:62, 277:57
BROWNIES (FAIRIES)
  Brownie 172:140, 173:26
BROWNIES (SCOUTS): see SCOUTS
BUCCANEERS: see PIRATES
BUCKINGHAM PALACE
  Buckingham Palace 172:128, 173:14
BUDDHISM
  Hymn to Buddha/Wou Liang 89:231
  Wou Liang/Hymn to Buddha 89:231
BUDS: see FLOWERS
BUFFALO: see BISON
BUGS: see INSECTS; names of insects, e.g.,
  LADYBUGS
BUILDERS AND BUILDING
  Bling Blang 130:74
  The Carpenters 245:59
  Castle in My City 296:8
  Tall Shop in the Town 165:66
  The Water Pipes 149:28
BULGARIA
  Elenka 89:191
  Oh, He Planted Ginger 114:54
BULULAND
  *Swinging Game 100:52
BUMBLEBEES: see BEES
BUMS: see TRAMPS
BURMA
  *Myan Myan 169:11, 269:17
  *Sein Kyu Kya Nyaung/Song of the
    Princess 89:221
  *Song of the Princess/Sein Kyu Kya
    Nyaung 89:221
BURROS: see DONKEYS
BUSES
  Big Yellow Bus 162:102
  The Bus Song 75:16, see also: 147:6,
    165:73, 291:46
  Look at Us 162:103
  The Wheels of the Bus Go Round and
    Round 147:6, 165:73, 291:46, see also:
    75:16
BUTTER
  Betty Botter 112:8, see also: 18:12
  Betty Botter's Batter 18:12, see also:
    112:8
  The King's Breakfast 172:93
  Little Tommy Tucker 17:99, 285:88, see
    also: 175:24
  Making Butter 191:76
  Tommy Tucker 175:24, see also: 17:99,
    285:88
BUTTERCUPS
  Buttercups and Daisies 17:109
BUTTERFLIES
  Butterflies 261:34

Butterfly 114:62 (Little butterfly, my
  friend)
The Butterfly 85:145 (I dance in the
  sunshine)
Dainty Little Butterfly 245:42
Fuzzy Wuzzy Caterpillar 162:20
BUYING AND SELLING: see also STORES;
  STREET CRIES
  At the Lemonade Stand 166:44
  Bafti Hindi 89:206, 114:52
  Buy a Broom 66:34
  Caller Herrin' 292:174
  Chairs to Mend 46:228, 71:104, 72:164,
    289:186, 293:64, 293:66, see also:
    111:58
  Cherries Ripe 17:27
  Clams 239:88
  Cockles and Mussels 22:22, 262:89
  Congo Tay 130:82
  The Crawfish Man 129:21, see also:
    262:35
  The Crow-fish Man 262:35, see also:
    129:21
  A Customer 154:22
  Doughnuts 239:88
  El Tortillero/The Tortilla-Seller 89:96,
    169:14, 216:24, 267:46
  Five Currant Buns in a Baker's Shop
    165:30
  Going Down to Town 232:158, see also:
    226:145
  Hippity Hop 17:47
  Hot Cross Buns 17:122, 135:105, 175:64,
    188:100, 285:54
  Hot Mutton Pies 71:103
  I'm Called Little Buttercup 252:8
  Junk Man 239:89
  Korobushka 178:60
  Les Belles Pommes D'Api! 227:9
  London Street Cries 71:102
  Mahiya Illa Zalab/Song of the Fig Ven-
    dors 89:246
  Market Man 41:40
  Market Square 172:136, 173:22
  The Muffin Man 14:365, 17:46, 129:99,
    135:27, 165:195, 168:107, 175:42,
    283:53, 289:99
  My Father Is Dead 188:44, see also:
    Swapping Song
  My Roadside Stand 154:20
  Old Chairs to Mend 111:58, see also:
    Chairs to Mend
  Ole Clo' 71:102
  The Peddler 72:150
  The Popcorn Man 207:90
  Portobello Road 275:84, 276:70
  The Roving Pedlar 36:98
  Simon's Song 58, see also: 17:31, 175:16,
    285:33

Simple Simon   17:31, 175:16, 285:33, see also: 58
Solas Market   130:85
Song of the Fig Vendors/Mahiya Illa Zalab   89:246
The Swapping Boy   143, see also: Swapping Song
The Swapping Song   37:174, 129:38, 213:10, see also: 18:36, 111:63, 143, 188:44
The Tortilla-Seller/El Tortillero   89:96, 169:14, 216:24, 267:46
White Sand and Gray Sand   62:18, 71:113, 293:68
Young Lambs to Sell   135:48
BUZZARDS
Song of the Buzzards   74:18

C

CABBAGES
Do You Know How to Plant Cabbages   217:53, see also: 165:85, 168:164
Do You Plant Your Cabbages in the Right Way   165:85, see also: 168:164, 217:53
Planting Cabbages/Savez-vous Planter les Choux?   168:164, 217:53, see also: 165:85
Savez-vous Planter les Choux?/Planting Cabbages   168:164, 217:10, see also: 165:85
CAKES AND COOKIES
Birthday Cake   207:10
Cakes and Custard   18:48
Christmas Cookies   207:48
The Gingerbread Boy   41:45
Our Cookie Jar   207:11
Pat-A-Cake   17:127, 75:60, 175:80, 188:162
CALENDARS
Chicken Soup with Rice   235:60
CALIFORNIA
Abalone   72:98, 226:333
Banks of Sacramento   226:112, see also: 33:210
Banks of the Sacramento   33:210, see also: 226:112
California   226:110
California Here I Come   170:46
Ho for California   239:64
Juanita   21:259, 61:144, 170:25
CALVES: see COWS
CAMBODIA
The Elephant   169:12
*Love Song/Prom Kut   89:222
*Prom Kut/Love Song   89:222

CAMP SONGS: see also ACTION SONGS; CLAPPING SONGS; NONSENSE; SINGING GAMES
Clementine   22:82, 25:76, 26:16, 61:100, 148:52, 195, 205:213, 230:27, 290:162
Down in the Valley   22:99, 24:902, 25:99, 46:224, 61:162, 148:70, 158:62, 205:79, 226:148, 230:33
Each Campfire Lights Anew   72:37
I Love the Mountains   26:21, 148:176
Mules   26:19, 289:148, 292:36
Once There Were Three Fishermen   148:294, see also: 26:13, 63:98, 290:50
Rabbit Ain't Got   292:96
Rise Up, O Flame   69:7, 71:11, 72:174
Scouting We Go   26:68
She'll Be Comin' 'Round the Mountain   20:36, 22:156, 25:14, 62:70, 148:324, 165:197, 170:33, 201, 205:175, 226:372, 232:90, 283:30, 290:24
Sing Your Way Home   46:217, 133:334
Skinamarink   290:114
Smile Song (S-M-I-L-E)   25:39, 26:12
Song of the Great Lakes Region   69:46
Taps   25:126, 26:92, 69:10, 71:12, 72:53, 148:370, 197:62, 277:45
Tell Me Why   25:122, 26:63, 148:372
There We Would Be   69:51
We're All Gonna Shine Tonight   290:206
We're Here Because We're Here   290:217
CAMPING
Around the Campfire Bright   25:121
CANADA
*Anio/On to War   89:32
As I Roll My Rolling Ball   262:49
The Bonny Banks of Virgie-O   134:52
Crocodile Song   89:33, 234:72, see also: 26:36
*Dans Les Chantiers Nous Hivernerons   176:62
Donkey Riding   71:81, 72:117, 78:11, 128:88
*D'où Viens-tu, Bergère?/Whence Art Thou, My Maiden?   54:133, see also: 279:96
*En Roulant Ma Boule Roulant   89:34
Here Comes a Knight A-Riding   168:152
I's the B'y   27:66, see also: 134:74
Isabeau S'y Promene   176:134
I'se the B'y That Builds the Boat   134:74, see also: 27:66
*Long Live the Girls of Canada/Vive la Canadienne   208:5
The Maid of Newfoundland   89:36
Mon Vieux Moine/My Old Top   189:138
My Old Top/Mon Vieux Moine   189:138
*On to War/Anio   89:32

CANADA—*Continued*
 *Vive la Canadienne/Long Live the Girls of Canada 208:5
 *Whence Art Thou, My Maiden?/D'où Viens-tu, Bergère? 54:133, *see also:* 279:96
 Where Have You Been Walking, Shepherdess? 262:170
CANARIES
 The Canary 41:20
CANDLES
 The Candle 67:83 *(A candle let me be)*
 The Candle 162:67 *(A little candle cries)*
CANDY
 End of a Lollypop 26:16
 Hippity Hop 17:47, *see also:* 165:139
 Hippity Hop to the Candy Shop 165:139, *see also:* 17:47
 Lollipop 118:21
CANOES AND CANOEING
 Bolumbu 100:77
 The Canoe 41:33
 Canoe Round 293:60, *see also:* 62:19
 My Paddle's Keen and Bright 62:19, *see also:* 293:60
 The Paddle Song 25:28
 The Young Voyageur 22:36
CANONS
 All Things Must Perish 293:6, *see also:* 62:20, 69:50
 Alleluia 55:255, 86:150, 241:224 *(Alleluia, Alleluia, Alleluia)*
 Ave Maria (Mozart) 241:225
 Canon of the Mimes 241:229
 Christmas Eve Canon 241:223
 Dona Nobis Pacem 55:254, 69:11, 176:47, 241:224, 262:34, 293:112
 Evening Hymn, Tallis's Canon 86:170, 189:60, *see also:* 71:106, 72:51, 176:104
 Greeting Song 262:27
 June, Lovely June 262:34
 Listen to the Bells 27:238
 The Red Herring 262:27
 The Song of the Ship-Builders 262:133
 Star of Bethlehem 140:119, *see also:* The Star of Bethlehem
 The Star of Bethlehem 197:114 *(The night a Child was born)*
 Tallis's Canon 71:106, 72:51, 86:170, 176:104, 189:60
 Thanksgiving Canon 72:63
 Wake Ev'ry Breath 140:109
 When Jesus Wept 140:112
 Willie, Willie Will 262:141
CAPS: *see* HATS
CAREERS: *see* OCCUPATIONS
CAREFULNESS: *see* SAFETY
CAROLINE ISLANDS
 *Ngai I Tanga I 89:305

CARPENTERS AND CARPENTRY
 The Carpenters 245:59
CARRIBBEAN SEA: *see* names of islands, e.g., CUBA
CAROLS: *see* CHRISTMAS CAROLS
CAROUSELS: *see* MERRY-GO-ROUNDS
CARRIAGES: *see* STAGECOACHES
CARROTS
 Donkeys and Carrots 293:92
 Donkeys Love Carrots 144:23
CASEY JONES
 Casey Jones 22:142, 158:264, 158:266, 176:148, 222, 226:366
CASTLES
 Buckingham Palace 172:128, 173:14
 Castle in My City 296:8
 Donde Están las Llaves?/Where Are the Keys of the Castle? 188:54, *see also:* 189:154
 Il Mio Bel Castello/I'm the King of the Castle 189:152
 I'm the King of the Castle/Il Mio Bel Castello 189:152
 I've a Fine, Bonny Castle/Yo Tengo un Castillo 189:154, *see also:* 188:54
 Where Are the Keys of the Castle?/ Donde Están las Llaves? 188:54, *see also:* 189:154
 Yo Tengo un Castillo/I've a Fine, Bonny Castle 189:154, *see also:* 188:54
CATALOG SONGS
 Aiken Drum 111:44, 162:36, 175:130, 188:104, 189:28, 289:96
 Hush, Little Baby 10, 59:52, 75:33, 178:56, 213:84, 232:147, 261:56, 274:20, 289:12, 298, *see also:* 63:90, 125:134, 129:97, 135:52, 197:57
 Lazy John 135:38, 213:16, 254:112
 Mama's Gonna Buy 197:57, *see also:* Hush, Little Baby
 A Man of Words 44:72
 Mrs. Murphy's Chowder 290:16
 The Mocking Bird 125:134, 129:97, *see also:* Hush, Little Baby
 The Mockingbird 135:52, *see also:* Hush, Little Baby
 Papa's Going to Buy Me a Mockingbird 93, *see also:* Hush, Little Baby
CATERPILLARS (LARVAE)
 The Caterpillar 191:36
 Caterpillars 261:32
 Fuzzy Caterpillar 296:34 *(Fuzzy, fuzzy caterpillar crawling, crawling by)*
 The Fuzzy Caterpillar 207:26 *(Fuzzy little caterpillar, why do you roam?)*
 Fuzzy Wuzzy Caterpillar 162:20
 Little Arabella Miller 75:44, 165:165
CATS
 Black Cats Come 166:34

Broder Manyo 89:66
The Cat Came Back 102
A Cat Came Fiddling Out of a Barn 111:51
Cat in the Plum Tree 144:11
Creep, Mouse, Creep 135:111
Daddy Wouldn't Buy Me a Bow Wow 197:68
Ding, Dong Bell 17:49, 147:13, 175:174
Don Gato/Sir Cat 295:4, see also: 216:3
El Señor don Gato/Sir Tomcat 216:3, see also: 295:4
Ev'rybody Wants to Be a Cat 275:70, 276:56
The Hungry Cat and the Grumbling Mouse 112:64
I Know a Little Pussy 165:94
I Love Little Pussy 17:116, 175:86, 283:15, 285:66
If You Were a Kitty 296:20
Il Etait une Bergère/There Was a Shepherdess 217:32
Johnny Doolan's Cat 84:39
Kitty and Puppy 162:86
Kitty White 14:357
La Mère Michel/Old Lady Mitchell 217:26
The Little Kitty 62:47
Little Robin Redbreast 17:67, 18:16
Long Time Ago 17:146, 129:26, 130:108, see also: 62:47
The Mice 296:10
The Mice and the Cat 291:78
Mrs. Pussy's Dinner 191:60
My New Baby Kitten 207:14
Night 59:13
Obedient Kitten 245:47
Old Lady Mitchell/La Mère Michel 217:57
The Owl and the Pussy Cat 112:26
The Presbyterian Cat 62:43
Pretty Little Pussy Cat 165:158
Pussy Cat 175:166, 188:28
Pussy Cat High, Pussy Cat Low 175:166, 188:28
Pussy Cat Mole 111:14
Pussy Cat Pussy Cat 17:108, 144:15, 175:110, 188:112, 285:70, 292:66
Pussycat Wussycat 111:65
The Shepherd Maid 227:6
The Siamese Cat Song 276:50
Sir Cat/Don Gato 216:41, 295:4
Sir Tomcat/El Señor don Gato 216:41, 295:4
Six Little Mice Sat Down to Spin 111:12, see also: 175:144
Softly, Silently 7:30
There Was a Shepherdess/Il Etait une Bergère 217:59

Three Little Kittens 17:12, 188:90, 283:18, 285:29, 292:64
Three Mice Went Into a Hole to Spin 175:144, see also: 111:12
CATTLE: see COWBOYS; COWS
CELEBRATIONS: see HOLIDAYS; names of holidays, e.g., HALLOWEEN
CENTRAL AMERICA: see LATIN AMERICA; names of countries, e.g., PANAMA
CEYLON
  Bubbles and Bubbles 114:10
  *Nature's Splendor/Varga Pavati 89:215
  *Vandura 169:13, 271:50
  *Varga Pavati/Nature's Splendor 89:215
CHAD
  *E Lala E Liyo 89:259
CHAIRS
  Chairs to Mend 46:228, 71:104, 72:164, 289:186, 293:64, 293:66, see also: 111:58
  Old Chairs to Mend! 111:58, see also: Chairs to Mend
CHANTEYS: see SEA SONGS
CHANTS
  Diller, Diller Dollar 110:18
  Sandpiper 69:24
  Sen Chain, Sen Chain, Sen Chain 215:8
  Vu-gu vu-gu vu-gu 215:17
  War Song/Yaya 89:282
  Yaya/War Song 89:282
CHANUKAH: see HANUKKAH
CHAPMAN, JOHN (JOHNNY APPLESEED)
  Johnny Appleseed's Grace 101:31
CHASE: see HUNTING
CHEERS AND CHEERLEADING
  Lead a Yell 166:20
CHEROKEE INDIANS
  Alknomook 273:114, see also: 61:116
  The Indian's Death Song 61:116, see also: 273:114
CHERRIES
  Cherries Are Ripe 262:26
  Cherries Ripe 17:27
  Cherries So Ripe 293:69
CHERUBS: see ANGELS
CHICAGO
  A Hot Time in the Old Town 126:57, 157:191, see also: 21:30, 184
  There'll Be a Hot Time 21:30, 184, see also: 126:57, 157:191
  They'll Be a Hot Time in the Old Town Tonight 203, see also: 21:30, 126:57, 157:191
CHICKENS
  Baile de los Pollos/The Chicken Dance 194:30
  Chick, Chick Little Chickies 114:48
  The Chicken/El Pollo 295:15

183

CHICKENS—*Continued*
The Chicken Dance/Baile de los Pollos 194:30
The Cock/Qhude 163:76
The Cock and the Fox/Le Coq et le Renard 243:36
The Duck and the Hen 17:73
El Pollo/The Chicken 295:15
He Moa Kane/A Strutting Rooster 87:17
The Hen and Chickens 191:20
The Hen Who Laid Golden Eggs/La Poule aux Oeufs d'Or 243:14
Hickety, Pickety, My Black Hen 188:50, 189:13, 285:73, *see also:* 175:137
Higgledy, Piggledy, My Black Hen 175:137, *see also:* 188:50, 189:13, 285:73
La Poule aux Oeufs d'Or/The Hen Who Laid Golden Eggs 243:14
La Poulette Grise/The Old Grey Hen 289:30
Le Coq et le Renard/The Cock and the Fox 243:36
The Little Red Hen 245:60
Mother Hen 207:102 (*Mother Hen walked proudly*)
Mother Hen 41:36 (*Mother Hen calls to her baby chicks three*)
My Old Hen 234:44, 289:42, 289:156
The Old Grey Hen/La Poulette Grise 289:30
The Old Hen Cackled and the Rooster Laid the Egg 234:42
Paul on the Hillside 79:76
Qhude/The Cock 163:76
The Rooster's Our Watchman 245:6
A Strutting Rooster/He Moa Kane 87:17
CHILDREN: *see also* BABIES; FAMILY AND FAMILY LIFE
Children Can 219:45
CHILDREN'S DAY
"Hosanna!" Be the Children's Song 86:186
On Children's Day We Sweetly Sing 86:185
CHILE
Beautiful Maiden 114:70
El Cuando/O When, O When? 22:122
*El Tortillero/The Tortilla-Seller 89:96, 169:14, 216:24, 267:46
*Flowing River/Rio, Rio 208:7
*Going to Bethlehem/Vamos a Belén 54:303
O When, O When?/El Cuando 22:122
*Perica 262:18
*Rio, Rio/Flowing River 208:7
*The Tortilla-Seller/El Tortillero 216:47, *see also:* 89:96, 169:14, 267:46

*The Tortilla Vender 267:46, *see also:* 89:96, 169:14, 216:47
*Vamos a Belén/Going to Bethlehem 54:303
CHIMES: *see* BELLS
CHIMNEY SWEEPS
Chim Chim Cher-ee 275:48, 276:51
CHINA
Baby's Birthday 125:12
*Bad Faith/Whai Lyang Shin 49:17
Chinese Baby Song 17:134, 59:27
A Chinese Christmas Cradle Song 209:68
Chinese Cradle Song 78:77, *see also:* 125:10
Come, Fellow Workers 22:228
*Cool Breezes/Liang Fung Lyao Lyao 49:18
*Dze (r) dzoo diow/Purple Bamboo Flute 208:12
The Fishermen's Song 114:15
*The Flower Drum/Hua Ku Ko 89:232
*Frogs/Show Ha Mo 49:14
*Fuhng Yahng Flower Drum/Fuhng Yahng Hwah Goo 208:10
*Fuhng Yahng Hwah Goo/Fuhng Yahng Flower Drum 208:10
*Gently Flowing Stream/Shao Hua Tang Shui 49:20
*Hua Ku Ko/The Flower Drum 89:232
*Hymn to Buddha/Wou Liang 89:231
*Liang Fung Lyao Lyao/Cool Breezes 49:18
*Lio Lang Jr Ge/The Vagabond's Song 49:13
Oh, Lily, Lily White 78:77, 125:10
*Poor Sz Bbei/Sz Bbei Shang Gung 49:16
*Purple Bamboo Flute/Dze (r) dzoo diow 208:12
*San Wu Yao/Song of the Three "Nots" 49:19
*Shao Hua Tang Shui/Gently Flowing Stream 49:20
*Show Ha Mo/Frogs 49:14
Song of the Great Wall 22:204
*Song of the Three "Nots"/San Wu Yao 49:19
*Sz Bbei Shang Gung/Poor Sz Bbei 49:16
*The Vagabond's Song/Lio Lang Jr Ge 49:13
*Wei Sha Bu Hwei Ja/Why Don't You Come Home? 49:12
*Welcome Spring/Yin Chuin Wha Ur Kai 49:15
*Whai Lyang Shin/Bad Faith 49:17
*Why Don't You Come Home?/Wei Sha Bu Hwei Ja 49:12

*Wou Liang/Hymn to Buddha   89:231
*Yin Chuin Wha Ur Kai/Welcome Spring
   49:15
CHIPMUNKS
   The Chipmunk's Day   44:30
CHIPPEWA INDIANS: *see* OJIBWA INDI-
ANS
CHIVALRY: *see* KNIGHTS AND KNIGHT-
HOOD; names of persons, e.g., ARTHUR,
KING
CHRISTIANITY: *see* CHRISTMAS CAROLS;
HYMNS; PRAYERS; RELIGION; SPIRITUALS
CHRISTMAS CAROLS: *see also* CHRISTMAS
SONGS
   A la Media Noche/At the Hour of Mid-
      night   54:286
   Above, On the Mountain/Da Droben
      vom Berge   54:174
   Adeste Fideles/O Come All Ye Faithful,
      22:245, 54:318, 92:171, 148:266,
      241:148, 279:18, 283:50, *see also:* O
      Come All Ye Faithful
   Aguinaldo/"Mary," Said Saint Joseph
      140:28
   Ain't That a Rocking All Night   233:42
   Al Quebrar la Piñata/On Breaking the
      Piñata   295:79
   Alegría/Happily Singing   54:293
   All Hail to the Morning   140:82
   All My Heart This Night   54:59, 184:50
   All Poor Men and Humble   96:1, 244:96
   All-the-Year-Carol   189:78, *see also:*
      220:94
   Alle Jahre Wieder/As Each Happy Christ-
      mas   86:44, 279:70
   Almost Day   130:41
   Als Ich Bei Meinen Schafen Wacht/While
      By My Sheep I Watched at Night
      54:146, 241:136
   Although You Are Still Weak and Help-
      less/Quoique Soyez Petit Encore
      54:116
   Amid the Roses Mary Sits   209:59
   The Angel Gabriel   220:72, 241:42, *see
      also:* 209:33
   Angels and Shepherds   220:100, *see also:*
      54:236, 279:116
   Angels From Heaven   54:240
   Angels, From the Realms of Glory   45:21,
      54:49, 96:2, 148:28, 210:12, 241:144,
      264:118
   Angels O'er the Fields Were Singing/Les
      Anges Dan Nos Campagnes   54:96, *see
      also:* 241:102, 279:89
   Angels We Have Heard On High   22:234,
      92:144, 241:102, 264:120, 279:89,
      284:123
   Arre, Burriquito/Hurry Little Donkey
      295:75

   As Each Happy Christmas/Alle Jahre
      Wieder   86:44, 279:70
   As I Was Watching By My Sheep
      244:274
   As Joseph Was A-Walking   86:36, 220:68,
      241:46, 279:44
   As Lately We Watched/Die Hirten auf
      dem Felde   54:170
   As the Frightened Baby Jesus/Como Bus-
      ca el Tierno Infante   54:298
   As with Gladness Men of Old   54:48,
      210:13
   At the Crèche   140:18, *see also:* 54:282
   At the Door a Babe Is Knocking   209:9
   At the Gates of Heaven Above/Sus in
      Poarta Raiului   54:238
   At the Hour of Midnight/A la Media
      Noche   54:286
   Away in a Manger   45:19, 54:60, 65:89,
      86:35, 92:146, 96:3, 125:102, 140:85,
      190:50, 190:52, 210:15, 241:166,
      264:110, 279:54, 283:49, 284:23
   The Babe   54:308, *see also:* 100:154,
      279:106
   The Babe in Bethlehem's Manger
      220:54, *see also:* 241:28
   A Babe Is Born   209:46, 241:39
   Babe of Bethlehem   140:74, 190:37,
      233:37
   Baboushka   214
   Baby Born Today   190:142, 233:28, *see
      also:* 67:28, 140:56
   A Baby in the Cradle/Ein Kindlein in der
      Wiegen   54:178
   Baile de Nadal   89:162, *see also:* Fum,
      Fum, Fum
   Ballad of Jesus Christ/Ballade de Jesus
      Christ   54:114
   Ballade de Jesus Christ/Ballad of Jesus
      Christ   54:114
   Baloo, Lammy   54:56, 241:14, *see also:*
      125:64
   Baloo Loo, Lammy   125:64, *see also:*
      54:56, 241:14
   Balulalow/A Cradle Song   210:88
   Barn Jesus/Child Jesus   54:190
   Bed of Hay   67:64
   Behold a Branch Is Growing/Es Ist ein
      Ros Entsprungen   279:58, *see also:*
      54:166, 210:30, 241:84, 264:86
   Behold How Many Lights/Miren Cuantas
      Luces   216:52
   Behold That Star   54:78, 140:62, 140:110,
      244:1
   The Bell   67:88
   The Bellman's Song   184:10, *see also:*
      208:72, 210:68, 220:92
   Bells Over Bethlehem/Campana Sobre
      Campana   54:278

CHRISTMAS CAROLS—*Continued*

The Beloved 67:40

Berger, Secoue Ton Sommeil Profond/ Shepherd, Shake Off Your Drowsy Sleep 54:122

Beside Thy Cradle Here I Stand/Ich Steh an Deiner Krippe Hier 54:163, 210:16, 241:156

Bethlehem 220:60, *see also:* 210:39

The Birds 184:18, *see also:* Carol of the Birds

The Birthday of a King 241:204

Birthday Presents 245:121

Blessed Be That Maid Marie 54:41

The Blessings of Mary 190:61, 233:58, *see also:* Seven Joys of Mary

Blow the Trumpet and Bang the Drum 96:4

Boar's Head Carol 54:34, 210:63, 241:18, 264:96, 292:112

Bohemian Carol 262:103

Born Is He, Little Child Divine 209:10

Born Is Jesus, the Infant King/Il Est Né, le Divin Enfant 279:92

A Boy Is Born in Bethlehem/Puer Natus in Bethlehem 54:316, *see also:* 220:111, 279:12

The Boys' Carol/Personant Hodie 220:104

Break Forth, O Beauteous Heavenly Light/Brich an, du Schönes Morgenlicht 54:162, 210:18, 241:124

Brich an, du Schönes Morgenlicht/Break Forth, O Beauteous Heavenly Light 54:162, 241:124

Brightest and Best 54:88, *see also:* 140:78, 210:20, 233:36

Bring a Torch, Jeannette, Isabella 3, 54:128, 217:64, 241:98, 264:72, 279:94, *see also:* 22:242, 184:36, 217:50

Calm on the Listening Ear of Night 241:143

Campana Sobre Campana/Bells Over Bethlehem 54:278

The Candle 67:83

Canon of the Mimes 241:229

Cantemos/We Are Singing 54:296

Cantique de Noël/O Holy Night 54:107, *see also:* 241:197

Canzone d'i Zampognari/Carol of the Bagpipers 54:242, 241:100, *see also:* 279:100

Carol for East and West 209:61

Carol of the Bagpipers/Canzone d'i Zampognari 54:242, 241:100, 279:100

Carol of the Beasts 128:62, *see also:* 13, 54:24, 86:47, 138:unpaged

Carol of the Birds 54:124, 54:268, 128:60, 140:96, 183:22, 184:18, 209:119, 241:61, 264:94, 284:61, 292:126

Carol of the Children of Bethlehem/Lied der Kinder zu Bethlehem 279:84

Carol of the Flowers 241:66, 284:93

Carol of the Hay/Sliczna Panienka 54:216

Carol of the Nuns of Saint Mary's, Chester 279:16

Carol of the Seekers 244:28

Carol to a Child 280:unpaged

Caux Carol 210:90

Celebrons la Naissance 54:92, 279:21

Charles Ives's Carol 190:82, 190:84

Cherry Tree Carol 140:26, 232:182, 264:76, 284:55, *see also:* 190:70, 233:24

The Child 67:37

Child in the Manger 209:11

A Child Is Born in Bethlehem/Et Barn er Fodt I Betlehem 54:192

A Child Is Born in Bethlehem/Puer Natus in Bethlehem 279:12, *see also:* 54:316, 220:111

Child Jesus/Barn Jesus 54:190 *(Child Jesus in a manger lay)*

The Child Jesus 241:88, *see also:* 54:284, 197:117, 209:110

Child of God 190:88, 233:40, *see also:* 140:64

A Child This Day Is Born 210:11, 241:4

Children's Song of the Nativity 184:39, *see also:* 96:7, 209:82

A Chinese Christmas Cradle Song 209:68

Chiquirriquiten/O My Loveliest One 54:280

The Christ-Child Lay on Mary's Lap 184:47, 209:117, 244:64

Christ Is Born This Evening/Gdy Się Chrystus Rodzi 54:210, *see also:* 279:124

Christ the Lord Most Glorious 140:40, 140:118

Christ Was Born in Bethlehem 86:41, 157:65

Christ Was Born on Christmas Day 241:68

Christians, Awake 210:21, 241:114

Christmas Bells Ring Out Glad News 86:43

Christmas Comes Anew/Noël Nouvelet 54:118, *see also:* 220:78

Christmas Cradle Song 100:154, *see also:* 54:308, 279:106 *(A la rururu, little boy)*

Christmas Cradle Song 210:92 *(Still and dark the night)*

Christmas Eve Canon 241:223

Christmas Every Day 67:50

Christmas Is Here Again 89:170, 262:42, *see also:* 54:193, 241:168, 279:112
Christmas Mouse 282
The Christmas Nightingale/Die Weihnachtsnachtigall 279:62
Christmas Piece 209:70
Christmas Polka 262:42 *see also:* 54:193, 89:170, 241:168, 279:112
A Christmas Song 220:86 *(Winds through the olive trees)*
Christmas Song/Zu Weihnachten 279:66 *(I stand beside Thy cradle here)*
A Christmas Spiritual 209:48
Chtic, Aby Spal, Tak Zpívala/Sweet Mary Sings Her Babe to Sleep 54:234
Come All Ye Shepherds/Nesem vam Noviny 220:100, 279:116, *see also:* 54:236
Come, Hear the Wonderful Tidings 54:236, *see also:* 220:100, 279:116
Come, My Dear Old Lady/Ya Viene la Vieja 54:254
Come, Oh Come, Dear Children All 244:166
Come Running, You Shepherds/O Laufet Ihr Hirten 54:154
Como Busca el Tierno Infante/As the Frightened Baby Jesus 54:298
Corde Natus Ex Parentis/Of the Father's Love Begotten 54:314
Coventry Carol 22:252, 54:19, 220:114, 241:26, 264:116, 279:32, *see also:* 190:105, 210:46
Cowboy Carol 210:96
Cradle Hymn 65:89, 125:102, *see also:* Away in a Manger
Cradle Hymn 233:41, *see also:* Hush, My Babe *(Hush, my babe, lie still and slumber)*
Cradle Song 184:62, *see also:* Hush, My Babe *(Hush! my dear, lie still and slumber)*
Cradle Song 220:24, *see also:* Joseph, Dearest Joseph
A Cradle Song/Balulalow 210:88
Da Droben Vom Berge/Above, On the Mountain 54:174
Dance Carol 279:112, *see also:* 54:193, 89:170, 241:168, 262:42
Dans Cette Etable/In That Poor Stable 210:39, *see also:* 220:60
The Darkness Is Falling/Es Wird Scho Glei Dumpa 279:82, *see also:* 54:172
De Nederige Geboorte/The Simple Birth 54:182
De Rommelpot/The Rommelpot 89:140
De Tierra Lejana Venimos/Song of the Wise Men 54:288, *see also:* 140:22

Dear Nightingale, Awake/Lieb Nachtigall, Wach Auf 54:158, *see also:* 279:62
Deilig Er dem Himmel Blaa/Lovely Is the Dark Blue Sky 54:188
Dere's a Star in de Eas' on Christmas Morn 209:22, *see also:* Rise Up, Shepherd and Follow
Det Kimer Nu Til Julefest/The Happy Christmas Comes Once More 54:186
Die Hirten auf dem Felde/As Lately We Watched 54:170
Die Kinder an der Krippe 86:42, *see also:* 54:142, 241:162, 279:72
Die Könige/The Kings 241:215, *see also:* 210:121
Die Weihnachtsnachtigall/The Christmas Nightingale 279:62
Din Dan Don It's Christmas 51
Dormi, Dormi, O Bel Bambin 54:248, 209:30, 241:94
Dors, Ma Colombe 54:120, *see also:* 184:44
D'où Viens-tu, Bergère?/Whence Art Thou, My Maiden 54:133, *see also:* 279:96
Down Came an Angel 157:65, *see also:* 86:41
Down in Yon Forest 27:82, 190:58, 210:23
Du Gronne, Glitrende Tre, God-Dag/You Green and Glittering Tree, Good Day 54:198
Dziasiaj w Betlejem/O Come Rejoicing 54:206
Ehre Sei Gott/Glory to God 241:233
Eia, Eia 241:207
Ein Kindlein in der Wiegen/A Baby in the Cradle 54:178
El Cant dels Ocells 54:268, *see also:* Carol Of the Birds
El Desembre Congalat/The Icy December 54:266
El Mino Jesús/The Child Jesus 241:88, *see also:* 54:284, 209:110
El Noi de la Mare/The Son of Mary 54:260
El Rei Herodes/King Herod 54:264
El Rorro 54:308, 100:154, 279:106
El Santo Niño/The Holy Child 54:284, *see also:* 209:110, 241:88
En Belén Tocan a Fuego 54:276, 295:76, *see also:* 89:276
En el Portal a Belén 54:282, 140:18
En Nombre del Cielo/Pray Give Us Lodging 54:306
Entre le Boeuf et L'âne Gris 54:100, 241:82

CHRISTMAS CAROLS—*Continued*

Es Ist ein Ros Entsprungen   54:166, 210:30, 241:84, 279:58

Es Wird Scho Glei Dumpa/The Twilight is Falling   54:172, 279:82

Esta Sí Que Es Nochebuena/Yes! It is Christmas Eve   295:78

Et Barn er Fodt I Betlehem/A Child is Born in Bethlehem   54:192

Falade Ben Baixo/We'll Speak Very Softly   54:271

Farmer's Carol   210:101

A Fire Is Started in Bethlehem   54:276, *see also:* 89:276, 295:76

The First Courier   86:37

The First Good Joy That Mary Had   22:262, 54:14, 148:322, 210:65, 240:30, 241:193, *see also:* Seven Joys of Mary

The First Noel   65:100, 264:102, 279:25, *see also:* First Nowell

The First Nowell   22:256, 54:26, 92:150, 96:12, 148:92, 184:30, 210:66, 220:20, 241:6, 242:unpaged, 284:51, *see also:* 65:100, 264:102, 279:25

Foom, Foom, Foom!   241:80, *see also:* Fum, Fum Fum!

Fraternal   209:80

The Friendly Beasts   13, 54:24, 86:47, 138:unpaged, *see also:* 128:62

From Heaven Above to Earth I Come   54:161, 86:30, 161:96, *see also:* 241:150, 279:64, 280:115

From Heaven High/Vom Himmel Hoch   241:150, 279:64, *see also:* 54:161, 86:30, 161:96, 280:115

From Heaven High I Come to You   280:115, *see also:* 54:161, 86:30, 161:96, 241:150, 279:64

From Out the Forest a Cuckoo Flew/Zezulka z Lesa Vylítla   54:230

From Sky Above   262:52

From Starry Skies Descending/Tu Scendi dalle Stélle   279:98, *see also:* 54:244

From Starry Skies Thou Comest/Tu Scendi dalle Stélle   54:244, *see also:* 279:98

From the Eastern Mountains   241:130

Fum, Fum, Fum!   54:258, 125:121, 197:115, 241:80, 279:104, 295:84, *see also:* 89:162

Gather Around the Christmas Tree   54:68

Gdy Sie Chrystus Rodzi/Christ Is Born This Evening   54:210, 279:124

Gebet an den Heiligen Christ/Prayer to the Christ Jesus   241:174

Gently Sleep   125:20

Gesu Bambin L'e Nato/Jesus, the New-Born Baby   54:246

Gloria   54:181

Gloria in Excelsis Deo!   244:10

Glory to God/Ehre Sei Gott   241:233

Go Tell It on the Mountain   31:7, 54:84, 92:156, 140:58, 148:112, 190:79, 197:116, 233:29, 241:34, 242:unpaged 261:50

Go to Bethlehem   245:118

God Rest You Merry Gentlemen   22:260, 54:18, 92:152, 148:114, 184:16, 210:24, 220:18, 241:10, 279:28, 284:67

Going to Bethlehem/Vamos a Belén   54:303

Golden Mornings   184:48

Good Christian Men, Rejoice   22:240, 54:12, 184:40, 210:26, 284:127

Good King Wenceslas   22:246, 54:17, 65:90, 92:154, 148:118, 184:22, 210:27, 220:22, 241:16, 279:38, 284:79

A Greater King than They   155:24

Guava Berry Song   114:90

Hail, Mary, Full of Grace   220:56

Hajej, Nynej, Ježišku/Rocking Carol   54:226, 279:118

Happily Singing/Alegría   54:293

Happy Christmas Comes Once More/Det Kimer Nu Til Julefest   54:186

Hark! The Herald Angels Sing   22:264, 54:46, 65:96, 92:158, 148:148, 210:28, 241:158, 242:unpaged, 264:88, 279:42, 284:75, *see also:* 273:156

Hark to the Angels   220:82

Hasten Now, O Shepherds/Vamos, Pastorcitos   54:310

He Is Born, the Holy Child/Il Est Né   54:94, 220:46, *see also:* 279:92

He Smiles Within His Cradle   184:51, 210:29

He, Whom Joyous Shepherds Praised/Quem Pastores Laudavere   279:14, *see also:* 54:317, 220:58

Hear All the Angels Singing   245:125

Hear, O Shepherds/Oj Pastiri   241:70

Heard from Heaven Today   233:53

Heaven Bell Ring   190:112, 233:77

Heaven's Gate Has Opened   244:187, 245:116

Her Kommer Dine Arme Smaa/Thy Little Ones, Dear Lord, Are We   54:196

Here a Torch   184:36, *see also:* Bring a Torch, Jeanette, Isabella

Here Is the Little Door   210:103

Herod Dead/Mòrto Erode   279:102

The Holly and the Ivy   54:22, 184:20, 210:67, 220:34, 241:40, 264:71, 279:34, 284:43

The Holy Boy   209:105, 241:210

The Holy Child   54:284, 197:117, 209:110, *see also:* 241:88

The Holy Family   189:76

Holy Joseph and Mary the Maid/Sant Josep i la Mare de Deu   54:262

How Brightly Shines The Morning Star/ Wie Schön Leuchtet der Morgenstern 54:164, 241:132

How Far Is't to Bethlehem   96:7, 184:39, 209:82

How Shall I Fitly Meet Thee?/Wie Soll Ich Dich Empfangen?   241:152

The Huron Indian Carol   140:38, see also: 2, 54:76, 161:79

Hurry, Hurry to the Stable   209:12

Hurry, Little Donkey/Arre, Burriquito 295:75

Hush! My Dear, Lie Still and Slumber 184:62, 190:43, 241:116, see also: Hush, My Babe

I Am So Glad on Christmas Eve/Jeg Er Saa Glad Hver Julekveld   54:202

I Go to Bethlehem/Sel Bych Rád K Betlému   54:232,   241:184,   see also: 245:120

I Know a Rose Tree Springing   210:30, see also: 54:166, 241:84, 264:86, 279:58

I Sing of a Maiden   209:84

I Sing the Birth Was Born Tonight 209:14

I Wonder As I Wander   140:90, 183:10, 190:96, 209:15

Ich Steh an Deiner Krippe Hier/Beside Thy Cradle Here I Stand   54:163, 241:156, 279:66

The Icy December/El Desembre Congelat   54:266

Ihr Kinderlein Kommet   54:142, 86:42, 241:162, 279:72

Il Est Né, le Divin Enfant/He Is Born, the Holy Child   54:94, 220:46, 279:92

In a Manger   241:111

In Bethlehem So Lowly/Zu Bethlehem Geboren   54:144

In Bethlehem They Light a Fire   295:76, see also: 54:276, 89:276

In Bethlehem's Cradle   54:282, see also: 140:18

In Midnight's Silence/Wsrod Nocnej Ciszy   54:218

In That Poor Stable   210:39, see also: 220:60

In the Town   241:90

In the Valley   140:31, see also: 190:100

Infant Holy, Infant Lowly   220:36

Inkosi Jesus/My Sovereign Jesus   209:87

Irish Carol   241:48

It Came Upon the Midnight Clear   54:62, 65:90,   92:161,   140:102,   148:190, 190:131,   210:40,   210:41,   241:122, 264:84, 279:48, 284:83

Jeannette, Isabella   22:242, see also: Bring a Torch, Jeannette Isabella

Jeg Er Saa Glad Hver Julekveld/I Am So Glad on Christmas Eve   54:202

Jerusalem   Guide/Jerusalem   Rejoice 279:9

Jerusalem   Rejoice/Jerusalem   Guide 279:9

Jesus Borned in Bethlea   86:34, 140:16, 140:114, 190:102, 232:181, 233:48

Jesus Christ Is Born/Gdy Się Chrystus Rodzi   279:124, see also: 54:210

Jesus Christ Is Born Tonight   220:66

Jesus Christ the Apple Tree   190:93

Jesus Holy, Born So Lowly/W Zlobie Lezy 54:204

Jesus, Jesus, Rest Your Head   140:86, 183:28

Jesus, Redeemer of the World   279:10

Jesus the Christ Is Born   183:16

Jesus, the New-Born Baby/Gesu Bambin L'e Nato   54:246

Josef, Lieber Josef Mein   54:148, see also: 21:326

Joseph and Mary   190:70, 233:24, see also: 140:26, 232:182, 264:76, 284:55

Joseph, Dearest Joseph   21:326, 54:148, 210:42, see also: 184:42, 220:24

The Journey/La Jornada   54:300

Joy to the World   22:258, 54:28, 65:95, 92:166, 148:212, 241:146, 242:unpaged, 264:100, 279:56, 284:31

Juda's Carol   190:100, see also: 140:31

Jungfru Maria Till Betlehem Gick/Mary the Virgin to Bethlehem Went 279:111

King Herod/El Rei Herodes   54:264

King Jesus Hath a Garden   96:10, 210:44

The Kings/Die Könige   241:215, see also: 210:121

Kings of Orient   92:168, 184:34, see also: We Three Kings

Kling,   Glöckchen/Ring,   Little   Bells 54:140

Kolyada   128:55

Kommet, Ihr Hirten   54:326

La Jornada/The Journey   54:300

La Marche des Rois/The March of the Kings   54:126, 241:105

Las Posadas/Thou Art Well Content 54:256

Last Month O' the Year When Was Jesus Born   190:119

Le Sommeil de l'Enfant Jésus/The Sleep of the Infant Jesus   54:100, 241:62

Led By a Star   209:88

L'Enfant Jésus S'Endort/While Jesus Sleeps   241:108

CHRISTMAS CAROLS—*Continued*

Les Anges Dans Nos Campagnes/Angels O'er the Fields Were Singing 54:96, 241:102, 279:89

Lieb Nachtigall, Wach Auf/Dear Nightingale, Awake 54:158, 279:62

Lied der Kinder zu Bethlehem/Carol of the Children of Bethlehem 279:84

The Linden Tree 67:21

Lippai 54:168, 241:78

The Little Carol 209:113

A Little Child on the Earth Has Been Born 210:12

The Little Cradle Rocks Tonight 140:64, *see also:* 190:88, 233:40

Little Drummer Boy 115

Little Jesus Sleeps in the Hay 245:122

Little Lamb 162:50

The Little Path 67:75

Lo! A Light Is in the East 244:260

Lo, How a Rose E'er Blooming 54:166, 241:84, 264:86, *see also:* 210:30, 279:58

Look, a Star Shines 220:13

Look Away to Bethlehem 233:21

The Lord of the Dance 140:36

Los Reyes Oriente/Song of the Wise Men 140:22, *see also:* 54:288

Love Came Down at Christmas 210:46

Lovely Is the Dark Blue Sky/Deilig Er den Himmel Blaa 54:188

Lowly Bethlehem 277:109

Lulajze Jezuniu/Polish Lullaby 54:220, 241:74, 279:122

Lullay My Liking 209:89, 210:109

Lulle Lullay 190:105, *see also:* Coventry Carol

Lully, Lullay 241:26, *see also:* Coventry Carol

Lully, Lullay (Haydn) 241:222

Lully, Lully, Lu 284:119

The Man 67:42

The Manger 67:14

The March of the Kings/La Marche des Rois 54:126, 241:105

María Lavava/Mary Washed Linen 188:156

Maria auf dem Berge/Marie on the Mountain 241:86, 279:74

Maria Durch ein Dornwald Ging/Maria Walks Amid the Thorn 279:60, *see also:* 54:160, 241:96

Maria Durch ein Dornwald Ging/Maria Wandered Through a Wood 241:96, *see also:* 54:160, 279:60

Maria on the Mountain/Maria auf dem Berge 241:86, 279:74

Maria Walks Amid the Thorn/Maria Durch ein Dornwald Ging 279:60, *see also:* 54:160, 241:96

Maria Wandered Through a Wood/Maria Durch ein Dornwald Ging 241:96, *see also:* 54:160, 279:60

Mary Had a Baby 31:15, 54:83, 140:54, 190:73, 209:17, 232:180, 233:47

Mary on the Mountain 241:86, *see also:* 279:74

"Mary," Said Saint Joseph/Aguinaldo 140:28

Mary the Virgin to Bethlehem Went/Jungfru Maria Till Betlehem Gick 279:111

Mary Washed Linen/María Lavava 188:156, *see also:* 189:76

Mary, What You Going to Name That Pretty Little Baby 233:44, *see also:* 140:66, 140:69, 190:114, 190:134, 209:26

Mary's Little Boy 130:38

Mary's Lullaby 7:6 *(Tiny precious child)*

Mary's Lullaby 245:123 *(Little dove, little darling)*

Masters in This Hall 22:268, 54:50, 210:47, 241:36, 241:230

May Day Carol 208:72, *see also:* 184:10, 210:68, 220:92

Menyböl Ar Angyal/Angels From Heaven 54:240

Midnight, Sleeping Bethlehem 241:72

Minuit, Chrétians/O Holy Night 241:197, *see also:* 54:107

The Miracle 67:94

Miren Cuantas Luces/Behold How Many Lights 216:38

Mizerna Cicha/Only a Manger Bed 54:214

The Moon Shines Bright 210:68, 220:92, *see also:* 184:10, 208:72

Mòrto Erode/Herod Dead 279:102

My Sovereign Jesus/Inkosi Jesus 209:87

Myn Lyking 210:112

Nar Juldagsmorgon Glimmar/When Christmas Morn Is Dawning 54:194

Naranjas y Limas/Oranges and Lemons 295:82

Neighbor, What Has You So Excited?/Quoi, Ma Voisine, Es-tu Fachée? 54:104

Nesem Vam Noviny/Come All Ye Shepherds 279:116, *see also:* 54:236, 220:100

Nesem Vam Noviny/Come, Hear the Wonderful Tidings 54:236, *see also:* 220:100, 279:116

The New-Born Baby 233:34

A New Year Carol 209:56

Nne N'eku Nwa/O Mary, Dear Mother 209:95

No Room In the Inn 241:24

Noel 209:123

Noel! A New Noel! 54:118, 220:78

Noël des Ausels/Whence Comes This Rush of Wings Afar 54:124, see also: Carol of the Birds

Noël Nouvelet/Christmas Comes Anew 54:118

Noel Sing We 264:108

Noel-Time 209:92

Nova, Nova 220:50

Now It Is Christmastime/Nu Ar Det Jul Igen 241:168, see also: 54:195, 89:170, 262:42, 279:112

Nu Ar Det Jul Igen 54:193, 89:170, 241:168, 262:42, 279:112

Nuns in Frigid Cells 241:44

Of the Father's Love Begotten/Corde Natus Ex Parentis 54:314

O Babe in the Manger 155:26

O Bethlehem/Oi Betlehem 54:274

O Christmas, You Season of Childlike Delight/O Jul Med Din Glede 54:200

O Come All Ye Faithful/Adeste Fideles 22:244, 25:113, 45:20, 54:318, 66:94, 86:29, 92:171, 148:264, 210:48, 241:148, 262:162, 264:113, 279:18, 283:50, 284:35

O Come Away, Ye Shepherds/Quittez, Pasteurs 54:98

O Come, Little Children/Ihr Kinderlein, Kommet 54:142, 86:42, 241:162, 279:22, 284:25

O Come Rejoicing/Dziasiaj w Betlejem 54:206

O Du Fröhliche/O How Joyfully 54:136, 86:31

O Gwiazdo Betlejemska/O Star O'er Bethlehem Shining 54:208

O Holy Night 54:107, 92:173, 241:197, 264:79, 284:103

O How Joyfully/O Du Fröhliche 54:136, see also: 86:31

O Jerus'lem in the Morning 140:56, see also: 67:28, 190:142, 233:28

O Jesu Most Kind 209:19

O Jul Med Din Glede/O Christmas, You Season of Childlike Delight 54:200

O Laufet Ihr Hirten/Come Running, You Shepherds 54:154

O Leave Your Sheep 210:49

O Little One 184:52

O Little Town of Bethlehem 22:236, 45:18, 54:63, 65:98, 86:33, 92:177, 140:100, 148:268, 161:18, 184:24, 190:98, 210:52, 210:53, 210:114, 241:128, 242:unpaged, 264:106, 279:50, 284:27

Oh, Mary and the Baby, Sweet Lamb 190:116, 233:35

O Mary, Dear Mother/Nne N'eku Nwa 209:95

O Mortal Man, Remember Well 210:54

O My Loveliest One/Chiquirriquitin 54:280

O Po' Little Jesus 54:86, see also: 140:60, 158:354, 190:90, 233:52

O Publish the Glad Story/Celebrons la Naissance 279:21, see also: 54:92

O Sanctissima/O Thou Joyful Day 22:253, 241:120

O Sing a Song of Bethlehem 86:48

O Star O'er Bethlehem Shining/O Gwiazdo Betlejemska 54:208

O Thou Joyful Day 22:253, 241:120

Oi Betlehem/O Bethlehem 54:274

Oj Pastiri/Hear, O Shepherds 241:70

Old Provençal Christmas Song 209:125

The Old Shepherd 67:53

On a Winter Morning 86:40

On Breaking the Piñata/Al Quebrar la Piñata 295:79

On Christmas Night 54:40, see also: 210:56

On Christmas Night All Christians Sing 210:56, see also: 54:40

On That Christmas Day Morn 210:116

Once in Royal David's City 65:101, 86:32, 189:72, 210:55, 241:186, 243:unpaged, 284:111

One Star Above All Stars 244:146

Only a Manger Bed/Mizerna Cicha 54:214

Ons Is Geboren Een Kindekin/Today We Welcome a Tiny Child 54:184

Oranges and Lemons/Naranjas y Limas 295:82

Our Blessed Lady's Lullaby 220:44

The Ox and the Ass 67:34

Oxen and Sheep/Entre le Boeuf et L'Ane Gris 241:82, see also: 54:100

Pásli Ovce Valaši/Shepherds Watched Their Flocks by Night 241:179

Past Three A Clock 210:58

Pastoral Symphony from "Messiah" 210:145

Pastorale from the Christmas Concerto 210:141

Pastores a Belén/Shepherds In Bethlehem 54:290

Pat-A-Pan 54:112, 129:60, see also: 210:80, 220:90, 241:176, 262:50

Patapan 220:90, 241:176, see also: 54:112, 129:60, 210:80, 262:50

Personent Hodie/The Boys' Carol 220:104

Philippine Carol 209:96

Po' Lil Jesus 158:354, 233:52, see also: 54:86, 140:60, 156:90

CHRISTMAS CAROLS—*Continued*

Pochvalen Bud, Jezis Kristus/Praise to Jesus, Our Salvation 54:222

The Poet 67:45

Polish Lullaby/Lulajze Jezuniu 54:220, 241:74, *see also:* 279:122

A Polish Tune 220:85

Poor Little Jesus 190:90, 233:52, *see also:* 54:86, 140:60, 158:354

Poverty Carol 244:96, *see also:* 96:1

The Praise of Christmas 184:32

Praise to Jesus, Our Salvation/Pochvalen Bud, Jezis Kristus 54:222

Pray Give Us Lodging/En Nombre del Cielo 54:306

Pray God Bless 262:68

Prayer to the Child Jesus/Gebet and den Heiligen Christ 241:174

Prelude 67:1

Przybrezeli do Betleem Pasterze/Shepherds, Come A-Running 245:119, 279:120, *see also:* 54:212

Przybiezeli do Betlejem/Shepherds Came to Bethlehem 54:212, *see also:* 245:119, 279:120

Psallite Unigenito/Sing, O Sing! 279:23

Puer Natus 220:111, *see also:* 54:316, 279:12

Puer Natus in Bethlehem/A Child Is Born In Bethlehem 54:316, 220:111, 279:12

Pujdem Spolu Do Betlema/We Are Going to the Stable 54:224

Quelle Est Cette Odeur Agréable?/Whence Is That Goodly Fragrance? 54:102, 210:76

Quem Pastores Laudavere/He, Whom Joyus Shepherds Praised 54:317, 220:58, 279:14

Quittez, Pasteurs/O Come Away, Ye Shepherds 54:98

Quoi, Ma Voisine, Es-tu Fachée?/Neighbor, What Has You So Excited 54:104

Quoique Soyez Petit Encore/Although You Still Are Weak and Helpless 54:116

Rejoice All the Heavens 244:232

Rejoice and Be Merry 209:121

Ring, Little Bells/Kling, Glöckchen 54:140

Ring Out, Wild Bells 210:118

Rise Up, Shepherd, an' Foller 22:266, 190:55, 209:22, *see also:* Rise Up, Shepherd, and Follow

Rise Up, Shepherd, and Follow 54:80, 129:66, 140:49, 233:16, 241:54, *see also:* 22:266, 190:55, 209:22

Rockabye Jesus/Lulajze Jezuniu 279:122, *see also:* 54:220, 241:74

Rocking 68:45, 184:66, 220:28, 241:64, *see also:* 54:226, 210:45, 279:118

Rocking Carol/Hajej, Nynej, Ježišku 54:226, *see also:* Rocking

Rocking Song/Hajej, Nynej, Ježišku 279:118, *see also:* Rocking

The Rommelpot/De Rommelpot 89:140

The Roof above the Manger 67:9

The Rose Bush 67:18

St. Joseph's Carol 189:74

Saint Stephen and Herod 190:140

Saint Stephen Was Riding/Staffansvisa 279:114

Sans Day Carol 96:11

Sant Josep i la Mare de Deu/Holy Joseph and Mary the Maid 54:262

The Savior's Work 220:54, 241:28

The Season for Singing 140:95

See, Amid the Winter's Snow 210:60

Sel Bych Rád k Betlému/I Go to Bethlehem 54:232, 241:184

The Seven Joys of Mary 22:262, 54:14, 140:14, 140:116, 148:322, 210:65, 220:30, 241:193, 279:46, *see also:* 190:61, 233:58

Shelter Where Ox and Ass Are One 209:24

Shepherd, Lonely Shepherd 155:23

Shepherds Came to Bethlehem/Przybiezeli do Betlejem 54:212, *see also:* 245:119, 279:120

Shepherds Come A-Running 245:119, 279:120, *see also:* 54:212

Shepherds' Cradle Song/Wiegenlied Der Hirten 54:156

The Shepherds' Farewell to the Holy Family 210:126

Shepherds in Bethlehem/Pastores a Belén 54:290

Shepherds in Judea 140:92, 190:108, 233:32

Shepherds Leave the Hillside 86:39

Shepherds Rejoice 190:47, 233:30

Shepherds! Shake Off Your Drowsy Sleep 54:122, 220:88, 284:59

The Shepherd's Song 67:80

Shepherds, Up!/Hirten, auf um Mitternacht! 279:80

Shepherds Watched Their Flocks By Night/Pásli Ovce Valaši 241:179

The Shepherds Went Their Hasty Way 220:52

Shiao Bao-Bao/A Chinese Christmas Cradle Song 209:68

Shout the Glad Tidings 241:140

Silent Night   22:267, 54:176, 65:97, 86:45, 92:181, 148:332, 148:333, 161:61, 184:26,   187,   210:61,   241:58, 242:unpaged, 264:90, 279:86, 282, 283:48, 284:71

The Simple Birth/De Nederige Geboorte 54:182

Sing Hallelu   233:46

Sing Lullaby! Lullaby Baby   209:25

Sing, O Sing!/Psallite Unigenito   279:23

Sing We Christmas   209:61

Sing We the Virgin Mary   140:20, 140:108

Sinhalese Carol/Ave Dutek Kalum Hela Hela   209:98

Sir Donkey   292:31

Sister Mary Had But One Child   140:66, 190:134, 209:26, see also: 140:69, 190:114, 233:44

Sleep, Little Dove   54:120, 184:44

Sleep, My Darling/Dormi, Dormi, O Bel Bambin   209:30, see also: 54:248, 241:94

Sleep, My Little Jesus   241:182

Sleep, My Savior, Sleep   220:107, 241:194

The Sleep of the Infant Jesus/Le Sommeil de l'Enfant Jésus   54:100, 241:82

Sleep, O Holy Child of Mine/Dormi, Dor- mi, O Bel Bambin   241:94, see also: 54:248, 209:30

Sleep, O Sleep, My Lovely Child/Dormi, Dormi, O Bel Bambin   54:248, see also: 209:30, 241:94

Sleep, Sweet Babe   125:132, see also: 209:124

Sliczna Panienka/Carol of the Hay 54:216

Slysèli Jsme V Betlemĕ/We Have Heard in Bethlehem   54:228

The Snow Lay on the Ground   54:54

The Son of Mary/El Noi de la Mare 54:260

Song for a New Baby   244:290

Song of the Crib   184:42, see also: Joseph, Dearest Joseph

The Song of the Three Wise Men   241:66, 284:93

The Song of the Wise Men/De Tierra Lejana Venimos   54:288, see also: 140:22

Song of the Wise Men/Los Reyes Oriente 140:22, see also: 54:288

Songs of Praise the Angels Sang   65:93

The Spider in the Corner   67:71

A Spotless Rose   210:82

The Stable   67:4

Staffan   238

Staffansvisa/Saint Stephen Was Riding 279:114

Star in the East   140:78, 233:36, see also: 54:88, 210:20

Star of Bethlehem   140:119, see also: The Star of Bethlehem

The Star of Bethlehem   197:114 (The night the Child was born)

Star of the East   54:88, see also: 140:78, 210:20, 233:36

The Stars and the Moon   67:26

Stars of Glory   209:32

Still, Still, Still   54:180

Stille Nacht/Silent Night   54:176, 86:45, 148:332, 241:58, 279:86, 282, 283:48

Stilly Night, Starry and Bright   125:76

Suo-Gan   220:80

Sus In Poarta Raiului/At the Gates of Heaven Above   54:238

Susani   54:152

Sussex Carol   54:40, see also: 210:56

Sussex Mummers' Carol   210:54

Sweet Mary Sings Her Babe to Sleep/ Chtic, Aby, Spal, Tak Zpívala   54:234

Sweet Was the Song the Virgin Sang 210:62

There Is No Rose   85:237, 220:48

There Was A Donkey Standing By 197:119

There's a Song in the Air   54:61, 148:384

The Thirteen Days of Yule   95

This Endris Night   54:16

Thou Art Well Content/Las Posadas 54:256

Thou Must Leave Thy Lowly Dwelling 210:126

The Three Kings   210:121, see also: 241:215 (Three kings from Persian lands afar)

Three Kings   245:124 (Three kings traveled long from lands far away)

Three Kings of Orient   190:75, see also: We Three Kings

Thy Little Ones, Dear Lord, Are We/Her Kommer Dine Arme Smaa   54:196

To Bethlehem I Would Go   54:232, 241:184, 245:120

To the Town of Bethlehem   220:112

Today We Welcome a Tiny Child/Ons Is Geboren Een Kindekin   54:184

Tomorrow Shall Be My Dancing Day 220:94, see also: 189:78

Touro-Louro-Louro   54:130

Tu Scendi Dalle Stélle/From Starry Skies Descending   54:244, 279:98

'Twas in the Moon of Winter Time   2, 54:76, 161:79, see also: 140:38

The Twilight Is Falling/Es Wird Scho Glei Dumpa   48:189, 279:82

INDEX TO CHILDREN'S SONGS

CHRISTMAS CAROLS—*Continued*

Un Flambeau, Jeannette, Isabelle 217:50

Unto Us a Boy Is Born 210:71, 220:74

Unto Us a Boy Was Born 241:60

Vamos a Belén/Going to Bethlehem 54:303

Vamos, Pastorcitos/Hasten Now, O Shepherds 54:310

Velkomin Vertu/We Welcome Thee Tonight 209:36

The Virgin Mary 274:14

The Virgin Mary Had a Baby Boy 209:34

Virgin Mary, Meek and Mild 190:126

A Virgin Most Pure 190:34, 210:14, 220:38, 220:40, 233:26, *see also:* 54:42, 140:88

A Virgin Unspotted 54:42, 140:88, *see also:* A Virgin Most Pure

The Virgin's Cradle Hymn 210:124, *see also:* 125:132

The Virgin's Slumber Song 209:59

Vom Himmel Hoch/From Heaven High 54:152, 241:150, 279:64

W Zlobie Lezy/Jesus Holy, Born So Lowly 54:204

Wasn't That a Mighty Day 140:53, 190:145, 233:49

Watts's Cradle Song 190:43, 190:45, *see also:* Hush My Babe

We Are Going to the Stable/Pujdem Spolu Do Betlema 54:224

We Are Singing/Cantemos 54:296

We Have Heard in Bethlehem/Slysèli Jsme V Betlemĕ 54:228

We Sing in Celebration/Celebrons la Naissance 54:92, *see also:* 279:21

We Three Kings 21:169, 54:66, 65:99, 86:46, 96:13, 140:98, 148:408, 241:188, 264:124, 279:52, 284:87, *see also:* 92:168, 184:34, 190:75

We Welcome Thee Tonight/Velkomin Vertu 209:36

We Would See Jesus 86:49

Weihnachtslied/Silent Night 279:86, *see also:* Silent Night

We'll Speak Very Softly/Falade Ben Baixo 54:271

Wer Klopfet An?/Who's Knocking There? 279:77

We've Been Told a Joyful Thing 86:36

What Child Is This? 21:238, 54:30, 92:188, 125:46, 148:412, 241:50, 242:unpaged, 261:52, 264:123, 279:40, 284:99

What Is This Fragrance? 54:102, 220:32, *see also:* 210:76

What Sweeter Music 241:20

What You Gonna Call Yo' Pretty Little Baby? 140:69, 190:114, *see also:* 140:66, 190:134, 209:26, 233:44

When Christ Was Born of Mary Free 54:20, 209:45, 210:134

When Christmas Morn Is Dawning/Nar Juldagsmorgon Glimmar 54:194

Whence Art Thou, My Maiden?/ D'où Viens-tu, Bergère? 54:133, *see also:* 279:96

Whence Comes This Rush of Wings 209:119, 241:62, 284:61, *see also:* Carol of the Birds

Whence Is That Goodly Fragrance?/ Quelle Est Celle Odeur Agréable? 54:102, 210:76, *see also:* 220:32

Whence, O Shepherd Maiden?/D'où Viens-tu, Bergère? 279:96, *see also:* 54:133

Where Have You Been Walking, Shepherdess? 262:170

While By My Sheep I Watch at Night/Als Ich Bei Meinen Schafen Wacht 54:146, 241:136

While Jesus Sleeps/L'Enfant Jésus S'endort 241:107

While Shepherds Watched Their Flocks by Night 54:31, 134:105, 140:80, 184:28, 210:79, 241:154, 264:104, 284:95

Whom of Old the Shepherds Praised/ Quem Pastores Laudavere 54:317, 279:14

Who's Knocking There?/Wer Klopfet An? 279:77

Wie Schön Leuchtet der Morgenstern/ How Brightly Shines the Morning Star 54:164, 241:132

Wie Soll Ich Dich Empfangen?/How Shall I Fitly Meet Thee? 241:152

Wiegenlied Der Hirten/Shepherds' Cradle Song 54:156

The Winter Season 27:250

The Wisemen 67:57

The Wisp of Straw 67:67

Within a Humble Stable 220:108

Workers' Carol 210:139

The World's Desire 184:47, 209:117, 244:64

Wsrod Nocnej Ciszy/In Midnight's Silence 54:218

Ya Viene la Vieja/Come, My Dear Old Lady 54:254

Yes! It Is Christmas Eve/Esta Sí Que Es Nochebuena 295:78

You Green and Glittering Tree, Good Day/Du Gronne, Glitrende Tre, God-Dag 54:198

Yuletide Is Here Again 54:193, 279:112, *see also:* 89:170, 241:168, 262:42

Zezulka Z Lesa Vylítla/From Out the Forest a Cuckoo Flew 54:230

Zu Bethlehem Geboren/In Bethlehem So Lowly 54:144

Zu Weihnachten/Christmas Song 279:66

CHRISTMAS SONGS: *see also* CHRISTMAS CAROLS

Al Quebrar la Piñata/On Breaking the Piñata 295:79

All Poor Men and Humble 96:1, 244:96

Almost Day 130:41

Am Weihnachtsbaum die Lichter Brennen/Christmas Tree With Its Candles Gleaming 54:150

Behold How Many Lights/Miren Cuantas Luces 216:52

Bird's Christmas Feast 207:55

Busy Christmas Time 207:47

Children, Go Where I Send Thee, 54:82, 132:unpaged, 140:46, 190:68, *see also:* 213:88, 23:69

Christmas 207:58

Christmas Bells 43:6

Christmas Cookies 207:48

Christmas Day 220:64, *see also:* 138:unpaged, 197:121

Christmas Day in the Morning 233:79, *see also:* I Saw Three Ships

Christmas Eve 65:92 *(Watching in the meadows)*

Christmas Eve 166:76 *(Candles are gleaming)*

Christmas in the Air 207:49

Christmas Is Coming 27:248, 68:8, 128:54, 178:23, 210:94, 241:225, 293:76 *(Christmas is coming, the goose is getting fat)*

Christmas Is Coming 162:49 *(Christmas is coming, Christmas is coming)*

A Christmas Lullaby 207:50

Christmas Shoes and Stockings 207:54

The Christmas Tree 241:164, *see also:* O Tannenbaum

Christmas Tree 162:52 *(Christmas tree, Christmas tree, beautiful sparkling Christmas tree)*

The Christmas Tree With Its Candles Gleaming/Am Weihnachtsbaum die Lichter Brennen 54:150

Cold Is the Morning 241:63

Come All You Worthy Gentlemen 210:22

Come Bring With a Noise 112:42

Dame Get Up 17:123, 129:52, 138:unpaged, 188:150

A Day of Joy and Feasting 241:8

De Rommelpot/The Rommelpot 89:140

Deck the Halls 22:254, 54:53, 92:148, 148:62, 220:102, 241:2, 262:165, 264:98, 279:30, 284:39

Ding-a-Ling-a-Ling 162:52

Ding Dong Merrily on High 96:5, 210:22

Esta Sí Que Es Nochebuena/Yes! It Is Christmas Eve 295:78

Everywhere, Everywhere, Christmas Tonight 54:64

Gloucestershire Wassail 54:32, 241:22, *see also:* 89:130, 184:12, 210:74, 220:96

Happy Holiday 97:unpaged

Here We Come A-Caroling 264:82, *see also:* Wassail Song

Here We Come A-Wassailing 96:6, 128:66, 148:154, 209:12, 220:62, 284:47, *see also:* Wassail Song

Hold, Men, Hold! 241:178

I Heard the Bells on Christmas Day 54:58, 148:172, 190:86, 241:126

I Saw Three Ships 17:52, 54:52, 92:160, 96:8, 129:58, 138, 140:25, 148:180, 184:15, 189:128, 210:31, 241:12, 262:166, 264:93, 284:91, *see also:* 188:168, 190:128, 233:79

I'll Play Something for You 27:252

I'm a Fairy Doll on the Christmas Tree 165:54

In the Bleak Mid-Winter 210:108

An Invitation 207:51

Jingle Bells 17:63, 54:70, 92:163, 127:220, 148:200, 241:171, 264:114, 283:64

Jolly Old Saint Nicholas 54:74, 197:122

King Herod and the Cock 96:9

Little Bitty Baby 193:88, 233:69, *see also:* 54:82, 132:unpaged, 140:46, 190:68

Little Jack Horner 17:111, 175:75, 188:178, 283:16

Longfellow's Carol 54:58, 148:172, 190:86, 241:126

Mama Bake the Johnny Cake, Christmas Comin' 130:42

Merry Christmas 241:232 *(Merry Christmas, ev'ryone!)*

A Merry Christmas 227:32, *see also:* We Wish You a Merry Christmas

Merry, Merry Christmas 66:142

Miren Cuantas Luces/Behold How Many Lights 216:38

Mummers' Song 220:116

Naranjas y Limas/Oranges and Lemons 295:82

New Toys 207:56

O Christmas Tree 54:138, 92:179, 129:51, 148:262, 197:118, 241:164, 279:68, *see also:* 21:196

CHRISTMAS SONGS—*Continued*

O Tannenbaum 21:196, 54:138, 92:179, 129:51, 148:263, 197:118, 241:164, 279:68

On Breaking the Piñata/Al Quebrar la Piñata 295:79

On Christmas Day in the Morning 138:unpaged, 197:121, *see also:* 220:64

On the Corner 241:228

Oranges and Lemons/Naranjas y Limas 295:82

Ring the Christmas Bells 167:54

The Rommelpot/De Rommelpot 89:140

Rudolph the Red-Nosed Reindeer 127:232

Santa Claus 41:4 *(Santa Claus will soon be here)*

Santa Claus 191:80 *(O, clap, clap the hands)*

Santa's Coming 26:43

The Seven Joys of Christmas 241:192

Sunny Bank 190:128, *see also:* I Saw Three Ships

Symphony from the Christmas Oratorio 210:147

The Three Ships 241:52

The Toy Shop 207:53

The Twelve Days of Christmas 22:248, 30, 50, 54:36, 87:91, 92:183, 113, 121, 148:400, 190:148, 197:120, 210:64, 233:72, 241:30, 264:66, 287, 290:26, 292:160

Up on the Housetop 54:72

Wassail 89:130, *see also:* Wassail, Wassail All Over the Town

Wassail Song 22:270, 27:6, 54:35, 92:186, 96:6, 128:66, 148:154, 184:8, 189:130, 197:8, 209:12, 220:42, 262:112, 279:36, 284:47, *see also:* 264:82

Wassail Wassail All Over the Town 184:12, 210:74, 220:96, *see also:* 54:32, 89:130, 241:22

Watchman, Tell Us of the Night 241:138

We Got a Lot for Christmas! 241:221

We Wish You a Merry Christmas 27:254, 54:10, 128:57, 148:57, 148:410, 209:37, 220:26, 241:220, 264:74, *see also:* 227:32

Will I Get A Christmas Present? 241:226

Winter Holiday 162:47

Yes! It Is Christmas Eve/Esta Sí Que Es Nochebuena 295:78

CIRCLE GAMES

Circle Singing Games 177:75

Come My Love 126:91

Comin' Round the Mountain One By One 178:40

Love Somebody, Yes I Do 162:53, 226:140

Ring-A-Ring o Roses 175:41, 188:108, 172:24, 227:23, *see also:* Ring Around a Rosy

Ring Around a Rosy 17:139, 63:11, 277:19, 283:31, 291:63, *see also:* 100:32, 175:41, 188:108, 189:24, 227:23

Ring Around the Rosie 100:32, *see also:* Ring Around a Rosy

Ring Around the Rosy 277:19, *see also:* Ring Around a Rosy

Ringel, Ringel 100:33, 168:95

CIRCULAR SONGS

John Jacob Jingleheimer Jones 62:67, *see also:* 25:37, 26:14, 253:106, 289:125

John Jacob Jingleheimer Schmidt 25:37, 26:14, 253:106, 289:125, *see also:* 62:67

Michael Finnegan 25:41, 36:80, 62:67, 197:30, 289:138

My Father Gave Me 62:69

The Ragman and the Bagman 62:68

Sandy's Mill 62:68, 262:32

CIRCUSES: *see also* CLOWNS; names of circus animals, e.g., ELEPHANTS

Casey Junior 275:26, 276:8

The Circus 207:112

The Circus Comes to Town 26:71

The Circus Seal 207:111

The Funniest Clown 207:109

Here Comes the Circus 119:102

The Man on the Flying Trapeze 21:191, 170:87, 198, 205:167

Si Hubbard 226:350

Trapeze Artists 207:108

CITIES AND TOWNS

The City 91:22

The City Rat and the Country Rat 17:96

City Time 91:28

Even in the City 261:44

A Little Town 91:21

CIVIL RIGHTS: *see also* FREEDOM; PROTESTS

Free at Last 31:21, 157:139

Goodbye, Old Glory 73:295

Lift Every Voice and Sing 108

We Are Marching On to Victory 64:165

We Can Overcome 197:12, *see also:* 64:33, 72:79

We Shall Overcome 72:79, *see also:* 64:33, 197:12

We Will Overcome 64:33, *see also:* 72:79, 197:12

CIVIL WAR (U.S., 1861-1865): *see also* SLAVERY; names of persons, e.g., LINCOLN, ABRAHAM

Abraham's Daughter 27:17, 73:102

The Alabama 73:186

The Alabama and Kearsarge 73:189

All Quiet Along the Potomac Tonight 73:197, 157:132

The Army Bean 73:168, *see also:* 99:47

Battle Cry of Freedom 73:36, 157:122, 160:56

Battle Cry of Freedom (southern version) 73:38

Battle Hymn of the Republic 21:145, 22:220, 25:94, 26:89, 64:172, 71:10, 72:30, 73:5, 99:53, 127:132, 138:34, 157:126, 160:64, 277:57

Beauregard 73:86

Bonnie Blue Flag 21:142, 73:16, 127:141, 157:124

The Bonnie Blue Flag with the Stripes and Stars 73:19

Boys, Keep Your Powder Dry 73:148

The Bright Sunny South 35:18

Brother, Tell Me of the Battle 73:280

Call'em Names, Jeff 73:53

Come in Out of the Draft 73:136

Corporal Schnapps 73:115

The "Cumberland" Crew 35:20, *see also:* 73:183

The *Cumberland's* Crew 73:183, *see also:* 35:20

Darling Nelly Gray 21:132, 126:59

Dixie 12:192, 25:101, 26:15, 99:53, 127:112, 157:120, 160:42, *see also:* 73:8

Dixie Land 73:8, *see also:* Dixie

Dixie, the Land of King Cotton 73:20

The Drummer Boy of Shiloh 73:200

Eating Goober Peas 99:48, *see also:* 27:132, 73:166, 157:128, 277:85

Ellsworth Avengers 73:180

Farewell Father, Friend and Guardian 73:72

The Flag of Columbia 73:12

Foes and Friends 73:264

For Bales 73:192

God Bless the Old Sixth Corps 73:176

God Save the South 73:30

Goober Peas 25:132, 73:166, 157:128, 277:85, *see also:* 99:48

Goodbye, Old Glory 73:295

Grafted into the Army 71:133

Hard Crackers Come Again No More 73:146

Here's Your Mule 73:160

He's Gone to the Arms of Abraham 73:126

Hold the Fort 73:214, 230:20

How Are You, Conscript 73:139

I Goes to Fight Mit Sigel 73:118

The Invalid Corps 73:142

Jeff Davis' Dream 73:66

John Brown's Body 22:222, 64:170, 73:7, 158:120, 230:62, 277:57

Johnny, Git Your Gun 157:45

Johnny Has Gone For a Soldier 22:69, 134:94, 157:24, 158:117, 240:87, 262:25, 273:84, *see also:* 73:104

Johnny Is Gone For a Soldier 73:104, *see also:* Johnny Has Gone for a Soldier

Jubilo 27:134

Just Before the Battle, Mother 21:153

Kingdom Coming 73:93

A Life on the Vicksburg Bluff 73:211

Lincoln and Liberty 27:14, 157:51, 226:167

Little Major 73:194

Lorena 73:231

Marching Along 27:146

Marching Through Georgia 73:223, 157:130

Maryland, My Maryland (a northern reply) 73:24

May God Save the Union 73:28

Melt the Bells 73:42

Mother Would Comfort Me 73:256

Never Forget the Dear Ones 73:238

O, I'm a Good Old Rebel 73:88

Our Comrade Has Fallen 73:206

Poor Kitty Popcorn 226:431

Pray, Maiden, Pray 73:262

The Prisoner's Hope 73:172, *see also:* 21:147

Riding a Raid 73:90

Sherman the Brave 73:75

Shoo, Fly Don't Bother Me 21:159, 46:208, 70:24, 126:85, 129:108, 178:20, 292:198

Short Rations to the Corn-Fed Army of Tennessee 73:163

Sister Carrie or the Compromise Song 73:60

The Soldiers' Life 27:130

Somebody's Darling 73:228

Song of Dixie 69:40

Song of the Six Hundred Thousand 73:130

The Songs We Sang Upon the Old Camp Ground 73:288

The Southern Girl 73:248

The Southern Soldier Boy 73:252

Stonewall Jackson's Way 73:84

Stonewall's Requiem 73:203

Strike For the South 73:32

The Sword of Robert E. Lee 73:78

Take Your Gun and Go, John 73:112

Tell Me, Is My Father Coming Home? 73:282

Tenting On the Old Camp Ground 73:152, 197:60, *see also:* 21:150, 127:157

Tenting Tonight 21:150, *see also:* 73:152, 127:157, 197:60

There Was an Old Soldier 226:432

CIVIL WAR—*Continued*
Think of Your Head in the Morning 73:156
To Canaan 73:130
Tramp! Tramp! Tramp! 21:147, 73:172, 197:62
Treasury Rats 73:68
'Twas At the Siege of Vicksburg 73:208
Uncle Sam, What Ails You? 73:62
The Union Wagon Couldn't Be Split 73:46
The Upidee Song 73:154
The Vacant Chair 73:286
Virginia Marseillaise 73:39
Wait For the Wagon—A Northern Parody 73:46
Wait For the Wagon—A Southern Parody 73:46, 73:48
Wake Nicodemus 21:160, 73:96
We Are Coming, Father Abra'am 73:120
We Are Marching on to Richmond 73:220
We Were Comrades Together in the Days of War 73:274
Wearing of the Grey 73:292
Weeping, Sad and Lonely 73:267
We'll Fight for Uncle Abe 73:123
We're Tenting Tonight 127:157, *see also:* 21:150, 73:152, 197:60
We've Drunk From the Same Canteen 73:276
What's the Matter? 73:56
When Johnny Comes Marching Home 22:196, 27:228, 66:82, 73:284, 117:unpaged, 128:92, 148:414, 157:134, 197:61, 205:251
When Sherman Marched Down the Sea 73:216
When the Cruel War Is Over 73:267
When the Cruel War Is Over—Answer 73:270
When Upon the Field of Glory 73:270
Where Are You Going, Abe Lincoln? 73:64
Who Will Care for Mother Now? 73:259
Write a Letter to My Mother 73:242
Year of Jubilo 73:93
The Yellow Rose of Texas 73:245, 205:392
You Are Going to the Wars, Willie Boy! 73:106
The Young Volunteer 73:109
CLAMS
Clams 239:88
A Real Nice Clambake 218:106
CLAPPING GAMES
Bingo 26:22, 39:52, 46:201, 63:91, 75:13, 126:93, 129:101, 147:16, 253:94, 289:54, *see also:* 17:131

Clap Singing Game 177:76
Clap Your Hands 232:86, 289:160 (*Clap, clap, clap your hands*)
Clap Your Hands 26:27 (*Clap your hands! Clap your hands!*)
Clapping Game 68:9
Come All You Playmates 63:95
Down By the Bay 63:98
Green Sally Up 109:26
Hambone 109:36, 274:36
Head and Shoulder, Baby 109:33
I Am a Pretty Little Dutch Girl 63:88
Jack, Can I Ride 234:76
Johnny Had a Little Dog 17:131, *see also:* Bingo
Juba 109:40, 232:91
Miss Mary Mack 107:62, 290:57
Momma, Momma, Have You Heard? 63:90
Nobody Likes Me 63:94, 290:190
Old Lady Mac 141:80
One Saw, Two Saw 109:30
One-ry, Two-ry 109:28
Pat-A-Cake 17:127, 75:60, 175:80, 188:162
Pease Porridge Hot 17:74, 162:89, 285:90, 291:58, *see also:* 175:90
Pease Pudding Hot 175:90, *see also:* 17:74, 162:89, 285:90, 291:58
Sandy Dow 63:91
Shimmy, Shimmy, Coke-Ca-Pop! 141:78
Three Jolly Fishermen 63:98
Tom, Tom Greedy-Gut 109:15
Who Stole My Chickens and My Hens? 63:93
CLEANLINESS: *see also* GROOMING
The Bathroom 149:22
Clean Hands 11:12
Cleano 130:16
The Cranky Soap 91:46
Mother's Washing 165:34
Over and Under 296:36
Pretty and Shiny-O 130:22
CLOCKS AND WATCHES: *see also* TELLING TIME
The Clock 288:22
The Clock Song 291:36
Hickory Dickory Dock 17:113, 75:32, 135:117, 175:68, 188:172, 283:10, 285:25, 292:196
The Hours of the Clock/Las Horas del Reloj 295:34
Las Horas del Reloj/The Hours of the Clock 295:34
Tick Tock 11:16
What Does the Clock in the Hall Say? 1:38
CLOSING SONGS
Girl Scout Goodbye Round 71:103

Good Night, Cub Scouts 26:91
Good Night, Cubbers 26:91
Good-Night Song 68:48
Now Comes the Hour 262:90
Scout Vesper 25:125, 26:94
Scout Vesper Song 25:125, 26:94
Scout's Good-Night Song 25:61, 26:93
Shalom Chaverim 55:255, 293:110
Softly Now the Light of Day 125:83
The Sun Be Warm 55:259
Taps 25:126, 26:92, 69:10, 71:12, 72:53, 148:370, 197:62, 277:45
CLOTHING AND DRESS: see also HATS; SHOES
Bafti Hindi 89:206, 114:52
Bubbles and Bubbles 114:10
The Chicken/El Pollo 295:15
Down the Avenue 288:8
Dressing 91:5
El Pollo/The Chicken 295:15
Growing Up 172:126, 173:17
Hanging Out the Linen Clothes 226:117, 232:137, see also: 71:42, 134:14, 176:30, 205:72
Happiness 172:117, 173:3
I Have a Little Doll/Yo Tengo una Muñeca 194:28
Lazy John 135:38, 213:16, 254:112
The Living Room 149:18
Mary Wore a Red Dress 129:12, see also: 130:15, 232:130
Mary Wore Her Red Dress 232:130, see also: 129:12, 130:15
Mi Pollera/My Hoopskirt 216:2
My Hoopskirt/Mi Pollera 216:41
My New Moccasins 207:39
My New Snowsuit 207:63
The New Dress 114:32
Oh, Oh, the Sunshine 232:64
Phoebe in Her Petticoat 135:57
Pink Pajamas 25:41
This Lady She Wears a Dark Green Shawl 232:133
Yo Tengo una Muñeca/I Have a Little Doll 194:28
CLOUDS: see also FOG
Clouds 261:38
The Clouds at Kona/Kona Kai Opua 87:27
How Sweet to Be a Cloud 172:21, 174:7
Kona Kai Opua/The Clouds at Kona 87:27
October's Clouds 207:31
White Sheep 245:79
CLOWNS: see also CIRCUSES
The Funniest Clown 207:109
Funny Clown 162:70
A Funny, Silly Clown 288:6
I Want to Be a Clown 167:12

COACHES AND COACHMEN: see STAGECOACHES
COAL: see MINERS AND MINING
COBBLERS: see SHOEMAKERS
COCKLES
Cockles and Mussels 22:22, 262:89
COCKROACHES
The Cockroach 21:110, 197:38, 226:291
La Cucaracha 21:110, 197:38, 226:291
COCOONS: see BUTTERFLIES; CATERPILLARS (LARVAE)
COINS: see MONEY
COLOMBIA
*Bundle San Antonio 169:16
*El Lobo/The Wolf 70:27
*El Zancudo/The Mosquito 216:28
*For a Tender Kiss/Por un Beso de Tu Boca 89:94
*Hasten Now, O Shepherds/Vamos, Pastorcitos 54:310
*Mi Compadre Mona/My Godfather Monkey 216:32
*The Mosquito/El Zancudo 216:48
*My Godfather Monkey/Mi Compadre Mono 216:50
*Por un Beso de Tu Boca/For a Tender Kiss 89:94
*Vamos, Pastorcitos/Hasten Now, O Shepherds 54:310
*The Wolf/El Lobo 70:27
Yesterday Morning 114:72
COLONIAL PERIOD IN AMERICA: see also PILGRIMS; THANKSGIVING
Old Colony Times 21:252, 157:30
COLOR
Grün, Grün, Grün 262:123
Jennie Jenkins 20:40, 69:20, 75:42, 129:22, 158:54, 257, 262:37, see also: 135:62, 291:28
Jenny Jenkins 291:28, see also: Jennie Jenkins
Mary Was a Red Bird 130:15, see also: 129:12, 232:130
Mary Wore a Red Dress 129:12, see also: 130:15, 232:130
Mary Wore Her Red Dress 232:130, see also: 129:12, 130:15
Miss Mary Mack 107:62, 290:57
One, Two, Three, and Around We Go! 204:27
Open the Window 212:18
This Lady She Wears a Dark Green Shawl 232:133
Will You Wear Red? 135:62, see also: Jennie Jenkins
COLTS: see HORSES
COLUMBUS DAY: see COLUMBUS, CHRISTOPHER

COLUMBUS, CHRISTOPHER
Christopher Columbo 27:200, *see also:*
197:88
He Knew the Earth Was Round-o
197:88, *see also:* 27:200
It's All Wrong 197:89
Sailing on the Sea 27:202
COMMUNICATION: *see* POSTAL SERVICE;
TELEPHONES
COMMUNITY HELPERS: *see also* OCCU-
PATIONS; names of specific helpers, e.g.,
MILKMEN
Big Mr. Small 151:8
El Tortillero/The Tortilla-Seller 89:96,
169:14, 216:24, 267:46
The People in Your Neighborhood
206:43
Somebody's Coming! 149:30
The Tortilla-Seller/El Tortillero 216:47,
see also: 89:96, 169:14, 267:46
The Tortilla Vender 267:46, *see also:*
89:96, 169:14, 216:47
CONFEDERATE STATES OF AMERICA:
see CIVIL WAR (U.S., 1861-1865)
CONGO
Bolumbu 100:77
Kee-Chee 69:15
*Tou Oua 89:272
The Whistle of the Train 114:38
CONSTELLATIONS: *see* STARS
CONTEMPORARY FOLK SONGS
Blowin' in the Wind 72:8
The Cruel War Is Raging 72:12
Five Hundred Miles 72:17, *see also:*
148:252, 158:254
Today 72:14
Where Have All the Flowers Gone? 72:5
COOKS AND COOKERY
Baking Apples 41:9
The Gingerbread Boy 41:45
The Kitchen 149:14
Making Bread 191:72
Old Aunt Kate 232:139
Pat-a-Cake 17:127, 75:60, 175:80,
188:162
Popcorn Balls 207:69
Quan' Patate La Cuite/When Your Pota-
to's Done 262:99, *see also:* 79:38
When Your Potato's Done 79:38, 262:99
COONS: *see* RACCOONS
CORN
Corn-Grinding Song/Ockaya 68:13,
89:38 *(Lovely! See the cloud, the cloud
appear)*
Corn Grinding Song 197:85 *(Ioho,
wonder water)*
Corn in the Wind 245:64
The Cornfields/Los Maizales 270:50, *see
also:* 169:55

For the Golden Corn 245:111
How the Corn Grew 191:64
Los Maizales/The Cornfields 169:55,
270:50
Ockaya/Corn-Grinding Song 68:13,
89:38
Shuckin' of the Corn 21:296, 27:196
When the Corn Is Planted 86:177
COSTA RICA
Anton Firulero 114:75
*El Toro Pinto/The Spotted Bull 216:1
*The Spotted Bull/El Toro Pinto 216:41
*Yes, I Love You/Yo Te Amo, Idalatro
89:75
*Yo Te Amo, Idalatro/Yes, I Love You
89:75
COTTON: *see also* BOLL WEEVILS
Cotton Field 189:142
Cotton-Picking Song 239:45
Eleven Cent Cotton 21:98, 64:104
Pick a Bale of Cotton 20:38, 21:128,
25:21, 75:62, 107:46, 130:80, 135:106,
148:302, 158:234, 230:54, 232:148,
277:51
COUNTING
The Angel Band 233:74
Ants Came Marching 63:82, 118:24, *see
also:* 147:10
Ants Go Marching 147:10, *see also:*
63:82, 118:24
The Blessings of Mary 190:61, 233:58, *see
also:* Seven Joys of Mary
By'm By 129:18, 226:453, *see also:*
135:44, 157:156, 232:71, 289:13
By'M Bye 157:156, 232:71, 289:13, *see
also:* 129:18, 135:44, 226:453
By'n Bye 135:44, *see also:* By'M Bye
Children, Go Where I Send Thee 54:82,
132:unpaged, 140:46, 190:68, *see also:*
213:88, 233:69
The Counting Lesson 191:56, *see also:*
162:23
Did You Ever, Ever, Ever? 226:329
Dos y Dos Son Cuatro/Two and Two Are
Four 194:36
Dumplin's 130:48
Elephants Marching 63:80
Five Little Ducks 75:26, 165:136
Five People and My Family 206:18
Going Over the Sea 63:84
Goneh 169:65
Green Bottles 290:32, *see also:* 82,
147:30, 148:376
Green Grow the Rushes, Ho! 22:116,
25:100, 27:76, 71:50, 72:112, 148:134,
190:64, *see also:* 129:63, 176:146,
233:66
Head and Shoulder, Baby 109:33

Here Is the Beehive 162:23, *see also:* 191:56

Hitori de Sabishii 16:30

How Many Raindrops 162:27

Ichi Kake, Ni Kakete 16:55

I've Got Two 206:22

John Brown Had a Little Indian 135:112, 165:135, *see also:* 107:24

John Brown Knew a Little Indian 107:24, *see also:* 135:112, 165:135

Johnny Works With One Hammer 178:28, *see also:* 75:61, 165:166

Knick Knack 20:44, *see also:* This Old Man

Leemwah 169:64

Little Bitty Baby 213:88, 233:69, *see also:* 54:82, 132:unpaged, 140:46, 190:68

Little White Daisies 291:38

Los Diez Perritos/The Ten Puppies 295:17

Making Rice Cakes/Mochi Tauki Odori 49:24

Mo' Yet 130:50

Mochi Tauki Odori/Making Rice Cakes 49:24

New River Train 62:126, 128:78, 148:250, 230:74, *see also:* 88

Nine Men Slept in a Boarding House Bed 148:254, 290:34, *see also:* 26:23, 63:13, 148:32, 254:110

Ninety-Nine Bottles of Beer 147:30, *see also:* 82, 148:376, 290:32

One Elephant Went Out to Play 178:14

One Little Brown Bird 68:17

One Little Elephant Balancing 63:42

One Man Shall Mow My Meadow 132:unpaged

One, One, One 296:12

One, Two, Buckle My Shoe 175:38

One, Two, Three, Four, Five 107:22, 175:114

One Was Johnny 235:35

Over in the Meadow 17:21, 116, 139, 178:32, 289:70, *see also:* 129:14

Peter Hammers 75:61, 165:166, *see also:* 178:28

Raindrops 162:29

Roll Over 63:131, 254:110, *see also:* 26:23, 147:32, 148:254, 290:34

Roll Over, Roll Over 290:34, *see also:* Ten in the Bed

"Sing," Said the Mother 129:14, *see also:* Over in the Meadow

Song of Five 206:31

Stars In the Heaven 233:12

The Story of Twelve 129:62, *see also:* Green Grow the Rushes, Ho!

Ten Green Bottles 82, 148:376, *see also:* 147:30, 290:32

Ten In the Bed 147:32, *see also:* 26:23, 63:131, 148:254, 254:110, 290:34

Ten Little Goblins 197:96

Ten Little Indians 17:144, 75:74

The Ten Puppies/Los Diez Perritos 295:17

That New River Train 88, *see also:* New River Train

There Were Ten in the Bed 26:23, *see also:* Ten in the Bed

This Old Man 6, 17:94, 75:82, 129:98, 135:104, 147:42, 148:386, 175:70, 197:34, 232:165, 289:85, *see also:* 20:44

Three Craws 62:55, 128:32, 134:17, 290:144, 292:144

Three Jelly Fish, Three Jelly Fish 165:110

Three Little Angels All Dressed In White 141:94

Three Little Pigeons 46:215

Three Wood Pigeons 25:9

The Twelve Apostles 176:146, 233:66, *see also:* Green Grow the Rushes, Ho!

We'll All Go Down the Meadow 262:46

When Buster Brown Was One 63:86

Who Knows One? 192

COURTESY: *see* ETIQUETTE

COWBOYS: *see also* COWS; PIONEERS AND PIONEER LIFE

An Afternoon Like This 61:107

Arizona Home 61:296

At a Cowboy Dance 61:287

Back in the Saddle Again 25:70

Bad Man from the Brazos 159:138, *see also:* 61:104

The Big Corral 128:84, 239:26

Bill Venero 157:197, *see also:* 61:129, 146:42

Billy Veniro 61:129, 146:42, *see also:* 159:197

Black Tail Range 60:86, 146:142, 159:292

Blood on the Saddle 61:112, 290:170, *see also:* 61:113, 159:288

The Bloody Cowboy 61:113, *see also:* 61:112, 159:288, 290:170

Blue Mountain 61:239

The Boasting Drunk in Dodge 159:135

Border Ballad 61:236, *see also:* 60:36, 146:53, 159:15, 159:281

Bow Down Your Head and Cry 159:159

Bronc Peeler's Song 159:83

Bucking Bronco 61:165, 159:267, *see also:* 61:166, 146:59

The Buffalo Range 61:341

The Bull Rider Song 61:189, *see also:* 61:187, 223, 225:32

COWBOYS—*Continued*

Bury Me Not on the Lone Prairie 158:208, *see also:* Oh, Bury Me Not on the Lone Prairie

Bury Me Out on the Prairie 159:300, *see also:* 61:177

Cattle Call 61:302

Cattleman's Prayer 61:338, *see also:* 159:329

Charlie Rutledge 159:82

Cheyenne 159:245

The Chisholm Trail 60:4, 146:20, 146:23, *see also:* Old Chisholm Trail

Chopo 61:191

Clear Rock's Chisholm Trail 159:37, *see also:* 234:70

Clinch Mountain 37:142, *see also:* 24:855, 158:218, 159:163, 226:307, 230:69

The Colorado Trail 159:7, 225:62, 226:462

A Cow Camp on the Range 159:71

The Cowboy 159:139 *(Oh, a man there lives on the western plains)*

The Cowboy 159:168 *(It was only a few short years ago)*

The Cowboy 60:90, 146:132, 159:67 *(All day on the prairie in the saddle I ride)*

Cowboy Again for a Day 61:313

The Cowboy and His Love 159:311

The Cowboy at Church 159:272

The Cowboy at Work 159:83

Cowboy Carol 210:96

A Cowboy Dance Song 159:241

Cowboy Jack 159:230

Cowboy Lullaby 277:135

Cowboy Song 83:466, 288:25

Cowboy Spring 189:116, *see also:* 27:50

Cowboy Tune 207:120

The Cowboy Up to Date 159:296

Cowboys 207:123

The Cowboy's Christmas Ball 159:246

The Cowboy's Dance Song 159:251, *see also:* 61:284

The Cowboy's Dream 158:210, 159:44, *see also:* Cowboy's Heaven

The Cowboy's Gettin'-Up Holler 159:3, *see also:* 289:24

The Cowboy's Heaven 60:72, 146:106, 225:66, *see also:* 25:74, 26:74, 158:210, 159:44

Cowboy's Home Sweet Home 61:243

The Cowboy's Lament 24:859, 60:16, 159:417, *see also:* Streets of Laredo *(As I walked out in the streets of Laredo)*

The Cowboy's Lament 146:30, *see also:* 60:16, 69:22, 159:421, 262:51 *(My home's in Montana)*

The Cowboy's Life 61:236, 159:281, *see also:* 60:36, 146:53, 159:15

The Cowboy's Meditation 61:327, 159:122

A Cowboy's Prayer 61:343

The Cowboy's Ride 61:298

The Cowboy's Soliloquy 61:332

The Cowboy's Sweet Bye and Bye 25:74, 26:74, *see also:* Cowboy's Heaven

The Cowboy's Vision 61:329

The Cowman's Prayer 159:329, *see also:* 61:339

The Crooked Trail to Holbrook 159:27

Cyclone Blues 159:294

Dan Taylor 159:261

Diamond Joe 159:65

The Dogie Song 25:84, 71:86, *see also:* Git Along Little Dogies *(As I was a walking, one morning for pleasure)*

Dogie Song 159:51 *(The cow-bosses are good-hearted chunks)*

Dona Gal 61:232, *see also:* 61:233, 159:8, 232:69

Doney Gal 61:232, 159:8, *see also:* 61:233, 232:69

Don't Fence Me In 170:72

Dreary Life 60:36, 146:53, *see also:* 61:236, 159:15, 159:281

The Drifter 159:76

Drinking Song 159:136

The Dry-Landers 159:306

The Dying Cowboy 25:78, 61:314, 159:48, 225:48, *see also:* Oh, Bury Me Not on the Lone Prairie

The Dying Cowboy of Rim Rock Ranch 61:325, 159:98

The Dying Outlaw 61:319

Educated Feller 61:195, *see also:* 60:30, 61:194, 146:50, 159:78, 159:81, 225:38

Eleven Slash Slash Eleven 61:212

Famed Are the Roughriders/Kilakila Na Roughrider 87:88

The Fightin' Booze Fighter 61:102

The Gal I Left Behind Me 159:58, *see also:* 42:604, 61:171, 66:112, 205:25

George Britton 159:18

Get Along, Cayuse, Get Along 33:226

Get Along, Little Dogies 225:18, *see also:* Git Along Little Dogies

Git Along, Little Dogies 24:853, 26:73, 60:60, 61:207, 146:98, 146:102, 158:204, 197:81, 292:41, *see also:* 22:162, 25:84, 71:86, 129:92, 159:4, 225:18, 226:268

The Glory Trail 61:335

Goin' to Leave Ol' Texas 69:21, *see also:* 21:108, 61:182, 159:57, 277:35

Going to Leave Old Texas 61:182, *see also:* 21:108, 69:21, 159:57, 277:35

Good-By Old Paint 25:77, 33:218, 158:214, 159:12, 239:28, see also: Goodbye Old Paint

Goodbye, Old Paint 33:218, 60:106, 61:227, 128:86, 135:14, 146:169, 158:214, 232:62, see also: 25:77, 158:214, 159:12, 239:28

The Great Round-Up 159:327, see also: 61:330

The Hell-Bound Train 61:337, 159:236

The High-Toned Dance 61:284, see also: 159:251

The Hills of Mexico 61:89

Home on the Range 22:164, 25:75, 26:72, 60:42, 61:296, 71:90, 72:97, 146:166, 158:212, 159:424, 170:101, 205:361, 230:26

Home, Sweet Home 159:124 (We were lying on a prairie)

The Horse Wrangler 159:119, see also: 61:198, 226:274, 277:67

I Ride an Old Paint 24:857, 60:24, 128:82, 146:34, 157:154, 158:216, 225:41, 226:12, 230:25, 292:26

I Will Tell You My Troubles 61:75

Idyl of the Plains 61:85

I'm a Cowboy A-Ropin' 167:26

I'm a Poor Lonesome Cowboy 60:76, 61:229, 61:230, 146:112, 159:290, 225:46, 226:273

I'm Gonna Leave Old Texas Now 159:57, 277:35, see also: 21:108, 61:182, 55:21

It Is Spring 27:50, see also: 189:116

Jess's Dilemma 159:86

Jim Farrow 159:112

Jim the Roper 146:164

The Jolly Cowboy 159:275

Just Like a Cowboy 154:34

A Kansas Cowboy 159:103

A Kansas Line 159:15, see also: 60:36, 61:235, 146:53, 159:281

Kilakila Na Roughriders/Famed Are the Roughriders 87:88

Lackey Bill 159:187

The Last Longhorn 61:310, 159:325

Last Roundup 61:330, see also: 159:327

The Lavender Cowboy 61:114, 159:304

Leadbelly's Chisholm Trail 159:39, see also: 61:86

Lily of the West 61:154

Little Darling 61:158

Little Joe, the Wrangler 61:215, 146:124, 159:91

The Lone Buffalo Hunter 159:342, see also: 159:291

Lone Driftin' Riders 159:307

The Lone Prairie 60:20, 146:38, see also: Oh, Bury Me Not on the Lone Prairie

The Lone Star Trail 61:307, 159:19, 226:266, see also: 60:114, 146:162

The Lonely Cowboy 61:242

The Lonesome Trail 61:233, see also: 61:232, 159:8, 232:69

Lost River Desert 61:159

The Lovesick Cowboy 159:268

Macaffie's Confession 159:201

A Man Named Hods 159:355

Me an' My Doney-Gal 159:11

The Melancholy Cowboy 159:220

The Moonshine Steer 61:199

Moving Picture Cowboy 61:313

My Home's in Montana 60:16, 55:22, 159:421, 262:51, see also: 146:30

My Ma Was Born in Texas 61:98

My Parents Raised Me Tenderly 61:173

New River Shore 61:160, see also: 37:152, 159:181

Night Herding Song 59:49, 60:10, 61:224, 69:23, 71:91, 89:44, 129:94, 146:27, 159:60, 225:21, 239:30, 274:24

No Use For the Women 61:177, see also: 159:300

O-Bar Cowboy 159:166

Oh, Bury Me Not on the Lone Prairie 25:78, 61:314, 61:315, 61:316, 158:208, 159:48, 225:48, 226:20, see also: 60:20, 146:38

Ol' Texas 21:108, 61:182, 69:21, 159:57, see also: 277:35

The Old Chisholm Trail 21:219, 24:851, 25:72, 60:4, 61:210, 61:211, 64:122, 146:20, 146:23, 158:200, 158:202, 225:14, see also: 159:37

Old Paint 61:227, see also: Goodbye, Old Paint

Old Paint 158:216, see also: I Ride an Old Paint

Old Rosin the Beau 61:10, 157:50, 159:278

The Old-Time Cowboy 159:191

On His Bronco the Gay Caballero 262:87

On Red River Shore 61:16, see also: 37:152, 159:181

On the Lake of the Poncho Plains 146:46

On the Trail to Idaho 159:24

Once You Git the Habit 159:289

Only a Cowboy 159:116

The Overlander 89:310

Panhandle Cob 159:105

Pattonio 61:184, 159:356, see also: 60:82, 128:46, 146:116

The Pecos Puncher 61:303, 159:95

The Peeler's Lament 159:189

A Philosophical Cowboy 61:32, see also: 61:30

Pinto 159:73

COWBOYS—*Continued*

Plantonio, The Pride of the Plain 60:82, 128:46, 146:116, *see also:* 61:184, 159:356

Poor Lonesome Cowboy 60:76, 61:229, 61:230, 146:112, 159:290, 226:273, *see also:* 225:46

Powderhorn 61:192

Prairie Music 207:122

Punchin' Dough 61:110

Ragtime Cowboy Joe 61:290

The Railroad Corral 61:208, 159:42, 225:24, 262:64

Rain or Shine 232:69, *see also:* 61:232, 61:233, 159:8

The Rambling Cowboy 159:192

Rambling Gambler 159:266

The Range Riders 159:185, 159:280

A Real Cowboy 207:121

Red River Shore 159:181, *see also:* 37:152, 61:161

Red River Valley 22:146, 25:73, 55:514, 61:157, 126:55, 158:220, 159:298, 205:380, 226:130

Ride Cowboy, Ride 162:80

Riding Round the Cattle 234:70, *see also:* 159:37

Rigby Johnson Chandler 61:26

Root Hog or Die 61:30, *see also:* 61:32

Rounded Up in Glory 159:330

Roving Cowboy 61:163

Roy Bean 159:147

The Rustler 159:105

Rusty Jiggs and Sandy Sam 146:76, *see also:* 61:202, 225:52

Rye Whisky 24:855, 158:218, 159:163, 230:69, *see also:* 37:142, 159:166, 226:307

St. James Hospital 157:157

Salty Dog 159:110

The Santa Fe Trail 159:308

The Skew-Ball Black 159:14

Snagtooth Sal 61:289

Son of a Gun 159:287

Song of the Border 61:81

Song of the Cactus Region 69:37

Soy Pobre Vaquero 61:230

Speaking of Cowboy's Home 159:315

Squeball 61:18, *see also:* 61:20, 234:68

The Stampede 159:99

The State of Arkansas 158:240, 159:283

The Strawberry Roan 223, 225:32, *see also:* 61:187, 61:189

The Streets of Laredo 21:212, 61:321, 148:262, 158:206, 225:56, 230:41, 272:18, 277:61, *see also:* 24:859, 60:16, 146:30, 159:417, 226:263

Sweet Lily 61:228

Ten Thousand Cattle 146:152, 159:128

Ten Thousand God-Damn Cattle 159:130

The Tenderfoot 61:198, 226:274, 277:67, *see also:* 159:121

The Texas Cowboy 61:107 *(With a sort of careless swagger)*

The Texas Cowboy 60:48, 61:91, 61:93, 146:66, 159:22 *(Oh, I'm a Texas cowboy far away from home)*

The Texas Cowboys 159:291, *see also:* 159:342

A Texas Idol 61:104, *see also:* 159:138

Texas Jack 61:125

Texas Rangers 33:234, 159:359, 159:361

The Texas Song 159:57, *see also:* 21:108, 61:182, 69:21, 277:35

To Midnight 159:327

Trail End 159:288, *see also:* 61:112, 61:113, 290:170

The Trail to Mexico 24:858, 61:179, 146:62, 159:52, 225:64, 226:285, 239:32

The Triple "R" Song 119:106

Tying Knots in the Devil's Tail 61:202, 225:52, *see also:* 146:76

The U-S-U Range 159:96

Utah Carl 61:217, *see also:* 146:120, 159:125

Utah Carroll 146:120, 159:125, *see also:* 61:217

The Wagoner's Lad 36:64, 37:181, 61:13, *see also:* 230:21, 232:110

Wake Up, Jacob! 289:24, *see also:* 159:3

Wake Up, You Lazy Bones 291:74

Walking John 146:79

The Wandering Cowboy 146:144, 159:305

Way Out West 159:333

Western Cowboy 61:87

Western Home 61:295

When I Was a Brave Cowboy 159:228

When I Was a Cowboy 61:86, 159:39

When I Went A-Courtin' 61:24

When the Curtains of Night Are Pinned Back 61:244, 83:468, 226:259

When the Work's All Done This Fall 27:112, 61:220, 126:79, 159:74, 226:260

Where the Bravest Cowboys Lie 61:155

The White Steed of the Prairies 159:227

Whoopee, To Yi Yo, Git Along, Little Dogies 22:162, 129:92, 159:4, 226:268, *see also:* Git Along Little Dogies

Whose Old Cow? 159:117

Wild Bronc Peeler 159:85

Wild Buckaroo 61:106

The Wild Montana Boy 159:167

A Wild Rattling Cowboy 159:221

The Wild Rippling Water 61:6, 159:183

Windy Bill 60:54, 61:204, 146:69, 159:113

Young Charlottie 24:825, 159:231, *see also:* 27:244, 35:50, 226:58
Young Companions 146:109, 159:212
The Zebra Dun 60:30, 146:50, *see also:* 61:194, 61:195, 159:78, 159:81, 225:38
COWS
Alpine Song 245:8
The Animals Go to Sleep 41:14
The Bell Cow 128:40
Come, Little Sennerin 245:12
The Cow 44:14 *(The friendly cow all red and white)*
The Cow 17:115 *(Thank you, pretty cow that made)*
Cow on the Railroad Track 118:28
Did You Feed My Cow? 107:18, *see also:* 232:112, 234:56, 292:20, 292:44
Did You Go to the Barney? 232:112, *see also:* 107:18, 234:56, 292:20, 292:44
El Toro Pinto/The Spotted Bull 216:1
Feed-My-Cow 172:108
Hoosen Johnny 129:34, 135:36, 226:164, *see also:* 234:54, 292:46
The Last Longhorn 61:310, 159:325
Little Black Bull 135:36, 234:54, 292:46, *see also:* 129:34, 226:164
The Old Cow Died 234:56, 292:44, *see also:* 107:18, 232:112, 292:20
The Old Cowboy 61:299, 159:93
The Spotted Bull/El Toro Pinto 216:41
The Tune the Old Cow Died On 62:34, 71:94
Wake Up, You Lazy Bones 291:74
CRABS
Buy My Dainty Fine Beans 292:70
Crab Is a Better Man 130:76
Sandy McNab 290:193, 293:54
CRANES (BIRDS)
Crested Crane/Ntuha-Ntuha 265:56, *see also:* 169:69
Ntuha Ntuha/Crested Crane 169:69, 265:56
CRAWFISH: *see* CRAYFISH
CRAYFISH
The Crawdad 21:106, 24:896, 27:160, 230:86, *see also:* 129:30, 148:58, 158:107, 292:182
The Crawdad Hole 129:30, *see also:* Crawdad
Crawdad Song 148:58, 158:107, 292:182, *see also:* Crawdad
The Crawfish Man 129:21, *see also:* 262:35
The Crow-Fish Man 262:35, *see also:* 129:21
CREATIVE DRAMATICS
All the Fish Are Swimming in the Water 128:30, 130:100
Dance Like a Lady 296:23

Grandfather Frog 162:12
Lazy John 135:38, 213:16, 254:112
One Little Brown Bird 68:17
Quite Different 68:26
What Can I Do? 206:58
CREOLES
*En Avant, Grenadiers/Forward March Grenadiers 89:45
*Forward March Grenadiers/En Avant, Grenadiers 89:45
*Lolotte 157:150
*Musieu Bainjo 157:152
Sweet Potatoes 290:198
CRICKETS
Cricket Voices/Mushi-no Koe 286:30
Mushi-no Koe/Cricket Voices 286:30
CRIME AND CRIMINALS: *see* OUTLAWS; PIRATES
CROCKETT, DAVID (DAVY)
Ballad of Davy Crockett 275:90, 276:86
Davy Crockett 33:106
CROCODILES
The Crocodile 62:48, *see also:* 26:36, 89:33, 234:72 *(She sailed away on a bright and sunny day)*
The Crocodile 59:29, *see also:* 112:39 *(How doth the little crocodile)*
The Crocodile 290:168 *(One day when I was sailing)*
The Crocodile 292:178 *(Come list ye, landsmen, all to me)*
Crocodile Song 26:36, 89:33, 234:72, *see also:* 62:48
How Doth the Little Crocodile 112:39, *see also:* 59:29
Look at the Terrible Crocodile 165:104
Never Smile at a Crocodile 276:34
The Roaring Crocodile 62:50
CROWS
The Crow 286:26
The Crow and the Fox/Le Corbeau et le Renard 243:2
Crows in the Garden 130:107
The Farmer and the Crow 262:43
The Frog and the Crow 188:72
Le Corbeau et le Renard/The Crow and the Fox 243:2
Poor Old Crow 232:121, *see also:* Three Ravens
Three Craws 62:55, 128:32, 134:17, 290:144, 292:144
Three Crows 62:54, *see also:* Three Ravens
CRYING
Cry a Pint 237:unpaged
It's All Right to Cry 260:93
CUB SCOUTS: *see* SCOUTS AND SCOUTING

CUB SCOUTS—_Continued_
CUBA
*Canto Lucumi de Iya/Lucumi Cult Song 89:59
*El Conejo de Esperanza/The Rabbit of Hope 194:20
*The Fountain/La Fuente 168:112, _see also:_ 194:24
*The Guajira/La Guajira 89:58
*Hay Aquí, Madre, un Jardin/Mother, There Is a Garden 216:11
*La Fuente/The Fountain 168:112, _see also:_ 194:24
*La Guajira/The Guajira 89:58
*La Punta y el Tacón/The Tip and Heel Dance 194:32
*Lucumi Cult Song/Canto Lucumi de Iya 89:59
*Ma Teodora 216:19
*Mother, There Is a Garden/Hay Aquí, Madre, un Jardin 216:44
*Para Subir al Cielo/To Get to Heaven 194:26
*Pepito 194:22
*The Rabbit of Hope/El Conejo de Esperanza 194:20
*The Tip and Heel Dance/La Punta y el Tacón 194:32
*To Get to Heaven/Para Subir al Cielo 194:26
CUCKOOS
Cuckoo 17:40, 289:66 _(Cuckoo, Cuckoo, calls from the wood)_
The Cuckoo/Le Cou-Cou 27:52, 157:77, 217:60, _see also:_ 59:23, 292:130 _(The cuckoo is a funny bird)_
The Cuckoo 71:107 _(Down yonder in the woodland, the cuckoo sings today)_
A Cuckoo and an Owl 144:13
The Cuckoo Is a Pretty Bird 59:23, 292:130, _see also:_ 27:52, 157:77, 217:60
Le Cou-Cou/The Cuckoo 217:35
My Bonnie Cuckoo 262:129
Schäferin und Kuckuck/The Shepherdess and the Cuckoo 78:59
The Shepherdess and the Cuckoo/Schäferin und Kuckuck 78:59
CUMULATIVE SONGS: _see also_ DIMINISHING SONGS
Alouette 20:84, 22:124, 25:90, 26:24, 27:68, 148:18, 262:73
The Barnyard Song 68:27, 75:10, 128:34, 129:76, _see also:_ 27:96, 37:171, 55:265, 109:193, 132:unpaged, 232:104, 254:108, 289:47, 292:13, 292:18
Biddy Biddy Burkey/Widewidewenne 188:126
Bog in the Valley-O 72:127, _see also:_ Green Grass Grows All Around

Bought Me a Cat 232:104, _see also:_ Barnyard Song
Children, Go Where I Send Thee 54:82, 132:unpaged, 140:46, 190:68, _see also:_ 213:88, 233:69
The Court of King Carraticus 290:10
Deep in the Woods 197:48, _see also:_ Green Grass Grows All Around
Farmer's Boy 212:48
Fiddle-I-Fee 37:171, 292:18, _see also:_ Barnyard Song
Found My Lost Sheep 233:20
The Green Grass Grows All Around 94, 175, 290:19, _see also:_ 27:90, 62:72, 72:127, 109:197, 132:unpaged, 134:11, 176:130, 197:48, 213:20
Green Grow the Rushes, Ho! 22:116, 25:100, 27:76, 71:50, 72:112, 148:134, 190:64, _see also:_ 129:63, 176:146, 233:66
Had a Little Rooster 128:34, _see also:_ Barnyard Song
Hi! Ho! The Rattlin' Bog 134:11, _see also:_ Green Grass Grows All Around
Hole in the Ground 62:72, _see also:_ Green Grass Grows All Around
Holy Babe 233:70
I Bought Me a Rooster 289:47, _see also:_ Barnyard Song
I Had a Little Cat 132:unpaged, _see also:_ Barnyard Song
I Had a Little Rooster 292:13, _see also:_ Barnyard Song
I Had an Old Rooster 109:193, _see also:_ Barnyard Song
I Know an Old Lady Who Swallowed a Fly 23, 75:34, 289:116, 292:216, _see also:_ 5, 120, 148:378
I Love My Rooster 55:265, 254:108, _see also:_ Barnyard Song
Little Bitty Baby 213:88, 233:69, _see also:_ 54:82, 132:unpaged, 140:46, 190:68
The Little Pig 79:23, 135:56, 232:102, 234:50, _see also:_ Old Woman and Her Pig
The Mallard 62:75
Mommy, Buy Me a China Doll 297
My Father Gave Me 62:69
My Twenty Pennies 262:22
Oh, He Planted Ginger 114:54
Old King Twine 62:76
Old MacDonald Had a Farm 4, 17:148, 26:20, 55:262, 75:56, 81, 199, 283:12, 291:30
The Old Woman and Her Pig 129:27, 178:16, 292:60, _see also:_ 79:23, 110:42, 135:56, 213:52, 232:102, 234:50
The Old Woman and the Pig 213:52, _see also:_ Old Woman and Her Pig

Once an Austrian Went Yodeling 290:22
One Man Shall Mow My Meadow 132:unpaged
Pretty Pear Tree 109:197, *see also:* Green Grass Grows All Around
The Story of Twelve 129:62, *see also:* Green Grow the Rushes, Ho!
There Was an Old Lady Who Swallowed a Fly 5, *see also:* I Know an Old Lady Who Swallowed a Fly
There was an Old Woman 120, 148:378, *see also:* I Know an Old Lady Who Swallowed a Fly
There's a Hole In the Bottom of the Sea 75:78, *see also:* 290:14
There's a Hole in the Middle of the Sea 290:14, *see also:* 75:78
Today Is Monday 84:28, 253:92
The Tree in the Forest 176:130, *see also:* Green Grass Grows All Around
The Tree in the Valley-O 213:20, *see also:* Green Grass Grows All Around
The Tree in the Wood 27:90, *see also:* Green Grass Grows All Around
A Tree in Yonder Field 132:unpaged, *see also:* Green Grass Grows All Around
The Twelve Apostles 176:146, 233:66, *see also:* Green Grow the Rushes, Ho!
The Twelve Days of Christmas 22:248, 30, 50, 54:36, 87:91, 92:183, 113, 121, 148:400, 190:148, 197:120, 210:64, 233:72, 241:30, 264:66, 287, 290:26, 292:160
When I First Came to This Land 27:138, 29, 230:13
Widewidewenne/Biddy Biddy Burkey 188:126
Wiggle the Wool 290:12
The Wild Man of Borneo 62:74
Yonder Tree 27:96, *see also:* Barnyard Song

CUSTER, GEORGE ARMSTRONG
Custer's Last Charge 61:127

CYPRUS
*To Tragothi to Gamo/The Wedding Song 89:195
*The Wedding Song/To Tragothi to Gamo 89:195

CZECHOSLAVAKIA
The Broken Troth 262:77
*Chtic, Aby Spal, Tak Zpívala/Sweet Mary Sings Her Babe to Sleep 54:234
Cold Is the Morning 241:63
*Come All Ye Shepherds/Nesem Vám Noviny 220:100, 279:116, *see also:* 54:236
*Come, Hear the Wonderful Tidings/ Nesem Vám Noviny 54:236, *see also:* 220:100, 279:116
*Dobrou Noc/Sweetheart, Good Night 208:13
Dog Jumps Through the Window 189:21
Don't Want to Go Home 68:37, 262:25
Father/Taticek 189:148
*Flow, Oh Water, Flow On/Teče Voda Teče 208:15
*From Out the Forest a Cuckoo Flew/ Zazulka Z Lesa Vylítla 54:230
Good Night, My Baby 125:24
*Hajej, Nynej, Jezisku/Rocking Carol 54:226, 279:118
Honza, I Love You 262:61
*I Go to Bethlehem/Sel Bych Rád K Betlému 54:232, 241:184, *see also:* 245:120
Little Red Handkerchief 70:19
The Mailman/Počtovsky Panáček 289:80
*Milínkej Pan Dekan/Our Village Deacon 89:184
*Near Breclav/Starej Breclavy 89:186
*Nesem Vam Noviny/Come All Ye Shepherds 279:116, *see also:* 54:236, 220:100
*Nesem Vám Noviny/Come, Hear the Wonderful Tidings 54:236, *see also:* 220:100, 279:116
*Our Village Deacon/Milínkej Pan Dékan 89:184
*Pásli Ovce Valaši/Shepherds Watched Their Flocks by Night 241:179
Pochvalen Bud', Jezis Kristus/Praise to Jesus, Our Salvation 54:222
Počtovsky Panáček/The Mailman 289:80
*Praise to Jesus, Our Salvation/Pochvalen Bud, Jezis Kristus 54:222
*Pujdem Spolu Do Betlema/We Are Going to the Stable 54:224
The Quest 71:53
Rock-A-Bye 125:25
Rocking 68:45, 184:66, 220:28, 241:64, *see also:* 54:226, 210:45, 279:118
*Rocking Carol/Hajej, Nynej, Ježišku 54:226, *see also:* Rocking
*Rocking Song/Hajej, Nynej, Ježišku 279:118, *see also:* Rocking
*Sel Bych Rád k Betlému/I Go to Bethlehem 54:232, 241:184
*Shepherds Watched Their Flocks By Night/Pásli Ovce Valaši 241:179
Shusti-Fidli 71:56, 72:138, *see also:* Musicians
*Slysèli Jsme V Betlemě/We Have Heard in Bethlehem 54:228
*Starej Breclavy/Near Breclav 89:186
Stodola Pumpa 148:360, *see also:* 25:88, 262:23

CZECHOSLAVAKIA—*Continued*
Stodole Pumpa   262:23, *see also:* 25:88, 148:360
*Sweet Mary Sings Her Babe to Sleep/ Chtic, Aby Spal, Tak Zpívala   54:234
*Sweetheart, Good Night/Dobrou Noc 208:13
Swiftly Flowing Labe   262:63
Tancuj   69:17, 71:76, 72:140
Taticek/Father   189:148
*Tece Voda Tece/Flow, Oh Water, Flow On   208:15
Walking at Night   25:88, 262:23, *see also:* 148:360
*We Are Going to the Stable/Pujdem Spolu Do Betlema   54:224
*We Have Heard in Bethlehem/Slysèli Jsme V Betlemé   54:228
Whirling Maiden   262:142
You, You, You   78:51, *see also:* 262:26
*Zezulka Z Lesa Vylítla/From Out the Forest A Cuckoo Flew   54:230

D

DAIRYING: *see* BUTTER; COWS
DAISIES
Buttercups and Daisies   17:109
DAKOTA INDIANS: *see* SIOUAN INDIANS
DANCERS AND DANCING: *see also* HULA; SQUARE DANCING
Brother, Come and Dance with Me 75:14, 227:28
Dance, Little Maiden   245:32
Dance to the Merry Piper's Sound 245:50
The Dancing Lesson   227:28, *see also:* 75:14
The Harrington Barn Dance   159:244
I Like to Do the Highland Fling   167:42
La Imilla   114:66
My Uncle Terwilliger Waltzes with Bears 237:unpaged
Ranky Tank   109:130
Sandy Ree   109:136
Sisken   83:499
Try a Spanish Dance   166:62
When You Sing   162:106
DANCES
Ain't Gonna Rain   226:141
Alabama Girl   126:107
As the Sun Goes Down   72:144
Bailando el Gato/Dancing the Gato 89:88
Boscastle   83:508
Chester Schottische   126:95

Chiapanecas   162:107
Click Your Heels/Podkóweczki Dajcie Ognia   89:182
Coonshine   109:132
The Cornfields/Los Maizales   169:55, 270:50
Cripple Creek   24:898, 134:48
Cuckoo Waltz   226:160
Dancing the Gato/Bailando el Gato 89:88
El Vito   295:26
Gerakina   169:25, 267:38
Give the Fiddler a Dram   134:42
Gūri Gūri Karayō/I Will Rock Thee 89:216
I Will Rock Thee/Gūri Gūri Karayō 89:216
I'm Going Away to See Aunt Dinah 109:142
Irish Washerwoman   126:109
I's the B'y   27:66, *see also:* 134:74
I'se the B'y That Builds the Boat   134:74, *see also:* 27:66
Korobushka   178:60
La Jesucita   22:78, 72:106, 295:66
La Punta y el Tacón/The Tip and Heel Dance   194:32
Lailaw/Lament for an Absent Lover 208:1
Lament for an Absent Lover/Lailaw 208:1
L'Autre Jour En Voulant Danser/While I Was Dancing the Other Day   89:152
Lilly Dale   157:108, *see also:* 66:128
Lily Dale   66:128, *see also:* 157:108
Los Maizales/The Cornfields   169:55, 270:50
Magtanim   169:57, 271:23, *see also:* Planting Rice
Magtanim Ay Di Biro   87:54, *see also:* Planting Rice
The Minuet   207:84
Old Brass Wagon   33:98, 55:506, 226:159
Pinnal Kolattam/Weaving Dance 89:217
Planting Rice/Magtanim   55:262, 64:102, 70:12, 87:54, 169:57, 271:23, *see also:* 286:78
Podkóweczki Dajcie Ognia/Click Your Heels   89:182
Possum-la   109:128
Reel   107:50
Rosa, Let Us Be Dancing   100:116
Slovak Polka   100:111
Song of Praise/Um Home   163:39
Sovu Dance   89:262
Sugar-Lump   24:810
Svensk Masquerade   83:498

The Tip and Heel Dance/La Punta y el Tacón 194:32
Troika 55:515
Tzena 72:151
Um Home/Song of Praise 163:39
Vorira 89:179
Weaving Dance/Pinnal Kolattam 89:217
While I Was Dancing the Other Day/ L'Autre Jour en Voulant Danser 89:152
Ya Tsa Tsa, Via La La 178:51
Zudie-O 109:139

DANDELIONS
Dandelion Buttons 207:93
O Dandelion, Yellow As Gold 245:24

DANIEL
Daniel Saw the Stone 123:305
Didn't My Lord Deliver Daniel 31:17, 157:140

DAVIS, JEFFERSON
Call 'em Names, Jeff 73:53
Jeff Davis' Dream 73:66

DAWN: see also MORNING
Almost Day 233:76 (Chicken crowing for midnight)

DAY: see also BEDTIME; DAWN; EVENING; MORNING; NIGHT
Day and Night 125:38

DAYS: see also BIRTHDAYS; CALENDARS; HOLIDAYS; names of special days, e.g., HALLOWEEN
Camp Menu Song 25:22
Charlie Is My Darling 71:42, 176:30, 205:72, see also: 134:14, 226:117, 232:137
Dashing Away With the Smoothing Iron 134:14, see also: Charlie Is My Darling
Days of the Week 104:52, see also: Here We Go Round the Mulberry Bush
Hanging Out the Linen Clothes 226:117, 232:137, see also: 71:42, 134:14, 176:30, 205:72
Haying Song 169:59, 268:61
Here We Go Round the Mulberry Bush 14:366, 17:90, 20:9, 63:16, 75:50, 168:108, 175:78, 188:66, 189:40, 289:172, see also: 104:52, 283:17, 291:2
How Many Days Has My Baby to Play 285:45
The Mulberry Bush 15:365, 17:90, 63:16, 75:50, 168:108, 175:78, 289:172, see also: Here We Go Round the Mulberry Bush
'Round the Mulberry Bush 283:17, see also: Here We Go Round the Mulberry Bush
Solomon Grundy 112:49

This Is the Way We Wash Our Hands 291:2, see also: Here We Go Round the Mulberry Bush
Today Is Monday 84:28, 253:92
A Week of Birthdays 18:44
When Is the Day? 161:72

DEATH
El Quele le/The White Hawk 262:118
The White Hawk/El Quele le 262:118

DECORATION DAY: see MEMORIAL DAY
DEEP SEA DIVING: see SKIN DIVING AND SCUBA DIVING

DEER
Child's Song 44:78
The Deer Begins His Travels 74:13
Hey Ho, to the Greenwood 176:99, 292:82, 293:96
The Keeper 71:74, 72:118, 176:9, 230:59, 290:86, see also: 148:216, 292:84
The Keeper Would A-Hunting Go 148:216, 176:9, 290:86, 292:84, see also: 71:74, 72:118, 230:59

DEMOCRACY
Fair and Free Elections 27:218

DENMARK
*Alle elsker Lordag Asten 148:84
*Barn Jesus/Child Jesus 54:190
*Cat in the Sack/Katten I Saekken 208:19
*A Child Is Born In Bethlehem/Et Barn er Fodt I Betlehem 54:192
*Child Jesus/Barn Jesus 54:190
Dance of Greeting 83:497
*Deilig Er den Himmel Blaa/Lovely Is the Dark Blue Sky 54:188
*Det Kimer Nu Til Julefest/The Happy Christmas Comes Once More 54:186
*Et Barn er Fodt I Betlehem/A Child Is Born in Bethlehem 54:192
*Gaaer Jeg Udi Skoven/In Forest and Meadow 89:166
*Happy Christmas Comes Once More/ Det Kimer Nu Til Julefest 54:186
*Harvest Is Over/Marken er Mejet 208:17, see also: 83:496
*In Forest and Meadow/Gaaer Jed Udi Skoven 89:166
*Katten I Saekken/Cat in the Sack 208:19
*Lovely Is the Dark Blue Sky/Deilig Er den Himmel Blaa 54:188
*Marken Er Mejet/Harvest Is Over 83:496, 208:17
*Mow the Meadow/Marken Er Mejet 83:496, 208:17
*Music Shall Live 69:50, see also: 62:20, 293:6
*Rosen Fra Fuhn 69:52

DENMARK—*Continued*
  *Sisken 83:499
  *Stork Lange Bein/Stork Long-o'-Leg 189:146
  *Stork Long-o'-Leg/Stork Lange Bein 189:146
THE DEPRESSION YEARS
  Beans, Bacon, and Gravy 64:132
  Last Winter Was a Hard One 35:66
  Out of Work 157:172
  Soup Song 64:130
DESERTS
  Ajjamal Wanna/Caravan Song 89:244
  Caravan Song/Ajjamal Wanna 89:244
  The Desert 91:20
  I Wanted to Die in the Desert 159:323
DEVILS
  The Devil's Nine Questions 27:214, *see also:* 37:110, 134:85
  The Devil's Questions 37:110, 134:85, *see also:* 27:214
  Rusty Jiggs and Sandy Sam 146:76, *see also:* 61:201, 225:52
  Some Say the Devil's Dead 134:43
  Tying Knots in the Devil's Tail 61:201, 225:52, *see also:* 146:76
DIALOGUE SONGS: *see* QUESTION AND ANSWER SONGS
DIET: *see* COOKS AND COOKERY; FOOD AND EATING
DIGGING: *see* MINERS AND MINING
DIMINISHING SONGS: *see also* CUMULATIVE SONGS
  Bingo 26:22, 39:52, 46:201, 63:91, 75:13, 126:93, 129:101, 147:16, 253:94, 289:54, *see also:* 17:131
  Five Little Ducks 75:26, 165:136
  Green Bottles 290:32, *see also:* 82, 147:30, 148:376
  Los Diez Perritos/The Ten Puppies 295:17
  Nine Men Slept in a Boardinghouse Bed 148:254, 290:34, *see also:* 26:23, 63:131, 147:32, 254:110
  Ninety-Nine Bottles of Beer 147:30, *see also:* 82, 148:376, 290:32
  Oh, the Horse Went Around 290:30
  Roll Over 63:131, 254:110, *see also:* 26:23, 147:32, 148:254, 290:34
  Ten Green Bottles 82, 148:376, *see also:* 147:30, 290:32
  Ten in the Bed 147:32, *see also:* Roll Over
  The Ten Puppies/Los Diez Perritos 295:17
  There Were Ten in the Bed 26:23, *see also:* Roll Over
DISCIPLES, TWELVE: *see* APOSTLES

DISCOVERY PERIOD IN AMERICA: *see* COLUMBUS, CHRISTOPHER
DISCRIMINATION: *see* CIVIL RIGHTS; WOMEN—EQUAL RIGHTS
DOES: *see* DEER
DOG SLEDS
  On a Dog Sled 207:71
DOGS
  Bingo 26:22, 39:52, 46:201, 63:91, 75:13, 126:93, 129:101, 147:16, 231:94, 266:54, *see also:* 15:131 (*There was a farmer had a dog*)
  Bingo 59:59 (*The miller's mill-dog lay at the door*)
  Bow-Wow-Wow 17:78
  Cumberland Mountain Bear Chase 292:103
  Daddy Wouldn't Buy Me a Bow Wow 197:68
  The Dog Who Sees His Reflection in the Water/Le Chien Qui Se Voit dans L'Eau 243:4
  The Hound and Her Neighbor/La Lice et sa Compagne 243:41
  I Found a Little Dog 296:40
  I Have a Dog 24:18
  I Have a Little Puppy Dog 112:10
  If You Were a Kitty 296:20
  Johnny Had a Little Dog 17:131, *see also:* Bingo
  Kitty and Puppy 162:86
  La Lice et sa Compagne/The Hound and Her Neighbor 243:41
  La Poulette Grise/The Old Grey Hen 289:30
  Le Chien Qui Se Voit dans L'Eau/The Dog Who Sees His Reflection in the Water 243:4
  Les Deux Chiens/The Two Dogs 243:46, 243:53
  Les Deux Chiens et Leur Maître/The Two Dogs and Their Master 243:8
  Little Dog 150:3
  Little Dog, Little Dog 112:4
  Little Dog Named Right 234:26
  Little Lap-Dog Lullaby 234:27
  The Longest Dog in the World 167:38
  Los Diez Perritos/The Ten Puppies 295:17
  My New Puppy 207:13
  Oh, Blue 234:30, *see also:* Old Blue
  Oh, Where, O Where Has My Little Dog Gone? 17:43, *see also:* 26:18, 285:92, 292:70
  Ol' Rattler 130:32
  Old Blue 158:24, 258, 261:58, 277:147, 289:55, 292:72, *see also:* 234:30
  Old Dog Tray 292:67

The Old Grey Hen/La Poulette Grise 289:30

Old Mother Hubbard 175:22, 285:95

Our Dog 149:12

The Ten Puppies/Los Diez Perritos 295:17

Tinker—Mr. Small's Dog 154:36

The Two Dogs/Les Deux Chiens 243:46

The Two Dogs and Their Master/Les Deux Chiens et Leur Maître 243:8

Where Has My Little Dog Gone? 26:18, *see also:* 17:43, 285:92, 292:70

Where, Oh, Where Has My Little Dog Gone? 26:18, 285:92, 292:70, *see also:* 17:43

DOLLS

Dolly's Lullaby 85:219

Don't Cry Little Dolly 162:78

Have You Seen My Dolly? 165:56

I Have a Little Doll/Yo Tengo una Muñeca 194:28

Miss Polly Had a Dolly 63:40

My Dolly 130:20

Sleepy Dolly 167:40

Yo Tengo una Muñeca/I Have a Little Doll 194:28

DOMINICAN REPUBLIC

*Adoración/Adoration 89:55

*Adoration/Adoración 89:55

DONKEYS

Donkey, Donkey Old and Gray 285:42

Donkeys and Carrots 293:92

Donkeys Love Carrots 293:23

The Happy Burro 97:unpaged

La Burriquita/The Little Donkey 216:6

The Little Donkey/La Burriquita 216:42

Mi Abuelo Tenía un Huerto/My Grandfather Had a Garden 295:21

Mi Burro/My Donkey 289:64

Mon Ane/My Donkey 217:16

My Donkey/Mi Burro 289:64, *see also:* 217:55

My Donkey/Mon Ane 217:55, *see also:* 289:64

My Grandfather Had a Garden/Mi Abuelo Tenía un Huerto 295:21

Sir Donkey 292:31

Sweetly Sings the Donkey 26:45, 62:17, 144:3, 148:366, 176:129, 254:116, 289:187, 292:32, 293:94

Tinga Layo 290:54

DOUGHNUTS

Doughnuts 239:88

DOVES: *see also* PIGEONS

The Dove 292:132

Four Little White Doves 33:202

La Paloma Azul/The Sky-Blue Dove 89:72

The Sky-Blue Dove/La Paloma Azul 89:72

Three Doves 72:145

DRAGONS

The Dieting Dragon 166:12

DRAMA: *see also* CREATIVE DRAMATICS; MOVING PICTURES; OPERAS AND OPERETTAS; PUPPETS

All at Once You Love Her (Pipe Dream) 218:286

The Man I Used to Be (Pipe Dream) 218:282

No Other Love (Me and Juliet) 218:278

So Far (Allegro) 218:268

You Are Never Away (Allegro) 218:272

DREAMS

Climb Ev'ry Mountain 218:246

A Dream Is a Wish Your Heart Makes 276:35

Dream Song 19:35

Happy Talk 218:163

Nearly Missed 206:86

Smoo 261:10

Wishes 261:14

You Tell Me Your Dreams, I'll Tell You Mine 170:99

DREIDELS: *see* TOPS (TOYS)

DRESS: *see* CLOTHING AND DRESS

DRILLING

Bob Stanford 159:295

Drill, Ye Tarriers, Drill! 22:138, 64:87, 72:88, 239:80, 290:52

Drivin' Steel 226:150

DRUMS

Oh, We Can Play on the Big Bass Drum 165:184

DUCKS

All the Ducks 135:25, *see also:* 227:37

Dicky Ducky Daddle 162:13

The Duck and the Hen 17:73

The Duck and the Kangaroo 112:53

The Ducks 227:37, *see also:* 135:25

Ducks on a Pond 290:197

En Roulant Ma Boule Roulant 89:34

Five Little Ducks 75:26, 165:136

Have You Seen the Little Ducks Swimming in the Water 165:81

La Tortue et les Deux Canards/The Tortoise and the Two Ducks 243:22

Mistress Bond 62:52, 175:72, 292:154, *see also:* 188:116

My Ducklings 68:21

Oh, What Have You Got for Dinner, Mrs. Bond? 188:116, *see also:* 62:52, 175:72, 292:154

On, Roll On 128:74, *see also:* 89:34

Playmates 162:73

Six Little Ducks 43, 55:271, 63:104, 148:342, 289:106

DUCKS—*Continued*
Swim, Little Ducks 162:15
The Tortoise and the Two Ducks/La Tortue et les Deux Canards 243:22
Two Ducks on a Pond 262:86
DUTCH LANGUAGE: *see* NETHERLANDS
DWARFS (FAIRIES)
Dwarf Song 245:63

E

EAGLES
The Eagle 44:48
Song of the Watchers 74:59
EARS: *see also* BODY, HUMAN
Do Your Ears Hang Low 63:139, 118:19
EARTH DAY
It's the Same the Whole World Over 197:50
EASTER
At the Dawn of Easter Day 86:64
The Careful Bunny 207:100
Christ Is Risen 86:63
Christ the Lord Is Risen Today; Alleluia 86:67, 197:40
Christ Was Born in Bethlehem 86:41, 157:65
Come, O Children, Sing to Jesus 86:66
Down Came an Angel 157:65, *see also:* 86:41
Down in Yon Forest 27:82, 190:58, 210:23
Easter 207:101
Easter Alleluya 262:156
Easter Basket 197:42
Easter Bells 162:57
Easter Bunny Song 245:114
Easter Carol 184:60 *(Cheer up, friends and neighbors)*
An Easter Carol 86:59 *(Easter flow'rs are blooming bright)*
Easter Greeting 245:113
The Easter Hare 245:115
Easter Hats 207:99
Easter Hymn 167:20 *(As we greet each Easter morn)*
Easter Hymn 197:40, *see also:* 86:67 *(Christ the Lord is risen today)*
Easter Is Here 7:18
An Easter Message 207:98
Easter Rabbit 162:58
Easter Time 86:61
Flower Carol 184:58
Jesus Christ Is Risen Today 45:42, 86:62
Jesus Walked in Galilee 37:166
Joyful Easter 86:65

The Little Bunny 41:39
Make a Hat for Easter 162:38
O Glorious Bells of Easter 197:41
That Great Getting-Up Morning 27:74
We Welcome Glad Easter 86:60
EATING: *see* FOOD AND EATING
ECHO SONGS
Little Sir Echo 68:18
O Dad O' Mine 25:7
Oh, You Can't Get to Heaven 147:46, 290:93
Sippin' Cider Through a Straw 148:338, 290:38, *see also:* 226:329
Suckin' Cider Through a Straw 226:329, *see also:* 148:338, 290:38
ECOLOGY: *see also* POLLUTION
Mr. Wolz 260:46
ECUADOR
*En Sumag Palacio/In My Spacious Palace 89:97
*In My Spacious Palace/En Sumag Palacio 89:97
The Speckled Bird 122:76
EGYPT
Dance With Gladness/Doos Ya Lellee 89:248
*Doos Ya Lellee/Dance With Gladness 89:248
*El-thahlib 169:19
The Fox 269:62
EIRE: *see* IRELAND
EL SALVADOR
Hay-Hoo! Hay-Hoo!/Jeu! Jeu! 216:51, *see also:* 89:79
*Jeu! Jeu!/Hay-Hoo! Hay-Hoo! 89:79, 216:36
ELECTIONS: *see also* POLITICAL SONGS
Fair and Free Elections 27:218
ELECTRICITY
Lights 11:14
One Happy Swede 64:110
ELEPHANTS
The Elephant 169:12
The Elephant Is Big and Strong 165:103
The Elephant Present 59:60
Elephant's Bath 207:107
Elephants Marching 63:80
Eletelephony 44:64
Le Rat et l'Eléphant/The Rat and the Elephant 243:13
One Elephant Went Out to Play 178:14
One Little Elephant Balancing 63:42
The Rat and the Elephant/Le Rat et l'Eléphant 243:13
When I See an Elephant Fly 275:23, 276:10
ELVES
The Painter Elves 7:32
Under Yonder Oaken Tree 78:19

EMANCIPATION PROCLAMATION
Emancipation 73:26
EMOTIONS: *see also* CRYING; FEAR
Carefully Taught 218:169
The Clown in Me 219:17
A Face 206:63
Hitori de Sabishii 16:30
I Like to Be Told 219:49
I Whistle a Happy Tune 218:184
If You're Happy and You Know It 25:16, 26:39, 63:44, 147:20, 253:91
It's Such a Good Feeling 219:35
Just for Once 219:40
Please Don't Think It's Funny 219:32
A Soft Answer 155:11
Sometimes People Are Good 219:24
Talk It Out 91:12
What Do I Do When I'm Alone? 206:70
What Do You Do? 219:27
When a Baby Comes 219:37
Wishes Don't Make Things Come True 219:14
ENGINEERS
Casey Jones 22:142, 158:264, 158:266, 159:148, 222, 226:366
ENGINES, RAILWAY: *see* ENGINEERS; RAILROADS; TRAINS
ENGLAND
As I Walked Through London City 134:60
As I Was Going to Banbury 134:88
The Baby and the Moon 125:36
Birds' Lullaby 125:48
Blow the Wind Southerly 72:126
Boscastle 83:508
The British Grenadiers 22:198, 240:142
Buckingham Palace 172:128, 173:14
The Chinese Fan 68:16
Cornish May Song 208:70
Day and Night 125:38
The Fly and the Bumblebee 68:29, 128:44, *see also:* 17:77, 59:28, 188:20, 292:200
God Save the King 22:208
Harvest Home 189:122
Hiking Song 227:34, *see also:* 25:65, 26:65
Lambs Are Sleeping 125:56
The Lame Crane 71:114, 72:170, *see also:* 62:19, 144:25, 176:152, 292:65, 293:52
A Lame, Tame Crane 144:25, *see also:* The Lame Crane
The Lincolnshire Poacher 117:unpaged, 176:44
My Aunt Has a Lame Tame Crane 62:19, *see also:* Lame Crane

My Dame Hath a Lame, Tame Crane 144:25, 176:152, 292:165, 293:52, *see also:* 62:19, 71:114, 72:170
My Mother Said 68:24, *see also:* 63:97
Now Robin, Lend to Me Thy Bow 71:57, 72:121
Oft in the Stilly Night 66:26, 125:44
Oh, Dear! What Can the Matter Be? 17:88, 36:6, 62:126, 135:22, 148:271, 175:50, 188:80, 205:41, 262:101, 273:110, 283:44
Oh, How Lovely Is the Evening 21:322, 62:11, 71:109, 72:173, 148:273, 241:232, 289:189, 293:22
Oh, Music, Sweet Music 293:8
The Old Home Guard 275:79, 276:66
The Old Woman and the Pedlar 68:14, 79:41, 188:132, *see also:* 17:64, 27:58, 259
On Christmas Night 54:40, *see also:* 210:56
Open the Window 212:18
Push the Business On 70:13
Queen Mary 227:30
The Red Flag 64:190
The Red Herring 262:27
Robin a Thrush 78:15
Rock the Cradle 125:54
The Roman Soldiers 39:26, 129:114, 135:88
St. Stephen's Day 212:12
Sheep Shearing 129:36, 134:102, 292:54
Since First I Saw Your Face 189:92
Sir Eglamore That Valiant Knight 71:72
Slumber Soundly 125:35
The Snow Lay On the Ground 54:54
Some Say the Devil's Dead 134:43
Sumer Is a-Cumen In 71:108, *see also:* 27:154, 176:144, 189:110, 293:80
Summer Is a-Coming In 27:154, 71:108, 176:144, 293:80, *see also:* 189:110
Summer Is I-cumen In 189:110, *see also:* 27:154, 71:108, 176:144, 293:80
Sussex Carol 54:40, *see also:* 210:56
Swansea Town 208:74
Sweet and Low 125:52
Sweet Be Your Sleep 125:34, 262:86
Sweetly Sings the Donkey 26:45, 62:17, 144:3, 148:366, 176:129, 254:116, 289:187, 292:32, 293:94
There Was a Donkey Standing By 197:119
They're Moving Grandpa's Grave 290:172
Thou Poor Bird 292:129, 293:88
Three Crows 62:54, *see also:* Three Ravens

ENGLAND—*Continued*
The Three Ravens 22:94, 37:115, 189:88, 292:140, *see also:* 62:54, 232:121, 290:70, 292:142
Time Sends a Warning Call 125:55
To Portsmouth 85:15, 176:103
Tom Pearce 292:24, *see also:* 22:50, 71:68, 190
Turn Again, Whittington 62:16, 175:11, 176:83, 262:69, 293:40
Turn the Glasses Over 20:56, 39:2, 70:9, 129:120, *see also:* 134:44
Twankydillo 262:24
The Twelve Days of Christmas 22:248, 30, 50, 54:36, 87:91, 92:183, 113, 121, 148:400, 190:148, 197:120, 210:64, 233:72, 241:30, 264:66, 287, 290:26, 292:160
Unite and Unite 130:28
Wassail 89:130, *see also:* Wassail Wassail All Over the Town
Wassail Song 22:270, 27:6, 54:35, 92:186, 96:6, 128:66, 148:154, 184:8, 189:130, 197:8, 209:12, 220:42, 262:112, 279:36, 284:47, *see also:* 264:82
The Water Is Wide 148:406, 230:77
We'll All Go Down the Meadow 262:46
What Child Is This? 21:238, 54:30, 92:188, 125:46, 148:412, 241:50, 242:unpaged, 261:52, 264:123, 279:40, 284:99
When Christ Was Born of Mary Free 54:20, 209:45, 210:134
Widdicome Fair 22:50, 71:68, 193, *see also:* 292:24
Won't You Go My Way? 134:68
The Wraggle-Taggle Gypsies, O! 22:70, 227:12, *see also:* 148:144, 211, 226:311
EQUALITY: *see* CIVIL RIGHTS; WOMEN—EQUAL RIGHTS
ERIE CANAL
E-RI-E 21:282, 158:146, 226:180, 290:44, *see also:* 230:87, 277:39
Erie Canal 230:87, 277:39, *see also:* 21:282, 158:146, 226:180, 290:44 (E-RI-E)
Erie Canal 22:37, 69:34, 197:78, 226:171, 239:60, 246, 262:74, 292:38, *see also:* 33:58 (Low bridge everybody down)
Low Bridge, Everybody Down 33:58, *see also:* Erie Canal
ESKIMOS
*Ajaaj/Drum Song 89:31
*Drum Song/Ajaaj 89:31
Eskimos 207:77
On a Dog Sled 207:71
Walrus Hunt Song 26:33

ETHIOPIA
*Mengedagnan/The Wanderer 169:21, 267:27
Thank You, Wati/Tole Ya Wati 89:261
*Tole Ya Wati/Thank You, Wati 89:261
The Wanderer/Mengedagnan 169:21, 267:27
ETIQUETTE
Hello 107:14
The Living Room 149:18
Thank You 11:26
EVENING
Evening Is a Little Boy 59:37
Müde Bin Ich, Geh Zur Ruh/Weary, Now I Close Mine Eyes 86:173
Oh, How Lovely Is the Evening 21:322, 62:11, 71:109, 72:173, 148:273, 241:232, 289:189, 293:22
O Wie Wohl Ist's Mir Am Abend/O, How Lovely Is the Evening 241:232
Thou Who Once on Mother's Knee 86:168
Weary, Now I Close Mine Eyes/Müde Bin Ich, Geh Zur Ruh 86:173
EXERCISE GAMES: *see also* ACTION SONGS; FINGER AND HAND PLAY; SINGING GAMES
Baile de los Pollos/The Chicken Dance 194:30
The Chicken Dance/Baile de los Pollos 194:30
Follow the Leader 162:63
Head, Shoulders, Knees and Toes 54:267
On a Rainy Day 162:31
Raise Your Hands Above Your Head 165:124
Stretch Your Arms 204:21
Up I Stretch on Tippy Toe 165:142
Wake Up 130:10
Wind the Bobbin Up 165:122
EZEKIEL
Ezekiel Saw the Wheel 148:86, *see also:* 226:488
Ezekiel, You and Me 226:488, *see also:* 148:86

F

FABLES
The Adopted Monkey/Le Singe Adopté 243:45
The Ant and the Grasshopper/La Fourmi et la Sauterelle 243:34, *see also:* 79:65
The Bear and the Two Gascons/L'Ours et les Deux Gascons 243:26

The Beggar's Double Sack/La Besace 243:50

The Boy and the Schoolmaster/L'Enfant et le Maître d'Ecole 243:35

The City Rat and the Country Rat 17:96

The City Rat and the Country Rat/Le Rat de Ville et le Rat des Champs 243:29

The Clay Pot and the Iron Pot/Le Pot de Terre et le Pot de Fer 243:2

The Cock and the Fox/Le Coq et le Renard 243:36

The Crow and the Fox/Le Corbeau et le Renard 243:2

The Dog Who Sees His Reflection in the Water/Le Chien Qui Se Voit dans L'Eau 243:4

The Fly and the Ant/La Mouche et la Fourmi 243:10

The Fly and the Coach/La Mouche et le Coche 243:48

The Fox and the Grapes/Le Renard et les Raisins 243:42

The Fox and the Wolf/Le Renard et le Loup 243:38

The Frogs Who Want to Have a King/Les Grenouilles Qui Demandent un Roi 243:18

The Grasshopper and the Ant/La Cigale et la Fourmi 79:65, see also: 243:34

The Hare and the Frogs/Le Lièvre et les Grenouilles 243:16

The Hare and the Tortoise/Le Levraut et la Tortue 243:24

The Hen Who Laid Golden Eggs/La Poule aux Oeufs d'Or 243:14

The Hound and Her Neighbor/La Lice et sa Compagne 243:41

La Besace/The Beggar's Double Sack 243:50

La Cigale et la Fourmi/The Grasshopper and the Ant 79:65, see also: 243:34

La Fourmi et la Sauterelle/The Ant and the Grasshopper 243:34, see also: 79:65

La Lice et sa Compagne/The Hound and Her Neighbor 243:41

La Mouche et la Fourmi/The Fly and the Ant 243:10

La Mouche et le Coche/The Fly and the Coach 243:48

La Poule aux Oeufs d'Or/The Hen Who Laid Golden Eggs 243:14

La Tortue et les Deux Canards/The Tortoise and the Two Ducks 243:22

Le Chien Qui Se Voit dans L'Eau/The Dog Who Sees His Reflection in the Water 243:4

Le Coq et le Renard/The Cock and the Fox 243:36

Le Corbeau et le Renard/The Crow and the Fox 243:2

Le Levraut et la Tortue/The Hare and the Tortoise 243:24

Le Lièvre et les Grenouilles/The Hare and the Frogs 243:16

Le Lion et le Rat/The Lion and the Rat 243:6

Le Loup Berger/The Shepherd Wolf 243:30

Le Loup et la Cicogne/The Wolf and the Stork 243:30

Le Pot de Terre et le Pot de Fer/The Clay Pot and the Iron Pot 243:2

Le Rat de Ville et le Rat des Champs/The City Rat and the Country Rat 243:29

Le Rat et l'Eléphant/The Rat and the Elephant 243:13

Le Renard et le Loup/The Fox and the Wolf 243:38

Le Renard et les Raisins/The Fox and the Grapes 243:42

Le Singe Adopté/The Adopted Monkey 243:45

L'Enfant et le Maître d'Ecole/The Boy and the Schoolmaster 243:35

Les Deux Chèvres/The Two Goats 243:23

Les Deux Chiens/The Two Dogs 243:46, 243:53

Les Deux Chiens et Leur Maître/The Two Dogs and Their Master 243:8

Les Deux Mulets/The Two Mules 243:20

Les Grenouilles Qui Demandent un Roi/The Frogs Who Want to Have a King 243:18

The Lion and the Rat/Le Lion et le Rat 243:6

L'Ours et les Deux Gascons/The Bear and the Two Gascons 243:26

The Rat and the Elephant/Le Rat et l'Eléphant 243:13

The Shepherd Wolf/Le Loup Berger 243:30

The Tortoise and the Two Ducks/La Tortue et les Deux Canards 243:22

The Two Dogs/Les Deux Chiens 243:46

The Two Dogs and Their Master/Les Deux Chiens et Leur Maître 243:8

The Two Goats/Les Deux Chèvres 243:23

The Two Mules/Les Deux Mulets 243:20

The Wolf and the Stork/Le Loup et la Cicogne 243:30

FACES
Eye Winker 75:24
I've Got Two 206:22

FACES—*Continued*
  Mouth and Eyes   204:19
  Nose, Nose   111:55
  Right in the Middle of My Face   206:28
  Who Has a Nose?   178:9
FACTORIES: *see also* MILLS
  Automation   64:146
FAIRIES: *see also* BROWNIES; DWARFS (FAI-
  RIES); ELVES; LEPRECHAUNS
  Bamboo Fairies   68:36
  Dance, Little Maiden   245:32
  The Fairies   227:40
  The Fairy Flute   245:30
  Go Away, Little Fairies   125:74
  In Fairyland   207:94
FALL: *see* AUTUMN
FAMILY AND FAMILY LIFE: *see also* BA-
  BIES; HOME
  All Of Us   149:6
  Bedtime Stories   207:21
  Children Can   219:45
  A Child's Song   85:222
  Come, Son   176:76
  Daddy's Whiskers I   197:70
  Daddy's Whiskers II   197:70
  Dance Like a Lady   296:23
  The Dining Room   149:16
  Don't Swat Your Mother (parody)
    290:176
  Five People in My Family   206:18
  Gentle Mother/Yasashii Okasan   286:54
  Grandpa and I   207:17
  I Like to Be Told   219:49
  I Want a Girl   25:33
  I'd Like to Be Like Dad   219:43
  I'd Like to Be Like Mom   219:43
  I'm Taking Care of You   219:58
  Johnny Jump Around   296:14
  The Kitchen   149:14
  The Living Room   149:18
  Love My Daddy, Yes I Do   197:71
  Luli, Deck the Crib   125:12
  Mama Small   154:37
  Mammy Don't 'Low   290:62, *see also:*
    197:58
  Mi Abuelo Tenía un Huerto/My Grandfa-
    ther Had a Garden   295:21
  Mother and I   207:22
  Mother Machree   170:40
  Mother's Day   86:151
  My Grandfather Had a Garden/Mi Abue-
    lo Tenía un Huerto   295:21
  My Mom Won't Allow   197:58, *see also:*
    290:62
  My Mother   207:117
  New Baby Brother   166:56
  O Dad O' Mine   25:7
  Parents Are People   260:48
  Pierre   235:43

Soliloquy   218:91
That's All About Mr. Small   154:40
There Are Dads (boys)   26:15
A Valentine for Grandma   207:78
Watching for Pa   197:69
What Do You Do, Papa Small   154:38
Where Are You Going Grandmama?
  68:39
Yasashii Okasan/Gentle Mother   286:54
Your Mother and Mine   276:31
FAREWELLS: *see also* CLOSING SONGS
  Aloha Oe/Farewell to Thee   87:99
  Farewell to Thee/Aloha Oe   87:99
  The Mail Boat   129:13
FARM LIFE: *see also* FARMERS; HARVEST;
  RANCH LIFE; names of farm products,
  e.g., CORN
  Alpine Song   245:8
  The Barnyard Song   68:27, 75:10, 128:34,
    129:76, *see also:* 27:96, 37:171, 55:265,
    109:193, 132:unpaged, 232:104,
    254:108, 289:47, 292:13, 292:18
  Bought Me a Cat   232:104, *see also:*
    Barnyard Song
  Can You Show Me How the Farmer
    17:32
  The Children's Zoo   162:19
  The City Rat and the Country Rat   17:96
  Come, Little Sennerin   245:12
  Come to the Farm   162:15
  Cotton-Picking Song   239:45
  The Crops Have Been Gathered   125:22
  A Customer   154:22
  Dakota Land   61:62, 159:410, 226:280,
    see also: 61:63, 61:64
  Did You Feed My Cow   107:18, *see also:*
    232:112, 234:56, 292:20, 292:44
  Did You Go to the Barney   232:112, *see
    also:* 107:18, 234:56, 292:20, 292:44
  Down on Penny's Farm   64:100
  Eleven Cent Cotton   21:98, 64:104
  The Farm Windmill   207:104
  The Farmer in the Dell   14:347, 17:8,
    20:70, 63:13, 157:46, 283:9, 289:180
  Farmer's Boy   212:48
  Farmer's Carol   210:101
  Fiddle-I-Fee   37:171, 292:18, *see also:*
    Barnyard Song
  Had a Little Rooster   128:34, *see also:*
    Barnyard Song
  Harvest Home   189:122
  Harvest Is Over/Marken er Mejet
    208:17, *see also:* 83:496
  How the Corn Grew   191:64
  I Had a Little Cat   132:unpaged, *see also:*
    Barnyard Song
  I Had a Little Rooster   292:13, *see also:*
    Barnyard Song

I Had an Old Rooster   109:193, *see also:* Barnyard Song
I Like to Live on the Farm   154:19
I Want to Be a Farmer   128:76
I Went to Visit a Farm One Day   165:77
If I Could Have a Windmill   55:267, 165:84
If I Had a Tractor   154:18
Little Boy Blue   17:10, 175:56, 188:32, 283:23, 285:38
The Little Vine-Clad Cottage   61:70
Marken Er Mejet/Harvest Is Over   83:496, 208:17
Mi Chacra/My Farm   262:19
Mow the Meadow/Marken Er Mejet   83:496, 208:17
My Farm/Mi Chacra   262:19
My Father Is Dead   188:44, *see also:* Swapping Song
My Roadside Stand   154:20
My Twenty Pennies   262:22
The Old Cow Died   234:56, 292:44, *see also:* 107:18, 232:112, 292:20
Old MacDonald Had a Farm   4, 17:148, 26:20, 55:262, 75:56, 81, 199, 283:12, 291:30
On the Farm   207:106
One Man Shall Mow My Meadow   132:unpaged
The Swapping Boy   143, *see also:* Swapping Song
The Swapping Song   37:174, 129:38, 213:10, *see also:* 18:36, 111:63, 188:44
The Tractor's Song   288:12
When I Was a Bachelor   18:36, *see also:* Swapping Song
When I Was a Little Boy   111:63, *see also:* Swapping Song
FARMERS
Ain't It Hard to Be a Farmer   109:212
Can You Show Me How the Farmer   17:32
The Farmer   226:282, *see also:* 24:879, 64:96, 230:57, 239:42
The Farmer and the Crow   262:43
The Farmer Comes to Town   24:879, 239:42, *see also:* 64:96, 226:282, 230:57
The Farmer in the Dell   14:347, 17:8, 20:70, 63:13, 157:46, 283:9, 289:180
The Farmer Is the Man   64:96, 230:57, *see also:* 24:879, 226:282, 239:42
The Jolly Thrasher   35:91
Men of the Soil   64:94
One Happy Swede   64:110
The Ploughboy   262:131
Poor Sz Bbei/Sz Bbei Shang Gung   49:16
Seven-Cent Cotton and Forty-Cent Meat   24:877

Sz Bbei Shang Gung/Poor Sz Bbei   49:16
Wayfaring Stranger   24:881
Whoa Buck   158:232
The Young Man Who Wouldn't Hoe Corn   24:874, 158:230, 230:42
FASHION: *see* CLOTHING AND DRESS
FATHERS: *see* FAMILY AND FAMILY LIFE
FAWNS: *see* DEER
FEAR
Night Noises   166:10
FEASTS: *see* FOOD AND EATING; names of holidays, e.g., THANKSGIVING DAY
FEBRUARY
Great Americans   207:80
January, February   233:50
FEET: *see* BODY, HUMAN
FERRIES
The Ferry   71:118
The Ferry Boat   41:31
FESTIVALS: *see* HOLIDAYS; names of festivals, e.g., HANUKKAH (FEAST OF LIGHTS)
FIDDLES: *see* VIOLINS
FILLING STATIONS: *see* SERVICE STATIONS
FINGER AND HAND PLAY: *see also* ACTION SONGS; CLAPPING GAMES; RHYTHMS; SINGING GAMES; SKIPPING MUSIC; SKIPPING ROPE
All for Baby   191:40
The Caterpillar   191:36
The Counting Lesson   191:56, *see also:* 162:23
Dance, Thumbkin, Dance   17:42, 111:29
Dancing   104:50
The Dicky-Bird Song   75:20, *see also:* Two Little Blackbirds
Do, Do, Pity My Case   24:805, 232:136
Down in the Grass, Curled Up in a Heap   165:95
Eency Weency Spider   20:81, 232:126, 289:92, 291:44, *see also:* 46:216, 63:103, 75:22, 147:26, 292:202
Eentsy Weentsy Spider   75:22, *see also:* Eency Weency Spider
Eye Winker   75:24
Fingers Like to Wiggle Waggle   165:120
Five Currant Buns in a Baker's Shop   165:30
Five Little Ducks   75:26, 165:136
Five Little Mice   191:44
Grandma's Spectacles   75:28
Help Me Wind My Ball of Wool   165:32
The Hen and Chickens   191:20
Here Is the Beehive   162:23, *see also:* 191:56
Here Is the Church   75:30
Hickory, Dickory, Dock   17:113, 75:32, 135:117, 175:68, 188:172, 283:10, 285:25, 292:196

FINGER AND HAND PLAY—*Continued*
How Does a Caterpillar Go? 165:44
How the Corn Grew 191:64
I Have Made a Pretty Nest 165:155
I Roll the Ball 75:37
I'm a Little Teapot 63:106, 75:36, 165:31, 291:50
Incy Wincy Spider 46:216, *see also:* Eency Weency Spider
Inky Dinky Spider 147:26, *see also:* Eency Weency Spider
Inky Pinky 'Pider 63:103, *see also:* Eency Weency Spider
Jack and Jill 17:83, 75:38, 175:18, 177:90, 188:124, 283:24, 289:88
Jack-O-Lantern 75:40
Knock At the Door 17:150
The Lambs 191:16
A Little Boy's Walk 191:32
The Little Plant 191:24
The Little Pony 291:53
Little White Duck 75:46, 289:56
Look At the Terrible Crocodile 165:104
Making Bread 191:72
Making Butter 191:76
The Merry Little Men 191:12
The Mill 191:68
Mrs. Pussy's Dinner 191:60
My Hat 83:471, *see also:* 291:54
My Hat It Has Three Corners 83:471, 291:54
Pat-A-Cake 17:127, 75:60, 175:80, 188:162
Pease Porridge Hot 17:74, 162:89, 285:90, 291:58, *see also:* 175:90
Pease Pudding Hot 175:90, *see also:* 17:74, 162:89, 285:90, 291:58
The Pigs 191:28
Santa Claus 191:80
Scraping Up Sand In the Bottom of the Sea 232:96
Shiloh 232:96
Six Little Snails 17:62, 165:48
The Sparrows 191:52
The Spider 46:216, *see also:* Eency Weency Spider
The Squirrel 191:48
The Teensy Weensy Spider 292:202, *see also:* Eency Weency Spider
Ten Fingers 75:72
Ten Little Indians 17:144, 75:74
There Was a Little Turtle 75:76
This Is My Little House 165:29
This Little Pig 17:71, 75:80, 285:14, *see also:* 175:48
This Pig Went to Market 175:48, *see also:* 17:71, 75:80, 285:14

Tommy Thumb, Tommy Thumb, Where Are You? 165:169, *see also:* 75:88, 289:110
Two Little Blackbirds 162:9, 178:18, 290:104, 291:40, *see also:* 75:20, 111:32
Two Little Dicky Birds 111:32, *see also:* Two Little Blackbirds
What Does the Clock In the Hall Say? 165:38
Where Is Thumbkin? 75:88, *see also:* 165:169, 289:110
Where's Mister Thumbkin 289:110, *see also:* 75:88, 165:169
With My Little Broom I Sweep, Sweep, Sweep 165:33
FINGERS: *see* HANDS
FINLAND
*The Finnish Forest/Suomen Salossa 89:172
God Is the Loving Father 86:20
*Kesailta/'Twas Summer and 'Twas Evening 208:21
Rocking the Cradle 125:26
Sandman Will Come 125:28
Sleep, My Duckling 245:87
*Suomen Salossa/The Finnish Forest 89:172
'Twas Summer and 'Twas Evening/Kesailta 208:21
The Wood Bird's Lullaby 125:29
FIRE DEPARTMENTS: *see* FIREFIGHTERS; FIRES
FIRE ENGINES: *see also* FIREFIGHTERS; FIRES
Fire Truck 154:30 *(Clang, clang! The firetruck comes)*
The Fire Truck 162:98 *(Hurry, hurry, drive the fire truck)*
Little Red Engine 162:99
FIREFIGHTERS: *see also* FIRE ENGINES; FIRES
Fireman Brave 154:31
Smokey the Bear 26:81
FIREFLIES
Come Fireflies/Hotaru Koi 286:24, *see also:* 16:32
Firefly 162:21 *(I'm a little firefly, flit, flit, fan)*
Firefly 245:48 *(A little light is going by)*
Glow Worm 21:72
Hotaru Koi/Come Fireflies 16:32, 286:24
Light My Way to Bed 19:21
FIRES: *see also* FIRE ENGINES; FIREFIGHTERS
Fire Down Below 98:34, 129:84, 232:162, *see also:* 134:64
Fire! Fire! 134:64, *see also:* 98:34, 129:84, 232:162

A Hot Time in the Old Town 126:57, 157:191, *see also:* 21:30, 203

London's Burning 25:30, 175:20, *see also:* 46:227, 148:321, 283:35, 289:188, 293:36

Scotland's Burning 46:227, 62:13, 148:321, 283:35, 289:188, 293:36, *see also:* 25:30, 175:20

There'll Be a Hot Time 21:30, 203, *see also:* 126:57, 157:191

They'll Be a Hot Time in the Old Town Tonight 203, *see also:* 21:30, 126:57, 157:191

FISH: *see also* names of fish, e.g., HERRING

All the Fish Are Swimming in the Water 128:30, 130:100

Farewell, Little Fishes 292:177

The Fishes 292:168, *see also:* 289:72

Fishy, Fishy 17:48

In Our Aquarium 162:85

La Poulette Grise/The Old Grey Hen 289:30

The Old Grey Hen/La Poulette Grise 289:30

Song of the Fishes 289:72, *see also:* 292:168

Swim, Little Fish, In Water Clear 165:112

The Water Bug Stands Upon a Fish 74:14

The Whizz-Fish Song 84:19

FISHERMEN AND FISHING

The Angler's Song 189:120

The Bold Fisherman 27:208, 128:116, 239:20, 256

The Carite Fish/El Carite 216:42

Cool Breezes/Liang Fung Lyao Lyao 49:18

The Crawdad 21:106, 24:896, 27:160, 230:86, *see also:* 129:30, 148:58, 158:107, 292:182

The Crawdad Hole 129:30, *see also:* Crawdad

Crawdad Song 148:58, 158:107, 292:182, *see also:* Crawdad

Dance to Your Daddy 27:142, 111:42, 281:56

Did You Ever Go Fishing? 112:28

El Carite/The Carite Fish 216:4

Ento Shinku/Faraway Island 49:32

Faraway Island/Ento Shinku 49:32

Father's At Sea 281:57

A Fish Net/He 'Upena 87:16

Fishermen's Evening Song 262:121

The Fishermen's Song 114:15

The Fishes 292:168, *see also:* 289:72

Fishin'Fun 167:28

Fishing Weather 281:58, *see also:* 18:26

Fishy, Fishy 17:48

The Four Winds 18:26, *see also:* 281:58

The Gallant Fisherman 89:158

He 'Upena/A Fish Net 87:16

The Herring Song 292:172

Hush-a-Bye 281:55

Hush Song 281:59

I Catch-a da Plenty of Feesh 226:409

Liang Fung Lyao Lyao/Cool Breezes 49:18

The Mist 281:60

Nantucket Lullaby 281:62

Okino Kamomeini/To the Sea Gull Offshore 49:27

The Oyster Fishers' Song 262:140

Pescator dell' Onda/The Gallant Fisherman 89:158

Song of the Fishes 289:72, *see also:* 292:168

Sponge Fishing 114:56

Three Jolly Fishermen 63:98, 290:50, *see also:* 26:13, 148:294

To the Sea Gull Offshore/Okino Kamomeini 49:27

FISHING: *see* FISHERMEN AND FISHING

FLAGS

A Flag Salute 207:83

Our Flag 207:42

Pledge of Allegiance to the Flag 32:28

The Stars and Stripes Forever 25:42

You're a Grand Old Flag 72:28, 197:66, 205:331

FLANDERS

*De Nederige Geboorte/The Simple Birth 54:182

*The Simple Birth/De Nederige Geboorte 54:182

FLEAS

The Flea and the Louse/La Pulga y el Piojo 295:12

La Pulga y el Piojo/The Flea and the Louse 295:12

FLIES

Baby Bye, Here's a Fly 59:14

The Fly and the Ant/La Mouche et la Fourmi 243:10

The Fly and the Coach/La Mouche et le Coche 243:48

La Mouche et la Fourmi/The Fly and the Ant 243:10

La Mouche et le Coche/The Fly and the Coach 243:48

Shoo, Fly Don't Bother Me 21:159, 46:208, 70:24, 126:85, 129:108, 178:20, 292:198

The Spider and the Fly 175:168

FLIGHT

Birds Have Wings 7:28

I Can Fly 162:101

FLIGHT—*Continued*
You Can Fly! You Can Fly! You Can Fly!
275:58, 276:30
FLOWERS: *see also* names of flowers, e.g.,
DAISIES
Bellflower Taryong/Toraji Taryong
49:36
Easter Greeting 245:113
Easter Hats 207:99
The First Bouquet 207:86
Hiraita, Hiraita/Open, Open 16:47,
286:36
I'm Little White Clover 245:36
A Lei for Our Queen/Makalapua 87:76
Lei Ilima 87:62
The Leis of Hawaii/Na Lei O Hawaii
87:60
Makalapua/A Lei for Our Queen 87:76
Marie in the Meadow 245:25
May Baskets 207:115
Na Lei O Hawaii/The Leis of Hawaii
87:60
Open, Open/Hiraita, Hiraita 16:47,
286:36
Out in Our Meadow/Uti Var Hage
262:39
Rose Red 46:229
Rose, Rose 262:159, 293:24
Summer Bouquet 97:unpaged
Toraji Taryong/Bellflower Taryong
49:36
Uti Var Hage/Out in Our Meadow
262:39
White Coral Bells 46:227, 62:13, 72:160,
148:416, 262:32, 293:18
FLUTE
Dze(r) dzoo diow/Purple Bamboo Flute
208:12
Purple Bamboo Flute/Dze(r) dzoo diow
208:12
Song of the Flute 74:27
FLYING: *see* FLIGHT
FOG: *see also* CLOUDS
Fog 162:30
FOOD AND EATING: *see also* names of
meals, e.g., BREAKFAST; specific foods,
e.g., BREAD
A-gardening We Will Go 26:84
Back of the Bread 72:44
Bellflower Taryong/Toraji Taryong
49:36
Bird's Christmas Feast 207:55
Busy Little Bushytail 207:28
Ca, Ca, Ca 236:77
Camp Menu Song 25:22
Can You Show Me How the Farmer
17:32
The City Rat and the Country Rat 17:96
Come Out to Play 18:46

The Cow 17:115
Cowboys' Gettin'-Up Holler 159:3, *see
also:* 289:24
Crows in the Garden 130:107
A Customer 154:22
Dame Get Up 17:123, 129:52,
138:unpaged, 188:150
The Dieting Dragon 162:12
The Dining Room 149:16
Doodle Dandy 134:92
East Coast Line 109:97
Eating Goober Peas 99:48, *see also:*
27:132, 73:166, 157:128, 277:85
The Farmer is the Man 64:96, 230:57, *see
also:* 24:879, 226:282, 239:42
Fishy, Fishy 17:48
Five Fat Turkeys Are We 178:42
Food 11:10
Give Me Three Grains of Corn, Mother
226:41
Goober Peas 27:132, 73:166, 157:128,
277:85, *see also:* 99:48
Good King Arthur 18:28, 112:7, 188:142,
see also: 17:100
Green Corn 130:46, 134:36
Greens 226:347
Ham and Eggs 25:26, 26:26
Harvest Home 189:122
Harvest Is Over/Marken Er Mejet
208:17, *see also:* 83:496
Hurry Up, Liza Jane 128:18
I'm Going Away to See Aunt Dinah
109:142
Isn't It Funny 172:17, 174:3
It's Very, Very Funny 172:25, 173:11
Jack Spratt 17:70, 175:15
Just From the Kitchen 109:52
King Arthur 17:100
The Kitchen 149:14
Les Belles Pommes D'Api! 227:9
Let's Go to the Sea/Vamos a la Mar
216:49
Let's Hike to the Woodlands Today
245:23
Little King Pippin 111:60
A Little Seed Lay Fast Asleep 86:8
Mahiya Illa Zalab/Song of the Fig Ven-
dors 89:246
The Mallard 62:75
Maple Sweet 33:50
Marken Er Mejet/Harvest Is Over
83:496, 208:17
Market Man 41:40
Mow the Meadow/Marken Er Mejet
83:496, 208:17
My Roadside Stand 154:20
Oh, John the Rabbit 232:100, 291:32
Old Aunt Kate 232:139
Skip to Market 162:63

Solas Market 130:85

Song of the Fig Vendors/Mahiya Illa Zalab 89:246

Today Is Monday 84:28, 253:92

Toraji Taryong/Bellflower Taryong 49:36

Vamos a la Mar/Let's Go to the Sea 216:30

What Shall We Do About Poor Little Tigger? 172:51, 174:37

FORESTS AND WOODS: see also LUMBERING; TREES

The Forest 91:19

4-H CLUBS

4-H Field Song 55:257

FOURTH OF JULY: see also FLAGS; NATIONAL SONGS

America 25:44, 26:88, 66:90, 69:4, 71:4, 72:32, 127:73, 148:22, 157:118, 160:32, 197:76 (My country tis of thee)

Fireworks for the Fourth 166:64

Whose Birthday 97:unpaged

Yankee Doodle Boy 157:212, 197:75, see also: 205:301

Yankee Doodle Dandy 205:301, see also: 157:212, 197:75

FOWLS: see CHICKENS; DUCKS; GEESE; TURKEYS

FOXES

A-Hunting We Will Go 17:134, 63:36, 135:118, 136, 165:192, see also: 14:349, 20:82, 42

All Ye Jolly Huntsmen 212:22

Catch a Little Fox 47, see also: A-Hunting We Will Go

The Cock and the Fox/Le Coq et le Renard 243:36

The Crow and the Fox/Le Corbeau et le Renard 243:2

The Fox 129:46, 148:100, 230:80, 292:86, see also: 62:41, 234:32, 247, 262:41

The Fox and the Goose/Fuchs, Du Hast Die Gans Gestohlen 289:60

The Fox and the Goose 62:41, see also: Fox Went Out on a Chilly Night

The Fox and the Grapes/Le Renard et les Raisins 243:42

The Fox and the Wolf/Le Renard et le Loup 243:38

The Fox Went Out on a Chilly Night 148:100, 230:80, 247, 292:86, see also: 62:41, 129:46, 234:32, 262:41

A Fox Went Out One Starry Night 262:41, see also: Fox Went Out on a Chilly Night

Fuchs, Du Hast Die Gans Gestohlen/The Fox and the Goose 289:60

Hunting 15:349, see also: A-Hunting We Will Go

Le Coq et le Renard/The Cock and the Fox 243:36

Le Corbeau et le Renard/The Crow and the Fox 243:2

Le Renard et le Loup/The Fox and the Wolf 243:38

Le Renard et les Raisins/The Fox and the Grapes 243:42

Old Fox 234:32, see also: Fox Went Out On a Chilly Night

The Three Foxes 172:132, 173:18

FRANCE: see also FRENCH LANGUAGE

*Ah! Vous Dirai-je, Maman/Oh! Shall I Tell You, Mother 217:12

*Ainsi Font, Font, Font/They Do Like This 217:23

Ali, Alo 72:130

*Although You Still Are Weak and Helpless/Quoique Soyez Petit Encore 54:116

The Apples 227:10

*Auprès de ma Blonde/Near to My Fair One 21:340

A Basque Lullaby 71:38, 125:114

Berceuse Française 78:41, see also: 59:51

*Berger, Secoue Ton Sommeil Profond/Shepherd, Shake Off Your Drowsy Sleep 54:122, 220:88, 284:59

The Butterfly's Wedding/Les Noces du Papillon 217:63

Cadet Rousselle 217:44

*Celebrons la Naissance/We Sing in Celebration 54:92, see also: 279:21

The Coward 227:11

Dodo, Baby Do 125:108, see also: 78:41

*D'où Viens-tu, Bergère?/Whence, O Shepherd Maiden? 279:96, see also: 54:133

Dreamland 125:107

*En Passant par la Lorraine/Passing Through Lorraine 176:66, 217:36, see also: 208:23

*French Slumber Song 78:41, 125:108

*Gentil Coquelicot/Pretty Poppies 217:20

*Il Etait une Bergère/There Was a Shepherdess 217:32

In the Town 241:90

*La Princesse Mariée à un Anglais/The Princess Wed to an Englishman 89:150

*L'Autre Jour En Voulant Danser/While I Was Dancing the Other Day 89:152

*Le Sommeil de l'Enfant Jésus/The Sleep of the Infant Jesus 54:100, 241:82

*Les Noces du Papillon/The Butterfly's Wedding 217:46

FRANCE—*Continued*
*Lullaby/Soum, Soum 208:25
*Ma Fille, Veux-tu un Bouquet/My Daughter, Would'st Have a Bouquet 80:66
Marche Lorraine 22:188
Margot, Dress the Vines 262:117
*Mon Ane/My Donkey 217:16
*My Daughter, Would'st Have a Bouquet?/Ma Fille, Veux-tu un Bouquet 79:66
*My Donkey/Mon Ane 217:55
*Near to My Fair One/Auprès de ma Blonde 21:340
*Neighbor, What Has You So Excited?/Quoi, Ma Voisine, Es-tu Fachée? 54:104
*Nous N'Irons Plus au Bois/We Will Go No More to the Woods 217:40
Obedient Kitten 245:47
*O Come Away, Ye Shepherds/Quittez, Pasteurs 54:98
*Oh! Shall I Tell You Mother/Ah! Vous Dirai-je, Maman 217:53
*Papa, les Petits Bateaux/Papa, the Little Boats 217:45
Papa, the Little Boats/Papa, les Petits Bateaux 217:63
Passing Through Lorraine/En Passant par la Lorraine 208:23, *see also:* 176:66, 217:60
Pat-A-Pan 54:112, 129:60, *see also:* 210:80, 220:90, 241:176, 262:50
Patapan 220:90, 241:176, *see also:* 54:112, 129:60, 210:80, 262:50
Pretty Poppies/Gentil Coquelicot 217:56
The Princess Wed to an Englishmen/La Princesse Mariée à un Anglais 89:150
*Quelle Est Cette Odeur Agréable?/Whence Is That Goodly Fragrance? 54:102, 210:76, *see also:* 220:32
*Quittez, Pasteurs/O Come Away, Ye Shepherds 54:98
*Quoi, Ma Voisine, Es-tu Fachée?/Neighbor, What Has You So Excited? 54:104
*Quoique Soyez Petit Encore/Although You Still Are Weak and Helpless 54:116
Robin Loves Me/Robin M'Aime 22:125, 189:94
Robin M'Aime/Robin Loves Me 22:125, 189:94
Shelter Where Ox and Ass Are One 209:24
The Shepherd Maid 227:6
*Shepherd, Shake Off Your Drowsy Sleep/Berger, Secoue Ton Sommeil Profond 54:122, 220:88, 284:59

*The Sleep of the Infant Jésus/Le Sommeil de l'Enfant Jésus 54:100, 241:82
*Soum, Soum/Lullaby 208:25
Spring Carol 27:54, 189:68
There Was a Shepherdess/Il Etait une Bergère 217:59
They Do Like This/Ainsi, Font, Font, Font 217:56
Three Drummer Boys/Trois Jeunes Tambours 217:58
Three Little Old Men/Trois Petits Bonshommes 217:58
*Touro-Louro-Louro 54:130
*Trois Jeunes Tambours/Three Drummer Boys 217:30
*Trois Petits Bonshommes/Three Little Old Men 217:29
*We Sing. in Celebration/Celebrons la Naissance 54:92, *see also:* 279:21
We Were Ten Maidens 227:38
We Will Go No More to the Woods/Nous N'Irons Plus au Bois 217:61
*Whence Is That Goodly Fragrance?/Quelle Est Cette Odeur Agréable? 54:102, 210:76, *see also:* 220:32
*Whence, O Shepherd Maiden?/D'où Viens-tu, Bergère? 279:96, *see also:* 54:133
*While I Was Dancing the Other Day/L'Autre Jour en Voulant Danser 89:152
FREEDOM
Adams and Liberty 157:28
America, Commerce, and Freedom 273:118
American "Heart of Oak" 273:38
Castle Island Song 273:26, *see also:* 28:22
Chester 21:242, 28:147, 157:20, 197:25, 240:83, 273:140
Come Swallow Your Bumpers 28:13, *see also:* 240:47, 273:24
Derry Down 27:164, *see also:* 28:51, 240:67, 273:36
Emancipation 73:26
Fair and Free Elections 27:218
The Federal Constitution and Liberty Forever 273:62
Follow Washington 27:32, 28:84
Free America 240:57, 273:28, *see also:* 27:120, 28:43
Free Amerikay 27:120, 28:43, *see also:* 240:57, 273:28
Free at Last 31:21, 157:139
Go Down, Moses 22:316, 31:13, 64:168, 148:108, 158:372, 197:45, 205:178
Green Grow the Lilacs 22:174, 148:132, 157:70, *see also:* 66:96
The Hammer Song 230:19
Huzza for Liberty 273:72

In Freedom We're Born   27:182, 28:9, *see also:* 21:238, 157:16, 240:44, 273:20

Independence Day   28:68, 240:84

I've Got No Strings   275:21, 276:12

Jefferson and Liberty   27:188, 64:188

The Liberty Song   21:238, 157:16, 240:44, 273:20, *see also:* 27:182, 28:9

The Liberty Tree   28:58

Lift Every Voice and Sing   108

Massachusetts Liberty Song   240:47, 273:24, *see also:* 28:13

Oh, Freedom   21:167, 31:53, 64:164, 157:138, 158:370

On Independence   240:84, *see also:* 28:68

A Song Made Upon the Election of a New Magistrate for This City   240:27

A Song Made Upon the Foregoing Occasion   240:28

FRENCH AND INDIAN WAR (1754-1763)

Brave Wolfe   158:118, 240:33, 273:16

Death of General Wolfe   273:18

Hot Stuff   240:145

How Stands the Glass Around   240:144, 273:14

FRENCH LANGUAGE: *see also* FRANCE

A la Claire Fontaine   217:42

Ah! Vous Dirai-je, Maman   217:12

Ainsi Font, Font, Font   217:23

Alouette   20:84, 22:124, 25:90, 26:24, 27:68, 148:18, 262:73

Au Clair de la Lune   22:74, 71:69, 148:30, 188:40, 217:13, 283:57

Auprès de ma Blonde   21:340

Ballade de Jésus Christ   54:114

Berceuse Française   78:41, *see also:* 59:51

Berger, Secoue Ton Sommeil Profond   54:122

Bethlehem   220:60, *see also:* 210:39

Bring a Torch, Jeannette, Isabella   3, 54:128, 217:64, 241:98, 264:72, 279:94, *see also:* 22:242, 184:36, 217:50

Cadet Rousselle   217:44

Canadian Friendship   107:16

Cantique de Noël   54:107, *see also:* 241:197

Celebrons la Naissance   54:92, 279:21

Chevaliers de la Table Ronde   176:98

Colin   262:147

Dans Cette Etable   210:39, *see also:* 220:60

Dans les Chantiers Nous Hivernerons   176:62

Derrière de Chez Mon Père   188:110

Dites-moi   218:134

Do, Do, L'Enfant Do   59:51, *see also:* 78:41

Donkeys and Carrots   293:92

Dors, Ma Colombe   54:120, *see also:* 184:44

D'où Viens-tu, Bergère?   54:133, *see also:* 279:96

En Avant, Grenadiers   89:45

En Passant par la Lorraine   176:66, 217:36, *see also:* 208:23

En Roulant Ma Boule Roulant   89:34

Entre le Boeuf et L'âne Gris   54:100, 241:82

Et Moi de M'Encourir   217:38

Fais Do-Do   33:130

Fais Dodo, Colin   59:71

French Cathedrals   71:101, 72:165, 293:38

French Slumber Song   78:41, 125:108

Frère Jacques   17:72, 62:11, 90, 148:102, 176:73, 188:180, 217:17, 283:21, 289:186, 293:42, *see also:* 25:31, 26:42

Gentil Coquelicot   217:20

Il Est Né, le Divin Enfant   54:94, 220:46, 279:92

Il Etait une Bergère   217:32

Il Pleut, Bergère   217:22

In That Poor Stable   210:39, *see also:* 220:60

Isabeau S'y Promène   176:134

J'ai du Bon Tabac   217:34

La Bersace   243:50

La Cigale et la Fourmi   79:65, *see also:* 243:34

La Fourmi et la Sauterelle   243:34, *see also:* 79:65

La Gue Declarée   89:61

La Lice et sa Compagne   243:41

La Marche des Rois   54:126, 241:105

La Marseillaise   22:223

La Mère Michel   217:26

La Mouche et la Fourmi   243:10

La Mouche et le Coche   243:48

La Poule aux Oeufs d'Or   243:14

La Poulette Grise   289:30

La Princesse Mariée à un Anglais   89:150

L'Autre Jour en Voulant Danser   89:152

Le Bon Roi Dagobert   217:28

Le Chien Qui Se Voit dans L'Eau   243:4

Le Coq et le Renard   243:36

Le Corbeau et le Renard   243:2

Le Cou-Cou   217:35

Le Furet de Bois Joli   217:48

Le Levrant et la Tortue   243:24

Le Lièvre et les Grenouilles   243:16

Le Lion et le Rat   243:6

Le Loup Berger   243:30

Le Loup et la Cicogne   243:30

Le Petit Chausseur   217:18

Le Petit Navire   89:62, 217:14

Le Pot de Terre et le Pot de Fer   243:2

FRENCH LANGUAGE—*Continued*
Le Rat de Ville et le Rat des Champs 243:29
Le Rat et l'Eléphant 243:13
Le Renard et le Loup 243:38
Le Renard et les Raisins 243:42
Le Singe Adopté 243:45
Le Sommeil de l'Enfant Jésus 54:100, 241:62
L'Enfant et le Maître d'Ecole 243:35
L'Enfant Jésus S'Endort 241:108
Les Anges Dans Nos Campagnes 54:96, 241:102, 279:89
Les Belles Pommes D'Api! 227:9
Les Deux Chèvres 243:23
Les Deux Chiens 243:46, 243:53
Les Deux Chiens et Leur Maître 243:8
Les Deux Mulets 243:20
Les Grenouilles Qui Demandent un Roi 243:18
Les Noces du Papillon 217:46
Lolotte 157:150
L'Ours et les Deux Gascons 243:26
Ma Fille, Veux-tu un Bouquet 79:66
Malbrouck 21:346, *see also:* 217:49
Malbrough 217:49, *see also:* 21:346
Meunier, Tu Dors 217:41
Minuit, Chrétiens 241:197, *see also:* 54:107
Mon Ane 217:16
Music Shall Live 69:50, *see also:* 62:20, 293:6
Musieu Bainjo 157:152
Noël des Ausels 54:124, *see also:* Carol of the Birds
Noël Nouvelet 54:118
Nous N'Irons Plus au Bois 217:40
Our Chalet Song 69:8, 71:15, 72:38
Papa, les Petits Bateaux 217:45
Quand J'étais Chez Mon Père 176:64
Quelle Est Cette Odeur Agréable? 54:102, 210:76
Quittez, Pasteurs 54:98
Quoi, Ma Voisine, Es-tu Fachée 54:104
Quoique Soyez Petit Encore 54:116
Rise Up, O Flame 69:7, 71:11, 72:174
Savez-vous Planter les Choux? 168:164, 217:10, *see also:* 165:85
Soum, Soum 208:25
Sur le Pont d'Avignon 78:39, 148:364, 188:76, 189:44, 217:24, *see also:* 14:372
Touro-Louro-Louro 54:130
Tout le Monde Samedi Soir 148:84
Trois Jeunes Tambours 217:30
Trois Petits Bonshommes 217:29
Un Flambeau, Jeannette, Isabelle 217:50
Vive la Canadienne 208:5
Vive l'Amour 25:124, 290:208, *see also:* 205:103

Vive la Compagnie 205:103, *see also:* 25:124, 290:208
FRIENDS: *see* FRIENDSHIP
FRIENDSHIP
Auld Lang Syne 22:76, 25:89, 27:2, 46:207, 148:32, 170:62, 197:10, 205:50, 290:216
Be Nice to Spiders 261:22
Can You Tell 261:16
The Caravan Song 69:54
Come All You Playmates 63:95
Each Campfire Lights Anew 72:37
Glad to Have a Friend Like You 260:119
Hello 91:4
It's a Small World 275:88
Just for Once 219:40
Lilliburlero 176:156
Make New Friends 68:38, 69:10, 262:34, 293:11
Merry-Go-Round 147:39, *see also:* 25:8, 26:10, 73:48
The More We Are Together 73:48, *see also:* 25:8, 26:10, 147:39
The More We Get Together 25:8, 26:10, *see also:* 73:48, 147:39
Playmates 162:73
Someone Nice 206:74
Vive l'Amour 25:124, 290:208, *see also:* 205:103
Vive la Compagnie 205:103, *see also:* 25:124, 290:208
What Do I Do When I'm Alone? 206:70
Won't You Be My Neighbor? 219:3
Yellow Fox 261:18
You Are Special 219:7
FROGMEN: *see* SKIN DIVING AND SCUBA DIVING
FROGS: *see also* TOADS
The Bullfrog 97:unpaged
The Foolish Frog 147:38, 231, *see also:* 290:164
The Frog and the Crow 188:72
The Frog and the Mouse 129:32, *see also:* Frog Went A-Courtin'
A Frog, He Would A-Wooing Go 17:34, 175:140, 188:34, 250, 283:28, *see also:* Frog Went A-Courtin'
The Frog in the Bog 63:134
The Frog in the Spring 292:118
The Frog in the Well 62:44, *see also:* Frog Went A-Courtin'
Frog Round 69:14, 71:107, 72:167, *see also:* 289:187, 293:100
The Frog Song 289:187, *see also:* 69:14, 71:107, 72:167, 293:100

Frog Went A-Courtin' 79:27, 131, 135:64, 205:30, 232:116, *see also:* 17:34, 20:62, 35:88, 62:44, 62:46, 129:32, 148:104, 162:11, 175:140, 188:34, 226:143, 230:56, 250, 261:62, 274:22, 283:28, 289:58, 292:116

A Frog Went Walking 162:11, *see also:* Frog Went A-Courtin'

Froggie Went A-Courtin' 20:62, 148:104, 230:56, 261:62, 292:116, *see also:* Frog Went A-Courtin'

Froggie Went Courting 274:22, *see also:* Frog Went A-Courtin'

The Frogs 293:100, *see also:* 69:14, 71:107, 72:167, 289:187

Frogs/Show Ha Mo 49:14

The Frog's Flute/Kaeru-no Fue 286:32

The Frogs Who Want to Have a King/Les Grenouilles Qui Demandent un Roi 243:18

The Hare and the Frogs/Le Lièvre et les Grenouilles 243:16

Kaeru-no Fue/The Frog's Flute 286:22

Keemo Kyemo/There Was an Old Frog 290:108, *see also:* 234:48

Le Lièvre et les Grenouilles/The Hare and the Frogs 243:16

Les Grenouilles Qui Demandent un Roi/The Frogs Who Want to Have a King 243:18

The Little Bullfrog 147:41

Missie Mouse 35:88, *see also:* Frog Went A-Courtin'

Mister Frog Went A-Courting 226:143, 289:58, *see also:* Frog Went A-Courtin'

Mr. Rat and Miss Mouse 62:46, *see also:* Frog Went A-Courtin'

Nothing Else to Do 290:164, *see also:* 147:38, 231

Show Ha Mo/Frogs 49:14

The Snake Baked a Hoecake 234:24, 292:115

Song of the Frog Waiting for Spring 19:29

There Was an Old Frog/Keemo Kyemo 234:48, *see also:* 290:108

FRONTIER LIFE: *see* PIONEERS AND PIONEER LIFE; names of frontiersmen, e.g., CROCKETT, DAVID (DAVY)

FROST

White Mornings 207:32

FRUIT: *see* names of specific fruits, e.g., APPLES

FUTURE

Someday Little Children 206:108

G

GABON

*Ka Tam Ma Wai/One Morning I Rose 89:264

*One Morning I Rose/Ka Tam Ma Wai 89:264

GAMES: *see* BALL BOUNCING; BALL ROLLING; CIRCLE GAMES; CLAPPING GAMES; FINGER AND HAND PLAY; GUESSING GAMES; SINGING GAMES; SKIPPING ROPE; names of games, e.g., BASEBALL

GARDENS AND GARDENERS: *see also* FLOWERS; VEGETABLES

Child's Song 44:78

The Garden of Paoakalani/Kuu Pua I Paoakalani 87:47

Hay Aquí, Madre, un Jardin/Mother, There Is a Garden 216:11

How Does My Lady's Garden Grow 17:98, 175:40, 188:92, *see also:* Mary Mary, Quite Contrary

In Our Garden 291:56

Kuu Pua I Paoakalani/The Garden of Paoakalani 87:47

Mary, Mary, Quite Contrary 175:171, 177:87, 188:52, 285:12, *see also:* 17:62, 17:98, 175:40, 188:92, 283:16

Mi Abuelo Tenía un Huerto/My Grandfather Had a Garden 295:21

Mistress Mary, Quite Contrary 17:62, 283:16, *see also:* Mary, Mary, Quite Contrary

Mother, There Is a Garden/Hay Aquí, Madre, un Jardin 216:44

My Grandfather Had a Garden/Mi Abuelo Tenía un Huerto 295:21

My Lady's Garden 17:98, 188:92, *see also:* Mary, Mary, Quite Contrary

Oh, John the Rabbit 232:100, 291:32

Purple Tulip Morning 261:30

To People Who Have Gardens 135:30

GASOLINE: *see* SERVICE STATIONS

GAUCHOS: *see* COWBOYS

GAZELLES: *see* ANTELOPES

GEESE

Aunt Rhody 230:45, *see also:* Go Tell Aunt Rhody

Bruce the Goose 91:39

The Fox and the Goose/Fuchs, Du Hast die Gans Gestohlen 289:60

Fuchs, Du Hast die Gans Gestohlen/The Fox and the Goose 289:60

GEESE—*Continued*
Go and Tell Aunt Nancy 135:61, *see also:* Go Tell Aunt Rhody
Go Tell Aunt Abbie 62:51, *see also:* Go Tell Aunt Rhody
Go Tell Aunt Nancy 158:16, *see also:* Go Tell Aunt Rhody
Go Tell Aunt Rhody 9, 17:104, 59:15, 72:89, 148:110, 196, 274:26, 289:69, 292:150, *see also:* 37:176, 62:51, 135:61, 158:16, 188:176, 230:45
Kari/Wild Geese 286:20
My Goose 128:101, 144:21, 176:91, *see also:* Why Shouldn't My Goose
Old Gray Goose 37:176, 135:61, *see also:* Go Tell Aunt Rhody
Ol Grey Goose 188:176, *see also:* Go Tell Aunt Rhody
Old Lady Goose 234:40
Why Shouldn't My Goose 148:420, 262:91, 289:189, 292:149, 293:90, *see also:* 128:101, 144:21, 176:91
Wild Geese/Kari 286:20
GENERALS: *see* names of generals, e.g., JACKSON, THOMAS JONATHAN STONEWALL
GEOGRAPHY: *see* names of countries, e.g., ENGLAND; natural phenomena, e.g., MOUNTAINS
GEOLOGY: *see* MOUNTAINS
GERMAN LANGUAGE: *see also* GERMANY
Ach Ja 55:510, 83:495, *see also:* 178:30
Ach Yah! 178:30, *see also:* 55:510, 83:495
All Is Silent 293:84
All Things Must Perish 293:6, *see also:* 69:50
Alle Jahre Wieder 86:44, 279:70
Als Ich Bei Meinen Schafen Wacht 54:146, 241:136
Am Weihnachtsbaum die Lichter Brennen 54:150
Brahms' Lullaby 17:33, 289:18, *see also:* 71:122, 72:58, 85:176, 125:89, 283:60
Brich an, du Schönes Morgenlicht 54:162, 241:124
Christ Was Born on Christmas Day 241:68
Da Droben Vom Berge 54:174
De Nederige Geboorte 54:182
Der Blaue Montag 89:147
Der Kuckuck 20:86
Die Abendglocke 21:322
Die Binschgauer Wallfahrt 89:149
Die Gedanken Sind Frei 64:178
Die Kinder an der Krippe 86:42, *see also:* 54:142, 241:162, 279:72
Die Könige 241:215, *see also:* 210:121
Die Lorelei 176:68
Die Weihnachtsnachtigall 279:62

Ehre Sei Gott 241:233
Ein Feste Burg 21:324, 45:10
Ein Jäger aus Kurpfalz 89:145
Ein Kindlein in der Wiegen 54:178
Es Ist ein Ros Entsprungen 54:166, 210:30, 241:84, 279:58
Es Ist ein Schnitter 89:142
Es Wird Scho Glei Dumpa 54:172, 279:82
Fuchs, Du Hast Die Gans Gestohlen 289:60
Gebet in den Heiligen Christ 241:174
Gelobet 69:52
Gloria 54:181
Gott Ist die Liebe 86:146
Grün, Grün, Grün 262:123
Haenschen Klein 168:94
Hexlein 78:63
I Know a Rose Tree Springing 210:30, *see also:* 54:166, 241:84, 264:86, 279:58
Ich Ging Emol Spaziere 89:144
Ich Steh an Deiner Krippe Hier 54:163, 241:156, 279:66
Ihr Kinderlein Kommet 54:142, 86:42, 241:162, 279:72
In Stiller Nacht 208:27
Jedermann Liebt Samstag Nacht 148:84
Jesus Liebt Mich Ganz Gewiss 86:97
Josef, Lieber Josef Mein 54:148, *see also:* 21:326
Kling, Glöckchen 54:140
Kommet, Ihr Hirten 54:326
Lieb Nachtigall, Wach Auf 54:158, 279:62
Lied der Kinder zer Bethlehem 279:84
Lippai 54:168, 241:78
Lo, How a Rose E'er Blooming 54:166, 241:84, 264:86, *see also:* 210:30, 279:58
Maria auf dem Berge 241:86, 279:74
Maria Durch ein Dornwald Ging 54:160, 241:96, 279:60
Mein Hands 20:88
Mozart's Lullaby 289:34
Müde Bin Ich, Geh Zur Ruh 86:173
Music Shall Live 69:50, 293:6
Musikanter 55:268
Müss I Denn? 22:112, 176:70
Noël Alsacien 54:120, *see also:* 184:44
Nun Danket Alle Gott 86:130
Nur Du 22:114
O Du Fröhliche 54:136, 86:31
O Laufet Ihr Hirten 54:154
O Tannenbaum 54:138, 92:179, 197:118, 241:164
O Wie Wohl Ist's Mir Am Abend 241:232, 293:22
Onkel Jakob, Onkel Jakob 148:102, 293:43

Praise and Thanksgiving Let Everyone Bring 86:210
Rätsel 79:71
Ringeltanz 188:144
Schäferin und Kuckuck 78:59
Schlaf, Kindlein, Schlaf 188:96, 289:16
Schneiderlied 208:2
Schönster Herr Jesu 86:116
Still, Still, Still 54:180
Susani 54:152
Süse, Liebe Süse 79:74
Vom Himmel Hoch 54:152, 241:150, 279:64
Vreneli 208:67
Wachet auf 241:118
Weihnachtslied 279:86
Wer Klopfet An? 279:77
Widewidewenne 188:126
Wie Schön Leuchtet der Morgenstern 54:164, 241:132
Wie Soll Ich Dich Empfangen? 241:152
Wiegenlied 86:139
Wiegenlied Der Hirten 54:156
Zu Bethlehem Geboren 54:144
Zu Weihnachten 279:66
GERMANY: see also GERMAN LANGUAGE
Ach Ja 55:510, 83:495, see also: 178:30
*Ach Yah! 178:30, see also: 55:510, 83:495
All is Silent 71:112, 72:168, 293:84
*All Things Must Perish 293:6, see also: 69:50
*Am Weihnachtsbaum die Lichter Brennen/The Christmas Tree With Its Candles Gleaming 54:150
*Behold the Reaper/Es Ist ein Schnitter 89:142
Can You Count the Stars 86:3, 125:80
The Children's Prayer 125:98, 262:149
The Christmas Nightingale/Die Weihnachtsnachtigall 279:62
*Christmas Song/Zu Weihnachten 279:66
The Christmas Tree 241:164, see also: O Tannenbaum
*The Christmas Tree With Its Candles Gleaming/Am Weihnachtsbaum die Lichter Brennen 54:150
Clapping Game 68:9
Come, Let Us Be Joyful 46:200, 70:15
Cradle Song 71:122, 72:58, 85:176, 125:89, see also: 17:63, 283:60, 289:18 (Lullaby and goodnight, in the sky stars are bright)
Cradle Song 85:101, see also: Lullaby (Lullay, my prince, lullaby)
*Der Kuckuck 20:86
*Die Gedanken Sind Frei 64:178

*Die Weihnachtsnachtigall/The Christmas Nightingale 279:62
*Ein Jäger aus Kurpfalz/A Hunter from Kurpfalz 89:145
*Es Ist ein Schnitter/Behold the Reaper 89:142
Evening Hymn 125:106
The Foot Traveler 71:45, 72:135
From Heaven High 241:150, 279:64, see also: 54:161, 86:30, 161:96, 280:115
From Sky Above 262:52
Good-Night 125:82
*Haenschen Klein/Little Hans 168:94
*Hexlein/Little Witch 78:63
*A Hunter from Kurpfalz/Ein Jäger aus Kurpfalz 89:145
*Ich Ging Emol Spaziere/One Day I Went A-Walking 89:144
In Bethlehem So Lowly/Zu Bethlehem Geboren 54:144
*Kling, Glöckchen/Ring, Little Bells 54:140
Lili Marlene 22:202
The Linden Tree 125:86
*Little Hans/Haenschen Klein 168:94
*Little Witch/Hexlein 78:63
Lovely Rosa/Schöne Rosa 189:144
Lullaby 125:85 (Hush-a-by, baby, and go to sleep)
Lullaby (Mozart) 71:123, 125:92, 125:96, see also: 85:101 (Sleep, my boy, go to sleep)
Müde Bin Ich, Geh Zur Ruh/Weary, Now I Close Mine Eye 86:173
*Music Shall Live 69:50, see also: 293:6
*Müss I Denn?/Must I Then? 22:112, 176:70
*Must I Then?/Müss I Denn? 22:112
My Ducklings 68:21
*Nur Du/Thou Only 22:114
*One Day I Went A-Walking/Ich Ging Emol Spaziere 89:144
The Peat-Bog Soldiers 22:212, 64:192
*Rätsel/A Riddle 79:71
*A Riddle/Rätsel 79:71
*Ring, Little Bells/Kling, Glöckchen 54:140
Ringel, Ringel 100:33, 168:95
*Ringeltanz/Round Dance 188:144
*Round Dance/Ringeltanz 188:144
*Savior, Hear Us, We Pray/Wiegenlied 86:139
*Schäferin und Kuckuck/The Shepherdess and the Cuckoo 78:59
*Schlaf, Kindlein, Schlaf/Sleep, Baby Sleep 188:96, 266:16
Schöne Rosa/Lovely Rosa 189:144
The Shepherd Moon 125:78

GERMANY—*Continued*
*The Shepherdess and the Cuckoo/Schäferin und Kuckuck 78:61
*Shepherds' Cradle Song/Wiegenlied Der Hirten 54:156
*Sleep, Baby, Sleep/Schlaf, Kindlein, Schlaf 188:96, 289:16
Softly Now the Light of Day 125:83
Spin, Spin 262:135
*Susani 54:152
*Süse, Liebe Süse/Suzy, Lovely Susy 79:74
*Susy, Lovely Susy/Süse, Liebe Süse 79:74
Ten Thousand Men Were Going On Manoeuvres 262:137
*Thou Only/Nur Du 22:114
Valleys Green, You Are My Joy 72:132
*Vom Himmel Hoch/From Heaven High 54:152, 241:150, 279:64
Weary, Now I Close Mine Eyes/Müde Bin Ich, Geh Zur Ruh 86:173
When Little Children Go to Sleep 125:100
*Wiegenlied/Savior, Hear Us, We Pray 86:139
*Wiegenlied Der Hirten/Shepherds' Cradle Song 54:156
*Zu Bethlehem Geboren/In Bethlehem So Lowly 54:144
*Zu Weihnachten/Christmas Song 279:66
GHANA
A-Fishing 168:26
Abena 114:41
*Che Che Koole 178:65, *see also:* 169:23
*Kye Kye Kole 169:23
*O Mane 266:25
*Sovu Dance 89:262
*Weaving the Kanti Cloth 266:25
GHOSTS: *see also* HALLOWEEN
Calliope 226:349
The Ghost of John 293:46, *see also:* 289:190
Have You Seen the Ghost of John 289:190, *see also:* 293:46
Little Ghost 197:95
My Good Old Man 20:68, 129:24, 274:40
The Peanut Stand 27:211
There Was a Li'l Woman Who Took a Stroll 197:92
GIPSIES: *see* GYPSIES
GLACIERS
Greenland Glaciers 166:52
GLOW WORMS: *see* FIREFLIES
GOATS: *see also* HERDING
Bahyahn Mongol/Rich Mongolia 208:45
Bill Grogan's Goat 289:151
Billy Goat 114:59

Counting The Goats 292:56
The Goat 62:38, *see also:* 171
The Goat Paths 44:52
The Hungry Goat 171, *see also:* 62:38
Les Deux Chèvres/The Two Goats 243:23
Mary Had a William Goat 62:39, 226:336
Rich Mongolia/Bahyahn Mongol 208:45
The Two Goats/Les Deux Chèvres 243:23
GOD: *see* HYMNS; JUDAISM; PRAYERS; RELIGION; SPIRITUALS
GOLD RUSH: *see* CALIFORNIA
GONGS: *see* BELLS
GOOD GROOMING: *see* GROOMING, PERSONAL
GOPHERS
The Cross-eyed Gopher 234:20
GOSPEL SONGS: *see* SPIRITUALS
GRACE AT MEALS: *see* PRAYERS
GRAIN: *see* names of grains, e.g., CORN
GRANDFATHERS: *see* FAMILY AND FAMILY LIFE
GRANDMOTHERS: *see* FAMILY AND FAMILY LIFE
GRAPES
The Fox and the Grapes/Le Renard et les Raisins 243:42
Le Renard et les Raisins/The Fox and the Grapes 243:42
GRASS
The Green Grass Grows All Around 94, 192, 290:19, *see also:* 27:90, 62:72, 72:127, 109:197, 132:unpaged, 134:11, 176:130, 197:48, 213:20
The Green Green Grass 149:42
GRASSHOPPERS
The Ant and the Grasshopper/La Fourmi et la Sauterelle 243:34, *see also:* 79:65
Grasshopper 292:210 *(The first grasshopper jumped over the second grasshopper's back)*
Grasshopper 177:84 *(Grasshopper, grasshopper, jumping up and down)*
The Grasshopper 288:10 *(A grasshopper hopped on a sweet potato vine)*
The Grasshopper and the Ant/La Cigale et la Fourmi 79:65, *see also:* 243:34
Grasshoppers Three 62:18, 292:208
La Cigale et la Fourmi/The Grasshopper and the Ant 79:65, *see also:* 243:34
La Fourmi et la Sauterelle/The Ant and the Grasshopper 243:34, *see also:* 79:65
Leap Frog 46:222
GREAT BRITAIN: *see* ENGLAND; SCOTLAND; WALES

GREECE
*Gerakina   169:25, 267:38
*Klahpsete/Oh, Weep Mine Eyes 89:194
Nani, Nani   125:128
*Oh, Weep Mine Eyes/Klahpsete 89:194
*Ohlee Ahgahpoon Toe Sahvahtoh 148:84
Seven Great Towns of Greece   293:34
Sponge Fishing   114:56
GREEN MOUNTAIN BOYS: see ALLEN, ETHAN
GREENLAND
Greenland Glaciers   166:52
GREETINGS
Buon Giorno   69:50
Good Morning   11:25 (Good morning, good morning, what is your name)
Good Morning   177:93 ("Good morning, good morning," it's such fun to say)
Good Morning   77:12 (Thank you for the sun)
Good Morning, Dear Children   245:5
Good Morning to You   17:123, 289:11
Goodbye, Julie   232:60
Greeting Song   262:27
Greetings   162:72
Hail, Hail the Gang's All Here   25:4, 26:7
Hello   107:14 (Hello, hello, hello, and how are you?)
Hello   91:4 (Hello, hello, hello, won't you be my friend?)
Hello! Hello!   25:6, 26:10, 69:10, 71:11, 72:160
Hevenu Shalom A'leychem   72:149, 169:39, 208:36, 266:36
Hi There, Cub!   26:7
How Do You Do   25:5, 24:8
How-D'Ye-Do   274:30
I Love That Word Hello   26:11
Little White Daisies   291:38
Merry-Go-Round   147:39, see also: 25:8, 26:10, 73:48
A Mince Pie or a Pudding   233:78
The More We Are Together   73:48, see also: 25:8, 26:10, 147:39
The More We Get Together   25:8, 26:10, see also: 73:48, 147:39
We Come to Greet You in Peace/Hevenu Sholom A'leichem   72:149, 169:39, 208:36, 266:36
Welcome Here!   140:41, 233:78
Welcome Song   68:4 (Come in! Come in! Come in!)
Welcome Song   77:19 (Your bright face makes us glad today)
We're All Together Again   25:7, 26:9, 71:12, 72:39
We're Glad to See You Here   26:11
We're Here For Fun   25:6, 26:9
When Ducks Get Up in the Morning 291:26
Yonder She Comes   232:50
GROOMING, PERSONAL
The Bathroom   149:22
The Cranky Soap   91:46
Here We Go Round the Mulberry Bush 14:366, 17:90, 20:9, 63:16, 75:50, 168:108, 175:78, 188:66, 189:40, 289:172, see also: 104:52, 283:17, 291:2
Johnny, Get Your Hair Cut   135:15, 226:158, 232:142, see also: 157:44, 226:158
The Mulberry Bush   14:365, 17:90, 63:16, 75:50, 168:108, 175:78, 289:172, see also: Here We Go Round the Mulberry Bush
'Round the Mulberry Bush   283:17, see also: Here We Go Round the Mulberry Bush
Rubber Duckie   206:121
This Is the Way We Wash Our Hands 291:2, see also: Here We Go Round the Mulberry Bush
GROUND HOGS: see WOODCHUCKS
GROWING UP
Everything Grows Together   219:12
Growing Up   172:126, 173:17 (I've got shoes with grown-up laces)
Growing Up   261:20 (How do you know when you've grown up)
Lily, Lily Wallflowers   291:76
Someday Very Soon   162:71
Song for a Boy   156:4
Song for a Girl   156:26
When We Grow Up   260:32
You're Growing   219:21
GUATEMALA
*Buenos Días Mi Señorio   169:27, 269:26
Let's Go to the Sea/Vamos a la Mar 216:49
*Matatero-tero-la   114:78, 169:27
*A Mountain High-Top/Naci En la Cumbre   89:76
*Naci en la Cumbre/A Mountain High-Top   89:76
*Vamos a la Mar/Let's Go to the Sea 216:30
GUESSING GAMES
Bo-san, Bo-san   16:16, 286:44
Hand Game Guessing Song   74:51
GUITARS
My Guitar   162:104
My Spanish Guitar   197:90
GYPSIES
A Hej te Cigany/Hey, You Gypsy   208:32

GYPSIES—*Continued*
Gypsy Davy 226:311, *see also:* 22:70, 148:144, 211, 227:12
The Gypsy Laddie 211, *see also:* 22:70, 148:144, 226:311, 227:12
Gypsy Rover 148:144, *see also:* 22:70, 211, 226:311, 227:12
Gypsy Song 69:14, 262:124
Hey You Gypsy/A Hej te Cigany 208:32
My Mother Said 68:24, *see also:* 63:97
The Wraggle-Taggle Gypsies, O! 22:70, 227:12, *see also:* 148:144, 211, 226:311

H

HAIR
Chippy, Get Your Hair Cut 157:44, 226:158, *see also:* 135:15, 226:158, 232:142
Johnny, Get Your Hair Cut 135:15, 226:158, 232:142, *see also:* 157:44, 226:158
HAITI
*Danse Juba/Juba Dance 89:57
*Feuilles, Oh/Leaves, Oh 208:29
*Juba Dance/Danse Juba 89:57
*Leaves, Oh/Feuilles, Oh 208:29
*Shango 208:30, 208:31
HALE, NATHAN
Hale in the Bush 28:80, *see also:* 240:98
Nathan Hale 240:98, *see also:* 28:80
HALLOWEEN: *see also* GHOSTS; PUMP-KINS; WITCHES AND WITCHCRAFT
At Halloween 207:24
Be a Cool Ghoul 167:44
The Ghost of John 293:46, *see also:* 289:190
Halloween 41:46
Halloween Goblins 207:34
Halloween Is Very Queer 7:38
Halloween Marching Song 207:33
Halloween Sounds 162:41
Have You Seen the Ghost of John 289:190, *see also:* 293:46
Here We Go to the Pumpkin Shop 7:36
I'm a Witch 162:38
Jack-o-Lantern 75:40 (*I'm a Jack-o-lantern with a great big grin*)
Jack-o-Lantern 97:unpaged (*Jack-o-lantern, Jack-o-lantern, big and yellow*)
Jack-o'-Lanterns 197:96
Little Ghost 197:95
The Little Pumpkin 162:40
One Two Three 162:40
A Pumpkin Man 162:42

Ten Little Goblins 197:96
Three Black Cats 162:39
Three Little Witches 68:46
Whippily, Whoppily, Whoop 197:93
The Witches 162:41
HAMMERS
Johnny Works With One Hammer 178:28, *see also:* 75:61, 165:166
Peter Hammers 75:61, 165:166, *see also:* 178:28
This Ol' Hammah 55:265, *see also:* 232:149
This Old Hammer 232:149, *see also:* 55:265
HAND PLAY: *see* FINGER AND HAND PLAY
HANDS
Keep Moving 14:352, *see also:* 26:37, 253:104
Mein Hands 20:88
One Finger Keep Moving 253:104, *see also:* 14:352, 26:37
One Finger, One Thumb 26:37, *see also:* 14:352, 253:104
Put Your Finger in the Air 75:66, 130:12, 253:108, 289:164
Tommy Thumb, Tommy Thumb, Where Are You? 165:169
Where Is Thumbkin? 75:88, *see also:* 289:110
Where's Mister Thumbkin? 289:110, *see also:* 75:88
With My Hands I Clap Clap Clap 178:29
HANUKKAH (FEAST OF LIGHTS)
Candles of Hanukkah 162:48
Dreidel Song 68:30
Hanukkah Song 22:292, 197:110
Happy Hanukkah 207:61
Let Us Light the Candles 129:56
Mi Y'malel 27:256
Rock of Ages (Hanukkah Hymn) 72:44, 197:112
Spin, Little Dreidel 207:62
Winter Holiday 162:47
HARES: *see* RABBITS
HARVEST: *see also* THANKSGIVING DAY
Autumn Is Here 245:109
Barley Harvesting/Mugi Kari 286:76
Bringing in the Sheaves 157:166
Come, Ye Thankful People, Come 45:44, 86:179
The Crops Have Been Gathered 125:22
For the Golden Corn 245:111
God Hath Given Us Harvest 86:178
Harvest Home 189:122
Harvest Is Over/Marken Er Mejet 208:17, *see also:* 83:496
How the Corn Grew 191:64
Indian Harvest 245:110

Marken Er Mejet/Harvest Is Over 83:496, 208:17

Mow the Meadow/Marken Er Mejet 83:496, 208:17

Mugi Kari/Barley Harvesting 286:76

Praise to God, Immortal Praise 86:175, 262:106

Sing to the Lord of Harvest 86:174

HATS

My Hat 83:471, *see also:* 291:54

My Hat It Has Three Corners 83:471, 291:54

Where Did You Get That Hat 205:219

HAWAII (state)

*Aia O Pele I Hawaii/Pele Is at Hawaii 87:14

*Ainahau 87:40

*Aloha Oe/Farewell to Thee 87:99

Bamboo Fairies 68:36

*Blue Flower/Lan Hua-Hua 87:50

*A Charge to Keep I Have/He Kihapai No Ka'u 87:30

*The Clouds at Kona/Kona Kai Opua 87:27

The Cockeyed Mayor of Kaunakakai 87:84

*Come Surfing With Me/Ku'u Ipo I Ka He'e Pu'eone 87:36

*E Hii E/I Rock Thee 87:18

*Famed Are the Roughriders/Kilakila Na Roughriders 87:88

*Farewell to Thee/Aloha Oe 87:99

*A Fish Net/He 'Upena 87:16

*Flying Carp/Koi Nobori 87:52, 286:74

*The Garden of Paoakalani/Kuu Pua I Paoakalani 87:47

*Hail, Waimea!/Hole Waimea 87:26

*Hawaii Ponoi/Hawaii's Own True Sons 87:58

*Hawaii's Own True Sons/Hawaii Ponoi 87:58

*He Kihapai No Ka'u/A Charge to Keep I Have 87:30

*He Mele O Ke Kahuli/Song of the Land Shell 87:15

*He Moa Kane/A Strutting Rooster 87:17

*He 'Upena/A Fish Net 87:16

*Hole Waimea/Hail, Waimea 87:26

*Hua-Hua'i/Wander Here With Me 87:34

*I Rock Thee/E Hie E 87:18

*Iesu No Ke Kahuhipa/Savior, Like a Shepherd Lead Us 87:97

*Imi Au Ia Oe/King's Serenade 87:66

*Kilakila Na Roughriders/Famed Are the Roughriders 87:88

*King's Serenade/Imi Au Ia Oe 87:66

*Koi Nobori/Flying Carp 286:74, *see also:* 87:52

*Kona Kai Opua/The Clouds at Kona 87:27

*Ku'u Ipo I Ka He'e Pu'eone/Come Surfing With Me 87:36

*Kuu Pua I Paoakalani/The Garden of Paoakalani 87:47

*Lan Hua-Hua/Blue Flower 87:50

*A Lei for Our Queen/Makalapua 87:76

*Lei Ilima 87:62

*The Lei's of Hawaii/Na Lei O Hawaii 87:60

*Like No A Like/Remembrance 89:299

*Makalapua/A Lei for Our Queen 87:76

*Na Lei O Hawaii/The Leis of Hawaii 87:60

*Na Lei O Hawaii/Song of the Islands 87:81

*Pahupahu/Who Is Knocking? 87:19

*Pele Is At Hawaii/Aia O Pele I Hawaii 87:14

*Puna Paia Aala/Puna's Bow'ry Walls 87:43

*Puna's Bow'ry Walls/Puna Paia Aala 87:43

*Pupu Hinu Hinu/Shiny Shells 87:68

*Remembrance/Like No A Like 89:299

Sandpiper 69:24

*Savior Like a Shepherd Lead Us 45:62, 87:97

*Shiny Shells/Pupu Hinu Hinu 87:68

*Song of the Islands/Na Lei Hawaii 87:81

*Song of the Land Shell/He Mele O Ke Kahuli 87:15

*A Strutting Rooster/He Moa Kune 87:17

*Sweet Lei Lehua 87:42

*Wai O Punalau/Waters of Punalau 87:71

*Waipio 87:73

*Wander Here With Me/Hua-Hua'i 87:34

*Waters of Punalau/Wai O Punalau 87:71

*Who Is Knocking?/Pahupahu 87:19

HAWKS

Song of the Nighthawk 74:22

Song of the Watchers 74:59

HAY AND HAYING

Haying Song 169:59, 268:61

HEALTH

Clean Hands 11:12

Cleano 130:16

HEALTH—*Continued*
 Here We Go Round the Mulberry Bush
  14:365, 17:90, 20:9, 63:16, 75:50,
  168:108, 175:78, 188:66, 189:40,
  289:172, *see also:* 104:52, 283:17, 291:2
 The Mulberry Bush 14:365, 17:90, 63:16,
  75:50, 168:108, 175:78, 289:172, *see
  also:* Here We go Round the Mulberry
  Bush
 Perfect Posture 26:43
 'Round the Mulberry Bush 283:17, *see
  also:* Here We Go Round the Mulberry
  Bush
 This Is the Way We Wash Our Hands
  291:2, *see also:* Here We Go Round the
  Mulberry Bush
HEBREW LANGUAGE: *see* YIDDISH LAN-
 GUAGE
HEBREWS: *see* ISRAEL; JUDAISM; YIDDISH
 LANGUAGE
HENS: *see* CHICKENS
HERDING: *see also* COWBOYS; COWS;
 GOATS; SHEEP; SHEPHERDS AND SHEP-
 HERD LIFE
 Dona Gal 61:232, *see also:* 61:231,
  61:233, 159:8, 232:69
 Doney Gal 61:231, 61:232, 159:8, *see
  also:* 61:233, 232:69
 Herdgirl's Song 68:21
 Herdsmaid's Song 176:78
 The Herdsman 25:93, 71:65, 72:119
 Little Bo Peep 17:87, 175:82, 188:60,
  189:18, 285:10
 Little Boy Blue 17:10, 175:56, 188:32,
  283:23, 285:38
 The Lonesome Trail 61:233, *see also:*
  61:231, 61:232, 159:8, 232:69
 Night Herding Song 59:49, 60:10,
  61:224, 69:23, 71:91, 89:44, 129:94,
  146:27, 159:60, 225:21, 239:30, 274:24
HERRING
 Caller Herrin' 292:174
 The Herring Song 292:172
HIGHWAYMEN: *see* OUTLAWS
HIKING: *see* WALKING
HILLS: *see* MOUNTAINS
HISTORY: *see* names of wars; names of
 countries, e.g., FRANCE; names of historic
 persons, e.g., JEFFERSON, THOMAS
HITLER, ADOLF
 Round and Round Hitler's Grave 158:88
HOBBYHORSES
 Aunt Hessie's White Horse/Tante Hessie
  Se Witperd 189:140
 Ride a Cock-Horse 17:79, 175:26,
  188:70, 283:37, 285:50
 Tante Hessie Se Witperd/Aunt Hessie's
  White Horse 189:140
HOBOS: *see* TRAMPS

HOGS: *see* PIGS
HOLIDAYS: *see also* names of specific holi-
 days, e.g., CHRISTMAS
 Barley Harvesting/Mugi Kari (Summer-
  Japan) 286:76
 Counting Song/Kazoe Uta (New Year's
  Day) 286:86
 Flying Carp/Koi Nobori (Spring Festivals)
  87:52, 286:74
 Kazoe Uta/Counting Song (New Year's
  Day) 286:86
 Koi Nobori/Flying Carp (Spring Festivals)
  286:74, *see also:* 87:52
 Mugi Kari/Barley Harvesting (Summer
  Holidays) 286:76
 Mura Matsuri/Village Festival (Japanese)
  286:82
 Now's the Time 85:202
 Soul Cakes (All Souls' Day) 293:72, *see
  also:* 134:26, 210:26
 The Souling Song (All Souls' Day)
  134:26, 210:26, *see also:* 293:72
 Star Festival/Tanabata (Japanese)
  286:81
 Tanabata/Star Festival (Japanese)
  286:81
 Village Festival/Mura Matsuri (Japanese)
  286:82
HOLLAND: *see* NETHERLANDS
HOLLYHOCKS
 Hollyhock Ladies 166:16
HOME: *see also* FAMILY AND FAMILY LIFE;
 HOUSES
 Arizona Home 61:296
 Beacon-Light of Home 66:12
 Beautiful Is Our Lodge 19:15
 Crab Is a Better Man 130:76
 Hajimete Karausu 16:41
 Halfway Down 172:122, 173:8
 Home on the Range 22:164, 25:75,
  26:72, 60:42, 61:296, 71:90, 72:97,
  146:166, 158:212, 159:424, 170:101,
  205:361, 230:26
 Home, Sweet Home 22:52, 127:61,
  157:98
 Hushabye Swing 207:91
 I Have a Little House 296:24
 I Have Made a Pretty Nest 165:155
 My Little New Log Cabin in the Hills
  61:70
HONDURAS
 *Canción del Marinero Hondureño/Song
  of the Honduran Sailor 89:74
 *El Sapo/The Toad 216:20
 *Song of the Honduran Sailor/Canción
  del Marinero Hondureño 89:74
 The Toad/El Sapo 216:46
HOPI INDIANS
 Hevebe Song 79:15

Little Prairie Dog   162:59
HORSE RACING
  Camptown Races   22:64, 66:36, 126:67,
    157:90, 205:126, 230:40
HORSES: *see also* HOBBYHORSES
  All the Pretty Li'l Horses   59:42, *see also:*
    All the Pretty Little Horses
  All the Pretty Little Horses   105, 129:53,
    158:14, 277:23, 289:22, *see also:* 59:42,
    176:54, 188:136, 189:90, 232:178
  Bonnie Black Bess   61:15, 159:217
  Cactus—Mr. Small's Pony   154:32
  Chopo   61:191
  Dona Gal   61:232, *see also:* 61:231,
    61:233, 159:8, 232:69
  Doney Gal   61:232, 159:8, *see also:*
    61:233, 232:69
  Educated Feller   61:194, *see also:* 60:30,
    61:194, 146:50, 159:78, 159:81, 225:38
  Galloping Horses   129:74
  Get Along, Cayuse, Get Along   33:226
  Giddiap   162:81
  Goodbye, Old Paint   33:218, 60:106,
    61:227, 128:86, 135:14, 146:169,
    158:214, 225:70, 232:62, *see also:* 25:77,
    158:214, 159:12, 239:28
  Here We Come on Our Ponies   135:102
  Here We Go on Our Ponies   178:6
  Hey, Little Boy   292:20
  Hop, Chop, My Little Horse   17:124
  Hop, Hop, Hop   17:121
  Horse Named Bill   226:340, 289:154,
    292:28
  The Horse Named Napoleon   62:35
  Horsey, Horsey   72:94
  Hush 'n' Bye   232:178, *see also:* All the
    Pretty Little Horses
  Hush-You-Bye   176:54, *see also:* All the
    Pretty Little Horses
  I Found a Horseshoe   226:382
  I Ride an Old Paint   24:857, 60:24,
    128:82, 146:34, 157:154, 158:216,
    225:41, 226:12, 230:25, 292:26
  John Cook   111:15
  The Little Horses   189:90, *see also:* All
    the Pretty Little Horses
  The Little Pony   291:53
  The Lonesome Trail   61:233, *see also:*
    61:232, 159:8, 232:69
  Mother Horse and Colt/Ouma   286:16
  My Little Horse   296:15
  Oh, the Horse Went Around   290:30
  The Old Gray Mare   226:102, 292:22
  Old Paint   61:227, *see also:* Goodbye, Old
    Paint
  Old Paint   143:216, *see also:* I Ride an
    Old Paint
  Ouma/Mother Horse and Colt   286:16

  Pattonio, the Pride of the Plain   61:184,
    159:356, *see also:* 60:82, 128:46,
    146:116
  Plantonio, The Pride of the Plain   60:82,
    128:46, 146:116, *see also:* 61:184,
    159:356
  Ploughboy   262:131
  Ponies   162:83
  The Pony   177:83
  Pony Song   41:42, 162:82
  Ponycart Driver/Song of the Delhi Ton-
    gawallah   262:150
  Pretty Little Horses   188:136, *see also:*
    All the Pretty Little Horses
  Rain or Shine   232:69, *see also:* 61:232,
    61:233, 159:8
  The Skew-Ball Black   159:14
  Song of the Delhi Tongawallah/Ponycart
    Driver   262:150
  Squeball   61:18, 61:20, *see also:* 234:68
  Stewball   234:68, *see also:* 61:18, 61:20
  The Strawberry Roan   223, 225:32, *see
    also:* 61:187, 61:189
  To Midnight   159:327
  Tom Pearce   292:24, *see also:* 22:50,
    71:68, 193
  Trot Old Joe   162:82
  Trot, Trot, Trot, Go and Never Stop
    165:17
  Walking John   146:79
  Widdicome Fair   22:50, 71:68, 193, *see
    also:* 292:24
  The Zebra Dun   60:30, 61:194, 146:50,
    159:78, 159:81, 225:38
HOSPITALS
  Take Me Out to the Hospital   63:97
HOUNDS: *see* DOGS
HOURS: *see* TELLING TIME; TIME
HOUSES: *see also* HOME
  The Bathroom   149:22
  The Bedroom   149:24
  Built My Lady a Fine Brick House
    232:170
  The Cellar   149:26
  The Dining Room   149:16
  The Green Green Grass   149:42
  The Kitchen   149:14
  The Little 'Dobe Casa   61:71
  The Little Old Sod Shanty   61:68, 61:72,
    159:405, 226:89
  The Little Vine-Clad Cottage   61:70
  The Living Room   149:18
  Our House   149:4
  Snail Snail   162:26
  This Is My Little House   165:29
HULA
  Aia O Pele I Hawaii/Pele Is at Hawaii
    87:14

HULA—*Continued*

He Mele O Ke Kahuli/Song of the Land Shell 87:15

Pele Is At Hawaii/Aia O Pele I Hawaii 87:14

Song of the Land Shell/He Mele O Ke Kahuli 87:15

HUMAN BODY: *see* BODY, HUMAN

HUMAN RIGHTS: *see* CIVIL RIGHTS; WOMEN—EQUAL RIGHTS

HUMMINGBIRDS

Song of the Hummingbird 74:20

HUNGARY

*Ablakomba/Through My Window 89:188

*Angels From Heaven/Menyböl Ar Angyal 54:240

*Azert Hogy én Huszár Vagyok/Look at Me, A Gallant Hussar 89:187

The Crops Have Been Gathered 125:22

*Debreczenbe K'éne Menni/The Turkey 289:86

Gently Sleep 125:20

*Hej, te Cigany/Hey, You Gypsy 208:32

*Hey, You Gypsy/Hej, te Cigany 208:32

*Look at Me, a Gallant Hussar/Azert Hogy én Huszár Vagyok 89:187

*Menyböl Ar Angyal/Angels from Heaven 54:240

Old Hungarian Round 71:111, 72:171

Out, Out, Out 78:55

*Ritka Búza/Thrifty Miss 208:33

*Thrifty Miss/Ritka Büza 208:33

*Through My Window/Ablakomba 89:188

*The Turkey/Debreczenbe K'éne Menni 289:86

HUNTING

A-Hunting We Will Go 17:134, 63:36, 135:118, 136, 165:192, *see also:* 14:349, 20:82, 47

All Ye Jolly Huntsmen 212:22

And We Hunted and We Hunted 234:36, *see also:* 27:62, 106, 128:122, 292:190

Boggy Creek 159:41, *see also:* Buffalo Skinners

The Buffalo Skinners 24:854, 64:120, 146:92, 158:174, 159:335, 226:270, 230:63, 277:137, *see also:* 159:41

Catch a Little Fox 47, *see also:* A-Hunting We Will Go

The Cheerful Horn 27:194

The Cheshire Hunt 71:41

Cumberland Mountain Bear Chase 292:103

The Deer Song 234:34, 292:80

Ein Jäger aus Kurpfalz/A Hunter from Kurpfalz 89:145

En Roulant Ma Boule Roulant 89:34

The Fox and the Goose/Fuchs, Du Hast Die Gans Gestohlen 289:60

Fox in a Box 20:82, *see also:* A-Hunting We Will Go

Fuchs Du Hast Die Gans Gestohlen/The Fox and the Goose 289:60

Herne the Hunter 85:188

A Hunter from Kurpfalz/Ein Jäger aus Kurpfalz 89:145

Hunting 14:349, *see also:* A-Hunting We Will Go

A Hunting Tale 61:8

Huntsman's Song 85:179

The Huntsmen 59:54

John Peel 22:92, 176:48, 205:374

The Keeper 71:74, 72:118, 176:9, 230:59, 290:86, *see also:* 148:216, 292:84

The Keeper Would A-Hunting Go 148:216, 176:9, 290:86, 292:84, *see also:* 71:74, 72:118, 230:59

Le Petit Chasseur/The Little Hunter 217:18

The Lincolnshire Poacher 117:unpaged, 176:44

A Little Brown Sparrow 111:18

A Little Cock-Sparrow 18:22, 175:148, 188:128

The Little Hunter/Le Petit Chasseur 217:55

The Man With the Gun 175:112

Oh, A-Hunting We Will Go 47, 135:118, 136, *see also:* A-Hunting We Will Go

Old Bangum and the Bear 37:126

Settin' On a Rail 78:91

Three Jolly Hunters 27:62, *see also:* 106, 128:122, 234:36, 292:190

Three Jovial Huntsmen 106, *see also:* 27:62, 128:122, 234:36, 292:190

Walrus Hunt Song 26:33

We Hunted and We Hunted 292:190, *see also:* 27:62, 106, 128:122, 234:36

We Whooped and We Hollered 128:22, *see also:* 27:62, 106, 234:36, 292:190

HURON INDIANS

*Anio/On to War 89:32

The Huron Indian Carol 140:38, *see also:* 2, 54:76, 161:79

*On to War/Anio 89:32

'Twas in the Moon of Winter Time 2, 54:76, 161:79, *see also:* 140:38

HYGIENE: *see* HEALTH

HYMNS: *see also* CHRISTMAS CAROLS; RELIGION; SPIRITUALS

Abide With Me 25:114, 45:61

Accept Our Offering 86:194

A'don Olom 25:120

All Creatures of Our God and King 161:29

All Glory, Laud, and Honor 22:294, 86:56, 161:106

All Hail the Power of Jesus' Name 22:283, 25:116, 157:32

All Things Bright and Beautiful 8, 45:32, 86:11

Am I a Soldier of the Cross 66:138

Amazing Grace 148:20, 157:56, 158:344, 272:10

And God Said 86:6

As Pants the Hart 45:24

At Work Beside His Father's Bench 86:51

Be Thou My Vision 86:136

Before the Lord We Bow 86:14

The Bible Helps Us 86:81

Blest Be the Tie That Binds 161:91

Bringing In the Sheaves 157:166

A Charge to Keep I Have/He Hihapai No Ka'u 87:30

Children of Jerusalem Sang the Praise 86:128

The Church of God Is Everywhere 86:68

Come, Holy Spirit, Come 86:71

Come, Thou Almighty King 45:31, 86:15, 161:85, 273:158

Come Thou Long Expected Jesus 161:54

Come Unto Me 155:31

Come with Hearts Rejoicing 86:124

Come Ye Children, Praise the Savior 86:129

Come, Ye Thankful People, Come 45:44, 86:179

Crown Him With Many Crowns 45:43

David's Lamentation 273:142

Day Is Dying in the West 22:288

Dear Lord and Father of Mankind 45:30, 148:60, 161:67

The Door of My Heart 155:15

The Doxology 21:312, 22:287, 45:7, 86:213, 148:74, 157:12, 161:11

Early in the Morning 155:2

An Easter Carol 86:59

Easter Time 86:61

Ein' Feste Burg/A Mighty Fortress Is Our God 21:324, 45:10

Fairest Lord Jesus 22:289, 45:36, 86:116, 148:90

Faith of Our Fathers 25:114, 45:35, 86:70

Far Away in Old Judea 86:52

Father, We Thank Thee for the Night 25:115, 45:40, 86:141

For the Beauty of the Earth 45:48, 86:10, 148:96, 262:151

From Greenland's Icy Mountains 157:55

The Garden Hymn 37:158

Gentle Jesus, Meek and Mild 86:24

Give to Our God Immortal Praise 86:9

A Gladsome Hymn of Praise 86:126

Glee Reigns in Galilee 22:284

Glorious Things of Thee Are Spoken 86:69

God Be in My Head 111:30, 161:124

God Did So Love the World 86:80

God Himself Is With Us 86:187

God Is Love/Gott Ist Die Liebe 86:146

God Is the Loving Father 86:20

God My Father, Loving Me 86:114

The God of Abraham Praise 86:13

God of Our Fathers 45:49

God Sees the Little Sparrow Fall 86:26

God the Master of All Pagans 273:134

God Who Made the Earth 86:25

God, Whose Name Is Love 86:17

God's a Father Kind and True 86:18

Gott Ist Die Liebe/God Is Love 86:146

Gracious Spirit, Dove Divine 86:72

Greenfields 21:354, 157:54, 226:154

Guide Me, O Thou Great Jehovah 22:286

He Kihapai No Ka'u/A Charge to Keep I Have 87:30

He Leadeth Me 45:52

Here in Our Father's House 86:74

Here We Come With Gladness 86:193

Holy, Holy, Holy 45:29, 86:127, 148:166, 161:102

"Hosanna!" Be the Children's Song 86:186

Hosanna, Loud Hosanna 86:57

How Firm a Foundation 21:352, 45:54

I Love God's Tiny Creatures 86:19

I Love to Tell the Story 45:38

I Love to Think That Jesus Saw 86:21

I Sing a Song of the Saints of God 86:111

I Sing the Mighty Power of God 86:12

I Think When I Read That Sweet Story of Old 45:8, 86:108

I Was Glad 86:73

I Would Follow Jesus 86:112

Iesu No Ke Kahuhipa/Savior, Like a Shepherd Lead Us 87:97

In Christ There Is No East or West 86:88

In Our Church We Gladly Sing 86:77

In the Sweet By and By 21:176, see also: 66:150

Jerusalem the Golden 45:55

Jesus, Friend of Little Children 86:96

Jesus From Thy Throne on High 86:143

Jesus Listens When I Pray 86:138

Jesus, Lover of My Soul 21:335

Jesus Loves Me 45:26, 86:97, 283:61

Jesus, Saviour, Pilot Me 22:291

Jesus, Tender Shepherd 45:27, 283:63, see also: 86:171

HYMNS—*Continued*

Joyful, Joyful, We Adore Thee 86:132
The King of Love My Shepherd Is 45:11
Lead, Kindly Light 45:14
Lead On, O King Eternal 45:16
Let All Mortal Flesh Keep Silence 86:190
Let the Savior's Gentle Call 86:91
Let Us With a Gladsome Mind 86:148
The Lord Is Ever Near 86:140
Lord Jesus, Thou Art Mine 86:137
Love Divine, All Love Excelling 45:60
The Many, Many Children 86:90
A Mighty Fortress Is Our God 21:324, 22:278, 45:10
Mother's Day 86:151
Müde Bin Ich, Geh Zur Ruh/Weary, Now I Close Mine Eyes 86:173
My Best Friend Is Jesus 86:105
My Body Is God's Temple 86:107
My Faith Looks Up to Thee 22:282, 148:244
My Father's House 25:119
Nearer, My God to Thee 21:174
New-Plymouth 273:146
Now Thank We All Our God 86:130, 161:119
Now the Day Is Over 45:64, 59:18, 71:124, 72:59, 125:39, 148:258, 161:74
Nun Danket Alle Gott/Now Thank We All Our God 86:130
O Come and Let Us Worship 86:191
O Come, Let Us Worship 86:188
O Come, O Come, Emmanuel/Veni, Emmanuel 54:312, 86:27, 241:134
O God of Love, O King of Peace 86:94
O God, Our Help In Ages Past 21:334, 45:47, 161:23
O Grant Us Lord, Thy Peace 86:93
O Jesus, Once a Nazareth Boy 86:122
O Lord, Turn Not Thy Face From Them 45:53
O Love That Wilt Not Let Me Go 45:37
O Master, Let Me Walk With Thee 45:25
O Master Workman of the Race 86:55
O Perfect Love 45:50
O Worship the King 25:115, 86:16
O Worship the Lord 86:189
The Old Rugged Cross 45:46
Omega 273:158, *see also:* 45:31, 86:15, 161:85
On Jordan's Bank the Baptist's Cry 86:28
Once to Every Man and Nation 45:63, 262:161
Once Upon a Hillside 86:53
Onward, Christian Soldiers 25:110, 161:113
Our Beautiful Earth 86:149

Our Father, You Have Given Me 86:148
Oxford 240:17
The People That In Darkness Walked 123:278
Praise Him, Praise Him 86:133
Praise, O Praise 72:55
Praise the Lord 86:156
Praise to God For Things We See 86:5
Praise to God, Immortal Praise 86:175, 262:106
Praise to God In the Highest 210:59
Psalm of Sion 184:72
Remember All God's Children 86:95
Rock of Ages 22:296, 45:13
Savior, Hear Us, We Pray/Wiegenlied 86:139
Savior, Like a Shepherd Lead Us 45:62, 87:97
Savior, While My Heart Is Tender 86:115
Saviour, Again to Thy Dear Name 45:23, 86:207
Schönster Herr Jesu/Fairest Lord Jesus 86:116
Shall We Gather at the River? 22:297, 157:164
Sing to God in Joyful Voice 86:1
Sing to the Lord of Harvest 86:174
Something Kind 86:101
Southwel New 273:130
Stand Up, Stand Up, For Jesus 22:290
The Strife Is O'er 161:47
Sun of My Soul 45:17
Sweep, Sweep and Cleanse Your Floor 190:138
Take My Life and Let It Be 86:123
Teach Us, Dear Lord, To Pray 86:22
Teach Us To Pray 86:142
Tell Me the Stories of Jesus 86:121
Thanksgiving Time Has Come 86:176
There Is a Green Hill Far Away 45:15, 86:58, 161:41
These Things Shall Be! 64:174, 71:28
This Is My Father's World 86:2
This Is the Day the Lord Hath Made 86:155
This Is the Truth Sent From Above 210:69
Thou Wilt Keep Him In Perfect Peace 86:79
Thus Saith the High, The Lofty One 273:138
Thy Word Is Hid 86:84
Thy Work, O God, Needs Many Hands 86:196
Thy Works of Love 83:50
To God's Most Holy House 86:82
To Thy Father and Thy Mother 86:154
Two Little Hands 86:120

Veni, Emmanuel/O Come, O Come, Emmanuel   54:312, 241:134, see also: 86:27
Vesper Hymn   262:171
Victory   273:148
Wachet auf/Wake, Awake for Night Is Flying   241:118
Wake, Awake, For Night Is Flying/Wachet auf   241:118
We Gather Together   45:56, 205:24, see also: 21:338, 27:234
We Give Thee But Thine Own   86:195
We Love Our Church, O God   86:75
We Pray For Children O'er the Sea 86:89
We Thank Thee, O Our Father   86:135
We Welcome Glad Easter   86:60
Weary, Now I Close Mine Eyes/Müde Bin Ich, Geh Zur Ruh   86:173
Welcome, Happy Morning!   45:41
When Morning Gilds the Skies   86:162
When the Master Calls Me Home   86:131
When to Church I Go   86:76
When Wilt Thou Save the People? 64:180
Who Is the Man?   22:295, 262:110
Who Made the Sky So Bright and Blue 86:4
Who Made the Stars   86:7
Wiegenlied/Savior, Hear Us, We Pray 86:139
Wondrous   Love   21:351,   37:160, 134:108, 140:76, 157:57, 158:348
Work For the Night Is Coming   25:116

I

ICE SKATING: see SKATING
ICELAND
   *Now the Winter Is Past/Nu Er Vetur Ur Boe   89:171
   *Nu Er Vetur Ur Boe/Now the Winter Is Past   89:171
   Velkomin Vertu/We Welcome Thee Tonight   209:36
   We Welcome Thee Tonight/Velkomin Vertu   209:36
IDAHO
   Way Out in Idaho   61:304, 146:87, 159:265
ILLINOIS
   El-a-noy   21:298, 226:162, see also: 35:62
   A Hot Time in the Old Town   126:57, 157:191, see also: 21:30, 203
   The Plains of Illinois   35:62, see also: 21:298, 226:162

There'll Be a Hot Time   21:30, 203, see also: 126:57, 157:191
They'll Be a Hot Time in the Old Town Tonight   203, see also: 21:30, 126:57, 157:191
IMAGINATION: see also MAKE-BELIEVE
   Clouds   261:38
   Imag-inat-ion   261:12
   The Magic Pony   245:28
   Smoo   261:10
IMPRISONMENT: see PRISONS AND PRISONERS
INDEPENDENCE: see FREEDOM
INDEPENDENCE DAY: see FOURTH OF JULY
INDIA
   *Guri Guri Karayo/I Will Rock Thee 89:216
   *Hush, My Baby/Ninni, Baba   169:30, 268:19
   *I Will Rock Thee/Guri Guri Karayo 89:216
   *Kolattam/The Stick Dance   70:10, 100:126, 168:57
   *Ninni, Baba/Hush, My Baby   169:30, 268:19
   *Pinnal   Kolattam/Weaving   Dance 89:217
   *Stick Dance/Kolattam   70:10, 100:126, 168:57
   *Weaving Dance/Pinnal Kolattam 89:217
   Who Is It?   168:56
INDIANA
   On the Banks of the Wabash   205:254, see also: 157:197
   On the Banks of the Wabash, Far Away 157:197, see also: 205:254
INDIANS OF NORTH AMERICA: see also names of tribes, e.g., HOPI INDIANS; linguistic families, e.g., SIOUAN INDIANS
   The Blue Juniata   66:92
   Death Song of an Indian Chief   273:108
   In the Forest Lonely   72:68
   Indian Lullaby   245:84
   Indian War Song   28:118
   The Indian's Death Song   61:116, see also: 273:114
   It's an Indian Village   166:14
   Little Mohea   24:824, 27:236, 37:128, 61:135, 263
   Rain Dance   178:62
   Red Wing   61:142
   The Redbird Sings   74:19
   Song of the Flute   74:27
INDONESIA
   *Bengawan Solo/Solo River   265:14
   Hand Shadow Song   114:16
   *Lir I Lir   169:34, 265:13

INDONESIA—*Continued*
  *Little Father Horse-washer/Man Paman Goejang Djarang 89:294
  *Man Paman Goejang Djarang/Little Father Horse-Washer 89:294
  *Solo River/Bengawan Solo 265:14
  *Ular Naga 169:32, 265:12
INDUSTRY
  Bread and Roses 64:70
  Hard Times in the Mill 64:68
INFANTS: *see* BABIES
INSECTS: *see also* names of insects, e.g., BUTTERFLIES
  Hojita de Guarumal/Little Leaf of the Guarumal 216:13
  Little Leaf of the Guarumal/Hojita de Guarumal 216:44
  Lots of Worms 296:26
  Space Bug 97:unpaged
  The Water Bug Stands Upon a Fish 74:14
INTERPLANETARY VOYAGES: *see* SPACE (OUTER)
IRAN
  Chick, Chick Little Chickies 114:48
  *Kouh Beh Kouh/On the Road 89:201
  *On the Road/Kouh Beh Kouh 89:201
  *Soroud-e-danesh Kade Afsari 169:36
  *Wedding Song/Ye Hahmoomee Sit Besahzum 208:35
  *Ye Hahmoomee Sit Besahzum/Wedding Song 208:35
IRAQ
  *Lovely Maiden/Yammil Abaya 89:202
  *Yammil Abaya/Lovely Maiden 89:202
IRELAND
  Ballinderry 42:596, 134:66
  Ballynure Ballad 42:593
  Barney and Katey 89:137
  Bold Brennan on the Moor 22:28, *see also:* 35:72
  Brennan on the Moor 35:72, *see also:* 22:28
  Cockles and Mussels 22:22, 262:89
  *Come, Oh Love/Shule Aroon 21:344, 89:136
  The Cork Leg 78:25
  The Cruiskeen Lawn 42:609
  Dumb, Dumb, Dumb 78:22
  Eileen Aroon 42:599
  Erin's Green Shores 35:86
  The Fair-Haired Child 42:598
  Finnegan's Wake 42:611
  The Foggy Dew 35:34
  Golden Cradle 125:60, *see also:* 42:613
  Green Grow the Lilacs 22:174, 148:132, 157:70, *see also:* 66:96
  I Know My Love 36:4, 42:601

  *I Wish I Had the Shepherd's Lamb 292:52
  John O'Dwyer of the Glens 42:591
  "Johnny, I Hardly Knew Ye" 42:605, *see also:* 148:204
  Johnny I Hardly Knew You 148:204, *see also:* 42:605
  Kevin Barry 21:116, 64:194, 226:42
  The Lamentation of Hugh Reynolds 42:607
  The Leprechaun 42:608, 79:61
  The Little Beggarman 117:unpaged
  The Maid of the Sweet Brown Knowe 42:610
  The Minstrel Boy 22:226
  Molly Brannigan 42:594
  Mother Machree 170:40
  My Gentle Harp 22:88
  My Wild Irish Rose 170:85, 205:263
  Nell Flaherty's Drake 290:179
  Night Is Coming 125:62
  Oro, My Little Boat 245:76
  Paisteen Fionn 42:598
  Rickety Tickety Tin 290:186
  Rory O'More 167:10
  Saint Patrick's Day 205:154
  The Shamrock and the Heather 262:75
  The Shan Van Vocht 42:592
  She Moved Through the Fair 42:600
  Shule Agra 21:344, *see also:* 89:136
  *Shule Aroon/Come, Oh Love 89:136, *see also:* 21:344
  The Snow Lay on the Ground 54:54
  The Snowy Breasted Pearl 42:597
  The Star of the County Down 42:610
  Suantree (Hush Song) 125:60, *see also:* 42:613
  "Thank You, Ma'am," Says Dan 42:603
  Three Craws 61:55, 128:32, 134:17, 290:144, 292:144
  The Tinker's Daughter 117:unpaged
  'Tis Pretty To Be in Ballinderry 42:596, 134:66
  Too-Ra-Loo-Ra-Loo-Ral 170:39
  Wearin' of the Green 21:286, *see also:* 205:163
  Wearing of the Green 205:163, *see also:* 21:286
  When Irish Eyes Are Smiling 170:84
  Wild Mountain Thyme 134:100
  The Wren Song 134:32
  Ye Banks and Braes 21:284, *see also:* 66:124
IRISH REPUBLIC: *see* IRELAND
ISLANDS OF THE PACIFIC: *see also* names of specific islands, e.g., SOLOMON ISLANDS
  E! E! E! 89:304
  *Like No a Like/Remembrance 89:299

*Lulay/Serenade 89:296
*Remembrance/Like No a Like 89:299
*Serenade/Lulay 89:296
ISRAEL: *see also* JUDAISM; PALESTINE; YIDDISH LANGUAGE
*Arbor Day Song 197:49
*Bring the Bricks/Hava L'Venim 89:203
*Cadima 107:42
*Greetings of Peace/Hevenu Shalom A'Leychem 266:36, *see also:* 72:149, 169:39, 208:36
*Hava L'Venim/Bring the Bricks 89:203
*Havah Nagilah 266:36
*Hevenu Shalom A'leychem 72:149, 169:39, 208:36, 266:36
How Good and Joyous 114:50
*Let Us Be Friends Again/Lomir Sich Iberbetn 89:205
*Lomir Sich Iberbetn/Let Us Be Friends Again 89:205
*Once/Pa'am Akhat 70:16, 266:35
*Pa'am Akhat/Once 70:16, 266:35
Tzena 72:151
*Uga, Uga, Uga 266:36
*We Come to Greet You in Peace/Hevenu Shalom A'leychem 72:149, 169:39, 208:36, 266:36
Ya Tsa Tsa, Via La La 178:51
*Zum Gali Gali 25:90, 64:106, 69:49, 148:424, 290:196
ITALY
*Cicerenella/Tarantella of Posilipo 78:47
*Ciu Ciu Bèllo 169:41, 265:24
*Dormi, Dormi, O Bel Bambin 54:248, 209:30, 241:94
*E Arrivato L'Ambasciatóre 188:118
*From Starry Skies Descending/Tu Scendi Dalle Stélle 279:98, *see also:* 54:244
*From Starry Skies Thou Comest/Tu Scendi Dalle Stélle 54:244, *see also:* 279:98
*The Gallant Fisherman/Pescator Dell' Onda 89:158
*Gesù Bambin L'e Nato/Jesus, the New-Born Baby 54:246
*Gira, Gira Tondo/Ring-A-Ring-Round-O 188:48, 189:25
*Golden Tresses/La Treccia Bionda 208:39
*Herod Dead/Mòrto Erode 279:102
*Il Mio Bel Castello/I'm the King of the Castle 189:152
*I'm the King of the Castle/Il Mio Bel Castello 189:152
In the Morning, When You Wake 125:116
*Jesus, the New-Born Baby/Gesù Bambin L'e Nato 54:246

La Biritullera 262:40
*La Treccia Bionda/Golden Tresses 208:39
*L'Avvelenato/The Poisoned Lover 89:156, *see also:* 157:71, 232:140
*Madame Dore 188:86, 265:23
*María Lavava/Mary Washed the Linen 188:156
*Mary Washed the Linen/María Lavava 188:156, *see also:* 189:76
*Mòrto Erode/Herod Dead 279:102
*Pescator dell 'Onda/The Gallant Fisherman 89:158
*The Poisoned Lover/L'Avvelenato 89:156, *see also:* 157:71, 232:140
*Ring-A-Ring-A Round-O/Gira, Gira Tondo 188:48, 189:25
Santa Lucía 22:30
The Silver Moon Is Shining 55:259, 72:133
Sleep, My Child 125:118, 194:16
*Sleep, My Darling/Dormi, Dormi, O Bel Bambin 209:30, *see also:* 54:248, 241:94
*Sleep, O Holy Child of Mine/Dormi, Dormi, O Bel Bambin 241:94, *see also:* 54:248, 209:30
*Sleep, O Sleep, My Lovely Child/Dormi, Dormi, O Bel Bambin 54:248, *see also:* 209:30, 241:94
Song of the Maremma 262:47
*Stornello Toscano/Tuscan Serenade 208:37
*Tarantella of Posilipo/Cicerenella 78:47
Three Doves 72:145
*Tiritomba 21:200
*Tu Scendi Dalle Stélle/From Starry Skies Descending 54:244, 279:98
*Tuscan Serenade/Stornello Toscano 208:37
*Zither and I 262:145

J

JACK-O-LANTERNS: *see* HALLOWEEN; PUMPKINS
JACKSON, ANDREW
The Hunters of Kentucky 157:34, 226:427
JACKSON, THOMAS JONATHAN (STONEWALL)
Stonewall Jackson's Way 73:84
Stonewall's Requiem 73:203
JAILS: *see* PRISONS AND PRISONERS

JAMAICA
 Chicken Hawk 100:108
 Cotton Field 189:142
 Dumplin's 130:48
 Hill an' Gully 134:20
 Isabella 65:60
 Mango Walk 134:40
 Water Come a Me Eye 72:107
JAMES, JESSE WOODSON
 The Death of Jesse James 61:258, *see also:* Jesse James
 I Went Down to the Depot 226:374
 Jesse James 21:224, 60:96, 61:255, 61:257, 61:259, 61:260, 146:154, 157:158, 158:296, 159:152, 159:155, 159:156, 159:157, 226:420, 230:36, *see also:* 61:256, 61:258
 Jesse James and His Boys 61:256, *see also:* Jesse James
JANUARY
 January, February 233:50
JAPAN
 *Aizu Komori Uta/Aizu Lullaby 49:22
 *Aizu Lullaby/Aizu Komori Uta 49:22
 *Antagata Dakosa/Where Do You Come From 286:50
 *Auntie Nextdoor/Tonari-mo Obasan 286:48
 *Barley Harvesting/Mugi Kari 286:76
 *Bird in the Cage/Kagome Kagome 169:45, 286:38, *see also:* 16:20, 266:46
 *Bo-san, Bo-san 16:16, 286:44
 The Border 114:18
 *Butsu Butsu Mame/Red Beans 286:39
 *Cherry Blossoms/Sakura Sakura 286:73, *see also:* 72:141
 *Cherry Trees/Sakura 72:141, *see also:* 286:73
 *Chi Chi Pappa, Chi Pappa 266:47
 *Come Fireflies/Hotaru Koi 286:24, *see also:* 16:32
 *Come Quickly, New Year/Hayaku Koi Koi Oshogatsu 286:85
 *Counting Song/Kazoe Uta 286:86
 *Cricket Voices/Mushi-no Koe 286:30
 *The Crow 286:26
 *Da Re Demo Do Yo Bi Gasuki 148:84
 *Dendenmushi/The Snail 286:21
 *Deta Deta/The Moon Is Coming Out 286:62
 *Doll's Festival/Hina Matsuri 286:70
 *Ento Shinku/Faraway Island 49:32
 *Evening Glow/Yu-Yake Koyake 286:64
 *Faraway Island/Ento Shinku 49:32
 *Flying Carp/Koi Nobori 87:52, 286:74
 *From Nippon Bridge/Kochae-Bushi 89:237
 *Gentle Mother/Yasashii Okasan 286:54

 *Gombei Is Sowing/Harvest Song 78:83
 *Hajimete Karausu 16:41
 *Hakone Hachiri/Hakone Mountain Road 49:30
 *Hakone Mountain Road/Hakone Hachiri 49:30
 *Haru Ga Kita 100:15, *see also:* 286:69
 *Harvest Song/Gombei Is Sowing 78:83
 The Hasty Crab Barber 286:34
 *Hato Popo/Pigeons 286:17
 *Hayaku Koi Koi Oshogatsu/Come Quickly, New Year 286:85
 *Hide and Seek/Kakurembo 286:41
 *Hina Matsuri/Doll's Festival 286:70
 *Hiraita, Hiraita/Open, Open 16:47, 286:36
 *Hitori de Sabishii 16:30
 *Hohai Bushi/Hohai Song 49:29
 *Hohai Song/Hohai Bushi 49:29
 *Hora Nero, Nen Nero 16:35
 *Hotaru Koi/Come Fireflies 16:32, 286:24
 *Ichi Kake, Ni Kakete 16:55
 *Kagome Kagome/Bird in the Cage 16:20, 169:45, 266:46, 286:38
 *Kakurembo/Hide and Seek 286:41
 *Kari/Wild Geese 286:20
 *Kariboshi Kiri Uta/Miscanthus Mowing Song 49:23
 *Kazoe Uta/Counting Song 286:86
 *Kimi-ga Yo 286:53
 *Kisha/The Train 286:58
 *Kochae-Bushi/From Nippon Bridge 89:237
 *Koganemushi/Mister Golden Beetle 286:23
 *Koi Nobori/Flying Carp 286:74, *see also:* 87:52
 *Komoriuta/Lullaby 286:63
 *Kutsu-ga Naru/Shoes Squeak 286:60
 *Lullaby/Komoriuta 286:63
 *Making Rice Cakes/Mochi Tauki Odori 49:24
 *Miscanthus Mowing Song/Kariboshi Kiri Uta 49:23
 *Mister Golden Beetle/Koganemushi 286:23
 *Mochi Tauki Odori/Making Rice Cakes 49:24
 *The Monkey Palanquin/O-Saru-no Kagoya 286:28
 *The Moon Is Coming Out/Deta Deta 286:62
 *Mother Horse and Colt/Ouma 286:16
 *Mountain Monkey/O-yama-no O-saru 286:22
 *Mugi Kari/Barley Harvesting 286:76
 *Mura Matsuri/Village Festival 286:82
 *Mushi-no Koe/Cricket Voices 286:30

*Nambu Ushiori Uta/Song of the Cattle Driver 49:28
*O-saru-no Kagoya/The Monkey Palanquin 286:28
*O-Tsuki-san Momo-Iro 16:23
*O-yama-no O-saru/Mountain Monkey 286:22
*Okino Kamomeini/To the Sea Gull Off Shore 16:27
*Open, Open/Hiraita, Hiraita 16:47, 286:36
*Ora No Omboko 16:37
*Ouma/Mother Horse and Colt 286:16
*Pass Through This Gate/Toryanse 16:61, 286:46
*Pigeons/Hato Popo 286:17
*Rabbits/Usagi 16:25, 286:18
*Rat in the Rice Sack/Zui, Zui, Zukorobashi 16:51, 286:42
*Red Beans/Butsu Butsu Mame 286:39
*Sakura/Cherry Trees 72:141, 286:73
*Sempuku-Yama 16:44
*Shoes Squeak/Kutsu-ga Naru 286:60
*The Snail/Dendenmushi 286:21
*Song of the Cattle Driver/Nambu Ushiori Uta 49:28
*Sparrow School/Su zu me No Gakko 266:47, see also: 286:14
*Sparrows' Music School/Suzume-no Gakko 286:14, see also: 266:47
*Spring Song/Haru-ga Kita 286:69, see also: 100:15
*Springtime Has Come 100:15, see also: 286:69
*Star Festival/Tanabata 286:81
*Suzume-no Gakko/Sparrows' Music 266:47, see also: 286:14
*Suzume-No Gakko/Sparrow's Music School 286:14, see also: 266:47
*Tanabata/Star Festival 286:81
*Teru, Terubozu/Wishing Dolls 286:56
*To the Sea Gull Offshore/Okino Kamomeini 49:27
*Tonari-no Obasan/Auntie Nextdoor 286:48
*Toryanse 16:61, 286:46
*The Train/Kisha 286:58
*Tsubodono 16:27
*Usagi/Rabbits 16:25, 286:18
*Village Festival/Mura Matsuri 286:82
Where Are You Going Grandmama? 68:39
*Where Do You Come From?/Antagata Dokosa? 286:50
*Wild Geese/Kari 286:20
*Wind in the Willows 125:14
*Wishing Dolls/Teru, Terubozu 286:56
*Yasashii Okasan/Gentle Mother 286:54
*Yonlyem Jinku 89:236

*Yu-Yake Koyake/Evening Glow 286:64
*Zui, Zui, Zukorobashi/Rat in the Rice Sack 16:51, 286:42
JEFFERSON, THOMAS
Jefferson and Liberty 27:188, 64:188
JESUS CHRIST: see APOSTLES; CHRISTMAS CAROLS; RELIGION; SPIRITUALS
JEWS: see ISRAEL; JUDAISM; PALESTINE; YIDDISH LANGUAGE; names of specific holidays, e.g., HANUKKAH (FEAST OF LIGHTS)
JOHN HENRY
Ever Since Uncle John Henry Been Dead 226:376
Every Monday Morning (More About John Henry) 232:156, see also: John Henry
John Henry 22:170, 33:178, 64:82, 89:40, 158:258, 158:260, 158:262, 226:24, 230:82, 232:154, 239:68, 272:15, 274:16, see also: 232:156
This Ol' Hammah 55:265, see also: 232:149
This Old Hammer 232:149, see also: 55:265
JOHNNY APPLESEED: see CHAPMAN, JOHN (JOHNNY APPLESEED)
JONAH
There Was an Old Fish 128:48
The Voice of God 123:273
JONES, JOHN PAUL
Paul Jones 35:16, see also: 240:132 (An American frigate from Baltimore came)
Paul Jones 240:134 (Of heroes and statesmen)
Paul Jones' Victory 240:132, see also: 35:16
The Yankee Man-of-War 240:130
JOSHUA
Joshua Fit the Battle of Jericho 22:304, 107:28, 158:374, see also: 148:208, 230:37
Joshua Fought the Battle of Jericho 148:208, 230:37, see also: 22:304, 107:28, 158:374
JOY
Ode to Joy 71:27, 72:54
JUDAISM: see also names of specific holidays, e.g., HANUKKAH (FEAST OF LIGHTS)
A'don Olom 25:120
All Men Are Brothers 77:20
And Thou Shalt Love 77:30
Autumn Song 77:50
Brethren in Peace Together 72:147
Dayenu 27:84, 197:46
Evensong 77:26
For Simhat Torah 77:46
For Sukkot 77:44
God Is Always With Us 77:28

JUDAISM—*Continued*
Good Morning 77:12
Grace After Meals 77:16
Grace Before Meals 77:14
Hanukkah Song 22:292, 197:110
Happy Hannukah 207:61
A Happy New Year 77:40
Hatikvah/The Hope 22:194
The Hope/Hatikvah 22:194
The Jewish Year 77:36
Let Us Light the Candles 129:56
New Moon 77:49
Pesah, Season of Cheer 77:57
Preparing for Seder 197:44
Purim Time Is Fun 77:55
Rock of Ages (Hanukkah Hymn) 72:44, 197:112
Sabbath Song 77:39
Sholom A'leychem 25:112
Torah, Torah-Torah 55:256
Who's the Hero? 77:53
Yom Kippur Day 77:43
JUGOSLAVIA: *see* YUGOSLAVIA
JUMPING ROPE: *see* SKIPPING ROPE
JUNE
June Is Bustin' Out All Over 218:85
June, Lovely June 262:34

K

KANGAROOS
The Duck and the Kangaroo 112:53
Jump, Jump! Kangaroo Brown 165:105
My Father Shot a Kangaroo 292:197, *see also:* 289:142
My Uncle Roasted a Kangaroo 289:142, *see also:* 292:197
KANSAS
In Kansas 61:96, *see also:* 61:97
Way Out West in Kansas 61:97, *see also:* 61:96
KENTUCKY
Down in the Valley 22:99, 24:902, 25:99, 46:224, 61:162, 148:70, 158:62, 205:79, 226:148, 230:33
Kentucky Babe 125:139
My Old Kentucky Home 21:134, 157:88, 205:135
KENYA
The Famine 114:43
*Giant Snake/Ssemusota 89:265
*Ssemusota/Giant Snake 89:265
KIDD, CAPTAIN WILLIAM
Captain Kidd 21:332
KINDNESS
Do Unto Others 155:10
The Good Samaritan 155:18
Kindness 155:13
KINGS AND RULERS
Buckingham Palace 172:128, 173:14
The Court of King Carraticus 290:10
God Save the King 22:208
Good King Dagobert/Le Bon Roi Dagobert 217:58
Il Mio Bel Castello/I'm the King of the Castle 189:152
I'm the King of the Castle/Il Mio Bel Castello 189:152
King William 39:4, *see also:* 63:24
King William Was King George's Son 63:24, *see also:* 39:4
The King's Breakfast 172:93
La Princesse Mariée à un Anglais/The Princess Wed To an Englishman 89:150
Le Bon Roi Dagobert/Good King Dagobert 217:28
A Lei for Our Queen/Makalapua 87:76
Makalapua/A Lei for Our Queen 87:76
Matarile 169:60, 269:38, 295:37
Matarile, Rile, Ro 169:60, 269:38, 295:37
The Princess Wed to an Englishman/La Princesse Mariée à un Anglais 89:150
Sein Kyu Kya Nyaung/Song of the Princess 89:221
Song of the Princess/Sein Kyu Kya Nyaung 89:221
There Was a Princess Long Ago 165:188
Three Kings A-Riding 63:36
KITES (TOYS)
Fly, Kite, Fly 207:89
Kite String 141:94
Let's Go Fly a Kite 275:55
Song of the Wind 162:33
KITTENS: *see* CATS
KNIGHTS AND KNIGHTHOOD
Sir Eglamore That Valiant Knight 71:72
The Spanish Knight 168:110
KNIGHTS OF THE ROUND TABLE: *see also* ARTHUR, KING
KNITTING
Help Me Wind My Ball of Wool 165:32
Warm Mittens 207:64
KOOKABURRA
Kookaburra 128:108, 148:218, 176:23, 178:55, 189:136, 262:148, 289:188, 293:86
KOREA
*Arirang 49:40, 72:153, 114:22
*Bellflower Taryong/Toraji Taryong 49:36
*Beside the Nodle River/Nodle Kangbyon 49:38
*Blue Bird/Parangsai 49:34
*Hung Taryong 49:35

*I-pal Chyongchyun Ka/Sweet Sixteen
49:42
*Kangwon Do Arirang   49:41
*Nodle Kangbyon/Beside the Nodle River   49:38
*Parangsai/Blue Bird   49:34
*Sa Tah Ryung/Song of Birds   208:41
*Song of Birds/Sa Tah Ryung   208:41
*Springtime/Yangsando   49:43
*Sweet Sixteen/I-pal Chyongchyun Ka
49:42
*Thul Tahryung   89:235
*Toraji Taryong/Bellflower Taryong
49:36
*Yangsando/Springtime   49:43
KRISS KRINGLE: see CHRISTMAS SONGS
KWAKIUTL INDIANS
Cradle Song   79:17 (Sleep, oh, sleep, oh, sleep, oh)

L

LABOR AND LABORERS: see also LABOR UNIONS; WORK; WORK SONGS
Bread and Roses   64:70
The Eight Hour Day   64:26
Eight Hours   21:215
Joe Hill   22:48, 64:20
LABOR UNIONS
A. R. U.   226:190
Anthem of the ILGWU   64:78
Brother John   64:29
Casey Jones (parody)   64:43
Commonwealth of Toil   64:14
The Death of Mother Jones   64:58
Get Thee Behind Me, Satan   64:28
Great Day (parody)   64:40
Hinky Dinky Parle Vous (parody)   64:31
Hold the Fort (parody)   64:36
Joe Hill   22:48, 64:20
Me Johnny Mitchell Man   24:865
The Mill Was Made of Marble   64:76
Old Ma Bell   64:42
On the Line   64:30
The Preacher and the Slave   64:155, 226:222, see also: 24:886
The Red Flag   64:190
Roll the Union On   64:44
The Scabs Crawl In   64:46
Solidarity Forever   64:12, 230:91
Song of the Guaranteed Wage   64:162
Talking Union   64:22
The Teacher's Lament   64:141
Too Old to Work   64:143
U.A.W.–C.I.O.   64:90
Union Maid   64:17

Union Man   64:62
Union Train   64:34
United Steelworkers Are We   64:92
We Are Building a Strong Union   64:72
We Shall Not Be Moved   64:38, 230:38
West Virginia Hills   64:56
Which Side Are You On?   64:54, 230:94, 239:90
You've Got to Go Down   64:25
LADYBIRDS: see LADYBUGS
LADYBUGS
Lady Bird, Lady Bird   285:58, 292:203, see also: 175:89
Ladybird   85:162
Ladybird, Ladybird   175:89, see also: 285:58, 292:203
Ladybug   166:22
LAMBS: see SHEEP
LAOS
*Most Adored/Thorum   89:223
*Thorum/Most Adored   89:223
LARKS
La Calandria/The Lark   295:7
The Lark   292:134 (The lark it is a handsome bird)
The Lark/La Calandria   295:7 (There was a lark hanging from a balcony)
The Merry Lark   71:110, 72:169
The Rising of the Lark   262:81
LATIN AMERICA: see also names of Latin American countries, e.g., PANAMA
*Al Animo/Cheer Up   194:24, see also: 168:112
*Cheer Up/Al Animo   194:24, see also: 168:112
*Riqui Ran   262:17, see also: 295:45
*Riquirran   295:45, see also: 262:17
LATIN LANGUAGE
Adeste Fideles   22:245, 54:318, 92:171, 148:266, 241:148, 279:18, 283:50
Carol of the Nuns of Saint Mary's, Chester   279:16
Corde Natus Ex Parentis   54:314
Dona Nobis Pacem   55:254, 69:11, 176:47, 241:224, 262:34, 293:112
O Sanctissima   22:253, 241:120
Personent Hodie   220:104
Psallite Unigenito   279:23
Puer Natus in Bethlehem   54:316, 279:12
Quem Pastores   54:317, 279:14
Veni, Emmanuel   54:312, 241:134, see also: 86:27
Viva la Musica   71:98, 72:170, 293:14
LATTER-DAY SAINTS: see MORMONS AND MORMONISM
LAW ENFORCEMENT: see POLICE
LAWYERS
When I Went to the Bar   252:38

LEAVES: *see also* AUTUMN; TREES
  The Autumn Leaves Have Fallen Down
    165:61
  Falling Leaves   41:44
  The Forest   91:19
LEBANON
  Ar-Rouzana   157:35
  *Bintil Shalabeya/Fairest Maid   89:206
  *Fairest Maid/Bintil Shalabeya   89:206
  *Ya Ghizayyel   169:46, 265:36
LEE, ROBERT EDWARD
  The Sword of Robert E. Lee   73:78
LEGS
  Our Legs   204:23
LEMONADE
  At the Lemonade Stand   166:44
LEPRECHAUNS
  The Leprechaun   42:608, 79:61
LESOTHO
  *Khoe Li/The Moon   89:256
  *The Moon/Khoe Li   89:256
LIBERIA
  I'm Goin' Chop Crab   89:266
LIBERTY: *see* FREEDOM
LIBYA
  *Ajjamal Wanna/Caravan Song   89:244
  *Caravan Song/Ajjamal Wanna   89:244
LICE
  The Flea and the Louse/La Pulga y el
    Piojo   295:12
  La Pulga y el Piojo/The Flea and the
    Louse   295:12
LIGHTNING BUGS: *see* FIREFLIES
LILACS
  Green Grow the Lilacs   22:174, 148:132,
    157:70, *see also:* 66:96
LIMERICKS
  The Golux's Song   59:19
  The Limerick Song   290:100
  Mister Crumpit   91:42
LINCOLN, ABRAHAM: *see also* CIVIL WAR
    (U.S., 1861-1865); EMANCIPATION PROC-
    LAMATION
  The Abe-iad   73:50
  Farewell Father, Friend and Guardian
    73:72
  Great Americans   207:80
  Lincoln and Liberty   27:14, 157:51,
    226:167
  Old Abe Lincoln   21:140, 27:12, 226:168
  To Honor Lincoln   207:82
LIONS
  Le Lion et le Rat/The Lion and the Rat
    243:6
  The Lion and the Rat/Le Lion et le Rat
    243:6
  Pierre   235:43
LITTER AND LITTERING
  The Garden   206:116

Litterbug Rag   26:83
Picture a World   206:90
LITTLE JOHN: *see also* ROBIN HOOD
  Robin Hood and Little John   164:10,
    262:132
LIZARDS
  Mole in the Ground   234:25, *see also:*
    24:900, 253:96
  The Snake Baked a Hoecake   234:24,
    292:115
LOCOMOTIVES: *see* RAILROADS
LOCUSTS: *see also* GRASSHOPPERS
  Hojita de Guarumal/Little Leaf of the
    Guarumal   216:13
  Little Leaf of the Guarumal/Hojita de
    Guarumal   216:44
LOGGING: *see* LUMBERING
LOONS
  The Loons Are Singing   19:19
LULLABIES: *see also* NIGHT; SLEEP
  A la Niñita, Nana   54:252, 279:108, *see
    also:* 89:161, 216:31
  A la Puerta del Cielo/At the Gate of
    Heaven   72:142
  A la Ru   277:149
  Aizu Komori Uta/Aizu Lullaby   49:22
  Aizu Lullaby/Aizu Komori Uta   49:22
  All the Pretty Lil' Horses   59:42, *see also:*
    All the Pretty Little Horses
  All the Pretty Little Horses   105, 129:53,
    158:14, 277:23, 289:22, *see also:* 59:42,
    176:54, 188:136, 189:90, 232:178
  All the World Is Sleeping   125:70
  All Through the Night   21:337, 59:20,
    125:72, 205:60, 289:26
  Armenian Lullaby   125:130
  At the Gate of Heaven/A la Puerta del
    Cielo   72:142
  Aunt Rhody   230:45, *see also:* Go Tell
    Aunt Rhody
  The Babe   54:308, *see also:* 100:154,
    279:106
  The Baby and the Moon   125:36
  Baby Bunting   59:33, *see also:* Bye Baby
    Bunting
  Baby Dear   232:141
  Baby Mine   114:60
  Baby Sitter's Lullaby/Vigndig A Fremd
    Kind   289:32
  Baloo, Lammy   54:56, 241:14, *see also:*
    125:64
  Baloo Loo Lammy   125:64, *see also:*
    54:56, 241:14
  A Basque Lullaby   71:38, 125:114
  Bears Are Sleeping   294
  Bed Is Too Small   69:48
  Berceuse Française   78:41, *see also:* 59:51
  Bird Song Ntyilo   163:36
  Birds' Lullaby   125:48

Bossy Cow   112:30

Brahms' Lullaby   17:63, 289:18, *see also:* 71:122, 72:58, 85:176, 125:89, 283:60

Buy a Pretty Pony   234:65, *see also:* 245:100

Bye, Baby Bunting   17:110, 125:40, 175:14, 188:14, 283:58, *see also:* 59:33, 285:102

Bye-lo, Baby Bunting   285:102, *see also:* Bye Baby Bunting

By'm By   129:18, 226:453, *see also:* 135:44, 157:156, 232:71, 289:13

By'M Bye   157:156, 232:71, 289:13, *see also:* 129:18, 135:44, 226:453

By'n Bye   135:44, *see also:* By'M Bye

Can You Count the Stars?   86:3, 125:80

The Children's Prayer   125:98, 262:149

Chinese Baby Song   17:134, 59:27

Chinese Cradle Song   78:77, *see also:* 125:10

The Christ Child's Lullaby   59:31

Christmas Cradle Song   100:154, *see also:* 54:308, 279:106 *(A la rururu, little boy)*

Christmas Cradle Song   210:92 *(Still and dark the night)*

A Christmas Lullaby   207:50

Close Your Eyes   59:77

Come to the Window   245:94

Cossack's Lullaby   262:93, *see also:* 125:18

The Cottager to Her Infant   59:61

Cotton Eyed Joe   128:20, 274:6, 289:25

Cradle Song   41:48 *(Baby mine, a star is peeping in the sky)*

Cradle Song   71:122, 72:58, 85:176, 125:89, *see also:* 17:63, 283:60, 289:18 *(Lullaby and goodnight, in the sky stars are bright)*

The Cradle Song   59:41 *(Sleep, sleep, beauty bright)*

Cradle Song   79:17 *(Sleep oh, sleep oh, sleep oh)*

Cradle Song   85:101, *see also:* Lullaby *(Lullay, my prince, lullaby)*

Cradle Song   85:140 *(Lulla, lulla, pretty little darling)*

The Crops Have Been Gathered   125:22

The Cuckoo Is a Pretty Bird   59:23, 292:130, *see also:* 27:52, 157:77, 217:60

Daddy's Gone to Town   125:30

Daisies   245:99

Dance to Your Daddy   27:142, 111:42, 281:56

Day and Night   125:38

Din Don   188:170

Do, Do L'Enfant Do   59:51, *see also:* 78:41

Do Not Cry, My Child/Yeke, Omo Mi   89:270, 267:14, *see also:* 169:50, 208:47

Dobrou Noc/Sweetheart, Good Night   208:13

Dodo, Baby Do   125:108, *see also:* 78:41

Dolly's Lullaby   85:219

Douglas Mountain   59:70

Dreamland   125:107

Duérmete Mi Niño/Sleep My Child   194:16

Dutch Lullaby   33:74

E Hie E/I Rock Thee   87:18

El Coqui   69:32

Evening Hymn   125:106

Evening Is a Little Boy   59:37

The Evening Is Coming   17:33, 289:38

Far in the Wood   245:97

Father's at Sea   281:57

Fiddle-Dee-Dee   17:77, 59:28, 188:20, 292:200, *see also:* 68:29, 128:44

The Fly and the Bumblebee   68:29, 128:44, *see also:* 17:77, 59:28, 188:20, 292:200

French Slumber Song   78:41, 125:108

The Frog's Flute/Kaeru-no Fue   286:32

Fum, Fum, Fum   54:258, 125:121, 197:115, 241:80, 279:104, 295:84, *see also:* 89:162

Gently Sleep   125:20

Gille Beag 'O/Little Lad Oh   89:133

Go and Tell Aunt Nancy   135:61, *see also:* Go Tell Aunt Rhody

Go Away, Little Fairies   125:74

Go Tell Aunt Abbie   62:51, *see also:* Go Tell Aunt Rhody

Go Tell Aunt Nancy   158:16, *see also:* Go Tell Aunt Rhody

Go Tell Aunt Rhody   9, 17:104, 59:15, 72:89, 148:110, 196, 274:26, 289:69, 292:150, *see also:* 37:76, 62:51, 135:61, 158:16, 188:176, 230:45

Go To Sleep   41:19 *(Little boys, little girls, go to sleep)*

Go To Sleep   107:68 *(Go to sleep, go to sleep, hush a bye and go to sleep)*

Go To Sleep   245:100, *see also:* 234:65 *(Go to sleep, go to sleep, go to sleep, little baby)*

Go To Sleepy   226:454, 232:176, 262:122, *see also:* 109:8

Go To Sleepy, Little Baby   109:8, *see also:* 226:454, 232:176, 262:122

Golden Cradle   125:60, 42:613

Golden Slumbers   71:120, 72:56, 79:53, 111:72, 175:34

Good-Night   125:82

Good Night, My Baby   125:24

Good Night to You All   125:34, 262:86, 293:106

LULLABIES—Continued
Great Big Dog 78:93
Heidschi Bumbeedschi 245:89
Hej Pada Pada/Raindrops 289:36
Highland Lullaby 85:169
The Holy Family 189:76
Hora Nero, Nen Nero 16:35
The Huntsmen 59:54
Hush-A-Baw Birdie 112:44, see also: 262:125
Hush-a-Bye 281:55
Hush-a-Bye, Baby 135:110 (Hush-a-bye, Baby, thy cradle is green)
Hush-a-Bye, Baby 175:85, 188:88 (Hush-a-bye, baby, on the tree top)
Hush, Little Baby 10, 59:52, 75:33, 178:56, 213:84, 232:147, 261:56, 274:20, 289:12, 298, see also: 63:90, 125:134, 129:97, 135:52, 197:57
Hush, My Babe 54:87, 140:24, 140:113, 283:62, see also: 184:62, 190:43, 190:45, 233:41
Hush, My Baby/Ninni, Baba 169:30, 268:19
Hush 'n' Bye 232:178, see also: All the Pretty Little Horses
Hush Now, My Children 208:47, see also: 89:270, 169:50, 267:14
Hush Song 281:59
Hush-You-Bye 176:54, see also: All the Pretty Little Horses
I Rock Thee/E Hie E 87:18
In the Morning, When You Wake 125:116
Indian Lullaby 245:84
The Journey 59:45
Jungle Mammy Song 226:455
Kaeru-no Fue/The Frog's Flute 286:32
Kentucky Babe 125:39
Kitty Alone 289:28
Komoriuta/Lullaby 286:63
La Poulette Grise/The Old Grey Hen 289:30
Lambs Are Sleeping 125:56
The Linden Tree 125:86
Little Brother in the Cradle 245:83
Little Cossack 125:18, see also: 262:93
Little Donkey Close Your Eyes 245:101
The Little Dustman 71:52, see also: 125:90
The Little Horses 189:90, see also: All the Pretty Little Horses
Little Lad, Oh/Gille Beag 'O 89:133
Little Lambkin Sweet 245:98
Little Red Bird 176:52, 245:86
Louisiana Lullaby 72:99, 79:37
Lulajze Jezuniu/Polish Lullaby 54:220, 241:74, 279:122
Luli, Deck the Crib 125:126

Lullaby 125:85 (Hush-a-by, baby, and go to sleep)
Lullaby/Komoriuta 286:63
Lullaby (Mozart) 71:123, 125:92, 125:96, see also: 85:101
Lullaby/Nhim Ne Nhim 89:225
Lullaby/Niña, Nana 216:49, see also: 54:252, 89:161, 279:108
Lullaby 114:44 (Ayo, ay, oh baby don't you cry)
Lullaby 177:92 (Sleep, my baby, slumber deep)
Lullaby/Soum, Soum 208:25
Lullaby 262:127 (Lula, baby, la, la)
Lullaby 19:11 (Way way way way way)
Lullaby for Mr. Benjamin B. Bickelbaum 237:unpaged
Lullaby, My Jamie 176:56
Lullaby of the Rain 162:31
Lullaby to the Animals 296:42
Lullay My Liking 209:89, 210:109
Mama's Gonna Buy 197:57, see also: Hush, Little Baby
Mammy Loves 157:68
Many Million Years Ago 59:32
Menominee Lullaby 19:37
Mighty Lak' a Rose 205:268, see also: 125:136
Mighty Like a Rose 125:136, see also: 205:268
Minnie and Winnie 59:34
The Mist 281:60
The Mocking Bird 125:134, 129:97, see also: Hush, Little Baby
The Mockingbird 135:52, see also: Hush Little Baby
Momma, Momma, Have You Heard? 63:90, see also: Hush, Little Baby
Moon and Sun 125:94
Mozart's Lullaby 289:34
My Son 125:124
Nani, Nani 125:128
Nantucket Lullaby 281:62
Nhim Ne Nhim/Lullaby 89:225
Night 59:13
Night Is Coming 125:62
The Night Will Never Stay 59:68
Niña Nana/Lullaby 89:161, 216:31, see also: 54:252, 279:108
Ninni, Baba/Hush, My Baby 169:30, 268:19
Now the Day Is Over 45:64, 59:18, 71:124, 72:59, 125:39, 148:258, 161:74
Ntyilo-Ntyilo/Bird Song 163:36
The Nut Tree 59:24, 227:5, see also: I Had a Little Nut Tree
Oft in the Stilly Night 66:26, 125:44
Oh, Can Ye Sew Cushions 71:82, 78:29, 125:68, see also: 27:110

O Hush Thee, My Babie   262:94, *see also:* 125:66
O Hush Thee, My Baby   125:66, *see also:* 262:94
Oh, Lily, Lily White   78:77, 125:10
Old Gray Goose   37:176, 135:61, *see also:* Go Tell Aunt Rhody
Old Grey Goose   188:176, *see also:* Go Tell Aunt Rhody
The Old Grey Hen/La Poulette Grise   289:30
Old Highland Cradle Song   71:82, 78:29, *see also:* 27:110, 125:68
Olilili/Lullaby   163:100
Ora No Omboko   16:37
Papa's Going to Buy Me a Mockingbird   93, *see also:* Hush, Little Baby
Polish Lullaby/Lulajze Jezuniu   54:220, 241:74, *see also:* 279:122
Pretty Little Horses   188:136, *see also:* All the Pretty Little Horses
Raindrops/Hej Pada Pada   289:36
Raisins and Almonds   59:67, 128:24
Rock-A-Bye   125:25
Rock-A-Bye Baby   59:36, 283:56, 289:20, *see also:* 17:68, 125:142
Rock-A-Bye, Boy   125:123
Rock the Cradle   125:54
Rockaby   17:141
Rockabye, Baby   17:68, 125:142, *see also:* 59:36, 283:56, 289:20
Rocking the Cradle   125:26
Russian Slumber Song   78:71
Schlaf, Kindlein, Schlaf/Sleep, Baby, Sleep   188:96, 289:16
Seal Lullaby   59:64
Señora Santa Ana/Lady Saint Anne   216:16
Sh-Ta-Ra-Dah-Dey   226:35, *see also:* 64:154
The Shepherd Moon   125:78
Sister's Lullaby   207:20
Sleep, Baby, Sleep   59:48, 285:62
Sleep, Baby, Sleep/Schlaf, Kindlein, Schlaf   17:84, 125:105, 185, 188:96, 289:16
Sleep, Little Daughter   19:17
Sleep, My Child   125:118, 194:16
Sleep, My Duckling   245:87
Sleep, My Son   123:56
Sleep Now and Rest   125:17
Sleep On, Little One   125:90, *see also:* 71:52
Sleep, Sweet Babe   125:132, *see also:* 210:124
Sleepy Dolly   167:40
Sleepytime   125:110
Slumber, Slumber   71:121, 72:60
Slumber Soundly   125:35

Soum, Soum/Lullaby   208:25
Spanish Lullaby   125:122
The Starlighter   59:16
Stars in the Sky   125:23
Suantree (Hush Song)   125:60, *see also:* 42:613
Sun Is Down   125:112
Sunset   125:32
Sunshine and Rain   245:78
Sweet and Low   125:52
Sweet Baby, Sleep   184:70
Sweet Be Your Sleep   125:34, 262:86
Sweetheart, Good Night/Dobrou Noc   208:13
The Telephone Book Lullaby   59:62
Time for Bed   125:58
Time Sends a Warning Call   125:55
Times Is Mighty Hard   64:154, *see also:* 226:35
Too-Ra-Loo-Ra-Loo-Ral   170:39
Trip a Trop a Tronjes   128:41
Tutu Maramba   262:15
Twilight Song   125:33
Vigndig A Fremd Kind/Baby Sitter's Lullaby   289:32
Wavvuuvuumira   236:18
Wee Little Piute   61:237
Western Lullaby   166:30
What Will We Do With the Baby-O?   75:86, *see also:* 110:26, 232:146
What'll We Do With the Baby?   232:146, *see also:* 75:86, 110:26
What'll We Do With the Baby-O?   110:26, *see also:* 75:86, 232:146
When Little Children Go to Sleep   125:100
Where Do You Sleep?   59:26
Wind in the Willows   125:14
Windy Nights   59:47
Winkum, Winkum   17:26
The Wood Bird's Lullaby   125:29
Woowooto   236:71
Wynken, Blynken and Nod   112:68, 245:92
Ye Ke, Omo Mi/Hush Now, My Children   208:47, *see also:* 89:270, 169:50, 267:14
Yeke Omo Mi/Do Not Cry, My Child   89:270, 169:50, 267:14, *see also:* 208:47
LUMBERING AND LUMBERJACKS
Blue Mountain Lake   158:168
Canaday-i-o   64:118
Cutting Down the Pines   35:8
Dans Les Chantiers Nous Hivernerons   176:62
Driving Saw-Logs on the Plover   226:396
Gerry's Rocks   24:847, *see also:* 21:222, 35:6, 158:170, 226:394
Here's a Tree With a Trunk So Brown   165:93

LUMBERING AND LUMBERJACKS
—*Continued*
Jack's Yak 91:41
The Jam on Gerry's Rocks 21:222, 35:6, 158:170, 226:394, *see also:* 24:847
The Logger's Boast 277:73
The Lumberman in Town 158:172
Once More a Lumb'ring Go 158:166
Oxen Song 21:250
The Pinery Boy 239:34
The Shanty-Boy and the Pine 239:36
The Shantyman's Life 33:242, 35:11, 226:390
Silver Jack 159:234
Timber 226:386
We Are Woodmen Sawing Trees 165:92
The Woodmen's Alphabet 35:12
LUXEMBOURG
*Dewdrops On Leaves/D'Purle Vum Da 89:146
*D'Purle Vum Da/Dewdrops On Leaves 89:146

M

MADAGASCAR
*Mifohaza 169:47
*Ny O L'on Nanacy/Song of the Orphan 89:267
*Song of the Orphan/Ny O L'on Nanacy 89:267
MADISON, DOLLEY
Pretty Dolly Madison 166:46
MAGIC
Bibbidi-Bobbide-Boo 275:39, 276:37
Magicians Do Tricks 166:58
The Two Magicians 145
MAGNETS
A Magnet Hung in a Hardware Shop 252:32
MAIL SERVICE: *see* POSTAL SERVICE
MAILMEN: *see* POSTAL SERVICE
MAIZE: *see* CORN
MAKE-BELIEVE: *see also* IMAGINATION
The Clown in Me 219:17
Don't You Push Me Down 130:54
Line and Squares 172:142, 173:28
Lines Written By a Bear of Very Little Brain 172:31, 157:17
Pretending 91:6
MALAWI: *see* NYASALAND
MALAYSIA
*Aroi Toyong/Oh, Beloved 89:295
*Oh, Beloved/Aroi Toyong 89:295
Suriram 114:24

MANDAN INDIANS
Dancing Song of the Skunk 74:29
The Kettle Is Burning 74:31
Song of the Captive Goose Woman 74:33
MANKIND
No Man Is an Island 72:116
MANNERS: *see* ETIQUETTE
MAORIS
Maori Indian Battle Chant 107:26
MARCHING
The Band 162:66
The Big Procession 135:103
Boom Boom 162:66
Marching Music 11:35
Marching Song 41:7
Marching to Pretoria 72:148, 254:118
Para Subir al Cielo/To Get to Heaven 194:26
Round Her Neck She Wore a Yellow Ribbon 205:384, *see also:* 170:22
She Wore a Yellow Ribbon 170:22, *see also:* 205:383
Swiftly Flowing Labe 262:63
To Get to Heaven/Para Subir al Cielo 194:26
MARES: *see* HORSES
MARION, FRANCIS (SWAMP FOX)
Marion's Men 28:144
MARIONETTES: *see* PUPPETS
MARMOTS: *see* WOODCHUCKS
MARRAKESH
*Night's Dark Shadows/Walla Zala Mudduja 89:245
*Walla Zala Mudduja/Night's Dark Shadows 89:245
MARYLAND
Maryland, My Maryland 73:22, 127:149, 160:50
MATHEMATICS: *see also* COUNTING; NUMBERS
I Can Figure Figures 237:unpaged
MATURING: *see* GROWING UP
MAXIMS: *see* PROVERBS
MAY (MONTH): *see also* MAY DAY
Let Us Go A-Maying 262:127
The May Carol 27:102, 213:80, *see also:* 128:70, 134:31
May Day Carol 128:70, 134:31, *see also:* 27:102, 213:80
May Time 207:119
Old Hungarian Round 71:111, 72:171
Three Children Sliding on the Ice 17:40, 188:16, *see also:* 68:5, 197:52
Three Little Girls 68:5, 197:52, *see also:* 17:40, 188:16
Unite and Unite 130:28
MAY DAY
All Around the Maypole 83:492
Come Lasses and Lads 79:51, 227:42

Cornish May Song 208:70
A Little Seed Lay Fast Asleep 86:8
May Baskets 207:115
The May Carol 27:102, 213:80, *see also:* 128:70, 134:31
The May Day Carol 128:70, 134:31, *see also:* 27:102, 213:80
May Day in the Morning 189:52, *see also:* 27:104
Now Is the Month of Maying 72:110, 85:19, 189:112, 197:53, 262:159
Today's the First of May 197:54
'Twas May Day in the Morning 27:104, *see also:* 189:52
MEALS: *see* names of meals, e.g., BREAKFAST
MELONS: *see* WATERMELONS
MEMORIAL DAY
On Memorial Day 207:118
MERCHANTS: *see* BUYING AND SELLING
MERMAIDS AND MERMEN
The Mermaid 71:78, 72:72, 117:unpaged, 290:160
Ringeltanz/Round Dance 188:144
Round Dance/Ringeltanz 188:144
MERRY-GO-ROUNDS
Carousel 20:59
Carrousels/Karusellen 89:168, 100:50
Crazy Carrousel 166:66
Karusellen/Carrousels 89:168
The Merry-Go-Round 17:92
Merry Go Round 162:70
METALS: *see* names of metals, e.g., GOLD
MEXICAN WAR (1846-1848)
The Maid of Monterey 157:114
Santy Anna 21:288, 24:835, 262:105, *see also:* 158:136
Santy Anno 158:136, *see also:* 21:288, 24:835, 262:105
Way Down in Mexico 159:365
MEXICO
*A la Víbora/To the Serpent 295:24
*Al Quebrar la Piñata/On Breaking the Piñata 295:79
*The Babe 54:308, *see also:* 100:154, 279:106
*Behold How Many Lights/Miren Cuantas Luces 216:52
*The Bumpkin 262:14
*The Chaparreras/Las Chaparreras 89:71
Christmas Cradle Song 100:154, *see also:* 54:308, 279:106
The Cockroach 21:110, 197:38, 226:291
*Doña Blanca 168:28, 295:30
*Doña María 295:55
*Early Mornings/Mañanitas 226:292, *see also:* 169:49, 262:21, 268:41, 295:62
El Abandonado 226:295

*El Charro/The Bumpkin 262:14
El Juego del Pañuelo/The Handkerchief Game 194:18
El Rorro 54:308, 100:154, 279:106
*En Nombre del Cielo/Pray Give Us Lodging 54:306
*Esta Sí Que Es Nochebuena/Yes! It Is Christmas Eve 295:78
*The Handkerchief Game/El Juego Del Pañuelo 194:18
*Juego de los Pavos/The Turkey Game 194:34
*La Calandria/The Lark 295:7
*La Chaparrita/Little Sweet One 262:21
*La Cucaracha 21:110, 197:38, 226:290
*La Jesucita 22:78, 72:106, 295:66
*La Pájara Pinta/The Spotted Bird 168:127
La Virgencita/The Little Maiden 70:14
*Lady Saint Anne/Señora Santa Ana 216:45
*The Lark/La Calandria 295:7
*Las Chaparreras/The Chaparreres 89:71
*Las Mañanitas/Morning Song 169:49, 226:292, 262:21, 268:41, 295:62
The Little Maiden/La Virgencita 70:14
*Little Sweet One/La Chaparrita 262:21
*Los Diez Perritos/The Ten Puppies 295:17
*Mambru Se Fué a la Guerra/Mambru Went to War 295:56
*Mambru Went to War/Mambru Se Fué a la Guerra 295:56
*Miren Cuantas Luces/Behold How Many Lights 216:38
*Morning Serenade/Las Mañanitas 295:63, *see also:* 169:49, 226:292, 262:21, 268:41
*Morning Song/Las Mañanitas 169:49, 226:292, 262:21, 268:41, *see also:* 295:63
*Naranja Dulce/Sweet Orange 295:36
*Naranjas y Limas/Oranges and Lemons 295:82
*On Breaking the Piñata/Al Quebrar la Piñata 295:79
On His Bronco the Gay Caballero 262:87
*Oranges and Lemons/Naranjas y Limas 295:82
Oranges Sweet 114:81
*Pray Give Us Lodging/En Nombre del Cielo 54:306
*The Rocking of the Child/El Rorro 279:106, *see also:* 54:308, 100:154
*Señora Santa Ana/Lady Saint Anne 216:16

MEXICO—*Continued*
The Spotted Bird/La Pájara Pinta 168:127
*Sweet Orange/Naranja Dulce 295:36
*Tecolote 27:70
*The Ten Puppies/Los Diez Perritos 295:17
*To the Serpent/A la Víbora 295:24
The Turkey Game/Juego de los Pavos 194:34
*Versos de Montalgo 226:303
*Yes! It Is Christmas Eve/Esta Sí Que Es Nochebuena 295:78
MICE
The Christening 172:138, 173:24
Complete Version of Ye Three Blind Mice 103, *see also:* 17:25, 25:29, 26:41, 62:10, 148:391, 175:52, 188:82, 189:14, 283:66, 292:192, 293:98
Creep, Mouse, Creep 135:111
Dormy Dormouse 144:17
Five Little Mice 191:44
The Frog and the Mouse 129:32, *see also:* Frog Went A-Courtin'
A Frog, He Would A-Wooing Go 17:34, 175:140, 188:34, 261, 283:28, *see also:* Frog Went A-Courtin'
The Frog in the Well 62:44, *see also:* Frog Went A-Courtin'
Frog Went A-Courtin' 79:27, 131, 135:64, 205:30, 232:116, *see also:* 17:34, 20:62, 35:88, 62:44, 62:46, 129:32, 148:104, 162:11, 175:140, 188:34, 226:143, 230:56, 250, 261:62, 274:22, 283:28, 289:58, 292:116
A Frog Went Walking 162:11, *see also:* Frog Went A-Courtin'
Froggie Went A-Courtin' 20:62, 148:104, 230:56, 261:62, 292:116, *see also:* Frog Went A-Courtin'
Froggie Went Courting 274:22, *see also:* Frog Went A-Courtin'
Hickory, Dickory, Dock 17:113, 75:32, 135:117, 175:68, 188:172, 283:10, 285:25, 292:196
The House of the Mouse 245:38
The Hungry Cat and the Grumbling Mouse 112:64
Kitty White 14:357
The Mic 296:10
The Mice and the Cat 291:78
Missie Mouse 35:88, *see also:* Frog Went A-Courtin'
Missing 172:118, 173:4
Mister Frog Went A-Courting 226:143, 289:58, *see also:* Frog Went A-Courtin'
Mr. Rat and Miss Mouse 62:46, *see also:* Frog Went A-Courtin'
Mousie, Mousie, Little Mousie 63:132

My New Pet Mouse 245:39
Six Little Mice Sat Down to Spin 111:12, *see also:* 175:144
The Tailor and the Mouse 75:70, 117:unpaged, 292:194
Three Blind Mice 17:25, 25:29, 26:41, 62:10, 103, 148:391, 175:52, 188:82, 189:14, 283:66, 292:192, 293:98
Three Mice Went Into a Hole to Spin 175:144, *see also:* 111:12
MIDDLE AGES: *see* KNIGHTS AND KNIGHTHOOD, names of persons, e.g., ROBIN HOOD
MILITARY LIFE: *see also* SAILORS; SOLDIERS
The Air Force 27:126
Captain Jinks 66:63, 70:28, 126:65, 135:96
The Marines' Hymn 197:102, 205:358, 277:121
The Old Navy 290:60
MILKMEN
It's the Milkman 107:20
MILLINERY: *see* HATS
MILLERS
Happy Is the Miller 20:35, *see also:* 17:118, 63:28, 135:82, 227:26
Hey, the Little Rusty Dusty Miller 111:59
Jolly Is the Miller Boy 17:118, 135:82, 227:26, *see also:* 20:35, 63:28
Jolly Miller 110:51, *see also:* 165:200
The Jolly Old Miller 63:28, *see also:* 17:118, 20:35, 135:82, 227:26
Meunier, Tu Dors/Miller, You Are Sleeping 217:41
The Mill 191:68
Miller, You Are Sleeping/Meunier Tu Dors 217:62
There Was a Jolly Miller 110:51, 165:200
MILLS: *see also* WINDMILLS
Hard Times in the Mill 64:68
The Mill 191:68
The Mill Was Made of Marble 64:76
Sandy's Mill 62:68, 262:32
The Winnsboro Cotton Mill Blues 64:74
MINERS AND MINING:
Acres of Clams 64:138
The Banks of Sacramento 226:112, *see also:* 33:210
The Banks of the Sacramento 33:210, *see also:* 226:112
The Blantyre Explosion 64:49
California 226:110
The Days of '49 158:180, 159:378
The Death of Mother Jones 64:58
Down, Down, Down 24:867, 158:188
Down in a Coal Mine 33:122, 64:47, 128:14

The Dreary Black Hills 61:65, 146:95, 159:372, 226:264, 277:125
The Fools of Forty-nine 159:381
Four Pence a Day 64:134, *see also:* 117:unpaged
Fourpence a Day 117:unpaged
The Happy Miner 159:383
Ho for California 239:64
I Don't Want Your Millions, Mister 64:160
Joe Bowers 61:33, 159:375, 230:47
Lousy Miner 24:863
Me Johnny Mitchell Man 24:865
A Miner's Life 64:65
My Sweetheart's the Mule in the Mines 24:864, 64:64
Sixteen Tons 64:52
Union Man 64:62
West Virginia Hills 64:56
What Was Your Name in the States? 21:307, 24:861, 226:106
Which Side Are You On? 64:54, 230:94, 239:90

MISSISSIPPI
The Cross-eyed Gopher 234:20

MISSOURI
Kansas City 218:24
Meet Me in St. Louis, Louis 205:296
Missouri Land 61:64, *see also:* 61:62, 61:63, 159:410, 226:280
St. Louis Blues 21:120

MOCCASINS
The New Moccasins 207:39

MOCKINGBIRDS
The Mockingbird 44:34

MOLES (ANIMALS)
Mole in the Ground 234:25, *see also:* 24:900, 253:96

MONARCHS: *see* KINGS AND RULERS

MONEY
Gum-Ball Machine 166:18
I Love Sixpence 188:46, *see also:* 175:97
O, Dear Sixpence 175:97, *see also:* 188:46

MONGOLIA
*Bahyahn Mongol/Rich Mongolia 208:45
*Five Hills/Tahleeng Tahvahng Toalgoy 208:43
*Ouliastai/The Waters of Ouliastai 89:230
*Rich Mongolia/Bahyahn Mongol 208:45
*Tahleeng Tahvahng Toalgoy/Five Hills 208:43
*The Waters of Ouliastai/Ouliastai 89:230

MONKEYS
The Adopted Monkey/Le Singe Adopté 243:45
Baboon Climbs the Hill 292:213, *see also:* 289:52
Dip and Fall Back Low 130:52
Le Singe Adopté/The Adopted Monkey 243:45
Mi Compadre Mono/My Godfather Monkey 216:32
The Monkey and the Skunk 166:26
Mountain Monkey/O-yama-no O-saru 286:22
My Godfather Monkey/Mi Compadre Mono 216:50
O-yama-no O-saru/Mountain Monkey 286:22
Stop Your Groaning 289:52, *see also:* 292:213
The Whizz-Fish Song 84:19

MONTALGO
Versos de Montalgo 226:303

MONTGOMERY, GENERAL RICHARD
A Song On the Brave General Montgomery 240:118

MONTHS: *see also* names of months, e.g., MAY
Chicken Soup With Rice 235:60
January, February 233:50

MOODS: *see* EMOTIONS

MOON
Aiken Drum 111:44, 162:36, 175:130, 188:104, 189:28, 289:96
The Baby and the Moon 125:36
Cancao a Lua/Song to the Moon 89:164
Deta Deta/The Moon Is Coming Out 286:62
The Early Morning 44:18
El Sol y la Luna/The Sun and the Moon 216:14
Good Evening, Shining Silver Moon 245:82
I See the Moon 111:80
Khoe Li/The Moon 89:256
Lazy Moon 21:84
Lullaby of the Rain 162:31
The Man in the Moon 17:107 *(The man in the moon came down too soon)*
The Man in the Moon 112:48 *(The man in the moon as he sails the sky)*
The Moon/Khoe Li 89:256
The Moon Is Coming Out/Deta Deta 286:62
New Moon 77:49
Oh, Mister Moon 148:278
Song to the Moon/Cancao a Lua 89:164
The Sun and the Moon/El Sol y la Luna 216:44
The Sun, It Rises 293:102

MOON—*Continued*
There's a Sun for the Morning 245:16
Willie Wood 111:46, *see also:* Aiken Drum
MORMONS AND MORMONISM
Brigham Young 159:399
Come, Come Ye Saints 21:300
The Handcart Song 277:107
The Mormon Bishop's Lament 159:401
A Mormon Immigrant Song 159:403
St. George and the Drag-on 61:78
That Is Even So 61:44
MORNING: *see also* DAWN; WAKE-UP SONGS
The Animals Wake Up 41:15
Bright Morning Stars Are Rising 233:15
The Cock Crows 114:37
Come Arise! 245:28
The Early Morning 44:18
Early Mornings/Mañanitas 226:292
Good Morning 177:93
Good Morning, Dear Children 245:5
Good Morning to You 17:123, 289:11
Hevenu Shalom A'leychem 72:149, 169:39, 208:36, 266:36
Las Mañanitas/Morning Song 169:49, 262:21, 268:41, 295:62
Lazy Mary 17:101, 289:17
Mañanitas 226:292
Merrily, Merrily 46:227, 71:110, 72:165, 293:12, *see also:* 62:12
Merrily, Merrily Greet the Morn 62:12, *see also:* 46:227, 71:110, 72:165, 293:12
Mifohaza 169:47
Morning Is Come 71:111, 72:169
Morning Serenade/Las Mañanitas 295:63, *see also:* 169:49, 262:21, 268:41
Morning Song 71:48, *see also:* 245:2 *(The sun is rising out of bed)*
Morning Song/Las Mañanitas 169:49, 262:21, 268:41, *see also:* 295:63 *(With a morning song we greet you)*
Now I Wake 86:167
Oh, What a Beautiful Morning 218:16
Singing Time 245:15
Sleepers, Arise! 71:60
The Sun 245:14
The Sun Is Rising Out of Bed 245:2, *see also:* 71:48
Sunny Morning 7:24
The Sweet Rosy Morn 245:11
Thanks to God 86:164
When Morning Gilds the Skies 86:162
MOSES
Go Down, Moses 22:316, 31:13, 64:168, 148:108, 158:372, 197:45, 205:178
Oh, Mary Don't You Weep 148:274, 230:78, *see also:* 226:476

Pharaoh's Army Got Drownded 226:476, *see also:* 148:274, 230:78
MOSQUITOES
El Zancudo/The Mosquito 216:28
The Mosquito/El Zancudo 216:48
MOTHER GOOSE (ABOUT)
Old Mother Goose 17:44
MOTHER GOOSE SONGS: *see* NURSERY RHYMES
MOTHERS: *see* FAMILY AND FAMILY LIFE
MOTHER'S DAY
Mother's Day 86:151
My Mother 207:117
MOTION PICTURES: *see* MOVING PICTURES
MOTTOES: *see* PROVERBS
MOUNTAINS
Glory to the Mountain 141:38
MOUTHS: *see* BODY, HUMAN
MOVING PICTURES
The Age of Not Believing (Bedknobs and Broomsticks) 276:65
Alice in Wonderland (Alice In Wonderland) 275:47
Bali Ha'i (South Pacific) 218:142
Ballad of Davy Crockett (Davy Crockett) 275:90, 276:86
Bare Necessities (Jungle Book) 275:68, 276:60
Beautiful Briny (Bedknobs and Broomsticks) 276:68
Bella Notte (Lady and the Tramp) 275:62, 276:49
Bibbidi-Bobbidi-Boo (Cinderella) 275:39, 276:37
Carefully Taught (South Pacific) 218:169
The Carousel Waltz (Carousel) 218:64
Casey Junior (Dumbo) 275:26, 276:8
Chim Chim Cher-ee (Mary Poppins) 275:48, 276:51
Climb Ev'ry Mountain (Sound of Music) 218:246
Dites-Moi (South Pacific) 218:134
Do-Re-Mi (Sound of Music) 218:234
A Dream Is a Wish Your Heart Makes (Cinderella) 276:35
Edelweiss (Sound of Music) 218:252
Eglantine (Bedknobs and Broomsticks) 275:81
Ev'rybody Has a Laughing Place (Song of the South) 275:36
Ev'rybody Wants to Be a Cat (Aristocats) 275:70, 276:56
Following the Leader (Peter Pan) 275:60, 276:28
Fortuosity (Happiest Millionaire) 276:73
Getting to Know You (The King and I) 218:200

Give a Little Whistle (Pinocchio) 275:19, 276:16

Happy Talk (South Pacific) 218:163

Heigh-Ho (Snow White and the Seven Dwarfs) 275:9, 276:1

Hello, Young Lovers (The King and I) 218:189

He's a Tramp (Lady and the Tramp) 276:48

A Hundred Million Miracles (Flower Drum Song) 218:296

I Cain't Say No (Oklahoma) 218:35

I Enjoy Being a Girl (Flower Drum Song) 218:308

I Have Confidence (Sound of Music) 218:230

I Wan'na Be Like You (Jungle Book) 276:62

I Whistle a Happy Tune (The King and I) 218:184

I Wonder (Sleeping Beauty) 276:40

If I Loved You (Carousel) 218:80

I'm Gonna Wash That Man Right Out of My Hair (South Pacific) 218:137

I'm Late (Alice in Wonderland) 275:42, 276:42

It Might As Well Be Spring (State Fair) 218:260

It's a Grand Night for Singing (State Fair) 218:264

I've Got No Strings (Pinocchio) 275:21, 276:12

Jolly Holiday (Mary Poppins) 276:55

June Is Bustin' Out All Over (Carousel) 218:85

Kansas City (Oklahoma) 218:24

Let's Go Fly a Kite (Mary Poppins) 275:55

Little April Shower (Bambi) 276:26

The Lonely Goatherd (The Sound of Music) 218:240

Love Is a Song (Bambi) 275:86, 276:24

Love, Look Away (Flower Drum Song) 218:304

March of the Siamese Children (The King and I) 218:195

Mister Snow (Carousel) 218:73

My Favorite Things (Sound of Music) 218:226

Never Smile at a Crocodile (Peter Pan) 276:34

Oh, What a Beautiful Morning (Oklahoma) 218:16

Oklahoma (Oklahoma) 218:54

The Old Home Guard (Bedknobs and Broomsticks) 275:79, 276:66

Once Upon a Dream (Sleeping Beauty) 275:64, 276:41

Oo-De-Lally (Robin Hood) 276:76

Out of My Dreams (Oklahoma) 218:50

Pastures Green (Scandalous John) 276:78

People Will Say We're in Love (Oklahoma) 218:40

Pore Jud (Oklahoma) 218:44

Portobello Road (Bedknobs and Broomsticks) 275:84, 276:70

A Real Nice Clambake (Carousel) 218:106

Second Star to the Right (Peter Pan) 276:33

Shall We Dance? (The King and I) 218:212

The Siamese Cat Song (Lady and the Tramp) 276:50

So This Is Love (Cinderella) 276:39

Soliloquy (Carousel) 218:91

Some Day My Prince Will Come (Snow White and the Seven Dwarfs) 275:14, 276:2

Some Enchanted Evening (South Pacific) 218:129

Something Good (Sound of Music) 218:249

Something Wonderful (The King and I) 218:208

The Sound of Music (The Sound of Music) 218:220

A Spoonful of Sugar (Mary Poppins) 276:54

Stay Awake (Mary Poppins) 275:53

Summer Sweet (Rascal) 275:76, 276:72

Supercalifragilisticexpialidocious (Mary Poppins) 275:50, 276:52

The Surrey With the Fringe on Top (Oklahoma) 218:19

There Is Nothin' Like a Dame (South Pacific) 218:173

This Nearly Was Mine (South Pacific) 218:47

The Unbirthday Song (Alice In Wonderland) 275:44, 276:45

Very Good Advice (Alice in Wonderland) 276:44

We Kiss in a Shadow (The King and I) 218:204

A Whale of a Tale (20,000 Leagues Under the Sea) 276:79

What's the Use of Wond'rin' (Carousel) 218:115

When I See an Elephant Fly (Dumbo) 275:23, 276:10

When You Wish Upon a Star (Pinocchio) 275:16, 276:14

Whistle While You Work (Snow White and the Seven Dwarfs) 275:12, 276:6

Who's Afraid of the Big Bad Wolf? (Three Little Pigs) 275:28, 276:20

MOVING PICTURES—*Continued*
Winnie the Pooh (Winnie the Pooh) 275:66, 276:82
With a Smile and a Song (Snow White and the Seven Dwarfs) 275:10, 276:4
A Wonderful Guy (South Pacific) 218:153
The Work Song (Cinderella) 276:36
You Are Beautiful (Flower Drum Song) 218:314
You Can Fly! You Can Fly! You Can Fly! (Peter Pan) 275:58, 276:30
You'll Never Walk Alone (Carousel) 218:118
Younger Than Springtime (South Pacific) 218:159
Your Mother and Mine (Peter Pan) 276:31
Zip-a-Dee Doo-Dah (Song of the South) 275:33

MOZAMBIQUE
*E, Ie, Ie 89:269

MUD
Mud! 245:73

MULES
Erie Canal 22:37, 69:34, 197:78, 226:171, 230:87, 239:60, 246, 262:74, 292:38, *see also:* 33:58
Kicking Mule 234:62, 292:34
Les Deux Mulets/The Two Mules 243:20
Low Bridge Everybody Down 33:58, *see also:* Erie Canal
Mule Skinner's Song 226:400
The Mule Song 35:80
Mules 26:19, 289:148, 292:36
Old Thompson's Mule 84:33
Peep Squirrel 109:216, 234:18
The Two Mules/Les Deux Mulets 243:20
Whoa, Mule! Can't Get the Saddle On 234:64
Whoa, Mule, Whoa! 110:32, 208:80

MUSIC AND MUSICIANS: *see also* BLUES; MUSICAL INSTRUMENTS; OPERAS AND OPERETTAS; SINGING; names of musical instruments, e.g., FLUTES
All Things Must Perish 293:6, *see also:* 62:20, 69:50
All Things on Earth 62:20, *see also:* 69:50, 293:6
Come Here and Sing 176:17
Dance to the Merry Piper's Sound 245:50
The Fairy Flute 245:30
The Fiddlers Are Playing 176:74
Fun With Music 119:96
Let's Have a Rhythm Band 166:28

Music Shall Live 69:50, *see also:* 62:20, 293:6
Musikanter 55:268
Oh, Music, Sweet Music 293:8
Oh, We Are Two Musicians 245:51
Sweet Music Enchanting 262:148
To Music 85:224
Viva la Musica 71:98, 72:170, 293:14

MUSICAL INSTRUMENTS: *see also* names of instruments, e.g., FLUTES
Herdgirl's Song 68:21
I Am a Fine Musician 75:52, *see also:* Musicians
I Am a Gay Musician 289:170, *see also:* Musicians
I Am a Musician 254:119, *see also:* Musicians
I'll Play Something for You 27:252
The Instrument Song 20:16, *see also:* Musicians
Let's Have a Rhythm Band 166:28
Music 104:53, *see also:* Musicians
The Musicians 75:52, *see also:* 20:16, 71:56, 72:138, 104:53, 254:119, 289:170
Quodlibet/What You Will 262:82
The School Band 177:79
Shusti-Fidli 71:56, 72:138, *see also:* Musicians
What Makes Music 206:36
You'll Sing a Song and I'll Sing a Song 107:12
Zither and I 262:145

MUSICIANS: *see* MUSIC AND MUSICIANS; MUSICAL INSTRUMENTS

MUSKRATS
Muskrat 234:21

MUSSELS
Cockles and Mussels 22:22, 262:89

N

NAMES
Among the Little White Daisies 110:48
The Christening 172:138, 173:24
Goodbye, Julie 232:60
Little White Daisies 291:38
Mary 197:56, *see also:* 205:327
Mary's a Grand Old Name 205:327, *see also:* 197:56
My Name 206:52

NATIONAL SONGS
Adams and Liberty 157:28
America 273:154 (*Amid surrounding foes*)

America   25:44, 26:88, 66:90, 69:4, 71:4, 72:32, 127:73, 148:22, 157:118, 160:32, 197:76, *(My country tis of Thee)*
America   240:49 *(To Thee the tuneful anthem soars)*
America the Beautiful   25:46, 26:86, 45:34, 69:2, 71:5, 72:24, 127:184, 148:24, 157:216, 160:70, 161:35, 197:74, 205:351
Chester   21:242, 28:147, 157:20, 197:25, 240:83, 273:140
The Children's Song   71:7
Columbia, the Gem of the Ocean   26:86, 157:116, 160:36, *see also:* 197:65
Finlandia   262:155
A Flag Salute   207:83
Forward America   25:49
God Bless America   25:45, 72:33
Hail, Columbia   21:266, 27:185, 66:84, 157:26, 160:26, 205:46, 240:187, 273:68
I Vow to Thee, My Country   71:8
In Freedom We're Born   27:182, 28:9, *see also:* 21:238, 157:16, 240:44, 273:20
The Land We Call Home   69:36
The Liberty Song   21:238, 157:16, 240:44, 273:20, *see also:* 27:182, 28:9
Make America Proud of You   26:87
O Beautiful Banner   69:4, 71:6, 72:36
Our Flag   207:42
Patriotic Medley   162:108
Pledge of Allegiance to the Flag   32:28
The Red, White and Blue   197:65, *see also:* 26:86, 157:116, 160:36
Sing a Song About the Flag   162:111
Soroud-e-danesh Kade Afsari   169:36
The Star-Spangled Banner   12, 21:272, 22:184, 25:48, 26:85, 27:151, 66:80, 69:2, 71:2, 72:26, 122, 127:39, 148:354, 160:14, 197:64, 240:207, 249, 283:67
The Stars and Stripes Forever   25:42
This Land Is Your Land   25:81, 26:90, 72:4, 130:116, 230:30
Uncle Sam's Farm   27:42, 66:87, 157:106
Yankee Doodle Boy   157:212, 197:75, *see also:* 205:301
Yankee Doodle Dandy   205:301, *see also:* 157:212, 197:75
You're a Grand Old Flag   72:28, 197:66, 205:331
NATIVITY: *see* CHRISTMAS CAROLS
NATURE
Ainahau   87:40
Birds' Lullaby   125:48
The Brooklet   262:72
The Earth Needs the Raindrops   245:80
The Forest   91:19
4-H Field Song   55:257
God, Our Loving Father   71:24, 72:46, 135:31

I Know a Place   72:45
I Like It   162:105
I Love the Mountains   26:21, 148:176
It's Going To Be a Long Vinter   55:260
John O'Dwyer of the Glens   42:591
Ka Tam Ma Wai/One Morning I Rose   89:264
Lambs Are Sleeping   125:56
Land of the Silver Birch   55:257
Let's Hike to the Woodlands Today   245:23
A Life That's Free   262:66
A Little Boy's Walk   191:32
Longing for Spring   85:107
Nature's Splendor/Varga Pavati   89:215
One Morning I Rose/Ka Tam Ma Wui   89:264
The Silver Moon Is Shining   55:259, 72:133
Song of the Great Lakes Region   69:46
There's a Sun for the Morning   245:16
Valleys Green, You Are My Joy   72:132
Varga Pavati/Nature's Splendor   89:215
NAVAJO INDIANS
Navajo Happiness Song   277:99
*Navajo Happy Song   69:26, 197:84, 262:107
NAVAL BATTLES
Perry's Victory   240:197
The *Shannon* and the *Chesapeake*   240:196
The Yankee Man-of-War   240:130
NEBRASKA
The Kinkaiders   159:412, 226:278
Nebraska Land   61:64, *see also:* 61:62, 61:63, 159:410, 226:280
NEEDLEWORK
Needle Sing   130:36
NEIGHBORS
The Good Samaritan   155:18
The People in Your Neighborhood   206:43
NEPAL
Daphe Bird   114:26
*Kana Ma Laune/My Husband   89:214
*My Husband/Kana Ma Laune   89:214
NETHERLANDS
All the Ducks   135:25, *see also:* 227:37
*De Bezem/The Broom   262:120
The Ducks   227:37, *see also:* 135:25
*In Kieldrecht/Te Kieldrecht   89:139
Little Dutch Girl, Sitting There   167:57
*Ons Is Geboren Een Kindekin/Today We Welcome a Tiny Child   54:184
*Prayer of Thanksgiving   21:338
Put on Your Wooden Shoes   167:57
*See My Wagon, It's Full Laden   21:318
*Shoe Game   55:250, 70:18, *see also:* 20:90, 83:491, 289:173

NETHERLANDS—*Continued*
*Te Kieldrecht/In Kieldrecht 89:139
*Today We Welcome a Tiny Child/Ons Is Geboren Een Kindekin 54:184
*We're Singing Our Praises/Wilt Heden Nu Treden 21:338, *see also:* 27:234, 45:56, 205:24
What Did I See? 68:20
*Wilt Heden Nu Treden/We're Singing Our Praises 21:228

NEW GUINEA
Guan Pazek/Stepping on the Dog 168:75
Mailong Sera 168:76
Stepping on the Dog/Guan Pazek 168:75

NEW YEAR
Auld Lang Syne 22:76, 25:89, 27:2, 46:207, 148:32, 170:62, 197:10, 205:50, 290:216
Bright New Year 97:unpaged
Come Let's Go A'Planting 100:64
Come Quickly, New Year/Hayaku Koi Koi Oshogatsu 286:85
Greensleeves 128:68, 220:42, *see also:* 210:68
Happy New Year 41:1 *(Happy New Year, everyone here)*
A Happy New Year 27:4 *(The old year now does pass away)*
Hayaku Koi Koi Oshogatsu/Come Quickly, New Year 286:85
Here We Come A-Caroling 264:82, *see also:* Wassail Song
Here We Come A-Wassailing 96:6, 128:66, 148:154, 209:12, 220:62, 284:47, *see also:* Wassail Song
New Year's Day in the Morning 188:168, *see also:* I Saw Three Ships
Sunny Bank 190:128, *see also:* I Saw Three Ships
Wassail Song 22:270, 27:6, 54:35, 92:186, 96:6, 128:66, 148:154, 184:8, 189:130, 197:8, 209:12, 220:42, 262:112, 279:36, 284:47, *see also:* 264:82

NEW YORK
East Side West Side 148:328, *see also:* 157:188, 205:240
Give My Regards to Broadway 205:307
New York 157:102
Oh, What a Charming City 157:102
The Sidewalks of New York 148:328, 157:188, 205:240

NEW ZEALAND
The Keel Row 135:16, 262:68, *see also:* 89:302
*Love Song/Waiata Aroha 89:301
*Waiata Aroha/Love Song 89:301

NICARAGUA
*Mr. Snail/Señor Caracol 168:129
*No, Never Can I Go With You/No Puedo, Tengo Otro Dueño 89:77
*No Puedo, Tengo Otro Dueño/No, Never Can I Go With You 89:77
*Señor Caracol/Mr. Snail 168:129

NIGERIA
*Bobo Waro Fero Satodeh 148:84
*Caney Mi Macaro 107:40
*Do Not Cry, My Child/Yeke, Omo Mi 89:270, 267:14, *see also:* 169:50, 208:47
Everybody Loves Saturday Night 64:200, 148:82, *see also:* 89:279
Hush Now, My Children 208:47, *see also:* 89:270, 169:50, 267:14
*O-um Anyu O-um Aruonwu 215:16
*Vu-gu vu-gu vu-gu 215:17
*Ye Ke, Omo Mi/Hush Now, My Children 208:47, *see also:* 89:270, 169:50, 267:14
*Yeke Omo Mi/Do Not Cry, My Child 89:270, 169:50, 267:14, *see also:* 208:47

NIGHT: *see also* BEDTIME; EVENING
All Through the Night 21:337, 59:20, 125:72, 205:60, 289:26
The Animals Go to Sleep 41:14
Bella Notte 275:62, 276:49
Bird of Night 44:44
Black Cats Come 166:34
Day and Night 125:38
Evening Glow/Yu-Yake Koyake 286:64
Evening Hymn 85:34
Follow the Drinking Gourd 33:162
From Daylight to Darkness 74:15
Gently the Breezes 71:47
Good Night 71:49
I Walk With My Little Lantern 245:91
In the Starlight 66:100
The Mockingbird 44:34
Night 59:13
The Night Will Never Stay 59:68
Night's Dark Shadows/Walla Zala Mudduja 89:245
Now the Day Is Over 45:64, 59:18, 71:124, 72:59, 125:39, 148:258, 161:74
The Starlighter 59:16
Tiptoe Night 59:76
Twilight 114:34
Walla Zala Mudduja/Night's Dark Shadows 89:245
Yu-Yake Koyake/Evening Glow 286:64

NIGHTINGALES
The Nightingale 262:48

NOAH
Oh, Mary Don't You Weep 230:78
One More River 22:308, 148:296, 290:42, 292:206, *see also:* 57
One Wide River 57, *see also:* 22:308, 148:296, 290:42, 292:206

Rise and Shine 148:312
Who Built the Ark 135:24, 232:128
NONSENSE SONGS: *see also* LIMERICKS
And We Hunted and We Hunted 234:36, *see also:* 27:62, 106, 128:122, 292:190
The Animal Fair 25:38, 26:17, 62:33, 226:348, 289:152, 292:188, *see also:* 254:121
Anna Elise 112:3
The Ants Come Marching 63:82, 118:24, *see also:* 147:10
The Ants Go Marching One By One 147:10, *see also:* 63:82, 118:24
The Baby Prune 63:134
Be Kind to Your Webfooted Friends 26:12, 118:32, 292:158
Beeper Booper 237:unpaged
Big-Eye Rabbit 128:36
The Bold Fisherman 27:208, 128:116, 239:20, 256
Boom, Boom, Ain't It Great to Be Crazy? 178:72, 289:143
Bruce the Goose 91:39
The Carrion Crow 89:131, 134:56, 175:160, 188:152, 292:148
The Cat Came Back 102
A Cat Came Fiddling Out of a Barn 111:51
Cat in the Sack/Katten I Saekken 208:19
The Chicken/El Pollo 295:15
Cottleston Pie 172:27, 174:13, 289:121
Cow on the Railroad Track 118:28
Crazy Song to the Air of "Dixie" 226:342
Crocodile Song 26:36, 89:33, 234:72
Daddy's Whiskers I 197:70
Daddy's Whiskers II 197:71
Do Your Ears Hang Low 63:139, 118:19
Drool Song 25:40, *see also:* 63:124
Dunderbeck 290:158
El Pollo/The Chicken 295:15
Eletelephony 44:64
Fiddle Hi Ho 97:unpaged
Fooba-Wooba John 289:136
Ford Song 118:16
Found a Peanut 63:138, 118:8, 147:24, 254:114
Glory Glory How Peculiar 118:6
Go Get the Ax 226:332, 289:150, *see also:* 197:33
The Goat 62:38 *see also:* 171
Goin' Down to Town 226:145, *see also:* 232:158
Going Down to Town 232:158, *see also:* 226:145
Good King Dagobert/Le Bon Roi Dagobert 217:58
Goody Bull 28:15, *see also:* 240:40, 273:58, 289:133

The Great Meat Pie 148:130
The Hearse Song 62:109, 226:444, *see also:* 290:178
A Horse Named Napoleon 62:35
The Horses Run Around 25:32
How Many Strawberries Grow in the Sea? 18:5, *see also:* 112:23
Hugh 91:31
The Hungry Goat 171, *see also:* 62:38
I Can't Do That Sum 289:130
I Know a Little Puppy 26:18, 254:111
I Know an Old Lady Who Swallowed a Fly 23, 75:34, 289:116, 292:216, *see also:* 5, 120, 148:378
I Went Downtown 112:46
I Went to the Animal Fair 254:121, *see also:* Animal Fair
I Went to the Movies Tomorrow 290:121
I'm a Nut 63:137
In a Cottage in Fife 112:6
In de Vinter Time 226:334, *see also:* 27:242
In Frisco Bay 118:13
In the Boardinghouse 290:174
In the Vinter 27:242, *see also:* 226:334
It's All Wrong 197:89
Jack, Can I Ride? 234:76
Jack's Yak 91:41
Jacky Jingle 18:34
Jennifer Gently 36:36, *see also:* 37:122, 62:143, 128:114
Jig Along Home 130:114
John Brown's Baby 20:32, 26:30, 118:31, 253:100, 289:114
John Brown's Ford 26:31
John Jacob Jingleheimer Jones 62:67, *see also:* 25:37, 26:14, 253:106, 289:125
John Jacob Jingleheimer Schmidt 25:37, 26:14, 253:106, 289:125, *see also:* 62:67
Johnnie Verbeck 25:18
Johnny Went Down in a Bucket 62:94
The Kangaroo 290:106
Katten I Saekken/Cat in the Sack 208:19
Keemo Kyemo 290:108, *see also:* 234:48
The Knickerbocker Line 35:94
The Lady and the Pig 46:226, *see also:* 175:76
The Lady and the Swine 175:76, *see also:* 46:226
Le Bon Roi Dagobert/The Good King Dagobert 217:28
A Leg of Mutton Went Over to France 62:100
Lena 91:34
Little Peter Rabbit 26:30
The Little Skunk 63:138
Liza Jane 128:124, 226:132
London Bridge 188:160, 290:124
Long Nail A-Grinding 118:26

NONSENSE SONGS—*Continued*

A Man in the Wilderness 112:23, *see also:* 18:5

Maverick the Two-Gun Cowboy 62:97

May Day in the Morning 189:52, *see also:* 27:104

Mi Burro/My Donkey 289:64

Michael Finnegan 25:41, 36:80, 62:67, 197:30, 289:138

Midnight on the Ocean 290:138

Mrs. Murphy's Chowder 290:16

My Body Lies Over the Ocean 63:145

My Donkey/Mi Burro 289:64

My Father Is Dead 188:44, *see also:* Swapping Song

My Gal's a Corker 290:98

My Nose Is Blue 290:139

Nickety Nackety 37:122, 62:143, *see also:* 36:36, 128:114

Nobody Likes Me 63:94, 290:190

Nothin' From Nothin' Leaves You 84:52

Old Grimes 66:68

Old Lady Mac 141:80

The Old Maid and the Burglar Bold 84:12

The Old Soldier 62:91

The Old Sow 234:52

The Old Sow Song 84:56

Old Thompson's Mule 84:33

The Old Woman and the Pedlar 68:14, 79:41, 188:132, 259 *see also:* 17:64, 27:58

On Top of Spaghetti 75:58, 76, 118:23, 147:29

One Fine October Morning 112:34

The Owl and the Pussy Cat 112:26

Papa, les Petits Bateaux/Papa, the Little Boats 217:45

Papa, the Little Boats/Papa, les Petits Bateaux 217:63

Polly-Wolly-Doodle 46:208, 66:70, 83:507, 205:139, 290:112

Putting on the Style 35:60, 148:306, 230:68

Rigby Johnson Chandler 61:26

Risseldy, Rosseldy 128:114, *see also:* 36:36, 37:122, 62:143

Robin the Bobbin 111:74

Sam, Sam, Tommy Trot, and Barber, Barber 112:24

Sandy Dow 63:91

The Snake Baked a Hoecake 234:24, 292:115

Song of the Plumber 84:36

The Speller's Fate 84:30

The Story the Crow Told Me 290:68

The Swapping Boy 143, *see also:* Swapping Song

The Swapping Song 37:174, 129:38, 213:10, *see also:* 18:36, 111:63, 143, 188:44

There Once Was a Maiden 62:96

There Was a Little Woman 17:64, *see also:* Old Woman and the Pedlar

There Was a Man and He Was Mad 232:76, 289:120

There Was a Man in Our Town 17:82, 111:36

There Was an Old Frog 234:48, *see also:* 290:108

There Was an Old Lady 27:58, *see also:* Old Woman and the Pedlar

There Was An Old Lady Who Swallowed a Fly 5, *see also:* I Know an Old Lady Who Swallowed a Fly

There Was an Old Woman 120, 148:378, *see also:* I Know an Old Lady Who Swallowed a Fly

There's a Flea in Lizzie's Ear 197:33, *see also:* 226:332, 289:150

Three Craws 62:55, 128:32, 134:17, 290:144, 292:144

Three Jolly Hunters 27:62, *see also:* 106, 128:122, 234:36, 292:190

Three Jovial Huntsmen 106, *see also:* 27:62, 128:122, 234:36, 292:190

Three Wise Old Women 62:95

Throw It Out the Window 25:24, 26:38, 290:102, *see also:* 175:22

Today Is Monday 84:28, 253:92

The Tune the Old Cow Died On 62:34, 71:94

'Twas May Day in the Morning 27:104, *see also:* 189:52

Twinkle, Twinkle, Little Bat 289:84

Watermelons 63:124, *see also:* 25:40

We Hunted and We Hunted 292:190, *see also:* 27:62, 106, 128:122, 234:36

We Three Kings of Orient Are, Tried to Smoke a Rubber Cigar 63:145

We Whooped and We Hollered 128:22, *see also:* 27:62, 106, 234:36, 292:190

Web-Footed Friends 118:32, *see also:* 26:12, 292:158

The Whale 62:49

What Did I See? 68:20

When I Was a Bachelor 18:36, *see also:* Swapping Song

When I Was a Little Boy 111:63, *see also:* Swapping Song

Where Was Moses When the Lights Went Out? 84:26

While Shepherds Washed Their Socks By Night 63:146

The Whizz-Fish Song 84:19

The Whole Dam Family 84:54

The Wicky Wacky Wocky Bird 97:unpaged
The Woodchuck 144:9
The World Turned Upside Down 28:159, 273:58, 289:133, *see also:* 240:40
The Worm Song 290:178, *see also:* 62:109, 226:444
Yon Yonson 63:135
Zizzy, Ze Zum, Zum! 84:42
NORTH AMERICAN INDIANS: *see* INDIANS OF NORTH AMERICA; names of tribes, e.g., NAVAJO INDIANS
NORWAY
*Astri, Mi Astri/Astri, My Astri 208:49
*Astri, My Astri/Astri, Mi Astri 208:49
Billy Goat 114:59
*Carrousel/Karusellen 89:168, 100:50
Cut the Oats 100:49, 168:100
Daddy's Gone to Town 125:30
Herdsmaid's Song 176:78
*I Am So Glad on Christmas Eve/Jeg Er Saa Glad Hver Julekvald 54:202
*Jeg Er Saa Glad Hver Julekveld/I Am So Glad on Christmas Eve 54:202
*Karusellen/Carrousel 89:168
*O Christmas, You Season of Childlike Delight/O Jul Med Din Glede 54:200
*O Jul Med Din Glede/O Christmas, You Season of Childlike Delight 54:200
Paa Vossevangen 83:490
Paul on the Hillside 79:76
*Per Spelemann/Pete Fiddler 208:52
*Pete Fiddler/Per Spelemann 208:52
Sunset 125:32
The Thief 55:504
*Tra, la, la Ja sas 83:501
Twilight Song 125:33
NOSES
Nose, Nose 111:55
Who Has a Nose 178:9
NUMBERS: *see also* COUNTING; MATHEMATICS
The Angel Band 233:74
The Ants Came Marching 63:82, 118:24, *see also:* 147:10
The Ants Go Marching 147:10, *see also:* 63:82, 118:24
By'm By 129:18, 226:453, *see also:* By 'M Bye
By 'M Bye 157:156, 232:71, 289:13, *see also:* 129:18, 135:44, 226:453
By'n Bye 135:44, *see also:* By 'M Bye
Children, Go Where I Send Thee 54:82, 132:unpaged, 140:46, 190:68, *see also:* 213:88, 233:69
The Clock 288:22
The Counting Lesson 191:56, *see also:* 162:23

Dos y Dos Son Cuatro/Two and Two Are Four 194:36
Elephants Marching 63:80
Five People in My Family 206:18
Going Over the Sea 63:84
Green Grow the Rushes, Ho! 22:116, 25:100, 27:76, 71:50, 72:112, 148:134, 190:64, *see also:* 129:63, 176:146, 233:66
Here Is the Beehive 162:23, *see also:* 191:56
How Many Raindrops 162:27
I Can Figure Figures 237:unpaged
I've Got Two 206:22
John Brown Had a Little Indian 135:112, 165:135, *see also:* 107:24
John Brown Knew a Little Indian 107:24, *see also:* 135:112, 165:135
Johnny Works With One Hammer 178:28, *see also:* 75:61, 165:166
Little Bitty Baby 213:88, 233:69, *see also:* 54:82, 132:unpaged, 140:46, 190:68
Little White Daisies 291:38
Mo' Yet 130:50
One Man Shall Mow My Meadow 132:unpaged
Peter Hammers 75:61, 165:166, *see also:* 178:28
Raindrops 162:29
Song of Five 206:31
The Story of Twelve 129:62, *see also:* Green Grow the Rushes, Ho!
That New River Train 88, *see also:* New River Train
The Twelve, Apostles 176:146, 233:66, *see also:* Green Grow the Rushes, Ho!
Two and Two Are Four 167:46
Two and Two Are Four/Dos y Dos Son Cuatro 194:36
NURSERY RHYMES
A B C Tumbledown D 17:138
A-Tisket, A-Tasket 14:351, 17:106, 20:51, 165:195, 283:20, 289:176, *see also:* 24:806, 63:11, 197:42
Baa, Baa, Black Sheep 17:147, 175:84, 188:102, 189:20, 283:24, 285:49
Baby Bunting 59:33, *see also:* Bye Baby Bunting
Bobby Shafto 255, 289:87, *see also:* Bobby Shaftoe
Bobby Shaftoe 17:105, 59:50, 135:34, 162:94, 175:30, 285:64, *see also:* 255, 289:87
Bow-Wow-Wow 17:78
Bye, Baby Bunting 17:110, 125:40, 175:14, 188:14, 283:58, *see also:* 59:33, 285:102
Bye-lo, Baby Bunting 285:102, *see also:* Bye Baby Bunting

NURSERY RHYMES—*Continued*

Christmas Is Coming   27:248, 68:8,
    128:54, 178:23, 210:94, 241:225, 293:76
Cobbler, Cobbler   17:47, 165:174, 285:84
Cock-a-Doodle-Doo   17:138,   111:76,
    135:50, 175:116, 285:86, 289:98
Cock Robin   37:177, 134:58, *see also:*
    135:32, 289:74, 292:138
Cock Robin and Jenny Wren   188:148
Cocky Robin   135:32, 289:74, *see also:*
    37:177, 134:58, 292:138
Cross Patch   112:16
Curly Locks   17:86, 175:106, 285:68
Dance a Baby, Diddy   17:74, 188:18
Diddle, Diddle Dumpling   285:97, *see
    also:* 162:88, 175:162
A Dillar, a Dollar   285:79
Doctor Faustus   112:18
Dog Jumps Through the Window   189:21
Donkey, Donkey, Old and Gray   285:42
Fiddle-Dee-Dee   17:77, 59:28, 188:20,
    292:200, *see also:* 68:29, 128:44
Fishy, Fishy   17:48
The Fly and the Bumblebee   68:29,
    128:44, *see also:* 17:77, 59:28, 188:20,
    292:200
Georgie Porgie   17:38, 175:152, 188:146
Goosey, Goosey Gander   17:7, 111:64,
    175:32, 285:60
Great A, Little A   285:61
Hark, Hark the Dogs Do Bark   59:57,
    111:41, *see also:* 17:70
Hector Protector   111:21
Hey Diddle Diddle   17:5, 175:67, 283:32,
    285:83
Hey Diddle Dumpling, My Son John
    162:88, 175:162, 285:97
Hickety, Pickety, My Black Hen   188:50,
    189:13, 285:73, *see also:* 175:137
Hickory, Dickory, Dock   17:113, 75:32,
    135:117,   175:68,   188:172,   283:10,
    285:25, 292:196
Higgledy, Piggledy, My Black Hen
    175:137, *see also:* 188:50, 189:13,
    285:73
Hippity Hop   17:47, *see also:* 165:39
Hippity Hop to the Candy Shop   165:39,
    see also: 17:47
Hot Cross Buns   17:122, 135:105, 175:64,
    188:100, 285:54
How Does My Lady's Garden Grow?
    17:98, 175:40, 188:92, *see also:* Mary,
    Mary, Quite Contrary
How Many Days Has My Baby to Play
    285:45
Humpty Dumpty   17:102,   175:104,
    188:174, 283:47, 285:56

I Had a Little Nut Tree   18:18, 135:41,
    175:92, 188:98, 189:12, 283:54, 285:16,
    see also: 17:145, 59:24, 227:5, 289:108
I Love Little Pussy   17:116,   175:86,
    283:15, 285:66
If All the Seas Were One Sea   53, 111:34
Itiskit, Itasket   14:351, 17:106, 197:42, *see
    also:* A-Tiskit, A-Tasket
Jack-a-Nory   111:39
Jack and Jill   17:83, 75:38, 175:18, 177:90,
    188:124, 283:24, 289:88
Jack Be Nimble   17:46, 162:88, 285:87
Jack Horner   17:11, 175:75,   188:178,
    283:16
Jack Spratt   17:70, 175:15
Jack Spratt, His Wife and Cat   112:43
Knock at the Door   17:150
Lady Bird, Lady Bird   285:58, 292:203,
    see also: 175:89
Ladybird, Ladybird   175:89, *see also:*
    285:58, 292:203
Lazy Sheep, Pray Tell Me Why   175:132
Little Bo Peep   17:87, 175:82, 188:60,
    189:18, 285:10
Little Boy Blue   17:10, 175:56, 188:32,
    283:23, 285:38
Little Miss Muffet   17:85,   175:74,
    188:134, 285:81
Little Mother Goose   167:34
Little Polly Flinders   17:150, 175:44,
    112:47, 285:100
Little Tommy Tucker   17:99, 285:88, *see
    also:* 175:24
London's Burning   25:30, 175:20, *see
    also:* 46:227, 148:321, 283:35, 289:188,
    293:36
Lucy Locket   17:38, 175:16,   188:84,
    285:22
A Man in the Wilderness   112:23, *see also:*
    18:5
Mary Had a Little Lamb   17:51, 162:7,
    175:58, 283:11, 289:77, 292:48
Mary, Mary, Quite Contrary   175:171,
    177:87, 188:52, 285:12, *see also:* 17:62,
    17:98, 175:40, 188:92, 283:16
Merrily Dance the Quaker's Wife
    188:120
Mistress Mary, Quite Contrary   17:62,
    283:16, *see also:* Mary, Mary, Quite
    Contrary
Mother, May I Go Out to Swim?   17:73
The Muffin Man   14:365, 17:46, 129:99,
    135:27,   165:195,   168:107,   175:42,
    283:53, 289:99
My Lady's Garden   17:98, 188:92, *see
    also:* Mary, Mary, Quite Contrary
Natural History   17:133, *see also:* 18:31,
    111:33, 175:102
Nick Spence   112:43

The North Wind Doth Blow 17:129, 18:25, 135:116, 175:88, 188:106, 189:124, 227:31, 285:34, 292:139

O, Dear Sixpence! 175:97

Old King Cole 17:28, 55:261, 71:96, 162:87, 175:142, 188:114, 283:34, 285:53

Old Mother Goose 17:44

Old Mother Hubbard 175:22, 285:95

The Old Woman of Norwich 175:164

Old Woman Tossed Up in a Basket 158:154, see also: 17:142, 18:20, 188:66, 285:30, 289:78

The Old Woman Tossed Up in a Blanket 188:166, see also: Old Woman Tossed Up in a Basket

Once I Saw a Little Bird 111:49, 285:99, see also: 18:32

One, Two, Buckle My Shoe 175:38

One, Two, Three, Four, Five 107:22, 175:114

Over the Hills and Far Away 17:45, 175:62, 188:36, 189:54, see also: 111:38

The Owl 18:10

Pat-A-Cake 17:127, 75:60, 175:80, 188:162

Paul's Steeple 175:46, see also: 17:26, 188:154

Pease Porridge Hot 17:74, 162:89, 285:90, 291:58, see also: 175:90

Pease Pudding Hot 175:90, see also: 17:74, 162:89, 285:90, 291:58

Peter Piper 112:61

Pippen Hill 18:14

Pitty Patty Polt 188:158, 189:33

Polly Put the Kettle On 17:54, 135:40, 175:12, 188:74, 283:59, 285:76

Pop! Goes the Weasel 17:136, 20:48, 21:302, 46:209, 55:508, 66:72, 75:64, 135:115, 157:45, 175:36, 200, 205:132, 283:33, 289:100, 292:88

Pussy Cat 175:166, 188:28

Pussy Cat High, Pussy Cat Low 175:166, 188:28

Pussy-Cat Pussy-Cat 17:108, 144:15, 175:110, 188:112, 285:70, 292:66

The Quaker's Wife 17:20

Rain, Rain, Go Away 17:48, 285:18

Ride A Cock-Horse 17:79, 175:26, 188:70, 283:37, 285:50

Ring-A-Ring O'Roses 175:41, 188:108, 189:24, 227:23, see also: Ring Around a Rosy

Ring Around a Rosy 17:139, 63:11, 277:19, 260:31, 291:63, see also: 100:32, 175:41, 188:108, 189:24, 227:23

Ring Around the Rosie 100:32, see also: Ring Around a Rosy

Ring Around the Rosy 277:19, see also: Ring Around a Rosy

Ringeltanz/Round Dance 188:144

Round Dance/Ringeltanz 188:144

Rub-a-dub-dub 175:138

Saint Paul's Steeple 17:126, 188:154, see also: 175:46

Sally Go Round the Moon 135:73, see also: 63:11, 130:90, 232:164

Sally Go Round the Sun 63:11, see also: 130:90, 135:73, 232:164

Sally Go Round the Sunshine 130:90, 232:164, see also: 63:11, 135:73

Scissors and String 175:156

See-Saw 17:103, 175:172, 188:68, 283:14, 285:40

See-Saw, Sacra-down 111:24, 135:124, 162:89

Simon's Song 58, see also: 17:31, 175:16, 285:33

Simple Simon 17:31, 175:16, 285:33, see also: 58

Sing a Song of Sixpence 17:24, 135:114, 175:122, 188:26, 189:16, 283:22, 285:47

Sing, Sing, What Shall I Sing? 111:17

Six Little Snails 17:62, 165:48

Sleep, Baby, Sleep 59:48, 285:62

Solomon Grundy 112:42

A Spider for Miss Muffet 166:24

Taffy Was a Welshman 17:135

Tell Tale, Tit 17:78

There Was a Crooked Man 17:19, 62:88, 111:67, 175:28, 285:37, 289:82

There Was a Little Girl 285:20

There Was a Little Man 17:119

There Was an Old Woman (who lived in a shoe) 175:120

There Was an Old Woman (lived under a hill) 177:87

There Was an Old Woman (tossed up in a basket) 17:142, 18:20, 285:30, 289:78, see also: 111:56, 175:154, 188:166

This Is the Way the Ladies Ride 17:91, 130:61, 175:158

This Little Pig 17:71, 75:80, 285:14, see also: 175:48

This Pig Went to Market 175:48, see also: 17:71, 75:80, 285:14

Three Blind Mice 17:25, 25:29, 26:41, 62:10, 103, 148:391, 175:52, 188:82, 189:14, 283:66, 292:192, 293:98

Three Children Sliding on the Ice 17:40, 188:16, see also: 68:5, 197:52

Three Jovial Huntsmen 106, see also: 27:62, 128:122, 234:36, 292:190

Three Little Girls 68:5, 197:52, see also: 17:40, 188:16

Three Little Kittens 17:12, 188:90, 283:18, 285:29, 292:64

NURSERY RHYMES—*Continued*

Three Wise Men of Gotham 112:57, 285:57

To Bed, To Bed 17:50, 112:54, 285:101

To Market, To Market 17:112, 285:74

Tom the Piper's Son 188:130, *see also:* 17:6, 175:100, 285:85

Tom, Tom, the Piper's Son 17:6, 175:100, 285:85, *see also:* 188:130

Tommy Snooks and Bessie Brooks 111:77

Tommy Tucker 175:24 *see also:* 17:99, 285:88

Tweedle-dum and Tweedle-dee 111:70, 285:26

Twinkle, Twinkle, Little Star 17:41, 130:91, 175:108, 205:193, 283:69, 289:84

Two Birds Sat on a Stone 18:38, 112:66

Wee Willie Winkie 59:73, 112:60, 162:91, 175:146

A Week of Birthdays 18:44

What Are Little Boys Made of? 18:31, 111:33, 175:102, *see also:* 17:133

What Are Little Girls Made of? 18:30, 111:33, 175:102, *see also:* 17:133

When I Was a Bachelor 18:36, *see also:* Swapping Song

Where Are You Going? (round) 293:62

Where Has My Little Dog Gone? 26:18, *see also:* 17:43, 285:92, 292:70

Where, Oh, Where Has My Little Dog Gone? 26:18, 285:92, 292:70, *see also:* 17:43

Who Comes Here? 18:11, 111:61

Who Killed Cock Robin? 62:56, 134:58, 292:138, *see also:* 37:177, 135:32, 289:74

Who Killed Cocky Robin? 289:74, *see also:* Who Killed Cock Robin?

Willie Wood 111:46, *see also:* Aiken Drum

NYASALAND

*Cruel Baboon/Mfene Sandhleni 89:286

*Mfene Sandhleni/Cruel Baboon 89:286

O

OCCUPATION: *see also* names of specific occupations, e.g., LAWYERS

Ha-Ha, This-A-Way 75:87, 128:11, 135:74, 289:166, *see also:* 17:110, 27:192, 130:86, 189:50, 232:168

Ha, Ha, Thisaway 27:192, 130:86, *see also:* Ha-Ha, This-A-Way

I Want to Be a Farmer 128:76

When I Was a Little Boy 27:192, 128:11, 189:50, *see also:* Ha Ha, This-a-Way

When I Was a Shoemaker 75:87, *see also:* Ha-Ha, This-A-Way

When I Was a Young Girl 17:110, 135:74, 289:166, *see also:* Ha Ha, This-a-Way

When I Was a Young Maid 232:168, *see also:* Ha-Ha, This-A-Way

OCEANIA: *see* ISLANDS OF THE PACIFIC

OCEAN: *see* SEA SONGS; SEAMEN; SEAS; SEASHORE; SHIPS

OIL: *see* SERVICE STATIONS

OJIBWA INDIANS

Beautiful Is Our Lodge 19:15

*Do Not Cry 19:43

Dream Song 19:35

Flute Song 19:25

Gonigetagina/I Wonder 89:37

I Wonder/Gonigetagina 89:37

Light My Way to Bed 19:21

The Loons Are Singing 19:19

*Lullaby 19:11

Menominee Lullaby 19:37

Sleep, Little Daughter 19:17

*Song of a Boy Growing Up 19:39

Song of Departure 69:27

*Song of the Deer Dancing 19:13

Song of the Frog Waiting for Spring 19:29

Song to Make a Baby Laugh 19:23

The Spirit Will Appear 19:41

*Very Much Afraid 19:33

What Is This I Promise You? 19:27

OKLAHOMA

Oklahoma 218:54

OPERAS AND OPERETTAS

Boys' Chorus (Carmen) 85:196

Brother, Come and Dance With Me (Hansel and Gretel) 75:14, 227:28

Carefully on Tiptoe Stealing (H.M.S. Pinafore) 252:16

The Children's Prayer (Hansel and Gretel) 125:98, 262:149

The Dancing Lesson (Hansel and Gretel) 227:28, *see also:* 75:14

Faint Heart Never Won Fair Lady (Iolanthe) 252:40

The Flowers That Bloom in the Spring (Mikado) 252:46

For He Is an Englishman (H.M.S. Pinafore) 252:12

I Am the Captain of the Pinafore (H.M.S. Pinafore) 252:10

I Am the Monarch of the Sea (H.M.S. Pinafore) 252:14

I Am the Very Model of a Modern Major-General (Pirates of Penzance) 252:26

I Can't Do That Sum (Babes in Toyland) 289:130

I Have a Song to Sing, O! (The Yeomen of the Guard) 252:56, 239:57

I'm Called Little Buttercup (H.M.S. Pinafore) 252:8

In Enterprise of Martial Kind (The Gondoliers) 252:62

A Magnet Hung in a Hardware Shop (Patience) 252:32

The Moon and I (The Mikado) 252:52

Nothing Whatever to Grumble At (Princess Ida) 290:182

Peasant Chorus (Faust) 262:97

A Policeman's Lot Is Not a Happy One (Pirates of Penzance) 252:22

Poor Wandering One (Pirates of Penzance) 252:24

Prithee, Pretty Maiden (Patience) 252:31

A Private Buffoon (The Yeomen of the Guard) 252:58

Sweet Music Enchanting (The Magic Flute) 262:148

Three Little Maids from School (The Mikado) 252:50

Titwillow (The Mikado) 252:48

A Wandering Minstrel (The Mikado) 252:44

We Sail the Ocean Blue (H.M.S. Pinafore) 252:6

When a Merry Maiden Marries (The Gondoliers) 252:64

When Frederic Was a Little Lad (Pirates of Penzance) 252:20

When I First Put This Uniform On (Patience) 252:29

When I Go Out of Doors (Patience) 252:34

When I Went to the Bar (Iolanthe) 252:38

With Cat-Like Tread (Pirates of Penzance) 252:25

OPOSSUMS
Possum-la 109:128

OUTER SPACE: see SPACE (OUTER)

OUTLAWS: see also PIRATES
The Bad Boy 159:161

The Ballad of Billy the Kid 61:266, 61:268, 159:140

Billy the Kid 61:266, 61:268, 159:140

Bold Brennen on the Moor 22:28, see also: 35:72

Bonnie Black Bess 61:15, 159:217, see also: 61:16

Brennan on the Moor 35:72, see also: 22:28

Bring Him Back Dead or Alive 61:250

Cole Younger 61:262

The Death of Jesse James 61:258, see also: Jesse James

The Desperado 159:137, 290:63

Down, Down Derry Down 226:118

The Dying Outlaw 61:319

I Went Down to the Depot 226:374

I've Been All Around This World 61:252

Jack Donahoe 159:209

Jesse James 21:224, 60:96, 61:255, 61:257, 61:259, 61:260, 146:154, 157:158, 158:296, 159:152, 159:155, 159:156, 159:157, 226:420, 230:36, see also: 61:256, 61:258

Jesse James and His Boys 61:256, see also: Jesse James

Juan Murray 159:158

Po' Laz'us 24:909, 158:308

Poor Lazarus 24:909, 158:308

Quantrell 159:142, 159:144

Queen of the Desperadoes 61:269, 61:270

Rowan County Troubles 24:891

The Rustler 159:105

Sam Bass 61:263, 146:159, 158:298, 159:150, 226:422

Sam Hall 159:422

The Streets of Forbes 176:80

Tom Dooley 148:392, 158:300, 205:402

The Wells and Fargo Line 61:46

The Wild Montana Boy 159:167

OWLS
Bird of Night 44:44

A Cuckoo and an Owl 144:13

If You Were a Kitty 296:20

I'm Wise 68:34

It Is I, the Little Owl 19:31

One Two Three 162:40

The Owl 18:10

The Owl and the Pussy Cat 112:26

The Owl Sings 74:21

Tecolote 27:70

Three Owls 162:10

Very Much Afraid 19:33

OXEN
The Oxen Song 21:250

P

PACIFIC ISLANDS: see ISLANDS OF THE PACIFIC

PAIUTE INDIANS
Wee Little Piute 61:237

PAKISTAN
*Angan Phuli/Jasmine Flowers in Bloom 89:218

PAKISTAN—*Continued*
  *Jasmine Flowers in Bloom/Angan Phuli 89:218
PALACES: *see* CASTLES
PALESTINE
  Come Let's Go A'Planting 100:64
  *Shalom Chaverim 55:255, 293:110
  Who Can Retell? 22:280
PANAMA
  *El Marido y la Piedra/The Husband and the Stone 89:78
  *Hojita de Guarumal/Little Leaf of the Guarumal 216:13
  *The Husband and the Stone/El Marido y la Piedra 89:78
  *Little Leaf of the Guarumal/Hojita de Guarumal 216:44
  *Mi Pollera/My Hoopskirt 216:2
  *My Hoopskirt/Mi Pollera 216:41
PANTHERS
  Of All the Beast-es 234:75
PAPAGO INDIANS
  I Bring the Rain 74:60
  I Will Toss Up the Sticks 74:61
  Song of the Watchers 74:59
  We Must Run 74:58
PARADES
  The Big Procession 135:103
  Marching Song 41:7
  On Parade 207:80
  Troy, the Drummer Boy 167:30
PARAGUAY
  *La Palomita/Little Dove 169:53, 265:45
  *La Tejedora de Nanduti/The Weaver of Nanduti 89:98
  *Little Dove/La Palomita 265:45, *see also:* 169:53
  *The Weaver of Nanduti/La Tejedora de Nanduti 89:98
PARAKEETS
  My Parakeet Talks 167:18
PARENT AND CHILD: *see* FAMILY AND FAMILY LIFE
PARODIES
  After the Ball Was Over 290:130
  Away Down South Where Grows the Cotton(Dixie) 73:11
  Banks of the Dee 240:62, 273:32, *see also:* 26:77
  Battle Cry of Freedom (southern version) 73:38
  The Bonnie Blue Flag With the Stripes and Stars 73:19
  Casey Jones 64:43
  Come Shake Your Dull Noodles 28:11, 240:45, 273:22
  Don't Swat Your Mother 290:176
  Everybody's Dixie 73:11

For Bales 73:192 *(When Johnny comes marching home)*
Ford Song 118:16
Glory Glory How Peculiar 118:6
Great Day 64:40
The Hills of Mexico 61:89
I Wish I Was in St. Law County 73:11
John Brown's Ford 26:31
Long Nail A-Grinding 118:26
Maryland, My Maryland (a northern reply) 73:24
Maverick the Two-Gun Cowboy 62:97
Mixed-Up Mother Goose 290:122
My Bonnie 290:128, *see also:* 55:272
New National Anthem 159:319
Oh Susanna 66:46
The Old Family Toothbrush 290:145
Old King Cole 27:122
A Parody of the Banks of the Dee 28:77, *see also:* 240:62, 273:32
Parody Upon a Well-Known Liberty Song 240:45
Scintillate 290:122
The Song of the Salvation Army 290:134
Springtime in the Rockies 290:132
Ta-Ra-Ra Boom-De-Ay 147:23
Take Me Out to the Hospital 63:97
Three Myopic Rodents 290:126
Two Little Blackbirds 290:104
The Union Wagon Couldn't Be Split 73:46
Wait for the Wagon (A northern parody) 73:46
Wait for the Wagon (A southern parody) 73:46, 65:48
We Three Kings of Orient Are, Tried to Smoke a Rubber Cigar 63:145
While Shepherds Washed Their Socks By Night 63:146
PARTIES (ENTERTAINMENTS)
  Party Parting 237:unpaged
PARTRIDGES
  The Squirrel 79:34, 128:38, 292:100, *see also:* 234:19
PASTRIES: *see* CAKES AND COOKIES; PIES
PATRICK, SAINT: *see* ST. PATRICK'S DAY
PATRIOTIC SONGS: *see* NATIONAL SONGS
PAWNEE INDIANS
  Bear Is Pointing at the Sun 74:49
  Hand Game Guessing Song 74:51
  I Am Like a Bear 74:50
  Song for Returned Pawnee Soldiers 74:54
  Song of the Coyote 74:48
  You Need Not Fear the Horse 74:53
PEACE
  Crow on the Cradle 292:146
  The Dove 292:132

Johnny, I Hardly Knew Ye 42:605, *see also:* 148:204
Johnny, I Hardly Knew You 148:204, *see also:* 42:605
Strangest Dream 230:32
PEANUTS
Found a Peanut 63:138, 118:8, 147:24, 254:114
Whoever Shall Have Peanuts 128:118
PEDDLERS AND PEDDLING: *see* BUYING AND SELLING
PENOBSCOT INDIANS
*Song of Greeting 79:8
PEOPLE: *see* BIOGRAPHY
PERRY, OLIVER HAZARD
Perry's Victory 240:197
PERU
*Al Canto de una Laguna/At the Edge of a Lagoon 216:22
*At the Edge of a Lagoon/Al Canto de una Laguna 216:46
Blow on the Sea Shell 262:13
*The Cornfields/Los Maizales 270:50, *see also:* 169:55
*Dime, Lluvia/Tell Me, Rain 216:17
The King May Pass/Que Pase el Rey 168:149
*Los Maizales/The Cornfields 169:55, 270:50
*Overflowing Torrent/Río de Avenida 89:99
*Que Pase el Rey/The King May Pass 168:149
*Río de Avenida/Overflowing Torrent 89:99
The River 114:84
Tell Me, Rain/Dime, Lluvia 216:45
PETROLEUM: *see* SERVICE STATIONS
PETS: *see also* names of animals, e.g., CATS
Cactus—Mr. Small's Pony 154:32
The Canary 41:20
I Found a Little Dog 296:40
Joseph Henry Alligator 166:70
The Monkey and the Skunk 166:26
Tinker—Mr. Small's Dog 154:36
PHILIPPINES
A Lad to Prove His Love 114:29
*Lulay/Serenade 89:296
*Magtanim 169:57, 271:23, *see also:* Planting Rice
*Nan Sob-oy/We Pray 89:298
*One Starlit Night/Sarong Banqui 208:55
Pagtatanim ng Palay/Planting Rice 70:12, *see also:* Planting Rice
Planting Rice/Magtanim 55:262, 64:102, 70:12, 87:54, 169:57, 271:23, *see also:* 286:78

*Sarong Banqui/One Starlit Night 208:55
*Serenade/Lulay 89:296
*We Pray/Nan Sob-oy 89:298
PICKETING: *see* LABOR UNIONS; PROTEST SONGS
PICNICS
Picnic Time 207:129
PICTURE BOOKS (AND ILLUSTRATORS)
All the Pretty Horses (Susan Jeffers) 105
All Things Bright and Beautiful (Leo Politi.) 8
Always Room for One More (Nonny Hogrogian) 179
Baboushka and the Three Kings (Nicholas Sidjakov) 214
Bears Are Sleeping (Nonny Hogrogian) 294
Billy Boy (Glen Rounds) 38
Bobby Shafto's Gone to Sea (Mark Taylor) 255
The Bold Fisherman (Mark Taylor) 256
The Boll Weevil (Glen Rounds) 221
Bring a Torch Jeannette, Isabella (Adrienne Adams) 3
A Capital Ship (Paul Galdone) 34
Casey Jones (Glen Rounds) 222
The Cat Came Back (Dahlov Ipcar) 102
Catch a Little Fox (Brinton Turkle) 47
Christmas Mouse (Barbara Remington) 282
Clementine (Robert Quackenbush) 195
Complete Version of Ye Three Blind Mice (Walton Corbould) 103
The Derby Ram (Rick Schreiter) 229
Din Dan Don It's Christmas (Janina Domanska) 51
The Erie Canal (Peter Spier) 246
The Foolish Frog (Miloslav Jagr) 231
The Fox Went Out on a Chilly Night (Peter Spier) 247
Frère Jacques (Lilian Obligado) 90
The Friendly Beasts (Nicholas Sidjakov) 13
A Frog He Would A-Wooing Go (William Stobbs) 250
Frog Went A-Courtin' (Feodor Rojankovsky) 131
Go Tell Aunt Rhody (Aliki) 9
Go Tell Aunt Rhody (Robert Quackenbush) 196
The Golden Vanity (David Gentleman) 133
The Green Grass Grows All Around (Hilde Hoffman) 94
The Gypsy Laddie (Dorothy Rice) 211
The Hungry Goat (Abner Graboff) 171
Hush Little Baby (Aliki) 10

PICTURE BOOKS (AND ILLUSTRATORS)
—*Continued*

Hush, Little Baby (Margot Zemach) 298

I Know an Old Lady (Abner Graboff) 23

I Saw a Ship A-Sailing (Janina Domanska) 52

If All the Seas Were One Sea (Janina Domanska) 53

Jennie Jenkins (Mark Taylor) 257

Kellyburn Braes (Evaline Ness) 180

The Laird of Cockpen (Adrienne Adams) 181

Little Drummer Boy (Ezra Jack Keats) 115

The Little Mohee (Joanna Troughton) 263

London Bridge Is Falling Down (Ed Emberly) 56

London Bridge Is Falling Down (Peter Spier) 248

The Man on the Flying Trapeze (Robert Quackenbush) 198

Mommy, Buy Me a China Doll (Margot Zemach) 297

Oh, A-Hunting We Will Go (Nancy Winslow Parker) 136

Ol' Dan Tucker (Joe Krush) 137

Old Blue, You Good Dog You (Mark Taylor) 258

Old Macdonald Had a Farm (Pam Adams) 4

Old MacDonald Had a Farm (Abner Graboff) 81

Old MacDonald Had a Farm (Robert Quackenbush) 199

The Old Woman and the Pedlar (Mark Taylor) 259

On Top of Spaghetti (Art Seiden) 76

One Is God (Christine Price) 192

One Wide River to Cross (Ed Emberley) 57

Over in the Meadow (Ezra Jack Keats) 116

Over in the Meadow (Feodor Rojankovski) 139

Over the River and Through the Woods (Brinton Turkle) 40

Papa's Going to Buy Me a Mockingbird (Don Higgins) 93

A Paper of Pins (Margaret Gordon) 80

Pop! Goes the Weasel (Robert Quackenbush) 200

A Promise to Our Country (James Daugherty) 32

She'll Be Comin' 'Round the Mountain (Robert Quackenbush) 201

Simon's Song (Ed Emberley) 58

Six Little Ducks (Chris Conover) 43

Skip to My Lou (Robert Quackenbush) 202

Sleep, Baby, Sleep (Trudi Oberhansli) 185

Soldier, Soldier, Won't You Marry Me? (Anita Lobel) 142

Staffan (Nicolas Sidjakov) 238

The Star Spangled Banner (Ingri and Edgar d'Aulaire) 12

The Star Spangled Banner (Paul Galdone) 122

The Star Spangled Banner (Peter Spier) 249

The Strawberry Roan (Glen Rounds) 223

The Swapping Boy (Beth and Joe Krush) 143

Sweet Betsy from Pike (Roz Abisch and Boche Kaplan) 1

Sweet Betsy from Pike (Glen Rounds) 224

Ten Green Bottles (Susanna Gretz) 82

That New River Train (Lucy Hawkinson) 88

There Was an Old Lady Who Swallowed a Fly (Pam Adams) 5

There Was an Old Woman (Steven Kellogg) 120

There'll Be a Hot Time in the Old Town Tonight (Robert Quackenbush) 203

The Thirteen Days of Yule (Nonny Hogrogian) 95

This Old Man (Pam Adams) 6

Three Jovial Huntsmen (Susan Jeffers) 106

'Twas in the Moon of Wintertime (Boche Kaplan) 2

The Twelve Days of Christmas (Robert Broomfield) 30

The Twelve Days of Christmas (DiGeorge) 50

The Twelve Days of Christmas (Ilonka Karasz) 113

Twelve Days of Christmas (Jack Kent) 121

The Twelve Days of Christmas (Brian Wildsmith) 287

Two Magicians (Fritz Eichenberg) 145

The Walloping Window Blind (Harry Devlin) 48

Waltzing Matilda (A. B. Paterson) 186

When I First Came to This Land (Doris Burn) 29

Widdecombe Fair (Christine Price) 193

Yankee Doodle (Ed Emberley) 228

Yankee Doodle (Steven Kellogg) 15

Yankee Doodle (Robert Quackenbush) 200

PIES

The Great Meat Pie 148:130

Hot Mutton Pies 71:103
Little Jack Horner 17:111, 175:75, 188:178, 283:16
Simon's Song 58, *see also:* 17:31, 175:16, 285:33
Simple Simon 17:31, 175:16, 285:33, *see also:* 58
Sing a Song of Sixpence 17:24, 135:114, 175:122, 188:26, 189:16, 283:22, 285:47
PIGEONS
Hato Popo/Pigeons 286:17
My Pigeon House I Open Wide 165:157
Pigeons/Hato Popo 286:17
Three Little Pigeons 46:215
PIGS
The Lady and the Pig 46:226, *see also:* 175:76
The Lady and the Swine 175:76, *see also:* 46:226
Little Dame Crump 17:130
The Little Pig 79:23, 135:56, 232:102, 234:50, *see also:* The Old Woman and Her Pig
The Old Sow 234:52
The Old Sow Song 84:56
The Old Woman and Her Pig 129:27, 178:16, 292:60, *see also:* 79:23, 110:42, 135:56, 213:52, 232:102, 234:50
The Old Woman and the Pig 213:52, *see also:* Old Woman and Her Pig
Sow Got the Measles 292:62, *see also:* 277:63
The Sow Took the Measles 277:63, *see also:* 292:62
Tale of a Pig 110:42, *see also:* Old Woman and Her Pig
This Little Pig 17:71, 75:80, 175:48, 285:14
Three Little Piggies 62:40, 289:50, 292:57, *see also:* 116:110
Three Pigs 130:110, *see also:* 62:40, 289:50, 292:57
Where Are You Going, You Little Pig? 112:19
PILGRIMS: *see also* THANKSGIVING
Pilgrims 207:44
PIÑATAS
Al Quebrar la Piñata/On Breaking the Piñata 295:79
On Breaking the Piñata/Al Quebrar la Piñata 295:79
PIONEERS AND PIONEER LIFE: *see also* COLONIAL PERIOD IN AMERICA; COWBOYS; names of frontiersmen, e.g., BOONE, DANIEL
Ballad of Davy Crockett 275:90, 276:86
Banks of Sacramento 226:112, *see also:* 33:210
Banks of the Little Eau Pleine 157:42

Banks of the Sacramento 33:210, *see also:* 226:112
Belle Brandon 61:138
Bill Peters, the Stage Driver 159:391
Bill Venero 159:197, *see also:* 61:129, 146:42
Billy Veniro 61:129, 146:42, *see also:* 159:197
Boggy Creek 159:41, *see also:* Buffalo Skinners
The Buffalo Hunters 61:4, 159:344
The Buffalo Skinners 24:854, 64:120, 146:92, 158:174, 159:335, 226:270, 230:63, 277:137, *see also:* 159:41
California 226:110
The California Stage Company 159:393
Covered Wagon Song 69:39
Cumberland Gap 33:154, 230:67, 277:79
Custer's Last Charge 61:127
Dakota Land 61:62, 159:410, 226:280, *see also:* 61:63, 61:64
Davy Crockett 33:106
The Disheartened Ranger 159:369
The Dreary Black Hills 61:65, 146:95, 159:372, 226:264, 277:125
El-a-noy 21:298, 226:162, *see also:* 35:62
Fair Lady of the Plains 61:121, 146:148
The Farmer 226:282, *see also:* 24:879, 64:96, 230:57, 239:42
The Farmer Comes to Town 24:879, 239:42, *see also:* 64:96, 226:282, 230:57
The Farmer Is the Man 57:96, 210:57, *see also:* 24:879, 226:282, 239:42
Four Little White Doves 33:202
Freighting from Wilcox to Globe 61:50, 159:394
Great-Granddad 27:140, 60:66, 89:41, 146:83, 159:302
Greer County 159:407
Hanging Out the Linen Clothes 226:117, 232:137, *see also:* 71:42, 134:14, 176:30, 205:72
The Harrington Barn Dance 159:244
Haunted Wood 61:118
Here's to the Ranger 159:371
In Kansas 61:96, *see also:* 61:97
In the Summer of Sixty 159:386
Johnny Cake 61:23
The Killer 159:172
The Kinkaiders 159:412, 226:278
The Lane County Bachelor 61:58, 226:120, 277:91
Life in a Prairie Shack 61:108
The Little 'Dobe Casa 61:71
Little Old Sod Shanty 61:68, 61:72, 159:405, 226:89
The Little Vine-Clad Cottage 61:70
Maiden on the Plains 61:121, *see also:* 146:148

PIONEERS AND PIONEER LIFE
—*Continued*
Missouri Land 61:64, *see also:* 61:62, 61:63, 159:410, 226:280
A Mormon Immigrant Song 159:403
Muster Out the Rangers 159:368
My Little New Log Cabin in the Hills 61:70
Nebraska Land 61:64, *see also:* 61:62, 61:63, 159:410, 226:280
New Nation Anthem 159:319
O Dakota 61:63, *see also:* 61:62, 61:63, 61:64, 159:410, 226:280
The Old Scout's Lament 159:354
Old Settler's Song 158:184
The Plains of Illinois 35:62, *see also:* 21:298, 226:162
The Railroad Corral 61:208, 159:42, 225:24, 262:64
The Road to Cook's Peak 159:384
The Rolling Stone 35:56
Root Hog or Die 61:30, *see also:* 61:32
St. George and the Drag-On 61:78
Sioux Indians 61:123, 159:344, 277:119
Song of the Emigrant Trail 61:124
Song of the Kansas Emigrant 157:36
Starving to Death on a Government Claim 158:238
Sweet Betsy from Pike 1, 22:62, 24:861, 61:48, 157:38, 158:176, 159:388, 205:122, 224, 226:107, 239:66
Texas Jack 61:125
That Is Even So 61:44
Uncle Sam's Farm 27:42, 66:87, 157:106
Way Out in Idaho 61:304, 146:87, 159:265
Way Out West in Kansas 61:97, *see also:* 61:96
Westward Ho 159:415
When I First Came to This Land 27:138, 29, 230:13
Whoa! Ha! Buck and Jerry Boy 61:54
Will You Go Out West? 35:54
PIRATES
Captain Kidd 21:332
The Coasts of High Barbary 22:166
Three Pirates Came to London Town 128:90, 262:76
When Frederic Was a Little Lad 252:20
With Cat-Like Tread 252:25
PIXIES: *see* ELVES; FAIRIES
PLANTS AND PLANTING: *see also* names of plants, e.g., CORN
A-Gardening We Will Go 26:84
Can You Show Me How the Farmer 17:32
Come Let's Go A'Planting 100:64
Gombei Is Sowing/Harvest Song 78:83
Harvest Song/Gombei Is Sowing 78:83

I Know a Little Pussy 165:94
In Our Garden 291:56
The Little Plant 191:24
Little Seed 130:92
Oats and Beans 135:76, 165:83, *see also:* Oats, Peas, Beans
Oats, Peas, Beans 14:369, 17:60, 20:80, 63:14, 283:27, 289:181, *see also:* 135:76, 165:83
Off to the Garden Patch 207:103
The Sower 155:16
PLAY: *see also* IMAGINATION; MAKE-BE-LIEVE; TOYS
As I Walked Out One Holiday 232:89
Children Can 219:45
Come All You Playmates 63:95
Come and Play With Me 162:75
Come Out and Play 245:19
Come Out to Play 18:46
Don't Cry Little Dolly 162:78
Don't You Push Me Down 130:54
Down By the Greenwood Sidey-O 232:87
Giddiap 162:81
Girls and Boys Come Out to Play 17:9, 175:60, 188:56, 189:32
Hide and Seek 41:16
Hoppity 172:124, 173:10
It Rained a Mist 162:30, 232:68
The Magic Pony 245:28
Our Yard 149:8
Playing in the Sand 162:77
Ride Cowboy, Ride 162:80
Roll the Ball 291:64
Somebody Come and Play 206:124
A Tea Party 162:76
What Shall We Do? 291:48, *see also:* 165:179, 232:59
What Shall We Do When We All Go Out? 165:179, 232:59, *see also:* 291:48
PLAYS: *see* DRAMA
PLUMBERS AND PLUMBING
Song of the Plumber 84:36
POETRY
Beautiful Soup 112:12
Bed in Summer 227:36
Bird of Night 44:44
Boats Sail on the Rivers 245:75
Brownie 172:140, 173:26
Buckingham Palace 172:128, 173:14
Child's Song 44:78
The Chipmunk's Day 44:30
The Christening 172:138, 173:24
Christopher Robin Is Going 172:79, 174:65
Cottleston Pie 172:27, 174:13, 289:121
The Cow 44:14
The Cradle Song 59:41
The Crocodile 59:29

The Eagle 44:48
The Early Morning 44:18
Eletelephony 44:64
Everywhere, Everywhere, Christmas To-
night 54:64
The Fairies 227:40
Feed-My-Cow 172:108
The Goat Paths 44:52
Good-Night 125:82
Growing Up 172:126, 173:17
Halfway Down 172:122, 173:8
Happiness 172:117, 173:3
Here Lies a Tree 172:75, 173:61
Hoppity 172:124, 173:10
How Sweet To Be a Cloud 172:21, 174:7
I Could Spend a Happy Morning 172:55,
174:41
I Heard the Bells on Christmas Day
54:58, 148:172, 190:86, 241:126
I Lay on My Chest 172:71, 174:57
If Rabbit Was Bigger 172:63, 174:49
In Just 44:22
In the Bleak Mid-Winter 210:108
In the Fashion 172:120, 173:6
Isn't It Funny 172:17, 174:3
It Was a Lover and His Lass 85:16,
176:137, 189:104
It's Very Very Funny 172:25, 173:11
Jump, Jump, Jump 68:6
The King's Breakfast 172:93
The Lamb 112:59, 189:62
Lines and Squares 172:142, 173:28
Lines Written By a Bear of Very Little
Brain 172:31, 174:17
Little Trotty Wagtail 44:10
Longfellow's Carol 54:58, 148:172,
190:86, 241:126
Love Came Down at Christmas 210:46
A Man of Words 44:72
Market Square 172:136, 173:22
Missing 172:118, 173:4
Mistress Bond 62:52, 175:72, 292:154,
see also: 188:116
The Mockingbird 44:34
The More It Snows 172:47, 174:33
Mud! 245:73
Nuns in Frigid Cells 241:44
Oh, the Butterflies Are Flying 172:59,
174:45
Oh, What Have You Got for Dinner, Mrs.
Bond 188:116, see also: 62:52, 175:72,
292:154
Old Doctor Wango Tango 111:68
The Owl and the Pussy Cat 112:26
Politeness 172:135, 173:21
Rain 17:117
Rules 290:142
Sing Ho! For the Life of a Bear 172:35,
174:21

Stonewall Jackson's Way 73:84
The Sword of Robert E. Lee 73:78
There Was a Little Turtle 75:76
They All Went Off to Discover the Pole
172:39, 174:25
This Warm and Sunny Spot 172:67,
174:53
3 Cheers for Pooh 172:43, 174:29
The Three Foxes 172:132, 175:18
'Tis the Voice of the Lobster 112:40
Twinkle, Twinkle, Little Bat 289:84
Twinkle, Twinkle Little Star 17:41,
130:91, 175:108, 176:193, 283:69,
289:84
Vespers 172:145, 173:31
What Shall We Do About Poor Little Tig-
ger? 172:51, 174:37
When That I Was and a Little Tiny Boy
71:71
Where Go the Boats? 69:43
White Fields 44:26
Who Has Seen the Wind? 112:25
Who's In 44:68
Will You Walk a Little Faster? 112:22
The Wind 44:4
POLAND
Ah, How the Moon Is Shining 262:69
*Belt Red as Flame/Czerwony Pas
208:58
*Carol of the Hay/Sliczna Panienka
54:216
*Christ Is Born This Evening/Gdy Się
Chrystus Rodzi 54:210, see also:
279:124
*Click Your Heels/Podkóweczki Dajcie
Ognia 89:182
*Czerwony Pas/Belt Red as Flame
208:58
*Dziasiaj w Betlejem/O Come Rejoicing
54:206
*Gdy Się Chrystus Rodzi/Christ Is Born
This Evening 54:210, 279:124
Haying Song 169:59, 268:61
*In Midnight's Silence/Wsrod Nocnej
Ciszy 54:218
In Poland 227:20
*Jésus Christ Is Born/Gdy Się Chrystus
Rodzi 279:124, see also: 54:210
*Jesus Holy, Born So Lowly/W Zlobie
Lezy 54:204
*Lata Ptaszek Po Uticy/The Little Bird
189:150
*The Little Bird/Lata Ptaszek Po Uticy
189:150
*Lulajze Jezuniu/Polish Lullaby 54:220,
241:74, 279:122
*Mizerna Cicha/Only a Manger Bed
54:214

POLAND—*Continued*
*O Come Rejoicing/Dziasiaj w Betlejem 54:206
*O Gwiazdo Betlejemska/O Star O'er Bethlehem Shining 54:208
*O Star O'er Bethlehem Shining/O Gwiazdo Betlejemska 54:208
*Only a Manger Bed/Mizerna Cicha 54:214
*Podkóweczki Dajcie Ognia/Click Your Heels 89:182
*Polish Lullaby/Lulajze Jezuniu 54:220, 241:74, *see also:* 279:122
*Przybiezeli do Betleem Pasterze/Shepherds Come A-Running 245:119, 279:120, *see also:* 54:212
*Przybiezeli do Betlejem/Shepherds Came to Bethlehem 54:212, *see also:* 245:119, 279:120
Quite Different 68:26
*Rockabye Jesus/Lulajze Jezuniu 279:122, *see also:* 54:220, 241:74
*Shepherds Came to Bethlehem/Przybiezeli do Betlejem 54:212, *see also:* 245:119, 279:120
*Shepherds Come A-Running/Przybiezeli do Betleem Pasterze 245:119, 279:120, *see also:* 54:212
*Sliczna Panienka/Carol of the Hay 54:216
Stars In the Sky 125:23
*W Zlobie Lezy/Jesus Holy, Born So Lowly 54:204
*Wsrod Nocnej Cisy/In Midnight's Silence 54:218
POLICE
Here Comes a Policeman, Riding a Bicycle 165:71
A Policeman's Lot Is Not a Happy One 252:22
POLITENESS: *see* ETIQUETTE
POLITICAL SONGS
The Abe-iad 73:50
Call 'em Names, Jeff 73:53
Jeff Davis' Dream 73:66
Lincoln and Liberty 27:14, 157:51, 226:167
Ma! Ma! Where Is Papa? 197:98
Old Abe Lincoln 21:140, 27:12, 226:168
Times Are Sadly Out of Joint 197:99
Tippecanoe and Tyler Too 157:112
POLLUTION: *see also* LITTER AND LITTERING
The Garden 206:116
I Love Trash 206:95
It's the Same the Whole World Over 197:50
Litterbug Rag 26:83
Picture a World 206:90

PONIES: *see* HORSES
POPPIES
Gentil Coquelicot/Pretty Poppies 217:20
Pretty Poppies/Gentil Coquelicot 217:56
PORTUGAL
*Cancao a Lua/Song to the Moon 89:164
*Emilia 89:165
Pico Serenico 189:156
*Song to the Moon/Cancao a Lua 89:164
POSSUMS: *see* OPOSSUMS
POSTAL SERVICE
I Got a Letter This Morning 232:144
Mail Myself to You 130:70
Mailman 130:73
The Mailman/Počtovsky Panáček 289:80
Počtovsky Panáček/The Mailman 289:80
The Postman 41:24 (*Ho, there you are, Mister Postman*)
The Postman 207:81 (*Good morning, Mister Postman*)
Postman, Postman 178:5
POSTMEN: *see* POSTAL SERVICE
POTATOES
Quan' Patate La Cuite/When Your Potato's Done 262:99, *see also:* 79:38
When Your Potato's Done/Quan' Patate La Cuite 79:38, 262:99
POULTRY: *see* CHICKENS; DUCKS; GEESE; TURKEYS
POVERTY
The Little Beggarman 117:unpaged
PRAIRIE DOGS
Little Prairie Dog 162:59
PRAYERS
All Good Gifts Around Us 86:197
Allelujah 55:254, 71:14, 72:175, 101:33
Back of the Bread 72:44
Bless This Table 72:173
Bless Us, O Jesus 124:148
The Board Is Spread 101:33
A Boy Scout's Prayer 25:62
Can a Growing Child Like Me 86:199
Children's Chorale 86:166
Child's Prayer 177:86 (*Dear Lord, look down upon us*)
Child's Prayer 86:202 (*We thank Thee, loving Father*)
Chinese Grace 86:212
Choral Grace 86:211
Dear Lord Jesus, Hear My Prayer 86:165
Do Unto Others 155:10
Evening Hymn 125:106
Evening Prayer 155:28
Evensong 155:29
Father/Taticek 189:148

Father, We Thank Thee for the Night 25:115, 45:40, 86:141
Father, We Thank You for Your Word 86:208
For All Thy Gifts   101:32
For Health and Strength   68:38, 71:13, 72:175, 101:32
Forgive Me, God   86:204
Foxlease Vesper   71:17, 72:41
Gebet an den Heiligen Christ/Prayer to the Christ Jesus   241:174
God is Great   55:253
Grace   25:111, *see also:* 262:174
Grace After Meals   77:16
Grace Before Meals   77:14
Grace Song   25:111, 101:34
Hark to the Chimes   71:13, 72:172, 101:32
Hear Our Prayer, O Lord   86:200
I Give Thee Thanks With All My Heart 86:92
I See the Moon   111:80
Invocation for Girl Scouts   69:5, 71:29
Johnny Appleseed's Grace   101:31
Listen to the Bells   27:238
A Little Child's Thanksgiving   7:8
The Lord Be With Us   86:209
Lord, Who Lovest All Thy Children 86:203
The Lord's Prayer   155:14
Matthew, Mark, Luke and John   111:16, 189:84
Modeh Ani   77:11
Morning, Ev'ning, Noon and Night 101:32, 262:172
Morning Prayer   155:3
My Savior, Hear My Prayer   86:169
New Moon   77:49
Now I Lay Me Down to Sleep   17:30
Now I Wake   86:167
Now Let Every Tongue Adore Thee 55:253
Now Thank We the Father   86:145
Oh, Give Thanks   71:13, 72:57, 101:31
Oh, Render Thanks   71:14
Philmont Grace   25:57
Praise and Thanksgiving Let Everyone Bring   86:210
Praise We the Father   86:210
Prayer for Each Day   86:163
Prayer for Peace   155:32
A Prayer to Jesus   86:113
Prayer to the Child Jesus/Gebet an den Heiligen Christ   241:174
Rana Djinak/We Have Come Here 89:243
Savior, Again to Thy Dear Name   45:23, 86:207
Scottish Grace   71:14, 101:33

Scout Benediction   26:94
Scout Leader's Prayer   25:55
Song of Praise   207:43
Spirit of the Living God   86:205
Table Graces   86:213
Taticek/Father   189:148
Thank Thee, Heav'nly Father   86:144
Thank You for the World So Sweet 55:253
Thank You for This Lovely Day   55:253
Thank You, Loving Father   86:206
Thanking God   86:201
Thanksgiving Canon   72:63
Thou Who Once on Mother's Knee 86:168
Traveler's Grace   69:11, 101:34
Vespers   172:145, 173:31
The Wayfarer's Grace   262:173
We Have Come Here/Rana Djinak 89:243
We Thank Thee, Lord   155:6
When I Say My Prayer   86:172
PREHISTORIC TIMES
In Prehistoric Times   167:22
PRESIDENTS—UNITED STATES: *see also* names of Presidents, e.g., LINCOLN, ABRAHAM
The Presidents   27:222
PRETENDING: *see* IMAGINATION; MAKE-BELIEVE
PRINCES AND PRINCESSES: *see* KINGS AND RULERS
PRISONS AND PRISONERS
Almost Done   158:324
Been in the Pen So Long   226:220
Bird in a Cage   226:213
The Boston Burglar   159:203
The Convict   159:90
The Durant Jail   158:316, 159:176
The Gray Goose   134:89, 234:38, 274:28, 292:152, *see also:* The Grey Goose
The Grey Goose   24:907, 129:48, 158:20, 277:49, *see also:* 134:89, 234:38, 274:28, 292:152
Grizzly Bear   274:10, 292:108
Hard Times in the Mount Holly Jail 24:887
It Takes a Worried Man   147:40, *see also:* 24:890, 148:422
Midnight Special   21:90, 24:908, 158:318, 226:26, 226:217, 230:55
Moonlight   226:216
The Newburgh Jail   35:64
The Peat-Bog Soldiers   22:212, 64:192
Po' Boy   226:30
Portland County Jail   226:214
A Prisoner For Life   159:88
Seven Long Years in State Prison 226:218

PRISONS AND PRISONERS—*Continued*
Shorty George 158:70
Work All de Summer 239:50
Worried Man Blues 24:890, 148:422, *see also:* 147:40
Yonder Comes the High Sheriff 226:213
PROCESSIONS: *see* PARADES
PROSPECTORS: *see* MINES AND MINING
PROVERBS
Early to Bed 71:105, 293:26
Paddle Your Own Canoe 66:40
PUERTO RICO
*A Cantar a una Niña/To Teach a Young Girl to Sing 216:12
*A la Media Noche/At the Hour of Midnight 54:286
*Aguinaldo/"Mary," Said Saint Joseph 140:28
*Alegría/Happily Singing 54:293
*Arroz Con Leche 168:136, *see also:* 216:10, 295:28
*At the Crèche 142:16, *see also:* En el Portal a Belén
*At the Hour of Midnight/A la Media Noche 54:286
The Child Jesus 241:88, *see also:* 54:284, 197:117, 209:110
*De Tierra Lejana Venimos/Song of the Wise Men 54:288, *see also:* 140:22
*El Coqui 69:32
*El Mino Jesús/The Child Jesus 241:88, *see also:* 54:284, 209:110
*El Santo Niño/The Holy Child 54:284, *see also:* 209:110, 241:88
*En el Portal a Belén 54:282, 140:18
*Era una Vez/There Was Once 89:62, 216:34
*Happily Singing/Alegría 54:293
*The Holy Child 54:284, 197:117, 209:110, *see also:* 241:88
*In Bethlehem's Cradle 54:282, *see also:* 140:18
*Los Reyes Oriente/Song of the Wise Men 140:22, *see also:* 54:288
*"Mary," Said Saint Joseph/Aguinaldo 140:28
*Once There Was/Era una Vez 89:62, 216:50, *see also:* 217:14
*Pastores a Belén/Shepherds in Bethlehem 54:290
*Rice Pudding/Arroz Con Leche 168:136, *see also:* 216:43, 295:28
*Rice With Milk/Arroz Con Leche 216:43, *see also:* 168:136, 295:28
*San Sereni 20:83, 262:16
*Shepherds in Bethlehem/Pastores a Belén 54:290
*Song of the Wise Men/De Tierra Lejana Venimos 54:288, *see also:* 140:22
*Song of the Wise Men/Los Reyes Oriente 140:22, *see also:* 54:288
*There Was Once/Era una Vez 89:62, 216:50
To Teach a Young Girl to Sing/A Cantar a una Niña 216:44
PUMPKINS: *see also* HALLOWEEN
Here We Go to the Pumpkin Shop 7:36
PUPPETS
Ainsi Font, Font, Font/They Do Like This 217:23
Dancing Dollies 128:98
Les Petites Marionettes 283:55
They Do Like This/Ainsi Font, Font, Font 217:56
PUPPIES: *see* DOGS

Q

QUAIL
The Quail 262:54
QUANTRELL
Quantrell 159:142, 159:144
QUEENS: *see* KINGS AND RULERS
QUESTION AND ANSWER SONGS
As I Walked Through London City 134:60
Awake, Awake 35:3
The Baby and the Moon 125:36
Billy Boy 17:66, 36:28, 38, 62:111, 62:112, 66:56, 71:38, 135:42, 197:22, 205:53, 283:52, *see also:* 27:22
Buffalo Boy 290:88
Butterfly 114:62
The Cutty Wren 64:175
Daughters, Will You Marry? 290:76
The Deaf Woman's Courtship 37:136, 69:19, 129:100, 213:72, 262:119, 290:75, *see also:* 20:26, 46:223, 83:470
The Devil's Nine Questions 27:214, *see also:* 37:110, 134:85
The Devil's Questions 37:110, 134:85, *see also:* 27:214
Did You Feed My Cow? 107:18, *see also:* 232:112, 234:56, 292:20, 292:44
Did You Go to the Barney? 232:112, *see also:* 107:18, 234:56, 292:20, 292:44
Donde Están las Llaves?/Where Are the Keys to the Castle? 188:54, *see also:* 189:154
Dumplin's 130:48
En Nombre del Cielo/Pray Give Us Lodging 54:306
Fiddler's Fair 110:40
The Fuzzy Caterpillar 207:26
The Gambling Suitor 37:146

Haste Away to the Wedding 46:225
Henery, My Boy 62:113, *see also:* 89:39
Henry, My Son 89:39, *see also:* 62:113
Here Come the Dukes 110:46, *see also:* Three Dukes
Here Come Two Dukes A-Riding 135:84, 213:40, *see also:* 39:16, 100:92, 110:46, 227:18
Hexlein/Little Witch 78:63
Hey, Little Boy 292:20, *see also:* 107:18, 232:112, 234:56, 292:44
A Hole in the Bucket 290:74, *see also:* 197:32
Home Came the Old Man 37:118
Honza, I Love You 262:61
I Took a Notion Now 62:129
I'll Give to You a Paper of Pins 17:93, 20:42, 62:114, 68:22, 80, 134:18, 148:300, 290:78
I've a Fine, Bonny Castle 189:154, *see also:* 188:54
Jennie Jenkins 20:40, 69:20, 75:42, 129:22, 158:54, 257, 262:37, *see also:* 135:62, 291:28
Jenny Jenkins 291:28, *see also:* Jennie Jenkins
Jimmy Randal 157:71, *see also:* 89:156, 232:140
Johnny's Jarmanie 37:179
The Kettle Is Burning 74:31
The Keys of Canterbury 27:26
Kind Miss 226:144
La Viudita del Conde Laurel/The Widow of Count Laurel 295:43
The Lady on the Mountain 39:20
Lamkin 176:153
L'Avvelenato/The Poisoned Lover 89:156, *see also:* 157:71, 232:140
Little Ghost 197:95
Little Witch/Hexlein 78:63
Lliw Gwyn Rhosyn Yr Haf/White Rose of My Heart 89:134
Lolly Too Dum 36:52, 37:138, 148:232, 158:46, 277:71
Ma! Ma! Where Is Papa? 197:98
Madam, I Have Come A-Courting 62:122
Madam, I Have Come to Court 62:120
Mary Was a Red Bird 130:15, *see also:* 129:12, 232:130
Mary Wore a Red Dress 129:12, *see also:* 130:15, 232:130
Mary Wore Her Red Dress 232:130, *see also:* 129:12, 130:15
Matarile 169:60, 269:38, 295:37
Matarile, Rile, Ro 169:60, 269:38, 295:37
Miss Jenny Jones 17:39, 68:12, 100:90, *see also:* 63:32

Mistress Bond 62:52, 175:72, 292:154, *see also:* 188:116
My Billy Boy 27:22, *see also:* Billy Boy
My Boy Billy 27:22, *see also:* Billy Boy
My Boy, Tammie 182:56
My Boy Willie 61:112, *see also:* Billy Boy
My Good Old Man 20:68, 129:24, 274:40
My Jo, Janet 182:21
My Pretty Maid 36:35, *see also:* Where Are You Going to, My Pretty Maid?
Oh, No, John 148:282
Oh, What Have You Got for Dinner, Mrs. Bond 188:116, *see also:* 61:52, 175:72, 292:154
Oh, Won't You Sit Down? 262:71, 290:84, *see also:* Set Down, Servant
The Old Cow Died 234:56, 292:44, *see also:* 107:18, 232:112, 292:20
Old Woman 20:26, 46:223, 83:470, *see also:* Deaf Woman's Courtship
One Bottle of Pop 290:202
Paper of Pins 20:42, 62:114, 80, 134:18, 148:300, 290:78, *see also:* 17:93, 68:22
The Poisoned Lover/L'Avvelenato 89:156, *see also:* 157:71, 232:140
Poor Jenny 212:42, *see also:* 165:196, 175:134
Poor Jenny Sits A-Weeping 165:196, 175:134, *see also:* 212:42
Pray Give Us Lodging/En Nombre del Cielo 54:306
Pretty Girls and the Shoemaker 68:44
Quite Different 68:26
The Rolling Stone 35:56
The Sailor's Return 262:78
Set Down, Servant 148:284, 158:362 *see also:* 22:312, 83:465, 128:26, 262:71, 290:84
Shoo, Turkey 109:54
Sit Down, Sister 22:312, 128:26, *see also:* Set Down, Servant
Soldier Boy 134:96
Soldier, Soldier 17:55, 290:80, *see also:* Soldier, Soldier, Won't You Marry Me?
Soldier, Soldier, Will You Marry Me? 17:55, 62:118, 148:348, 290:80, *see also:* Soldier, Soldier, Won't You Marry Me?
Soldier, Soldier, Won't You Marry Me? 21:186, 142, 157:72, 227:24, *see also:* 17:55, 62:118, 79:32, 148:348, 290:80
Soldier, Won't You Marry Me? 79:32, *see also:* Soldier, Soldier, Won't You Marry Me?
Spin, Spin 262:135
Ten Thousand Men Were Going On Manoeuvres 262:137
"Thank You, Ma'am," Says Dan 42:603
There's a Hole in Our Bucket 197:32, *see also:* 290:74

QUESTION AND ANSWER SONGS
—*Continued*

Three Dukes 39:16, 100:92, 227:18, *see also:* 110:46, 135:84, 213:40

Walking on the Green Grass 134:96

What Did You Have for Your Supper? 232:140, *see also:* 89:156, 157:71

Where Are the Keys of the Castle?/ Donde Están las Llaves? 188:54, *see also:* 189:154

Where Are You Going Grandmama? 68:39

Where Are You Going, My Pretty Maid? 62:116, 290:79, 293:62, *see also:* Where Are You Going To, My Pretty Maid?

Where Are You Going To, My Pretty Maid? 17:114, 128:110, 175:118, 188:140, 262:53, *see also:* 36:3, 36:35, 62:116, 290:79, 293:62

Where Have You Been Walking, Shepherdess? 262:170

Whippily, Whoppily, Whoop 197:93

Whistle, Mary, Whistle 72:95

White Rose of My Heart/Lliw Gwyn Rhosyn Yr Haf 89:134

Who Comes Here? 18:11, 111:61

Who Did? 129:102, 289:102

The Widow of Count Laurel/La Viudita del Conde Laurel 295:43

Wild Americay 35:44

Won't You Go My Way? 134:68

Won't You Sit Down 83:465, *see also:* Set Down, Servant

R

RABBITS

Big-Eye Rabbit 128:36

Brother Rabbit 135:28

Easter Basket 197:42

Easter Bunny Song 245:114

The Easter Hare 245:115

Easter Is Here 7:18

Easter Rabbit 162:58

The Hare and the Frogs/Le Lièvre et les Grenouilles 243:16

The Hare and the Tortoise/Le Levraut et la Tortue 243:24

Le Levraut et la Tortue/The Hare and the Tortoise 243:24

Le Lièvre et les Grenouilles/The Hare and the Frogs 243:16

The Little Bunny 41:39

Little Peter Rabbit 26:30

Market Square 172:136, 173:22

Mistah Rabbit 78:95, *see also:* Mister Rabbit

Mister Rabbit 71:83, 129:80, 158:22, 234:16, 253:102, 292:94, *see also:* 78:95

Old Mister Rabbit 232:98

Old Molly Hare 232:99, 289:44, 292:91

Rabbit 162:16

Rabbit Ain't Got 292:96

Rabbits/Usagi 16:25, 286:18

See the Little Bunny Sleeping 165:154

Song of the Bunnies 245:45

Usagi/Rabbits 16:25, 286:18

RACCOONS

Coonie's Got a Pretty Tail 292:97

Raccoon and Possum 234:15

Settin' on a Rail 78:91

RAGTIME

Bill Bailey, Won't You Please Come Home 21:88, 148:42, 170:44, 205:272

Hello, Ma Baby 157:194, 205:258

RAILROADS

A. R. U. 226:190

Big Black Train 162:96

Big Rock Candy Mountains 21:112, 24:884, 158:278, 230:66

C. C. Rider 226:246, *see also:* 158:68, 226:247

Can'Cha Line 'Em 158:274

Casey Jones 22:142, 158:264, 158:266, 176:148, 222, 226:366

Casey Junior 275:26, 276:8

The Choo-Choo Train 289:94

Chug-a-Lug-a-Lug 291:20

Chug Chug Chug 162:96

Cow on the Railroad Track 118:28

Down at the Station Saga 55:263, *see also:* 25:30, 26:45, 75:21, 165:67

Down By the Station 25:30, 26:45, 75:21, 165:67, *see also:* 55:263

Down By the Station (adaptation) 41:28

Drill, Ye Tarriers, Drill! 22:138, 64:87, 72:88, 239:80, 290:52

Drivin' Steel 226:150

The Dying Hogger 226:186

Easy Rider 158:68, *see also:* 226:246, 226:247

Engine, Engine 112:16

Ever Since Uncle John Henry Been Dead 226:376

Every Monday Morning (More About John Henry) 232:156, *see also:* John Henry

Fillimeeoooreay 230:43, *see also:* Pat Works on the Railway

Goin' for a Ride 206:48

The Gospel Train 72:85, 148:126

Hammer Man 226:139

Hurry Up, Liza Jane 128:18

I Been Wukkin' on de Railroad 22:148, *see also:* I've Been Workin' on the Railroad
I Don't Like No Railroad Man 226:326
If I Die a Railroad Man 226:362
I've Been Workin' on the Railroad 25:35, 26:78, 83:506, 129:86, 148:192, 162:95 197:80, 205:196, *see also:* 22:148, 27:174
Jay Gould's Daughter 226:364
Jerry, Go an' Ile That Car 64:88, 226:360
John Henry 22:170, 33:178, 64:82, 89:40, 158:258, 158:260, 158:262, 226:24, 230:82, 232:154, 239:68, 272:15, 274:16, *see also:* 232:156
Kisha/The Train 286:58
Little Black Train 232:152, *see also:* 24:914, 148:228
Little Black Train Is A-comin' 24:914, 148:228, *see also:* 232:152
Little Red Caboose 46:213, 162:97
The Little Train 154:14
Long John 107:52
Mama Have You Heard the News? 226:368
The Midnight Train 226:325
My Old Hammah 226:458
Nine Hundred Miles 148:252, 158:254, *see also:* 72:17
O, Lula! 158:272
On the Charlie So Long 226:365
On the Train 227:21
Out in the Country 154:16
Paddy Works on the Erie 22:150, 158:270, *see also:* Pat Works on the Railway
Pat Works on the Railway 27:40, 64:84, 239:72, 277:115, *see also:* 22:150, 62:90, 158:270, 226:356, 230:43
Patsy on the Railroad 62:90, *see also:* Pat Works on the Railway
Poor Paddy Works on the Railway 226:356, *see also:* Pat Works on the Railway
Puffer Train, Puffer Train 165:109
Railroad Bill 226:384
The Railroad Cars Are Coming 226:358
Rainbow Round My Shoulder 158:323
The Rock Island Line 35:52, 129:90, 130:64, 148:314, 274:12
The Runaway Train 26:80
She'll Be Comin' 'Round the Mountain 20:36, 22:156, 25:14, 62:70, 148:324, 165:197, 170:33, 201, 205:175, 226:372, 232:90, 283:30, 290:24
Steve Is the Engine 232:151, *see also:* 232:150
Take This Hammer 21:210, 24:913, 64:80, 158:322, 239:48, 277:87

There's a Train 296:38
There's Many a Man Killed on the Railroad 226:371
This Ol' Hammah 55:265, *see also:* 232:149
This Old Hammer 232:149, *see also:* 55:265
This Train 72:86, 75:84, 148:388
Track-Lining Chant 239:74
The Train 41:29 *(Choo, choo, choo, the train will soon be going)*
The Train/Kisha 286:58 *(When we think the train is running)*
The Train Is Carrying Coal 165:69
Train Song 26:77
The Wabash Cannon Ball 21:208, 157:163, 205:368, 230:85
The Whistle of the Train 114:38
RAIN: *see also* WEATHER
April Rain 97:unpaged
Dime, Lluvia/Tell Me, Rain 216:17
Doctor Foster 175:126
El Patio de Mi Casa/The Patio of My House 295:40
Happiness 172:117, 173:3
Hej Pada Pada/Raindrops 289:36
Hevebe Song 79:15
How Many Raindrops 162:27
I Bring the Rain 74:60
If All the Raindrops 289:140
Il Pleut, Bergère/It Is Raining, Shepherdess 217:22
It Is Raining, Shepherdess/Il Pleut, Bergère 217:56
It Rained a Mist 162:30, 232:68
Little April Shower 276:26
Lullaby of the Rain 162:31
On a Rainy Day 162:31
The Patio of My House/El Patio de Mi Casa 295:40
Pit, Pat, Pat 245:67
Pray Open Your Umbrella 165:62
Rain 11:28 *(Little drops of rain)*
Rain 17:117 *(The rain is raining all around)*
Rain/Yagmur 266:57 *(Rain, rain, you rain)*
Rain, Come Wet Me 232:67
Rain Dance 178:62 (music only)
Rain Dance 197:86 *(Rain now is here with us)*
Rain Falls 206:102
Rain in the Night 245:70
Rain, Oh Rain 296:18
Rain, Rain, Go Away 17:48, 285:18
Rain Song 41:38
The Rainbow 207:125
Raindrop Round 72:161

RAIN—*Continued*

Raindrops 162:29 *(One little raindrop riding on a cloud)*

Raindrops/Hej Pada Pada 289:36 *(Raindrops a falling from the skies)*

Rainy Day in Utica, N. Y. 237:unpaged

Rainy Day Lady 296:30

Rainy Day Round 71:114

Spring Puddles 207:88

Spring Rain 261:28

Tell Me, Rain/Dime, Lluvia 216:45

Teru, Terubozu/Wishing Dolls 286:56

Wishing Dolls/Teru, Terubozu 286:56

Yagmur/Rain 266:57

RAIN CROWS: *see* CUCKOOS

RAINBOW

The Rainbow 207:125

RAMS: *see* SHEEP

RANCH LIFE: *see also* COWBOYS; COWS; SHEEP

The Big Ranch/El Rancho Grande 216:47

El Rancho Grande/The Big Ranch 216:23

RATS

Broder Manyo 89:66

The City Rat and the Country Rat 17:96 *(Once a rat who loved the city)*

The City Rat and the Country Rat/Le Rat de Ville et le Rat des Champs 243:29 *(Le rat de ville au rat des champs)*

Le Lion et le Rat/The Lion and the Rat 243:6

Le Rat de Ville et le Rat des Champs/The City Rat and the Country Rat 243:29

Le Rat et l'Eléphant/The Rat and the Elephant 243:13

The Lion and the Rat/Le Lion et le Rat 243:6

The Rat and the Elephant/Le Rat et l'Eléphant 243:13

RATTLESNAKES: *see* SNAKES

RAVENS

Billy Magee Magaw 290:70, 292:142, *see also:* Three Ravens

The Three Ravens 22:94, 189:88, 292:140, *see also:* 37:115, 62:54, 232:121, 290:70, 292:142

The Two Ravens 37:115, *see also:* Three Ravens

RAVIOLI

Ravioli 26:25

RECONSTRUCTION: *see* CIVIL WAR (U.S., 1861-1865)

RELATIVES: *see* FAMILY AND FAMILY LIFE

RELIGION: *see also* CHRISTMAS CAROLS, HYMNS, JUDAISM, MORMONS, PRAYERS, SPIRITUALS; names of people, e.g., NOAH

All Night Long 226:448, *see also:* 66:136

Alleluia 86:134

Allelujah 55:254, 71:14, 72:175, 101:33

And Thou Shalt Love 77:30

The Angel's Song 155:22

Angelus ad Virginem/Carol of the Annunciation 189:70

Ave Maria (Mozart) 241:225

Awake 233:62

The Best Book of All 86:85

Bethel 123:72

Bible Stories 36:109, 290:156, *see also:* 178:70

Blind Man Lay Beside the Way 226:452

Bound for the Promised Land 21:256, 158:350, *see also:* 157:58

Brethren in Peace Together 72:147

The California Brothers 61:38

Carol of Beauty 184:64

Carol of the Annunciation/Angelus ad Virginem 189:70

The Child of God 155:27

Children From Everywhere 124:152

Children of the Heavenly King 233:62

The Children's Friend 86:104

The Christian Year 86:161

Church in the Wildwood 25:117, *see also:* 21:164

Come, Come, Ye Saints 21:300

Come, O Sabbath Day 25:113

Come, Saints and Sinners 21:349

The Creation 123:22

Dear Lord, We Give Our Youth to Thee 86:118

Don't You Hear the Lambs A-Crying? 233:19

Evening Hymn, Tallis's Canon 86:170, 189:60, *see also:* 71:106, 72:51, 176:104

Exultation 140:84, 233:61, *see also:* 190:41

Father Bless Our School Today 86:158

First Day of the Week 124:243

Following Christ 86:109

For All the Love 72:43

For Stories Fine and True 86:83

Found My Lost Sheep 233:20

The Garden of Jesus 184:56

The Gentle Shepherd 189:86

Glory to Thee 176:104, *see also:* 71:106, 72:51, 86:170, 189:60

God Made the Shy, The Wild Ones 245:34

God, Our Loving Father 71:24, 72:46, 135:31

God's Garden 123:26

The Golden Rule 86:87

Good Night Canon 71:106, 72:51, *see also:* 86:170, 176:104, 189:60
The Good Samaritan 155:18
Grace Song 25:111, 101:34
Hail, Mary 124:26
Hallelu 55:280
Hark to the Chimes 71:13, 72:172, 101:32
Hatikvah/The Hope 22:194
He Shall Feed His Flock 241:201
Heard From Heaven Today 233:53
The Heavenly March 157:58, *see also:* 21:256, 158:350
The Heavens Resound 262:157
Here Is the Church 75:30
Highbridge 226:155
His Jewels 189:66
Hold the Wind 124:104
Holy Babe 233:70
The Holy Baby 124:68
Holy Bible, Book Divine 86:78
The Home of the Soul 66:140
Homes 86:152
The Hope/Hatikvah 22:194
Hosanna in the Highest 124:192
The House on the Rock 155:20
How Shall the Young Direct Their Way 86:86
Hush, My Babe 54:87, 140:24, 140:113, 283:62, *see also:* 184:62, 190:43, 190:45, 233:41
I Don't Want to Be a Gambler 226:465
I Got a Letter From Jesus 226:487
I Know the Lord's Laid His Hands on Me 83:469
I Never Felt Such Love 55:276
I Want to Be Like Jesus 155:5
In Dulci Jubilo 21:328, 210:32, 220:98, 241:76
In Our Work and in Our Play 86:117
In the Sweet By and By 21:176, *see also:* 66:150
Jehovah Hallelujah 233:23
Jerusalem 124:316
Jesus, Lead Me Day by Day 86:102
Jesus Liebt Mich Ganz Gewiss/Jesus Loves Me 86:97
Jesus Loves Me, Jesus Loves Me 86:103
Jesus Loves Me 45:26, 86:97, 283:61
Jesus, Our Friend 86:100
Jesus Walked in Galilee 37:166
Jesus Was a Loving Teacher 86:99
Kindness 155:13
Kum-Ba-Ya 25:108, 55:276, 72:143, 86:198, 107:36, 148:220, *see also:* 261:54
Kumbaya 261:54, *see also:* Kum-Ba-Ya
Let Me Learn of Jesus 86:98
Let the Words of My Mouth 86:192

Little Brown Church in the Vale 21:164, *see also:* 25:117
The Little Family 37:183
Lord, I Want to Be a Christian 83:477, 86:106
The Lord Is My Shepherd 155:30, *see also:* 72:50, 86:23
Lord This Day Thy Children Meet 86:159
The Lord's My Shepherd 72:50, 86:23, *see also:* 155:30
The Lost Sheep 155:17
Loving Shepherd of Thy Sheep 189:64
Magnificat 262:113
María Lavava/Mary Washed Linen 188:156
Mariner's Hymn 233:55
Martyrs Tune 273:128
Mary Washed Linen/María Lavava 188:156, *see also:* 189:76
Mary Wore Three Links of Chain 157:147, 226:474, *see also:* 158:376
May I Speak Peace 155:12
Michael, Row the Boat Ashore 25:95, 72:84, 148:242, 230:75
Millions of Snowflakes 86:181
The Miraculous Meal 124:147
Morning Hymn 189:59
Morning Star 128:64
My Neighbor 155:18
My Sabbath Home 66:144
Never Weather-Beaten Saile 176:142
The Ninety and Nine 66:146
O Be Joyful 155:8
Oh, Give Thanks 71:13, 72:57, 101:31
O God, Who Art the Only Light 262:98
O Jesu So Kind 85:86
Oh, Render Thanks 71:14
The Old Chariot 66:148, *see also:* 226:196
Old Hundredth 21:312, 22:287, 45:7, 86:213, 148:74, 157:12, 161:11
Old Ship of Zion 21:262, *see also:* 35:58
On Children's Day We Sweetly Sing 86:185
100 Psalm Tune New 273:132
148th Psalm 273:126
Our Father 155:14
Passing Through 230:31
Pilgrims' Melody 21:313
A Poor Wayfaring Stranger 22:34, 35:68, 148:304, *see also:* Wayfaring Stranger
Pull for the Shore 66:152
Rejoice My Friends 233:65
The Resurrection 35:70
The Rich Man and the Poor Man 62:101, 64:148, *see also:* 36:70
Roll the Chariot 226:196, *see also:* 66:148

RELIGION—*Continued*
Salve, O Jesus   124:29
Satan's a Liah   226:250
Shanghai Chicken   135:21
The Shepherd Boy's Song   112:62
Shepherds Awake   124:27
Shine Like a Star in the Morning   233:14
Ship of Zion   35:58, *see also:* 21:262
Simple Gifts   157:62, 176:92
Singing in the Land   233:64
Sinner Man   134:82, 148:336, 157:60
Slumber, Dear Jesus   184:54
Slumber Song   77:34
The Smallest Man in Jericho   124:182
A Soft Answer   155:11
Song of Baptism   124:89
Song of Pentecost   124:251
Song of Praise   155:7 *(Let us now our voices raise)*
Song of Praise   85:81 *(Thou, Thou, Jehova, hear my singing)*
Song of the Children   124:31
Song of the Followers   124:99
Song of the Sacred Stones   74:37
Song of the Seasons   86:184
Song of the Wind and Water   124:126
The Sower   155:16
The Spacious Firmament on High   262:100
Standin' on the Walls of Zion   226:484
Sunday Morning Song   86:157
Sweet By and By   66:150, *see also:* 21:176
Tallis's Canon   71:106, 72:51, 86:170, 176:104, 189:60
Thanks to God   86:164
There Is a Happy Land   66:155
Things I Used to Do   226:482
This Is God's House   86:160
This Is the Day   245:103
'Twas a Wonder in Heaven   233:54
Wakan'tanka Hears Me   74:36
Wayfaring Stranger   24:880, 27:45, 37:162, 158:346, 205:56, 230:15, 262:47, 277:41, *see also:* 22:34, 35:68, 148:304
We Are Thy Children   155:1
We're All Here: The Song of the Freed Man   66:136, *see also:* 226:448
When I Can Read My Title Clear   66:139
When I Go to Bed   124:148
When Jesus Was a Little Boy   154:4
When Jesus Wept   140:112, 157:13, 273:136
When the Corn Is Planted   86:177
Where God Hath Walked   71:32, 72:52
Where O Where Is Old Elijah?   226:92
Who Can Retell?   22:280
Who Did?   129:102, 289:102
Who Knows One?   192
Windsor   21:315

Winter Song   86:180
The Word of God   124:17
Yonder Comes Sister Mary   233:57
Yonlyem Jinky   89:236
York   21:314
Young Folks, Old Folks   178:70, *see also:* 36:109, 290:156
Zek'l Weep   226:449
REPTILES: *see* names of specific reptiles, e.g., SNAKES
REVOLUTIONARY WAR IN AMERICA (1776-1781)
Adam's Fall   240:79, *see also:* 28:49
Affair at Newport   28:114, *see also:* 240:155
America (To Thee the Tuneful Anthem Soars)   240:49
An American Frigate   27:124, 28:123
American "Heart of Oak"   273:38
American Hero   240:115, 273:40
American Rule Britannia   240:58
American Taxation   28:4, 240:36
American Vicar of Bray   240:157
Anthony Wayne   28:126, *see also:* 240:100
Arnold Is As Brave a Man   28:55
Ballad of Bunker Hill   240:114
Ballad of Jane McCrea   28:96
Ballad of Sergeant Champe   28:150, *see also:* 240:107, 273:52
Ballad of the American War   240:170
Ballad of Trenton   28:86, *see also:* 240:121
Banks of the Dee   28:74, 240:61, 273:30
Banks of the Dee (parody)   240:62, 273:32, *see also:* 28:77
Battle of Saratoga   240:124
Battle of the Kegs   28:94, 240:93, 273:46
Battle of Trenton   240:121
Begone, Pernicious Tea   28:29
The Bold Volunteer   27:36, 28:141
The Bombardment of Bristol   240:119
The Boston Massacre   28:20
Boston Tea Tax Song   240:53, *see also:* 28:26
Brave Paulding and the Spy   240:104, *see also:* 28:138
The British Grenadiers   22:198, 240:142
The British Light Infantry   240:153
Bunker Hill   28:46
Burgoyne's Defeat   28:100
Burgoyne's Disgrace   240:128
The Burrowing Yankees   28:63, 240:152
The Capture of Major Andre   28:138, *see also:* 240:104
Capture of Burgoyne   273:44
Castle Island Song   273:26, *see also:* 28:22
The Charleston Song   28:131

Chester   21:242, 28:147, 157:20, 197:25, 240:83, 273:140

Collinet and Phebe   273:82

Come Out, Ye Continentalers   27:34, 28:107

Come Shake Your Dull Noodles   28:11, 240:45, 273:22

Come Soldiers All in Chorus Join   240:118

Come Swallow Your Bumpers   28:13, see also: 240:47, 273:24

The Congress   240:150

Cornwallis Burgoyned   240:137, 273:56

The Cornwallis Country Dance   28:156, 240:135, 273:54, 277:16

The Cow Chase   28:134

Derry Down   27:164, see also: 28:51, 240:67, 273:36

The Destruction of the Tea   240:52

Doodle Dandy   134:92

A Dose for the Tories   240:162

The Dying British Sergeant   240:148

The Escape of Old John Webber   240:25

The Etiquette   240:168

The Farce   28:112

Fare Thee Well, You Sweethearts   28:153

The Fate of John Burgoyne   240:127

Felix the Soldier   240:32

The Female Patriots   28:109

Fish and Tea   240:67, see also: 27:164, 28:51, 273:36

Follow Washington   27:32, 28:84

Free America   240:57, 273:28, see also: 27:120, 28:43

Free Amerikay   27:120, 28:43, see also: 240:57, 273:28

A Funeral Dirge on the Death of General George Washington   273:74

Gage's Proclamation   28:31

God Save America   240:81

God Save Our States   28:166, see also: 240:82, 273:50

God Save the Thirteen States   240:82, 273:50, see also: 28:166

Good Bye to America   28:165

Goody Bull   28:15, see also: 240:40, 273:58, 289:133

Granny Wales   28:7

The Green Mountaineer   28:40

Hail, Columbia   21:266, 27:185, 66:84, 157:26, 160:26, 205:46, 240:187, 273:68

The Halcyon Day of Old England   240:167

Hale in the Bush   28:80, see also: 240:98

The Heads   240:165, see also: 28:82

Hearts of Oak Are We Still   240:42

The Hobbies   240:183

How Happy the Soldier   240:143, 273:86

In Freedom We're Born   27:182, 28:9, see also: 21:238, 157:16, 240:44, 273:20

Independence Day   28:68, 240:84

The Indian's Over the Border   28:116

An Invitation to North America   240:18

The Irishman's Epistle   240:64, see also: 28:53

It Is I, the Little Owl   19:31

Johnny Has Gone for a Soldier   22:69, 134:94, 157:24, 158:117, 240:87, 262:25, 273:84, see also: 73:104

A Junto Song   240:66

The King's Own Regulars   240:89, see also: 27:166, 28:89

The Liberty Song   21:238, 157:16, 240:44, 273:20, see also: 27:182, 28:9

Liberty Tree   28:58

The Little Sergeant   28:70

Mad Anthony Wayne   240:100, see also: 28:126

Marion's Men   28:144

The Maryland Resolves   28:33

Massachusetts Liberty Song   240:47, 273:24, see also: 28:13

Nathan Hale   240:98, see also: 28:80

A New Song, Written By a Soldier   240:111

A New Tory Ballad   240:177, see also: 28:104

Ode for American Independence   273:64

The Old Soldiers of the King   27:166, 28:89, see also: 240:89

The Old Woman Taught Wisdom   240:40, see also: 28:15, 273:58, 289:133

On Independence   240:84, see also: 28:68

A Parody of the Banks of the Dee   28:77, see also: 240:62, 273:32

Parody Upon a Well-Known Liberty Song   240:45

Paul Jones   35:16, see also: 240:132

Peter Parker   28:66, see also: 240:91

The Revolutionary Alphabet   28:36

Revolutionary Tea   157:18, 240:55

Riflemen of Bennington   20:14, 240:102

Rivington's Reflections   28:163

Rouse, Britons   28:104, see also: 240:177

The Sailors' Address   240:164

The Savannah Song   28:129

Sergeant Champe   240:107, 273:52, see also: 28:150

Sir Peter Parker   240:91, see also: 28:66

The Soldier's Lamentation   240:116

A Song Made Upon the Election of New Magistrates for this City   240:27

A Song Made Upon the Foregoing Occasion   240:28

Song of the Heads   28:82, 240:165

REVOLUTIONARY WAR IN AMERICA
(1776-1781)—*Continued*
　Song of the Minute Man　240:86
　A Song on the Brave General Montgomery　240:118
　The Sons of Liberty　240:147
　The Surrender of Cornwallis　240:139
　The Tea Party　28:26, *see also:* 240:53
　To the Commons　240:161
　To the Ladies　240:38
　To the Troops in Boston　28:53, *see also:* 240:64
　The Toast　157:22, 240:96, 273:48
　The Trip to Cambridge　28:49, *see also:* 240:79
　Unhappy Times　28:161
　War and Washington　240:97
　What a Court　28:51, *see also:* 27:164, 240:67, 273:36
　What a Court Hath Old England　273:36, *see also:* 27:164, 28:51, 240:67
　The Wicked Rebels　27:168, 28:17
　The World Turned Upside Down 26:159, 250:58, 289:133, *see also:* 240:40
　Yankee Doodle　17:80, 21:240, 26:14, 46:225, 127:14, 157:21, 160:20, 162:108, 188:22, 197:24, 200, 205:36, 228, 230:71, 240:71, 240:74, 240:76, 273:42, 277:15, 283:40, *see also:* 15, 28:61
　Yankee Doodle Doodle Doo　28:61, *see also:* Yankee Doodle
　Yankee Doodle's Expedition to Rhode Island　28:114, 240:155
　A Yankee Federal Song　240:181
　The Yankee Man-of-War　240:130
　The Yankee Privateer　28:120
　The Yankee's Return from Camp 240:76, *see also:* Yankee Doodle
　Ye Sons of North Britain　28:91
　You Simple Bostonians　28:22, *see also:* 273:26
RHODESIA
　*Manthi'Ki/Spirit Song　89:273
　*Spirit Song/Manthi'Ki　89:273
RHYTHMS
　A-Jump　162:105
　Apple Dumplings　166:22
　At the Lemonade Stand　166:44
　Baby-Sitter Sense　166:50
　Be a Cool Ghoul　167:44
　Black Cats Come　166:34
　Call Me on the Telephone　166:36
　Christmas Eve　166:76
　The Clock　288:25
　Cowboy Song　83:466, 288:25
　Crazy Carousel　166:66
　Dance in a Circle　162:62

Dieting Dragons　166:12
Dip and Fall Back Low　130:52
Dos y Dos Son Cuatro/Two and Two Are Four　194:36
Down the Avenue　288:8
Easter Hymn　167:20
Falling Snow　167:48
Fireworks for the Fourth　166:64
Fishin' Fun　167:28
Follow the Leader　162:63
Frogman, Frogman　167:32
A Funny, Silly Clown　288:6
Galloping Horses　129:74
The Gondolier's Song　166:48
The Grasshopper　288:10
Greenland Glaciers　166:52
Gum-Ball Machine　166:18
Hey Dee Roon　72:105, *see also:* 291:8
Hi-Dee-Roon　291:8, *see also:* 72:105
Hippity Hop　17:47, *see also:* 165:39
Hippity Hop to the Candy Shop　165:139, *see also:* 17:47
Hollyhock Ladies　166:16
Hop, Skip and Sing　167:8
Hopping Music　11:34
I Can Fly　162:101
I Like to Do the Highland Fling　167:42
I Want to Be a Clown　167:12
I'm a Cowboy A-Ropin'　167:26
In Prehistoric Times　167:22
Indian Song　288:28
It's an Indian Village　166:14
Joseph Henry Alligator　166:70
Jumping, Jumping, Jumping Jumping 178:12
Keeping Time　104:51
Lead a Yell　166:20
Let's Have a Rhythm Band　166:28
Little Dutch Girl, Sitting There　167:57
A Little Girl　162:61
Little Mother Goose　167:34
Little Shadow　162:64
The Longest Dog in the World　167:38
Magicians Do Tricks　166:58
Make a Hat for Easter　166:38
Marching Music　11:35
Message from the Medicine Man　166:42
The Monkey and the Skunk　166:26
My Polite Panda　166:60
New Baby Brother　166:56
Night Noises　166:10
Play Ball　166:32
Pretty Dolly Madison　166:46
Red Riding Hood's Hood　166:72
Scraping Up Sand in the Bottom of the Sea　232:96
Shiloh　232:96
Shoot an Arrow　166:8
Skip to Market　166:63

Skipping Music 11:33
The Snappy Turtle Says 166:40
A Spider for Miss Muffet 166:24
Swimmin' Fun 166:74
Thanks for Thanksgiving 167:50
Toy Soldier Sam 166:54
Try a Spanish Dance 166:62
Two and Two Are Four/Dos y Dos Son Cuatro 194:36
Walking Music 11:32
We'll Land on the Moon 166:68
Western Lullaby 166:30
RICE
Magtanim 169:57, 271:23, see also: Planting Rice
Magtanim Ay Di Biro 87:54, see also: Planting Rice
Planting Rice/Magtanim 55:262, 64:102, 70:12, 87:54, 169:57, 271:23, see also: 286:78
Rice Planting/Taue 286:78, see also: Planting Rice
Taue/Rice Planting 286:78, see also: Planting Rice
RIDDLES
The Devil's Nine Questions 27:214, see also: 37:110, 134:85
The Devil's Questions 37:110, 134:85, see also: 27:214
A Fish Net/He Upena 87:16
Funny Money Riddle 68:42
He Moa Kane/A Strutting Rooster 87:17
He 'Upena/A Fish Net 87:16
I Gave My Love a Cherry 277:105, see also: Riddle Song
I Had Four Brothers 17:22, 189:26, see also: Riddle Song
I Will Give My Love an Apple 27:28, see also: Riddle Song
I'm a Person 204:9
King Henry Has Set Me Free 62:31
Rätsel/A Riddle 79:71
A Riddle/Rätsel 79:71
The Riddle 22:25, 205:39, see also: Riddle Song
The Riddle Song 37:156, 69:21, 135:46, 148:310, 205:39, 230:72, 262:152, 277:105, see also: 17:22, 22:25, 27:28, 188:24, 189:26, 205:39
A Strutting Rooster/He Moa Kane 87:17
RIGHTS, CIVIL: see CIVIL RIGHTS
RIVERS
Afton Water 176:26, see also: 22:106, 205:95
Autumn Nights By the River 261:40
Barges 72:96
Flow Gently Sweet Afton 22:106, 205:95, see also: 176:26
Peace 69:7, see also: 55:255, 262:91

Peace of the River 262:91, see also: 55:255, 69:7
Raftsman Jim 24:840
The River 114:84
Swanee River 230:83, see also: 22:86, 127:99
Where Does This River Go? 91:17
ROBBERS: see OUTLAWS
ROBIN HOOD
Bold Robin Hood 37:124
Now Robin, Lend to Me Thy Bow 71:57, 72:121
Oo-De-Lally 276:76
Robin Hood and Allen A Dale 164:42
Robin Hood and Guy of Gisborne 164:68
Robin Hood and Little John 164:10, 262:132
Robin Hood and Maid Marian 164:48
Robin Hood and the Bishop 164:52
Robin Hood and the Bishop of Hereford 164:94
Robin Hood and the Bold Pedlar 164:64
Robin Hood and the Butcher 164:58
Robin Hood and the Curtal Friar 164:36
Robin Hood and the Golden Arrow 164:76
Robin Hood and the Prince of Aragon 164:28
Robin Hood and the Ranger 164:82
Robin Hood and the Stranger 164:16
Robin Hood and the Tanner 164:22
Robin Hood Rescuing Three Squires 164:104
Robin Hood Rescuing Will Stutly 164:88
Robin Hood's Death 164:110
Robin Hood's Golden Prize 164:98
ROBINS
Cock Robin 37:177, 134:58, see also: 135:32, 289:74, 292:138
Cocky Robin 135:32, 289:74, see also: 37:177, 134:58, 292:138
Little Robin Redbreast 17:67, 18:16
The Lonely Robin 207:87
The Merry Little Robin 245:10
The North Wind Doth Blow 17:129, 18:25, 135:116, 175:88, 188:106, 189:124, 227:31, 285:34, 292:139
The Robin 41:22
The Robin's Last Will 262:45
Who Killed Cock Robin? 62:56, 134:58, 292:138, see also: 37:177, 135:32, 289:74
Who Killed Cocky Robin? 289:74, see also: Who Killed Cock Robin?
ROCKING RHYMES: see LULLABIES
ROOSTERS: see CHICKENS
ROSES
The Hedge-Rose 85:141
Rose Red 46:229

ROSES—*Continued*
Rose, Rose 262:159, 293:24
ROUND TABLE: *see* ARTHUR, KING
ROUNDS
All Is Silent 71:112, 72:168, 293:84
All Things Must Parish 293:6, *see also:* 62:20, 69:50
All Things on Earth 62:20, *see also:* 69:50, 293:6
Alleluia (Version I) 55:255, 86:150, 241:224
Allelujah 55:254, 11:14, 72:175, 101:33
The Apple Tree 189:58
Are You Sleeping 25:31, 26:42, 62:11, 293:43, *see also:* Frère Jacques
At Summer Morn 262:125
Baa, Baa, Black Sheep 17:147, 175:84, 188:102, 189:20, 283:24, 285:49
Banbury Ale 290:194
The Bell 71:105, 72:172, *see also:* 293:16 (*The bell doth toll, its echoes roll*)
The Bell 67:88 (*I ring it far and near*)
The Bell Doth Toll 71:105, 72:172, 293:16
Billy Pringle 175:150
Birthday Roundelay 245:107
Bless This Table 72:173
A Boat, A Boat 290:192, 293:58
Buon Giorno 69:50
Buy My Dainty Fine Beans 293:70
Call John the Boatman 71:99, 72:162
Canoe Round 293:60, *see also:* 62:19
Cat in the Plum Tree 144:11
Chairs to Mend 46:228, 71:104, 72:164, 289:186, 293:64, 293:66, *see also:* 111:58
Cherries So Ripe 293:69
Christmas Bells Ring Out Glad News 86:43
Christmas Eve Canon 241:223
Christmas Is Coming 27:248, 68:8, 128:54, 178:23, 210:94, 241:225, 293:76
The Clocks 68:48, 262:33
Cock-A-Doodle-Doo 17:138, 111:76, 135:50, 175:116, 285:86, 289:98
Come-A-Hunting 26:43
Come and Let Us Dance 71:106
Come, Follow 71:104, 72:163, 148:57, 293:78
Coo, Coo 71:107
The Crocodile 62:48, *see also:* 26:36, 89:33, 234:72
The Crocodile Song 26:36, 89:33, 234:72, *see also:* 62:48
The Cuckoo 71:107
A Cuckoo and an Owl 144:13
Dame, Lend Me a Loaf 293:74
De Bezem 262:120

Die Abendglocke/The Evening Bells 21:322
Ding, Dong Bell 17:49, 147:13, 175:174
Dona Nobis Pacem 55:254, 69:11, 176:47, 241:224, 262:34, 293:112
Donkeys and Carrots 293:92
Donkeys Love Carrots 144:23
Dormy Dormouse 144:17
Down at the Station Saga 55:263, *see also:* 25:30, 26:45, 75:21, 165:67
Down By the Station 25:30, 26:45, 75:21, 165:67, *see also:* 55:263
Ducks on a Pond 290:197
Early to Bed 71:105, 293:26
Echo Yodel 55:254
Ego Sum Pauper 69:53
Ehre Sei Gott/Glory to God 241:233
Epigram on Singers 176:141
The Evening Bells/Die Abendglocke 21:322
Evening Hymn/Tallis's Canon 86:170, 189:60, *see also:* 71:106, 72:51, 176:104
Fare Thee Well 46:228, 69:10, 71:12, 72:172
Fie, Nay, Prithee, John 176:51
Fire's Burning 62:14
Flowers Are Dying 71:113
Follow, Follow 62:15
For Health and Strength 68:38, 71:13, 72:175, 101:32
The Four Loves 175:66, *see also:* 71:112, 292:90
Fray Felipe, Fray Felipe 148:102, 293:43
French Cathedrals 71:101, 72:165, 293:38
Frère Jacques/Are You Sleeping 17:72, 62:11, 90, 148:102, 176:73, 188:180, 217:17, 217:55, 283:21, 289:186, 293:42, *see also:* 25:31, 26:42
Frog Round 69:14, 71:107, 72:167, *see also:* 289:187, 293:100
The Frog Song 289:187, *see also:* 69:14, 71:107, 72:167, 289:100
The Frogs 293:100, *see also:* 69:14, 71:107, 72:167, 289:187
Gelobet 69:52
The Ghost of John 293:46, *see also:* 289:190
Girl Scout's Goodbye Round 71:103
Girl Scout's Round 71:104
Gloria, Gloria 71:17
Glory to God/Ehre Sei Gott 241:233
Glory to Thee 176:104, *see also:* 71:106, 72:51, 86:170, 189:60
Go to Jane Glover 71:103, 293:50
Gone Is Autumn 71:113, 72:175
Good Night 71:106

Good Night Canon 71:106, 72:51, *see also:* 86:170, 176:104, 189:60

Good Night to You All 125:34, 262:86, 293:106

Grasshoppers Three 62:18, 292:208

Great Tom Is Cast 71:103, 176:29, 293:21

The Hart He Loves 292:90, *see also:* 71:112, 175:66

The Hart He Loves the High Wood 71:112, *see also:* 175:66, 292:90

Haste Thee, Nymph 71:101

Have You Seen the Ghost of John? 289:190, 293:46

Hello! Hello! 25:6, 26:10, 69:10, 71:11, 72:160

Hey, Ho! 25:29, 26:43, 62:14, 64:201, 71:105, 72:163, 148:158, 293:30

Hey, Ho, To the Greenwood 176:99, 292:82, 293:96

Hi Ho! Nobody Home 25:29, 26:43, 62:14, 64:201, 71:105, 72:163, 148:158, 293:30

Ho! Every Sleeper Waken 262:67, 293:104

Hot Mutton Pies 71:103

I Love Little Pussy 17:116, 175:86, 283:15, 285:66

Jack and Jill 17:83, 75:38, 175:18, 177:90, 188:124, 283:24, 289:88

Jack, Boy, Ho, Boy 71:100, 293:48

Jane Glover 293:50, *see also:* 71:103

Johnny! Johnny! 71:100, 72:164

Joyful Greetings 245:107

Kookaburra 128:108, 148:218, 176:23, 178:55, 189:136, 262:148, 289:188, 293:86

The Lady and the Swine 175:76, *see also:* 46:226

The Lame Crane 71:114, 72:170, *see also:* 62:19, 144:25, 176:152, 292:65, 293:52

A Lame, Tame Crane 144:25, *see also:* The Lame Crane

Let Simon's Beard Alone 290:192

Let Us Go A-Maying 262:127

Let Us Sing Together 55:256

Let's Have a Peal 71:100

Lightsome Heart 262:128

List to the Bells 46:228

The Little Bells 71:101, 72:164, 293:20

Little Bells of Westminster 71:101, 72:164, 293:20

Little Tommy Tinker 26:44, 290:192

Lock the Dairy Door! 144:27

London Street Cries 71:102

London's Burning 25:30, 175:20, *see also:* 46:227, 148:321, 283:35, 289:188, 293:36

Lovely Evening 71:109, 72:173

Lully, Lullay (Haydn) 241:222

Make New Friends 68:38, 69:10, 262:34, 293:11

Man's Life 62:20, *see also:* 293:28

Man's Life's a Vapor 62:20, 293:28

Merrily, Merrily 46:227, 71:110, 72:165, 293:12, *see also:* 62:12

Merry Are the Bells 111:40

Merry Christmas 241:232

The Merry Lark 71:110, 72:169

Morning Is Come 71:111, 72:169

Music Shall Live 69:50, *see also:* 62:20, 293:6

My Aunt Has a Lame Tame Crane 62:19, *see also:* Lame Crane

My Dame Hath a Lame, Tame Crane 144:25, 176:152, 292:165, 293:52, *see also:* 62:19, 71:114, 72:170

My Ducklings 68:21

My Goose 128:101, 144:21, 176:91, *see also:* Why Shouldn't My Goose

My Paddle's Keen and Bright 62:19, 293:60

Now Comes the Hour 262:90

Now We'll Make the Rafters Ring 148:260, 290:195, 293:10

O Hark I Hear Those Pealing Bells 62:12, *see also:* 71:98, 72:166

Oh, How Lovely Is the Evening 21:322, 62:11, 71:109, 72:173, 148:273, 241:232, 289:189, 293:22

Oh, Music, Sweet Music 293:8

Oh, Render Thanks 71:14

O Wie Wohl Ist's Mir Am Abend/O, How Lovely Is the Evening 241:232, 293:22

Old Hungarian Round 71:111, 72:171

Ole Clo' 71:102

On the Corner 241:228

Onkel Jakob, Onkel Jakob 148:102, 293:43

The Paddle Song 25:28

Peace 69:7, *see also:* 55:255, 262:91

Peace of the River 262:91, *see also:* 55:255, 69:7

The Pealing Bells 71:98, 72:166, *see also:* 62:12

Perfect Posture 26:43

The Ploughboy 262:131

Poor Algy 144:19

A Poor and Carefree Stranger 69:53

Praise and Thanksgiving Let Everyone Bring 86:210

Pray God Bless 262:68

Pussy-Cat Pussy-Cat 144:15

Quodlibet/What You Will 262:82

Raindrop Round 72:161

Rainy Day Round 71:114

Rally Song 262:144

ROUNDS—*Continued*
Rheumatism 26:42, *see also:* 62:16
Rise Up, O Flame 69:7, 71:11, 72:174
Rose Red 46:229
Rose, Rose 262:159, 293:24
Rosen Fra Fuhn 69:52
Round—About Round 68:19
Rounds About Rounds 293:114
Row, Row, Row Your Boat 17:117, 25:30, 26:44, 62:10, 148:320, 165:116, 283:10, 289:185, 293:56
Sandy McNab 290:193, 293:54
Sandy's Mill 62:68, 262:32
Santa's Coming 26:43
Scotland's Burning 46:227, 62:13, 148:321, 283:35, 289:188, 293:36, *see also:* 25:30, 175:20
Seven Great Towns of Greece 293:34
Shaker Life 293:108
Shalom Chaverim 55:255, 293:110
Sing Together 71:99, 72:41
The Snake 144:7
Star Bright 162:37, *see also:* 59:58, 68:8
Star Wish 59:58, *see also:* 68:8, 162:37
Starlight, Starbright 68:8, *see also:* 59:58, 162:37
Sumer Is a-Cumen In 71:108, *see also:* 27:154, 176:144, 189:110, 293:80
Summer Is a-Coming In 27:154, 71:108, 176:144, 293:80, *see also:* 189:110
Summer Is I-Cumen In 189:110, *see also:* 27:154, 71:108, 176:144, 293:80
The Sun It Rises 293:102
The Swan Sings 262:35
Sweetly Sings the Donkey 26:45, 62:17, 144:3, 148:366, 176:129, 254:116, 289:187, 292:32, 293:94
Thou Poor Bird 292:129, 293:88
Three Blind Mice 17:25, 25:29, 26:41, 62:10, 103, 148:391, 175:52, 188:82, 189:14, 283:66, 292:192, 293:98
Time Sends a Warning Call 125:55
The Tinker 71:102
To Ope Their Trunks 62:15
To Portsmouth 85:15, 176:103
Torah, Torah-Torah 55:256
Turn Again, Whittington 62:16, 175:11, 176:83, 262:69, 293:40
Two Ducks on a Pond 262:86
Tzena 72:151
Viva la Musica 71:98, 72:170, 293:14
We Got a Lot for Christmas! 241:221
We Wish You a Merry Christmas 27:254, 54:10, 128:57, 148:410, 209:37, 220:26, 241:220, 264:74, *see also:* 227:32
Whene'er You Make a Promise 68:38, 69:6, 71:30, 72:25
Where Are You Going? 293:62
Where Is John? 144:5, 262:67, 293:44

Whip-Poor-Will 262:35
White Coral Bells 46:227, 62:13, 72:160, 148:416, 262:32, 293:18
White Sand and Gray Sand 62:18, 71:113, 293:68
Who Comes Here? 18:11, 111:61
Who Comes Laughing? 262:143
Who's the Hero? 77:53
Why Shouldn't My Goose 148:420, 262:91, 289:189, 292:149, 293:90, *see also:* 128:101, 144:21, 176:91
Will I Get a Christmas Present? 241:226
The Wind in the Willows 71:113, 72:170
The Wind Mill 262:85
The Wise Men Were But Seven 293:32
The Woodchuck 144:9
Zum Gali Gali 25:90, 64:106, 69:49, 148:424, 290:196
ROUNDUPS: *see* COWBOYS
ROWING: *see* BOATS AND BOATING
ROYALTY: *see* KINGS AND RULERS
RULERS: *see* KINGS AND RULERS
RUMANIA
*At the Gates of Heaven Above/Sus in Poarta Raiului 54:238
*Bucura t'e Tintirim/Oh, Rejoice, Thou Frightful Grave 89:192
*Happy Bride/Tarancuta 208:60
*Oh, Rejoice, Thou Frightful Grave/Bucura t'e Tintirim 89:192
*Sus In Poarta Raiului/At The Gates of Heaven Above 54:238
*Tarancuta/Happy Bride 208:60
RUSSIA
*Ah, My Beloved Dunaii/Ai Dunaii Moy 89:176
*Ai, Dunaii Moy/Ah, My Beloved Dunaii 89:176
*Bakhchalarda/In My Garden 89:178
The Birch Tree 71:80, 72:152
*The Captured Bird/Poymanaya Pteechka 289:62
*Chi Ya V'luzi Ne Kalina Bula?/Was I Not a Flower in the Meadow 89:177
*Dagestan 89:179
*Diw' Laiwinas/Two Little Boats 89:174
Duck of the Meadow 70:23
The Fiddlers Are Playing 176:74
*Gray Clouds Engulf the Sky/Yehrgeenkun Ahmbel Eh 89:181
In a Manger 241:111
*In My Garden/Bakhchalarda 89:178
*Kabak da Boynuma/Striking a Tune 89:180
*Kol Jauns Nevedes Buvau/Quite Young and Carefree Was I 89:175
Kolyada 128:55
Korobushka 178:60

*Kui Mina Alles Noor Veel Olin/When I Was But a Small Young Laddie   89:173
The Little Birch Tree   78:69
Little Cossack   125:18, *see also:* 262:93
Meadowlands   22:200
Moscow   22:206
The Peddler   72:150
*Poymanaya Pteechka/The Captured Bird   289:62
*Quite Young and Carefree Was I/Kol Jauns Nevedes Buvau   89:175
Russian Slumber Song   78:71
Sleep Now and Rest   125:17
Song of the Sea   72:129
*Striking a Tune/Kabak da Boynuma 89:180
Tachanka   22:214
*Taw Nye Vyetyer/'Tis No Wind   208:78
*'Tis No Wind/Taw Nye Vyetyer   208:78
Troika   55:515
*Two Little Boats/Diw Laiwinas   89:174
Vesper Hymn   262:171
*Vorira   89:179
*Was I Not a Flower in the Meadow?/Chi Ya V'luzi Ne Kalina Bula?   89:177
*When I Was But a Small Young Laddie/Kui Mina Alles Noor Veel Olin   89:173
The Wooing of the Titmouse   79:80
*Yehrgeenkun Ahmbel Eh/Gray Clouds Engulf the Sky   89:181
RWANDA
*Imandwa   89:278

S

SAFETY
I'm No Fool   119:108
Safety First   207:114
Safety Song   177:90
SAILING: *see also* BOATS AND BOATING; SHIPS
Allee Allee-o   39:46, 135:54, 289:118, *see also:* 63:37, 165:113, 291:16
Australia   71:34
A Big Ship Sailing   291:16, *see also:* Allee Allee-o
A Big Ship Sails Through the Alley, Alley O   165:113, *see also:* Allee Allee-o
Blow, Boys, Blow   33:42, 232:161
Blow, Ye Winds   24:829, 71:84, 72:71, *see also:* 64:112, 158:44
Blow Ye Winds, Westerly   128:50, *see also:* Boston Come All-Ye
The Boatman Dance   33:114
The Bold Fisherman   27:208, 128:116, 239:20, 256

The 'Bold Trellitee'   35:46, 35:48, *see also:* 22:172, 89:128, 133
Boston Come All-Ye   22:154, 33:18, 69:33, 71:85, 72:70, *see also:* 128:50
The Coasts of High Barbary   22:166
Down the River   20:75, 27:156, 197:82
The Duck Dance   14:346, *see also:* A Ship A-Sailing
The Fairy Ship   17:61, 68:25, *see also:* A Ship A-Sailing
Going Over the Sea   63:84
The Golden Vanity   22:172, 89:128, 133, *see also:* 35:46, 35:48
I Love to Row in My Big Blue Boat 165:111
I Saw a Ship A-Sailing   18:6, 52, *see also:* A Ship A-Sailing
Leave Her, Bullies, Leave Her   226:412
Lowlands Low   33:186
Merrily We Roll Along   17:113
Over the Sea in My Boat With Me   227:16
The Sail Boat   41:32
A Ship A-Sailing   33:66, 130:97, 188:58, *see also:* 14:346, 17:61, 18:6, 52, 68:25
SAILORS: *see* SEAMEN
SAINT PATRICK'S DAY
Saint Patrick Was a Gentleman   197:28
Saint Patrick's Day   162:55 *(We're wearing green for the Irish)*
Saint Patrick's Day   205:154 *(Though dark are our sorrows)*
Saint Patrick's Day Jig   97:unpaged
SAINT STEPHEN'S DAY
St. Stephen's Day   212:12
The Wren Song   134:32
SAINT VALENTINE'S DAY: *see* VALENTINE'S DAY
SAINTS: *see also* APOSTLES; names of specific saints' days, e.g., SAINT PATRICK'S DAY
Bunde San Antonio (St. Anthony)   169:16
Lady Saint Anne/Señora Santa Ana 216:45
Señora Santa Ana/Lady Saint Anne 216:16
SALESMEN: *see* BUYING AND SELLING
SAMSON
Samson   123:178
SAND: *see* SEASHORE
SANDMAN
The Sandman   91:47
The Sandman Comes   17:78
Sandman Will Come   125:28
SANDPIPERS
Sandpiper   69:24
SANTA ANNA, ANTONIO LOPEZ DE
Santy Anna   21:288, 24:835, 262:105, *see also:* 158:136

SANTA ANNA, ANTONIO LOPEZ DE
—*Continued*
  Santy Anno 158:136, *see also:* 21:288, 24:835, 262:105
  Way Down in Mexico 159:365
SANTA CLAUS: *see* CHRISTMAS SONGS
SAUDI ARABIA
  *Bafti Hindi 89:206, 114:52
SCARECROWS
  The Scarecrow 188:164
  When All the Cows Are Sleeping 165:86
SCHOOL LIFE
  Big Yellow Bus 162:102
  A Dillar, A Dollar 285:79
SCOTLAND
  Aiken Drum 111:44, 162:36, 175:130, 188:104, 189:28, 289:96
  All the Blue Bonnets Are Over the Border 66:50
  Ally Bally 135:35
  Always Room for One More 179
  Annie Laurie 22:110, 205:85
  Auld Lang Syne 22:76, 25:89, 27:2, 46:207, 148:32, 170:62, 197:10, 205:50, 290:216
  The Auld Man 182:41
  Aye, Wakin' O! 182:25
  Baloo, Lammy 54:56, 241:14, *see also:* 125:64
  Baloo Loo, Lammy 125:64, *see also:* 54:56, 241:14
  Bide Ye Yet 182:47
  The Blue Bells of Scotland 22:60, 205:66
  Bonnie George Campbell 22:24
  Bonnie Maggie Lauder 182:15
  The Bonny Earl O' Moray 134:54
  The Border Lament 89:132
  The Broom O' the Cowdenknowes 182:37
  The Campbells Are Coming 66:48, 184:204, 205:106
  Charlie Is My Darling 71:42, 176:30, 205:72, *see also:* 134:14, 226:117, 232:137
  The Cooper of Fife 20:25, *see also:* Wee Cooper of Fife
  The Dens of Yarrow 35:40
  Dumbarton's Drums 99:35
  Flow Gently, Sweet Afton 22:106, 205:95, *see also:* 176:26
  The Flowers O' the Forest 182:28
  Four Nights Drunk 230:22
  The Gaberlunzie Man 182:9
  *Gille Beag 'O/Little Lad, Oh 89:133
  Here Awa', There Awa' 182:34
  A Herring in Salt 182:31
  The Hills of Glenshee 35:92
  Hush-A-Baw Birdie 112:44, *see also:* 262:125

  I Like to Do the Highland Fling 167:42
  Jennie Dang the Weaver 182:50
  *Little Lad, Oh/Gille Beag 'O 89:133
  Loch Lomond 27:80
  Mactavish 134:49, 290:175
  Mingulay Boat Song 134:70
  My Bonnie Lad 134:72
  My Boy, Tammie 182:56
  My Jo, Janet 182:21
  Oh, Can Ye Sew Cushions 71:82, 78:29, 125:68, *see also:* 27:110
  The Piper Came to Our Town 182:59
  Sandy McNab 290:193, 293:54
  Scotland's Burning 46:227, 62:13, 148:321, 283:35, 289:188, 293:36, *see also:* 25:30, 175:20
  Skye Boat Song 22:18, 71:58, 72:115
  The Spanish Knight 168:110
  There's Nae Luck About the House 176:38, *see also:* 262:138
  The Thirteen Days of Yule 95
  The Three Ravens 22:94, 189:88, 292:140, *see also:* 37:115, 62:54, 232:121, 290:70, 292:142
  Turn Ye to Me 71:64, 72:122, 208:76
  Wee Cooper of Fife 59:44, 71:66, 72:120, 78:33, 176:24, *see also:* 20:25
  When the Kye Comes Home 182:43
  Wi' a Hundred Pipers 71:61
  Will Ye No Come Back Again? 176:32, 262:144
  The Yellow-Haired Laddie 182:18
SCOUTS AND SCOUTING
  Be Prepared 25:56
  The Beanie Song 68:23
  Bless Our Cub Scouts 26:93
  Boom! Boom! Gee It's Great to Be Scouting 25:53
  Boy Scouts of America 25:50
  A Boy Scout's Prayer 25:62
  Brownie Friend–Maker Song 68:32
  Brownie Hiking Song 68:28
  Brownie Magic 68:7
  Brownie Smile Song 68:47
  The Brownies' Song 68:10
  By the Blazing Council Fire 25:126
  Camporee or Jamboree Hymn 25:64
  Cub Days 26:51
  Cub Pledge 26:62
  Cub Scout Advancement Song 26:46
  Cub Scout Booster Song 26:46
  The Cub Scout Circus Comes to Town 26:71
  The Cub Scout Hymn 26:64
  Cub Scout Marching Song 26:59
  Cub Scout Prayer 26:95
  Cub Scout Travelers 26:77
  Cub Scout Welcome Song 26:8
  Cub Scouting Song 26:57

Cub Scouting We Will Go   26:57
Cub Scouts All   26:57
Cub Scouts in Blue   26:63
Cub Scouts U. S. A.   26:61
Cubbing Along Together   26:60
Cubbing in the Morning   26:56
Cubs Are Always Happy   26:50
Cubs Are Fair   26:52
Cubs Whistle While They Work   26:58
Girl Scouts Are We   71:18
Girl Scouts' Goodbye Round   71:103
Girl Scouts' Round   71:104
Girl Scouts Together   69:6, 71:22, 72:34
Good Night, Cub Scouts   26:91
Good Night, Cubbers   26:91
Good-Night Song   68:48
A Grand Time in Cubbing   26:52
Hail! Hail! Scouting Spirit   25:67
Hail to Cubbing   26:62
Hail to the Scouts   71:26
Here's to the Boy Scouts   25:69
Hiking   25:57
I'm Happy When I'm Hiking   25:65, 26:65, see also: 227:34
I've Got That Cub Scout Spirit   26:53
I've Got That Scouting Spirit   25:54
Old Akela Had a Pack   26:48
On My Honor   25:63
Our Cabana Song   69:9
Our Chalet Song   69:8, 71:15, 72:38
Pacific Northwest Girl Scout Regional Song   69:47
The Pack Meet   26:51
Pack Up Your Troubles   25:59
Philmont Hymn   25:58
Pinewood Derby Song   26:75, 26:76
The Promise and the Law   26:62
Recognition Song   26:11
Round-About Round   68:19
Scout Benediction   26:94
Scout Chant   71:30, 72:40
Scout Hearted Men   25:68
Scout Law Version of Kum Ba Yah   25:109
Scout Leader's Prayer   25:55
Scout Vesper   25:125, 26:94
Scout Vesper Song   25:125, 26:94
Scouting We Go   26:68
Scout's Good-Night Song   25:61, 26:93
Sharp Den Song   26:54
Space Derby Song   26:76
There Are Boys   26:15
There Are Cubs   26:52
There Are Dads (Boys)   26:15
There's Something About a Boy Scout   25:52
This Little Cubbing Light   26:49
The Torch of Scouting   25:60
Trail the Eagle   25:59

Up the Ladder   26:47
We Are Cub Den Number One   26:54
Weblos on Parade   26:66
We'll Be Loyal Scouts   26:67
We're on the Upward Trail   25:56, 26:69
Where Has My Little Boy Gone?   26:54
Yonder Lies the World Before Us   71:16, 72:42
You Can Tell a Scout   25:68
SEA CHANTEYS: see SEA SONGS
SEA SHELLS: see SHELLS (MOLLUSKS)
SEA SONGS: see also SEAMEN; SEAS; SHIPS
A-Roving   22:168, 36:24, 71:77, 72:78, 98:29, 176:34
Across the Western Ocean   226:412
Away to Rio   78:9, see also: 22:140, 176:110, 239:14
Blow the Man Down   22:152, 25:105, 36:54, 71:40, 72:77, 78:7, 87:22, 98:24, 148:46, 176:106, 197:79, 205:116, 226:404, 230:39, 277:113
The 'Bold Trellitee'   35:46, 35:48, see also: 22:172, 89:128, 133
Boney   98:17
Can't You Dance the Polka?   22:160
Cape Cod Chantey   129:82, see also: 290:110
Cape Cod Girls   290:110, see also: 129:82
Captain's Shanty   290:118
Clear the Track   239:18
The Dead Horse   98:39, 226:406
Fire Down Below   98:34, 129:84, 232:162, see also: 134:64
Fire! Fire!   134:64, see also: 98:34, 129:84, 232:162
The Golden Vanity   22:172, 89:128, 133, see also: 35:46, 35:48
Goodbye, My Lover, Goodbye   162:92, 290:214
Hanging Johnny   98:24
Haul Away, Joe   22:145, 98:18, 128:87, 134:69, 272:13, 290:48
Haul Away the Bowlin'   98:12, see also: 227:12, 239:13, 274:34
Haul on the Bowline   227:12, 239:13, 274:34, see also: 98:12
Johnny Come to Hilo   128:22, see also: 37:157, 157:40
Johnny's Gone to Hilo   37:157, see also: 128:22, 157:40
Leave Her, Johnny   64:114, 98:40, 134:73
Lowlands   22:132, 158:142
Mingulay Boat Song   134:70
Old Horse   290:220
One More Day   22:158
Paddy Doyle   134:76, see also: 37:150
Paddy O'Doyle   37:150, see also: 134:76
The Rio Grande   22:140, 176:110, 239:14, see also: 78:9

SEA SONGS—*Continued*
A Ripping Trip 61:36, 159:387
Rolling Home 69:44
See My Wagon, It's Full-Laden 21:318
Shanadoah 157:40, *see also:* Shenandoah
Shanandar 134:77, *see also:* Shenandoah
Shenandoah 22:136, 25:85, 61:2, 69:35, 98:30, 148:326, 158:138, 176:113, 205:82, 230:17, 239:16, 277:55, *see also:* 134:77, 157:40, 226:408
Song of the Sea 72:129
Spanish Ladies 21:330, 27:204, 262:65
Steamboat Bill 61:42
Tommy's Gone to Hilo 157:40, *see also:* 37:157, 128:22
We're Bound for Rio 71:70, 72:76
Whisky Johnnie 21:246, *see also:* 98:24, 226:403
Whisky Johnny 98:24, 226:403, *see also:* 21:246
The Wide Mizzoura 226:408, *see also:* Shenandoah
Won't You Go My Way? 134:68
Yeo, Heave Ho! 22:134
SEALS (ANIMALS)
The Circus Seal 207:111
Seal Lullaby 59:64
SEAMEN: *see also:* SEA SONGS; SEAS; SHIPS
A-Roving 22:168, 36:24, 71:77, 72:78, 98:29, 176:34
Across the Western Ocean 226:412
Ali, Alo 72:130
America, Commerce, and Freedom 273:118
Away to Rio 78:9, *see also:* 22:140, 176:110, 239:14
Bell Bottom Trousers 205:371
Bigerlow 226:174, *see also:* 24:843, 158:149
The Bigler 158:149, *see also:* 24:843, 226:174
The Bigler's Crew 24:843, *see also:* 158:149, 226:174
Blow, Boys, Blow 33:42, 232:161
Blow the Man Down 22:152, 25:105, 36:54, 71:40, 72:77, 78:7, 87:22, 98:24, 148:46, 176:106, 197:79, 205:116, 226:404, 230:39, 277:113
Blow the Wind Southerly 72:126
Blow, Ye Winds 24:829, 71:84, 72:71, *see also:* 64:112, 158:44
Blow Ye Winds, Westerly 128:50, *see also:* Boston Come All-Ye
Bobby Shaftoe 17:105, 59:50, 135:34, 162:94, 175:30, 285:64, *see also:* 255, 289:87
Boney 98:17
Boston Come All-Ye 22:154, 33:18, 69:33, 71:85, 72:70, *see also:* 128:50

A British Tar 98:52
Canción del Marinero Hondureño/Song of the Honduran Sailor 89:74
Can't You Dance the Polka 22:160
The Captain's Shanty 290:118
The Dead Horse 98:39, 226:406
Deep Blue Sea 230:76
The Drunken Sailor 22:176, 176:108, 205:33, *see also:* 39:35, 98:25, 239:10
The Flying Cloud 24:845
The Greenland Fisheries 24:832, 292:170
Hanging Johnny 98:24
Haul Away, Joe 22:145, 98:18, 128:87, 134:69, 272:13, 290:48
Haul Away the Bowlin' 98:12, *see also:* 227:12, 239:13, 274:34
Haul on the Bowline 227:12, 239:13, 274:34, *see also:* 98:12
Heart of Oak 98:51
The Hog-Eye Man 24:836, 226:410
I Am the Captain of the Pinafore 252:10
I Am the Monarch of the Sea 252:14
I Catch-a da Plenty of Feesh 226:409
Jackaro 213:64
The John B. Sails 226:22, *see also:* 148:344
Johnny Todd 212:38
Johnny's Jarmanie 37:179
Leave Her, Bullies, Leave Her 226:412
Leave Her, Johnny 64:114, 98:40, 134:73
The Limejuice Ship 98:45
Lowlands Low 33:186
The Mermaid 71:78, 72:72, 117:unpaged, 290:160
The Merry Golden Tree 37:120
Mister Crumpit 91:42
My Lovyer Is a Sailor Boy 262:130
My Spanish Guitar 197:90
Raging Canawl 226:178
The "Rainbow" 35:36
Red Iron Ore 226:176
The Rio Grande 22:140, 176:110, 239:14, *see also:* 78:9
Rock About My Saro Jane 158:151
Sacramento 21:306, 158:140, 262:38
A Sailor Went to Sea 63:79
The Sailor's Return 262:78
The Sailor's Song 85:109
Song of the Honduran Sailor/Canción del Marinero Hondureño 89:74
Steamboat Bill 61:42
Swansea Town 208:74
Ten Thousand Miles Away 226:100
We Sail the Ocean Blue 252:6
A Whale of a Tale 276:79
White Wings 21:227
SEAS
At the Beach 207:129

Barges 72:96
Beautiful Briny 276:68
A Capital Ship 34, 289:126, *see also:* 48
Come Surfing With Me/Ku'u Ipo I Ka
    He'e Pu'eone 87:36
Deep Blue Sea 230:76
Frogman, Frogman 167:32
Ku'u Ipo I Ka He'e Pu'eone/Come
    Surfing With Me 87:36
Little Shell 162:24
The Maid on the Shore 36:8
The Mist 281:60
My Love Is Gone to Sea 273:94
Nantucket Lullaby 281:62
Ocean Go 130:98
On the Beach 207:127
SEASHORE
    At the Beach 207:129
    On the Beach 207:127
    Pupu Hinu Hinu/Shiny Shells 87:68
    Sand Castle 91:27
    Shiny Shells/Pupu Hinu Hinu 87:68
SEASONS: *see* names of seasons, e.g., AU-
    TUMN
SEEDS: *see* PLANTS AND PLANTING
SEESAWS
    See Saw 177:91
    See-Saw, Margery Daw 17:103, 175:172,
        188:68, 283:14, 285:40
SELF-CONCEPT
    All By Myself 204:25
    Astonishing, Astonishing 91:10
    Be Alive 261:6
    Bein' Green 206:82
    The Clown in Me 219:17
    Everybody's Fancy 219:10
    Everyone Makes Mistakes 206:78
    Everything Grows Together 219:12
    Free to Be . . You and Me 260:16
    Gabriel 261:8
    Glad to Have a Friend Like You 260:119
    Growing Up 172:126, 173:17
    Honey, You Look So Sweet 130:26
    The Hungry Cat and the Grumbling
        Mouse 112:64
    I Am Quite Big, But My Lisbeth Is Wee
        245:21
    I Have Confidence 218:230
    I'm a Person 204:9
    I'm Taking Care of You 219:58
    It's Fun to Be a Person Yes–Sir–ee!
        204:31
    It's Such a Good Feeling 219:35
    My Name 206:52
    Others Are Special 204:29
    Special 206:112
    Walk Down the Street (With Your Head
        Up High) 206:98
    William's Doll 260:78

You Are Special 206:7
SEPTEMBER
    September Days 97:unpaged
SERVICE STATIONS
    The Gas Station 154:31
SEWING: *see* NEEDLEWORK
SHADOWS
    Little Shadow 162:64
    Shadows 207:128
SHANTEYS: *see* SEA SONGS
SHAPES: *see* SIZES AND SHAPES
SHARING
    I'm Taking Care of You 219:58
SHARKS
    The Chivalrous Shark 176:126
SHEEP: *see also* HERDING; SHEPHERDS AND
    SHEPHERD LIFE
    Baa, Baa, Black Sheep 17:147, 175:84,
        188:102, 189:20, 283:24, 285:49
    Bahyahn Mongol/Rich Mongolia 208:45
    The Big Sheep 234:58, *see also:*
        Darby Ram
    The Darby Ram 27:60, 37:134, 129:44,
        192:47, *see also:* 62:36, 229, 234:58
    Derby Ram 229, *see also:* Ram of Darby
    Don't You Hear the Lambs A-Crying?
        233:19
    The Gentle Shepherd 189:86
    I Held a Lamb 245:40
    The Lamb 112:59, 189:62
    The Lambs 191:16
    Lazy Sheep, Pray Tell Me Why 175:132
    Little Bo Peep 17:87, 175:82, 188:60,
        189:18, 285:10
    Mary Had a Little Lamb 17:51, 162:7,
        175:58, 283:11, 289:77, 292:48
    Old Bell'd Yoe 234:60
    Ram of Darby 234:58, *see also:* Darby
        Ram
    Rich Mongolia/Bahyahn Mongol 208:45
    Sheep Shearing 129:36, 134:102, 292:54
    Wee Lambie 62:37
    Young Lambs to Sell 135:48
SHELLS (MOLLUSKS)
    Little Shell 162:24
    Pupu Hinu Hinu/Shiny Shells 87:68
    Shiny Shells/Pupu Hinu Hinu 87:68
SHEPHERDS AND SHEPHERD LIFE: *see
    also* CHRISTMAS CAROLS; HERDING;
    SHEEP
    Il Etait une Bergère/There Was a Shep-
        herdess 217:32
    Los Pastores/The Shepherds 295:70
    Sheep Shearing 129:36, 134:102, 292:54
    The Shepherd Maid 227:6
    The Shepherd Maiden 245:56
    Shepherd, Shepherd 233:18
    The Shepherds/Los Pastores 295:70

SHEPHERDS AND SHEPHERD LIFE
—*Continued*
There Was a Shepherdess/Il Etait une Bergère 217:59
SHERMAN, WILLIAM T.
Sherman the Brave 73:75
When Sherman Marched Down to the Sea 73:216
SHIPS: *see also* BOATS AND BOATING
Across the Western Ocean 226:412
The *Alabama* 73:186
The *Alabama* and *Kearsarge* 73:189
Allee Allee-O 39:46, 135:54, 289:182, *see also:* 63:37, 165:113, 291:16
An American Frigate 27:124, 28:123
Away to Rio 78:9, *see also:* 22:140, 176:110, 239:14
A Big Ship Sailing 291:16, *see also:* Allee Allee-O
The Big Ship Sails Through the Alley, Alley O 165:113, *see also:* Allee Allee-O
Blow, Boys, Blow 33:42, 232:161
Boats Sail on the Rivers 245:75
The 'Bold Trellitee' 35:46, 35:48, *see also:* 22:172, 89:128, 133
A British Tar 98:52
A Capital Ship 34, 289:126, *see also:* 48
Captain Kidd 21:332
The Captain's Shanty 290:118
Clear the Track 239:18
The Coasts of High Barbary 22:166
The "Cumberland" Crew 35:20, *see also:* 73:183
The "Cumberland's" Crew 73:183, *see also:* 35:20
Donkey Riding 71:81, 72:117, 78:11, 128:88
The Drunken Sailor 22:176, 176:108, 205:33, *see also:* 39:35, 98:25, 239:10
The Duck Dance 14:346, *see also:* A Ship A-Sailing
The Fairy Ship 17:61, 68:25, *see also:* A Ship A-Sailing
The Flying Cloud 24:845
The Gallant Ship 62:98, 291:73, *see also:* 135:79
Going Over the Sea 63:84
The Golden Vanity 22:172, 89:128, 133, *see also:* 35:46, 35:48
The Greenland Fisheries 24:832, 292:170
Haul Away, Joe 22:145, 98:18, 128:87, 134:69, 272:13, 290:48
Haul Away the Bowlin' 98:12, *see also:* 227:12, 239:13, 274:34
Haul on the Bowline 227:12, 239:13, 274:34, *see also:* 98:12
Heart of Oak 98:51

I Am the Captain of the Pinafore 252:10
I Am the Monarch of the Sea 252:14
I Saw a Ship A-Sailing 18:6, 52, *see also:* A Ship A-Sailing
The John B. Sails 226:22, *see also:* 148:344
Le Petit Navire/The Little Ship 89:62, 217:14
Leave Her, Bullies, Leave Her 226:412
Leave Her, Johnny 64:114, 98:40, 134:73
The Limejuice Ship 98:45
The Little Ship/Le Petite Navire 217:54, *see also:* 89:62, 216:50
Lowlands Low 33:186
The Merry Golden Tree 37:120
Our Gallant Ship 135:79, *see also:* 62:98, 291:73
Raging Canawl 226:178
Red Iron Ore 226:176
Reuben James 230:84
Sacramento 21:306, 158:140, 262:38
A Ship A-Sailing 33:66, 130:97, 188:58, *see also:* 14:346, 17:61, 18:6, 52, 68:25
The Ship That Never Returned 226:147
The Ship Titanic 290:153, *see also:* 226:254
The Sloop John B. 148:344, *see also:* 226:22
The Song of the Ship-Builders 262:133
There Was Once a Little Ship 262:62
The Three Ships 241:52
De Titanic 226:254, *see also:* 290:153
The Walloping Window Blind 48, *see also:* 34, 289:126
The White Ship Sails 63:37, *see also:* Allee Allee-O
White Wings 21:227
The Yankee Privateer 28:120
SHIRLEY, MYRA BELLE: *see* STARR, BELLE
SHOEMAKERS
Cobbler, Cobbler 17:47, 165:174, 285:84
El Zapatero/The Shoemaker 78:88
The Shoemaker/El Zapatero 78:88
The Shoemaker 239:52
Shoemaker, Shoemaker 75:69
SHOES: *see also* MOCCASINS
Down The Avenue 288:8
New Shoes 207:12
Put on Your Wooden Shoes 167:57
SHOPPING: *see* BUYING AND SELLING
SHOPS AND SHOPKEEPERS: *see* STORES
SICILY
*Canzone d'i Zampognari/Carol of the Bagpipers 54:242, 241:100, *see also:* 279:100
*Carol of the Bagpipers/Canzone d'i Zampognari 54:242, 241:100, 279:100

SIERRA LEONE
*Ev'rybody Loves Saturday Night/Mofe Moni S'mo Ho Gbeke 89:279, *see also:* 64:200, 148:84
*Mofe Moni S'mo Ho Gbeke/Ev'rybody Loves Saturday Night 89:279, *see also:* 64:200, 148:84
SINGAPORE
The New Dress 114:32
SINGING
Ahora Voy a Cantarles/Now I'm Going to Sing 216:8
Brightly, Brightly Gleam the Sparkling Rills 262:153
Come Here and Sing 176:17
Do-Re-Mi 218:234
Epigram on Singers 176:141
4-H Field Song 55:257
The Gondolier's Song 166:48
Hey Dee Roon 72:105, *see also:* 291:8
Hi-Dee-Roon 291:8, *see also:* 72:105
High Middle Low 206:66
I Have a Song to Sing, O! 252:56, 262:57
I'll Sing You a Song 111:11
In the Morning, When You Wake 125:116
Let Us All Sing 237:unpaged
Let Us Sing Together 55:256
Now I'm Going to Sing/Ahora Voy a Cantarles 216:43
Sing 206:104
Sing Little Birdie 162:10
Sing Together 71:99, 72:41
When Is the Day? 162:72
When You Sing 162:106
SINGING GAMES: *see also* ACTION SONGS; BALL BOUNCING; BALL ROLLING; CIRCLE GAMES; CLAPPING GAMES; FINGER AND HAND PLAY; RHYTHMS; SKIPPING ROPE
A Canoa Virou/My Little Boat 168:139
A-Hunting We Will Go 17:134, 63:36, 135:118, 122, 165:192, *see also:* 14:349, 20:82, 47
A la Víbora/To the Serpent 295:24
A-Tisket, A-Tasket 20:51, 165:195, 283:20, 289:176, *see also:* 14:351, 17:106, 24:806, 63:11, 197:42
Ach Ja 55:510, 83:495, *see also:* 178:30
Ach Yah! 178:30, *see also:* 55:510, 83:495
Adam Had Seven Sons 129:99, 232:174
Ain't Gonna Rain 226:141
Ain't It Hard to Be a Farmer 109:212
Airplanes, Airplanes All in a Row 165:72
Al Animo/Cheer Up 194:24, *see also:* 168:112
All Around the Kitchen 128:100, 130:44, 232:94, 291:6
All Around the Maypole 83:492
All By Myself 204:25

All Hid 109:185
Allee Allee-O 39:46, 135:54, 289:182, *see also:* 63:37, 165:113, 291:16
Allee Galloo 291:72
Among the Little White Daisies 110:48
Annie the Miller's Daughter 20:19
Antagata Dakosa/Where Do You Come From 286:50
Anton Firulero 114:75
Arroz Con Leche 168:136, *see also:* 216:10, 295:28
As I Was Walking Down the Street, Heigh-ho, Heigh-ho, Heigh-ho 165:182, 178:124, *see also:* 283:41
Auntie Nextdoor/Tonari-no Obasan 286:48
The Autumn Leaves Have Fallen Down 165:61
Awo 236:42
Bear Went Over the Mountain 17:16, 75:12, 147:14, 290:72, 292:110
Betsy Liner 83:510
Bicycle Built for Two 21:19, 148:40, *see also:* 26:19, 83:493, 205:234
A Big Ship Sailing 291:16, *see also:* Allee Allee-O
The Big Ship Sails Through the Alley, Alley O 165:113, *see also:* Allee Allee-O
Billy Barlow 232:80, 274:18, *see also:* 20:11
Bird in the Cage/Kagome, Kagome 169:45, 286:38, *see also:* 16:20, 266:46
Blue Bird 141:35, *see also:* 20:20, 63:24, 110:44, 168:184, 232:118, 289:174
The Blue Tail Fly 27:10, 129:42, *see also:* 22:72, 178:26, 205:110, 230:12, 232:124
The Blue-Tail Fly 22:72, 205:110, 230:12, *see also:* 27:10, 129:42, 178:26, 232:124
Bluebell, Bluebell 20:20, *see also:* Blue Bird
Bluebird 289:174, *see also:* Blue Bird
Bluebird, Bluebird 168:184, *see also:* Blue Bird
Bob-a-Needle 109:164
Bow Belinda 126:105, *see also:* 39:32, 135:93, 178:52
Bow Bow Bow Belinda 178:52, *see also:* 39:32, 126:105, 135:93
Bow Down, O Belinda 135:93, *see also:* 39:32, 126:105, 178:52
Brother, Come and Dance With Me 75:14, 227:28
Brother Rabbit and Mister Railroad's Taters 109:207
Buffalo Gals 20:28, 24:841, 61:278, 66:58, 126:97, 148:50, 158:104, 205:119, 230:34, *see also:* 63:12, 128:80, 157:86, 283:41

SINGING GAMES—*Continued*

Built My Lady a Fine Brick House 232:170

Bunkhouse Orchestra 61:282

The Bus Song 75:16, *see also:* 147:6, 165:73, 291:46

Butsu Butsu Mame/Red Beans 286:39

Cabin in the Wood 26:32, *see also:* 55:270

Can You Show Me How the Farmer 17:32

Can You Tell Me What the Boys Do 165:178

Can You Walk on Two Legs, Two Legs, Two Legs? 165:143

Captain Jinks 66:63, 70:28, 126:65, 135:96

Carousel 20:59

Carrousel/Karusellen 89:168, 100:50

Catch a Little Fox 47, *see also:* A-Hunting We Will Go

Charlie Over the Water 75:18

Che Che Koole 178:65, *see also:* 169:23

Chebogah 83:494

Chechekoolay, Chechekoolay 169:23, 178:65

Cheer Up/Al Animo 194:24, *see also:* 168:112

Chicken Hawk 100:108

Chinene Nye?/What Is Big? 168:18

The Chinese Fan 68:16

Chip-Chop, Chip-Chop, Chipper, Chopper Joe 165:173

Christmas Is Coming 27:248, 68:8, 128:54, 178:23, 210:94, 241:225, 293:76

Chug-a-Lug-a-Lug 291:20

Chum, Chummy Lou 83:489

Ciranda/Dancer, Little Dancer 168:141, 169:9, 266:13

Clap Singing Game 177:76

Clap Your Hands 232:86, 289:160 *(Clap, clap, clap your hands)*

Clap Your Hands 26:27 *(Clap your hands! Clap your hands!)*

The Clock Song 291:36

The Closet Key 232:169

Cobbler, Cobbler 17:47, 165:174, 285:84

Cobbler's Dance 245:58

Cocky Doodle Doodle Do 130:44, *see also:* 128:100, 232:94, 291:6

Coffee Grows on White Oak Trees 39:42, 158:100

Come All You Playmates 63:95

Come, Let Us Be Joyful 46:200, 70:15

Come On and Join in to the Game 75:19, 289:158, 291:4

Come On Boys and Girls and Hush Your Talkin' 178:13, *see also:* 232:134

Come On, Girls (Boys), We're Going to Boston 178:36, *see also:* Going to Boston

Congo Tay 130:82

Coonie's Got a Pretty Tail 292:97

The Cooper of Fife 20:25, *see also:* Wee Cooper of Fife

The Cornfields/Los Maizales 270:50, *see also:* 169:55

Counting the Goats 292:56

Crocodile Song 26:36, 89:33, 234:72

Cuckoo Waltz 226:160

The Cushion Dance 176:57

Cut the Oats 100:49, 168:100

Daisy Bell 21:19, 205:234, *see also:* 26:19, 83:493, 148:40

Daisy, Daisy 26:19, 83:493, 148:40, *see also:* 21:19, 205:234

The Damper Song 26:34, *see also:* 253:90

Dance of Greeting 83:497

Dancer, Little Dancer/Ciranda, Cirandenha 168:141, *see also:* 169:9, 266:13

Dancing Dollies 128:98

The Dancing Lesson 227:28, *see also:* 75:14

The Deaf Woman's Courtship 37:136, 69:19, 129:100, 213:72, 262:119, 290:75, *see also:* 20:26, 46:223, 83:470

Deep and Wide 26:27

Der Kuckuck 20:86

Did You Ever See a Lassie? 14:344, 17:36, 20:33, 63:21, 165:180, 283:36, 289:162

Dixie Girls 141:90

Do, Do, Pity My Case 24:805, 232:136

Do You Know How to Plant Cabbages 217:53, *see also:* 165:85, 168:164

Do You Plant Your Cabbages in the Right Way 165:85, *see also:* 168:164, 217:53

Dollar, Dollar 20:10, 110:31

Don-Don Ba Ji 169:63, *see also:* 269:50

Doña Blanca 168:28, 248:30

Down at the Station Saga 55:263, *see also:* 25:30, 26:45, 75:21, 165:67

Down By the Bay 63:98

Down By the Old Millstream 290:66

Down By the Station 25:30, 26:45, 75:21, 165:67, *see also:* 55:263

Down Came a Lady 232:51

Down the River 20:75, 27:156, 197:82

Draw a Bucket of Water 14:345, 39:24, 109:80, 135:78

The Duck Dance 14:346, *see also:* A Ship A-Sailing

Duck of the Meadow 70:23

Dumplin's 130:48

East Coast Line 109:97

El Conejo de Esperanza/The Rabbit of Hope 194:20
El Lobo/The Wolf 70:27
El Patio de Mi Casa/The Patio of My House 295:40
El-thahlib 169:19
Elephant Fair 109:62
The Elephant Is Big and Strong 165:103
The Elfin Cap 245:56
The English Soldiers 63:34
Farm Boy's Bonny 20:66
The Farmer in the Dell 14:347, 17:8, 20:70, 63:13, 157:46, 283:9, 289:180
Fiddler's Fair 110:40
First He Walks Upon His Toes 165:146
Five Fat Turkeys Are We 178:42
Floating Down the River (Jump Josie) 135:94, see also: 128:97
The Fountain/La Fuente 168:112, see also: 194:24
Four in a Boat 20:23, 71:31
Four Jolly Blacksmiths 72:90
The Fox 269:62
Fox in a Box 20:82, see also: A-Hunting We Will Go
Free Little Bird 232:120
The Gallant Ship 62:98, 291:73, see also: 135:79
Gathering Nuts in May 128:102, see also: Nuts in May
The Gazelle/Gbodi 89:281
Gbodi/The Gazelle 89:281
Gira, Gira, Tondo/Ring-A-Ring-A-Round-O 188:48, 189:25
The Girl I Left Behind Me 42:604, 61:171, 66:112, 205:27, see also: 159:58
Girls and Boys Come Out to Play 17:9, 175:60, 188:56, 189:34
Glory to the Mountain 141:38
Go In and Out the Window 63:22, 75:27, 109:77, 110:52, see also: Round and Round the Village
Goin' to Boston 39:36, 157:47, see also: 63:39, 129:78, 135:98, 178:36
Going Down to Town 232:158, see also: 226:145
Going to Boston 63:39, 129:78, 135:98, see also: 39:36, 157:47, 178:36
Going to Chicago 63:26
The Grand Old Duke of York 26:25, 63:37, see also: Noble Duke of York
Green Corn 130:46, 134:36
The Green Grass Grows All Around 94, 192, 290:19, see also: 27:90, 62:72, 72:127, 109:197, 132:unpaged, 134:11, 176:130, 197:48, 213:20
Green Gravel 63:25, 110:54, 135:80, 175:124, see also: 109:70

Green, Green, The Crab Apple Tree 109:70, see also: 63:25, 110:54, 135:80, 175:124
Guan Pazek/Stepping on the Dog 168:75
Gustaf's Toast 46:204, 70:39
Ha-Ha, This-A-Way 75:87, 128:11, 135:74, 289:166, see also: 17:110, 27:192, 130:86, 189:50, 232:168
Ha, Ha, Thisaway 27:192, 130:86, see also: Ha-Ha, This-A-Way
Haenschen Klein/Little Hans 168:94
Halkada Boynundan/Here We Go Loop the Loop 266:57
Hanging Out the Linen Clothes 226:117, 232:137, see also: 71:42, 134:14, 176:30, 205:72
Happy Is the Miller 20:35, see also: 17:118, 63:28, 135:82, 227:26
Hark the Robbers 291:82
Harry McGarry 291:22
Harvest Is Over/Marken Er Mejet 208:17, see also: 83:496
Have Courage to Say No 109:204
Have You Seen My Dolly? 165:56
Have You Seen the Little Ducks Swimming in the Water 165:81
Help Me Wind My Ball of Wool 165:32
Hen Fell Out of the Roost/O-LU-WE 265:57
Here Come the Dukes 110:46, see also: Three Dukes
Here Come Two Dukes A-Riding 135:84, 213:40, see also: 39:16, 100:92, 110:46, 227:18
Here Comes a Knight A-Riding 168:152
Here Comes a Policeman, Riding a Bicycle 165:71
Here Comes Sally 135:87
Here Sits a Monkey 232:175
Here Stands a Red Bird 63:20
Here We Go Looby-loo 17:14, 63:18, 147:18, 165:194, see also: 39:6, 188:42, 189:42, 283:46
Here We Go Loop the Loop/Halkada Boynundan 266:57
Here We Go on Our Ponies 178:6
Here We Go Over the Mountain Two By Two 168:183, see also: 63:17, 70:11
Here We Go Round the Mountain 63:17, 70:11, see also: 168:183
Here We Go Round the Mulberry Bush 14:366, 17:90, 20:9, 63:16, 75:50, 168:108, 175:78, 188:66, 189:40, 289:172, see also: 104:52, 283:17, 285:2
Here's a Tree With a Trunk So Brown 165:93
Hey, Betty Martin 129:72, 135:120, 157:44, 226:158, see also: 33:194

INDEX TO CHILDREN'S SONGS

SINGING GAMES—*Continued*

Hey Dee Roon 72:105, *see also:* 291:8
Hey, Little Boy 292:20, *see also:* 107:18, 232:112, 234:56, 292:44
Hey, Little Lassie 70:21
Hi-Dee-Roon 291:8, *see also:* 72:105
Hi, Marsha Peter 55:260
Hide and Seek/Kakurembo 286:41
High, Betty Martin 33:194, *see also:* 129:72, 135:120, 157:44, 226:158
The High-Toned Dance 61:284, *see also:* 159:251
Hippity Hop 17:47, *see also:* 165:39
Hippity Hop to the Candy Shop 165:139, *see also:* 17:47
Hiraita, Hiraita/Open, Open 16:47, 286:36
Hog Drovers 27:24, *see also:* 24:810
Hokey-Pokey 148:164, 178:34, 289:168
Hole in the Ground 62:72, *see also:* Green Grass Grows All Around
Hop, Chop, My Little Horse 17:124
Hop, Old Squirrel 232:109
Hop, Skip, and Sing 167:8
Hop Up, My Ladies 128:23, 130:68, 135:18, 234:66
Horse and the Buggy 109:175
Hos Bilezik/Pretty Bracelet 70:20
Hotte, Hotte Reiterpferd 188:30
The Hours of the Clock/Las Horas del Reloj 295:34
Hullabaloo 39:6, *see also:* Looby-Loo
Hunt the Squirrel 24:806, *see also:* A-Tisket, A-Tasket
Hunting 14:349, *see also:* A-Hunting We Will Go
I Am a Fine Musician 75:52, *see also:* Musicians
I Am a Gay Musician 289:170, *see also:* Musicians
I Am a Musician 254:119, *see also:* Musicians
I Am a Pretty Little Dutch Girl 63:88
I Built My Love a Big Fine House 213:24
I Can Knock With My Two Hands 165:119
I Got a Gal at the Head of the Holler 24:897, 226:320, *see also:* Sourwood Mountain
I Got a Letter This Morning 232:144
I Had a Little Cat 132:unpaged, *see also:* Barnyard Song
I Had a Little Engine 165:70
I Know a Little Pussy 165:94
I Love to Row in My Big Blue Boat 165:111
I See You/Jag Ser Dig 189:134
I Spy 177:85
I Want to Be a Clown 167:12

I Was Riding Through the Country 141:36
I Went to School One Morning 165:145
I Went to Visit a Farm One Day 165:77
I Will Toss Up the Sticks 74:61
I Wish I Had the Shepherd's Lamb 292:52
I Would Like to Be As Tall As the Moon/Quisiera Ser Tan Alta Como la Luna 295:47
I Wrote a Letter to My Love 63:11, *see also:* A-Tisket, A-Tasket
If I Could Have a Windmill 55:267, 165:84
If I Had the Wings of a Turtledove 290:90
If I Were a Little Bird 165:153
If You Were a Beech Tree 165:96
If You're Happy and You Know It 25:16, 26:39, 63:44, 147:20, 253:91
Il Mio Bel Castello/I'm the King of the Castle 189:152
I'm a Fairy Doll on the Christmas Tree 165:54
I'm a Little Dutch Girl 63:40
I'm a Little Teapot 63:106, 75:36, 165:31, 291:50
I'm Gonna Pat My Little Old Head 204:17
I'm the King of the Castle/Il Mio Bel Castello 189:152
I'm Very, Very Tall 291:86
In a Cabin in the Wood 26:32, 55:270
In and Out the Bonnie Bluebells 245:54
In and Out the Window 39:14, 63:22, *see also:* Round and Round the Village
In Our Garden 291:56
The Instrument Song 20:16, *see also:* Musicians
It Doesn't Really Matter 63:46
Itiskit, Itasket 14:351, 17:106, 197:42, *see also:* A-Tiskit, A-Tasket
It's Fun to Be a Person, Yes–Sir–ee! 204:31
It's Love That Makes the World Go Round 55:269
I've a Fine, Bonny Castle 189:154, *see also:* 188:54
I've Been to Haarlem 20:56, 70:9, 129:120, 134:44, *see also:* 39:2
Jag Ser Dig/I See You 189:134
Jennie Jenkins 20:40, 69:20, 75:42, 129:22, 158:54, 257, 262:37, *see also:* 135:62, 291:28
Jenny Jenkins 291:28, *see also:* Jennie Jenkins
Jeremiah, Blow the Fire 135:119, 291:34
Jim Along, Josie 63:38, 135:108, 232:72

Jim Crack Corn 232:124, *see also:* Blue Tail Fly

Jimmy Crack Corn 178:26, *see also:* Blue Tail Fly

Jimmy Rose He Went to Town 232:58

Jingle at the Windows 232:173

Jinny Jo 63:32, *see also:* 17:39, 68:12, 100:90

John Brown's Baby 20:32, 26:30, 118:31, 253:100, 289:114

John Brown's Ford 26:31

Johnny Cuckoo 109:73

Johnny Works With One Hammer 178:28, *see also:* 75:61, 165:166

Jolly Is the Miller Boy 17:118, 135:82, 227:26, *see also:* 20:35, 63:28

Jolly Miller 110:51, *see also:* 165:200

The Jolly Old Miller 63:28, *see also:* 17:118, 20:35, 135:82, 227:26

Josephine 109:60

Juba 109:40, 232:91

Jubilee 134:39, 213:36

Juego de los Pavos/The Turkey Game 194:34

Jump, Jump! Kangaroo Brown 165:105

Jumping, Jumping, Jumping, Jumping 178:12

The Juniper Tree 27:88, 232:82

Just From the Kitchen 109:52

Kagome Kagome/Bird in the Cage 16:20, 169:45, 266:46, 286:38

Kakurembo/Hide and Seek 286:41

Karusellen/Carrousel 89:168

Kee-Chee 69:15

The Keel Row 135:16, 262:68, *see also:* 89:302

Keep Moving 14:352, *see also:* 26:37, 253:104

Keeping Time 104:51

The King May Pass/Que Pase el Rey 168:149

The King of France 14:355, 17:120, 83:505

King William 39:4, *see also:* 63:24

King William Was King George's Son 63:24, *see also:* 39:4

Kitty White 14:357

Knick Knack 20:44, *see also:* This Old Man

Knock Jim Crow 109:57

Kolattam/The Stick Dance 70:10, 100:126, 168:57

Kye Kye Kole 169:23

La Chacarera/The Little Farm Girl 70:17, 197:37

La Fuente/The Fountain 168:112, *see also:* 194:24

La Pájara Pinta/The Spotted Bird 168:127

La Palomita/Little Dove 169:53, 265:45

La Raspe/Mexican Clap Dance 178:45

La Virgencita/The Little Maiden 70:14

La Viudita del Conde Laurel/The Widow of Count Laurel 295:43

The Lady on the Mountain 39:20

Las Horas del Reloj/The Hours of the Clock 295:34

Last Evening Cousin Peter Came 165:170

Lata Ptaszek Po Uticy/The Little Bird 189:150

Leap Frog 46:222

Les Belles Pommes D'Api! 227:9

Let the Feet Go Tramp 14:359

Lilly Dale 157:108, *see also:* 66:128

Lily Dale 66:128, *see also:* 157:108

Lily, Lily Wallflowers 291:76

Little Arabella Miller 75:44, 165:165

Little Betty Martin 135:120, *see also:* 33:194, 129:72, 157:44, 226:158

The Little Bird/Lata Ptaszek Po Uticy 189:150 (*Little birdie, hopping gaily*)

The Little Bird 18:32, *see also:* 111:49, 285:99 (*Once I saw a little bird*)

Little Bird, Little Bird 232:118, *see also:* Blue Bird

Little Brown Jug 20:61, 21:198, 62:93, 126:50, 170:104, 205:172

Little Dove/La Palomita 265:45, *see also:* 169:53

The Little Farm Girl/La Chacarera 70:17, 197:37

Little Hans/Haenschen Klein 168:94

Little Johnny Brown 109:94

Little Lady from Baltimore 128:104

The Little Maiden/La Virgencita 70:14

Little Peter Rabbit 26:30

Little Red Caboose 46:213, 162:97

Little Red Handkerchief 70:19

The Little Red Wagon 129:70

Little Sally Walker 109:109, 109:110, 109:111, 291:68, *see also:* Little Sally Water

Little Sally Water 17:132, 100:89, 130:45, 141:34, 169:43, 271:63, *see also:* 109:109, 109:110, 109:111, 291:68

Little White Daisies 291:38

London Bridge 14:360, 17:37, 20:7, 37:189, 56, 63:30, 100:31, 109:181, 165:190, 175:98, 248, 283:43

London Hill 135:122, 291:15

Long Legs, Long Legs, Slowly Stalking 165:144

Looby-Loo 14:363, 17:14, 63:18, 147:18, 165:194, 188:42, 189:42, 283:46, *see also:* 39:6

Los Maizales/The Cornfields 169:55, 270:50

SINGING GAMES—*Continued*

Lou, Lou Skip to My Lou 37:193, 61:275, 129:104, 289:178, *see also:* Skip to My Lou

Love Somebody, Yes I Do 162:53, 226:140

Madame Dore 188:86, 265:23

Mailong Sera 168:76

Marken Er Mejet/Harvest Is Over 83:496, 208:17

Matatero-tero-la 114:78, 169:27

Matarile 169:60, 269:38, 295:37

Matarile, Rile, Ro 169:60, 269:38, 295:37

Mazoo 55:503

Mein Hands 20:88

Merry-Go-Round 70:22

Mexican Clap Dance/La Raspe 178:45

The Mice and the Cat 291:78

Miss Jenny Jones 17:39, 68:12, 100:90, *see also:* 63:32

Miss Polly Had a Dolly 63:40

Mr. Snail/Señor Caracol 168:129

Monkey See and Monkey Do 63:17

Mow the Meadow/Marken Er Mejet 83:496, 208:17

The Muffin Man 14:365, 17:46, 129:99, 135:27, 165:195, 168:107, 175:42, 283:53, 289:99

The Mulberry Bush 14:365, 17:90, 63:16, 75:50, 168:108, 175:78, 289:172, *see also:* Here We Go Round the Mulberry Bush

The Musicians 75:52, *see also:* 20:16, 71:56, 72:138, 104:53, 254:119, 289:170

My Little Boat/A Canoa Virou 168:139

My Mother Said 68:24, *see also:* 63:97

My Mother Sent Me Unto You 291:12

My New Toy 177:73

My Ole Man 46:206

My Parakeet Talks 167:18

Myan Myan 169:11, 269:17

Nana, Thread Needle 109:83

Naranja Dulce/Sweet Orange 295:36

The Needle's Eye 17:75, 68:31

Nnoonya Mwana Wange 236:8

No Bears Out Tonight 63:42

The No Laugh Race 237:unpaged

The Noble Duke of York 39:10, 70:30, 126:103, 128:107, 130:63, 135:90, 289:184, *see also:* 26:25, 55:520, 63:37, 165:193

The North Wind Doth Blow 17:129, 18:25, 135:116, 175:88, 188:106, 189:124, 227:31, 285:34, 292:139

Nuts in May 14:367, 63:32, 128:102, 165:191, 175:78, 188:38, 189:36

O-Lu-We/Hen Fell Out of the Roost 265:57

Oats and Beans 135:76, 165:83, *see also:* Oats, Peas, Beans

Oats, Peas, Beans 14:369, 17:60, 20:80, 63:14, 283:27, 289:181, *see also:* 135:76, 165:83

O Belinda! 39:32, *see also:* 126:105, 135:93, 178:52

Oh Green Fields, Roxie 109:75

Oh, John the Rabbit 232:100, 291:32

Oh, We Are Two Musicians 245:51

Old Bald Eagle 135:72

Old MacDonald Had a Farm 4, 17:148, 26:20, 55:262, 75:56, 81, 199, 283:12, 291:30

Old Roger 39:54, 63:27, 129:112, 135:86, 165:185, 168:154, 213:32, *see also:* 176:12

The Old Soap-Gourd 213:48

Old Woman 20:26, 46:223, 83:470, *see also:* Deaf Woman's Courtship

On the Bridge at Avignon/Sur le Pont d'Avignon 78:39, 148:364, 165:199, 189:44, 217:57, *see also:* 14:372, 168:162, 188:76

On the Bridge of Avignon/Sur le Pont D'Avignon 14:372, 168:162, 188:76, *see also:* On the Bridge at Avignon

Once/Pa'am Akhat 70:16, 266:35

One Elephant Went Out to Play 178:14

One Finger Keep Moving 253:104, *see also:* 14:352, 26:37

One Finger, One Thumb 26:37, *see also:* 14:332, 253:104

One Little Elephant Balancing 63:42

Open, Open/Hiraita, Hiraita 16:47, 286:36

Open the Gates as High As the Sky 283:31

Oranges and Lemons 17:58, 63:31, 165:198, 175:94, 188:78, 189:38, 227:17, *see also:* 295:82

The Organ Grinder Man 83:487

Our Gallant Ship 135:79, *see also:* 62:98, 291:73

Over in the Meadow 17:21, 116, 139, 178:32, 289:70, *see also:* 129:14

Paa Vossevangen 83:490

Pa'am Akhat/Once 70:16, 266:35

Pagtatanim ng Palay/Planting Rice 70:12, *see also:* Planting Rice

Pass the Shoe 20:90, 289:173, *see also:* 55:250, 70:18, 83:491

Pass Through This Gate/Toryanse 16:61, 286:46

The Patio of My House/El Patio de Mi Casa 295:40

The Pawpaw Patch 20:52, 25:20, 39:40, 46:212, 129:116, 189:48, 291:80, *see also:* 33:138, 178:38, 232:172

Peek-a-Boo 165:20, 291:62
Peep Squirrel 109:216, 234:18
A Penny in My Pocket 288:20
Pepito 194:22
Peter Hammers 75:61, 165:166, see also: 178:28
Pick a Bale of Cotton 20:38, 21:128, 25:21, 75:62, 107:46, 130:80, 135:106, 148:302, 158:234, 230:54, 232:148, 277:51
Pico Serenico 189:156
The Pig in the Parlor 20:50, 63:28, 291:66
Planting Cabbage/Savez-Vous Planter des Choux? 168:164, 217:53, see also: 165:85
Polly Perkin 135:109
Polly-Wolly-Doodle 46:208, 66:70, 83:507, 205:139, 290:112
Pop! Goes the Weasel 17:136, 20:48, 21:302, 46:209, 55:508, 66:72, 75:64, 135:115, 157:45, 175:36, 200, 205:132, 283:33, 289:100, 292:88
Postman, Postman · 178:5
Pretty Bracelet/Hos Bilezik 70:20
The Princess Was a Lovely Child 245:53
Punchinello 63:14, 109:106, 128:96, 135:113, 178:7
Push the Business On 70:13
Put on Your Wooden Shoes 167:57
Put Your Finger in the Air 75:66, 130:12, 253:108, 289:164
Que Pase el Rey/The King May Pass 168:149
Queen Mary 227:30
Quisiera Ser Tan Alta Como la Luna/I Would Like To Be As Tall As the Moon 295:47
The Rabbit of Hope/El Conejo de Esperanza 194:20
Rain/Yagmur 266:57
Rat in the Rice Sack/Zui, Zui, Zukorobashi 16:51, 286:42
Red Beans/Butsu Butsu Mame 286:39
Reel 107:50
A Rhyme and a Riddle 288:3
Rice Pudding/Arroz Con Leche 168:136, see also: 216:43, 295:28
Rice with Milk/Arroz Con Leche 216:43, see also: 168:136, 295:28
Ride, Charley, Ride 109:11
Riflemen of Bennington 20:14, 240:102
Ring-A-Ring-A-Round-O/Gira, Gira Tondo 188:48, 189:25
Ring-A Ring O' Roses 175:41, 188:108, 189:24, 227:23, see also: Ring Around A Rosy

Ring Around A Rosy 17:139, 63:11, 277:19, 283:31, 291:63, see also: 100:32, 175:41, 188:108, 189:24, 227:23
Ring Around the Rosie 100:32, see also: Ring Around A Rosy
Ring Around the Rosy 277:19, see also: Ring Around A Rosy
Ring on a String 20:11, see also: 232:80, 274:18
Ring the Christmas Bells 167:54
Ringel, Ringel 100:33, 168:95
Rise, Sally, Rise 63:26
The Robbers Coming Through 63:31
Roll the Ball 291:64
The Roman Soldiers 39:26, 129:114, 135:88
Rory O'More 167:10
Roselil 20:46
Round and Round the Village 14:375, 17:140, 165:189, 283:25, see also: 36:191, 38:14, 63:22, 75:27, 83:504, 109:77, 110:52
Round the Mountain 63:17, 70:11, see also: 168:183
'Round the Mulberry Bush 283:17, see also: Here We Go Round the Mulberry Bush
Round the Village 283:25, see also: Round and Round the Village
Rowing Song 288:18
Run, Children, Run 291:70, see also: 232:92
Run, Chillen, Run 232:92, see also: 291:70
Sailing at High Tide 24:812, 75:68, see also: 232:160
Sailing in the Boat 232:160, see also: 24:812, 75:68
Sally Down Our Alley 110:50, see also: 55:507
Sally Down the Alley 55:507, see also: 110:50
Sally Go Round the Moon 135:73, see also: 63:11, 130:90, 232:164
Sally Go Round the Sun 63:11, see also: 130:90, 135:73, 232:164
Sally Go Round the Sunshine 130:90, 232:164, see also: 63:11, 135:73
San Sereni 20:83, 262:16
Sandy Land 46:211, 70:25, 135:75
Santy Maloney 135:123
Savez-vous Planter les Choux?/Do You Know How to Plant Cabbages? 168:164, 217:10, see also: 165:85
Sea Lion 100:54, 168:161
See How I'm Jumping 135:107
See-Saw, Sacra-down 111:24, 135:124, 162:89

SINGING GAMES—*Continued*

Send My Brown Jug Down to Town 20:64, *see also:* 128:113

Señor Caracol/Mr. Snail 168:129

The Shepherd Maiden 245:56

Shoe Game 55:250, 70:18, *see also:* 20:90, 83:491, 289:173

Shoo, Fly Don't Bother Me 21:159, 46:208, 70:24, 126:85, 129:108, 178:20, 292:198

Shusti-Fidli 71:56, 72:138, *see also:* Musicians

Sir Mister Brown 109:99

Sissie in the Barn 178:59

Six Little Ducks 43, 55:271, 63:104, 148:342, 289:106

Six Little Girls A-Sliding Went 83:502

Skate With Me 167:52

Skating Away 39:48, 126:87

Skip to My Lou 17:128, 20:55, 37:193, 61:275, 70:32, 107:48, 129:104, 158:98, 188:94, 189:46, 202, 205:76, 230:90, 232:166, 289:178

Skip-a to My Lou 232:166, *see also:* Skip to My Lou

Sleepy Dolly 167:44

Smack Aunt Julie Down 83:489

Smoke Goes Up the Chimney 253:90, *see also:* 26:34

Snail 14:378, 100:96

Sometimes I'm Very, Very Small 165:187

Song of the Moccasin Game 74:45

Soup, Soup 109:103

Space Rocket Rick 167:16

The Spanish Knight 168:110

Spoon 100:38

The Spotted Bird/La Pájara Pinta 168:127

Steal Up, Young Lady 109:119

Stepping on the Dog/Guan Pazek 168:75

Steve Is the Engine 232:151, *see also:* 232:150

Stick Dance/Kolattam 70:10, 100:126, 168:57

Sur le Pont d'Avignon/On the Bridge at Avignon 78:39, 148:364, 188:76, 189:44, 217:24, *see also:* 14:372

Susie's Sitting Sewing 178:10

Sweet Orange/Naranja Dulce 295:36

Swine Herders 24:810, *see also:* 27:24

Swing on the Corner 55:509

Swinging in the Swing 227:44

Sycamore Tree 288:4

There She Stands, a Lovely Creature 24:804, *see also:* 39:20, 63:66, 135:70

There Stands a Lady on a Mountain 135:70, *see also:* 24:804, 39:20, 63:66

There Was a Jolly Miller 110:51, 165:200

There Was a Princess Long Ago 165:188

There's a Hole in the Bottom of the Sea 75:78, *see also:* 290:14

The Thief 55:504

This Is the Way We Wash Our Hands 291:2, *see also:* Here We Go Round the Mulberry Bush

This Is What I Can Do 291:10

This Lady She Wears a Dark Green Shawl 232:133

This Old Man 6, 17:94, 75:82, 129:98, 135:104, 147:42, 148:386, 175:70, 197:34, 232:165, 289:85, *see also:* 20:44

This Way, That-a Way 189:50, *see also:* Ha-Ha This-a-Way

Three Dukes 39:16, 100:92, 227:18, *see also:* 110:46, 135:84, 213:40

Three Jolly Fishermen 63:98, 290:50, *see also:* 26:13, 148:294

Three Kings A-Riding 63:36

Three Little Girls 68:5, 197:52, *see also:* 17:40, 188:16

Tideo 232:173

Tiptoe 291:60

To the Serpent/A La Víbora 295:24

Tommy Was a Soldier 291:11

Tonari-no Obasan/Auntie Nextdoor 286:48

Toodala 232:54, 291:14

Toryanse 16:61, 286:46

Tra, la, la, Ja sas 83:501

The Tractor's Song 288:12

Treasure Hunt 167:36

Troy, the Drummer Boy 167:30

The Turkey Game/Juego de los Pavos 194:34

Turn the Glasses Over 20:56, 39:2, 70:9, 129:120, *see also:* 134:44

The Turtle 177:85

Two and Two Are Four 167:46 *(One and one are two)*

Two and Two Are Four/Dos y Dos Son Cuatro 194:36

Two Dukes a'Riding 213:40, *see also:* Three Dukes

Two in a Boat 135:92

Two in the Middle 128:97, *see also:* 135:94

Two Valentines for You 167:14

Ular Naga 169:32, 265:12

Uncle Jessie 109:114

Uncle John 66:74

Up on the Mountain 129:110

Vacation's Here 167:24

Varsang 20:92

Wake Up, You Lazy Bones 291:74

Walk Along, John 178:13, 232:134

Walking on the Green Grass 24:807

Way Down in the Paw-Paw Patch 33:138, *see also:* Pawpaw Patch

Way Down Yonder in the Brickyard 109:116

Way Down Yonder in the Pawpaw Patch 178:38, *see also:* Pawpaw Patch

Way Down Yonder, Sometimes 109:101

Way Go, Lily 109:118

Way Up in the Holler 20:76

We Are All Nodding 291:18

Weasel's Nest 46:210

Weaving Cloth 70:26

We've Come From Spain 63:34

What Is Big?/Chinene Nye? 168:18

What Shall We Do? 291:48

What Shall We Do When We All Go Out? 165:179, 232:59

What Use Are You 41:34, 291:35

The Wheat 46:203, 55:521

When Ducks Get Up in the Morning 291:26

When I Was a Baby 63:22

When I Was a Shoemaker 75:87, *see also:* Ha-Ha, This-A-Way

When I Was a Young Maid 232:168, *see also:* Ha-Ha, This-A-Way

When I Was Single 20:30

Where Are the Keys of the Castle?/ Donde Están Las Llaves? 188:54, *see also:* 189:154

Where Do You Come From?/Antagata Dokosa? 286:50

Where, Oh, Where 75:89

Where Oh Where Is Pretty Little Susie? 232:172, *see also:* Pawpaw Patch

The White Ship Sails 63:37, *see also:* Allee Allee-o

Who Has a Nose? 178:9

Who Is It? 168:56

Who's That Knocking at My Door? 291:84, *see also:* 232:52

Who's That Tapping at the Window? 232:52, *see also:* 291:84

Whose Bag Is My Gold Ring? 109:165

The Widow of Count Laurel/La Viudita del Conde Laurel 295:43

Willowbee 129:106

Wind Up the Apple Tree 39:30, 100:114

With My Hands I Clap Clap Clap 178:29

The Wolf/El Lobo 70:27

Won't You Let the Birdie Out? 109:177

Yagmur/Rain 266:57

Yo Tengo un Castillo/I've a Fine, Bonny Castle 189:154, *see also:* 188:54

You Must Pass This Spoon 83:491, *see also:* 20:90, 55:250, 70:18, 289:173

Zui, Zui, Zukorobashi/Rat in the Rice Sack 16:51, 286:42

SIOUAN INDIANS
Dakota Hymn 69:25, 71:88, 72:69
The Horsemen in the Cloud 74:42
I Sing for the Animals 74:40
Sioux Night Song 197:84
Song of the Moccasin Game 74:45
Song of the Old Wolf 74:44
Song of the Sacred Stones 74:37
Song of the Young Wolves 74:43
Wakan'tanka Hears Me 74:36

SISTERS: *see* FAMILY AND FAMILY LIFE

SIZE AND SHAPE
Circles 206:14
Little Things 17:98, 86:119

SKATING
Six Little Girls A-Sliding Went 83:502, *see also:* 17:40, 68:5, 188:16, 197:52
Skate With Me 167:52
The Skaters' Song 207:72
Skating 7:14
Skating Away 39:48, 126:87
Three Children Sliding on the Ice 17:40, 188:16, *see also:* 68:5, 83:502, 197:52
Three Little Girls 68:5, 197:52, *see also:* 17:40, 83:502, 188:16

SKIING
A Day to Ski 207:73

SKIN
Skin 91:16

SKIN DIVING AND SCUBA DIVING
Frogmen, Frogmen 167:32

SKIPPING MUSIC
Billy Barlow 232:80, 274:18, *see also:* 20:11
Skip to the Barbershop 109:50
Skipping Music 11:33

SKIPPING ROPE
All the Boys in Our Town 63:69
Boom, Boom, Ain't It Great to Be Crazy 178:72, 289:143
Doctor, Doctor 63:68
Landlord 141:56
Miss Lucy 109:173
Oh, Marguerite! Go Wash Your Feet 24:796
On a Mountain 63:66, *see also:* 24:804, 39:20, 135:70
On the Hill 20:94
Rosy Apple, Lemon, and Pear 63:68
See Each India Rubber Ball 165:55
Some Love Coffee, Some Love Tea 110:38
Somebody, Nobody, Walks Down the Aisle 63:70
There Came a Girl from France 63:52
Up and Down Jamaica Plain 141:58
The Wind, the Wind 63:65
Yoki and the Kaiser 63:72

SKUNKS
Dancing Song of the Skunk 74:29
The Little Skunk 63:138
The Monkey and the Skunk 166:26
SLAVERY
Abolitionist Hymn 64:167
Bound to Go 157:136
Carry Me Back to Old Virginny 22:84,
127:176, 205:186
Darling Nelly Gray 21:132, 126:59
Emancipation 73:26
Follow the Drinking Gourd 33:162
Free at Last 31:21, 157:139
Good Bye to America 28:165
I'm Gwine to Alabamy 24:904
Kingdom Coming 73:93
Many Thousan' Gone 22:187, see also:
64:173
Massa Had a Yaller Gal 24:903
Wake Nicodemus 21:160, 73:96
SLED AND SLEIGHS
Jingle Bells 17:63, 54:70, 92:163,
127:220, 148:200, 241:171, 264:114,
283:64
My Red Sled 207:70
SLEEP: see also BEDTIME; DREAMS; LULLA-
BIES; SANDMAN
The Animals Go to Sleep 41:14
Are You Sleeping? 25:31, 26:42, 62:11,
293:43, see also: Frère Jacques
Bed in Summer 227:36
The Bedroom 149:24
Brother James 188:180, 217:55, see also:
Frère Jacques
Diddle, Diddle Dumpling 285:97, see
also: 162:88, 175:162
Fray Felipe, Fray Felipe 148:102,
293:43
Frère Jacques/Are You Sleeping? 17:72,
62:11, 90, 148:102, 176:73, 188:180,
217:17, 217:55, 283:21, 289:186, 293:42,
see also: 25:31, 26:42
Good Night 59:53 (Here's a body, there's
a bed)
Good Night 71:49 (Good night, good
night, companions all)
Good Night, Beloved 71:58
Night Noises 166:10
Onkel Jakob, Onkel Jakob 148:102,
293:43
Sleep Is a Pillow 91:48
Soft Falls the Dew 262:53
Stars of the Summer Night 71:124, 72:61
Stay Awake 275:53
SMILES
A Smile Is Quite a Funny Thing 26:20
Smile Song (S-M-I-L-E) 25:39, 26:12
Smiles 170:37

SNAILS
Chinese Baby Song 17:134, 59:27
Dendenmushi/The Snail 286:21
Six Little Snails 17:62, 165:48
Snail 14:378, 100:96 (Hand in hand you
see us well)
The Snail/Dendenmushi 286:21 (Here
comes the snail)
Snail Snail 162:26
SNAKES
Down in the Grass, Curled Up in a Heap
165:95
Giant Snake/Ssemusota 86:265
On Springfield Mountain 24:828, see
also: 21:254, 72:91, 157:49, 158:28,
290:51, 292:114
The Pesky Sarpent 21:254, 157:49,
292:114, see also: 24:828, 72:91, 158:28,
290:51
The Rattlesnake 159:194
The Snake 144:7
The Snake Baked a Hoecake 234:24,
292:115
Springfield Mountain 72:91, 158:28,
290:51, see also: 21:254, 24:828, 157:49,
292:114
Ssemusota/Giant Snake 89:265
SNEEZING
Ah-a-a-a-a-a-h 237:unpaged
SNOW: see also WINTER
A Day to Ski 207:73
Falling Snow 167:48
The First Snowfall 207:66
In the Snow 207:77
Making a Snowman 207:77
Millions of Snowflakes 86:181
The More It Snows 172:47, 174:33
She Perished in the Snow 35:50, see also:
24:825, 27:244, 159:231, 226:58
A Sliding Song 207:74
Snow 162:35 (The snow is piled so high)
Snow 11:30 (Snow is falling on the
ground)
Snow Boy 207:75
Snow Feathers 7:11
Snow Flakes 41:3
The Snowflakes 177:88
The Snowman 41:5
Snows 261:42
The Trees Have Put Their Nightgowns
On 7:12
White Fields 44:26
Winter 91:30
A World of Snow 162:34
SOLDIERS
Abraham's Daughter 27:17, 73:102
All Quiet Along the Potomac Tonight
73:197, 157:132
Beauregard 73:86

The Bonnie Blue Flag 21:142, 73:16, 127:141, 157:124
Boys' Chorus 85:196
Boys, Keep Your Powder Dry 73:148
Brave Wolfe 158:118, 240:33, 273:16
The British Grenadiers 22:198, 240:142
Brother, Tell Me of the Battle 73:280
The Caissons Go Rolling Along 197:103
Come in Out of the Draft 73:136
Come, Oh Love/Shule Aroon 21:344, 89:136
Come Out, Ye Continentalers 27:34, 28:107
Corporal Schnapps 73:115
The Cruel War Is Raging 72:12
Doodle Dandy 134:92
The Drummer Boy of Shiloh 73:200
Dumbarton's Drums 99:35
The English Soldiers 63:34
Gee, But I Want to Go Home 158:124, see also: 27:226
Gee, Mom, I Want to Go Home 27:226, see also: 158:124
God Bless the Old Sixth Corps 73:176
Goodbye, Old Glory 73:295
Grafted into the Army 73:133
Hard Crackers Come Again No More 73:146
Here's Your Mule 73:160
He's Gone to the Arms of Abraham 73:126
Hinky Dinky, Parlee-voo 126:61, 158:122, 170:61, 205:348, 226:440
Hold the Fort 73:214, 230:20
How Are You, Conscript? 73:139
How Happy the Soldier 240:143, 273:86
The Hunters of Kentucky 157:34, 226:427
I Don't Want No More of Army Life 63:140
I Goes to Fight Mit Sigel 73:118
I'm Going to Join the Army 232:95
The Invalid Corps 73:142
Johnny Has Gone for a Soldier 22:69, 134:94, 157:24, 158:117, 240:87, 262:25, 273:84, see also: 73:104
Johnny, I Hardly Knew Ye 42:605, see also: 148:204
Johnny, I Hardly Knew You 148:204, see also: 42:605
Johnny Is Gone for a Soldier 73:104, see also: Johnny Has Gone for a Soldier
A Life on the Vicksburg Bluff 73:211
Lili Marlene 22:202
Little Major 73:194
Malbrouck 21:346, see also: 217:49
Malbrough 217:49, see also: 21:346
March of the Men of Harlech 21:188

Marines' Hymn 197:102, 205:358, 277:121
Marlborough 217:64, 295:56
The Mulligan Guard 157:177
My Buddy 158:20
On Memorial Day 207:118
The Patriotic Diggers 27:172, see also: 240:205
A Pretty Fair Maid 226:68, see also: 35:32, 213:60
Pretty Fair Miss 213:60, see also: 35:32, 226:68
Rabble Soldier 159:253, 226:284
Reveille 197:104
The Roman Soldiers 39:26, 129:114, 135:88
Round Her Neck She Wore a Yellow Ribbon 205:384, see also: 170:22
Santy Anna 21:288, 24:835, 262:105, see also: 158:136
Santy Anno 158:136, see also: 21:288, 24:835, 262:105
The Sergeant, He Is the Worst of All 226:435
The Shan Van Vocht 42:592
Shule Agra 21:344, see also: 89:136
Shule Aroon/Come, Oh Love 89:136, see also: 21:344
Soldier Boy 134:96
Soldier, Soldier 17:55, 290:80, see also: Soldier, Soldier, Won't You Marry Me?
Soldier, Soldier, Will You Marry Me? 17:55, 62:118, 148:348, 290:80, see also: Soldier, Soldier, Won't You Marry Me?
Soldier, Soldier, Won't You Marry Me? 21:186, 142, 157:72, 227:24, see also: 17:55, 62:118, 79:32, 148:348, 290:80
Soldier, Won't You Marry Me? 79:32, see also: Soldier, Soldier, Won't You Marry Me?
Soldier's Song 85:167
Ten Thousand Men Were Going On Manoeuvres 262:137
Tenting on the Old Camp Ground 73:152, 197:60, see also: 21:150, 127:157
Tenting Tonight 21:150, see also: 73:152, 127:157, 197:60
This, This My Lad's the Soldier's Life 99:47
Three Days/Tri Dni 89:189
Three Drummer Boys/Trois Jeunes Tambours 217:58
Tramp! Tramp! Tramp! 21:147, 73:172, 197:62
Tri Dni/Three Days 89:189
Trois Jeunes Tambours/Three Drummer Boys 217:30
The Two Grenadiers 85:155

SOLDIERS—*Continued*
  Walking on the Green Grass 134:96
  Way Down in Mexico 159:365
  We Are Soldiers Marching Along 165:140
  We're Tenting Tonight 127:157, *see also:* 21:150, 73:152, 197:60
  When I First Put This Uniform On 252:29
  When Johnny Comes Marching Home 22:196, 27:228, 66:82, 73:284, 117:unpaged, 128:92, 148:414, 157:134, 197:61, 205:251
  Where They Were 226:442
  Whirling Maiden 262:142
  The White Army Bean 99:47, *see also:* 73:168
  Who Comes Here? 18:11, 111:61
  Wrap Me Up in My Tarpaulin Jacket 226:436
  You're in the Army Now 197:104
SOLOMON ISLANDS
  *My Son/Nuri 89:305
  *Nuri/My Son 89:305
SOMALIA
  *Our Great Leader/Shellila Shek 89:280
  *Shellila Shek/Our Great Leader 89:280
SONS: *see* FAMILY AND FAMILY LIFE
SORCERY: *see* WITCHES AND WITCHCRAFT
SOUDAN: *see* SUDAN
SOUNDS
  Little Sir Echo 68:18
  Sounds Are Fun 91:26
SOUP
  Beautiful Soup 112:12
  Chicken Soup With Rice 235:60
  Mrs. Murphy's Chowder 290:16
  Pease Porridge Hot 17:74, 162:89, 285:90, 291:58, *see also:* 175:90
  Pease Pudding Hot 175:90, *see also:* 17:74, 162:89, 285:90, 291:58
  Soup Song 64:130
SOUTH AFRICA, REPUBLIC OF
  As the Sun Goes Down 72:144
  Aunt Hessie's White Horse/Tant Hessie Se Witperd 189:140
  The Baboon Climbs the Hill 292:213, *see also:* 289:52
  Enkomo Zee-Gah-Baba 107:38
  *Fhola Li Na Mulanda/Snuff Is Very Guilty 89:275
  *Iga'ma Lo Ta'ndo/Song of Love 89:274
  *Mamma, 'Kwill 'N Man He'/Mother, I Want a Husband 89:276
  Marching to Pretoria 72:148, 254:118
  *Mother, I Want a Husband/Mamma, 'Kwill 'N Man He' 89:276
  *Snuff Is Very Guilty/Fhola Li Na Mulanda 89:275

  *Song of Love/Iga'ma Lo Ta'ndo 89:274
  Stop Your Groaning 289:52, *see also:* 292:213
  Tant Hessie Se Witperd/Aunt Hessie's White Horse 189:140
SOUTH AMERICA: *see* names of countries, e.g., BRAZIL
SOVIET UNION: *see* RUSSIA
SPACE (OUTER)
  Jackson Scott, the Astronaut 112:56
  Space Rocket Rick 167:16
  We'll Land on the Moon 166:68
SPAGHETTI
  On Top of Spaghetti 75:58, 76, 118:23, 147:29
SPAIN
  *A la Niñita, Nana 54:252, 279:108, *see also:* 89:161, 216:31
  *Al Olivo Subí/I Climbed the Olive Tree 216:26
  *Arre, Burriquito/Hurry, Little Donkey 295:75
  *Baile de Nadal 89:162, *see also:* Fum, Fum, Fum
  *The Baker Maiden/La Panaderita 89:160, *see also:* 216:45
  *The Ball/El Baile 208:62
  *The Bird/El Pájaro 295:10
  *Canco de's Batre/Threshing Song 89:163
  *The Chicken/El Pollo 295:15
  *Don Gato/Sir Cat 295:4, *see also:* 216:3
  *El Baile/The Ball 208:62
  *El Pájaro/The Bird 295:10
  *El Patio de Mi Casa/The Patio of My House 295:40
  *El Pollo/The Chicken 295:15
  *El Quele le/The White Hawk 262:118
  *El Señor don Gato/Sir Tomcat 216:3, *see also:* 295:4
  *El Sol y la Luna/The Sun and the Moon 216:14
  *El Tesoro de Santa Clara/The Treasure of the Santa Clara 295:68
  *El Vito 295:26
  *En Belén Tocan a Fuego 54:276, 295:76, *see also:* 89:276
  *En Salamanca/In Salamanca 295:51
  *The Flea and the Louse/La Pulga y el Piojo 295:12
  The Four Generals/Los Cuatro Generales 22:218
  *The Girl Warrior/La Doncella Guerrera 295:53
  *The Hours of the Clock/Las Horas del Reloj 295:34
  *Hurry, Little Donkey/Arre, Burriquito 295:75

I Climbed the Olive Tree/Al Olivo Subí 216:47

*I Have a Little Doll/Yo Tengo una Muñeca 194:28

*I Would Like to Be As Tall As The Moon/ Quisiera Ser Tan Alta Como la Luna 295:47

*In Bethlehem They Light a Fire 295:76, see also: 54:276, 89:276

*In Doncella Guerrera/Girl Warrior 295:53

*In Salamanca/En Salamanca 295:51

I've a Fine, Bonny Castle 189:154, see also: 188:54

*La Doncella Guerrera/The Girl Warrior 295:53

*La Molinera/The Miller's Wife 295:59

*La Panaderita/The Baker-Girl 89:160, 216:18

*La Pulga y el Piojo/The Flea and the Louse 295:12

*La Tarara 295:61

*La Torre de Alicante/The Tower of Alicante 216:7

*La Viudita del Conde Laurel/The Widow of Count Laurel 295:43

*Las Horas del Reloj/The Hours of the Clock 295:34

Los Cuatro Generales/The Four Generals 22:218

*Los Pastores/The Shepherds 295:70

*Mambru Se Fué a la Guerra/Mambru Went to War 295:56

*Mambru Went to War/Mambru Se Fué a la Guerra 295:56

*Mi Abuelo Tenía un Huerto/My Grandfather Had a Garden 295:21

*The Miller's Wife/La Molinera 295:59

*My Grandfather Had a Garden/Mi Abuelo Tenía un Huerto 295:21

*Niña Nana/Lullaby 89:161, 216:31, see also: 54:252, 279:108

*The Patio of My House/El Patio de Mi Casa 295:40

Pretty Girls and the Shoemaker 68:44

*Quisiera Ser Tan Alta Como la Luna/I Would Like to Be As Tall As the Moon 295:47

*Riqui Ran 262:17, see also: 295:45

*Riquirran 295:45, see also: 262:17

Salute to Freedom/Freiheit 22:210

*The Shepherds/Los Pastores 295:70

*Sir Cat/Don Gato 216:41, 295:4

*Sir Tomcat/El Señor don Gato 216:41, 295:4

*The Sky-Blue Dove/La Paloma Azul 89:72

*The Son of Mary/El Noi de la Mare 54:260

Spanish Lullaby 125:122

The Sun and the Moon/El Sol y la Luna 216:44

*Threshing Song/Canco de's Batre 89:163

The Tower of Alicante/La Torre de Alicante 216:43

*The Treasure of the Santa Clara/El Tesoro de Santa Clara 295:68

*We'll Speak Very Softly/Falade Ben Baixo 54:271

The White Hawk/El Quele le 262:118

*The Widow of Count Laurel/La Viudita del Conde Laurel 295:43

Yo Tengo un Castillo/I've a Fine, Bonny Castle 189:154, see also: 188:54

Yo Tengo una Muñeca/I Have a Little Doll 194:28

SPANISH AMERICA: see LATIN AMERICA

SPANISH-AMERICAN WAR (1898)
Break the News to Mother 21:41
A Filipino Hombre 226:434

SPANISH LANGUAGE
A Cantar a una Niña 216:12
A la Media Noche 54:286
A la Niñita, Nana 54:252, 279:108, see also: 89:161, 216:31
A la Puerta del Cielo 72:142
A la Rue 277:149
A la Víbora 295:24
Adelita 226:300, 226:301
Adoración 89:55
Aguinaldo 140:28
Ahora Voy a Cantarles 216:8
Al Animo 194:24, see also: 168:112
Al Canto de una Laguna 216:22
Al Olivo Subí 216:26
Al Quebrar la Piñata 295:79
Alegría 54:293
Arre, Burriquito 295:75
Arroyo Claro 188:62
Arroz Con Leche 168:136, see also: 216:10, 295:28
Bailando el Gato 89:88
Baile de los Pollos 194:30
Baile de Nadal 89:162, see also: Fum, Fum, Fum
Bogando a la Luz del Sol 89:103
Bunde San Antonio 169:16
Campana Sobre Campana 54:278
Canción del Marinero Hondureño 89:74
Canco de's Batre 89:163
Canto Lucumi de Iya 89:59
Cantemos 54:296
Chiquirriquitín 54:280
Cielito Lindo 197:36, 216:27, 226:298, 230:23
Ciranda 168:141, 169:9, 266:13
Como Busca el Tierno Infante 54:298

SPANISH LANGUAGE—*Continued*

Danse Juba   89:57

De Blanca Tierra   89:90, 262:19

De Tierra Lejana Venimos   54:288, *see also:* 140:22

Dime, Lluvia   216:17

Din Don   188:170

Don Gato   295:4, *see also:* 216:3

Doña Blanca   168:28, 295:30

Doña Maria   295:55

Donde Están las Llaves?   188:54, *see also:* 189:154

Dos y Dos Son Cuatro   194:36

Duérmete Mi Niño   194:16

Dulce, Dulce   107:44

El Abandonado   226:295

El Baile   208:62

El Cant dels Ocells   54:268, *see also:* Carol of the Birds

El Carite   216:4

El Conejo de Esperanza   194:20

El Coqui   69:32

El Desembre Congalat   54:266

El Juego del Pañuelo   194:18

El Lobo   70:27

El Marido y la Piedra   89:78

El Mino Jesús   241:88, *see also:* 54:284, 209:110

El Noi de la Mare   54:260

El Pájaro   295:10

El Patio de Mi Casa   295:40

El Pollo   295:15

El Rancho Grande   216:23

El Rei Herodes   54:264

El Rorro   54:308, 100:154, 279:106

El Santo Niño   54:284, *see also:* 209:110, 241:88

El Sapo   216:20

El Señor don Gato   216:3, *see also:* 295:4

El Sol y la Luna   216:14

El Tesoro de Santa Clara   295:68

El Toro Pinto   216:1

El Tortillero   89:96, 169:14, 216:24, 267:46

El Zancudo   216:28

En Belén Tocan a Fuego   54:276, 295:76, *see also:* 89:276

En el Portal a Belén   54:282, 140:18

En Nombre del Cielo   54:306

En Salamanca   295:51

Era una Vez   89:62, 216:34

Esta Sí Que Es Nochebuena   295:78

Estilo   89:100

Falade Ben Baixo   54:271

A Filipino Hombre   226:434

A Fire Is Started in Bethlehem   54:276, *see also:* 89:276, 295:76

Foom, Foom, Foom!   241:80, *see also:* Fum, Fum, Fum!

Fray Felipe, Fray Felipe   148:102, 293:43

Fum, Fum, Fum   54:258, 125:121, 197:115, 221:80, 279:104, 295:84, *see also:* 89:162

Hay Aquí, Madre, un Jardín   216:11

Hojita de Guarumal   196:13

The Holy Child   54:284, 197:117, 209:110, *see also:* 241:88

In Bethlehem They Light a Fire   295:76, *see also:* 54:276, 89:276

In Bethlehem's Cradle   54:282, *see also:* 140:18

In Doncella Guerrera   295:53

Jeu! Jeu!   89:79, 216:36

Juego de los Pavos   194:34

La Burriquita   216:6

La Calandria   295:7

La Chacarera   70:17, 197:37

La Chaparrita   262:21

La Cucaracha   21:110, 197:38, 226:290

La Doncella Guerrera   295:53

La Fuente   168:112, *see also:* 177:24

La Guajira   89:58

La Jesucita   22:78, 72:106, 295:66

La Jornada   54:300

La Molinera   295:59

La Pájara Pinta   168:127

La Paloma Azul   89:72

La Palomita   169:53, 295:45

La Panaderita   89:160, 216:18

La Pulga y el Piojo   295:12

La Punta y el Tacón   194:32

La Tarara   295:61

La Tejedora de Nanduti   89:98

La Torre de Alicante   216:7

La Viudita del Conde Laurel   295:43

Las Chaparreras   89:71

Las Horas del Reloj   295:34

Las Mañanitas   169:49, 226:292, 262:21, 268:41, 295:62

Las Posadas   54:256

Lo Que Digo   226:294

Los Diez Perritos   295:17

Los Maizales   169:55, 270:50

Los Pastores   295:70

Los Reyes Oriente   140:22, *see also:* 54:288

Ma Teodora   216:19

Mambru Se Fué a la Guerra   295:56

Matatero-tero-la   114:78, 169:27

Matarile   169:60, 269:38, 295:37

Matarile, Rile, Ro   169:60, 269:38, 295:37

Mi Abuelo Tenía un Huerto   295:21

Mi Burro   289:64

Mi Chacra   262:19

Mi Compadre Mono   216:32

Mi Pollera   216:2

Miren Cuantas Luces   216:38

My Twenty Pennies 262:22
Nací en la Cumbre 89:76
Naranja Dulce 295:36
Naranjas y Limas 295:82
Niña Nana 89:161, 216:31, *see also:* 54:252, 279:108
No Puedo, Tengo Otro Dueño 89:77
Oi Betlehem 54:274
Para Subir al Cielo 194:26
Pastores a Belén 54:290
Pepito 194:22
Perica 262:18
Por un Beso de Tu Boca 89:94
Que Bonita Bandera 230:14
Que Pase el Rey 168:149
Quisiera Ser Tan Alta Como la Luna 295:47
Río de Avenida 89:99
Río, Río 208:7
Riqui Ran 262:17, *see also:* 295:45
Riquirran 295:45, *see also:* 262:17
San Sereni 20:83, 262:16
San Sereni del Monte 188:138
Sant Josep i la Mare de Deu 54:262
Señora Santa Ana 216:16
Soy Pobre Vaquero 61:230
Tecolote 27:70
Vamos a Belén 54:303
Vamos a la Mar 216:30
Vamos, Pastorcitos 54:310
Versos de Montalgo 226:303
Ya Viene la Vieja 54:254
Yo Te Amo, Idolatro 89:75
Yo Tengo una Muñeca 194:28

SPARROWS
A Little Brown Sparrow 111:18
A Little Cock-Sparrow 18:22, 175:148, 188:128
Wake Up Little Sparrow 107:66

SPIDERS
Eency Weency Spider 20:81, 232:126, 289:92, 291:44, *see also:* 46:216, 63:103, 75:22, 147:26, 292:202
Eentsy Weentsy Spider 75:22, *see also:* Eency Weency Spider
Incy Wincy Spider 46:216, *see also:* Eensy Weensy Spider
Inky Dinky Spider 147:26, *see also:* Eensy Weensy Spider
Inky Pinky 'Pider 63:103, *see also:* Eensy Weensy Spider
Little Miss Muffet 17:85, 175:74, 188:134, 285:81
The Spider 46:216, *see also:* Eency Weency Spider
The Spider and the Fly 175:168
A Spider for Miss Muffet 166:24
The Spider Makes a Road 74:16

The Teensy Weensy Spider 292:202, *see also:* Eency Weency Spider

SPINNING
Spin, Spin 262:135
Spinning Chorus 85:209

SPIRITUALS
Ain' Go'n to Study War No Mo' 226:480, *see also:* Down By the Riverside
All God's Children Got Shoes 148:14, *see also:* 25:103, 31:9, 129:16
All God's Chillun Got Wings 129:16, *see also:* 25:103, 31:9, 148:14
All Night, All Day 55:278, 69:28
Band of Angels 129:54
By and By 157:149
Come and Go With Me 148:54
Daniel Saw the Stone 123:305
Deep River 31:27, 157:142
Dere's a Star in de Eas' on Christmas Morn 209:22, *see also:* Rise Up, Shepherd and Follow
Dese Bones Gwine to Rise Again 89:42, 197:94, 226:470, *see also:* 290:40
Didn't My Lord Deliver Daniel? 31:17, 157:140
Do, Lord, Remember Me 55:279, 148:64
Down By the Riverside 27:230, 148:66, *see also:* 57:202, 83:473, 226:480, 230:50
Every Time I Feel the Spirit 148:78
Ezekiel Saw the Wheel 148:86, *see also:* 226:488
Ezekiel, You and Me 226:488, *see also:* 148:86
Free at Last 31:21, 157:139
Go Down, Moses 22:316, 31:13, 64:168, 148:108, 158:372, 197:45, 205:178
Go Tell It on the Mountain 31:7, 54:84, 92:156, 140:58, 148:112, 190:79, 197:116, 233:29, 241:34, 242:unpaged, 261:50
God's Goin' to Set This World on Fire 226:478
Going to Study War No More 64:202, *see also:* Down By the Riverside
Good-bye, Brother 226:477
Good News 148:122
The Gospel Train 72:85, 148:126
Gwine to Ride Up in the Chariot 55:277
Hal-Le-Lu 277:47
Heaven Is So High 148:150
He's Got the Whole World in His Hands 25:102, 31:19, 55:278, 72:83, 75:31, 148:156, 205:399
I Ain't Gwine Study War No More 83:473, *see also:* Down By the Riverside
I Am a Pilgrim 148:168

SPIRITUALS—*Continued*

I Am a Poor Wayfaring Stranger 22:34, 35:68, 148:304, *see also:* Wayfaring Stranger

I Can't Stay in Egypt Lan' 89:54

I Couldn't Hear Nobody Pray 148:170

I Got Shoes 25:103, 31:9, *see also:* 83:476, 129:16, 148:14

I Know Moonlight 226:451

I'm Gonna Sing When the Spirit Says Sing 148:182

I'm on My Way 148:184

In His Hands 31:19

In My Father's House 226:483

Is There Anybody Here? 31:25

I've Got Shoes 83:476, *see also:* 25:103, 31:9, 129:16, 148:14

Jacob's Ladder 21:130, 25:97, 31:11, 69:29, 86:110, 148:198

Jesus, Won't You Come B'm-By? 226:469

Joshua Fit the Battle of Jericho 22:304, 107:28, 158:374, *see also:* 148:208, 230:37

Joshua Fought the Battle of Jericho 148:208, 230:37, *see also:* 22:304, 107:28, 158:374

Just a Closer Walk With Thee 148:214

Keep Your Hand on the Plow 158:376, *see also:* 157:147, 226:474

King of Kings 31:51

Let Me Fly 148:222, *see also:* 22:300

Let Us Break Bread Together 31:23, 55:274, 72:82

Little Black Train Is A-Comin' 24:914, 148:228, *see also:* 232:152

Little David 31:3, 123:210

Little Wheel A-Turnin' in My Heart 157:146, 227:27, *see also:* 129:10

Lonesome Valley 86:54, 148:238, 158:352, *see also:* 226:486

Lord, Remember Me 24:915

Mary and Martha 148:240

Mary Had a Baby 31:15, 54:83, 140:54, 190:73, 209:17, 232:180, 233:47

My Good Lord's Done Been Here 31:5

My Lord, What a Morning 22:314, 140:51, 262:42

My Lord's Writing All the Time 55:275

My Sins Are Taken Away 83:472

Never Said a Mumblin' Word 158:356

No Hiding Place 31:49, 262:145

Nobody Knows the Trouble I See 22:302, 31:45, 71:92, 72:81, 148:256, 157:137

Now Let Me Fly 22:300, *see also:* 148:222

Oh, a-Rock-a My Soul 22:306, 72:80, *see also:* 55:278

Oh, Dem Golden Slippers 21:205, 157:160, 205:189, *see also:* 126:63

Oh, Freedom 21:167; 31:53, 64:164, 157:138, 158:370

Oh Jerus'lem in the Morning 140:56, *see also:* 67:28, 190:142, 233:28

O Lord, How Long? 37:169

Oh, Mary, Don't You Weep 148:274, 230:78, *see also:* 226:476

O Mary, Where Is Your Baby? 190:123, 233:56

O Po' Little Jesus 54:86, *see also:* 140:60, 158:354, 190:90, 233:52

O What a Beautiful City 31:33, 230:81

Oh, Won't You Sit Down 262:71, 290:84, *see also:* Set Down, Servant

The Old Ark's A-Moverin' 83:475, 148:288

Old-Time Religion 157:165

Over Yonders Ocean 37:170

Po' Lil Jesus 158:354, 233:52, *see also:* 54:86, 140:60, 190:90

Poor and Foreign Stranger 22:34, 35:68, 148:304, *see also:* Wayfaring Stranger

Poor Little Jesus 190:90, 233:52, *see also:* 54:86, 140:60, 158:354

A Poor Wayfaring Stranger 22:34, 35:68, 148:304, *see also:* Wayfaring Stranger

The Resurrection 35:70

Rise and Shine 148:312

Rise Up, Shepherd, an' Foller 22:266, 190:55, 209:22, *see also:* Rise Up, Shepherd, and Follow

Rise Up, Shepherd, and Follow 54:80, 129:66, 140:49, 233:16, 241:54, *see also:* 22:266, 190:55, 209:22

Rock-a My Soul 55:278, *see also:* 22:306, 72:80

Rocking Jerusalem 31:35

Roll, Jordan, Roll 21:261, 25:95, 31:37, 148:318, 290:96

Set Down, Servant 148:284, 158:362, *see also:* 22:312, 83:465, 128:26, 262:71, 290:84

The Ship of Zion 35:58, *see also:* 21:262

Sinner Man 134:82, 148:336, 157:60

Sister Mary Had But One Child 140:66, 190:134, 209:26, *see also:* 140:69, 197:114, 233:44

Sit Down, Sister 22:312, 128:26, *see also:* Set Down, Servant

Skeleton Bones 197:94, *see also:* 89:42, 226:470, 290:40

Sometimes I Feel Like a Motherless Child 158:368, 230:49, 277:95

Soon One Mornin' 158:358

Stand the Storm 55:273

Standing in the Need of Prayer 148:350

Steal Away 22:298, 148:358, 277:21

Swing Low Sweet Chariot   22:310, 25:106, 31:43, 69:30, 83:474, 148:368, 157:144, 205:354, 230:16
That Great Getting-Up Morning   27:74
There Was an Old Fish   128:48
These Bones Gonna Rise Again   290:40, see also: 89:42, 197:94, 226:470
This Little Light o'Mine   135:20, see also: 148:224
This Train   72:86, 75:84, 148:388
The Train Is A-Coming   68:33, 232:150, see also: 232:151
Trampin'   83:464, 148:394
Twelve Gates to the City   230:81, see also: 31:33
Two White Horses   226:472
Two Wings   262:36
The Virgin Mary   274:14
Walk Together Children   31:28
Wasn't That a Mighty Day   140:53, 190:145, 233:49
Way Over in the New Buryin'Ground   226:473
Wayfaring Stranger   24:880, 27:45, 37:162, 158:346, 205:56, 230:15, 262:47, 277:41, see also: 22:34, 35:68, 148:304
We Can Overcome   197:12, see also: 64:33, 72:79
We Shall Overcome   72:79, see also: 64:33, 197:12
We Will Overcome   64:33, see also: 72:79, 197:12
Were You There?   21:264, 31:39
What You Gonna Call Yo' Pretty Little Baby?   140:69, 190:114, see also: 140:66, 190:134, 209:26, 233:44
When My Blood Runs Chilly an' Col'   158:360
When the Saints Go Marching In   25:104, 72:87, 148:416, 157:148, 205:377
Where Shall I Be?   31:47
Who Built the Ark?   135:24, 232:128
Who Did?   129:102, 289:102
Won't You Sit Down?   83:465, see also: Set Down, Servant
You Can Dig My Grave   25:96
You Got to Cross It Foh Yohself   226:486, see also: 86:54, 148:238, 158:352
SPORTS: see names of specific sports, e.g., SWIMMING AND DIVING
SPRING (SEASON): see also names of months, e.g., APRIL
April Rain   97:unpaged
Buttercups and Daisies   17:109
Cambridgeshire May Song   212:76
Cherry Blossoms/Sakura Sakura   286:73, see also: 72:141
Cherry Trees/Sakura   72:141, see also: 286:73

Come Gentle Spring   85:120
Come Lasses and Lads   79:51, 227:42
Cowboy Spring   189:116, see also: 27:50
Doll's Festival/Hina Matsuri   286:70
Easter Greeting   245:113
An Easter Message   207:98
The First Bouquet   207:86
Flower Carol   184:58
The Flowers That Bloom in the Spring   252:46
Fly, Kite, Fly   207:89
Flying Carp/Koi Nobori   37:52, 286:74
Gathering Nuts in May   128:102, see also: Nuts in May
Greeting   85:178
Haru Ga Kita/Spring Song   100:15, see also: 286:69
Hina Matsuri/Doll's Festival   286:70
Hushabye Swing   207:91
I Know It's Spring   162:58
In Just   44:22
It Is Spring   27:50, see also: 189:116
June, Lovely June   262:34
Lo, the Winter Is Past   86:182
The Lonely Robin   207:87
Longing for Spring   85:107
May Time   207:119
Now Is the Month of Maying   72:110, 85:19, 189:112, 197:53, 262:159
Nuts in May   14:367, 63:32, 128:102, 165:191, 175:78, 188:38, 189:36
Oh, the Butterflies Are Flying   172:59, 174:45
Out in the Open Air   85:165
Purple Tulip Morning   261:30
Sing O Sing   41:11
Spring   91:32
Spring Carol   27:54, 189:68
Spring Is Coming   112:50
Spring Puddles   207:88
Spring Rain   261:28
Spring Song   41:10 (Snowflakes and winter winds)
Spring Song   97:unpaged ("Hello, Mister Robin in the tree")
Spring Song/Haru-ga Kita   286:69, see also: 100:15 (Springtime has come)
Springtime   91:33 (Eggs in nests turn into birds)
Springtime   207:94 (Apple blossoms pink and white)
Springtime/Yangsando   49:43 (Springtime, springtime, beautiful springtime)
Springtime Has Come   100:15, see also: 286:69
Welcome Spring/Yin Chuin Wha Ur Kai   49:15
Yangsando/Springtime   49:43

SPRING (SEASON)—*Continued*
  Yin Chuin Wha Ur Kai/Welcome Spring
    49:15
SQUARE DANCING
  At a Cowboy Dance   61:287
  Chicken Reel   226:116
  Farmer Gray   126:75
  The Girl I Left Behind Me   42:604,
    61:171, 66:112, 205:27, *see also:* 159:58
  Golden Slippers   126:63
  I Got a Gal at the Head of the Holler
    24:897, 226:320, *see also:* Sourwood
    Mountain
  Life on the Ocean Wave   126:73
  Little Brown Jug   126:50
  Lucy Long   126:77
  The Mexican Waltz   126:99
  Miss McLeod's Reel   126:51
  Molly Brooks   37:202
  Old Bald Eagle   135:72
  Old Brass Wagon   33:98, 55:506, 226:159
  Old Joe Clark   20:78, 24:814, 134:46,
    158:86, 230:35, 232:84, 261:60
  Red River Gal   61:279
  Reel   107:50
  Sally Ann   230:53
  Sandy Land   46:211, 70:25, 135:75
  Shoot the Buffalo   61:272, 61:273, 61:274,
    158:103
  Sicilian Circle   126:101
  Sing a Little Hoe-Down Jordan   110:20
  Soldier's Joy   126:49
  Square Dance   178:46
  Star Promenade   83:500
  Tucker's Waltz   126:71
  Turkey in the Straw   20:72, 22:66,
    126:48, 197:107, 226:94
  Up and Down the Railroad Track   61:276
  Weevily Wheat   24:813, 66:76, 226:161,
    see also: 213:28
SQUIRRELS
  Busy Little Bushytail   20:28
  Hop, Old Squirrel   232:109
  Peep Squirrel   109:216, 234:18
  The Squirrel   79:34, 128:38, 292:100, *see
    also:* 234:19
  The Squirrel   191:48 (*Little squirrel
    living there in a hollow tree*)
  Squirrel Nutkin   245:44
  Whisky Frisky   112:55
STAGECOACHES
  The Road to Cook's Peak   159:384
STAIRWAYS
  Halfway Down   172:122, 173:8
  Upstairs and Down   149:20
STARR, BELLE
  Queen of the Desperadoes   61:269,
    61:270

STARR, RINGO
  Ringo, Ringo, Ringo Starr   141:16
STARS
  Bright Morning Stars Are Rising   233:15
  By'm By   129:18, 226:453, *see also:*
    135:44, 157:156, 232:71, 289:13
  By 'M Bye   157:156, 232:71, 289:13, *see
    also:* 129:18, 135:44, 226:453
  By'n Bye   135:44, *see also:* By 'M Bye
  The Child and the Star   17:11
  Daisies   245:99
  The Evening Star   262:109
  Follow the Drinking Gourd   33:162
  Great Big Stars   233:14
  Oh, Watch the Stars   233:13
  Second Star to the Right   276:33
  Star Bright   162:37, *see also:* 59:78, 68:8
  Star Wish   59:78, *see also:* 68:8, 162:37
  Starlight, Starbright   68:8, *see also:* 59:78,
    162:37
  Stars In the Heaven   233:12
  Twinkle, Twinkle, Little Star   17:41,
    130:91, 175:108, 205:193, 283:69,
    289:84
THE STATES: *see* UNITED STATES; names of
  states, e.g., ALABAMA
STEALING: *see* OUTLAWS
STEEL
  Drivin' Steel   226:150
  Hammer Man   226:139
  John Henry   22:170, 33:178, 64:82, 89:40,
    158:258, 158:260, 158:262, 226:24,
    230:82, 232:154, 239:68, 272:15, 274:16,
    see also: 232:156
STEERS: *see* COWS
STOATS: *see* WEASELS
STORES: *see also* BUYING AND SELLING
  A Customer   154:22
  Five Currant Buns in a Baker's Shop
    165:30
  Going Down to Town   232:158, *see also:*
    226:145
  Hippity Hop   17:47, *see also:* 165:139
  Hippity Hop to the Candy Shop   165:139,
    see also: 17:47
  The Quartermaster's Store   25:36
STORIES
  "A" Alligators All Around   235:39
  Bluebeard   290:148
  Chicken Soup With Rice   235:60
  The City Rat and the Country Rat   17:96
  Davi Ayele No Bu Lo   215:44
  The Grasshopper and the Ant/La Cigale
    et la Fourmi   79:65, *see also:* 243:34
  John Grumblie   79:57, *see also:* Old
    Grumbler
  Kaleeba   236:11
  La Cigale et la Fourmi/The Grasshopper
    and the Ant   79:65, *see also:* 243:34

The Little Red Hen 245:60
Old Cromwell 71:93, *see also:* Old Grumbler
Old Farmer Grumble 110:28, *see also:* Old Grumbler
Old Grumbler 27:115, *see also:* 62:138, 71:93, 79:57, 110:28, 128:120, 213:56
The Old Man in the Woods 62:138, 128:120, 213:56, *see also:* 27:115, 71:93, 79:57, 110:28
One Was Johnny 235:35
Pierre 235:43
Red Riding Hood's Hood 166:72
There Was a Li'l Woman Who Took a Stroll 197:92
The Wife Who Was Dumb 36:72
STORKS
Le Loup et la Cicogne/The Wolf and the Stork 243:30
Stork Lange Bein/Stork Long-o'-Leg 189:146
Stork Long-o'-Leg/Stork Lange Bein 189:146
The Wolf and the Stork/Le Loup et la Cicogne 243:30
STORMALONG
Stormalong 24:834, 33:34
STORMS
Hi, Thunder 245:72
STREAMS: *see* RIVERS
STREET CRIES
Buy My Dainty Fine Beans 293:70
Chairs to Mend 46:228, 71:104, 72:164, 289:186, 293:64, 293:66, *see also:* 111:58
Cherries So Ripe 293:69
Doughnuts 239:88
Junk Man 239:89
London Street Cries 71:102
Old Chairs to Mend! 111:58, *see also:* Chairs to Mend
Watermelons 239:87
STRIKES: *see* LABOR UNIONS
STUART, J. E. B.
Riding a Raid 73:90
SUDAN
*Don-Don Ba Ji 169:63, *see also:* 269:50
*The Gazelle/Gbodi 89:281
*Gbodi/The Gazelle 89:281
SUMMER
At the Beach 207:129
Autumn Voices 72:136
Barley Harvesting/Mugi Kari 286:76
Brightly, Brightly Gleam the Sparkling Rills 262:153
Come Out and Play 245:19
Dandelion Buttons 207:93
In Summer the Sunshine Is Brightest 72:131

In the Good Old Summertime 21:76, 25:98, 205:277
June Is Bustin' Out All Over 218:85
Now the Winter Is Past/Nu Er Vetur Ur Boe 89:171
Nu Er Vetur Ur Boe/Now the Winter Is Past 89:171
On a Summer Day 154:6
The Rainbow 207:125
Summer Is a-Cumen In 71:108, *see also:* 27:154, 176:144, 189:110, 293:80
Summer Bouquet 97:unpaged
Summer Is a-Coming In 27:154, 71:108, 176:144, 293:80, *see also:* 189:110
Summer Is I-cumen In 189:110, *see also:* 27:154, 71:108, 176:144, 293:80
Summer Puddles 261:26
SUN
Dearest Sun 245:4
El Sol y la Luna/The Sun and the Moon 216:14
Hi, Thunder! 245:72
The Sun 245:14
The Sun and the Moon/El Sol y la Luna 216:44
The Sun It Rises 293:102
Sunny Day 11:22
There's a Sun for the Morning 245:16
SUNRISE: *see* DAWN; MORNING
SUNSET: *see* EVENING
SUPERNATURAL: *see* DEVILS; GHOSTS; WITCHES AND WITCHCRAFT
SUPPER
Little Tommy Tucker 17:99, 285:88, *see also:* 175:24
Mistress Bond 62:52, 175:72, 292:154, *see also:* 188:116
Oh, What Have You Got for Dinner, Mrs. Bond? 188:116, *see also:* 62:52, 175:72, 292:154
Tommy Tucker 175:24, *see also:* 17:99, 285:88
SURFING
Come Surfing With Me/Ku'u Ipo I Ka He'e Pu'eone 87:36
Ku'u Ipo I Ka He'e Pu'eone/Come Surfing With Me 87:36
SURINAM
*Leba Gado/Leba God 89:102
*Leba God/Leba Gado 89:102
SWANS
The Swan Sings 262:35
Swan Swum 112:63
SWEDEN
*The Child's Testament/Den Lillas Testamente 89:169
*Christmas Is Here Again 89:170, 262:42, *see also:* 54:193, 241:168, 279:112

SWEDEN—*Continued*
*Christmas Polka 262:42, *see also:* 54:193, 89:170, 241:168, 279:112
*Dance Carol 279:112, *see also:* 54:193, 89:170, 241:168, 262:42
*Den Lillas Testamente/The Child's Testament 89:169
*Du Gronne, Glitrende Tre, God-Dag/ You Green and Glittering Tree, Good Day 54:198
Gently the Breezes 71:47
*Gladjens Blomster/Joyful Blossoms 208:65
Gustaf's Toast 46:204, 70:39
*Her Kommer Dine Arme Smaa/Thy Little Ones, Dear Lord, Are We 54:196
Herdgirl's Song 68:21
Hey, Little Lassie 70:21
*I See You/Jag Ser Dig 189:134
In Summer the Sunshine Is Brightest 72:131
*Jag Ser Dig/I See You 189:134
*Joyful Blossoms/Gladjens Blomster 208:65
*Jungfru Maria Till Betlehem Gick/Mary the Virgin to Bethlehem Went 279:111
*Mary the Virgin to Bethlehem Went/ Jungfru Maria Till Betlehem Gick 279:111
The Merry-Go-Round 17:92 *(Oh, camels and bears and ponies are found)*
Merry-Go-Round 70:22 *(Young maid, young maid, young maid, young maid dear)*
*Nar Juldagsmorgon Glimmar/When Christmas Morn Is Dawning 54:194
*Now It Is Christmastime/Nu Ar Det Jul Igen 241:168, *see also:* 48:193, 78:170, 262:42, 279:112
*Nu Ar Det Jul Igen 54:193, 89:170, 241:168, 262:42, 279:112
Out in Our Meadow/Uti Var Hage 262:39
*Saint Stephen Was Riding/Staffansvisa 279:114
*Staffan 228
*Staffansvisa/Saint Stephan Was Riding 279:114
Svensk Masquerade 83:498
*Thy Little Ones, Dear Lord, Are We/ Her Kommer Dine Arme Smaa 54:196
Uti Var Hage/Out in our Meadow 262:39
*Varsang 20:92
Weaving Cloth 70:26
*When Christmas Morn Is Dawning/Nar Juldagsmorgon Glimmar 54:194

*You Green and Glittering Tree, Good Day/Du Gronne, Glitrende Tre, God-Dag 54:198
*Yuletide Is Here Again 54:193, 279:112, *see also:* 89:170, 241:168, 262:42
SWIMMING AND DIVING: *see also* SKIN DIVING AND SCUBA DIVING
Aunt Jemima 46:226
Frogman, Frogman 167:32
Swimmin' Fun 166:74
SWINE: *see* PIGS
SWINGS AND SWINGING
The Swing 245:20
Swing Song 41:37
Swinging 288:16
Swinging Game 100:52
Swinging in the Swing 227:44
SWITZERLAND
*E Mi Son Chi in Barchetta/In My Little Boat 89:155
The Herdsman 25:93, 71:65, 72:119
*In My Little Boat/E Mi Son Chi in Barchetta 89:155
A Little Town in Switzerland 107:34
*Mir Senne Heil's Lustig/We Are Happy and Merry 89:154
Tra, La, La 25:15
Vreneli 208:67
*We Are Happy and Merry/Mir Senne Heil's Lustig 89:154
SYRIA
*Al Ya Zane/Oh Thou Zane 89:207
*Oh Thou Zane/Al Ya Zane 89:207

T

TAILORS
Schneiderlied/Song of the Tailor 208:2
Song of the Tailor/Schneiderlied 208:2
The Tailor and the Mouse 75:70, 117:unpaged, 292:194
TALL TALES: *see also* names of specific persons, e.g., JOHN HENRY
The Crocodile 292:178
Goin' Down to Town 226:145, *see also:* 232:158
The Herring Song 292:172
A Hunting Tale 61:8
Little Brown Dog 234:28, *see also:* 274:32
Taddle-o-Day 274:32, *see also:* 234:28
TAMBOURINES
My Tambourine 41:23
TANZANIA
*Goneh 169:65

*Leemwah 169:64
*War Song/Yaya 89:282
*Yaya/War Song 89:282
TEA
I'm a Little Teapot 63:106, 75:36, 165:31, 291:50
Polly Put the Kettle On 17:54, 135:40, 175:12, 188:74, 283:59, 285:76
TEA PARTIES: see PLAY
TEACHERS AND TEACHING
The Teacher's Lament 64:141
TEDDY BEARS: see TOYS
TEETH
In My Bureau Drawer 237:unpaged
TELEPHONES
Call Me on the Telephone 166:36
Eletelephony 44:64
Old Ma Bell 64:42
The Telephone 227:14
The Telephone Book Lullaby 59:62
Telephones 162:74
TELEVISION SHOWS
A Alligators All Around 235:39 (Really Rosie)
Anything Can Happen Day 119:100 (Mickey Mouse Club)
The Ballad of Chicken Soup 235:56 (Really Rosie)
Chicken Soup with Rice 235:60 (Really Rosie)
Do I Love You Because You're Beautiful 218:290 (Cinderella)
Fun with Music 119:96 (Mickey Mouse Club)
Here Comes the Circus 119:102 (Mickey Mouse Club)
A Lovely Night 218:293 (Cinderella)
The Merry Mousketeers 119:94 (Mickey Mouse Club)
Mickey Mouse March 119:92, 275:92, 276:85 (Mickey Mouse Club)
Mickey Mouse Theme Song 119:90 (Mickey Mouse Club)
Mousekartoon Time 119:109 (Mickey Mouse Club)
One Was Johnny 235:35 (Really Rosie)
Sesame Street 206:7 (Sesame Street)
Talent Roundup 119:104 (Mickey Mouse Club)
Today Is Tuesday 119:98 (Mickey Mouse Club)
TELLING TIME: see also CLOCKS AND WATCHES
The Clock 288:22
The Clock Song 291:36
The Hours of the Clock/Las Horas del Reloj 295:34
Las Horas del Reloj/The Hours of the Clock 295:34

Telling Time 41:18
Tick Tock 11:16
TERRAPINS: see TURTLES
TEXAS
Bob Stanford 159:295
The Dying Ranger 159:366
I'd Like to Be in Texas When They Round-Up in the Spring 159:321
I'm Gonna Leave Old Texas Now 159:57, 277:35, see also: 21:108, 61:182, 69:21
The Lone Star Trail 61:307, 159:19, 226:266, see also: 60:102, 146:162
Song of the Border 61:81
West Texas 159:413
The Yellow Rose of Texas 73:245, 205:392
THAILAND
*Ah! Ah! Ah! 89:224
*Chaw Mah Lee/My Beloved 169:67, 267:54
*Moonlight/Ngarm Saeng Duen 267:54
*My Beloved/Chaw Mah Lee 169:67, 267:54
*Ngarm Saeng Duen/Moonlight 267:54
Twilight 114:34
THANKSGIVING DAY
Autumn Is Here 245:109
Come, Ye Thankful People, Come 45:44, 86:179
The Coming Feast 207:41
Five Fat Turkeys Are We 178:42
For the Beauty of the Earth 45:48, 86:10, 148:96, 262:151
For the Golden Corn 245:111
Gobble, Gobble 162:46
God Hath Given Us Harvest 86:178
Hymn of Thanksgiving 27:234, see also: 21:338, 45:56, 205:24
On the First Thanksgiving Day 148:290, 197:108
Over the River and Through the Woods 17:56, 40, 148:298, 197:106
Praise to God, Immortal Praise 86:175, 262:106
Prayer of Thanksgiving 21:338
Sing to the Lord of Harvest 86:174
Thanks for Thanksgiving 167:50
Thanksgiving Day 17:56, see also: 40, 148:298, 197:106 (Over the river and through the woods)
Thanksgiving Day 97:unpaged (We have Thanksgiving Day as did the Pilgrims long ago)
Thanksgiving Prayer 205:24, see also: 21:338, 27:234, 45:56
Thanksgiving Time Has Come 86:176
Three Turkeys 162:44
We Are Thankful 162:46

THANKSGIVING DAY—*Continued*
We Gather Together 45:56, 205:24, *see also:* 21:338, 27:234
We're Singing Our Praises/Wilt Heden Nu Treden 21:338, *see also:* 27:234, 45:56, 205:24
Wilt Heden Nu Treden/We're Singing Our Praises 21:338
THIEVES: *see* OUTLAWS
THUNDERSTORMS
Hi, Thunder 245:72
TIBET
*The Dew Is Dry at Midday/Seba Alaso Trodje 89:234
*Seba Alaso Trodje/The Dew Is Dry at Midday 89:234
TICKS (INSECTS)
Dog Tick 232:127
TIGERS
Stepping Tigers 207:110
TIME: *see also* CALENDARS; CLOCKS AND WATCHES; TELLING TIME
I'm Late 275:42, 276:42
TINKERS
Jolly Old Roger 262:60, 239:83
The Tinker 71:102
The Tinker's Daughter 117:unpaged
The Tinker's Song 239:83, *see also:* 262:60
TITANIC (SHIP)
The Ship Titanic 290:153, *see also:* 226:254
De Titanic 226:254, *see also:* 290:153
TOADS: *see also* FROGS
El Sapo/The Toad 216:20
The Toad/El Sapo 216:46
The Tottenham Toad 135:49
TONGUE TWISTERS
Betty Botter 112:8, *see also:* 18:12
Betty Botter's Batter 18:12, *see also:* 112:8·
Counting the Goats 292:56
Grasshopper 292:210
The Lame Crane 71:114, 72:170, *see also:* 62:19, 144:25, 176:152, 292:65, 293:52
A Lame, Tame Crane 144:25, *see also:* The Lame Crane
Mules 26:19, 289:148, 292:36
My Aunt Has a Lame Tame Crane 62:19, *see also:* Lame Crane
My Dame Hath a Lame Tame Crane 144:25, 176:152, 292:165, 293:52, *see also:* 62:19, 71:114, 72:170
Peter Piper 112:61
She Sells Sea Shells 112:37
Swan Swum 112:63
Tongue Twisters 97:unpaged
Willie 91:37

The Woodchuck 144:9
TOOLS
Bling Blang 130:74
TOPS (TOYS)
My Dreydl 128:59, 197:111
Spin, Little Dreidel 207:62
TORTOISES: *see* TURTLES
TOWNS: *see* CITIES AND TOWNS
TOYS: *see also* names of specific toys, e.g., TOPS (TOYS)
I'm a Fairy Doll on the Christmas Tree 165:54
My New Toy 177:73
My Old Bear 91:45
My Rolling Wagon 207:15
New Toys 207:56
Our Yard 149:8
The Toy Shop 207:53
Toy Soldier Sam 166:54
TRADE UNIONS: *see* LABOR UNIONS
TRADES: *see* OCCUPATIONS
TRAINS: *see* RAILROADS
TRAMPS
Big Rock Candy Mountains 21:112, 24:884, 158:278, 230:66
Goin' Down the Road Feeling Bad 64:128, 148:116, 158:242
Hallelujah, I'm a Bum 22:102, 24:882, 64:126, 226:184, 239:54
Hard Traveling 64:124, 230:89
I Walked the Road Again 35:4
Jay Gould's Daughter 226:364
Tramp, Tramp, Tramp, Keep on A-Tramping 226:185
TRANSPORTATION: *see also* various means of transportation, e.g., RAILROADS
Goin' for a Ride 206:48
Gus 112:14
Horsey, Horsey 72:94 (Horse and Buggy)
I Had a Little Engine 165:70
Jingle Bells 17:63, 54:70, 92:163, 127:220, 148:200, 241:171, 264:114, 283:64 (Sleigh)
The Knickerbocker Line 35:94 (Trolleys)
Riding in the Buggy, Miss Mary Jane 232:78 (Horse and Buggy)
The Surrey With the Fringe on Top 218:19 (Horse and Buggy)
Wheels 91:23
The World Is Big, The World Is Small 107:32
TREES: *see also* APPLE TREES; ARBOR DAY
Al Olivo Subí/I Climbed the Olive Tree 216:26
Arbor Day Song 197:49
Bend With the Wind 162:32
The Birch Tree 71:80, 72:152

Bog in the Valley-O 72:127, *see also:* Green Grass Grows All Around

Cherry Blossoms/Sakura Sakura 286:73, *see also:* 72:141

Cherry Trees/Sakura 72:141, *see also:* 286:73

Deep in the Woods 197:48, *see also:* Green Grass Grows All Around

Derrière de Chez Mon Père/My Father's Apple Tree 188:110

The Forest 91:19

The Green Grass Grows All Around 94, 192, 290:19, *see also:* 27:90, 62:72, 72:127, 109:197, 132:unpaged, 134:11, 176:130, 197:48, 213:20

Hi! Ho! The Rattlin' Bog 134:11, *see also:* Green Grass Grows All Around

Hole in the Ground 62:72, *see also:* Green Grass Grows All Around

I Climbed the Olive Tree/Al Olivo Subí 216:47

If You Were a Beech Tree 165:96

The Juniper Tree 27:88, 232:82

The Linden Tree 67:21 *(Pardon, I'm the linden tree)*

The Linden Tree 125:86 *(A linden tree is standing beside a running stream)*

The Little Birch Tree 78:69

The Little Nut Tree 17:145, 175:92, 289:108, *see also:* I Had a Little Nut Tree

My Father's Apple Tree/Derrière de Chez Mon Père 188:110

The Oak and the Ash 71:54

Sakura/Cherry Trees 72:141, *see also:* 286:73

Sakura Sakura/Cherry Blossoms 286:73, *see also:* 72:141

To Ope Their Trunks 62:15

The Tree in the Forest 176:130, *see also:* Green Grass Grows All Around

The Tree in the Valley-O 213:20, *see also:* Green Grass Grows All Around

The Tree in the Wood 27:90, *see also:* Green Grass Grows All Around

A Tree in Yonder Field 132:unpaged, *see also:* Green Grass Grows All Around

Tree Song 71:25, 72:62

Tree Tree Tree 219:57

Woodman, Spare That Tree 157:104

TRINIDAD
Man Smart-Woman Smarter 89:64

TROBRIAND SUNSET ISLES
*The Gathering/Kaduguwai 89:303
*Kaduguwai/The Gathering 89:303

TULIPS
Tip-Toe Thru the Tulips With Me 170:79

TUNISIA
*Mahiya Illa Zalab/Song of the Fig Vendors 89:246
*Song of the Fig Vendors/Mahiya Illa Zalab 89:246

TURKEY
*Akhsham Oldu/Behold the Sun 89:208
Baby Mine 114:60
*Behold the Sun/Akhsham Oldu 89:208
*Halkada Boynundan/Here We Go Loop the Loop 266:57
*Here We Go Loop the Loop/Halkada Boynundan 266:57
Hos Bilezik/Pretty Bracelet 70:20
Pretty Bracelet/Hos Bilezik 70:20
*Rain/Yagmur 266:57
*Teen, Teen, Teeny Weeny Lady/Tin Tin Tini Mini Hanim 169:72, 243:58
*Tin Tin Tini Mini Hanim/Teen, Teen, Teeny Weeny Lady 169:72, 243:58
*Uskudar 89:209
*Yagmur/Rain 266:57

TURKEYS
Debreczenbe Kene Menni/The Turkey 289:86
Five Fat Turkeys Are We 178:42
Hay-Hoo! Hay-Hoo!/Jeu! Jeu! 216:51, *see also:* 89:79
Jeu! Jeu!/Hay-Hoo! Hay-Hoo! 89:79, 216:36
Juego de los Pavos/The Turkey Game 194:34
Shoo, Turkey 109:54
The Turkey/Debreczenbe Kene Menni 289:86
The Turkey Game/Juego de los Pavos 194:34
Turkey Song 234:46

TURTLES
The Hare and the Tortoise/Le Levraut et la Tortue 243:24
La Tortue et les Deux Canards/The Tortoise and the Two Ducks 243:22
Le Levraut et la Tortue/The Hare and the Tortoise 243:24
Mr. Turtle 162:84
The Snappy Turtle Says 166:40
There Was a Little Turtle 75:76
The Tortoise and the Two Ducks/La Tortue et les Deux Canards 243:22
The Turtle 177:85

TWELVE DISCIPLES: *see* APOSTLES

La Vidalita 22:108

U

U.S.S.R. (UNION OF SOVIET SOCIALIST REPUBLICS): *see* RUSSIA

UGANDA
*Akanyonyi 236:54
*Awo 236:42
*Bwalobera Nkere/The Frogs 89:283
*Ca, Ca, Ca 236:77
*Crested Crane/Ntuha Ntuha 265:56, *see also:* 169:69
Dipidu 114:46
*The Frogs/Bwalobera Nkere 89:283
Hen Fell Out of the Roost/O-Lu-We 265:57
*Kaleeba 236:11
*Nnoonya Mwana Wange 236:8
*Nnyonyi 236:27
*Nsangi 236:45
*Ntuha Ntuha/Crested Crane 169:69, 265:56
O-Lu-We/Hen Fell Out of the Roost 265:57
*Purrrrr Ce! 236:34
*Ttimba 236:63
*Twerire 236:23
*Wavvuuvuumira 236:18
*Woowooto 236:71

UNDERGROUND RAILROAD: *see* SLAVERY

UNION OF SOVIET SOCIALIST REPUBLICS: *see* RUSSIA

UNITED STATES: *see also* NATIONAL SONGS; names of states, e.g., ALABAMA
The Big Ranch/El Rancho Grande 216:47
Cielito Lindo/Pretty Skies Above 197:36, 216:27, 226:298, 230:23
El Rancho Grande/The Big Ranch 216:23
New England, New England 33:26
Pretty Skies Above/Cielito Lindo 216:48, 226:298, 230:23, *see also:* 197:36
Song of the Big Tree Region 69:42
Song of the Southland 69:45
The State Song 26:79
A Stately Song 290:136

URUGUAY
*Estilo 89:100

V

VAGABONDS: *see* GYPSIES; TRAMPS

VALENTINE'S DAY
Counting Valentines 162:53
Let's Make Valentines 97:unpaged
Pretty Valentines 207:79
Two Valentines for You 167:14
Valentine Dance 162:54
A Valentine From Grandma 207:78
Valentine's Day 7:16

VEGETABLES: *see also* GARDENS AND GARDENING; names of vegetables, e.g., POTATOES
Oh, John the Rabbit 232:100, 291:32

VENEZUELA
*As the Frightened Baby Jesus/Como Busca el Tierno Infante 54:298
*Bogando a la Luz del Sol/Rowing Toward the Sunlight 89:103
*Cantemos/We Are Singing 54:296
Carite Fish/El Carite 216:42
*Como Busca el Tierno Infante/As the Frightened Baby Jesus 54:298
Donana 114:86
*El Carite/The Carite Fish 216:4
*The Journey/La Jornada 54:300
*La Burriquita/The Little Donkey 216:6
*La Jornada/The Journey 54:300
The Little Donkey/La Burriquita 216:42
*My Twenty Pennies 262:22
*Rowing Toward the Sunlight/Bogando a la Luz del Sol 89:103
*We Are Singing/Cantemos 54:296

VIET NAM
*Lullaby/Nhim Ne Nhim 89:225
*Nhim Ne Nhim/Lullaby 89:225
*Quoc Ca Viet Nam 100:143

VIOLETS
White Violets 227:8

VIOLINS
Jacky, Come Give Me the Fiddle 112:58
Per Spelemann/Pete Fiddler 208:52
Pete Fiddler/Per Spelemann 208:52

VIRGIN ISLANDS (ST. CROIX)
Broder Manyo 89:66
Guava Berry Song 114:90

VIRGINIA
Carry Me Back to Old Virginny 22:84, 127:176, 205:186
Virginia Marseillaise 73:39

VOCATIONS: *see* OCCUPATIONS

VULTURES: see BUZZARDS

W

WAKE-UP SONGS: see also MORNING
The Animals Wake-Up   41:15
Cowboy's Gettin'-Up Holler   159:3, see also: 289:24
Ho! Every Sleeper Waken   262:67, 293:104
Lazy Mary   17:101, 289:17
Ma Fille, Veux-tu un Bouquet?/My Daughter, Would'st Have a Bouquet? 79:66
Morning Song   71:48, see also: 245:2
My Daughter, Wouldst Have a Bouquet?/ Ma Fille, Veux-tu un Bouquet?   79:66
Oh! How I Hate to Get Up in the Morning 25:39
Rose, Rose, and Up She Rises   232:145, 289:14
Singing Time   245:15
Sleepers, Arise!   71:60
The Sun Is Rising Out of Bed   245:2, see also: 71:48
The Sun Worshippers   69:26, 262:136
The Sweet Rosy Morn   245:11
Up Little Hans   245:13
Wake Up   130:10
Wake Up, Jacob!   289:24, see also: 159:3
WALES
All the World Is Sleeping   125:70
All Through the Night   21:337, 59:20, 125:72, 205:60, 289:26
*Lliw Gwyn Rhosyn Yr Haf/White Rose of My Heart   89:134
Under Yonder Oaken Tree   78:19
*White Rose of My Heart/Lliw Gwyn Rhosyn Yr Haf   89:134
WALKING
The Happy Wanderer   25:80, 26:70
Hiking Song   227:34, see also: 25:65, 26:65
I'm Happy When I'm Hiking   25:65, 26:65, see also: 227:34
Jog on, Jog on   262:129
Pack Up Your Troubles   25:59
A Song of the Open Air   262:84
Swinging Along   69:55
WAR OF 1812: see also names of historic persons, e.g., JACKSON, ANDREW
Battle of New Orleans   240:213
Come All You Bold Canadians   240:194
The Constitution and the Guerrière 240:191
Gunpowder Tea   240:189

Hey, Betty Martin   129:72, 135:120, 157:44, 226:158, see also: 33:194
High, Betty Martin   33:194, see also: 129:72, 135:120, 157:44, 226:158
James Bird   240:200
The Noble Lads of Canada   240:209
Old England Forty Years Ago   240:214
The Patriotic Diggers   27:172, see also: 240:205
Perry's Victory   240:197
The Shannon and the Chesapeake 240:196
Ye Parliament of England   21:270, 240:203
WAR SONGS AND CRIES: see also specific wars, e.g., CIVIL WAR (U.S., 1861-1865)
E! E! E!   89:304
A Filipino Hombre   226:434
The Minstrel Boy   22:226
War Song/Yaya   89:282
Where Have All the Flowers Gone?   72:5
Wi' a Hundred Pipers   71:61
Yaya/War Song   89:282
WASHINGTON, GEORGE
Follow Washington   27:32, 28:84
A Funeral Dirge on the Death of General George Washington   273:74
Great Americans   207:80
Hail, Columbia   21:266, 27:185, 66:84, 157:26, 160:26, 205:46, 240:187, 273:68
The Minuet   207:84
Mount Vernon   273:76
The Toast   157:22, 240:96, 273:48
War and Washington   240:97
Washington the Great   197:26
WATCHES: see CLOCKS AND WATCHES
WATER: see also BROOKS; RIVERS; SEAS
Arroyo Claro   188:62
Bring Me Li'l Water, Silvy   72:74, 130:79
Sweet Water Rolling   232:65
Sylvie   72:74, see also: 130:79
Water Song   91:24
WATERMELONS
Drool Song   25:40, see also: 63:124
I Planted Watermelons/Ja Posejah Lubenice   169:71, 270:63
Ja Posejah Lubenice/I Planted Watermelons   169:71, 270:63
Watermelons   63:124, see also: 25:40 (Just plant a watermelon on my grave)
Watermelons   239:87 (Watermelons off de vine)
WAYNE, ANTHONY
Anthony Wayne   28:126, see also: 240:100
Mad Anthony Wayne   240:100, see also: 28:126

WEASELS
Le Furet du Bois Joli/The Weasel from the Lovely Woods 217:48
The Weasel from the Lovely Woods/Le Furet du Bois Joli 217:64
WEATHER: *see also* specific types of weather, e.g., RAIN
Ain't Gonna Rain 226:141
Guess Who 207:65
Lines Written By a Bear of Very Little Brain 172:31, 174:17
Sunny Day 11:22
WEEVILS: *see* BOLL WEEVILS
WELCOMES: *see* GREETINGS
WESTWARD MOVEMENT: *see* PIONEERS AND PIONEER LIFE
WHALES AND WHALING
Blow Ye Winds 24:829, 71:84, 72:71, *see also:* 64:112, 158:44
The Greenland Fisheries 24:832, 292:170
In Frisco Bay 118:13
The Whale 62:49
WHIP-POOR-WILLS
Whip-Poor-Will 262:35
WHISTLES AND WHISTLING
Give a Little Whistle 275:19, 276:16
Grandma Grunts 79:21, 262:51
Whistle, Mary, Whistle 72:95
Whistle While You Work 275:12, 276:6
WINDMILLS
The Farm Windmill 207:104
The Wind Mill 262:85
WINDS
Bend With the Wind 162:32
Blow, Blow Thou Winter Wind 85:50
Corn in the Wind 245:64
Fishing Weather 281:58, *see also:* 18:26
Fly, Kite, Fly 207:89
The Four Winds 18:26, *see also:* 281:58
Poor Mister Wind 162:33
Song of the Wind 162:33
Which Is the Way the Wind Blows? 245:95
Who Has Seen the Wind? 112:25
Who Loves the Wind on a Stormy Night 245:68
The Wind 177:86 *(The wind is crying: "ooh-ooh o-o-h")*
The Wind 44:4 *(I saw you toss the kites on high)*
The Wind and I 207:29
The Wind and I Went Dancing 7:34
The Wind Blow East 130:95, 232:66
The Wind in the Willows 71:113, 72:170
The Wind It Blew Up the Railroad Track 226:379
Windy Day 296:19

Windy Nights 59:47
WINNEBAGO INDIANS
*Song of the Sun 79:9
Wai-Kun 79:12
WINTER: *see also* SNOW
Bird's Christmas Feast 207:55
Blow, Blow Thou Winter Wind 85:50
Come Out and Play 245:19
A Day to Ski 207:73
Even in the City 261:44
Falling Snow 167:48
Feed the Birds 97:unpaged
The First Snowfall 207:66
The Frozen Girl 27:244, *see also:* 24:825, 35:50, 159:231, 226:58
Guess Who 207:65
I Like Winter 152
In Summer the Sunshine Is Brightest 72:131
In the Snow 207:77
Lo, the Winter Is Past 86:182
Making a Snowman 207:77
Millions of Snowflakes 86:181
Nature's Goodnight 125:50
The North Wind Doth Blow 17:129, 18:25, 135:116, 175:88, 188:106, 189:124, 227:31, 285:34, 292:139
Skating 7:14
The Sleepy Bear 207:30
A Sliding Song 207:74
Snow 162:35 *(The snow is piled so high)*
Snow 11:30 *(Snow is falling on the ground)*
Snow Boy 207:75
Snow Feathers 7:11
Snow Flakes 41:3
The Snowflakes 177:88
The Snowman 41:5
Snows 261:42
Song of the Frog Waiting for Spring 19:29
The Trees Have Put Their Nightgowns On 7:12
White Fields 44:26
Winter 91:30
Winter Has Come 27:240
Winter Song 86:180
Winter Walks 207:67
Winter's Birthday Cake 207:68
A World of Snow 162:34
WISHES
Star Bright 162:37, *see also:* 59:58, 68:8
Star Wish 59:58, *see also:* 68:8, 162:37
Starlight, Starbright 68:8, *see also:* 59:58, 162:37
Sunsets of Smiles 261:24
When You Wish Upon a Star 275:16, 276:14
Wishes 261:14

Wishes Don't Make Things Come True 219:14
Wishing Song   110:23
WITCHES AND WITCHCRAFT: *see also* HALLOWEEN
Hexlein/Little Witch   78:63
I'm a Witch   162:38
Little Witch/Hexlein   78:63
Whippily, Whoppily, Whoop   197:93
The Witches   162:41
WOLFE, JAMES
Brave Wolfe   158:118, 240:33, 273:16
WOLVES
The Fox and the Wolf/Le Renard et le Loup   243:38
Le Loup Berger/The Shepherd Wolf 243:30
Le Loup et la Cicogne/The Wolf and the Stork   243:30
Le Renard et le Loup/The Fox and the Wolf   243:38
The Shepherd Wolf/Le Loup Berger 243:30
The Wolf and the Stork/Le Loup et la Cicogne   243:30
WOMEN—EQUAL RIGHTS
Let Us All Speak Our Minds   64:195
WOODCHUCKS
Ground Hog   24:893, 158:26, 213:68, 289:46, 292:98
Old Ground Hog   234:22
The Whistle Pig Song   110:19
The Woodchuck   144:9
WOODPECKERS
Oh, Three Pega/O, Tres Pega   89:92
O, Tres Pega/Oh, Three Pega   89:92
WOODS: *see* FORESTS AND WOODS
WOOL: *see also* SHEEP
Baa, Baa, Black Sheep   17:147, 175:84, 188:102, 189:20, 283:24, 285:49
Sheep Shearing   129:36, 134:102, 292:54
WORK
Days of the Week   104:52
The Grasshopper and the Ant/La Cigale et la Fourmi   79:65, *see also:* 243:34
The Green Green Grass   149:42
Helping   260:60
La Cigale et la Fourmi/The Grasshopper and the Ant   79:65, *see also:* 243:34
Over and Under   296:36
Pick a Bale of Cotton   20:38, 21:128, 25:21, 75:62, 107:46, 130:80, 135:106, 148:302, 158:234, 230:54, 232:148, 277:51
The Poor Working Girl   226:195
Timber   226:386
We'll All Work Together   27:178
WORK SONGS
Almost Done   158:324

Bolsum Brown   226:355
Can 'cha Line 'Em   158:274
Cap'n I Believe   226:363
Commonwealth of Toil   64:14
Dark As a Dungeon   64:49
Don' Let Yo' Watch Run Down   226:370
Ever Since Uncle John Henry Been Dead 226:376
Hammer Man   226:139
Heave Away   226:407
I Been Wukkin' on de Railroad   22:148, *see also:* I've Been Workin' on the Railroad
I've Been Workin' on the Railroad   25:35, 26:78, 83:506, 129:86, 148:192, 162:95, 197:80, 205:196, *see also:* 22:148, 27:174
John Grumblie   79:57, *see also:* Old Grumbler
The Kitchen   149:14
The Levee Song   27:174, *see also:* I've Been Workin' on the Railroad
Making Rice Cakes/Mochi Tauki Odori 49:24
Men of the Soil   64:94
A Miner's Life   64:65
Mochi Tauki Odori/Making Rice Cakes 49:24
Mule Skinner's Song   226:400
My Old Hammah   226:458
My Sister She Works in a Laundry 226:381
Ox Driving Song   61:35
Rainbow Round My Shoulder   158:323
Roll Out, Heave Dat Cotton   277:101
Shovellin' Iron Ore   226:183
Take This Hammer   21:210, 24:913, 64:80, 158:322, 239:48, 277:87
This Ol' Hammah   55:265, *see also:* 232:149
This Old Hammer   232:149, *see also:* 55:265
Track-Lining Chant   239:74
West Virginia Hills   64:56
Which Side Are You On?   64:54, 230:94, 239:90
Whistle While You Work   275:12, 276:6
The Winnsboro Cotton Mill Blues   64:74
Work All de Summer   239:50
WORLD WAR (1939-1945)
Gee, But I Want to Go Home   158:124, *see also:* 27:226
Gee, Mom, I Want to Go Home   27:226, *see also:* 158:124
The Old Home Guard   275:79, 276:66
WORMS
Lots of Worms   296:26
The Worm Song   290:178, *see also:* 62:109, 226:444

WORMS—*Continued*
Worms 246:42
WRENS
The Wren Song 134:32

Y

YIDDISH LANGUAGE
Dayenu 27:84, 197:46
For Sukkot 77:44
Grace After Meals 77:16
Grace Before Meals 77:14
Greetings of Peace 266:36, *see also:*
72:149, 169:39, 208:36
Hava L'Venim 89:203
Havah Nagilah 266:36
Hevenu Shalom A'leychem 72:149,
169:39, 208:36, 266:36
Jeder Eyne Hot Lieb Shabas Ba Nacht
148:84
The Jewish Year 77:36
Lomir Sich Iberbetn 89:205
Mi Y'malel 27:256
Modeh Ani 77:11
Onkel Jakob, Onkel Jacob 148:102,
293:43
Pa'am Akhat 70:16, 266:35
Pesah, Season of Cheer 77:57
Sabbath Song 77:39
Shalom Chaverim 55:255, 293:110
Sholom A'leychem 25:112
Slumber Song 77:34
Tumbalalaika 148:398
Uga, Uga, Uga 266:36
Vigndig A Fremd Kind 289:32
Yom Kippur Day 77:43
Zum Gali Gali 25:90, 64:106, 69:49,
148:424, 290:196
YODELS
The Lone Star Trail 61:307, 159:19,
226:266, *see also:* 60:102, 146:162
Yodeling Song 25:92
YOUNGER, COLE
Cole Younger 61:262
YUCATAN
*Baile de los Pollos/The Chicken Dance
194:30
*The Chicken Dance/Baile de los Pollos
194:30
*Dos y Dos Son Cuatro/Two and Two Are
Four 194:36
*Two and Two Are Four/Dos y Dos Son
Cuatro 194:36
YUGOSLAVIA
Butterfly 114:62
Come, Son 176:76

*Hear Me, Dearest/Kad Se Jangin
89:190
*Hear, O Shepherds/Oj Pastiri 241:70
*I Planted Watermelons/Ja Posejah
Lubenice 169:71, 290:63
*Ja Posejah Lubenice/I Planted Water-
melons 169:71, 290:63
*Kad Se Jangin/Hear Me, Dearest
89:190
*Oj Pastiri/Hear, O Shepherds 241:70
*Three Days/Tri Dni 89:189
*Tri Dni/Three Days 89:189
YULE: *see* CHRISTMAS CAROLS; CHRISTMAS
SONGS
YUMA INDIANS
The Deer Begins His Travels 74:13
From Daylight to Darkness 74:15
The Owl Sings 74:21
Song of the Blackbirds 74:17
Song of the Buzzards 74:18
Song of the Hummingbird 74:20
Song of the Nighthawk 74:22
The Spider Makes a Road 74:16
The Water Bug Stands Upon a Fish
74:14

Z

ZAMBIA
*O, Dance Like That!/Ozibane! Ozibane!
Ozibane! 89:284
*Ozibane! Ozibane! Ozibane!/O, Dance
Like That! 89:284
ZITHER
Zither and I 262:145
ZOOS
The Children's Zoo 162:19
The Elephant Is Big and Strong 165:103
Elephant's Bath 207:107
Let's Go to the Zoo 128:42
ZUNI INDIANS
Corn-Grinding Song/Ockaya 68:13,
89:38 *(Lovely! See the cloud, the cloud
appear)*
Corn Grinding Song 197:85 *(Ioho,
wonder water)*
Ockaya/Corn-Grinding Song 68:13,
89:38
Rain Dance 197:86
The Sun Worshippers 69:26, 262:136